SPIRITUAL DIVERSITY IN
SOCIAL WORK PRACTICE

SPIRITUAL DIVERSITY IN SOCIAL WORK PRACTICE

The Heart of Helping

Second Edition

Edward R. Canda

Leola Dyrud Furman

OXFORD
UNIVERSITY PRESS

2010

OXFORD
UNIVERSITY PRESS

Oxford University Press, Inc., publishes works that further
Oxford University's objective of excellence
in research, scholarship, and education.

Oxford New York
Auckland Cape Town Dar es Salaam Hong Kong Karachi
Kuala Lumpur Madrid Melbourne Mexico City Nairobi
New Delhi Shanghai Taipei Toronto

With offices in
Argentina Austria Brazil Chile Czech Republic France Greece
Guatemala Hungary Italy Japan Poland Portugal Singapore
South Korea Switzerland Thailand Turkey Ukraine Vietnam

Published by Oxford University Press, Inc.
198 Madison Avenue, New York, New York 10016

www.oup.com

Library of Congress Cataloging-in-Publication Data
Canda, Edward R.
Spiritual diversity in social work practice : the heart of helping / Edward R. Canda
and Leola Dyrud Furman. — 2nd ed.
p. cm.
Includes bibliographical references and index.
ISBN 978-0-19-537279-3
1. Social service—Religious aspects.   2. Social workers—Religious life.   3. Spiritual life.
4. Spirituality.   I. Furman, Leola Dyrud.   II. Title.
HV530.C27 2010
361.3'2—dc22
2009006897

9 8 7 6 5 4

Printed in the United States of America
on acid-free paper

I dedicate this work to my wife and partner in all things, Hwi-Ja Canda; to my parents, Frank and Anne Canda, who set me on the spiritual path; to my siblings Frank (in memorium), Tom (in memorium), Nancy and Greg; and to the well-being of all who are touched by this book.

- Edward R. Canda

I dedicate this work to my grandchildren Yara and Philip Furman, to my sons, Erik and Jon Furman and their spouses, to my four brothers, Chet, Loiell, Connely, and Clark Dyrud, and their spouses, and to the memory of my late husband, Philip J. Furman.

- Leola Dyrud Furman

ACKNOWLEDGMENTS

I thank the Shumaker Family Foundation of Kansas for generous funding that supported the development of this second edition. I offer special appreciation to Shantivanam, Forest of Peace House of Prayer, in Easton, Kansas, for providing me with an inclusive Catholic contemplative community of support. I am very grateful to all my teachers who have inspired me along my spiritual path of service, especially those whose guidance directly influenced this book: Joan Halifax Roshi of Upaya Zen Center in Santa Fe, New Mexico; Korean Percussion Master Byong-Sup Kim (in memorium); Professor Daniel B. Lee at Loyola University, Chicago; Seung Sahn Dae Seon Sa Nim, founder of the Kwan Um School of Zen (in memorium); and Dong Jun Yi, Professor Emeritus of Sungkyunkwan University, Seoul, Korea. Thanks to Professor Daniel B. Stevenson, Chair of the Department of Religious Studies at the University of Kansas (KU), for many years of friendship and interdisciplinary collaborations that have fed this book. Thanks likewise to my longtime friend and colleague, Professor Michael Yellow Bird of Global Indigenous Nations Studies of KU, for advice about the content on Indigenous religions. Sachiko Gomi, doctoral student in social work at KU, deserves special recognition for her extensive help as my research assistant on this book project. I am grateful to Orville Milk for the gift of his drawing (Illustration 2.4) and Amanda Blackhorse for the gift of the weaving (Illustration 4.1). Most of all, I thank my wife, Hwi-Ja Canda, for continuous support and encouragement and for her social work practice wisdom that infuses this book.
                                                              - Edward R. Canda

I thank the following people: Perry W. Benson, database manager/analyst at the University of North Dakota School of Medicine and Health Sciences, Department of Clinical Neuroscience, National Study of Health and Life Experiences of Women (NSHLEW): A 20-year National Study, for editorial assistance, statistical consultation and analysis, website design, and for preparing the web version of the survey instrument; Cordell Fontaine, Director, Social Science Research Institute, University of North Dakota, for assistance with data design, mailing, coding and data entry; John Hoover, Associate Dean of the College of Education, St. Cloud State University, for assistance in redesigning the original 1997 survey instrument and for his consultation regarding statistical analysis; Mari-Ann Zahl (in memorium), formerly Associate Professor of Social Work, Norwegian University of Science and Technology, Department of Social Work and Health Science, Trondheim, Norway for managing our survey in Norway and for spearheading the Spirituality and Social Work movement in Norway and Northern Europe; Cordelia Grimwood, faculty member in social work at the University of East London in Dagenham, Essex, United Kingdom, for managing our survey there; Blair Stirling, Doctoral candidate, Lecturer and Tutor in Social Work, within the Department of Social Work and Community Development at the University of Otago, Dunedin, Aotearoa New Zealand, for modifying the survey to meet demographic differences in New Zealand and for conducting our survey there; Bernard Moss, Professor of Social Work Education and Spirituality, Staffordshire University, UK, for his diligence and enthusiasm in promoting spirituality and religion in social work practice across the United Kingdom and for encouraging our work; Gale Valtinson, Clinical Psychologist, St. Paul, Minnesota, for her consultation regarding religion, spirituality, and professional ethics. All of these people provided great help and inspiration.

- Leola Dyrud Furman

We are very grateful to Maura Roessner and Lynda Crawford at Oxford University Press for their encouragement of this project and for their skill guiding the book through production. We thank all the OUP and Newgen editorial staff who worked so quickly and proficiently.

Permissions' Acknowledgments

We are grateful to Michael J. Sheridan, Ph.D., Research Associate Professor and Director of Research, Center for Spirituality and Social Work, National Catholic School of Social Service, Catholic University of America in Washington, DC, for her pioneering survey studies on spirituality in social work and for allowing us to build on her work in developing our survey instruments.

We gratefully acknowledge permission to revise and adapt material from the following works:

Canda, E. R. (1988). Conceptualizing spirituality for social work: Insights from diverse perspectives. Social Thought, 14(1), 30–46.

Canda, E. R. (1988). Spirituality, religious diversity, and social work practice. Social Casework, 69(4), 238–247. Reprinted with permission from Families in Society (FamiliesInSociety.org), published by the Alliance for Children and Families.

Table 9.2. Ethical considerations for using spiritually based activities in social work, from Canda, E. R. (1990). An holistic approach to prayer for social work practice. Social Thought, 16(3), 3–13.

All figures, including photographs, are by Edward R. Canda.

PREFACE

In the 10 years since we (EC and LF) wrote the first edition of this book, we have been gratified at the many positive comments we have received about it. We are also amazed at the growth of interest about spirituality in social work and allied helping professions around the world. During that time, both of us extended our commitments to cross-cultural and international networking and collaborations. This second edition retains the major organization and content of the first edition, since that has seemed to work well. However, in order to reflect growth in ourselves and the profession, we revised and expanded the book significantly.

The main new features of the second edition are:

- Slight reorganization of content to enhance flow of ideas and guidelines for practice
- More illustrations, figures, and tables to amplify major points
- More attention to the empirical evidence base for practice and debates about the nature of evidence in the study of spirituality
- More attention to meso- and macropractice
- More examples from social work practice, teaching, and daily life
- More content on ecophilosophical approaches to social work
- More detailed guidelines for use of spiritual assessment, meditation, ritual, and forgiveness in practice
- More exercises to engage the reader in personal and professional growth

- Major increase of interdisciplinary knowledge applicable to social work
- Major increase of international knowledge and worldwide view
- New sections on Confucian and Indigenous North American approaches to social work
- New information from our 2008 replication of the first edition's U.S. national survey on religion and spirituality in social work as well as surveys in Aotearoa New Zealand, Norway, and the United Kingdom
- New appendix with list of professional standards, publications, and websites for addressing spirituality in social work generally and within nine fields of practice
- Extensive use of internet-based resources

We hope that students, practitioners, researchers, and educators in social work and allied helping professions around the world will find this book useful as a trail guide on your spiritual paths of service. But, as the adage attributed to the anthropologist Gregory Bateson goes, "the map is not the territory." If the map offers guidance, carry it forward. If it leads you astray, disregard it. On the basis of your experience, redraw the map to help others coming later. And with each step, pay attention to the amazing view along the trail.

CONTENTS

A NOTE TO THE READER

Welcome.
Please enter
the reading of this book
as a journey of discovery and growth.

May you test
what you find herein
by your deepest wisdom,
by the guidance of those you respect, and
by your daily experiences
on the spiritual path of service.

PART I

Central Values and Concepts for Spiritually Sensitive Social Work

Guiding Principles

Human beings live not on bread alone.

Matthew 4:4, Christianity (Jerusalem Bible)

Spirituality is the heart of helping. It is the heart of empathy and care, the pulse of compassion, the vital flow of practice wisdom, and the driving energy of service. Social workers know that our professional roles, theories, and skills become rote, empty, tiresome, and finally lifeless without this heart, by whatever names we call it. We also know that many of the people we serve draw upon spirituality, by whatever names they call it, to help them thrive, to succeed at challenges, and to infuse the resources and relationships we assist them with to have meaning beyond mere survival value. We all have many different ways of understanding and drawing on spirituality. And in social work practice, all these ways come together, knowingly or unknowingly. In this book, we provide a framework of values, knowledge, and skills to bring together the many religious and nonreligious forms of spirituality together in a creative helping process.

Spirituality and religion have become very popular topics in the general public. For example, news media often have stories about the competing religious views and affiliations of politicians; moral and social policy debates over abortion, homosexuality, and human cloning; religiously motivated war and terrorism; breakthroughs in holistic forms of healing and therapy in medicine and psychotherapy; and inspirational spiritual lives of world leaders such as the Dalai Lama of Tibetan Buddhism and former South African President Nelson Mandela. In the publishing industry, spirituality is a major sector of the market. Movies and TV documentaries carry stories about angels, near death experiences, sexual abuse by clergy, quasi-religious encounters with extraterrestrial beings, miracles, and extra-sensory phenomena. In this new millennium of the information age, the Internet is replete with videos, music, and informational websites about virtually every spiritual tradition, fad, and controversy. Indeed, for the first time in human history, nearly all religions, cultures, and secular worldviews are in contact—sometimes harmoniously and sometimes conflictually. Yet all this talk about spirituality and religion can cast as much shadow and confusion as light and understanding.

Within North American social work and allied helping professions, there are movements to shed light on the many ways that spirituality impacts individuals, society, and world. Recently, these movements have begun to connect across disciplines such as social work, medicine, nursing, psychology, psychiatry, anthropology, pastoral counseling, sociology, and religious studies. There are international movements emerging as well. This is an exciting time of innovation and expansion as social workers stretch farther the reaches of human nurture (Canda, 2005a). As we shall explain, there is mounting empirical evidence and practice wisdom that a person's sense of positive spiritual meaning, purpose, and connectedness along with participation in supportive aspects of religious communities are associated with enhanced well-being. Yet, while momentum for spiritually sensitive social work has grown rapidly in the past 15 years, many practitioners, students, educators, and researchers remain unaware or suspicious about it.

This book draws on a wide range of interdisciplinary and international insights to present the state of the art of spiritually sensitive social work that is respectful and competent in response to the diverse forms of spirituality that is expressed in clients' lives and communities. It weaves this wide and scattered material into a comprehensive framework for practice. It builds on our professional heritage, from our roots in religious ideologies and institutions of social service to the most current work in cross-cultural study of religions, transpersonal theory, spiritually oriented psychotherapy, and social and environmental activism. It draws on insights from a wide range of religious, philosophical, scientific, and human service perspectives. While the focus of the book is on social work in the United States, wisdom about spiritually sensitive practice from other countries is included to encourage a worldwide view.

The book also incorporates ideas concerning spirituality and religion from social workers in direct practice, based on our national and international surveys. In 2008, we conducted a national survey of members of the National Association of Social Workers (NASW) who are engaged in direct practice (hereafter referred to as the National Survey). This is a replication of our original 1997 national survey, which was reported in the first edition of this book (Canda & Furman, 1999). Appendix B presents technical details about the study methodology. These comprehensive national surveys of NASW practitioner members on spirituality show their attitudes and range of relevant practices across a span of more than 10 years. We also draw on findings from international replication surveys we conducted with colleagues in the United Kingdom, Norway, and New Zealand.

At the outset, please be assured (or forewarned, depending on your viewpoint) that this book does **not** advocate for a religious sectarian view of spirituality or social work. It is not about proselytizing or converting anyone to any particular religious faith or spiritual path. Nor is it about stereotyping or putting down any particular religious faith. As will be explained with detail in Chapter 3, our use of the term *spirituality refers to a universal quality of human beings and their cultures related to the quest for meaning, purpose, morality, transcendence, well-being, and profound relationships with ourselves, others, and ultimate reality.* Spirituality expresses in diverse religious and nonreligious forms that are crucial to understand for contemporary social work. So this book is about social workers self-reflecting, searching for meaning, and sincerely striving to link our spiritual paths (of whatever kind) to professional values and settings. It is about learning to respond sensitively to the diverse religious and nonreligious forms of spirituality found among the individuals, families, groups, and communities whom social workers have dedicated to serve. In a nutshell,

> spiritually sensitive practice is attuned to the highest goals, deepest meanings, and most practical requirements of clients. It seeks to nurture persons' full potentials through relationships based on respectful, empathic, knowledgeable, and skillful regard for their spiritual perspectives, whether religious or nonreligious. It promotes peace and justice for all people and all beings. (Canda, 2008d, pp. x–xi)

This book proposes a guide for social work practice. However, it is only a proposal. We hope that the reader will reflect carefully and critically on our framework and then do the most important work of all—develop a personal framework that is congruent with your own values, professional commitments, and areas of practice. This book can be considered a success only if it helps the reader to accomplish this.

Why Bother with Spirituality?

Attending to spirituality can help us put clients' challenges and goals within the context of their deepest meanings and highest aspirations. Since social workers are committed to a whole person in environment perspective, we need to take a bio-psycho-social-spiritual view. On a pragmatic level, by considering the religious and spiritual facets of clients' lives, we may identify strengths and resources that are important for coping, resilience, and optimal development. Most societies include religions with pervasive influence on personal health, family relations, economics, and politics. Most Americans (and most people in the world) are concerned with matters of religion and spirituality. Many clients raise issues pertaining to religion and spirituality (Canda & Furman, 1999; Kvarfordt & Sheridan, 2007). People's sense of spiritual well-being and their participation in religious communities and practices influence their health, mental health, and social relations for better or worse (Koenig, 2007). This book explains how we can be prepared to respond to spirituality in a professional manner.

There are some objections to addressing spirituality in social work and the helping professions (see Canda and Furman, 1999 and Moss, 2005 for detailed discussions). Opponents tend to assume that there are defects in the nature of religious institutions and individuals (Clark, 1994; Sullivan, 1994; Weisman, 1997). They view connection of religion and spirituality to social work as problematic. Moreover, they identify logistical and practical difficulties of dealing with spirituality and religion in practice or education as discouraging or insurmountable. For example, some people view religion as inherently conservative and oppressive or spirituality as a personal preoccupation that diverts attention from issues of justice. Some are concerned about inappropriate proselytization, confusion between personal and professional boundaries, blurring role distinctions between clergy and social workers, inappropriate moralistic judgments, and separation of church and state in governmentally sponsored social welfare. Some people mistrust religious or philosophical understandings of human behavior (Canda, 2008a, 2008b). Some are concerned that there is insufficient and contradictory empirical evidence about the helpful and harmful effects of religion and spirituality (Powell, Shahabi, & Thoreson, 2003; Sloan, et al., 2000; Thyer, 2007).

In contrast, this book recognizes challenges surrounding spirituality and responds to them by building knowledge and skills for practice within the context of professional values and ethics. We recognize the positive contributions of religion and spirituality that should be engaged in the helping process. We also recognize the ways spirituality and religion can express in harmful ways, so that social workers can be prepared to prevent, ameliorate, or overcome unhealthy, discriminatory, or oppressive impacts. Indeed, as you will discover throughout this book, American and international standards for professional social work in general and for practice in many American fields (e.g., health, mental health) recognize the importance of religion and spirituality (see Appendix C).

In Table 1.1, we summarize concerns about studying religion and spirituality along with our responses. This provides a summary of our rationale for addressing this topic. The reader could reflect on the concerns and responses in order to identify his/her own position and also to formulate responses to objections one might encounter from clients, colleagues, supervisors, professors, and members of the general public.

Our contention that spirituality is relevant to practice is well supported by the 2008 National Survey (NS) findings. Most social workers in our study believed that it is appropriate to raise the topic of spirituality in a nonsectarian manner with clients on every issue we explored, but especially regarding terminal illness, bereavement, substance abuse, and suffering effects of a natural disaster (see Table 1.2). Most respondents also believed that it is appropriate to raise the topic of religion in cases of terminal illness, bereavement, adoptive and foster parenting, substance abuse, and suffering the effects of a natural disaster.

Table 1.1. Resolving the Debate about Studying Religion and Spirituality (R/S) in Social Work.

Opposing Views	Supporting Views
Inherent Deficiencies of R/S	**Responding to Challenges and Strengths of R/S**
Institutional Problems	*Institutional Challenges*
• Sectarian views are too limiting or biased for the profession	• Use inclusive view of spirituality and religion (s/r)
• Rigidity, dogmatism, and judgmentalism of religions are worrisome	• Engage diverse ideological and spiritual perspectives in dialogue; avoid negative stereotyping
• Religions are basically status quo maintaining	• Address the role of s/r in both restricting and promoting well-being and justice
• Spiritual perspectives are overly focused on personal issues rather than macro justice	• Identify both micro and macro implications of s/r perspectives
Personal Deficits	*Personal Strengths*
• Religion is an expression of psychopathology	• Identify the role of s/r in both restricting and promoting mental health
• Spirituality is inherently personal and idiosyncratic	• Compare diverse s/r perspectives for similarities, differences, and mutual understanding
Religion and Spirituality Are Inconsistent with the Nature of the Profession	**Religion and Spirituality Express the Nature of the Profession**
Professional Boundary Concerns	*Domain Implications*
• Religion and social work are separate and mutually exclusive domains	• Religion, spirituality, and social work are interrelated and can be complementary
• S/r are not important for understanding clients	• Evidence shows that s/r are crucial for understanding many clients and their cultures
• Addressing s/r would undermine the status of the profession	• Addressing s/r competently enhances the status of the profession
• S/r are the responsibility of clergy	• Prepare workers to address s/r or refer and collaborate with clergy as client prefers
Value Conflicts	*Value Dilemmas*
• Involving religion increases the danger of proselytization and violation of clients' self-determination	• Address s/r in a manner consistent with professional values and ethics
• Addressing religion weakens church/state separation	• Support church/state separation, freedom of religious practice, and respect for diversity
• Social work should be value free or objective	• Social work is inherently value based
• S/r are inconsistent with a scientific base for practice	• Addressing spirituality is consistent with current scientific evidence
• Social workers tend to be irreligious or uninterested	• Social workers are often religious and always spiritual
Logistical Problems	**Logistical Solutions**
Inadequate State of the Art	*Emerging State of the Art*
• Concept of spirituality is too vague for use	• Create clear definitions and conceptual models
• Efforts to combine s/r and social work are not adequately developed	• Utilize extensive available knowledge for linking s/r to service
• Supporting evidence is not yet adequate	• Explore extensive interdisciplinary research and expand social work research
• Workers are unprepared to address, so better to ignore or refer	• Enhance education of workers

(continued)

7

Table 1.1.   Continued.

Opposing Views	Supporting Views
Curriculum Concerns • Curriculum is already too crowded to include s/r • Educators are unprepared to teach, so better to ignore	**Curriculum Opportunities and Responsibilities** • Implement both infusion and specialization in curriculum • Engage educators in continuing education and curriculum development

Table 1.2.   Appropriate to Raise Topic of Religion/Spirituality by Client Issue.

Raise Topic of Religion/Spirituality with…	Religion			Spirituality		
	% Agree	$\bar{x}$	S	% Agree	$\bar{x}$	S
Terminal illness	74.9	3.81	1.06	86.1	4.15	0.92
Substance abuse	53.1	3.37	1.10	72.8	3.84	0.99
Foster parent	56.8	3.43	1.09	63.6	3.66	1.03
Adoptive parent	58.2	3.45	1.10	64.7	3.67	1.03
Difficult child or adolescent development	37.5	3.09	1.06	55.2	3.51	1.02
Sexual abuse	46.6	3.24	1.11	64.6	3.67	1.05
Partner violence	44.4	3.20	1.09	61.9	3.62	1.04
Suffering effects of natural disaster	56.3	3.43	1.08	71.2	3.78	1.02
Bereaved	72.1	3.75	1.03	81.9	4.05	0.91
Chronic mental disorder	36.5	3.06	1.08	52.2	3.45	1.06
Loss of job	37.1	3.08	1.06	54.0	3.48	1.05
Difficulty in family relations	43.7	3.19	1.05	59.6	3.56	1.01
Criminal justice	37.5	3.09	1.07	52.8	3.46	1.03

Note: A *t*-test of means showed a significant difference between religion and spirituality with clients presenting the same problem, with $p < 0.001$. Respondents were significantly more likely to believe it is appropriate to raise the topic of nonsectarian spirituality than religion.

However, for every issue, fewer believed it was appropriate to raise the subject of religion than nonsectarian spirituality. These findings indicate that many social workers recognize the importance of spirituality and religion while also making a distinction in applying them to practice.

Social workers in the 2008 National Survey were asked new questions to indicate their level of agreement regarding the appropriateness of raising the topic of religion and spirituality with clients from vulnerable populations (see Table 1.3). A large majority of respondents agreed that it is appropriate to raise the topic of spirituality with clients who are dealing with oppression. Although fewer believed it was appropriate to raise the subject of religion than nonsectarian spirituality, a large majority of respondents agreed that it is appropriate to raise the topics of religion and spirituality with clients who are experiencing religious oppression.

Table 1.3.   Appropriate to Raise Topic of Religion/Spirituality with Vulnerable
Populations.

Raise Topic of Religion/Spirituality with...	*Religion*			*Spirituality*		
	% Agree	$\overline{x}$	*S*	*% Agree*	$\overline{x}$	*S*
Race, ethnicity, or national origin	42.7	3.18	1.09	59.2	3.56	1.03
Gender	40.6	3.13	1.09	56.1	3.51	1.05
Sexual Orientation	45.2	3.21	1.11	59.8	3.56	1.06
Older adulthood	42.7	3.17	1.11	60.1	3.58	1.04
Political beliefs	34.6	3.03	1.07	50.7	3.41	1.05
Religious beliefs	79.8	4.00	1.01	82.2	4.05	0.93
Disability	40.7	3.14	1.10	58.5	3.55	1.05
Poverty	39.3	3.10	1.10	55.9	3.51	1.03

Note: A t-test of means showed a significant difference between religion and spirituality with clients presenting the same issue, with $p < 0.001$, except for religious beliefs ($p < 0.05$). Respondents were significantly more likely to believe it is appropriate to raise the topic of nonsectarian spirituality than religion.

Although the same general patterns emerged in the 2008 National Survey as in 1997, the respondents were significantly less likely ($p < 0.05$, based on mean ratings) to feel that it is appropriate to raise the topic of religion with certain client issues than in 1997: terminal illness, foster parenting, bereavement, and difficult family relations. On the other hand, 2008 respondents were significantly more likely ($p < 0.001$) to view raising the topic of religion with substance abuse issues as appropriate. Overall, 2008 respondents were significantly less likely ($p < 0.05$) than 1997 respondents to believe that it is appropriate to raise the topic of spirituality with all client issues except for substance abuse and chronic mental disorder. This might be because social workers have become even more cautious about imposing their agendas on clients (since this question involved raising the topic rather than responding to the client's initiative), which would be a development consistent with professional ethics (Canda, Nakashima, & Furman, 2004). In any case, it is clear that most social workers are positively disposed toward addressing spirituality and religion in practice.

Unfortunately, our 2008 National Survey showed that nearly 65% of respondents did not receive content on spirituality or religion in their social work education. On a positive note, this was 8% less than the 73% who reported no educational content in 1997. Among those who had received educational content on religion and spirituality in 1997 (27%) and 2008 (35%), there were few differences between the two groups regarding raising the topic of religion. A majority of the 2008 National Survey responders agreed that social workers should become more knowledgeable about spiritual matters (66.1%, $n = 1{,}167$) and religious matters (51.3%, $n = 906$). Nearly 25%, however, agreed that workers do not have the skill to assist clients in religious and spiritual matters. This finding is much lower than the 39% reported in 1997, which might reflect a promising trend of increased sense of competence. Yet it appears that many social work practitioners do not feel adequately prepared to address religion or spirituality, even though they recognize the importance.

It should be noted, however, that given the mean age of 58 for 2008 respondents, many received their education and training before religion and spirituality were acceptable subjects in the social work curriculum. It is perhaps not surprising then that respondents at or above the mean age of 58 had significantly lower mean ratings on all of the issues related to raising the topic of religion and of spirituality, except for raising the topic of religion with foster and adoptive parenting, than those respondents below the mean age. This reinforces the inference that over the past 10 years, openness to spirituality in social work has increased.

Imagine the following practice scenario. It illustrates the importance of preventing mistakes in practice due to neglect of spiritual and cultural factors. We are confident that you will have increased sense of competence and confidence to address this and other issues of spirituality by the time you complete reading this book.

Several years ago, a mental health consumers' advocacy group in Kansas discovered that a Mexican American woman had been kept in a psychiatric hospital for more than 10 years, without adequate review of her case. The woman originally had been taken to the hospital by police, who found her rummaging in a garbage bin and acting strangely. Hospital staff considered her to have a severe and persistent mental disorder, as evidenced by semi-incoherent speech, repetitive walking motions and gestures, unsociability, and bizarre beliefs and perceptions. The diagnosis had been confirmed by a Spanish-speaking psychiatrist. Upon further investigation, the advocates discovered a series of cultural and religious misunderstandings by helping professionals. They learned that the woman was wandering the streets due to poverty and severe grief after the death of her husband; she had no social support system. The psychiatrist who diagnosed her was Cuban American; he could not correctly understand the woman, who spoke a blend of Mexican Spanish, Tarahumara (an Indigenous language), and English. Some of the woman's initial disorientation was due to being overwhelmed by adversity and grief. Some of the ongoing supposedly bizarre beliefs and behaviors were rooted in her Tarahumara religious tradition and practices for self-protection. The woman's mental health status was reassessed. Through cooperation with the Mexican embassy, she was assisted to return to her home village in Mexico. If you were a social worker at the hospital, how could you have prevented these cultural and religious misunderstandings?

Principles That Guide the Writing of This Book

Seven principles have guided our writing: demonstrating value clarity, respecting spiritual diversity, being reflective, supporting strengths and empowerment,

Table 1.4. Guiding Principles.

1. Demonstrating Value Clarity
   • Self-reflection
   • Appropriate self-disclosure
   • Dialogue
   • Inclusive and transcendent perspective
2. Respecting Diversity
   • Appreciation of all types of human diversity
   • Nondiscrimination
   • Interreligious, interdisciplinary, and international collaboration
   • Affirmation of human rights and responsibilities
   • Provisional approach to spiritually sensitive practice
   • Engagement with locality-specific and culturally specific approaches
3. Being Reflective
   • Introspection and reflection between self and world
   • Silent mindfulness
   • Transformational learning
4. Supporting Strengths and Empowerment
   • Relating to people as whole beings
   • Emphasizing strengths, resources, capacities, aspirations
   • Overcoming personal, interpersonal, and structural obstacles
   • Action for well-being and justice
   • Considering helpful and harmful impacts of religion and spirituality
5. Taking a Holistic Perspective
   • Understanding person/environment wholeness
   • Engaging thinking, feeling, sensing, intuiting, and relating
   • Focusing on direct practice within wider systems and transpersonal view
   • Connecting local and global
6. Applying Best Practices
   • Competence
   • Evidence from an expanded view of inquiry
   • Multiple ways of knowing
   • Theoretical sophistication
   • Grounding in professional mission and values
   • Client-centered determination of "best"
7. Comparing within and between Vantage Points on Spirituality and Religion
   • General or universal aspects of human experience and culture
   • Particular religious and nonreligious expressions of spirituality
   • Underlying assumptions, strengths, and weaknesses of views
   • Process of reflection and communication

taking a holistic perspective, applying best practices, and comparing within and between vantage points on spirituality.

Demonstrating Value Clarity

In our writing, we do not claim or wish to be value free or bereft of moral standards, nor do we wish to impose our own values as absolute or superior truths. We promote another way that we call *value clarity*. First, value clarity means that each of us must be clear about our own values and how they shape us. Only in this way can we engage in conscientious self-reflection and growth. Second, whenever relevant and appropriate, we need to make our value positions explicit to colleagues and clients so that we can engage together in dialogue, sorting out the value dilemmas and possible conflicts involved. Through dialogue, our formation of values, ethics, and morals can be enriched, broadened, and refined. When educators and practitioners make their value positions explicit, then students, clients, and colleagues can scrutinize them and make choices about whether to agree or disagree. Only then is informed consent possible. In this way, we can examine how our values may affect the course of research, teaching, or practice, and we can take steps to engage them constructively or to change them.

This does not mean we should engage in self-revelation merely for our own purposes, out of self-preoccupation or grandiosity. As in all social work practice, we should engage in self-disclosure at times and in ways that are appropriate to the needs and circumstances of those we serve. However, not to self-disclose at all, or to hold major areas of who we are in secrecy, restricts our participation in helping as full human beings. In addition, it replaces the danger of openly imposed agendas with the danger of subtly imposed hidden agendas.

Discussion of religious and spiritual matters intensifies concerns about value openness precisely because people sometimes claim ultimate and absolute truth status for their religiously or ideologically based opinions. For social work purposes, *absolutism* is inappropriate. Social workers are not trained as theologians, philosophers, or metaphysicians; nor are they authorized by their profession or society to dictate absolute truths to clients. Although absolutism stems from a praiseworthy desire to know what is true, it is unworkable for professional helpers because it is based on an unrealistic and conceited assumption that the helper knows all and knows what is best for everyone. It excludes alternatives that may be important to the well-being of clients and their communities. It precludes dialogue and mutual understanding. For example, a social worker who believes that his or her religion proclaims with absolute authority that homosexuality is merely a matter of choice for people (and a sinful choice at that) likely will not be amenable to dialogue and revision of the value position. Scientific evidence or professional admonishments notwithstanding, the social worker might believe it is her or his duty to so-called fix the gay or lesbian client through religious conversion or psychotherapeutic manipulations.

This kind of rigid thinking is not the exclusive province of religion. Value rigid positions can be found among ideologues of every stripe, whether political, theoretical, or religious. The clinician who fervently believes in the dictates of Erik Erikson's stage theory of human development might try to evaluate every client in terms of developmental tasks achieved and ego functions mastered, no matter what gender, ethnic background, sexual orientation, or type of ability or disability. The Bowenian family therapist who is inattentive to cultural variation might misinterpret the Confucian filial piety of a Korean American eldest son and his wife, who live in an extended family household, as a form of immature enmeshment. The community organizer who is a strict classical Marxist might ignore or denigrate the potentially empowering spiritual and religious aspects of community life.

Another value pitfall appears at first to be the opposite of absolutism, that is, *relativism*. Relativism is more typical of certain secular ideologies, such as extreme forms of postmodernism, than religions. By this we mean a stance that social workers should hold no value positions or morals and should not judge clients on any basis, because (it is claimed) there are no universally valid values and no universal qualities of human beings. Relativism stems from a praiseworthy desire to avoid imposing irrelevant or harmful beliefs and standards on diverse clients, cultures, and varied situations (Mullaly, 2006). However, strictly speaking, relativism is unworkable for social work because it implies that it is impossible to understand, evaluate, or help across differences of culture, gender, religion, and other human variations. It inhibits the search for common ground and solidarity within and between groups working toward well-being and social justice. By focusing exclusively on situation-specific rights and empowerment, it sheds little insight on universal human rights and responsibilities. When difference and separation are overly emphasized, empathic connection is hampered. By confounding judgment with judgmentalism and discriminating thinking with negative discrimination, the exercise of careful discernment and assessment fails.

In fact, relativism is another variety of absolutism because it claims as absolute truth that there are no absolute or universal truths. Indeed, as the integral theorist Ken Wilber (2000a & b) pointed out, an extreme postmodern position that no perspective is better than any other is a self-contradiction in that it claims itself to be better than absolutism and other perspectives. Further, to claim that there is no absolute truth is a self-contradicting absolute claim of truth. Practically speaking, social workers are necessarily involved in matters of values and (at least provisional) truth claims, such as in professional codes of ethics, human rights accords, laws for public rights and responsibilities, and uses of helping practices supported by empirical research. Social workers must find common ground with clients in order to communicate and collaborate. We must be able to "step into others shoes," to take their perspectives, and to connect our minds and hearts with clients if we are to have rapport in the helping relationship. We need to be able to assist clients in many kinds of discernment such as strengths assessment, mental health diagnosis, and identifying counterproductive client behaviors, and oppressive environmental conditions. We need to assist clients when they wish to examine the helpful and harmful influences of religions and nonreligious spiritual perspectives. For example, Shim (in press) critiqued the so-called cultural defense used by some abusive Asian American men to legitimize abuse of their wives. This defense did not take into account the wives' perspectives on what is appropriate, nor did it examine the philosophical foundations (such as Confucianism) claimed to support wife abuse. Indeed, original Confucian teachings emphasize reciprocal care and responsibilities in families, not violence.

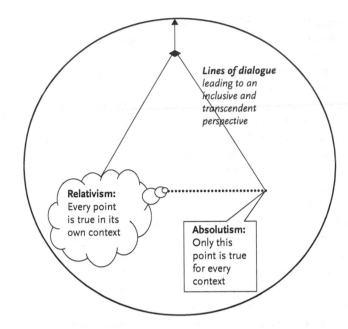

Figure 1.1. Transperspectival view: transcending absolutism and relativism.

We wish to avoid the extremes of absolutism and relativism. We also accept the importance of seeking truth, appreciating the contextual nature of truth claims, and avoiding the unjust domination of certain views over others. So we recommend the alternative of value clarity: to be clear and open about our various value positions, to continuously reflect within ourselves, and to engage in ongoing respectful dialogue (commune-icating) with others (Figure 1.1). In addition, we need to do this in a way that encourages mutual growth. Thus we can learn to appreciate the various truths of clients and their communities and we can facilitate collaborative connection in the helping process. We can move to a vaster perspective that includes the positive contributions of a variety of truths, while transcending their limitations. This book is designed to encourage readers' development toward such a widely inclusive perspective for spiritually sensitive practice.

This is consistent with the wisdom of a great social activist, Mahatma Gandhi. While he believed that there is a divine truth that transcends yet informs all cultures and religions, he felt that this truth is beyond the ability of anyone to know completely, given our limitations as human beings. Humility was a virtue he praised. He believed that every person and every human group is seeking truth, but that no one has exclusive possession or full understanding of truth. Even in conflict with oppressors, Gandhi sought to discover the opponents' understanding of truth. He avoided dehumanizing anyone, even when he was unjustly persecuted. His philosophy of nonviolence was made dynamic by the principle of *satyagraha*, or Truth Force. If each person strives continually to understand the truth, and opens up to others and helps others in their search for truth, we can all move closer to realization of truth (Erikson, 1969; Fischer, 1950; Gandhi, no date; Walz & Ritchie, 2000). This is spiritually sensitive and peace promoting social activism.

While we do not claim to achieve this profound level of value clarity, we commit ourselves to strive toward it. We hope that our own self-disclosures and our juxtapositioning of many different spiritual perspectives will help the reader on his or her own search for truth.

In order to encourage value clarity, we will use two literary devices in our writing style. One literary device is the traditional academic style of *third person*. This allows us to present ideas without making personal comments about them. It helps us present the thinking of others in their own terms and also to adhere to the rigors of academic scholarship. The other literary device is the narrative style of *first and second person*. Sometimes we will make explicit where we are giving voice to our joint personal views (*we*) or the views of just one of us (*I*). When writing in the first person, we will specify our initials (EC or LF). For example, it seems to us rather awkward and artificial to write "the authors believe..." It is more direct to say "we believe." We include autobiographical accounts of our personal and professional experiences for two reasons. First, we do this to illustrate how we strive to integrate spirituality into our lives and work. We do this also to expose aspects of our backgrounds and assumptions that shape this book and should be available for critical scrutiny. You will notice that we have similarities and differences between our spiritual perspectives. Our writing models dialogue and collaboration by honoring differences and finding commonalities. We hope this encourages you to work out your own integration between the personal and professional aspects of your lives.

Respecting Diversity

The social work profession promotes appreciation for all aspects of human diversity. Diversity is often discussed in the social work literature in terms of race, ethnicity, national origin, culture, religion, social class, gender, marital status, sexual orientation, political belief, and variations of ability. In particular, the Council on Social Work Education's (CSWE) Educational Policy and Accreditation Standards (2001 and 2008, retrieved from www.cswe.org on August 9, 2008) identify that education and practice should reflect nondiscrimination on the basis of religion and that students learn about religion as an aspect of human diversity as well as spiritual development. The National Association of Social Workers' (NASW) Code of Ethics is opposed to discrimination on the basis of religion or creed and expects social workers to obtain education and understanding about religion (Ethical Standards 1.05.c and 4.02, 1999). The International Federation of Social Workers' (IFSW)/ International Association of Schools of Social Work (IASSW) "Ethics in Social Work, Statement of Principles" (Principle 4.2, 2005, retrieved from www.ifsw.org on August 9, 2008) states that social workers should not engage in negative (i.e., harmful) discrimination on the basis of spiritual beliefs. Many different spiritual perspectives shape American society, the global community, and the clients and communities whom social workers serve; therefore, social workers must be prepared to understand and relate with them in a respectful manner (e.g. Bullis, 1996; Canda, 1988a & 1988b; Canda & Chambers, 1994; Coates, Graham, Swartzentruber, & Ouellette, 2007; Crompton, 1998; Lindsay, 2002; Loewenberg, 1989; Moss, 2005; Nash & Stewart, 2002; Patel, Naik, & Humphries, 1997; Van Hook, Hugen, & Aguilar, 2001). Genuine respect is more than just tolerance. Respect for diversity should extend to a genuine appreciation for diversity and to a competent response to the diverse backgrounds and situations of clients.

This raises a difficult issue. Some religions and secular ideologies propose that their way is the only true and correct way. From these exclusivist perspectives, spiritual diversity is seen as a problem. Variations from their beliefs are viewed as heresies, dangerous deceptions, or at best, misguided views that should be corrected. From an exclusivist view, the only acceptable kind of social work would be one that is sectarian, based on one's own religious or ideological beliefs.

This is not our position. We are committed to inclusiveness in spiritually sensitive social work and we encourage interreligious, interdisciplinary, and international dialogue and cooperation for human service. Exclusivists may not be comfortable with this, but we submit our position for consideration by all. Perhaps our greatest challenge is how we can be inclusive of exclusivist spiritual perspectives. For example, there has been a debate within the Council on Social Work Education about whether social work programs in certain religiously affiliated schools should be able to apply for an exemption from the requirement of nondiscrimination against people on the basis of sexual orientation (Parr & Jones, 1996; Van Soest, 1996). More recently, there have been claims and counterclaims that the social work profession systematically discriminates against people of conservative religious views in education and practice due to a predominance of elitist, liberal, and secular views (e.g., see Hodge, 2002 and subsequent letters to the editor in *Social Work*, 2003, volume 48, number 2).

Our position affirms social work professional standards of nondiscrimination as well as international human rights accords, such as the United Nations Universal Declaration on Human Rights, while realizing that concepts of ethics and human rights are continuously unfolding and that they must be adapted and developed situationally (Ife, 2001). We appreciate Ife's broad statement of moral principles for social work: "Act so as always to affirm and realize the human rights of all people. Do nothing to restrict, deny or violate the human rights of anyone" (p. 111). At the same time, we recognize the importance of responsibilities and reciprocity, which, we believe, are relevant to all cultures, but are especially emphasized in more communalistic (rather than individualistic) cultures (Yip, 2004). For example, we do not support any form of discrimination against gay or lesbian people or any other groups. And we also do not support restriction of religious freedom, discrimination on the basis of religion or creed, forced religious conversions, or discrimination against nonreligious people. The right to engage in religion goes together with the right of not engaging in religion. Thus, religious and nonreligious people have a responsibility to respect those who differ from them and to promote the common good of society and world. Therefore, our approach is to encourage discussion and debate in a respectful manner about such contentious issues and dilemmas. We will return to this complex issue in the next chapter.

Further, while we advocate our approach to spiritually sensitive practice as a provisional guide for social work, we emphasize that practitioners need to consider carefully what may or may not be relevant to particular clients' situations, locales, and cultural contexts. Population-specific, locality-specific, and culturally specific approaches to social work need to be developed from the ground up; they also need to be connected in mutual affirmation and scrutiny (Gray & Fook, 2004). Indeed, we have pulled together many of these context-specific insights with insights from general theories and cross-cultural and interdisciplinary views to form our approach. However, we realize that our approach, as all approaches, is limited. Please adapt what is useful and throw away what is not. We hope that this book spurs dialogue and collaborations within and across many approaches to social work.

Being Reflective

In writing the two editions of this book, we have engaged in a long process of self-reflection in order to link our own personal and professional experiences with others' work and to cull out implications for spiritually sensitive practice. In doing so, we changed and grew. Personal engagement in learning is a transformative experience that requires reflectivity, the practice of introspective self-reflection, and reflection about how one's inner life and the outer world reflect on each other. The capacity for reflection is necessary for the development of insight into self and others and to form empathic and intuitive connection with others.

Our responsibility is to present this book in a way that encourages and catalyzes the reader's continuing development through reflectivity (Ashencaen Crabtree, Husain, & Spalek, 2008). This can only be successful if there is a willingness by each reader to approach the reading of this book as an opportunity for growth. We have written this book with a stance of value clarity in a format that encourages reflectivity in the reader. We include our own self-reflections in autobiographical passages and provide exercises for the reader to engage in self-reflection and critical thinking in response to the text. In addition, we wish to offer here some suggestions for how to read this book in a reflective manner.

The prerequisite for *reflective reading* is silence. Silence means quieting in order to know oneself, the inner stirrings of the heart, and the discerning wisdom of the intellect. This is the starting place for the cultivation of intuition and practice wisdom that make social work an empathic connection with clients, rather than mere technical manipulation and rule enforcement (Keefe, 1996; Koenig & Spano, 1998; Krill, 1990). Intuition and practice wisdom involve the ability to respond spontaneously at just the right moment in just the right way to a client. This requires clear awareness focused in the moment.

Reflective silence does not necessarily require absence of external noise or internal mental chatter. But it does require a willingness to become introspective, to "get centered," and to pay gentle consistent attention to oneself and one's situation. The Vietnamese Buddhist meditation teacher, Thich Nhat Hanh (1987, p. 14), refereed to this as mindfulness:

> Keep your attention focused on the work, be alert and ready to handle ably and intelligently any situation which may arise—this is mindfulness. There is no reason why mindfulness should be different from focusing all one's attention on one's work, to be alert and to be using one's best judgment. During the moment one is consulting, resolving, and dealing with whatever arises, a calm heart and self-control are necessary if one is to obtain good results... Mindfulness is the miracle by which we master and restore ourselves... it is the miracle which can call back in a flash our dispersed mind and restore it to wholeness so that we can live each moment of life.

Therefore, we invite you to pause for a moment before sitting to read this book. Take a gentle breath, relax, center yourself, and prepare to read with a quiet and clear mind.

Mindful, reflective reading opens the possibility of discovering passages that seem to jump out at us, as if they were meant just for the reader. It allows readers to reflect sincerely and intelligently on the implications of the reading for personal and professional development. In effect, mindful reading can become a dialogue between ourselves and the text in which we discover important insights about ourselves and our work with clients.

This is quite contrary to a common academic way of reading. Often when we read a book for purposes of academic study, we read as if we are doing a heavy chore. We sift the text for facts, analyze and categorize, and try to pick out what we need to know for a class test or a professional licensing exam. Analytical reading is necessary but not sufficient for growth. If we read with brain but no heart, then we can master the facts but miss the implications for our own personal and professional transformation.

The Confucian tradition of East Asia emphasizes scholarship as a means of cultivating wisdom to apply to social service (Canda, 2002a). The traditional Chinese concept of mind (shim) combines the Western ideas of thinking mind and feeling heart. The Korean Neo-Confucian sage T'oegye (lived 1501–1570) said, "What is the meaning of 'thought'? It is seeking the matter out in one's own mind-and-heart and having a personal experience and grasp of it." (quoted in Kalton, 1988, p. 108). Kalton summarized the Neo-Confucian ideal of learning this way: "This reminds us once again that learning in this context is a spiritual project, and the essential exercise of the mind is not speculative knowledge but personal transformation through a profound personal understanding and appropriation of what is studied" (p. 108).

Reflectivity requires discerning the difference between our own projected biases, fantasies, and assumptions and the world as it is given to us. Therefore, reflection offers both peril of distortion and promise of insight. For example, when I (EC) was a young boy, I was both fascinated and frightened by looking from my bright room at reflections in dark windows at night. Sometimes I thought I saw surreal and frightening faces looking back at me. Looking closer, I realized that I was seeing my own distorted reflections mixed with others. "This was an important lesson, because it alerted me to be wary of distorted reflections of myself, seen in the faces and actions of clients and students, loved ones, and acquaintances. What is menacing is not the reflection itself, but rather my mistaking the reflection for reality. Just like the dark window reflection, our perception of clients is often a confused mix of their reality and our reflections" (Canda, 1995b, p. 3).

But mysterious reflections can also be wonderful. My colleague and friend, Professor Seung-Hee Park of Sungkyunkwan University in Seoul, Korea, traveled and taught me and my students during four study abroad trips. Often, when we visited a lovely palace or temple pond, he would exclaim enthusiastically to the students: "Look at the water! See the reflections—aren't they beautiful? Fish are swimming in the clouds! What is real? What is real?"

This book presents beliefs and helping practices from many spiritual perspectives. It advocates for particular values and questions others. It raises controversies and dilemmas. There is surely something here for everyone to feel: agreement or disagreement, comfort or discomfort, as well as confusion and clarity. In reflective reading, your reaction is not a matter of right or wrong. It is crucial first to be aware of your reaction. Second, you need to reflect on where the reaction comes from. A reaction is as much a result of what one brings to the reading as whatever is in the book. So pay gentle but keen attention to your reactions. What do they tell you about your own personal history, professional experience, biases, assumptions, spiritual beliefs and commitments, strengths, and limitations? Each strong reaction, favorable or unfavorable, is a message to pay attention to whatever it is in oneself that gives rise to the reaction. When this is understood, the third step is to consider what one's reaction implies for continued personal and professional growth. If a limitation of attitude, skill, or knowledge is identified, what can one do to correct the limitation and move beyond it? If a strength or resource within oneself or the environment is newly identified or the appreciation is heightened, how can it be used more effectively in practice?

Supporting Strengths and Empowerment

We support a strengths perspective on social work in general and spirituality in social work in particular (Saleebey, 2009). Strengths based social work means that people are viewed as whole beings, with inherent capacities for resilience and creativity. When they seek help for problems, they are never reduced to those problems. Problems are just one facet of their situation, not the defining facet. Problems are opportunities for growth and challenges for creativity. For example, if a person has a disability, the disability is one aspect of his or her situation. It is not the whole person. The client should never be reduced to a pathology or deficit label or negative expectations that come along with it. To define a person or situation only in terms of problems, defects, barriers, or deficiencies is to dehumanize and to dull our awareness of the strengths, resources, capacities, and resiliencies the person has used successfully to deal with having a disability. These inner strengths, environmental resources, and empowering actions need to be the focus of helping in order to support the actualization of people's goals and aspirations (Kim & Canda, 2006).

We also believe that empowerment is an important complement to the strengths perspective (Gutierrez, Parsons, & Cox, 2003; Lee, 2001; Saleebey, 2009). Empowerment requires that people become aware of obstacles to individual hopes and collective justice. This awareness then becomes shared with others in solidarity, so that mutual support and collective wisdom and action can lead to proactive response. Action for personal and social change is the next step. Awareness is not enough. Ironically, if a person only ventilates painful feelings about injustice, the feelings of hurt and anger may dissipate leading to temporary relief but no lasting benefit. So empowerment requires developing and implementing an action plan for change in oneself and the environment.

Respecting diversity and demonstrating value clarity and reflectivity are crucial ingredients for identifying strengths and empowering action. This is why we suggested in the previous section that the reader should engage in a reflective process of reading that moves from self-awareness of strengths and limitations and aspirations to actions supporting personal and professional growth. We encourage you to discuss your growth process with family, friends, and colleagues, to the extent it is comfortable and secure to do so. Make the most of any spiritual support group or religious community in which you already participate or develop new ones. Work out explicit plans for further implementation of learning in social work practice. Where obstacles or injustices are identified, perceive them as challenges and opportunities for creative transformative action. Make common cause and cooperation with others as you work for peace and justice through spiritually sensitive practice.

In writing this book, we focus on the strengths and resources available by incorporating spirituality and religion into social work practice. We also consider the obstacles and pitfalls that they may involve for people. As with any aspect of human life, religion and spirituality can be used to support or impede individual fulfillment and social justice. For example, I (EC) once visited the Catholic basilica in Mexico City. For me, this basilica was an intense symbol for the complexity of religion and spirituality. The beautiful religious artwork and architecture were inspiring. The images of Christ's compassion and the gentleness of his mother Mary, especially as Our Lady of Guadeloupe, patron saint of the Americas, illustrate virtues to which I aspire. Indeed, Our Lady of Guadalupe is believed to have appeared to Juan Diego Cuauhtlatoatzin, an Aztec convert, in 1531, and is therefore regarded by some as a sign of respect for Indigenous peoples. However, at the same time, there is something terrible about the history of the basilica. The guide explained that the original basilica was built upon the ruins of Aztec sacred temples, destroyed by the conquistadors, in order to show the might and victory of the Spanish colonialists and their church. The very people who were subjugated by this colonization were forced to build this church on the remains of their desecrated sites. The beauty and grandeur of the basilica cannot be denied and neither can the inhumanity and injustice of its origin. Both of these qualities coexist in the history of the Catholic Church and pose a dilemma for the Catholic faithful, as the contemplative activist monk, Thomas Merton (1968a) pointed out. As a member of the Catholic tradition myself, I must confront this paradox openly and honestly. Indeed, the late Pope John Paul II, in an effort to promote reconciliation, made apologies on behalf of the church for more than 100 forms of oppression and abuse, including of Indigenous peoples, during his pontificate (http://en.wikipedia.org/wiki/Pope_John_Paul_II#Apologies, Retrieved August 9, 2008).

In various ways, we all face this paradox. It is not unique to the Catholic Church. I have seen similar situations in every ideology and religious tradition I have explored around the world. Within every country there are religious and spiritual experiences, practices, and groups that provide great solace, strength, beauty, wisdom, and empowerment; there are also the harmful manifestations of religion and spirituality gone awry (Demerath, 2007; Derezotes, 2006; Koenig, 2007). In this book, we acknowledge both, seeking to actualize the strengths and resources of people and communities, while striving to transform problems and obstacles into challenges and opportunities for working through to ever-greater levels of well-being and justice.

Taking a Holistic Perspective

In social work, we often say that we wish to understand the whole person-in-the-environment. It is necessary to learn about the roles of religion and spirituality if we are to have such an understanding. In our conceptualization of spirituality, we will address the inextricable interrelationship between spirituality and the biological, psychological, social, and larger ecological dimensions of human experience (Coates, 2007; Robbins, Chatterjee, & Canda, 2006).

We also wish to engage the whole person in the process of learning about spirituality and social work. For this reason, we present features of this book that engage thinking, feeling, sensing, intuiting, and relating with ourselves and others, human and nonhuman. We encourage analytical, critical thinking. We evoke feelings using images, metaphors, and self-reflection exercises. We provide guidance for practices that help to cultivate intuition, such as meditation and empathy when relating with clients. We review current developments for practice in a variety of fields and with a wide range of populations. Although the main focus is on direct practice, we consider larger meso and macro social systems as well.

We focus on spiritually sensitive practice in the United States and interweave it with insights and concerns of the wider social and planetary environment. The United States is like a microcosm of the world in that it includes people representing many of the languages, cultures, and religions of the world. American social workers can learn from social workers around the world how to enhance practice with this internal diversity, work with refugee and immigrant groups, and collaborate in international social welfare efforts. Likewise, there may be lessons to learn around the world from American social work successes and failures. This connection of local and global perspectives extends to human/ nature interdependency as informed by ecophilosophy and spiritual traditions of service that respect the Earth and all beings. Finally, we consider how various spiritual perspectives understand the nature of ultimate reality, in theistic, nontheistic, animistic, atheistic, or other terms and the implications for human service. All of this includes appreciation for spiritual experiences and transpersonal development that bring people through and beyond limitation to the individual body-ego into profound connection and compassion with other people, all beings, and the ground of being itself, however understood and beyond understanding (Canda & Smith, 2001; Wilber, 2006).

Applying Best Practices

A major concern in social work and related helping professions is how to know whether our helping practices are effective. Practitioners wish to engage the practices that best benefit our clients. The NASW Code of Ethics rightfully mandates that social workers must be competent in their areas of practice. We concur that spiritually sensitive practice implies that social workers must accurately evaluate their qualifications to employ specific practices and further, they must assess whether the processes and outcomes of their work genuinely serve the purposes of clients. The most prevalent current manifestation of this concern for *best practice* is *empirically based practice or evidence-based practice* (Petr & Walter, 2005), influenced by medical and social scientific research. Indeed, empirical research is showing through hundreds of studies in several disciplines that positive sense of spiritual meaning and religious participation are related to reduced levels of depression, anxiety, substance abuse, and risk behaviors along with an increased sense of well-being and mutual support (Koenig, 2007; Koenig, McCullough, & Larson, 2001; Miller, 1999; Miller & Thoreson, 2003; Pargament, 2007; Richards & Bergin, 2005; Sperry & Shafranske, 2005). Specific spiritually based practices, such as forgiveness, meditation, and spiritually oriented cognitive-behavioral therapy are also showing promise.

However, we do not limit ourselves to common narrow assumptions of empirically or evidence-based practice. We wish to remain true to our professional values, tradition, and perspective even as we draw on methods and knowledge from other disciplines. As Petr and Walter (2005) point out, empirically based practice is often construed to mean practice that is restricted to activities that have been supported as effective by specific types of quantitative research designs. Although the word "empirical" simply means "based on experience," the type of evidence allowed in conventional empirically based research is limited to sensory perception, logic, and rationality within a positivist worldview (Lincoln & Guba, 1985; Patton, 2002; Rodwell, 1998; Wilber, 1998). "Evidence-based practice" is often given a slightly wider meaning that emphasizes the importance of linking empirically derived evidence (which may supplement quantitative methods with qualitative) with client concerns, professional discretion, and professional ethical priorities. Petr and Walter make the helpful recommendation to expand inquiry to include even greater involvement of qualitative studies, consumer perspectives, practice wisdom, program descriptions, professional standards of practice, and consideration of whether practices are accessible, affordable, accountable, and linked to other services in the community.

We suggest that the concept of *useful evidence* be expanded further to include information from any systematic and disciplined form of inquiry, the methods and results of which are subject to scrutiny by others, and for which there is sufficient current support to merit application in practice and further study. As we will explain in Chapter 3, the concept of spirituality includes certain quantifiable and measurable aspects (such as frequency of church attendance or level of self-assessed sense of meaning); various processes, experiences, and systems that are best explored through qualitative methods of observation (such as the subjective experience of meditation or the communal patterns of mutual support in religious groups); and certain transpersonal experiences and levels of consciousness that can best be explored through contemplative and transpersonal methods (Braud & Anderson, 1998). While we recognize the utility of the scientific method as it has derived from European and American cultures, we also respect the forms of knowledge and wisdom found among the elders, mentors, and adepts of religious traditions and culturally specific healing systems around the world. We value understanding that comes from a convergence of sensory, rational, emotional, and intuitive ways of knowing. For a truly integral approach, we need to combine inquiry approaches that address both the subjective and objective dimensions of individual and collective phenomena of spirituality (Wilber, 2006). Further, there are many metaphysical claims about the nature of reality, sacredness, and the divine that we make no attempt to either support or refute, since they are beyond our purview as social work researchers and educators. However, we respectfully convey many of these claims in the context of particular spiritual perspectives, so that you may understand adherents' views.

Research methods and evidence are formed by people who hold worldviews and theoretical assumptions that shape their research questions, methods, and resultant evidence. Therefore, we also consider how practices connect with theoretical frameworks that are attentive to spirituality. To adapt the criteria for evaluation of theories set out by Robbins et al. (2006), we appreciate a range of spiritually oriented practices that (1) take into account the whole person in relationship; (2) foster positive development through the life span; (3) promote well-being for individuals, families, organizations, institutions, communities, and world; (4) are consistent with social work values and ethics; (5) are consistent with a holistic view of the person-in-environment; and (6) emphasize strengths and resources in attaining full human potential while addressing intrapersonal and environmental barriers.

It is beyond the scope of this book to discuss these research issues in detail. Although empirical research on spirituality in social work and allied fields is still relatively new, it is growing quickly. We have drawn on the latest findings on best practices from many fields, using our broad understanding of evidence and research. Please keep in mind, though, that what is considered "best" should always change as more information comes to light and as practitioners identify through client feedback exactly what is or is not working in a particular situation. We ask the reader to look to our extensive references to find more information about the practices and their support by formal research, practice wisdom, client/consumer views, theory, and professional value and ethical standards. We also refer you to the *Spiritual Diversity and Social Work Resource Center* (www.socwel.ku.edu/canda/). This online resource center includes extensive information about spirituality in relation to social work and health, including links to other websites with information on relevant scientific research.

Comparing within and between Vantage Points

The prior six principles lead us to our seventh and final principle: comparing within and between vantage points on spirituality and religion in social work (Canda, 1989a). Throughout this book we weave comparison of spiritual perspectives and practice approaches from a variety of vantage points so they can shed light on each other (Sharma, 2005) in relation to social work. The first vantage of comparison examines *religion and spirituality as general or universal aspects* of human experience and culture. For example, in Chapter 3, we will consider general conceptions of spirituality and religion, from many different disciplines. From the second vantage, we consider *particular religious and nonreligious expressions of spirituality* as they effect social work practice. For example, in Part II we consider how various contrasting religious and non-sectarian spiritual traditions provide frameworks for social service. From the third vantage, we step back from both general theory and particular accounts of spirituality to examine their *underlying assumptions, strengths, and weaknesses,* and how these relate to practice. For example, Maslow (1968) critiqued the ways religions can promote or impede peak experiences and optimal human development. Part III presents detailed guidelines for understanding and applying spiritually relevant practices. From the fourth vantage, we reflect on the assumptions, values, implications for practice, and communication dynamics that *underlay the reflective process itself.* For instance, at the end of each chapter, we offer suggestions for various experiential and self-reflective exercises that promote insight of the reader and constructive communication dynamics when this book is used within courses or workshops.

Preview of Chapters

This book is organized in three parts. Part I (Chapters 1–3) presents key values and concepts for spiritually sensitive practice. Part II (Chapters 4–6) explores diverse spiritual perspectives on service and their implications for social work. Part III (Chapters 7–11 and Appendices A and C) offers conceptual understanding and practical guidelines for spiritually sensitive social work helping activities.

In the remainder of Part I, Chapter 2 explores fundamental values and ethical principles to guide spiritually sensitive practice. Chapter 3 offers definitions and conceptual models of spirituality.

In Part II, Chapter 4 reviews the history of spiritual diversity and related controversies in the United States and the social work profession. Chapter 5 presents an introduction to seven types of religious traditions of service: Buddhist, Christian, Confucian, Hindu, Indigenous, Islamic, and Judaic. Chapter 6 introduces nonsectarian existentialist and transpersonal/ecophilosophical spiritual perspectives on service. It also compares all nine perspectives and offers suggestions for finding commonality and engaging in dialogue across spiritual perspectives.

In Part III, Chapter 7 explains how to create a spiritually sensitive context in the helping relationship and process, and in human service organizations. Chapter 8 provides a theoretical basis and practical tools for assessing spiritual development of individuals throughout the life span. Chapter 9 offers guidelines for ethical use of religious or spiritual support systems and activities. Chapter 10 provides conceptual understanding and detailed practical suggestions for employing specific spiritually oriented helping activities, such as meditation, ritual, and forgiveness. Finally, Chapter 11 considers future directions for spiritually sensitive practice within a worldwide view.

This book is intended to be thought provoking and soul searching. It is designed to promote personal and professional growth in the reader. In doing so, it will be challenging, sometimes uncomfortable, but also exciting. The mind, heart, and action of the reader will be engaged. This book raises profound spiritual questions in religious and nonreligious guises. They are questions that every social worker must face somehow. Therefore, this book is not just about a specialized area of practice or theory. It is about the nature of the helping situation itself. Every social worker is involved in a spiritual journey, in his or her own private life, as well as in the course of professional work. This book is about that journey, that way of compassion.

EXERCISES

1.1. What Is Your Position?

You may be reading this book for many different reasons. Perhaps you already have a strong interest in spirituality and you want to learn more about applying this to practice. Perhaps you are unsure about the relevance of spirituality, but you are willing to consider it. Alternatively, you might believe that it is not appropriate to address spirituality in social work, but you are reading this because of a class requirement or because you want to find out what your pro-spirituality colleagues are thinking. In any of these cases, it is important for you to clarify your position, both in your own mind and in being able to articulate your views to people who disagree with you.

Look back to Table 1.1 which lists the rival positions. Review each position, con and pro, and consider the extent to which you agree. Think of an example and an explanation, based on your own personal and professional experience, for each point that strikes you as especially important. Then write a short essay that articulates your position. If the position you had before you read this chapter remains the same, explain why. If it has changed, also explain why. Once your position is well formulated, have a conversation about this with a trusted social work colleague who is likely to have a different position from yours. Try to reach mutual understanding, whether or not you end up agreeing.

1.2. How Well Does This Fit?

This first chapter presented seven principles that guide our approach to writing the book. Reflect back on your reactions to these principles in Table 1.4. How do they fit with your own views? Did you have any strong reactions of agreement or disagreement? Whatever your reactions, consider what it is about yourself that predisposes you to have these reactions. What does this indicate about your personal experience, professional training, cultural background, and religious or spiritual perspective? Based on these reactions, become aware of what your expectations are for the rest of this book. Do you expect to enjoy this? Do you expect to feel a sense of conflict with our approach? Write a brief essay about these reflections and expectations. Finally, put all these expectations aside and promise yourself that you will read with an open mind.

1.3. Journaling about Spirituality and Social Work

When quiet time and attention are set aside for regular self-reflection, personal and professional growth can be enhanced significantly. One method for doing this is to keep a growth journal. Journaling provides a format for dialogue with yourself about reactions to the reading, insights and implications about spiritual growth, and actions you take to support growth. A journal can be informal and unstructured, consisting of a free flowing dialogue with yourself. This has the advantage of spontaneity and flexibility. However, some structure can encourage regularity, consistency, and self-discipline. Following is a suggested structure for journaling in response to reading this book. The structure should provide consistency, but it should not hamper creativity. So feel free to modify it as needed.

The main purpose of this format is to encourage systematic self-reflection that moves all the way from awareness of reactions to actions planned or implemented to support growth. It is important to start with an accurate reading of the material, but reflective journaling is not just a matter of restating what was said. Reflective journaling incorporates intellectual analysis, but it should not be limited to detached, unfeeling thinking. Thinking, feeling, sensing, intuiting, and acting should all be joined.

After reading each chapter, relax and center yourself. Take a few minutes to page back through and recall your reactions, especially reactions of strong agreement or disagreement or any strong feelings and opinions. Identify which aspects of the chapter struck you as having the most significance for your personal and professional growth. If you made notes or underlined text, review those to refresh your memory. Then, take 15–30 minutes to write a commentary about your reactions and implications for growth.

A fictitious example will be given for each step. Since this example is fictitious, there is not as much personal detail as would be likely in a real journal entry. In addition, there will be great variation of style and content for each person. Find your own style of comfort with this journal process. Use the following format:

1. **Title of the chapter, date read, and date of journal entry**
2. **Insight in the Reading**

Summarize one idea contained in the reading of most significance to you. Choose this as your focus for the journal entry. Be sure this is an accurate summary of what you read. Keep it brief, not more than about 50 words.

Example: In the introduction, the authors mentioned that one of the greatest challenges to an inclusive approach to spirituality in social work is how to include people who have an exclusive viewpoint and do not wish to dialogue or are not open to change.

3. **Self-Reflection**

Explain in detail how this is significant to you. Include the following levels of reflection.

a) What was your immediate reaction at the time of reading? What is your reaction as you think back on it now?

Example: When I first read this, I wondered if they were talking about people like me, a committed Christian. I felt angry and defensive, as though they were insulting me. Now that I think about it, I recall they said rigid exclusivist thinking could apply to any spiritual perspective or ideology, so they were not singling Christians out. I realize that my feelings are easily hurt when the subject of religion or spirituality comes up in social work settings.

b) *Explain what it is **about you** that predisposes you to this reaction.* For example, what is the relevance of this insight to your personal and professional interests; special strengths and talents; any prejudices, biases, or lack of knowledge; significant faith or value commitments; religious or nonreligious upbringing; cultural heritage and patterns?

   Example: I became a born-again Christian 4 years ago. This made a tremendous impact on changing my life for the better. In addition, after my conversion, I felt called to follow Christ's example by serving others in social work. However, I've sometimes been stereotyped and insulted by other social workers as a right-wing fundamentalist. They imply that I should not be a social worker if I have such a strong Christian commitment.

c) Identify specific strengths and limitations of your personal and professional development that are revealed by this self-reflection.

   Example: My Christian commitment and support from my church are important sources of strength for me. They give me the energy and motivation to live a life of service. However, some of my fellow social workers do not share the same beliefs as me. I can see that this difference is sometimes hard to get past, both for them and for me. I understand why I feel defensive, considering my past hurts. However, I should not let this get in the way of communicating well with others. I need to figure out how to build on the strength of my faith and also how to join this with the values, ethics, and ways of communicating within the social work profession.

d) For each strength or limitation identified, list an implication for further growth.

   Example: My strength is my faith. I need to explore more how to join my faith with social work.

   My limitation is my defensiveness. I need to avoid assuming negative intentions when I receive constructive criticism. If someone raises questions about my faith, I need to learn how to relax and respond clearly. I need to learn how to listen to their concerns with empathy and learn from their position. I also need to learn how to encourage them to listen to me. This way we could have a dialogue and learn from each other. This after all is consistent both with my commitment to Christian love of neighbor and to the social work professional principle of "starting where the person is."

e) For each implication, list a specific action that you could take to support your growth.

   Example: For strength: I could explore the website of the North American Association of Christians in Social Work (NACSW, www.nacsw.org) and then decide whether to attend their meetings and join. I could also read articles and books about the history of Christian social work and the professional dilemmas and conflicts that sometimes arise around religion and social work. I could also learn about a different religious approach to social work, and talk with social workers of this religion, to help me broaden my perspective.

For limitation: When I meet other Christian social workers, we could form a support group to discuss our experiences in social work, positive and negative. This would provide interesting conversation, mutual support, and an opportunity to work through my feelings. When I meet with the social worker from another religious background, we could discuss how we each try to connect our spiritual ways to social work and find not only the differences but also the commonalities between us.

f) *Select at least one action that you commit to carrying out within the next month.* Make a promise to yourself in writing to do this. Make a practical plan for how it can be accomplished.

Example: Based on my review of the NACSW website, I decided to join within the next 2 weeks. I will find out the schedule for the next regional or national conference and make plans to attend. I will also invite my colleague who practices conservative religious Judaism to join me for lunch during the next week. We have already developed a friendly working relationship and gone to lunch a few times. However, the next time, I will ask if it would be all right to talk about our religious backgrounds and how we relate them to social work.

g) After this action is carried out, create an entry in your journal that discusses what happened, how you felt about it, and what you gained. If new areas for growth are identified from this, repeat the process of taking new actions and reporting to yourself about the results.

Example: I joined NACSW and eagerly await the conference scheduled for next month. I have already read their online materials and plan to order some of their publications. I felt affirmed to find out about the ways social work can be linked to church settings. I am excited to learn more about this. I am especially interested to explore how to abide by professional ethics while practicing as a Christian social worker.

This afternoon, I had lunch with my Jewish friend. She was surprised that I brought up the topic of religion, but she said she was glad. We had a good conversation. Although we have different faith commitments, we also discovered many commonalities of belief and experience as religiously committed social workers. We plan to discuss this more in the near future.

2

Compassion, the Call to Service, and Ethical Principles for Social Work

Strive constantly to serve the welfare of the world;
by devotion to selfless work one attains the supreme goal
of life.

The Bhagavad Gita 3:19, Hinduism
(trans. Easwaran, 1985)

In this chapter, we explore spiritually sensitive service as a matter of heart, as a vocation of compassion. *Compassion* literally means passion-with-others. It is commiseration in empathy with others. It is solidarity of response to suffering. Spiritually sensitive social work is a courageous (literally, from French, "of the heart") commitment to a spiritual path of action to promote the well-being of all people and all beings. This chapter reflects on the deep motivations that lead people into social work and considers some inspirational religious symbols of compassion. Finally, we use these insights about compassion to elaborate upon ethical principles for spiritually sensitive social work practice.

The theme of compassionate heart to heart connection in service is well expressed in traditional Chinese philosophy. The primary virtue emphasized in Confucianism is *ren* (Chinese) which means benevolence or humaneness. This Chinese character is formed by adding two strokes, signifying connection, to the symbol for "person." This means that to be a genuine human being (i.e. a true person) is to be connected (Canda, 2002a, 2002b). As we grow in sense of connection and responsibility with other people, other beings, and the ground of being, we have a natural drive to search for ways to help and heal ourselves and the world. All spiritual traditions and all people struggle with experiences of suffering, injustice, mortality, and death. Moreover, all seek means of remedy and transcendence.

The Chinese Confucian sage, Mencius (lived 372–289 BCE) said that everyone has a heart that cannot bear to see others suffer. "Suddenly seeing a baby about to fall into a well, anyone would be heart-stricken with pity...without a heart of compassion we aren't human" (trans. Hinton, 1998, p. 55). In fact, the Chinese character for mind is shaped like a heart, indicating that human mind is a font of feeling, thought, and caring concern (Lee, Ng, Leung, Chan, & Leung, 2009). Fittingly, the Center for Behavioral Health at the University of Hong Kong, which promotes a holistic East/West integrated approach to social work, has adapted this character for its logo (Figure 2.1).

Dass and Gorman (1985) said that when we let natural compassion express in our work, there is a mutual benefit to ourselves and to others. "The reward, the real grace, of conscious service, then, is the opportunity not only to help relieve suffering but to grow in wisdom, experience greater unity, and have a good time while we're doing it" (p. 16). The insights to come in this chapter remind us, as professionally trained social workers, to reflect back on the fundamental humanity and compassion that were already within us before the imposition of our learned rules, roles, theories, eligibility requirements, diagnostic schemes, and professional boundaries. By returning to this and cultivating this, we can keep our service full of vital energy and inspiration. This requires consistent attention to our personal and professional growth. Indeed, an empirical study showed that those who were more religiously or spiritually engaged rated higher in compassionate love for strangers and humanity in general (Sprecher & Fehr, 2005). Underwood's studies (2002) identified key aspects of compassionate love: freely choosing to care for the other; cognitively understanding the situation, including religious and nonreligious frameworks; knowing oneself; valuing others for their inherent worth; being open and receptive, including to inspiration; and responding from emotions, not just thinking. Trappist monks advise that it is important for people to engage in a sustained spiritually attuned way of life, including regular practices like prayer, in order to deepen understanding of self and given situations, and to integrate thinking and feeling for the expression of compassionate love (Underwood, 2005).

Figure 2.1. Logo, Centre for Behavioral Health, Hong Kong, Chinese character for mind.

The Virtue of Compassion in Professional Social Work

The Profession's Historical Commitment to Compassion

Social work is a caring profession, a vocation, guided by explicit values, morals, and codes of ethics (Graham, Coholic, & Coates, 2007; Reid & Popple, 1992). Insofar as moral and value systems constitute one of the main components of spirituality, we can say that *social work is fundamentally a spiritual profession*—one that sets its reason for existence and its highest priorities upon service (Siporin, 1986). In most of the world, core professional morals, values, and ethics are stated in nonsectarian terms without reference to concepts of the sacred or divinity. However, some social workers link their personal religious and spiritual values to these professional values (Brackney & Watkins, 1983; Coughlin, 1970; LeCroy, 2002; Sherwood, 2002; Spano & Koenig, 2007).

Jewish and Christian values of love of neighbor, charitable service, and justice directly shaped the formation of the profession's values in North America and in many other parts of the world influenced by the Judeo-Christian heritage (Boddie, 2008; Coates et al., 2007; Constable, 1983; Leiby, 1985; Lindsay, 2002; Moss, 2005; Siporin, 1983). In North America and in other parts of the world, the profession has also been influenced by the virtue of compassion (*karuna*, Sanskrit) found in Buddhism; benevolence found in Confucianism; the responsibility of almsgiving (*zakat,* Arabic) in Islam (Nadir & Dziegielewski, 2001); the value of harmony among people, the earth, and Creator among Indigenous peoples (Beatch & Stewart, 2002); and all the myriad other expressions of the true heart. Our profession's commitment to compassion could be reinforced through greater acknowledgment of and solidarity between the wide range of cultures and spiritual traditions in North America and around the world. This is exemplified by the bicultural Code of Ethics of the Aotearoa New Zealand Association of Social Workers which fully engages respect for the indigenous Maori worldview (http://www.anzasw.org.nz/excerpt-from-code-of-ethics.html, retrieved August 11, 2008).

The social work professional value system is promulgated through education of students and enforced through procedures of professional certification, licensure, and ethical adjudication (Reamer, 2001). This demonstrates a very high level of organizational commitment to moral and ethical reflection and action. Indeed, the social work profession can be considered to be a nonsectarian spiritual community. While professional bonds and mutual understanding of values are likely to be most strong within a given country, efforts of international organizations such as International Federation of Social Workers (IFSW) and International Association of Schools of Social Work (IASSW) are encouraging a global professional view.

The preamble to the current National Association of Social Workers' Code of Ethics (1999, p. 1) states:

The mission of the social work profession is rooted in a set of core values. These core values, embraced by social workers throughout the profession's history, are the foundation of social work's unique purpose and perspective:

- service
- social justice
- dignity and worth of the person
- importance of human relationships
- integrity
- competence

This mission, the core values, and the ethical standards that flow from them require the social worker to move beyond the bounds of egotism, prejudice, and ethnocentrism (Siporin, 1983). They even require putting the needs and interests of clients and the general welfare of society above one's own needs, as in support for client self-determination. They mandate that people are regarded as having inherent dignity and worth. They call for professionals to place a priority on the interests of the oppressed and to enhance social justice. All these commitments imply a stance of compassion with a transpersonal, that is, egotism transcending orientation a profound and challenging spiritual ideal.

Early in the history of the American profession, under the influence of religious charitable organizations and the Charity Organization Society, the religious and spiritual implications of this were explicit (Reamer, 1992). Indeed, there was a struggle between different views of compassion or charity. Unfortunately, sometimes charity was (and is) associated with condescending pity, moralistic judgmentalism, and paternalistic control. How far this is from its biblical meaning as love (*caritas*, Latin): "Love is patient and kind; love is not jealous or boastful; it is not arrogant or rude. Love does not insist on its own way; it is not irritable or resentful; it does not rejoice at wrong, but rejoices in the right. Love bears all things, believes all things, hopes for all things, endures all things" (1 Corinthians 13: 4–7, Revised Standard Version).

Already in 1967, Salomon cautioned that social workers should not abandon a moral view of life, but also should not fall into moralistic prejudice and judgmentalism. Rather, she recommended that we relate with clients through a spiritual encounter of whole person to whole person, so that both worker and client will experience change and healing. Siporin (1982) said that we need to regain moral vision and idealism, whether expressed in religious or secular terms, that combine concern for individual and social well-being. Constable (1983) summarized the ideal as reciprocity between values of social justice, freedom and opportunity for choice by individuals, and unconditional love and mutual respect.

Reamer (1992) warned about the lures of prestige, wealth, and power or simply a survival-based defensive emphasis on inter-professional competition and turf protection. These lures have grown as the profession increased its social acceptance and pressure by federal and state policies, insurance reimbursement regulations, and economic incentives from private clinical practice. In a religious context, these might be called temptations. So Reamer said, "To reclaim its enlightened view of the public good, social work must once again resemble a (secular) calling. One serves—primarily because one cares deeply about matters of social justice—those who are disadvantaged and oppressed, and those who are at risk. Gratification is primarily derived from knowing that one has responded to one of life's principal duties to others" (p. 28). He cautioned that social workers should keep their focus on our core values rather than on mere self-protecting ethical risk management (e.g. following rules to avoid litigation). We should delve more into *virtue theory*, "which entails analysis of core professional virtues such as honesty, respect, trust, fairness, responsibility, autonomy, nonmalfeasance, beneficence, justice, fidelity, faithfulness, forgiveness, generosity, compassion, and kindness" (Reamer, 2005, p. 27).

Social Workers' Personal Commitments to Service

Although there are many reasons that motivate service (Coles, 1993; LeCroy, 2002), those who make a commitment for a long time and are able to avoid the pitfalls of cynicism and self-promotion are likely to have a compassionate orientation. This makes sense not only because of the professional values social workers espouse formally, but also because of personal motivations to join the profession. Why should we commit ourselves to a profession often derided in media portrayals? Why are we often willing to work long hours in stressful conditions with caseloads beyond belief? What motivates us to a path of service when we live in a society driven largely by consumerism and glorification of economic profit or political power? We invite readers to reflect on your own experience and to consider how it matches this discussion of social work as a vocation expressing the virtue of compassion. Compare the following scenarios with your own experience.

* * *

My older brother died from AIDS 2 years ago. He was a gay activist, well known in his community for championing the rights of gay and lesbian people. As he drew close to death, his courage and continued caring for others inspired me and many other people. Although he was severely ill physically, he had a remarkable sense of spiritual vitality. His family and friends offered much support, but it really seemed more like he was helping us. I decided that I would like to carry on his example by becoming a social worker, with a special interest in hospice programs.

* * *

As my meditation practice deepened, I found a quality of peace and clarity that soothed my grief and pains and gave me the capacity to respond to life's challenges with greater energy and compassion. I realized that my own struggles are mirrored in the struggles of all people and all living beings. In my Buddhist tradition, we take a vow "to save all beings from suffering." In some small way, I hope that my practice as a social worker can help others to find their way from suffering to peace and joy.

* * *

When I was a teenager, my parents divorced. My father was abusive and alcoholic. Our family fractured under the strain. At the time, I felt my life was coming to an end. But support from members of my Christian church helped me get through it. Eventually, I found a source of inner strength and resilience that helped me to put the broken pieces of my life back together in a way that is healthier than I ever had as a child. There is something mysterious to me about this "resurrection" experience, but my religious teachings and community support made it possible. Now I would like to help other people find meaning and resiliency through difficult times.

These stories, though fictional, are similar to the accounts we have heard from social workers in private conversations, classroom discussions, and in autobiographical statements within applications to enter social work programs. Some surveys of social workers show not only that we are more likely than the general public to have experienced abuse, mental disorders, or substance abuse within our families of origin, but also that many of us have seen a way through this, a way toward personal recovery and service for others (Black, Jeffreys, & Hartley, 1993). Sometimes a life event or situation wakes a person up to the prevalence of human suffering and generates a drive to help relieve it, not only in oneself but also in others. This may be something positive, like inspiration from loving parents who demonstrate a commitment to public service. It might be a situation that is painful at first, like a crisis that shatters the foundations of meaning and security, but that leads eventually to positive personal growth. Some people come to this awareness through a gentle inner stirring, a gradual heightening of awareness and empathy. A person may develop a keen realization of suffering and the possibility of transformation that awakens the motivation to help others.

Some of us use religious ideas and metaphors to explain this vocation; some do not. But we expect that this theme of awakening from egotism and defeatism and then feeling called to a path of service and justice may not be uncommon among social workers. This is a spiritual developmental process that puts us in touch with our deepest insights into the meaning and purpose of life. Thus we respond to a calling. In traditional Christian and Judaic terms, a vocation is a stirring of the heart by the divine to go beyond the limits of the little ego and ordinary social conventions in order to follow a more profound way of life. A vocation is the use of one's talents, abilities, and assets in one's life to do the work that is consistent with God's will (Canda, 1990b; Singletary, Harris, Myers, & Scales, 2006).

Social work in its best sense can be considered a spiritual vocation. This does not mean that all social workers follow the beliefs of the Judeo-Christian tradition or that they are religious. Rather, it means that there is an awareness of suffering and the possibility of transformation. It means that there is a motive of compassion to work together with other people to help everyone to overcome obstacles and to achieve aspirations. In addition, it means that spiritually sensitive social workers practice unconditional positive regard for clients and live by hope in the possibilities of resiliency, reconciliation, and realization of social justice. Of course, it is difficult to "walk this talk."

In a qualitative study, 18 social work scholars discussed the values that motivated their work in the profession (Canda, 1990b). The interviewees identified themselves as being influenced by seven spiritual perspectives, which were combined for some people: atheist, Christian, existentialist, Jewish, shamanic, theistic humanist, and Zen Buddhist. Three main motivations were expressed: sense of a mandate to serve; a personal desire to promote social justice; and a quest for personal fulfillment.

Ten respondents said they have a feeling that they are mandated to serve. Some derived this sense of mandate from learned religious or cultural values, such as the Zen Buddhist commitment to help all beings attain enlightenment, Jewish community values for mutual support and social justice, Christian gospel values of love and service, and traditional First Nations Indigenous values of cooperation, sharing, and mutual helping. Some added that this mandate came from a transpersonal or divine source. For example, a Zen practitioner said that compassion and an imperative to help others arises naturally from meditative experiences of one's interconnectedness with other beings. Two Jewish respondents said that they felt mandated to serve out of the awareness that God appointed humanity as custodians of the earth. Four Christians said that they felt a sense of calling from God, sometimes at an early age. One respondent put it this way: "I am impelled not by my own volition, not on making a conscious choice, but that is the way the Lord wants, to use me" (Canda, 1990b, p. 12). Many respondents mentioned that they had a strong personal concern for people who are distressed and oppressed and that this impelled them to action.

All of the respondents said that their experience of personal fulfillment from service motivates them to persevere. Personal satisfactions are derived from meeting religious and cultural expectations for service, from viewing the beneficial changes in clients' lives as a result of service, and also from having a career that provides sustenance for their own families. In the experience of these social work scholars, compassionate service creates a situation of mutual benefit for themselves, their clients, and the larger society.

LeCroy's (2002) interviews with 34 social work practitioners revealed the prevalence of compassion and spirituality in their work. Many found value in connectedness with clients, their communities, and the larger universe. Many felt privileged to be invited into the intimacy of clients' lives, their troubles, and joys. Daily work encounters with suffering, crime, violence, and injustice evoked questions of the meaning and purpose of life. Many were committed to a spiritual lifestyle and felt that social work helped fulfill their spiritual goals and explore moral issues. He says that, "Compassion and caring can be promoted by the social workers who have accepted this as an important value in pursuing their purpose in life" (p. 158). Consider some other examples of social workers' call to service. Interviews with 10 Christian social work students illustrate how this is expressed in a particular faith context (Singletary et al., 2006). Some

students said that their decision to enter social work reflected their desire to follow God's direction for their lives or to follow the example of Jesus who helped
the poor, oppressed, the sick, and the dying. For some, this was a developmental
process while early in the social work major. One student said that the immersion in the program brought up more dreams and passions in the heart and a
sense of "...God moving me and calling me to do it" (p. 194).

Nakashima (1995) became fascinated with death and dying as a teenager
in Japan when her aunt and grandmother died unexpectedly, not long apart.
Buddhist, Confucian, and Shinto beliefs influenced her view that there is a soul
that reincarnates. However, she began to wonder about the purpose of reincar-
nation. Later experiences and study in Japan and the United States showed her
that many older people faced challenges preparing to die and many died feeling
unfulfilled. She saw that peaceful resolution of life issues requires introspection,
a search for meaning, and acceptance of life. This led her to become a hospice
worker and then to research the role of spirituality in positive ways of preparing
for death (2007).

Kreutziger (1995) journeyed in and out and back again to Christianity along
her path of social work. Her journey was shaped by membership in the United
Methodist Church and its concern for the social responsibility message of the
gospels. "This is the call to act on behalf of others in response to God's unre-
lenting love and action in our lives....I had tried for a while to ignore 'my Jesus
thing.' I went into social work because it allowed me 'to save the world' as a
secular missionary during a long period in early adulthood as I rotated among
cycles of agnosticism/atheism/agnosticism" (p. 29). But she said she was not a
good atheist because,

> I couldn't quit going to church. Despite my best efforts to disengage, I still
> loved the feel of the church: the rituals, the symbolism, the music, the peo-
> ple, the fellowship, the shared values, "the going into perfection"....My patients
> forced me to confront my own existential anxieties in order to help them face
> theirs. I had to move beyond my youth and inexperience and wobbly religious
> faith in order to fortify my practice and knowledge for their benefit....Most of
> all, I had to learn to support the courage that comes from staying the course
> minute by minute, day by day, just as the accumulated wisdom of my religion
> teaches me to do (p. 34).

Banerjee's (2005) path into social work was shaped by her childhood growing up as a Hindu in India, especially through her cousin's and grandmother's
teachings about spirituality within everyday life. She said, "Granny taught us to
pray to different Gods and Goddesses—Shiva, Vishnu, Krishna, Rama, Durga,
Lakshmi, Saraswati, Kartika, Ganesha, and Kali, as well as any and every God
or Goddess that may exist!" (p. 49). She learned how the Gods and Goddesses
bestow virtues such as strength, love, kindness, mercy, wisdom, justice, peace,
and prosperity. She learned that religion and spirituality are together integral to
living. Later, she tried to reconcile this with the scientific and materialist view of

Western thinking. After moving to the United States, study of the Bhagavad Gita helped her in an ongoing process of reconciling these different sides through the teaching of *karma yoga* (Sanskrit, action for union) to unify wisdom with action and to focus and dedicate oneself to one's work without egotistic attachment to results. These teachings helped prepare her for social work research into the role of spirituality as a source of strength for women of various religions who deal with poverty in both India and the United States.

Nelson-Becker (Letendre, Nelson-Becker, & Kreider, 2005) described a repeated experience during childhood in which she "felt a warmth that quickly glided through the core of my body, leaving me with an inner peace and a sense of relatedness to something Transcendent" (pp. 12–13). Such experiences and her upbringing and ministry in a Christian faith with a history of persecution, have shaped her life, her sensitivity to diversity, and her approach to teaching social work. She tries to remain open to the presence of Spirit permeating life as she opens her mind to relate with students of varied backgrounds in her classes.

These stories illustrate that the call to service is a call to a continuing spiritual journey of growth. As social workers help clients, we are also being helped. The expression of empathy and compassion makes us stretch ourselves into clients' worlds of suffering and meaning and thereby our own worlds are changed. *To the extent that we remain alert to this continuing call to service as a spiritual journey, we retain a sense of purpose, excitement, and vitality.* This is a very personal and compelling reason to keep the connection between spirituality and social work alive and well within our work as students, practitioners, educators, and researchers. Mother Teresa put this simply and directly: "The fruit of love is service. The fruit of service is peace" (Vardey, 1995, p. xxxviv).

Next, we would like to tell you some stories about our own spiritual journeys into social work. In part, this is to give you additional examples of the routes people may take and the roles of religion and spirituality. Also, we want you to be aware of the spiritual perspectives that shape us, because they also shape this book. You can then make better-informed analyses of how our perspectives aid or limit the inclusive approach to spiritual diversity that we promote. You will see that we have different personal and professional backgrounds. In writing this book we have continued a dialogue that engaged the contrasts, as well as the commonalities, between our spiritual perspectives. We hope that this exemplifies the ideals of respect and nonjudgmentalism that are so critical in spiritually sensitive social work.

A Call to Social Work

I (LF) became a social worker because of my religious upbringing and my personal faith. My Lutheran heritage provided clear messages to guide me. I was put on earth to serve God and humanity and not to waste time about it. My vocation was to do the will of God and no excuses. "And from every one who has been given much shall much be required" (Luke 12:48, New American Standard Bible).

Although my family of origin in northern Minnesota did not have a great deal of material goods, I knew even when I was young that I was privileged simply because of having loving parents with a strong religious faith, along with a large extended family who were concerned about my spiritual, physical, and emotional well-being. I realized that there were many who did not have their childhood needs met. I had been given much so I must return it. But I wondered how.

I saw my family's faith lived out every day unchanging and each Sunday that same faith was emphasized by others. I remember as a little girl hearing my uncles or great-uncles, and long-time family friends present sermons that spoke of heeding the call of God, even if it takes you "to the remotest part of the earth" (Acts 1:8, NASB). Indeed, many of these clergy had heeded the call of God that took them to remote places. A great-uncle and his wife were missionaries in mainland China. My mother's best friend from college was also a missionary teacher in China, and an uncle and his nurse wife were missionaries and health care workers in Madagascar. These clergy friends and relatives wrote often, their letters bearing colorful stamps from around the world. They brought slides of these countries when they were home for visits and told of political upheavals and cultural aspects of the people they served. They provided a rich education regarding human diversity, common human needs, and cross-cultural religious awareness.

As a child, I would sit in the church pew in a little log church that my immigrant Norwegian grandparents helped to build on the Minnesota prairie. I kept wondering when my call from God would come and what it would be. Would I too be called to go to the ends of the earth, learn another language, eat strange food, say goodbye to Mother and Father, and come back to the United States by ship only every 7 years like these clergy? I shivered at the thought!

My call came while I was attending a summer Bible Camp. There was a special session on careers. Social work was defined as a profession that served the poor, people of color who are experiencing prejudice, children having problems in schools, adults having troubled marriages and job loss, and those with physical or mental illnesses. Christ's teaching became clear to me: "Truly I say to you, to the extent that you did it [charity] to one of these brothers of Mine, even to the least of them, you did it to Me" (Matthew 25:40 NASB). I had seen the evidence of compassion in my family home and through the experiences of missionary relatives and friends. At 12 years of age, my call came to become a social worker.

When I attended Augsburg College in Minneapolis, Minnesota, I was overwhelmed by this call and wondered if I could accomplish this task as well as my heart and soul wanted. My family, my church, and my college showed me that the source of power to follow this call was not in myself ("Do not lean on your own understanding," Proverbs 3:5, NASB), but in my faith in God ("I can do all things through Christ who strengthens me," Philippians 4:13). It was at this point that Martin Luther's call to vocation became clear to me (Wingren, 1994). Alternatively, in the words of the present President of Augsburg College,

Paul Pribbenow (2008), "We believe we are called to Serve Our Neighbor" (p. 1). Pribbenow explains that our belief grounds our faith in a "deep and confident Christian and Lutheran faith" (p. 1). The theological concept of vocation or calling is central to how I was educated at Augsburg College, where this concept was articulated repeatedly. The gifts of *faith and call* lead us to serve our neighbor in the city, country, and around the world.

Since my first awareness of my call to compassionate service, I obtained MSW and PhD degrees. I worked in direct practice in school social work, psychiatric and medical social work, and family and marriage counseling. Then I felt a call that brought me to the academic world to teach and conduct research about religion, spirituality, and social work practice, first on the state level, then nationally, and finally internationally. I was also called to serve my neighbor on the policy level. In 1992, I was a University Summer Fellow in the Washington DC office of North Dakota Senator Kent Conrad, where I researched national health care and mental health treatment for potential legislation.

A little over a decade ago, however, this deep sense of compassion was tested. My faith was challenged to further growth as I encountered compassion firsthand as its recipient during a "once-in-two-hundred years" flood that inundated the town of Grand Forks, North Dakota, where I lived at the time. In 1997, swollen by winter snowstorms and April snowmelt, the Red River of the North inundated Grand Forks. The water forced all 50,000 people from their homes. Up to that point in time, no other major city in the history of the United States had been forced by a natural disaster to evacuate its entire population. There was no time for good-byes or for closures with school friends or graduations. We all experienced temporary homelessness, scattering to 50 states and two foreign countries. Everything closed, including the hospital, a vital link for any community.

Safe from the flood in my brother's home, I sat glued to the television thinking that we had seen the worst. Then I saw that the downtown was burning. I watched in horror as building after building burned. I saw my bank building in flames, then my attorney's office; the newspaper headquarters was next. The firefighters could not extinguish the fires because there was no pressure in the fire hydrants, and the fire engines could not get through the flooded streets. How ironic to be in the middle of so much water and not to have water available to put out a fire.

The call to compassion during this flood was answered by people in many different ways. Family and friends offered words of consolation. One of my brothers called and left me this Japanese haiku: "Now that my barn has burned down; I can see the moon more clearly." In other words, when you lose material things, you have a clearer view of what is really important in life. That message was brought home to me by my son Jon's call. He said, "Mom, don't forget you still have your faith, your family, and your friends." His words were comforting. It was also comforting that he had incorporated my value system and was now reminding me of what I had always deemed to be important in life.

Over and over, the people of Grand Forks experienced great compassion from the world. One day as I was cleaning, my doorbell rang, and there stood two of my former graduate social work students whom I had taught about compassion in our classes. They had been hired as outreach social workers who went door to door to every home to inquire about social, psychological, and financial needs. Their visit was comforting and placed me in the new position of receiving their compassion and their services.

A headline in the *Grand Forks Herald* read: "Goodness of God Flows into Grand Forks Churches." Area religious organizations handled flood relief donations exceeding $11 million, which helped people rebuild their lives, their homes, and their places of worship. B'nai Israel Synagogue received support from Jewish congregations in 49 states. Regional and national church bodies made donations. Distribution was directed through an interfaith coalition within Grand Forks. Banding together, this interfaith coalition supported a Billy Graham Crusade and door-to-door volunteers who were available to listen to people's concerns and to help them with their spiritual struggles. Never once did they proselytize. "Receiving so much help has been overwhelming," said many clergy and church members. "It's a wonderful display of God's great goodness to us." They voiced the feelings of all. Although we gladly helped each other—and every neighborhood had stories of kindness and pitching in together—it was humbling to receive from other hands.

The safety deposit box with my property deeds, kept at my bank, was filled with mud from the floodwaters. Even after experts tried to salvage the deeds, they looked like a tattered heap of brittle paper ready to crumble at the least touch. They represented the fragility of material things, and that is the real lesson I learned from this flood. Money, position, and power meant little the night we all evacuated. The only real treasures we have are spiritual ones. The one constant for me was my faith in the abiding presence of God. When I would look at my property deeds in a heap on a chair in my living room, awaiting a new safety deposit box, I would be reminded: "But lay up for yourselves treasures in heaven, where neither moth nor rust destroys" (Matthew 6:20, NASB).

The grace of God gives me hope to endure and to adjust. It gives me compassion to help others. It also provides me the opportunity to receive compassion from others with humility. This flood gave me a deeper understanding of compassion—not just good works to help others but compassion that dignifies the recipient. Since the occurrence of that flood, millions of Americans have been affected by natural disasters as bad as, or worse than, what I experienced. For myself and many others, our individual and collective faith has helped us adjust to the dramatic changes that such events engender.

An Awakening of Compassion

I (EC) was raised within a devout Roman Catholic Czech American family. My parents have attended daily Mass and have been active workers, volunteers, and supporters in their parishes as long as I can remember. In my family, being a Catholic meant a life style and worldview much more than just performing a set of religious obligations or attending church on Sunday. I was raised to put spirituality as the first priority in life and to shape my decisions and relationships accordingly.

My family's spiritual perspective emphasized the importance of discerning a vocation through which I could use my talents for the benefit of others and for the glory of God. My parents modeled an ideal of service through their attentive child raising, by their assistance for the parish, and in care for their own parents as they became ill. Through religious education from my parents and my Catholic elementary school, I also learned to admire the life of Jesus and the saints who gave of themselves selflessly.

I have a vivid memory of an event from the second grade of elementary school that awakened a keen sense of compassion. As a young boy, I sometimes played games with violent content, from imitation war to contact competitive sports to killing bugs for fun. To that point, I had little compunction about these things, except for occasional pangs of guilt or admonitions from my mother.

My second grade teacher, a Catholic nun, had taken a special liking to me and made special efforts to draw me out of my shyness. What she said and did made a strong impression on me. One spring day, the classroom windows were open. Flies were buzzing around the room, providing distraction and entertainment. Some boys were trying to catch or swat the flies. The sister interrupted the class not so much to complain about our misbehavior as to give us a life lesson. She asked us not to harm the flies, because they were her friends. That quite surprised me—that someone could regard these ugly little irritating bugs as friends and serve as their protector. Suddenly I realized that they were living things that merit caring treatment. The sister's friendly pleading woke me up to a sense of compassion that extended out beyond my family and friends to all creatures. The biblical teaching that God made the world and saw it was good suddenly struck home deep in my heart. From that day on, I began to look at things differently.

Much later, when I turned 16 years old, I had another awakening to compassion. By this time, I had begun to explore the philosophical teachings of many religious traditions, hoping they would help me understand the nature of things and the purpose of life more broadly than my Catholic upbringing. I was also quite upset about the violence of the Vietnam War, the injustices exposed by the civil rights movement, and the materialistic consumerism I saw rampant around me. Readings of Western and Eastern mystics guided me to develop a personal meditation practice which helped me to obtain some sense of peace in the midst of this. The writings of Thomas Merton (1961, 1968a, 1968b), who was a Catholic contemplative monk committed to social justice and interreligious dialogue, were especially important to me.

My Catholic high school economics teacher assigned us to write a paper based on some current economic issues. I chose to read a book by the NeoMarxist psychoanalyst, Erich Fromm, *Marx's Concept of Man* (1966). This book contained

Karl Marx's Economic and Philosophical Manuscripts. Considering that Marx was avidly opposed to conventional religions, I was surprised to find a description of communism as an ideal that fit well my sense of Christian love applied to social justice. Marx described the ideal of communism as a society in which all forms of alienation and exploitation between human beings and humans and nature would be overcome. This sounded to me like heaven on earth, or the realization of Christ's beatitudes. Ironically, Marx's words spurred me in a direction that did not fit either the conventional thinking of Marxists or capitalists.

One evening, I sat in meditation on my bed, facing a portrait of the Sacred Heart of Jesus. In this picture, Jesus is portrayed with heart exposed, aflame with compassion. I posed the question to myself, "What would it be like for every form of alienation and exploitation to be transcended?" Suddenly my mind opened to a sense of profound communion with the universe in which all separations disappeared. There was a sense of all pervasive love.

When I pondered this experience soon afterward, it was clear to me that my life and cultural conditioning were far from this ideal. I examined the problems, prejudices, and obstacles in my thinking, feelings, and relationships in order to bring myself more into congruence with this sense of union with others. Since society is characterized by many forms of separation, alienation, and suffering, I felt that I should begin to work toward actualizing this unity through social service. But I did not have any practical guidance about how to do this. I was a young person, confused in many ways, groping toward a light.

This sense of a call to service prompted me to begin volunteer work during summer vacations. For the last two summers of high school, I assisted children with severe developmental disabilities in a nearby residential hospital and war veterans at a Veterans Administration psychiatric facility. I was also active in socially concerned student activism at my high school.

In college at Kent State University in Ohio, I majored in cultural anthropology, especially anthropology of religions, in order to explore how people in various cultures have come to understand the nature of reality and the meaning of life. When I was a senior, an anthropology professor who specialized in Korean culture and religion connected me with a graduate exchange study program at Sungkyunkwan University in Seoul, so that I could study East Asian philosophy and religion there immediately after graduation. My Korean teachers exposed me to the 2500-year long Confucian tradition that links scholarly study with political action and social administration. I also studied about Buddhism and shamanism. After 15 months, I returned to the United States to complete a Master's degree in religious studies focusing on East Asian religions at the University of Denver.

Throughout these studies, I saw a common theme among religious traditions East and West. All identified suffering as a fundamental problematic feature of human existence and all recommended remedies for this problem, that is, some form of helping, healing, salvation, or enlightenment. But it struck me as odd that in the academic study of religion, few scholars went beyond description and analysis of religious phenomena to actually apply these various approaches to helping in direct service.

After a year of discernment, I realized that the study of religions was not sufficient to meet my calling to a life of service. For this reason, I changed fields to study social work. Throughout my MSW and Ph.D. programs at The Ohio State University, and my direct practice, I brought the cross-cultural study of religion and spirituality into social work.

Social work has been a wonderful way for me to link my spiritual call to service with a profession and tradition of service-oriented scholarship. But I found that many other social workers were struggling with a similar desire to link their spiritual vision into professional helping and that there was little guidance in education for how to do so. Once I realized that, I found a way I could be of service to the profession itself. As a professor at the University of Iowa (1986–1989) and the University of Kansas (1989–present), I dedicated my scholarly research, teaching, and community service to developing a spiritually sensitive approach to social work that would be inclusive and respectful of diverse spiritual perspectives. It has been extremely satisfying to find many other kindred souls around the world and to work together from our various spiritual and professional views on this common goal.

Symbols of Compassion in Religious Traditions

In this section, we begin to examine particular religious traditions through their symbols of compassion. This is not to say that people from these traditions always behave in a compassionate manner, as that would be very unrealistic; but it is to say that religious traditions identify ideals for compassion that are offered to their adherents. Here, we only touch on these symbols from three widely influential religious perspectives; there is much more depth and detail and variation in these symbols and how they are used. We explore more information about specific religious and nonsectarian forms of spiritually-based service in Part II.

We hope that these religious symbols of compassion will stir readers' recollections and meditations on symbols and ideals of compassion that motivate and inspire you. Consider how you respond to each of these symbols. If you feel a sense of comfort and resonance, consider why. What other symbols are important to you? Reflect also on the extent to which you keep symbols vital to inspire and sustain your practice. If you feel discomfort or unfamiliarity, also consider why. This kind of reaction suggests opportunities for you to explore greater understanding by connecting with people from these religious perspectives. By working through feelings of discomfort and by addressing gaps in our knowledge, we can deepen our capacity to empathize with people for whom these symbols are important.

We present symbols from contrasting religious perspectives: Buddhist, Christian, and shamanistic. Buddhism, from Asian origins, can be considered nontheistic in that it does not maintain belief in God in the sense of a personal supreme being; but neither is it concerned to deny it. Christianity, of Middle Eastern origins, is a monotheistic religion that shares with Judaism and Islam belief in a personal supreme being and certain scriptures (i.e. the Pentateuch). Shamanism is the name for a wide range of animistically oriented religious systems of spirit-guided healing found throughout the world, especially in many Indigenous cultures. The word "shaman" was adapted from the Tungus language of North Central Asia and generalized cross-culturally by anthropologists and scholars of religion (Eliade, 1964). These three types of religious traditions share ideals of compassion, but each has a different nuance. By reflecting on the differences and commonalities, we can expand our own understanding of compassion.

Kuan Yin, The Bodhisattva of Compassion

Mahayana Buddhism is the most common form of Buddhism found in East Asia (especially China, Korea, Japan, and Vietnam). One of the most widely known schools of Mahayana in the West is Zen (aka *chan*, Chinese or *seon*, Korean; see de Bary, 1969; Canda, 2001; Sheng-Yen & Stevenson, 2001). The term Mahayana means literally, Great Vehicle, meaning it is a vehicle large enough to move all beings toward enlightenment. In Mahayana, many Zen practitioners take a vow of great compassion: "Sentient beings are numberless; I vow to save them all." This vow encompasses a commitment to serve all beings, human and nonhuman.

Bodhisattvas have deeply awakened to their true nature, but postpone entering Nirvana so that they can help others until all beings are enlightened. Thus, devotees may regard them as divine beings and appeal to them for help in special circumstances of need, such as a time of death or crisis. In the Zen context, Bodhisattvas can be considered symbolic expressions of the Buddha-nature of virtue and enlightenment inherent within each person (Sheng-Yen & Stevenson, 2001; Venerable Chong Mu, personal communication, Seoul, Korea). Reflection on the ideal and symbol of a Bodhisattva should inspire a person to realize that quality within himself or herself and to express it in action (Cheng Yen, 1999).

One of the most popular Bodhisattvas is Kuan Yin, also named *Kuan Shi Yin* (Chinese; *Gwanseum*, in Korean), the Bodhisattva of Compassion (Blofeld, 1988; Canda, 1995a). The name of this Bodhisattva means literally, "to perceive the sound of the world." The Korean Zen Master, Seung Sahn (personal communication), said that this represents the ideal of having a mind and heart clear and open to perceive the cries of all suffering beings so that we can respond with help. Kuan Yin is an East Asian adaptation of an earlier Indian figure named Avalokitesvara who is portrayed with male gender (Schumacher & Woerner, 1994). Since at least the 10th century, Kuan Yin has been portrayed variously as male, female, or androgynous. In essence, the Bodhisattva is beyond gender distinctions or any conceptions, but may manifest in various forms as needed to help people.

Sometimes Kuan Yin is depicted as having a thousand eyes and hands. This symbolizes a compassionate mind that perceives all suffering and is able to reach out in all directions with help. Kuan Yin is also sometimes shown with 12 heads depicting various aspects of compassion. Often there are 11 faces on a crown above the main face of the Bodhisattva (Figure 2.2). According to one explanation, three faces symbolize praise for people of good heart (Canda, 1995a). Three faces represent rightful anger toward those who do harm. Three faces smile with encouragement and praise for people who do good. One face in the middle indicates nonjudgmental acceptance of all kinds of people. And one face (often a standing figure on the forehead or crown of the head) represents the Buddha of Infinite Light or unlimited consciousness, which is the culmination of spiritual development. These 11 faces are above the main face of Kuan Yin, which represents the face of wisdom beyond any of the other conditional compassionate reactions. The ideal here is that compassion may be expressed in many different ways and circumstances, but the direction should always be to help others in a nonjudgmental way. In fact, Kuan Yin is sometimes used to illustrate the ideal of social work in Korean Buddhist settings (Canda, Shin, & Canda, 1993).

Figure 2.2.   Eleven headed Kuan Yin Bodhisattva, Korea.

The Passion of Jesus

The passion of Jesus is one of the most common devotional themes in Christian theology and art. Christians regard Jesus Christ as God incarnate, joining the fullness of divinity with a complete experience of human suffering and death (Nielsen, Hein, Reynolds, & Miller, 1993; Smith, 1995). In the context of the Trinitarian doctrine, Jesus' incarnation represents the boundless love of God for human beings, since God sent his only son, knowing that Jesus would be crucified as an atonement for the sins of humanity. The conjunction of the glory of God with the abject suffering of human beings is itself a main theme of the passion of Jesus.

Various Christian traditions of iconography depict the passion of Jesus in many ways (Gieben, 1980; van Os, 1994; Weitzmann, 1978). In portrayals of the crucifixion, Jesus is often shown with explicit marks of pain and torture, such as starvation exposed ribs, nails in hands and feet, and blood and water flowing from the sword wound in his side. The divinity of Jesus is also portrayed, such as God looking on or weeping angels hovering above. Often the cross is shown with no figure at all, or with a resplendent Jesus figure, in order to emphasize the resurrection of Christ. When Christians contemplate these symbols of the suffering Jesus, they may immerse themselves vicariously in his pain in order to work through to a catharsis in the mystery of Jesus' resurrection from the dead. During the season of Lent and Easter, Christian communities follow the various stages of Jesus' passion, death, and resurrection. This is both a commemoration of past events and a process linking individuals' and communities' experiences of suffering and mortality into the redemptive model, so that hope and healing may be experienced. This refreshes Christians' understanding of the rite of communion (or Eucharist), which commemorates the Passover meal that Jesus shared with his disciples shortly before his crucifixion. In the rite of communion, the community shares bread and often wine, representing the body and blood of Jesus.

Jesus' suffering, death, and resurrection were the culmination of many gospel stories about his compassion for people. Jesus defied social conventions to care for the sick, the poor, and disrespected members of society, such as tax collectors and prostitutes. Jesus' compassion for the poor and oppressed has been the primary model for Christian-based medical and social services. A popular Catholic depiction of Jesus' compassion is the Sacred Heart (Figure 2.3) as mentioned in my (EC) story of a call to service.

The Shaman as Wounded/Healed Healer

Shamanism is not the name of a particular religion, as Buddhism or Christianity. Rather, *shamanism* is a name made up by anthropologists and religious studies scholars for a set of religiously based themes and practices that are found in many distinct cultures on all continents and in Oceania (Bowie, 2006; Canda, 1983;

Figure 2.3. Sacred Heart of Jesus, Street Mural, Chicago.

Walsh, 1990). Shamanism is connected to a worldview that honors connectedness between humans, nature, and the spiritual qualities within and around us (Figure 2.4). This will be explained further in Part II. For now, our focus is the shaman, a person who learns culturally prescribed ways of communicating with spiritual beings and forces in order to heal people of afflictions, to overcome crises, and to maintain or restore personal, social, and cosmic harmony. A shaman uses intensified, ecstatic states of consciousness in order to communicate with these spiritual forces and to engage in healing with their guidance (Eliade, 1964).

In many cultures, a person becomes a shaman through a process of initiation in which the initiate is symbolically wounded, dismembered, sickened, or killed by envisioned spirits so that he or she can be reconstructed beyond the ordinary limits of social roles and conventions as a healer (Halifax, 1982). A period of spontaneous sacred calling and disruption is followed by rituals of transformative death and rebirth, as well as training by master shamans, in order to help the initiate learn how to use trance and to communicate with spirits in a culturally prescribed and disciplined manner. In some cultures, people who eventually become shamans have often gone through severe experiences of illness, oppression, or mistreatment that fracture their psychosocial status quo and open them up to spirit influences. Thus, the shaman is able to use the learning from his or her own experiences of crisis and resolution as a pattern for the process of helping other people.

The Korean myth of Princess Pari illustrates this pattern (Canda, 1982, 1995a). In a version of the Seoul area, the princess was born as the seventh daughter in a royal family long ago. Given the patriarchal context, the king was angry

Figure 2.4. Untitled, by Orville Milk, Lakota, gift from the artist.

that he had not yet had a son to inherit the throne, so he locked the princess in a box and cast her out to sea. Miraculously, she was discovered by a loving couple who adopted her. As a young woman, she learned of her true identity. But her royal parents were gravely ill. Despite their mistreatment of her, she decided to seek a magic cure for them which could only be found in the Western Paradise by a heroic journey through mountains full of dangerous monsters. With the help of spirit beings, she found the cure and returned, only to find her parents dead. Nonetheless, the medicine restored them to life. In the process, Princess Pari's suffering was resolved through reconciliation with her parents and fulfillment of the role of healer.

This theme of the wounded/healed healer may inspire potential shamans as well as general members of the community. For example, the sweat lodge purification ritual is one of the most widely shared spiritual practices among First Nations peoples of North America (Lyon, 1996; Schiff & Pelech, 2007). It is used to help people clarify and purify themselves, often in preparation for other ceremonies, to gain insight into one's life purpose and mission, or to gain wisdom and strength to deal with personal or community crises. The sweat lodge is usually constructed of saplings bowed over and tied to form a dome shaped support structure. The frame is covered with hides or blankets so that the inside is completely dark, even during daylight. This lodge is the sacred womb of the earth to which people return to be renewed and reborn. Red-hot rocks are brought from a sacred fire and placed in a pit in the middle of the lodge. Water and sometimes healing herbs are placed on the rocks to release their hot healing steam. The structure of the lodge and the sacred materials used in the ritual all reflect a prayerful recognition of the participants' connection with all things, and an invocation of healing and help from the spirit powers of earth and sky.

These stones share their hot purifying energy as people pray and sing for the well-being of themselves, loved ones, the community, and all things. The hot steam may cause some suffering, but when the suffering is offered to help others, it becomes a sacrifice of compassion that also heals oneself. Literally, from the Latin roots, the word *sacrifice* means "to make sacred."

Black Elk, who was a Lakota shaman and Catholic catechist, shared this prayer from a sweat lodge (Brown, 1971, p. 40). "O Wakan-Tanka, Grandfather, above all, it is thy will that we are doing here. Through that Power which comes from the place where the giant Waziah lives, we are now making ourselves as pure and as white as new snow. We know that we are now in darkness, but soon the Light will come. When we leave this lodge may we leave behind all impure thoughts and all ignorance. May we be as children newly born! May we live again, O Wakan-Tanka!" In the Lakota tradition, when people enter or leave the lodge, they say "All my relatives." This is a prayer to honor all the beings and powers that support us and to share the benefit of the ritual for all.

A Common Heart of Compassion

The religious views implied in these symbols might seem to be vastly different, even irreconcilable. Certainly, in the understanding of many adherents, this would be the case. But there is also a deep commonality. As social workers striving to develop a moral and ethical framework that honors diversity while finding common ground, we should consider whether there might be a common heart of compassion underlying the differences. This is not something that can be discerned scientifically, but it is a philosophical and moral question about which we need to take a clear position as a basis for formulating general ethical principles for spiritually sensitive social work. In order to do this, it is helpful to return to the study of social work scholars' diverse spiritual perspectives (Canda, 1990c).

Although there were significant contrasts in the content of beliefs among the participants, there was a surprising commonality of core values. Participants from atheist, humanist, Christian, Buddhist, existentialist, Jewish, and shamanistic perspectives agreed that each human being has inherent dignity and worth and deserves unconditional positive regard. They agreed that social workers should strive to complement both individual well-being and social justice. They also indicated that human beings should extend care and responsibility to the nonhuman world, because of our interdependence with it, or because it is seen as an expression of God's creativity, or because it is understood that all things are alive with their own personality and sacred power. All agreed that people should cultivate a moral perspective that goes beyond egotism, ethnocentrism, and human exploitation of the environment. Respondents of all perspectives felt a basic congruence between professional values and their personal values, but also felt points of tension where professional ideals of justice and service to the poor and oppressed seemed to be eroding.

This commonality of core values among people of diverse spiritual perspectives is probably related to the fact that they were all American social workers. It suggests that when social workers of diverse spiritual backgrounds enter into dialogue and share their deepest commitments and ideals, it may be possible to find our common heart of compassion. This humane heartedness can become a point of mutual respect and cooperation as we dialogue and collaborate, even when dealing with very different and conflicting details of spiritual beliefs, values, and practices. This common humane heartedness can be found by looking deeply into each of our own hearts and by communicating deeply with each other heart to heart. Huston Smith (1991) has extensively studied the similarities and differences among the world's major wisdom traditions. He concludes that we must all listen to each others' understandings of truth, religious and secular, because we live in an interconnected global community.

> Those who listen work for peace, a peace not built on ecclesiastical or political hegemonies but on understanding and mutual concern. For understanding, at least in realms as inherently noble as the great faiths of humankind, brings respect; and respect prepares the way for a higher power, love—the only power that can quench the flames of fear, suspicion, and prejudice, and provide the means by which the people of this small but precious Earth can become one to one another...So we must listen to understand, but we must also listen to put into play the compassion that the wisdom traditions all enjoin..." (p. 390).

Ethical Principles for Spiritually Sensitive Social Work

By intention, this chapter has not proceeded in a linear analytical way. We introduced themes, stories, and symbols from various personal, professional, and religious perspectives associated with compassion and the call to service. Now, drawing on these moral and value reflections, we would like to state a set of broad ethical principles for spiritually sensitive social work. These build on the principles within the NASW Code of Ethics and the IFSW/IASSW Statement of Principles. We believe that they are consistent with the broad mission, values, and ethical principles of the social work profession. However, these principles are tailored to focus on spirituality.

We intend our statement of ethical principles to serve two purposes: (1) to clarify the values and ethical principles that guide us in our particular version of spiritually sensitive practice and (2) to raise questions and controversies that stimulate readers to engage in your own formulation of ethical principles. Although the principles are stated as prescriptions, they are, of course, not binding on anyone. They are meant to be encouragements and challenges for each of us to decide whether these are helpful for various professional settings and cultural and national contexts. In agreement with Kreitzer (2006) and Yip (2004), we hope that our principles incorporate appreciation for responsibility and rights, social stability and change, and empowerment and interrelationship through an attitude of dynamic exchange between the views of people with diverse spiritual perspectives and social–political locations. We realize that any set of ethical principles reflect limitations based in the culture, spiritual beliefs, and political context of the framers. In Part III, we will consider more detailed ethical guidelines with regard to the application of spiritually or religiously based ideas and helping activities in social work. The values and ethical principles stated here shape the contents and perspective of the rest of this book.

We describe them in relation to the six ethical principles set forth in the current NASW Code of Ethics (1999, pp. 5–6). In the Code of Ethics, the six core values are matched with an explanatory ethical principle and a brief text that elaborates on the principle. In our presentation, we quote the core value and ethical principle from the Code and then add our own elaboration that highlights how this principle could be expressed in the context of spiritually sensitive social work practice. We also take into account the IFSW/IASSW principles on human rights and dignity, social justice, and professional conduct as well as challenges to universal standards for social work (e.g. Keitzer, 2006; Yip, 2004). *Note that original wording from the NASW Code will be italicized.*

Actually, the real guide for day to day behavior is a social worker's personal code of ethics based on her or his core values. These values are determined through experience and personal reflection as to which teachings and values one wishes to incorporate into one's own worldview and to translate into one's behavior. Realistically, people do not accord a professional standardized code of ethics authority over their moral and ethical decisions unless it is incorporated into the personal code.

My students and I (LF) often get into discussions about the importance of having a personal code of ethics and that this is necessary before one can adopt a professional code of ethics. We discuss the influences on a personal code of ethics, such as teachings about right and wrong given by parents, clergy, teachers and peers; professional standards such as the NASW Code of Ethics; as well as one's own moral standards developed through our life experiences. Students must then arrive at decisions about which of these teachings and experiences they truly believe and wish to incorporate into their own personal code of ethics and conduct. This way, students can make well-informed decisions about whether they can assent to the professional code of ethics. If a student decides that she or he cannot assent to the professional code, then a serious question arises as to whether one should be a professional social worker or pursue another type of helping vocation. The professional code is at a very general level. The details of a personal code integrate professional values and apply it to the specifics of day to day life.

Value: Service

Ethical Principle: *Social workers' primary goal is to help people in need and to address social problems.*

Spiritually sensitive social workers rise above personal interests to serve and benefit others. They recognize that serving others is itself a spiritual path that promotes the well-being of both worker and client. Spiritually sensitive social workers apply knowledge, values, and skills to help people attain their goals by attending to material, biological, psychological, relational, and spiritual needs, according to the priorities and aspirations of clients. They support clients to utilize their personal strengths and environmental resources in a socially and ecologically responsible manner. They work with individuals, families, groups, communities, and the wider world to promote peace and justice.

Spiritually sensitive social workers support people who wish to clarify their understanding of life purpose, ultimate concerns, and the nature of reality. When clients identify religious or nonreligious forms of spiritual support, such as religious communities or sacred beings, related beliefs and practices are respected by the worker and included in the approach to helping as relevant to clients' own preferences. As relevant to the client, religious and nonreligious spiritual systems are considered for their helpful and harmful impacts. When harm is identified, clients are assisted to change the quality of their relationship with them in a respectful manner.

Spiritually sensitive social workers should strive to make services accessible, affordable, and relevant. They are encouraged to volunteer time with no expectation of remuneration. They continually reexamine how the conduct of their professional roles is congruent with the virtue of compassion and their deepest sense of calling to a life of service.

Value: Social Justice

Ethical Principle: *Social workers challenge social injustice.*

Spiritually sensitive social workers pursue positive social change and social justice, particularly with and on behalf of vulnerable and oppressed individuals and groups of people, including targets of negative spiritual discrimination. Their social change activities also address individuals and groups who are motivated by spiritual beliefs to perpetuate harm, such as intrafamilial abuse or neglect, negative discrimination against individuals and groups, or personal and collective violence. They promote empowerment in relation to all aspects of human diversity, including by encouraging clients' own proactivity and by working to eliminate environmental barriers and harmful social policies while expanding availability of and access to resources. They do not place clients in harm or engage in activities designed to undermine the integrity of families, communities, or nations.

Spiritually sensitive social workers recognize that social justice and human well-being are closely interrelated with the well-being of nonhuman beings and the total planetary ecology. Therefore, they strive to overcome environmental racism, international social injustice, war between cultures and nations, and human activities that are destructive to local and planet-wide ecological systems. This concern extends to any place humans traverse, on this Earth or beyond.

Value: Dignity and Worth of the Person

Ethical Principle: *Social workers respect the inherent dignity and worth of the person.*

Spiritually sensitive social workers treat everyone with compassion and respect, mindful of individual and cultural differences, including religious and spiritual diversity. Spiritually sensitive social workers address clients as whole persons, applying professional roles, rules, and assessment labels in a flexible and collaborative way that is responsive to the values of the client and his or her community. They also strive to make respectful connections across differences and to find common ground for cooperation. They honor the common and universal human needs for a sense of meaning, purpose, morality, and fulfilling relationships.

Spiritually sensitive social workers promote individuals', cultures', and nations' self-determination in the context of social and global responsibility. Spiritually sensitive social workers enhance clients' capacity and opportunity to live harmoniously and to change and grow, including through crises and experiences of spiritual transformation.

Spiritually sensitive social workers are responsible to both clients and the broader society and world. They seek to resolve conflicts between clients' and others' interests in a socially responsible peaceful manner consistent with the values of the profession. They do not assist inhumane practices, such as torture, terrorism, or genocide.

Value: Importance of Human Relationships

Ethical Principle: *Social workers recognize the central importance of human relationships.*

Spiritually sensitive social workers understand that healthy relationships between and among people and other beings are important for growth. Social workers engage people as partners in the helping process, including collaboration with religious and nonreligious spiritual support systems as relevant to clients. Spiritually sensitive social workers seek to strengthen relationships among people and other beings in order to promote, restore, maintain, and enhance the well-being of individuals, families, social groups, organizations, communities, the global community, and all the ecosystems in which these are embedded. They identify and respect clients' various ways of construing social relations, such as individuality, family centered identity, or communality.

Although the primary focus of social work is on humans, spiritually sensitive social workers recognize human interdependency with all beings and ecosystems. The natural world and all the beings within it are granted respect for their intrinsic worth and not just for utilitarian purposes. Spiritually sensitive social workers understand that many people believe in and claim to experience relationship with sacred, supernatural, or transcendent aspects of reality. Therefore, when such beliefs and experiences are important to clients, spiritually sensitive social workers explore how clients' relationships with these spiritual aspects may influence their sense of well-being and the development of fulfilling relationships.

Value: Integrity

Ethical Principle: *Social workers behave in a trustworthy manner.*

Spiritually sensitive social workers remain aware of the profession's values and ethics and practice in a manner consistent with them. They promote ethical and spiritually sensitive practices and policies in the human service organizations with which they are affiliated.

Spiritually sensitive social workers are honest about the moral, professional, religious, theoretical, ideological, political, cultural, and other assumptions of themselves and their organizations that are germane to the helping process. Whenever necessary, they provide this information to clients in a way that encourages informed consent and freedom of choice for the client to decide whether to maintain a professional relationship with the worker or the organization with which the worker is affiliated. Professional self-disclosure is done for the benefit of clients, rather than for egocentric, judgmental, or discriminatory reasons.

Value: Competence

Ethical Principle: *Social workers practice within their areas of competence and develop and enhance their professional expertise.*

Spiritually sensitive social workers continually strive to increase their professional wisdom, knowledge, and skills for effective practice. Especially in regard to explicit use of religious or nonreligious spiritual beliefs, symbols, rituals, therapeutic practices, or community support systems, spiritually sensitive social workers obtain relevant knowledge and skills. Social work practice across different spiritual traditions, communities, and cultures is performed with respect for the values and preferences of clients and relevant members of those groups. Spiritually sensitive social workers learn how to cooperate and collaborate with community-based spiritual support systems, helpers, and healers in a culturally competent manner.

Spiritually sensitive social workers should aspire to contribute to the knowledge base of the profession, especially in relation to innovations in spiritually sensitive social work practice, theory, policy, research, and education.

Conclusion

In this chapter, we reviewed core values in the history of the profession and in diverse spiritual perspectives of social workers. We considered common themes and various symbolic expressions of compassion and the call to service. Finally, we offered a framework of values and ethical principles for spiritually sensitive practice by elaborating upon the NASW Code of Ethics and IFSW/IASSW Statement of Principles. These value themes and ethical principles will pervade the remainder of the book.

EXERCISES

2.1. What Does Compassion Mean to You?

During the discussion of the virtue of compassion in social work history, some rival views were discussed. For example, compassion as unconditional love and care was contrasted with moralistic judgmentalism and condescending pity. Compassion as a commitment to social justice was contrasted with individual-istic gratification. Compassion as an altruistic and generous way of service was contrasted with professional preoccupation with prestige, profit, and personal advantage. Consider how these different concepts of compassion play out in your personal and professional life. What kind of value conflicts and dilemmas occur when different motives for service come into conflict? Clarify what is your own understanding of compassion and how this is reflected in your professional work.

2.2. Writing a Vocational Autobiography

Return to the discussion of social work as a vocation, including the personal accounts of how social work scholars and practitioners, including us, understand the call to service. What is your reaction to these stories? Which can you iden-tify with? Which are incongruent with your sense of vocation? What does your reaction tell you about your own core values, motives, and developmental expe-riences that guide you in the social work profession?

Whether you are a student, a seasoned practitioner, an agency administra-tor, an educator, researcher, or policy analyst, think back to when this motive to serve originated. What happened to you and within you that woke you up to this vocation? Were there any inspiring figures in your life? Were there any religious or moral teachings that influenced you? Did you have any experiences of struggle and resolution that pointed you in this direction? In case you have lost the original fresh sense of vocation, take this opportunity to recall it, to rest in it, and to restore it. By returning to our original inspiration, we are not only recalling, but we are being recalled. This gives us an opportunity to answer once again, perhaps by restoring an earlier sense of vitality, or by appreciating where we are now, or even by finding new ways to live according to our deepest life aspirations.

Now you are prepared to write an autobiography of your call to service. Organize your insights according to a time line, dividing the phases of your life in whatever way makes sense for you—for example early childhood, school years, graduate education, beginning of professional practice, significant personal transitions or crises, your current situation. Tell stories to friends about important events and people. Discuss the key themes that run through your professional development. Consider how your present situation represents growth, stasis, or loss of original inspiration. Then write an essay that recounts this development.

2.3. Symbols of Compassion

Take out three sheets of paper. Label one sheet "Early Childhood"; one sheet "Now"; and one sheet "My Ideal for the Future." On each sheet, use colorful markers or other decorations to draw or depict a representation of what compassion means to you. First think back to your earliest childhood memories of compassionate people or symbols of compassion from your cultural or religious heritage. Create a picture that represents your feelings, thoughts, or symbols about this. Next, do the same for your current understanding of compassion as you express it in our personal and professional lives. Then imagine your ideal of compassion as you would like to achieve it in the future. Finally, compare the three pictures and reflect on the changes and opportunities for further growth that they suggest. As an alternative to making pictures, write down key words or phrases that represent your symbols of compassion at each stage of life.

2.4. A Common Heart of Compassion

Think of occasions in which you were involved with friendships or professional relationships that bridged significant cultural or religious differences. What qualities in yourself and the other person made this connection possible? If you discovered a sense of common purpose and common humanity together with the differences, explain what that involved. Consider how these qualities can be applied within social work practice to enhance empathy, respect, and cooperation with clients who come from spiritual backgrounds very different from your own. Write an essay based on these insights.

2.5. Ethical Principles for Spiritually Sensitive Social Work: Personal Fit

Statements of core values and ethical principles are necessarily very broad and leave much room for interpretation. Each professional needs to consider the extent to which they feel fit with these values and principles.

First, review each ethical principle that we presented. Consider your agreement or disagreement with each principle and explain why you have this reaction.

Consider whether you believe our principles are consistent with the social work Code of Ethics in your country or the IFSW/IASSW Principles. Consider also how they fit with your personal code.

Next, reflect on the social work Code of Ethics in your country or the IFSW/ IASSW Principles. Consider areas of agreement or disagreement. How do these agreements or disagreements affect your practice as a social worker? If you feel a basic incompatibility with the relevant Code, consider whether it makes sense for you to continue to identify as a social worker, to change to another helping profession, or to advocate for changes or clarifications in the Code of Ethics.

3

The Meaning of Spirituality

The Tao that can be told is not the eternal Tao.

Tao te Ching, Daoism
(trans. Feng & English, 1972)

In Chinese Daoism, the term *Tao* (currently often spelled, *Dao*) means "way of life" or the natural flow of the universe. Daoist philosophy emphasizes that there is something mysterious about the Tao that cannot be captured in words. The nameless Tao gives rise to all things, but it cannot be reduced to them. Spirituality also has an irreducible dynamic and holistic quality. It connects us with conceptions and experiences of profound, transcendent, sacred, or ulti-mate qualities. Its deepest meaning cannot be expressed, but its expressions and names are numerous. In this chapter, we provide definitions of spirituality and related terms, but we also recognize its mysterious quality.

Contemporary social work scholars usually distinguish between spirituality and religion as related but distinct concepts (Canda, 2008a). Here is a restatement of our preliminary definitions from Chapter 1. *Spirituality* refers to a universal and fundamental human quality involving the search for a sense of meaning, purpose, morality, well-being, and profundity in relationships with ourselves, others, and ultimate reality, however understood. In this sense, spirituality may express through religious forms or it may be independent of them. *Religion* is an institutionalized (i.e. systematic) pattern of values, beliefs, symbols, behaviors, and experiences that are oriented toward spiritual concerns, shared by a com-munity, and transmitted over time in traditions. Notice that spirituality (like emotionality or physicality) is a type of word that connotes a process and way of being.

In order to develop a framework for spiritually sensitive social work that respects and appreciates diverse expressions, we need to refine and amplify these definitions. Sometimes disputes between colleagues or between social workers and clients result from lack of clear definitions and unspoken but contradictory assumptions about the nature of religion and spirituality. In order to communicate clearly among helping professionals and others about spirituality, we need to form clear explicit definitions. In order to conduct research about the impacts of religion and spirituality on human behavior, we need to apply clearly defined concepts in a consistent manner. In order for practitioners to do assessments of clients' spiritual development, strengths and challenges, we need to explain the key concepts underlying our standards for assessment. Researchers sometimes need to employ even more tightly defined terms.

This chapter identifies difficulties inherent in trying to define spirituality and religion; it presents our approach to meet the challenge. It reviews the current definitions of spirituality and related terms in social work and allied fields and the common themes among them. By integrating these insights, we develop formal definitions of spirituality and related terms, and amplify the meaning of spirituality through two conceptual models. For readers who wish to be familiar with the interdisciplinary background and resources that lead to our definitions, the entire chapter is important. For those who wish to focus on final definitions and conceptual models, you may skip to the last major section of the chapter on Definitions and Models Related to Spirituality.

The Challenges of Defining Spirituality

A definition of spirituality that will be acceptable for the common base of the profession needs to be inclusive of diverse religious and nonreligious expressions. This poses two challenging dichotomies involved in disagreements around this topic: the particular versus the universal and the expressible versus the inexpressible.

Particular versus Universal

There are three strategies for defining spirituality. One is to focus on spirituality in particular contexts, times, places, persons, and cultures. This means defining spirituality (or using the term at all) only in situation-specific ways. This is sometimes referred to as an *emic* approach, which means using the insider's or believer's perspective (Bowie, 2006). It emphasizes contextual understanding, or in extreme cases, relativism, as discussed in Chapter 1. The advantage of this approach is avoiding concepts and assumptions that are irrelevant or inappropriate for clients and particular communities. One can develop rich detailed descriptions and accounts of particular beliefs, experiences, and patterns from the ground up. As context-specific accounts from many different people and communities are collected or brought into dialogue, people can learn about each other on their own terms. This is consistent with the movement to indigenize or localize social work, that is, to develop approaches to social work by, with, and for particular groups, cultures, and nations (Gray & Fook, 2004).

People who support the emic approach are highly suspicious of general definitions or theories of religion and spirituality because they run the risk of oversimplification, stereotypes, and even imperialistic impositions of spiritual assumptions and agendas. In the postmodern world of tremendous cultural and spiritual diversity, competing value systems, and calls for the empowerment of disenfranchised individuals and groups, this emic approach is very appealing (Griffin, 1988; Scherer, 2006). For example, in clinical practice, the client's beliefs, behaviors, values, symbols, and rituals should be paramount rather than any preconceptions on the part of the practitioner. In community empowerment work, social workers should be members or allies of the community and should build upon local spiritual perspectives and priorities in collaboration with all its constituencies, under advice from spiritual elders, mentors, and leaders.

In contrast, the *etic* approach utilizes general concepts and theories that are thought to be applicable across various cultures and situations. We can use such general theories and concepts to describe, compare, and analyze the variety of spiritual perspectives and common human needs and goals. They provide a shared language for discussion among people coming from a variety of spiritual perspectives. For example, if an atheistic social worker is assisting a charismatic Christian client, it would be useful to have a general framework for discussing spiritual matters that can bridge the differences and find common ground.

Some etic approaches are universalistic, that is, they claim that there is a fundamental level of reality to which all religions and spiritual perspectives point, such as a Supreme Being or Ultimate Truth, even if some believers don't recognize that (Paden, 2003). This view is suspicious of emic approaches, because they may be ethnocentric or idiosyncratic barriers to universal human understanding and cooperation. Some see the search for commonality as a balm for the postmodern situation of value relativism, moral confusion, and interreligious conflict (Cave, 1993; Rennie, 1996). In extreme cases, the etic approach becomes absolutism, as discussed in Chapter 1. Absolutism is prone toward chauvinism, imperialism, and proselytism.

Our strategy in this book is a third option that includes the insights and transcends the limitations of emic and etic approaches. We appreciate diversity by remaining faithful to particular spiritual experiences and traditions and by seeking common ground for understanding and communication. For this, we coin the term, *transperspectival approach*. In other words, we bring various particular (emic) perspectives into interaction and dialogue with each other to affirm both the particular and the shared aspects of human experience. Claims of universal truth or panhuman aspects of spirituality (given by others or ourselves) are themselves recognized as particular spiritual claims. Theories of human behavior and practice models (etic approaches) can help us to compare spiritual perspectives and understand their impacts on clients. Yet they are also scrutinized for their limitations and for their relevance (or lack thereof) to particular clients and communities.

We advocate for continuing self-reflection and dialogue between helping professionals, consumers, and community members of many spiritual perspectives, so that we can move toward continuously greater mutual understanding and cooperation. The social worker needs to have a wide mind and repertoire of knowledge and skills in order to understand and mediate between multiple spiritual perspectives without being stuck within any of them. This wide transperspectival view is represented by the encompassing circle that we showed in Figure 1.1.

For example, in a study of Buddhist mutual assistance associations among Southeast Asian refugees in the United States, Canda and Phaobtong (1992) used a general (etic) social work classification of physical, mental, social, and spiritual supports to examine culture-specific community strengths and resources. Particular (emic) Theravada Buddhist terms and practices, based on field observation and interviews within refugee communities, were presented to illustrate this. Thus a common base for mutual understanding and cooperation between Southeast Asian American Buddhists and others was established. As another example, a series of studies about how adults with a chronic illness, cystic fibrosis, respond with resilience came from an opposite direction of analysis (Canda, 2009). It focused on particular individuals' (emic) understandings of spirituality as a source of strength and resources in order to identify both distinctive and shared patterns of meaning among participants and then relate them to strengths-based social work (etic). Indeed, the search for strengths and resources in religious communities and spiritually focused individuals is consistent with the strengths perspective, which is an etic approach to social work that values emic (i.e. client-based) perspectives (Saleebey, 2009).

This transperspectival approach retains an unavoidable challenge. Whenever general definitions of spirituality are developed that can be inclusive of all possible versions, such as theism, polytheism, atheism, animism, and nontheism, they might become vague (Canda, 1990b). When too much is included, a definition does not aid in making important distinctions. In order to address this concern, we develop a broad and inclusive conceptualization of spirituality, as well as a holistic conceptual model, by taking into account insights of many spiritual traditions and scholarly disciplines. We also provide a detailed operational model of spirituality that includes many observable and measurable components useful for application in practice and research.

Expressible versus Inexpressible

Many scholars of religion and spirituality say that they can be studied scientifically only if they can be expressed, observed, and even measured. How else could a practitioner know when a client is being religious, exhibiting signs of a spiritual development crisis, or is affected beneficially or adversely by a spiritual practice like prayer? Other scholars and mystics emphasize that the most distinctive features of religion and spirituality are ineffable, that is, beyond description, expression, or intellectual analysis. Some scholars object that the claim of ineffability is simply a strategy to avoid critical scrutiny of truth claims and to invest personal experiences or traditional doctrines with an aura of supreme unquestionable authority (Proudfoot, 1985). There are two major debates involved: the ineffability of mystical experience and the irreducibility of the nature of religion or spirituality.

Mystical experiences or experiences of *the sacred* are direct personal encounters with aspects of reality that are beyond the limits of language and reason to express. They transcend human capacity for thinking and expression. They are described in various religious traditions as experiences of supernatural or paranormal powers, events, spirits, and ghosts (Hollenback, 1996); deep spiritual communion with God (Johnston, 1995); or ego transcending expansions of consciousness (Wilber, 2006). Experiencers typically claim that mystical experiences are ineffable, meaning that they are so private and profound that they cannot be communicated to another (Dupre, 1987; James, 1982). They surpass rational understanding and the capacity of words. Further, the sacred referents of spiritual devotion and belief, such as God or Tao, are considered ineffable in many religious traditions, because they are supernatural, mysterious, or beyond human understanding. As the eminent historian of religions, Mircea Eliade (1959) said, experience of the sacred is a fundamental experience that can only be understood through sensitivity to the sacred and its experienced qualities of absoluteness, mysteriousness, awesomeness, and ultimate priority.

For these reasons, many scholars of religion and religious adherents claim that the mystical, sacred, or transcendental aspects of spirituality and religion are beyond scientific understanding or proof. This does not mean that mystical experiences or divine realities cannot be talked about. But it means that their reality will always be beyond whatever one says about them. It also means that much religious and spiritual language will be paradoxical, metaphorical, poetic, symbolic, and allegorical.

Our position is that key terms pertaining to spirituality and religion should be defined carefully in order to encourage mutual understanding and consistency of usage, which are prerequisites for research and practice about spirituality. However, the definitions are for the sake of convenience. Concepts never should be mistaken for their referents. Referents cannot be fully captured by labels and definitions, in regards to any phenomenon, spiritual or otherwise. Even on a mundane level, the address is not the place. On a deeper level, one's love for a lover is far more than countable caresses.

As the Jewish, Christian, and Islamic traditions emphasize, the image of God is not to be confused with God. Our definitions function like a pointing finger. As a Zen analogy puts it, it is good to point at the moon to share the lovely sight with your friend. But once your friend has seen the moon, the finger no longer needs to point.

An Open Conceptualization of Spirituality

We aim to be precise, yet open in our definition of spirituality and related terms. For example, there are numerous competing definitions of religion in the fields of religious studies and anthropology (Lehmann & Myers, 2001; Winzeler, 2008). Hill and colleagues (2000) have shown that the concepts of religion and spirituality take on many different nuances in the social sciences and helping professions. Debates have continued for decades about these definitions or whether there even should be any definitions (Braun & McCutcheon, 2000; Scherer, 2006). Exactitude and consensus remain elusive. We feel that this is not necessarily a problem. It is understandable that a complex and highly diverse phenomenon will evade capture by limited categories and definers. In such a case, it is better to develop an open working definition, which takes into account previous scholarly work and invites continued dialogue and debate. Thus, definition is a continuous process, not a final act. Open working definitions need to be clear but not rigid.

Cox (1996) and Hick (1990) have suggested that this can be accomplished by presenting a variety of definitions of religion and spirituality and then considering the family semblance among them. In other words, certain common patterns and themes emerge even with difference and disagreement. In the following discussion, we will integrate insights from many disciplines in order to achieve this. We will construct a comprehensive conceptualization of spirituality and related terms. We will compare this conceptualization to findings from national and international surveys of social workers to consider how well it reflects actual usage in the field.

These definitions and conceptual models are primarily for the purpose of professional discourse. They provide a provisional set of terms and meanings for common understanding among practitioners, educators, and researchers. They give pointers for how to approach the topic of spirituality with clients. But social workers should use them flexibly. We need to adapt our terms and definitions to fit particular contexts. In fact, we do not even need to use the words "spirituality or religion" to get at the meanings behind them. Whenever the terms or definitions do not fit purposes well, please throw them away.

The Concept of Spirituality in the Helping Professions

Definitions of Spirituality and Religion in Social Work

Since professional social work in North America developed partially out of religious movements for charity and community service, the early discussions of spirituality and religion hinged on particular theological terms and beliefs, mainly Christian and Jewish. However, social workers increasingly recognize that spirituality should be addressed in a manner that includes diverse religious and nonreligious expressions because of the tremendous increase of religious diversity and secularization, the legal principle of church/state separation, and the professional ethical standards of client self-determination, respect for diversity, and cultural competence (Bullis, 1996; Canda, 2008a, 2008b; Crompton, 1998; Derezotes, 2006; Ellor, Netting, & Thibault, 1999; Nash & Stewart, 2002; Van Hook, Hugen, & Aguilar, 2001).

The earliest formal attempts to define spirituality inclusively were done by Christian social work scholars who felt that basic Christian values could be extended universally by presenting them in nonsectarian terms. For example, in 1945, Charlotte Towle (1965) said that a complete understanding of the person should involve material, psychological, social, and spiritual aspects. She highlighted spiritual needs as including use of church-based resources, developing a sense of meaning and purpose in life, and formation of value frameworks and sense of social responsibility. Spencer (1956) felt that Christian values of freedom, love, and service were fully compatible with a nonsectarian approach to social work. Later (1961), she defined spirituality as aspects of individual feelings, aspirations, and needs concerned with a search for life meaning and purpose, not necessarily connected to a church or systematic beliefs and practices (i.e. religion).

During the 1970s and 1980s, the profession generally neglected education or research about religion or spirituality outside of religious settings for practice. However, during the same period, prominent scholars advocated for a return of professional attention to spirituality. In addition to Christian and Jewish perspectives, existentialist, humanist, Zen Buddhist, and shamanistic perspectives joined in the effort to define spirituality in an inclusive manner (Canda, 1988a, 1988b). For example, Max Siporin (1985) said that the spiritual is a moral aspect of the person, called the soul, which strives for relatedness with other people and supernatural powers, seeks knowledge of ultimate reality, and forms value frameworks. He emphasized that spirituality may be expressed inside or outside of religious institutional frameworks. Later, he clarified that the definition of spirituality should not be limited to ideas of God or the soul, since not all spiritual perspectives share these (Siporin, 1990). Faver (1986) called for social work to include multiple ways of knowing in research and practice in order to take into account the roles of religion and faith in human experience. She defined religion in terms of institutional cumulative traditions of faith. She used Fowler's definition of faith (see Part III) which is personal and, like Siporin's idea of spirituality, relates to a universal aspect of human beings, by which we orient ourselves to ourselves and the universe. Joseph (1987) similarly defined spirituality as "the underlying dimension of consciousness which strives for meaning, union with the universe, and with all things; it extends to the experience of the transcendent or a power beyond us" (p. 14).

In 1986, I (EC) completed a study of the diverse definitions of spirituality presented in American social work publications to that time (Canda, 1986, 1988a, 1988b, 1990b). In addition, I interviewed 18 authors (the most prominent contributors who could be reached) to cull more detailed personal insights about spirituality and social work. These included participants who identified with atheist, Christian, existentialist, Jewish, shamanistic, and Zen Buddhist perspectives, some including more than one of these. The main purpose of this qualitative philosophical study was to develop a comprehensive and inclusive conceptualization of spirituality that built on all the work that had gone before. I summarized the conceptualization as follows (1990b):

> I conceptualize spirituality as the gestalt of the total process of human life and development, encompassing biological, mental, social, and spiritual aspects. It is not reducible to any of these components; rather, it is the wholeness of what it is to be human. This is the most broad meaning of the term. Of course, a person's spirituality is concerned significantly with the spiritual aspect of experience. In the narrow sense of the term spirituality, it relates to the spiritual component of an individual or group's experience. The *spiritual* relates to the person's search for a sense of meaning and morally fulfilling relationships between oneself, other people, the encompassing universe, and the ontological ground of existence, whether a person understands this in terms that are theistic, atheistic, nontheistic, or any combination of these.

In this definition, spirituality is distinguished from religion in that a religion involves patterns of spiritual beliefs and practices formed in social institutions and traditions that are maintained by a community over time.

Carroll (1998) reviewed the various definitions in social work literature and identified three common features of spirituality: an *essential or holistic quality* of the human being that cannot be reduced to any part of a person; an *aspect* of the person concerned with development of meaning and morality and relationship with a divine or ultimate reality; as *transpersonal experiences*, in which consciousness transcends the ordinary limits of ego and body boundaries, such as in mystical experiences.

Some authors emphasize that spirituality relates primarily to individuals' inner experiences in contrast to religion as a community-based phenomenon (Hugen, 2001). Others point out that spirituality includes both individual and collective dimensions for several reasons (Brenner & Homonoff, 2004; Canda, 2008a, 2008b; Canda & Furman, 1999; Coates, 2007; Derezotes, 2006; Nash & Stewart, 2002). First, the developmental thrust of spirituality is toward connectedness with oneself, other people, other nonhuman beings, the universe, and (for many) the sacred or divine. Second, individuals may communicate about their spiritual experiences with friends, relatives, and mentors. Third, most people in the United States, and many people throughout the world, engage spirituality in part, or primarily, within religious communities or informal spiritual support groups. Fourth, in many traditional cultures as well as mystical traditions, spirituality infuses all of daily life and relationships. Fifth, regarding the social work helping relationship, it is especially important to be aware of the relational quality of spirituality as it can engage empathetic connection, understanding of others' perspectives, partnership, connection across diversities, and striving for justice for individuals and communities. Indeed, this is what we intend by spiritually sensitive practice.

Practitioners' Definitions of Spirituality, Religion, and Faith

In our series of national surveys in the United States (U.S.), the United Kingdom (U.K.), Norway, and Aotearoa New Zealand (ANZ), we explored how social workers who were members of the respective national professional organizations understood the terms spirituality, religion, and faith. We asked people to identify which of 16 descriptors (meaning, purpose, belief, ritual, meditation, organization, community, personal, morality, values, ethics, miracles, prayer, personal relationship with higher power, sacred texts, scripture) they relate to the terms. These findings provide insight into the fit between our use of terms and practitioners' use.

Among the top eight descriptors selected in every country, *spirituality* was most often associated with "meaning, personal, purpose, values, belief, and ethics." For all countries, 60% or more of responders selected "meaning, personal, and values." For the U.S. responders, the top six selections (listed most to least frequent) remained consistent from 1997 to 2008: "meaning, personal, purpose, values, belief, personal relationship with a Divine or Higher Power." "Meditation and ethics" were both selected as the 7th or 8th most common descriptors in both years in the United States. The frequencies for all eight selections remained within 5% over these years. Interestingly, the United States (the least secularized of the countries) is the only country in which the descriptor "personal relationship with a Divine or Higher Power" was in the top six most frequent selections.

Among the top eight descriptors selected in every country, *religion* was most often associated with "belief, ritual, community, values, prayer, and scripture." For all countries, 60% or more of responders selected "belief, ritual, values, prayer, and scripture," with "community" being selected by at least 59%. For the U.S. responders, the top six selections (listed most to least frequent in 2008) remained within 5% frequency from 1997 to 2008: "ritual, belief, organization, scripture, prayer, and community."

Among the top eight descriptors selected for every country (excluding ANZ), *faith* was most often associated with "meaning, belief, personal, values, prayer, and personal relationship with a Divine or Higher Power." For all countries, 60% or more of responders selected "belief." Interestingly, the term "faith" was omitted from the ANZ survey at the advice of local consultants, who saw the term as irrelevant to social work and biased toward a Judeo-Christian perspective that does not reflect Indigenous views (Blair Stirling, University of Otago, personal communication). For the U.S. responders, the top eight selections (listed most to least frequent) remained consistent from 1997 to 2008: "belief, personal relationship with a Divine or Higher Power, personal, meaning, purpose, prayer, values, and ethics." The frequency of selection for "belief, personal, and personal relationship with a Divine or Higher Power" remained within 5% over these years.

We can conclude from this that many social work practitioners across the four countries would be able to relate to the contrasts and overlap between the concepts of spirituality and religion made often in the literature and in our definitions. We can also conclude that individual practitioners vary in their definitions of these terms, even though there are common patterns. Religion had contrasting emphases to spirituality. The descriptors "meaning and personal" were higher for spirituality (i.e. more than 67%) and lower for religion (i.e. less than 56%) in every country. The descriptors "ritual, scripture, and prayer" were higher for religion (i.e. more than 66%) and lower for spirituality (i.e. less than 47% in every country). In all countries but ANZ, at least 24% more respondents associated "community" with religion than spirituality. This may be because Indigenous Maori worldview, which is highly integrated into social work there, views spirituality as infused in culture and community life.

There was a high level of agreement to associate faith with "belief" in all countries (more than 81% of responders) except for ANZ for which we were advised not to include the concept. Fifty-four percent or more in all included countries also associated faith with "personal" and "personal relationship with a Divine or Higher Power." Thus, it shared similarity with religion in terms of "belief" and "personal relationship with a Divine or Higher Power." It shared similarity with spirituality in terms of "belief" in all countries. It is also noteworthy that the pattern of distinction and overlap between the concepts spirituality, religion, and faith remained consistent in the 1997 and 2008 U.S.A. National Surveys.

Interestingly, the three terms are connected by the descriptor "belief" which was selected by at least 39% of responders in all countries (excluding ANZ). In addition, many descriptors cut across all three terms for some respondents in every country. For example, in every country, at least 4% of responders chose all descriptors in relation to spirituality and religion (and faith, excluding ANZ). These findings show that many social work practitioners would likely find our definitions, distinctions, and interrelatedness of spirituality and religion understandable in the United States, United Kingdom, Norway, and ANZ even though there are significant differences of history, language, and cultures. (We will discuss this further in the concluding chapter.)

This is even clearer for U.S. social workers, since the trend of meanings has remained consistent for 11 years. This observation is supported by a smaller ($n = 303$) national exploratory survey of USA-NASW affiliated graduate students, in which the descriptions of spirituality and religion show distinction as well as overlap (Hodge, 2006). Responders most commonly associated spirituality with a "personally constructed view without reference to the transcendent" (33%) and "belief in/experience of a higher power" (23%). They most commonly associated religion with "organized beliefs or doctrines" (25%) and "the practice of spirituality/faith" (23%). Eleven percent or more of responders associated "personally constructed," "belief in/experience of God," and "belief in/experience of a higher power" for both terms. Earlier studies by Derezotes and Evans (1995) and Sheridan and Bullis (1991) showed a similar distinction between concepts.

In my (EC) experience teaching, collaborating with scholars, and presenting at conferences in more than 15 countries around the world, I have found that most social workers are able to relate usefully to the distinction between spirituality and religion, even if this is rather new to them. For example, in Japan, social workers, educators, and mental health professionals are beginning to adopt the word English word "spirituality," transliterated into *katagana*, to make this distinction (Yoshiharu Nakagawa & Sachiko Gomi, personal communications). My Japanese colleagues have said this is helpful because most Japanese people do not have formal membership in a religion, though many utilize and connect ideas and practices from Buddhism, Christianity, Confucianism, Daoism, and Shinto for various purposes. In the Republic of Korea, some social workers are making this distinction as well. Some transliterate the English word "spirituality" into Korean (*hangeul*). Others translate it as *yeong seong* (literally, "sacred or spiritual quality") which is often contrasted with *jonggyo* (literally, "central learning," often used to mean religion). One scholar created a new word, *eulal* (literally, "spiritual essence"; see Canda and Furman, 1999, translation by Seung-Hee Park, Sungkyunkwan University Press, 2003) in order to avoid connotations associated with a specific religion. This is important for South Korea because only about 53% of the population identified affiliation with a religion. Among these, about 55% are Christians and 43% are Buddhists. Others are Confucians, or practice indigenous religions like shamanism; and many blend various religions (see www.korea.net, "Religion", retrieved 7/1/08). My Chinese colleagues in Hong Kong, where English is a common language, also make a distinction between religion and spirituality (e.g. Lee, et al., 2009). This is useful to accommodate religious diversity in China as well as prevalent atheism and agnosticism.

I believe that these various international trends support the utility of the distinctions between the concepts of spirituality and religion in social work. On the other hand, the variability of usage in the literature and among individual practitioners reinforces the need for clarifying the concepts.

Definitions of Spirituality and Religion in Related Fields

In health care fields, such as medicine, hospice care, psychiatry, pastoral counseling, and nursing, clinical and research interest in spirituality has accelerated significantly in the past 15 years. Koenig (2007) gives the following reasons why health professionals should include spirituality in patient care. Research has shown that many patients are religious or spiritual and wish to include spirituality in health care. Religion and spirituality may influence (for better or worse) coping with illness, use of medical treatments, mental and physical health outcomes, and community-based supports. Indeed, JCAHO (Joint Commission for the Accreditation of Hospital Organizations) requires that health care organizations address spiritual issues.

Hill et al. (2000) pointed out that there has been a narrowing of the definition of religion within the public and within the social and psychological sciences, especially since the 1980s. Over this time, the concept of spirituality has become used commonly as a broader term than religion, with distinctions similar to those in social work. Religion is commonly associated with formal organizations, communities, doctrines, and rituals. Spirituality is commonly associated with the search for meaning and truth, encounter with transcendence or the sacred, and connectedness. As in social work, scholars commonly recognize that spirituality can express in religious and nonreligious forms. Hill and colleagues recommend that the concept of spirituality should include a focus on *the sacred*. In their view, "The sacred is a person, an object, a principle, or a concept that transcends the self" and that invokes "feelings of respect, reverence, devotion, and may, ideally, serve an integrative function in human personality" (p. 64). This in fact is very close to what the eminent historian of religions, Mircea Eliade (1959), said is the hallmark of religious experience. For Eliade, as is common in the field of religious studies, the term religion has a broad meaning similar to spirituality.

Miller and Thoreson (2003) point out that spirituality often implies an *animating or vital principle*, as reflected by the Latin meaning of *spiritus*, which means breath or spirit. Religion is an institutionalized pattern that involves spirituality as well as other economic, political, and social goals that are not necessarily spiritual in focus. The concept of spirituality does involve observable practices (such as when manifested in religious participation), but it focuses on an experiential level related to immaterial aspects. It may involve salutary qualities such as love, well-being, and peace. Similarly, Frey, Daaleman, and Peyton (2005) agree that spirituality may or may not express in religion and that it relates to good health status, subjective well-being, meaningful life, self-efficacy, and personal agency. Koenig, McCullough, and Larson (2001) conducted a massive review of studies about spirituality and religion in relation to health. They arrived at the following definitions: "Spirituality is the personal quest for understanding answers to ultimate questions about life, about meaning, and about relationship to the sacred or transcendent, which may (or may not) lead to or arise from the development of religious rituals and the formation of community" (p. 18). In contrast, "Religion is an organized system of beliefs, practices, rituals, and symbols designed to (a) facilitate closeness to the sacred or transcendent (God, higher power, or ultimate truth/reality) and (b) foster an understanding of one's relationship and responsibility to others in living together in a community." They also view spirituality as the more encompassing concept. Their review of studies shows that related terms (such as religiosity, religiousness, and spiritual well-being) are defined and operationalized in various ways by researchers. On an international level, the World Health Organization's Quality of Life Measure for assessment of spirituality, religion and personal beliefs includes eight facets: meaning of life, awe, wholeness and integration, inner peace/serenity/harmony, hope and optimism, connectedness to a spiritual being or force, spiritual strength, and faith (Moreira-Almeida & Koenig, 2006). As Moreira-Almeida and Koenig point out, the latter three facets may relate more directly to spirituality itself while the others may be outcomes of spiritual involvement.

Nursing has come to make similar distinctions between spirituality and religion. An analysis of the concept of spirituality in 90 health related publications between 1983 and 2005 (Sessana Finnell & Jezewski, 2007) found four ways of relating spirituality with religion: (1) spirituality and religion are equivalent; (2) spirituality refers to meaning, purpose, and connection; (3) spirituality is separate from religion; and (4) spirituality relates to metaphysical or transcendent phenomena. They recommend improving consistent usage by defining spirituality in terms of four themes: search; meaning; unifying and integrating; and basis for community. In this sense, spirituality may or may not be religious. Similarly, Berry (2005) views spirituality as the broader concept, focused on experience, and religion as related to groups and doctrines. Delgado (2005) defines spirituality as related to a belief system, search for purpose, harmonious interconnectedness, and self-transcendence that may result in inner peace and successful adaptation and good health. Buck (2006, p. 289) defines spirituality as "that most human of experiences that seeks to transcend self and find meaning and purpose through connection with others, nature, and/or a Supreme Being, which may or may not involve religious structures and traditions." O'Brien (2008) finds no uniformity in definitions of spirituality in the nursing literature. However, it is associated commonly with values, meaning, purpose, transcendence, positive virtues (such as love and compassion), ultimate concerns, sense of the sacred, harmonious relationships, and integration of body, mind, and spirit. She views spirituality as central to holistic nursing practice. McSherry and Cash (2004) caution that nurses must be open to the diverse meanings to these terms given by patients.

In a review of the field of the psychology of religion, Emmons and Paloutzian (2003) indicate that spirituality may refer to a search for the sacred that is dynamic and infused in daily life. They believe that spirituality and religion (or religiousness) should not be treated as dichotomous concepts (e.g. individual vs. collective or good vs. bad). Psychological studies address feeling states (such as love, gratitude, devotion), virtues (such as forgiveness, hope, love, humility, wisdom), spiritual transcendence (such as prayer joy through divine contact, sense of the unitive nature of life, or connectedness across groups and generations), ultimate concerns (such as life-orienting goals and priorities), and spiritual transformation (such as conversion or gradual and sudden changes in spirituality). The positive psychologists Snyder and Lopez (2007, p. 262) define spirituality as, "the thoughts, feelings, and behaviors that fuel and arise from the search for the sacred." Pargament (2007) views the sacred as the core of spirituality. The sacred relates to concepts of God, the divine, transcendent reality, and other aspects of life that are associated with the divine or transcendence. Zinnbauer and Pargament (2005) emphasize that spirituality and religiousness both relate to three key concepts: significance, search, and the sacred. *Significance* relates to "valued, meaningful, or ultimate concerns." "These concerns may be psychological (e.g. growth, self-esteem, comfort), social (e.g. intimacy, social justice), physical (e.g. health, fitness), material (e.g. money, food, cars), or related to the divine (e.g. closeness with God, religious experience)" (p. 33). *Search* refers to the life process of discovering and conserving what is significant. *The sacred*, as already described, when added to significance and search, distinguishes religion and spirituality from other phenomena. They go on to explain how they differ in seeing spirituality or religiousness as the broader concept, but both agree that spirituality and religion are related.

In the field of counseling psychology, Faiver, Ingersoll, O'Brien, and McNally (2001) associate spirituality with "a deep sense of wholeness, connectedness, and openness to the infinite" (p. 2). Spirituality is an innate quality, our vital life force, and our experience of that. It expresses in religious and nonreligious forms. Frame (2003) and Miller (2003) recount definitions of spirituality involving a search for harmony and wholeness, connectedness with a higher power, a growth tendency toward meaning, hope, transcendence, connectedness, compassion, and formation of value systems. Frame summarizes, "*Spirituality* includes one's values, beliefs, mission, awareness, subjectivity, experience, sense of purpose and direction, and a kind of striving toward something greater than oneself" (p. 3) that may or may not be expressed through religious institutional participation.

Ken Wilber (2000a), an integral philosopher who is also highly influential in transpersonal psychology, summarizes five common definitions of spirituality. His Integral Institute is developing applications of integral theory for many fields, including medicine, business, psychotherapy, and social work. Wilber's ideas will be explained further in Parts II and III. (1) Spirituality involves the transpersonal (i.e. beyond ordinary limitations of body and ego) levels of human development in any line of development, such as in cognition (transrational intuition), affect (transpersonal love), morality (compassion for all beings), and self-identity (the transpersonal or True Self). (2) Spirituality is the overall path of development of the transpersonal levels. (3) Spirituality is a distinctive developmental line of consciousness that moves from prepersonal to personal to transpersonal levels. (4) Spirituality involves profound attitudes such as openness or love. (5) Spirituality involves states or peaks of consciousness that temporarily propel one into transpersonal awareness.

This literature review makes it obvious that the term spirituality now is used commonly in the helping professions and health related research. Although there is no uniformity of definitions, it is common to use spirituality as a broader concept and to assert that it may express in religious or nonreligious forms. However, as Praglin (2004) and Canda and Furman (1999) pointed out, within the fields of religious studies, anthropology, and sociology, the term spirituality is not so common. These fields study religion as a broad phenomenon of human behavior embedded in history, traditions, and communities. The term spirituality is used most often in the context of Christian theology, in which it refers to the way a person develops a personal relationship with God (Barry & Connoly, 1982; Jones, Wainwright, & Yarnold, 1986; Van Kaam, 1983). So when scholars of religion write about spirituality it is often about particular Christian beliefs and practices, or other meditative and contemplative practices, rather than about a general or universal aspect of all people. They may also study people's conceptions and practices of spirituality as religious phenomena (e.g. Erricker & Erricker, 2001).

In Greco-Roman antiquity, the Latin term *religio* (noun) referred to fulfillment of duties in the state religion, while *religiosus* (adjective) connoted preoccupation with superstition (Scherer, 2006). Cicero (1st century before the Common Era, BCE) posited that *religio* referred to carefully pondering sacred matters. In Christian antiquity, Lactantius (305 CE) shifted the meaning to reconnecting to God and a sense of wholeness.

As Paden (2003) pointed out, the term religion in Europe grew from a narrowly restricted meaning (e.g. Christianity) to become much broader since the 17th century, as Western scholars engaged in comparative religious studies and tried to encompass tremendous variety of worldviews. For example, definitions of religion often connect to concepts of the sacred, the transcendent, and the supernatural. Religions abound in various, sometimes contradictory, concepts of God, gods, spirits, ghosts, vital energies, numinous power, universal consciousness, and ultimate reality (Capps, 1995; Paden, 1994, 2003; Pals, 1996). Scherer (2006) summarizes seven dimensions of religion, based on the work of Ninian Smart: ritual/practical, doctrinal/philosophical, mythic/narrative, experiential/emotional, ethical/legal, organizational/social, and material/artistic. Some definitions of religion focus on particular features distinctive to religions; some focus on social and psychological functions of religions; and some deconstruct the term as a problematic if not useless product of overgeneralization and ethnocentrism (Arnal, 2000).

Clearly the term religion is given a wide range of meanings in religious studies, often with broad inclusion (e.g. pertaining to ultimate concern, transcendence of ordinary limits of physical space and time, or sacredness) similar to the variety of conceptions of spirituality (including religious expressions) in the helping professions. Many scholars of religion examine the particular historical and cultural forms of religion and may compare between them. It is important to note that many scholars of religion dispute the usefulness of abstract terms, such as religion or the sacred, because they are thought to be vague, ambiguous, and culturally and theologically biased (Braun & McCutcheon, 2000). Studies of religions from many disciplines will inform the remainder of this book, especially the conceptual models of spirituality in the next section of this chapter and the accounts of various religions in Part II. Given that most people's spirituality expresses through religion, insights from studies of religion can shed light on spirituality and social work (Lee & Gorman, 2005; Praglin, 2004).

Major Insights about Spirituality

To summarize insights from current thinking in the helping professions and religious studies, we can identify *12 commonly mentioned attributes of the concept of spirituality*:

1. An essential quality of a person that is inherently valuable, sacred, or immaterial. This is sometimes associated with beliefs about soul, spirit, vital energy, life force, consciousness, true self, or core nature.
2. An innate drive of persons to search for meaning.
3. A developmental process of searching and moving toward a sense of wholeness and connectedness in oneself and with others.
4. The contents of beliefs, values, moral frameworks, practices and relationships with self and others, including ultimate reality, involved in this process.
5. Transpersonal levels of consciousness.
6. Particular experiences and states of consciousness of a profound, transpersonal or sacred nature, such as out of body experiences, revelatory visions, sense of connection with spirits, communing with God, or cosmic consciousness.
7. Participation in spiritual support groups that may or may not be religious.
8. Engagement in particular beliefs and behaviors that support growth toward wholeness or contact with the sacred, such as prayer or meditation, in a religious or nonreligious context.
9. Central priorities that orient life toward what is considered ultimate, sacred, or transcendent.
10. Virtues that may arise from development of spirituality, such as compassion, love, sense of justice, forgiveness, and humility.
11. Qualities of well-being that may arise from spiritual development, such as resilience, joy, peace, contentment, and clear life purpose.
12. A holistic quality of the entire person in relationship, not reducible to parts, that includes yet transcends all the parts. Holistic awareness may emerge as one becomes aware of all one's aspects and relationships and works out a sense of integration and connectedness.

In the following section, by drawing on these insights, we develop formal definitions of spirituality as an aspect of the person along with related terms (such as religion and faith) and present two interrelated conceptual models of spirituality. The first, *an operational model of spirituality*, deals with spirituality as an aspect of human experience in more detail, including categories of drives, experiences, functions, developmental processes, and contents of spiritual perspectives. The second, *a holistic model of spirituality*, deals with spirituality in relation to the bio-psycho-social model of the person and environment.

Definitions and Models Related to Spirituality

Spirituality as an Aspect of the Person

As the review of definitions of spirituality showed, spirituality is most often defined as an aspect of the person that is distinctively human, namely the search for a sense of meaning, purpose, connectedness, and morality with special reference to what is considered sacred, transcendent, or ultimate. We concur with most helping professional definitions that regard spirituality as a broader concept than religion and that it may express in religious and nonreligious forms. On the basis of these considerations, we propose formal definitions of spirituality and religion as follows.

Spirituality Is:

A process of human life and development

- focusing on the search for a sense of meaning, purpose, morality, and well-being;
- *in relationship* with oneself, other people, other beings, the universe, and ultimate reality however understood (e.g. in animistic, atheistic, nontheistic, polytheistic, theistic, or other ways);
- orienting around centrally significant priorities; and
- engaging a sense of transcendence (experienced as deeply profound, sacred, or transpersonal).

Individuals and groups may express spirituality in religious and nonreligious ways. A religious or nonreligious *spiritual perspective* is an individual's or group's worldview or ideology rooted in spirituality. Spirituality always has a private and individual expression in a person's life. Individuals may or may not connect their spirituality to explicit public expression or participation in groups (such as religions or informal spiritual support groups). However, there are always implications of an individual's spirituality for relationships. Spirituality may or may not permeate an individual's daily life and a group's culture. Transcendence refers to experiences and interpretations of events as profound, breaking through banality and limitedness by time and space. For example, transcendence could involve a sense of divine revelation; an awareness of the sacredness immanent within the self and nature; a breaking through the body/self boundary with expanded consciousness; a sense of great clarity and wonder within ordinary activities; a deep human engagement of intimacy with people and the physical world; or strong dedication to ideals of peace and justice that have no divine or sacred referent. As a universal feature of persons and cultures, everyone has spirituality, though people vary in amount of focus on it.

Healthy spirituality encourages individuals to develop a sense of meaningfulness, purposefulness, personal integrity, wholeness, joy, peace, contentment, coherence of worldview, and overall well-being. It fosters transpersonal experiences, the emergence of transpersonal levels of consciousness, and an expanded sense of identity and connectedness. Healthy spirituality engenders individuals' virtues, such as compassion and justice, as well as relational webs of caring, respect, and support extending outward to other people and beings (Canda, 2008b). It encourages groups to develop mutual support, philanthropic activity, appreciation of diversity, and actions for the common good of society and world. Unpleasant yet authentic feelings (such as existential despair, grief, or pangs of conscience), developmental crises or emergencies (such as disruptive transpersonal experiences), and difficult group dynamics (such as working toward mutual understanding and reconciliation during times of conflict) can be significant and valuable components of healthy spirituality.

Unfortunately, spirituality—like any aspect of human behavior—does not always manifest in healthy ways (Moss, 2005 and see his paradigm at http://www.bernardmoss.org.uk/new%20_paradigm.htm, retrieved October 17, 2008). Spirituality can be distorted and misdirected into beliefs, attitudes, and behaviors that are harmful to self or others, such as feelings of inappropriate guilt, shame, and hopelessness and discrimination and oppression. On a collective level, religions and informal spiritual groups may not help members to achieve their full spiritual potential. They may be hostile and violent toward some of their members and toward other individuals and groups who do not conform to their perspective.

Our definition of spirituality does not presume (or exclude) belief in an incorporeal, immaterial, or supernatural realm or entities. We make no claims about that in our capacity as social workers. However, we promote helping professionals' respect and knowledge regarding the diverse metaphysical beliefs among our clients and communities. The word "spirit" does not necessarily presume that either. "Spirit" comes from the Latin, *spiritus*, referring to breath, spirit, and life force. This is similar to Greek *pneuma*, Hebrew *ruach*, Sanskrit *prana*, and Chinese *qi* (or *ch'i*). In contemporary English usage, people can be "inspired" or have "team spirit" without literally being possessed or controlled by a spirit. People can understand "spirit" literally or metaphorically to refer to that which gives them vitality and drive for meaning and transcendence.

Religion Is:

An institutionalized (i.e. systematic and organized) pattern of values, beliefs, symbols, behaviors, and experiences that involves

- spirituality
- a community of adherents
- transmission of traditions over time and
- community support functions (e.g. organizational structure, material assistance, emotional support, or political advocacy) that are directly or indirectly related to spirituality.

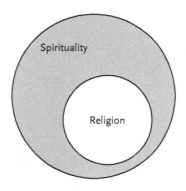

Figure 3.1. Spirituality including and transcending religion.

Religion always involves some degree of both private and public community experience for individual members of a religious group and for the group as a whole. A religion may operate with or without centralized and bureaucratized organizational structures. It may or may not permeate a person's daily life and a group's culture. Not all individuals or societies are religious. *Religiousness* (or religiosity) refers to the degree and style of someone's religious involvement. *Healthy religiousness*, as an expression of spirituality, encourages a person's and a religious group's sense of well-being, coherent worldview, transpersonal development, virtues, and relational webs of caring, respect, and support that extend toward fellow adherents and toward community, society, and world. Unpleasant authentic feelings (such as appropriate guilt or shame), developmental crises or emergencies (such as severe doubt or distress during conversion), and difficult religious group dynamics (such as holding religious leaders accountable for misuse and abuse of authority) can be significant components of healthy religiousness. However, religiousness does not always manifest in healthy ways, as we discussed in reference to spirituality. For example, religiously based delusions, hallucinations, low self-esteem, abuse, oppression, and violence are lamentable expressions of unhealthy religiousness.

Given these definitions, spirituality is the source of religion, but it is not limited to religion. Spirituality includes and transcends religion (see Figure 3.1).

Alternative Views of Spirituality and Religion

Of course, clients (and colleagues and members of the public) vary in their definitions of religion and spirituality. Professional definitions set themes for possible exploration with clients, but client's own terms, definitions, and interests relating to these themes should set the tone for communication in the helping relationship. It is not necessary to use the terms religion or spirituality in order to get at the themes explained above. Here are some alternative meanings of spirituality and religion that can alert us to variations we may find among clients (see Figure 3.2). Note that our definition of spirituality includes and transcends all these alternatives.

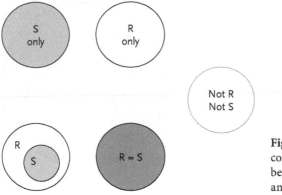

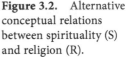

Figure 3.2. Alternative conceptual relations between spirituality (S) and religion (R).

Spirituality only.

- "I am spiritual but not religious." This person likely does not participate in a religious group, but is concerned about matters of meaning, purpose, and morality. This is most common among people who disavow traditional forms of religion or are atheist or agnostic. In the United States, this is most common among those in the baby boomer generation and younger (Roof, 1993). Some people may have had negative experiences with religion and therefore reject it. Some might view religion as inherently bad and spirituality as inherently good.
- "Spirituality is my whole life." For this person, spirituality totally infuses daily life. This may be more likely for those who have a fervent dedication to spiritual development, such as adults who view all of life, including dealing with adversities, as a spiritual path (e.g. Canda, 2001, 2009).
- "Spirituality is my culture." This is most likely in traditional and Indigenous cultures that view all of life as sacred. For example, among the Maori of Aotearoa New Zealand, *wairuatanga*, (the spiritual dimension) is inseparable from collective everyday awareness and culture, as everything is imbued with spirit (Nash & Stewart, 2002).

Religion only.

- "I am religious but not spiritual." This person might participate in religious activities (such as church going) but mainly for personal or social benefits, unconcerned with deep matters of meaning, purpose, or experience of the sacred. Or, a traditionally religious person might view spirituality as something unfamiliar, unorthodox, or nebulous. This latter view is more likely among American older adults (Nelson-Becker, 2003).

- "Religion is my whole life." This person might identify intensely with a particular religious tradition and engage frequently in its activities, such as prayer, scripture reading, and church attendance. She or he may view all of life as a spiritual path, but name it in terms of a specific religion.
- "Religion is my culture." This is most common in traditional or Indigenous cultures in which all of life is viewed as sacred and in which the sacred is associated with the concept of religion. For example, in traditional Islam, religion and faith are infused throughout culture and daily life, as demonstrated by submission (or dedication) of oneself to God, daily prayers, and application of Shari'a law to community relations (Ashencaen Crabtree, Husain, & Spalek, 2008).

Religion includes spirituality.

- "I practice spiritual prayers or meditation as part of my religion." This view may reflect the idea that activities directed toward the divine or toward attaining enlightenment are spiritual and that these function within a particular religion.
- "Religion is my whole life and spirituality is part of that." This person might identify with a particular religious tradition that completely imbues daily life. Activities such as worship, prayer, or meditation may be considered spiritual within the religious context.
- "Religion is my culture and spirituality is part of that." This is most common in traditional or Indigenous cultures that view all of life as sacred and in which the sacred is associated with the concept of religion. Activities such as worship, prayer, meditation, or ritual might be seen as spiritual within that religious and cultural context.

Religion and spirituality are the same.

- "I express my spirituality completely through my religion, so there is no difference between them." This person might recognize a difference of meanings between spirituality and religion, but his or her religion is a total and sufficient means for the expression of spirituality.
- "Religion is my whole life, so spirituality is not different from that." This person might identify with a particular religious tradition and that tradition completely imbues daily life. He or she views all related activities as religious so there is no useful distinction from spirituality.
- "Spirituality and religion are one in my culture." This is most common in traditional or Indigenous cultures in which all of life is viewed as sacred and in which the sacred is associated with both the concepts of religion and spirituality.

Neither religion nor spirituality.

- "I do not consider myself to be religious or spiritual." This statement is most likely if a person is not interested in matters of sacredness and is also not participating in a religious group. Some atheists or agnostics might hold this view. However, this does not mean that the person does not have spirituality according to our definitions; it simply means that she or he might not focus on it or might not use that term.

Defining Faith

The term faith is not used as often as the terms spirituality or religion in the secular helping professions, except for two situations. One situation is when clients or research participants use the term faith to describe an aspect of their spiritual or religious perspective. In this case, as we have seen in our Multi-National Surveys of social workers, the term *faith* is usually associated with (1) the beliefs of one's religion; (2) assent to those beliefs; and (3) experience of relationship with God or other sacred powers. Ai (2006) and Williams and Smolek (2007) use the term "faith matters" broadly to refer to spiritual practices, values, and attitudes that are commonly related to a religion.

In popular American discourse, the term faith most commonly implies Christianity or Judaism. In some religious contexts, the term "people of faith" implies particular religious standards of orthodoxy or conformance with denominational norms. Since the third meaning of the term faith is used most commonly in theistic religions, especially in the Judeo-Christian-Islamic (i.e. Abrahamic) traditions, it can lead to confusion when applied to other spiritual perspectives. For example, in Zen Buddhism, it can make sense to say one has faith or confidence in the teachings of the Buddha, in meditation techniques that help one toward enlightenment, or in the inherent nonduality of mind—but that has a very different connotation from a Christian faith relationship with a personal God (Sheng-yen, 1987). As another example, consultants for the ANZ survey felt that the term faith was too closely associated with the colonially intruded religion of Christianity and was not well suited to Indigenous perspectives

The second situation in which the term "faith" is used commonly regards so-called "faith-based human services". These refer to social services provided under the auspices of religiously affiliated agencies or congregations, such as Lutheran Social Services or a local church-based soup kitchen. As we will discuss in Part III, this term became popular due to its use in social policies promoting greater involvement of religiously affiliated community-based programs during the Clinton and G. W. Bush administrations. Tangenberg (2005) suggests that the term "faith-related" more accurately captures the wide variety of settings and styles of such programs. These range from those that have explicitly religious mission statements, affiliations, purposes, priorities, and hiring practices (described as *faith-permeated*) to those that have implicit reference to religious values, weaker connections to religious institutions, few religious expectations of staff, and varied levels of support from denominations (described as *faith-background*). There are also *faith-secular* partnerships. In our parlance, all these programs are *religiously affiliated* to various degrees. This implies that religiously affiliated programs are involved with spirituality in various ways. However, they may or may not be spiritually sensitive or congruent with social work professional values.

In order to be consistent with our formal definitions of spirituality and religion, and most common usage in our profession, we subsume the concept of faith within spirituality and religion. We also wish to avoid unintended theistic connotations when referring to spirituality or religion in general. We sometimes use the term faith as defined above or in reference to authors and religious believers who employ it.

An Operational Model of Spirituality as an Aspect of the Person

An operational model of spirituality supports more precise and practical use of concepts in social work practice and research (see Figure 3.3). This model depicts spirituality as an aspect of the person regarding its various religious and nonreligious manifestations. On the basis of insights from social work and the other disciplines related to the study of religion and spirituality, we identify five interrelated categories of manifestations of spirituality: spiritual drives, spiritual experiences, functions of spirituality, spiritual development, and contents of a spiritual perspective including religious expressions. Part II introduces details of a variety of religious and nonreligious perspectives along with social work implications. In Part III, we consider healthy and unhealthy expressions of spirituality and possible helping practices associated with these manifestations of spirituality.

Spiritual Drives

When we acknowledge that spirituality involves a search for meaning, purpose, morally fulfilling relationships, significance, and transcendence, we imply underlying drives for this search. We summarize these as the *drive for profound experiences* that enrich, vitalize, and orient life; the *drive for a sense of meaning and purpose*; and the *drive for connectedness, integrity, and wholeness*. The ways we choose to express or inhibit these drives set our spiritual priorities and motivations.

Human nature involves reaching out and encountering the world, not only in banal ways but also in ways that yield a sense of intrinsic significance, authority, compellingness, ultimacy, and sacredness (Davis, 1989; Eliade, 1959; Jung, 1938; Maslow, 1970; Nielsen et al., 1993). As we grow in empathic relationship with the world, our natural sense of compassion blossoms.

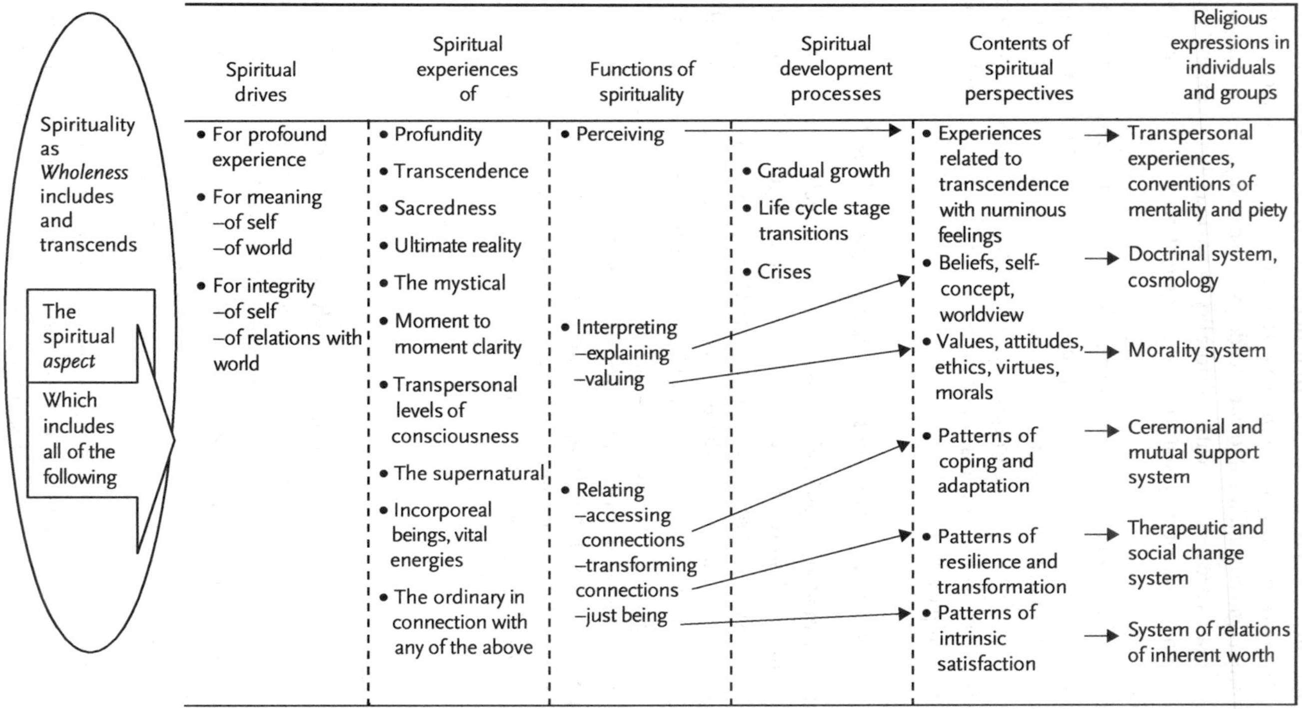

Spiritual drives	Spiritual experiences of	Functions of spirituality	Spiritual development processes	Contents of spiritual perspectives	Religious expressions in individuals and groups

• For profound experience
• For meaning
  –of self
  –of world
• For integrity
  –of self
  –of relations with world
	• Profundity
	• Transcendence
	• Sacredness
	• Ultimate reality
	• The mystical
	• Moment to moment clarity
	• Transpersonal levels of consciousness
	• The supernatural
	• Incorporeal beings, vital energies
	• The ordinary in connection with any of the above
		• Perceiving
		
		• Interpreting
		  –explaining
		  –valuing
		
		• Relating
		  –accessing connections
		  –transforming connections
		  –just being
			• Gradual growth
			• Life cycle stage transitions
			• Crises
				• Experiences related to transcendence with numinous feelings
				• Beliefs, self-concept, worldview
				• Values, attitudes, ethics, virtues, morals
				• Patterns of coping and adaptation
				• Patterns of resilience and transformation
				• Patterns of intrinsic satisfaction
					→ Transpersonal experiences, conventions of mentality and piety
					→ Doctrinal system, cosmology
					→ Morality system
					→ Ceremonial and mutual support system
					→ Therapeutic and social change system
					→ System of relations of inherent worth

Spirituality as *Wholeness* includes and transcends

The spiritual *aspect*

Which includes all of the following

Figure 3.3. An operational model of spirituality.

It is human nature to try to make sense of self and world. Who am I? Why do I exist? What is my purpose? What is the nature of reality? How did things get to be the way they are? How do I fit in the world? On what should I base my life? Everyone struggles with these questions of meaning in various ways. Even if we accept religious or culturally prescribed answers to these questions, at certain points of life crisis, when our neat worlds are shattered, we ask again: Why?

We also need a sense of integration, wholeness, and connectedness within ourselves and in relation with the world. Do I know myself? How can I reach a place of clarity and calm within? Do I feel attuned to myself? Do I behave as if "the right hand doesn't know what the left hand is doing"? How do I relate with others? How can I love and be loved? What is my place in the scheme of things? How am I interrelated with other people, other things, and the source of existence? What is of greatest significance to me? We strive for a sense of integrity; literally, we seek integration with ourselves, the world, and what we hold to be most dear or sacred.

Spiritual Experiences

These drives motivate us to experience things in profound ways and to orient our experiences around central priorities. Usually people describe experiences as spiritual when they involve a sense of contact with powers and meanings of profound, transcendent, transpersonal, sacred, or ultimate significance (Angel, 1994; Griffin, 1988; Grof, 1988; James, 1982; Johnston, 1995, 2004; Otto, 1950; Roberts, 2004; Wilber, 2006; Zinnbauer & Pargament, 2005). Indeed, people can experience any event of an ordinary or extraordinary kind as a reflection, manifestation, or reminder of transcendent concerns, values, and reality. For example, for the Zen practitioner, simply washing dishes with mindfulness can be an experience of beautiful clarity and appreciation for the extraordinariness of the mundane and the preciousness of each moment. There is a common Zen saying that Zen is nothing special, or, Zen mind is ordinary mind. In other words, clarity makes everything special. Agnostics and atheists do not describe the experience of transcendence in terms of divinity or supernaturalism. Nonetheless, as we will see in the discussion of the existential spiritual perspective (Chapter 6), there can be a sense of ultimate guiding principles that transcend egotism, such as freedom, responsibility, compassion, and justice, rooted in profound experiences of connection with humanity and the universe.

Functions of Spirituality

Spiritual perceiving. The drive for experience of ultimacy engages and edifies all human faculties and capacities. For example, a biological imperative such as sexual craving can express through loving communion with another person. The senses can be engaged in a way that opens awareness of the wonder of each moment or the immanent presence of the divine. Transpersonal theory

and mystical traditions suggest there are other faculties of perception that enable
people to experience a level of reality that transcends the limits of ego, physical
boundary, space, and time (Braud & Anderson, 1998; Grof, 1988; Wilber, 1998).

Spiritual interpreting. The drive for meaning engages people's cognitive sym-
bolizing and story-making abilities in order to explain and to grant value. We create representations for the phenomena of our inner experience and the external
world and create myths (sacred stories) for why things are this way (Anderson,
1996; Eliade, 1959, 1963; Fowler, 1996; Lehmann & Meyers, 2001; Nielsen et al.,
1993; Paden, 2003; Pals, 1996; Proudfoot, 1985; Smith, 2001; Winzeler, 2008).
We establish priorities, goals, and systems for moral decision-making. Studies of
resilient people show that they are able to interpret crises, loss, and adversity in
terms of challenges and opportunities for meaning and transcendence (Canda,
2009).

Spiritual relating. The drive for integrity engages us in relationship with
ourselves, other beings, and the ultimate ground of reality however a person
understands it. We *access and maintain connections* to nourish our development as individuals and groups, including inner resources of wisdom and outer
resources of social support and, for some, divine grace or revelation (Bellah,
1991; Johnstone, 2004; Jones, Wainwright, & Yarnold, 1986; Lehmann & Meyers,
1997; Lessa & Vogt, 1972; Roberts, 2004). We also *transform connections* with
ourselves and others through conflict, conflict management, growth and crises.
Natural compassion and ideals of justice shape individual's and groups' efforts
to advance the well-being of other people and all in the world. While these first
two functions of relating imply extrinsic goals to benefit ourselves or others, the
third function, *just being,* is a nonacquisitive, nonegoistic, and non-goal-oriented
way of communing and being in the moment. For example, a parent might hold
her or his baby and quietly rest in awareness of the loving bond. A person deep
in prayer can simply dwell in communion with God. A lover of the earth may sit
by a brook, just listening, and imbibe a sense of harmony.

Spiritual development. Our creativity and efforts to adapt to or make
changes in the environment and in ourselves take place through many kinds of
developmental processes that challenge and expand our established frameworks
of meaning (Barry & Connoly, 1982; Erikson, 1962, 1969; Fowler, 1996; Robbins,
Chatterjee, & Canda, 2006; Wilber, 2006). As we will discuss extensively in
Part III, spiritual development flows through periods of relatively smooth gradual growth; life cycle stage transitions affected by physical maturation (such as
birth, puberty, and death) and culturally prescribed life transition points (such
as becoming an adult, marrying, and divorcing); and spiritual crises (such as
sudden loss of faith in one's religion of upbringing). Spiritual experiences can
propel our development into peaks of insight and sometimes into pits of despair.
And our ongoing developmental challenge is to integrate all our experiences into
a sense of self as a whole person in fulfilling relations with others. As we grow
in healthy spirituality, we are more able to integrate our highest insights and
wisdom into daily consciousness, relationships, and the practical details of life

and death. If we derail in spiritual development, we might become lost in triviality, meaninglessness, despair, or torment. Societies also develop spiritually. In healthy spiritual development, societies develop more and more widely embracing views of justice and human rights and responsibilities.

Contents of an Individual's or Group's Spiritual Perspective

Spiritual experiences, functions, and processes of development interact to form particular contents of an individual's or group's spiritual perspective. The function of perceiving can yield *experiential spiritual contents* of transcendence, profundity, ultimacy, the supernatural, the sacred, the transpersonal, or the mystical and the ordinary in relation with these. In a religious context, the experiential spiritual contents relate to understandings of God, spirits, ancestors, vital energies, and consciousness upheld by an adherent's community. Experiences of nondual consciousness are beyond the limits of thinking, feeling, and images. Paradoxically, such contents are empty of specific form.

Numinous feelings of profound significance, awesomeness, lovingness, mysteriousness, and compelling authority commonly accompany spiritual experiences (Eliade, 1959; James, 1982; Otto, 1950). Individual personality and group norms can shape spiritual feelings into certain emotional styles, such as effusive emotional intensity (e.g. charismatic Christian prayer) or serene nonjudgmental awareness (e.g. Zen Buddhist mindfulness meditation). In a religious context, these feelings and emotional styles may link to *conventions of mentality, piety, reverence,* and *devotion.*

The interpretive function blends experiences with cognitive and emotional responses. The cognitive explanatory component of interpretation results in *spiritual beliefs* about self and world in an overall worldview and influences our feeling reactions to spiritual experiences. Beliefs express in both literal language and creative complex communications, such as symbols, metaphors, parables, and many art forms. Worldview changes in response to new insights into self and world. If this occurs in the context of religious language and institutions, people organize doctrines and ideas about a sacred cosmology (Beane & Doty, 1975; Bellah, 1991; Hick, 1990; Johnstone, 2004; Nielsen et al., 1993; Paden, 1994, 2003). The emotive valuing component of interpretation leads to the formation of *value systems,* including priorities, life goals, attitudes, ethical guidelines, and moral positions. If this occurs in a religious context, people form a moral framework, vested by a community with a sense of ultimate moral authority coming from a transcendent source.

The relational function of accessing and maintaining connections leads to *spiritual patterns of coping and adaptation* to maintain or acquire physical, mental, social, spiritual, and environmental strengths and resources for ongoing personal and community survival and growth in accord with spiritual priorities. This might include intrapersonal strategies for self-reflection and self-understanding, such as prayer and meditation. This might also include interpersonal strategies for affirming and protecting oneself and community and for connecting with external supports, including family, friends, spiritual support groups, and communication with supernatural forces. In a religious context, the person learns ceremonies of affirmation and celebration, patterns of mutual help, forms of worship, techniques for prayer, magic, or meditation, and ways of examining conscience that have been formed by a religious community.

The relational function of transforming connections produces *spiritual patterns of resilience* and *transformation* for breaking through significant life challenges, promoting significant personal and social change, and transcending the ego/body bound limits of self and world. The drive to connect with other beings and the ground of being brings constant challenges as our self-concepts and worldviews stretch and snap due to life crises and experiences of sacred revelation or inspiration. Resources and strategies for helping, healing, and seeking justice are applied to strive toward ideals of well-being (such as harmony, salvation, or enlightenment) and to respond to physical, mental, social, or spiritual distress. In the religious context, the transforming function leads to community sanctioned therapeutic and social service systems for religiously motivated helping, healing, saving, reconciliation, and social activism (Beckford & Demerath, 2007; Bellah, 1991; Dossey, 1993; Fuller, 2008; Matthews, Larsen & Barry, 1993; Niebuhr, 1932; Sobrino, 1988).

The relational function of just being produces *patterns of intrinsic satisfaction*. Experience of the preciousness or sacredness of our connectedness and aliveness carries with it intrinsic joy, contentment, peace, and wonder (Maslow 1968, 1970). We can also engage in action dedicated to the well-being of others, yet without attachment to results. As Mohandas Gandhi put it, "He is a true devotee…who has dedicated mind and soul to God…who renounces all fruits of action, good or bad, who treats friend and enemy alike, who is untouched by respect or disrespect" (Mitchell, 2000, pp. 214–215). In transpersonal experience of unitive nondualistic consciousness, there is no division between self or other and no object to be attained. Wilber (2006, p. 74) describes this as "ever-present Nondual awareness, which is not so much a state [of consciousness] as the ever-present ground of all states (and can be experienced as such)." Within religious contexts, people can engage in ceremonies, rituals, social gatherings, meditation, prayer, and altruism just for the inherent worth of human community and communing with the sacred, without seeking rewards or benefits. Paradoxically, just being without ulterior motive can be its own profound reward.

For the sake of simplicity, we described how functions of spirituality lead to particular contents of a spiritual perspective. This is not a one-way process, however. The expression of spiritual drives, the nature of spiritual experiences, and spiritual functioning and development interact and are all shaped by a person's or group's contact with established spiritual perspectives. In a very profound way, just being can infuse all aspects of life with meaning, significance, and transcendence. We intend our model to serve as a heuristic device that suggests the components, complexity, and subtlety of spirituality, rather than specific causal pathways. For example, Bradley, Maschi, and Gilmore (2007) adapted the 1999 version of this model to illustrate in real life rich detail the spiritual development of an 80 year old peace activist.

A Holistic Model of Spirituality

Social work parlance commonly understands the whole person in environment in terms of biological, psychological, and sociological aspects. In addition, scholars sometimes describe spirituality as the wholeness or gestalt of the human being, irreducible to any part. Figure 3.4, A Holistic Model of Spirituality, depicts spirituality in relation to the bio-psycho-social model, using three metaphors: spirituality as the wholeness of the person, spirituality as the center of the person, and spirituality as the spiritual aspect of the person.

Spirituality as an *aspect* of the person completes a quaternity—the biological, psychological, sociological, and spiritual aspects each have their necessary functions (Robbins et al., 2006). In Figure 3.4, we illustrate the spiritual aspect as one piece among four, but it is a very special piece. As we discussed above, the spiritual aspect motivates experience and action to engage self with the world and symbolic reflection to interpret self and world. It orients the person and groups toward meaning, purpose, connectedness, and transcendence. This spiritual aspect is fundamental to human nature and infuses the other bio-psycho-social aspects. Indeed, the spiritual aspect impels us to give meaning and purpose to our bodies and biological functions, to our thoughts and feelings, and to our relationships with other people and the rest of the universe.

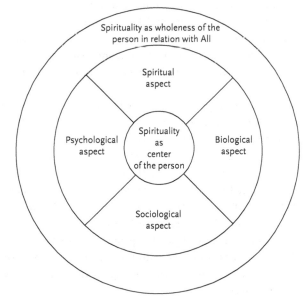

Figure 3.4. A holistic model of spirituality.

For example, when human beings try to understand one of the most significant bodily events—death—we raise deeply spiritual questions about the reason for sickness and mortality, especially for untimely deaths. Spirituality probes the meaning of death, what happens after death, how to come to terms with the deaths of ourselves and loved ones, how to process feelings of grief, and how to acknowledge death through rituals and prayer. Spirituality infuses all our aspects and helps to weave them together into a sense of integrity (i.e. integratedness), connectedness, and wholeness.

Accordingly, many scholars have suggested that spirituality should refer to a quality of human being that is not reducible to any part. This is spirituality as the *wholeness* of what it is to be human. This wholeness is sometimes referred to as that which is sacred or transcendent (Angel, 1994; Eliade, 1959; Imre, 1971). So each person is worthy of respect and care regardless of any of his or her particular qualities or conditions. This is the basis of the value of unconditional positive regard, common in humanistic psychology, pastoral counseling, and social work. In religious contexts, this mysterious and holistic quality of the person may be described as a divine nature within humanity, "made in the image of God," the Buddha Nature of the person, or the true Self (Atman), which is one with Brahman in Vedantic Hinduism. Indeed, the root meanings of the words *whole, holy,* and *heal* are related. Even when people reject these religious or metaphysical ideas, as with atheistic existentialists, the notion of human wholeness and irreducibility is strongly valued.

Further, this wholeness is not limited to an individual, because individuals achieve wholeness of self only through meaningful and respectful relations with others. The quest for personal integration and wholeness brings individuals into a quest for mutually satisfying relations with other individuals and communities, the rest of the world, and the ultimate ground of reality however a person understands that (Assagioli, 1965; Helminiak, 1996; Jung, 1938). Contemporary ecophilosophy and many traditional Indigenous worldviews emphasize that human wholeness is inextricable from awareness of our interdependency with all the earth and cosmos (Besthorn, 2001; Besthorn & Canda, 2002; Coates, 2007).

As a person grows in personal and relational integrity, the sense of responsibility for and connection with others also grows. She or he defines and experiences self in relation to other people, other beings, and the ground of being itself (Faver, 2004). Further, a person may experience a sense of unity with the divine or all that exists. Then, the whole self is experienced not only as a separate entity limited by body and ego, but also as a transpersonal Self at one with all (Wilber, 2000a). This transpersonal Self includes and transcends all particular aspects. Figure 3.4 represents it by the outer circle that encompasses the person in relation with all things. The spiritual journey toward wholeness, or expansion of consciousness to union with the divine or ultimate reality that enfolds all, is a movement of transcendence, going upward and beyond the limits of the ordinary body/ego.

However, this journey can also be a movement of immanence, going inward to "the center" of the person. This *center* is sometimes described as soul or the seat of consciousness, which is the connection and orientation point between all aspects of the person. This metaphor is used in the context of introspection, going inside oneself to find a center point of unity and integration. Many traditions of prayer, meditation, and contemplation employ centering techniques such as awareness of the breath, which literally flows through our central channel, or focus on a central energy point below the navel (*tantien*, Chinese) or at the heart. Even aside from particular religious beliefs and practices, most people can relate to this metaphor as in the idiomatic expression, "to get centered." "Becoming centered" is to find a place of quiet within oneself that provides a sense of connection, integration, and clear awareness of self and world. Both the metaphors of the center and the wholeness of the person are different ways of coming to the same realization. Indeed, centering actually opens us up to clear awareness and empathy in connection with others. By going within, we find unity with others. By going without, we find a scope of consciousness that embraces all.

Whereas the notion of spirituality as an aspect of the person is widely accepted in scholarly circles, the notion of spirituality as wholeness or center is not as widely used in academic writing of the helping professions. This is probably because these metaphors are difficult to state in operational terms for use in research and clinical assessment. However, as these three ways of experiencing and understanding spirituality are quite common both within and without religious contexts, it is certainly appropriate to be aware of them and to be able to use them as metaphors with people for whom they make sense. Although we wish to refrain from making metaphysical claims, we do feel that these metaphors of spirituality as wholeness and as center are very consistent with the social work professional perspective, which makes a commitment to honor all people with unconditional positive regard. When we take together the three vantage points on spirituality (aspect, wholeness, and center), we have a more complete and rich understanding of the concept.

Spirituality and Religion of Groups

The drives, functions, experiences, developmental processes, and contents of spirituality occur in individuals as well as social systems, such as families, small groups, communities, organizations, cultures, and the global community. A religion emerges when a group shares spiritual experiences, beliefs, values, and behaviors and decides to create enduring patterns of religiousness. However, it is possible for a group to interact for relatively brief amounts of time concerning spiritual matters without forming into a religion. Therefore, there are *spiritual support groups* that do not constitute religions. In addition, members of a religion could depart from it and shift toward a private or individually tailored forms of nonreligious spirituality (Brinkerhoff & Mackie, 1993; Dowdy, 1991).

Realistically, since every culture has some form of religious institutions and most people experience them, nonreligious and religious individuals often influence each other. For example, even people who participate in small informal spiritual support groups, and borrow eclectically from diverse religious traditions to form new beliefs and practices, could not do so without interacting with those religious traditions. Further, if a nonreligious spiritual support group begins to regularize and institutionalize its spiritual ways, it becomes a new alternative religious movement.

Mainstream religions are those that predominate in a society because of their numbers of adherents and economic and political influence (Corbett, 1997). *Alternative religions* have smaller membership and have marginal economic and political influence on a society. There is no absolute dividing line between these types, since this is partly a matter of perception and there is so much variation among religions. Some commonly cited identifying features of alternative religions are: charismatic, lay leadership; less bureaucratic organization; relatively small size; emphasis on conversion and voluntary membership; spontaneous forms of worship; pervasive influence over members' daily lives; frequently an appeal to people who are marginalized, poor, or oppressed (Miller, 1995, pp. 3–4). Sometimes alternative religions are called "cults" or "new religious movements." The term cult has become pejorative and vague, so we will not use it. The term new religious movement is nonjudgmental, but not all alternative religions have originated recently.

Some sociologists also identify cultural patterns that resemble religion and derive from it but are not limited to formal organized religion (Cristi & Dawson, 2007). Bellah (1991) called this civil religion. *Civil religion* involves values and beliefs about the relation between people and sacred powers that become pervasive through a society, even beyond the bounds of a particular religious institution. For example, the American government appropriates Judeo-Christian concepts of God and morals and applies them to support a sense of social coherence and confidence in public life and political governance. The U.S. Constitution refers to God for its notion of human rights and many political groups appeal to divine legitimacy for their policies. Presidents of any political party often end a speech with "God bless America."

There are also social systems built around meanings and values given ultimate significance that do not pertain to organized religions and may not use ideas of the sacred or supernatural. Smith (1994) called these *quasi-religions*. Quasi-religions are ideologies that provide elaborate structures of belief, ritualized behavior, and symbols related to a compellingly profound, often utopian, ideal. They may require supreme commitment from followers, even unto death. For example, Marxism gives ultimate priority to establishing utopian communism. Some countries, like North Korea, have transformed communism into a state sanctioned quasi-religion. Following Griffin (1988), in order to avoid confusion in our definition of religion, we will refer to a system of meaning (or a group) built around an ultimate concern without reference to religious institutions, as a *nonreligious spiritual perspective or group*.

Key Issues in Research about Spirituality

As noted previously, the concept of spirituality is difficult to define in part because it involves aspects of reality that transcend words or measures. However, social workers also need to have concepts, methods, and practical tools for use in assessment and research. We will focus on assessment in Part III. For now, we overview some issues in researching and measuring spirituality, so that the reader is aware of how research could inform spiritually sensitive practice.

Whether spirituality can be *operationalized*, that is, reduced to phenomena that can be directly observed and measured, depends on what one means by the term. By definition, spirituality as wholeness cannot be measured or reduced to any component for measurement without violating the very concept of spirituality as wholeness. As this chapter's opening quote suggested, for those who uphold a holistic or mystical view of spirituality, there is something mysterious, and perhaps sacred, that cannot and should not be violated by reductionist empirical prying and intellectual analysis. However, even here, mystics would say that spirituality as wholeness not only *can* be experienced, but also *should* be experienced. This is a kind of empiricism (i.e. knowledge by direct experience) based on ways of knowing (e.g. prayer, meditation, contemplation, ritual process) that go beyond the limits of the physical senses and ways of thinking or feeling that are bound by ego, space, and time (Braud & Anderson, 1998; Wilber, 1998, 2006). Some meditative and contemplative traditions, such as Zen Buddhism or Christian centering prayer, have systematic instructions for how to engage in spiritual inquiry (methods), standards for legitimacy of insights derived from the methods, and authorized teachers and mentors who guide practitioners, compare experiences, and write up results in religious texts. Yet when mystics talk about this realm of experience, they often use metaphors, paradoxes, parables, and cautions to remind us that the Reality of which they speak is beyond any words or concepts.

Of course, people whose own worldview rejects the possibility of sacredness, ego-transcendence, and mystical experiences will view such claims as mere delusions, self-deceptions, or mistaken beliefs. Thus, for them, the claim of immeasurability or inexpressibility is merely a hiding strategy; they view mysticism as a mystification. This debate rests on fundamentally different ways of experiencing and interpreting the world.

Note that whether or not a researcher accepts metaphysical ideas within a spiritual perspective, the researcher can study its contents and effects. For example, we can study people's accounts of the holistic, transcendent, and immanent qualities of spirituality through interviews and through examination of the symbols, narratives, poetry, music, paintings, ceremonies, and rituals they may be used to communicate about it.

In our operational model of spirituality as an aspect of the human being, the situation becomes more clear. Although researchers or social work practitioners cannot directly observe drives, they can infer them from observation of pervasive human activities that strive for profundity, meaning, transcendence, and integrity. We can also document people's description of their spiritual motivations and purposes.

It is possible to operationalize functions and contents of spirituality in terms of observable and measurable things and events. We can observe, describe, and analyze the way people perceive, interpret, and relate within the context of their spiritual perspectives. We can also study developmental processes and relate them to ways of analyzing life cycle stages and crises of transformation. We can observe and measure the contents of a person's spiritual perspective. For example, we can listen to people's accounts of transpersonal experiences and use biofeedback equipment to measure physiological states and changes that correspond to subjective reports of alterations of consciousness and mystical experiences. This does not measure the subjective experience directly, but it does document its correlations with observable physical events.

Researchers can classify and rate aspects of spirituality and religiousness and examine their correlations with other attitudes, behaviors, and outcomes for personal and social well-being (Benson, Donahue, & Erikson, 1993; Brown, 1994; Hill & Pargament, 2003; Shafranske, 1996; Watts & Williams, 1988; Wulff, 1991). For reviews of hundreds of studies of spirituality and religion along with numerous examples of measuring tools, see the Fetzer Institute's 1999 report on multidimensional measurement of religiousness/spirituality for use in health research (http://www.fetzer.org/PDF/total_fetzer_book.pdf, retrieved September 21, 2008), Hill and Hood (1999), Koenig, McCullough, and Larson (2001), and Paloutzian and Park (2005). Numerous measures and scales are available to explore spiritual development and all the contents of spiritual perspectives listed in our operational model. These very often focus on religious forms of spirituality, both those engaged in religious community (such as worship and ceremony) and those that are private (such as solitary prayer rooted in a religious tradition).

Religiousness can be measured by rating such factors as *religious preference*, or sense of belonging to a particular religious group; *formal religious organizational affiliation*; *credal assent* to particular religious beliefs; *personal religious behavior*, or how often a person prays or engages in other religious activities privately; frequency of *attendance at places of religious* practice; religious *organizational activity* other than at places of religious practice; *amount of financial support* for religious groups; *sense of religious despair or hope*; *religious commitment/motivation* regarding the level of importance given to religion by a person; the extent of *growth seeking or searching for meaning* through religious contexts; types of *religious experiences*; processes of *religious conversion*; *religious coping behaviors and styles*; *religious or spiritual well-being*, such as feelings of fulfillment and meaningfulness in relation to God or to life in general; amount of *religious knowledge* regarding one's own or others' religions; *religious functionality*, such as perceived closeness to God, degree of support by a religious community, or sense of religious or spiritual struggle; and *philanthropic consequences* of religious involvement, such as volunteerism or donation to social causes. All of these features of religiousness have corresponding nonreligious forms, for example, in private nonreligious spiritual activity and in informal spiritual support groups.

Research on spirituality in the field of positive psychology is useful for social workers because it draws on interdisciplinary perspectives, it addresses impacts of spirituality on personal and social functioning, and focuses on positive contributions of spirituality, similar to the strengths perspective in social work. A brief review of this field of research on spiritual well-being illustrates contributions and limitations of prevalent empirical research on spirituality.

Spiritual well-being is a quality of developing and being oriented toward ultimate or sacred concerns that alleviates personal and collective suffering, provides a sense of meaning and purpose to life and death, and fosters optimal human development and fulfilling relationships (Canda, 2009, in press). Spiritual well-being **as a process** is healthy spirituality. Spiritual well-being **as outcome** refers to salutary effects on health, mental health, and social relationships from healthy spirituality. Unfortunately, process and outcome are not always distinguished in the concepts and measures of spirituality and well-being, leading to circular thinking in research (i.e. healthy living results in healthy living).

The Spiritual Well-being Scale (Ellison & Paloutzian, 2007) includes 10 items each for existential well-being (i.e. related to a person's level of life perspective, meaning, and purpose) and religious well-being (i.e. view of God and sense of positive relationship with God). The concept "religious" is distinguished and limited here by belief in God or a higher power. The Spiritual Well-being Questionnaire (Moberg, 2001), includes items about meaning and purpose as well as specifically religious matters of beliefs, attitudes, activities, feelings, and identity. Some items are limited by Christian terms. The Spirituality Index of Well-being (Daaleman & Frey, 2004) addresses self-assessments of insight, ability to solve problems, and sense of purpose and meaning in life. Peterson and Seligman (2004) developed the VIA classification of virtues and strengths, including transcendence, which they defined as strengths that forge connections to the universe and that provide meaning. This category includes appreciation of beauty and excellence, gratitude, hope, humor, and spirituality. Spirituality is defined as "Having coherent beliefs about the higher purpose and meaning of the universe." The Authentic Happiness website (www.authentichappiness.sas.upenn.edu, retrieved September 13, 2007), hosted by Martin Seligman, includes The Authentic Happiness Inventory, The Approaches to Happiness Questionnaire, and The Meaning in Life Questionnaire with questions about sense of meaning, purpose, and benefit to others. VIA Signature Strengths includes a self-rating of degree of being spiritual. These various tools can be used for clinical assessment, self-assessment, and research measurement.

Unfortunately, variability of terms, definitions, and measures among tools can be confusing. For example, the most commonly used features of the concept of spiritual well-being are positive sense of meaning and purpose in life. Some instruments focus exclusively on meaning and purpose; some include related-ness with the sacred, transcendence, and a general sense of positive connect-edness. Some items use religiously limited terms, but are applied to everyone. Some scholars prefer a broad conceptualization of spiritual well-being without reference to religion or sacredness. Others believe that a reference to particu-lar religious contexts or sacredness is crucial. Practitioners who use such tools, or use the findings from research, need to examine the strengths and limita-tions of the tools and be cautious about comparing results based on different tools. Or practitioners can refer to careful reviews of the research such as Hill and Hood (1999), Koenig (2007), Koenig, McCullough, and Larson (2001), and Paloutzian and Park (2005). Websites on spirituality and health (see the link listed in Exercise 3.3) provide helpful information as well.

These tools can be helpful for simple assessments or statistically based research. However, they are limited by a structure that does not allow deep or detailed engagement with people's spiritual perspectives on their own terms. Open-ended questions, interview methods, and field studies of daily life suit this purpose better. When structured tools are needed for specific religions or cul-tures, it would be useful to tailor them to the relevant spiritual perspectives.

There is a questionable assumption implicit in common measures of spiri-tual well-being that a clear sense of life meaning and purpose is positive and that it contributes to other aspects of well-being, such as coping with illness. While this can be true, it is not necessarily true. Development of spiritual well-being is a process that may involve unpleasant feelings (such as authentic guilt and shame motivating personal change and restitution for wrongs) and crises of meaning, purpose, and faith. Further, development of transpersonal consciousness involves questioning and transcending egocentric pleasures, meanings, and purposes. Some approaches to spiritually based social and environmental activism view spiritual well-being as an ideal for loving and just communities that attend to the well-being of self, other people, and all beings of the earth and beyond. These insights suggest that we need to find measures of spiritual well-being that include the potential positivity of negativity and the transpersonal levels of individual consciousness, societies, and world community. We will bring these consider-ations to bear in our guidelines for spiritual assessment in Part III.

Conclusion

In the remainder of this book, we will remain consistent in our use of these terms. Our specific meaning should be clear from the context of usage, or else, we will specify it. For example, if the terms "spiritual" or "spirituality" are used without qualification, they should be understood to include both religious and nonreligious expressions. If we say "spiritual and/or religious," this is a short form for saying "religious and/or nonreligious forms of spirituality." Use of the terms religion or religious will always refer to an individual's or group's expressions of spirituality that connect with institutionalized religions.

In this chapter, we developed detailed definitions and holistic and operational models of spirituality. Our conceptualization assists understanding of spirituality in practice and research. As we saw in chapters one and two, if we are to remain consistent with professional values and a moral vision of compassion and justice, we need to address spirituality in social work. In the remainder of this book, we present a foundation of knowledge and skills for how to do this.

EXERCISES

3.1. What Does Spirituality Mean to You?

You are likely to have had some strong reactions to the various ideas about spirituality and religion presented in this chapter. Strong reactions often stem from feelings of congruence or conflict between one's own beliefs and others. In order to identify where these are coming from, try the following self-reflection exercise to determine your own definitions and issues related to the terms spirituality and religion. This exercise also makes clear that our definitions are affected by our life situation, sociocultural conditioning, and self-understandings. Since these change over time, our personal definitions of spirituality and religion may change over time as well.

Take out five blank sheets of paper. Label the top of each sheet with the headings that follow. Then, following the suggestions, record your reflections on each topic.

Understanding of Spirituality and Religion in Early Childhood

Take a moment to relax and be quiet. Think back to your earliest memories of hearing discussions or having experiences that relate to an understanding of aspects of reality that are ultimate, sacred, or supernatural. What words to label them did you learn to use at the time? Did parents teach you to believe or not believe in a God, spirits, or some other divine forces? Did you participate in a spiritual group or religious community? What kinds of stories did you learn to explain the nature of life and death? What rituals and symbols do you recall vividly? In association with these experiences and words, what mental pictures and feelings come to mind? What were the feelings of affirmation and strength related to this? What were feelings of confusion or distress related to this? Do not judge yourself about any of this. Simply be aware of these memories and accept them gently, without any discomfort.

Draw a picture or diagram, or write down some key words, that sum up your insights about this.

Understanding of Spirituality and Religion Now

Consider the same questions as above. However, identify the terms that are meaningful to you now. What are the thoughts, images, and feelings that you now associate with the terms religion, spirituality, faith, or any others that are important to you? What are the strengths and struggles you now experience in regard to this?

Draw a picture or diagram, or write down some key words, that sum up your insights about this.

How Did You Get Here?

Be aware of the developmental process that you have gone through to move from your childhood experience of spirituality to your current experience. What were the key events that signaled change points? Who were inspirational or troubling figures in your life who have shaped your understanding of spirituality?

Again, depict your insights through a picture or key words.

Where Do You Want to Go?

Look over what you have written and drawn so far. Get a sense of the flow of your spiritual development to this point in time. Now, imagine where you would like to go with your spiritual development. What are your overall life aspirations? How would you describe your images and feelings that are associated with your ideal of spiritual growth? How can you build on your spiritual strengths and resources? If you have identified limitations or conflicts, how could you address them to grow toward your aspirations? Draw a picture or diagram, or write down key words that depict your spiritual ideals and aspirations.

Reflection on the Reading

Now, think back to your reactions to reading this chapter. If there were specific passages that provoked a strong response, consider whether there is any relation between what you have learned about yourself from this exercise and your reaction.

3.2 Alternative Meanings of Spirituality and Religion

We defined spirituality and religion, including the relationship between these concepts. Figure 3.1 depicts spirituality as a broader concept than religion. Figure 3.2 depicts alternative meanings and relationships that clients, colleagues, and people in the public might use. Re-examine all the options and choose the one that best fits your own preferred understanding of the meanings of spirituality and religion and how they relate. If none of them fit, describe your own understanding. Also, consider how faith relates to these terms for you. Write a brief summary.

Recall a client (or a close acquaintance) who had a different understanding of spirituality, religion, or faith from yours. Explain the person's view and how it was different from yours. Write a brief account comparing your views and how these differences impacted your relationship and communication. Did you listen carefully to the person and adjust your communication to join in a helpful way? Was the relationship constrained by misunderstanding? How could you have improved your communication with the person? What did you learn from what you did well or less well to apply to future work with clients?

3.3 Exploring Resources on Spirituality and Social Work Online

There has been an explosion of information and resources about spirituality in relation to social work and health in the past 15 years. Explore the Spiritual Diversity and Social Work Resource Center to discover many of these developments. (via www.socwel.ku.edu/canda) This website complements the material in this book. Initially, spend 20 minutes exploring links in the Resource Center. Write a brief essay about implications for your practice based on what you find there. Make a commitment to spend more time exploring any of the resources that are relevant to your practice and personal interests.

Exploring Spiritual Diversity for Social Work Practice

4

Human Diversity, Spirituality, and Social Work Practice

(I hope for a) Cathedral of Humanity
which should be capacious enough
to house a fellowship of common purpose.

Jane Addams, Settlement House Movement
(cited in Oakley, 1955, p. 27)

Human spirituality is like an intricate tapestry of all aspects of human diversity woven together with spiritual experiences, values, beliefs, and practices. In order to establish the context for this discussion of spiritual diversity in Part II, it will be helpful to consider how the universal and particular qualities of spirituality relate to human experience. As we saw in Chapter 3, there are a variety of opinions among theorists as to whether there is an essential or universal quality of religion or spirituality or whether the concepts are merely social constructions (Scherer, 2006). While we avoid making a definite claim about this, we believe that it is important for social workers to find ways of understanding patterns of difference and similarity among diverse spiritual perspectives in order to encourage a sense of common humanity as a basis for dialogue and connection with clients and communities. We offer the metaphor of weaving to highlight this.

Spirituality as *wholeness of the person-in-relation* is like the frame of a loom. The frame provides a structure and support for the interweaving of warp and woof fibers. Before weaving begins, the frame is empty; it represents a potential for form and beauty that is not yet actualized. This is like the universal potential for spiritual development of all people and cultures. The frame must be strong in order to hold taut the warp fibers that are the necessary foundation for weaving a wonderful fabric. The frame (wholeness) is the intrinsic and universal (transpersonal, transcultural, or transcendent) human nature that provides for the possibility of particular spiritual experiences and expressions. It encompasses and holds all the fibers of particular spiritual expressions, but it also transcends them. Without this intrinsic nature, the weaving of spirituality would not occur so pervasively around the world. This is similar to the notion of a "universal grammar of religion" that recognizes common properties of humanity reflected in sacred texts, rituals, and other spiritual manifestations around the world (Rosemont, 2008, p. 89–90).

Before weaving upon the loom frame can begin, a warp of parallel lengthwise fibers must be strung across the structure. This warp is the central threading that pervades the entire tapestry, hidden within it. This is like the universal (panhuman) *spiritual drives* for profound experience, sense of meaning, and integrity. The warp fiber must be strong and durable. This dimension of spirituality is universal, like the frame, but it is immanent rather than transcendent. It pervades the tapestry, courses throughout it, and gives it shape. The warp threads connect to the frame, from which they derive the necessary tautness and support.

The woof consists of fibers woven through and around the warp (see Figure 4.1). The woof can be composed of many colors and textures. These woof patterns form the outer particular appearance of the tapestry of an individual or group's spirituality. The woof of spirituality results from the complex weaving together of many diverse strands deriving from *spiritual experiences* as shaped by such factors as gender, ethnicity, sexual orientation, age, religious or spiritual perspective, socioeconomic class, and various physical and mental abilities and disabilities. The act of weaving is the spiritual creativity of the person-in-relation. We each weave a life tapestry by *functions of perceiving, interpreting, and relating* as they proceed through *developmental processes.* As we weave our

Figure 4.1. Navajo weaving, anonymous artist, gift to author.

lives in relation with the world, we form particular *contents of religious or non-religious spiritual perspectives.*

The woof represents spiritual diversity. The intricate patterns represent a person's or group's way of life woven upon the universal warp of spiritual drives while the warp connects to the transcendent frame. When the weaving is complete, the formerly empty frame of spiritual potential displays a particular and distinctive fabric associated with each person. Each individual weaves her or his spiritual tapestry in relation with other people and beings. Collectively, we are all weaving a cosmic tapestry that connects all people and all things. In this way, we mutually shape our spiritual patterns of life together in families, groups, organizations, societies, and world. This metaphor expresses the integral connectedness between differentness, distinctness, and diversity, as one quality of spirituality, and commonality and universality, as another quality.

In this chapter, we give an overview of spiritual expressions and forms in relation to human diversity. We discuss the history of religious diversity in American society and the social work profession. We consider links between ethnic diversity and the variety of religions. We also consider some concerns and controversial issues that arise from the intersection between religious diversity and other aspects of human diversity, in particular for women and for lesbian, gay, bisexual, and transgender (LGBT) people. A pervasive theme of this chapter is that religious and spiritual diversity in the United States has always been characterized by a perplexing and challenging blend of religious freedom and religious persecution. The current world situation also reflects this ambiguity. Therefore, spiritually sensitive practice necessarily calls for a commitment to both personal well-being and social and environmental justice.

History of Spiritual Diversity in the United States

Historical Trends

For at least tens of thousands of years, hundreds of Indigenous cultures in North America have maintained distinct patterns of religious beliefs, rituals, and organizations influenced by relationship to the sacred earth and cosmos. For example, peoples of the eastern woodlands, the southwestern deserts, the northern plains, and the northwestern coastal rain forests developed distinctive spiritual ways in relation to the particular characteristics of the land, weather, and beings of the place. Europeans began to colonize North America in large numbers during the 1600s. The English pilgrims, other Puritans, and later, many other groups such as Quakers and Catholics came to North America seeking freedom from religious persecution (Chalfant, Beckley, & Palmer, 1987). Unfortunately, the Christian settlers often did not extend respect of religious freedom to members of rival Christian denominations and often engaged in denigration and persecution of First Nations peoples (Brave Heart, 2001; Bullis, 1996; Canda, 2008b; Canda, Carrizosa, & Yellow Bird, 1995; Gaustad & Schmidt, 2002; Johnstone,

2004). Religious competition was compounded by nationalistic rivalries between French and Spanish territories (primarily Catholic) and English colonies (primarily Protestant) (Keller, 2000). During the American revolutionary war, many colonists in the northeast sought freedom from both tyranny of the English government and the control of the Church of England. Christians both for and against revolution used religious justifications for their actions (Weber & Jones, 1994).

During this period, Euro-American forms of Christianity predominated in the political and economic processes of the government and the general public. However, according to Melton (1993), many of the masses did not display strong church-based religiosity. In 1776, only about 5% of the colonial population were regular participating members of churches. In reaction to interreligious competition and the desire to free governmental control from any particular Christian denomination, formal church–state relations on the federal level were cut at the time of the revolution with the First Amendment to the Constitution and again at the state level with the Fourteenth Amendment in 1868 (Johnstone, 2004). This may also have been influenced by the First Great Awakening, beginning in 1734, which was a widespread Protestant evangelical movement that emphasized salvation by personal relation with Christ and reliance on the Bible, while de-emphasizing the importance of religious affiliation (Chalfant, Beckley, & Palmer, 1987). During this period, enslaved Africans and free Black people began to convert to Christianity in significant numbers, with or without the approval of White enslavers (Martin & Martin, 2002). However, separation of church and state did not challenge the predominance of Protestant Christianity in public life. In the formerly English colonies, out of a population of about 3.5 million, about 20,000 were Roman Catholic and about 6,000 were Jewish. Limited religious pluralism was recognized, but Protestant Christianity was given privilege.

The 19th century involved forces that expanded significantly the religious diversity of the United States (Chalfant, Beckley & Palmer, 1987; Gaustad & Schmidt, 2002; Johnstone, 2004; Keller, 2000). Expansion of European settlers and colonialism westward to the Pacific coast brought contact with hundreds more Indigenous cultures and religions. It also incorporated French and Spanish Catholic territories into the predominantly Protestant nation. With the separation of church and state, Christian churches expanded private voluntary organizations and self-support systems while protecting their privileged position with the state. This opened more room to newer immigrant religious groups, such as the Moravians, Amish, Mennonites, and many more Catholics. In addition, theological disputes among longer established Protestant groups increased the number of denominations.

The civil war involved splits between Christian abolitionists and proslavery Christians (Gaustad & Schmidt, 2002; Jones, 1991; Martin & Martin, 2002; Weber & Jones, 1994). Many Protestant denominations split into northern and southern branches. In the 1750s, slave-owners began to allow proselytization among enslaved laborers (Morris, 1991; Newsome, 1991). After the 1770s, voluntary participation of African Americans in Christianity increased, and they began to form separate congregations. Separate and independent African American Protestant denominations formed in the 1800s, such as the African Methodist Episcopal Church (est. 1816). Free African Americans, slaves, and emancipated African Americans formed religious movements that combined influences from traditional African religions, Christianity, and liberationism (Corbett, 1997; Logan, 2001; Logan, Freeman & McRoy, 1990). In the early 1800s, the Second Great Awakening movement led to the predominance of evangelical and revivalist Christian groups in the south and southwest.

Between 1815 and 1920, about five and a half million Irish (mainly Catholic) people emigrated to the United States. By 1850, there were 1.6 million Catholics (Takaki, 1993). The Catholic Church had become the largest single denomination. This rapid increase of Catholics was met with opposition by many Protestant groups (Gaustad & Schmidt, 2002).

The small percentage of the population who were Jewish in the 1700s were mostly of Spanish, Dutch, German, and Portuguese descent. In the 1880s and early 1900s, the first large Jewish emigration occurred from Germany and Russia, largely in response to anti-Semitic pogroms in Russia (Gaustad & Schmidt, 2002). Many were secularized and urbanized and some were political activists. Some of the German Jews established the more liberal humanistic branch of Reform Judaism. Others established the Conservative Judaism branch, which emphasizes Jewish traditions without strict orthodoxy. During the late 19th century, the more orthodox Eastern European Jews established Orthodox Judaism. Throughout this period, the Jewish emphasis on ethnic solidarity as well as constraints on Jews imposed by anti-Semitism maintained a distinct Jewish subculture, albeit with many religious and secular variations.

The 1800s also involved a period of religious innovation among Christians leading to major new denominations, such as the Church of Jesus Christ of Latter-day Saints, Christian Science, and Jehovah's Witnesses. Each of these groups experienced organized opposition from preestablished Christian groups and sometimes the U.S. government.

During the 1800s, there were three major areas of social justice-related religious debates in addition to the conflict between proslavery and abolitionist forces. First, the alcohol prohibition period (1860s–1933) involved intense opposition to alcohol, primarily by some Protestant groups, while many people of Catholic background supported alcohol consumption (Weber & Jones, 1994). Second, the Social Gospel movement, from 1880–1910, arose primarily among liberal northern churches in urban areas to link efforts for personal salvation with religiously based social justice advocacy (Gaustad & Schmidt, 2002; Johnstone, 2004). For example, Jane Addams' settlement house work and peace activism were influenced by the social gospel orientation of her Quaker father. The social gospel movement led to the founding of the Federal Council of Churches, later named the National Council of Churches. The third debate related to the continuation and intensification of religious and cultural persecution of Indigenous peoples (Deloria, 1994; Johnstone, 2004). Westward expansion of Euro-Americans brought territorial, military, economic, religious, and other forms of imperialistic destruction. By the time of the Allotment Act of 1887 (Dawes Act), which further destroyed the land base of Native peoples, virtually every form of traditional religion was banned on reservations. Although some Christians objected to this behavior, the majority actively supported this process through missionization and support of federal policies or else remained silent about it.

Trends of diversification continued to expand in the 20th century. Antidiversity forces also rose in reaction. For example, by 1925 the anti-Catholic, anti-Jewish, and anti-Black Ku Klux Klan was operating in all states and had a membership of about 8 million. In contrast, ecumenical and interreligious movements also began to grow, especially after World War II. For example, the National Council of Churches in Christ expanded formal cooperation between the more inclusive and liberal Protestant denominations in the 1950s and 1960s. Trends of unification increased within Lutheran, Methodist, and Presbyterian denominations. Interreligious dialogue between Protestants, Catholics, Jews, and members of other religions increased after the Second Vatican Council of the Catholic Church (1962–1965). Another post World War II trend involved a revival of Evangelical, Fundamentalist, and Pentecostal Protestant groups, including major denominations (such as Southern Baptists) and numerous non-denominational churches.

Three major themes of religiously related social justice debate flowed through the 20th century. First, during the two world wars, religious rationales for just war were elaborated. But religiously based pacifism and the antiwar movement also expanded. Second, in the post World War II period, religious debates concerning the civil rights movement and Vietnam War increased the social activist agendas of many religious groups. Third, since the 1960s, there have been counter trends of increased Christian conservatism and evangelicalism with highly organized political action on the one hand, and, on the other hand, greater calls for ecumenical and interreligious cooperation, feminist approaches to spirituality, gay liberation, and liberation theology among more politically and theologically liberal groups.

Contemporary Spiritual Diversity

This section includes statistics and observations compiled from estimates provided by several sources (primarily the Association of Religion Data Archives [ARDA], [http://www.thearda.com/about/, retrieved October 25, 2008] plus Chalfant, Beckley & Palmer, 1987; Corbett, 1997; Famighetti, 1995; Gaustad & Schmidt, 2002; Lippy & Williams, 1988; Keller, 2000; Melton, 1993; Williamson, 1992). These researchers relied on surveys, reports of membership by religious organizations, and review of religious organization directories. They sometimes arrive at rather different demographic figures. This means that figures for groups without formal organizations or membership reporting procedures (e.g. the New Age Movement or traditional Indigenous spiritualities) are not represented or are based on inferences. Further, membership reports by religious organizations are not always accurate. This summary serves as a broad picture of spiritual diversity in the United States.

According to Melton (1993), from 1800–1988, the number of Christian denominations grew from 20 to more than 900. About 82% of Americans identify as Christian; about 60% are Protestant; about 22% are Catholic. ARDA illustrates diversity and groupings among Christians by denominational "families" including Adventist, Anglicanism, Baptist, Christian Science, Communal, Eastern Orthodox, European Free-Church (e.g. Mennonite, Quakers, Amish), Holiness, Independent Fundamentalist, Latter-day Saints, Liberal, Lutheran, Methodist, Pentecostal, Presbyterian-reformed, Spiritualist, Western Catholic and others. Further, within these families and the specific denominations, there are variations of specific spiritual perspectives and behaviors across congregations, families, and individuals.

Jewish Americans (about 2% of the U.S. population) reflect many variations of conservative, orthodox, reform, secular, and other spiritual styles. Islam (about 1.6% of the U.S. population) is one of the fastest growing religions in the United States due to emigration from the Middle East, Africa, and Asia, growth of the Nation of Islam among African Americans, and interest by Euro-Americans (including Sufism). Emigration from Asia, especially in the 1970s and 1980s, brought many ethnic-specific forms of Hinduism and Buddhism. In addition, many Euro-Americans have become converts to offshoots of Hinduism (such as the Hare Krishna movement) and Buddhism (such as Tibetan Buddhism and East Asian forms of Zen and Pure Land Buddhism). Buddhism now represents nearly 1% of the U.S. population. The New Age movement of the 1970s and 1980s brought about many sectarian and nonsectarian blendings of humanism, new paradigm scientific thinking, and Eastern and Western spiritual practices. There are hundreds of Indigenous cultures, each with a variety of spiritual perspectives from culture-specific traditionalism to blending with Protestant and Catholic denominationalism, to completely new forms. Other than Christians, Jews, Muslims, and Buddhists, about 11% of the population are nonreligious and about 2.24% are other religious.

These facts highlight three cautions for social workers. First, given the 900 plus Christian denominations, we need to avoid assuming any particular religious beliefs or practices when meeting a Christian client. We need to find out from the client what Christian affiliation means to her or him. Secondly, because most social workers are influenced by Christianity, we must be especially cautious not to impose religious assumptions or beliefs upon non-Christian clients. Thirdly, since non-Christian minorities may be more likely to experience negative social stigma and prejudice, we must be especially attentive to issues of religious freedom and social justice for these groups. This is especially evident in the post 9/11 period in which Muslims are at increased risk of negative stereotyping, discrimination, and oppression due to suspicions in the general public. These points are actually salient for every combination of worker/client spiritual perspective. We must always find out the significance (if any) of a religious or nonreligious spiritual perspective from the client's point of view. We must always avoid imposing our own view. And we must always be alert to client's experiences of harmful discrimination or oppression based on their spiritual perspective.

Contemporary Trends of Spiritual Belief and Practice

Although spirituality in the United States involves great diversity, there is also a high level of consensus. According to ARDA figures, most Americans share the following characteristics: Christian (82%), belief in God (95.6%), belief in a human soul (95.6%), belief in life after death (81.2%; heaven, 87.5%; hell, 74.6%). Most say that religion is important (82.5%) and that it provides comfort and strength (79.5%); 78.5% belong to a denomination. Most say that church provides answers for spiritual needs (74.5%) and family problems (61%). Most meditate or pray (89.3%), praying more than once a week (71.1%). Evangelical Protestants now make up the largest religious category at 30% of the population (Pew Research Center for the People and the Press, 2003).

In American contemporary society, more people place first priority on private, personal, individualized faith rather than on institutional religious participation (Corbett, 1997; Greeley, 1989 & 1995). Religious group membership often involves crossing boundaries set by expectations of family, ethnic group, and social class. In many congregations, there is a stronger focus on local issues and religious group particularism, rather than on global issues and ecumenism. There is great interest in application of religion and spirituality to healing, alternative therapies, social action, and other practical "this worldly" benefits. Emotional and experiential approaches to spirituality have grown more popular than intellectual approaches. Concern about women's issues and gay rights has grown among religious people. Increased population movements across national boundaries have led to increasingly complex variations of religious traditionalism, conversion or loss of religion, spiritual exploration, and blending of religious and nonreligious spiritual perspectives (Ammerman, 2007). In the past 10 years, cyberspace of the internet has dramatically increased opportunities for learning and communicating about one's own and others' spiritualities around the world (Lovheim, 2007). Some people revel in these opportunities for spiritual flexibility, some reinforce adherence to their singular perspective, and some foment intolerance and violence.

These patterns are influenced by age, with American baby boomers (born from 1946–1962) emphasizing more spiritual questing and flexibility in contrast to elders (65 or older) who may reflect more traditional religious beliefs, even though private spiritual activities may become more common than formal religious group participation as health and mobility decline (Nelson-Becker, Nakashima, & Canda, 2006; Roof, 1993). Many contemporary youth conceptualize spirituality as distinct from, and more significant than, religion and institution-alized authority, even though they may participate in religions (Smithline, 2000; Steen, Kachorek & Peterson, 2003; Wilson, 2002). Among Generation Nexters (18–25 year olds), 44% are Protestant, 25% are Roman Catholic, less than 10% are other religious. Although a similar proportion identify as Evangelical to older adults, 20% are nonreligious, atheist, or agnostic. This generation is the least likely to attend church regularly.

The current world situation of intense interdependency and interaction between societies impacts spiritual perspectives and spiritual perspectives impact the process of globalization (Roberts, 2004). On the one hand, partic-ular religious denominations can be enriched by connection among members from different languages and nationalities on the basis of common beliefs and practices. The potential for interreligious dialogue and understanding increases as well. On the other hand, differing cultural traditions and political leanings among fellow believers and between different believers of various cultures and nations can lead to confusion and conflict.

History of Connections between Spirituality and Social Work

The previous discussion of religion and spirituality in the United States illus-trates some of the ways that religious groups vied for influence in public life, social policy, and social activism. In this section, we consider briefly the shifting trends of connection between spirituality and the social work profession.

Five broad overlapping historical phases characterize the development of connections between spirituality and social work in America (Table 4.1). These provide a simplified heuristic overview of complex trends (Canda, 2005a): *Indigenous social welfare* (precolonial period); *sectarian origins* (colonial period through early 20th century); *professionalization and secularization* (1920s through 1970s); *resurgence of interest in spirituality* (1980s to mid-1990s); and *transcending boundaries* (mid-1990s to present).

The first phase, *Indigenous social welfare*, covers tens of thousands of years during which Indigenous cultures in North America (as everywhere else) had distinctive spiritually based patterns of helping, healing, and mutual support extending to social welfare and respect for the earth. There are no written records for most of this period. However, certain features can be inferred from archeological evidence, oral traditions, current practices, and written records of the past 500 years. Many of these continue to the present, separate from or in connection with professional social work, as will be discussed in Chapter 5. As mentioned previously, there were hundreds of distinct cultures with their own languages and worldviews. Precolonial Indigenous helping likely occurred in the context of holistic worldviews emphasizing: (1) individual development of harmony between spiritual, emotional, physical, and mental aspects or persons; (2) a strong web of family, clan, and community relations; (3) family, clan, and community-based identity; (4) sense of respect for and interdependency with all

Table 4.1. Historical Phases in Connection between Spirituality and American Social Work.

Phase	Characteristics
One: Indigenous precolonial times	Hundreds of Indigenous cultures with spiritually based social welfare systems Discrimination, oppression, and mass destructive impacts from European colonial contact and expansion
Two: Sectarian origins (colonial period to early 20th century)	Primarily Christian and Jewish sectarian professional services Sectarian ideologies in governmental services Beginnings of nonsectarian humanistic spiritual ideologies for social services
Three: Professionalization and Secularization (1920s–1970s)	Professionalization and secularization of social work ideologies and institutions Increased professional skepticism of religiously based social work Separation of church and state more strictly enforced in social service delivery Tacit religious ideologies continue in governmental social services Social work education detaches from religion and spirituality Sectarian private social service agencies and educational institutions continue Beginnings of existential, humanistic, and new nonsectarian approaches to social work
Four: Resurgence of interest in spirituality (1980–1995)	Continuation of private sectarian social work Calls for inclusive approach to spirituality Increasing diversity of religious and nonreligious spiritual perspectives in social work Rapid increase of related research, publication, and networking Beginnings of systematic international collaborations Return of attention to religion and spirituality in social work education
Five: Transcending boundaries (1995 to present)	Escalation of previous trends General and context-specific definitions and research on spirituality refined Curriculum guidelines, courses, textbooks widely established Postmodern perspectives increased Faith-based social services policies formalized Interdisciplinary and international networking and collaborations increased Empirical studies increased Whole earth perspectives on spirituality introduced

of nature; (5) rootedness in particular places and special relationship with the sacred beings thereof; and (6) a sense of sacredness and connectedness of person, family, clan, nation, world, mother earth, and universe (Baskin, 2006; Brave Heart, 2001; Bucko & Iron Cloud, 2008; Deloria, 1994; Fire, 2006; McKenzie and Morrisette, 2003; O'Brien, S., 2008; Smith, 2005). Therefore, help provided by community leaders, herbalists, spiritual healers, peacemakers, respected elders, and ritualists sought to maintain or restore the web of harmonious relations within and among persons, communities, and cosmos. Unfortunately, these Indigenous helping systems were assaulted during the colonial period and they were largely ignored by the Euro-American founders of professional social work.

In our view, all social workers should hold Indigenous ways of helping with special esteem and appreciation. In particular, social workers who are immigrants or descendents of immigrants should respect those who are the first caretakers of this land. We should also be cognizant of the unpaid debt for our intrusion upon this land and its original peoples. Further, contemporary social work is rediscovering many insights of Indigenous worldviews, such as holistic understanding of the person/environment whole, the interrelatedness of all things, and the sacredness of the Earth. We believe that the ANZ professional social worker organization's recognition of Indigenous people's rights, colonists' treaty obligations, and appreciation for their spiritual perspective is a good model for American social work (Nash & Stewart, 2002).

In the second phase, *sectarian origins*, voluntary social services and governmental social welfare related policies were largely influenced, directly or indirectly, by Christian and Jewish conceptions of charity and community responsibility (Axinn & Levin, 1982; Boddie, 2008; Brower, 1984; Bullis, 1996; Cnaan, Wineburg, & Boddie, 1999; Garland, 1992; Gelman, Andon, & Schnall, 2008; Kreutziger, 1998; Leiby, 1985; Loewenberg, 1988; Marty, 1980; Niebuhr, 1932; Reid & Popple, 1992; Van Hook, 1997). These involved rival applications of theological ideas to social life, such as emphasizing individual moral blame or merit (e.g. distinction between worthy and unworthy poor) versus social justice and communal responsibility (e.g. Jewish communal service and the Christian social gospel). During this phase, Indigenous, African American, and French and Spanish Catholic spiritual perspectives also shaped social work, though these have not been acknowledged widely (Martin & Martin, 2002; Van Hook, Hugen, & Aguilar, 2001).

There were also social work pioneers who had strong spiritual motivations for service, but did not focus on religious terminology or institutions to express them. For example, in 1888, Jane Addams, the Nobel Prize winning pioneer of the settlement house and peace movements, used the metaphor of a "Cathedral of Humanity which should be capacious enough to house a Fellowship of common purpose, and which should be beautiful enough to persuade men to hold fast to the vision of human solidarity" (as cited in Oakley, 1955, p. 27). An article in a Christian magazine in the 1930s, The Churchman, expressed it this way (Simkhovitch, 1950, p. 139): "The settlement, made up as America is made up, of various types of people with varying points of view, cannot fasten upon any one aspect of truth, political or religious, and, regarding it as the solely valid key to life, insist upon its acceptance by others." Cnaan, Wineburg, and Boddie (1999) pointed out that while religions had significant influence on the formation of American social work, there were also significant nonreligious and governmental influences.

During the third phase, *professionalization and secularization*, as social work professionalized in competition with and along medicine and law, secular humanistic and scientific perspectives, such as socialism, social functionalism, Freudianism, and behaviorism became more influential than theology. It was hoped that these scientific views would provide a more reliable base for practice. Increased involvement of federal and state governments in social work and social welfare brought greater concerns about separation of church and state within the arena of social services. In general, many social workers grew wary of the tendency of some religious providers of services to engage in moralistic judgmentalism, blaming the victim, proselytization, and exclusivism. During this period, the National Association of Social Workers and the Council on Social Work Education (CSWE) formed as inclusive, secular, professional organizations, in contrast to earlier sectarian social work organizations. Curriculum policy guidelines of CSWE in the 1950s and 1960s referred to the spiritual needs of people, in nonsectarian terms. But the CSWE guidelines of the 1970s and 1980s eliminated even these nonsectarian references to spirituality (Marshall, 1991; Russel, 1998).

However, religious and nonreligious spiritual perspectives influenced social work throughout the third phase. Many religiously related agencies continued to provide social work services, such as through Catholic Social Services, Lutheran Social Services, Jewish Family Services, and the Salvation Army. Nonsectarian spiritual perspectives grew in influence, such as in 12 Step programs. Social workers brought their own personal spiritual views and values into practice, at least implicitly. Some social work scholars continued to call attention to spirituality in publications (e.g. Spencer, 1956; Towle, 1965). Ideas from Asian religions began to enter social work literature (e.g. Brandon, 1976; Krill, 1978). Humanistic, Jungian, and other nonsectarian spiritual perspectives grew within social work, often without explicit mention of religion or spirituality (Robbins, Chatterjeee, & Canda, 2006).

The fourth phase, *resurgence of interest in spirituality*, expanded on the ecumenical, interreligious, and nonsectarian spiritual undercurrents that existed in the profession from its beginning. During the 1980s, publications called for a return to our profession's historic commitment to spirituality. The significant innovation was addressing spirituality in a way that includes and respects the diverse range of religious and nonreligious spiritual perspectives among clients (Borenzweig, 1984; Brower, 1984; Canda, 1988b, 1988c, 1989; Constable, 1983; Joseph, 1987; 1988; Loewenberg, 1988; Marty, 1980; Meystedt, 1984; Siporin, 1982, 1985).

Up to the mid-1990s, this trend continued to expand rapidly. Numerous articles and books appeared dealing with spirituality and social work, including a wider range of religious and nonsectarian approaches such as Buddhism, Confucianism, Hinduism, Shamanism, Taoism, and transpersonal theory (Canda,

Nakashima, Burgess, Russel, & Barfield, 2003). I (EC) founded the Society for Spirituality and Social Work in 1990 (based on informal networking begun in 1986) to bring together scholars and practitioners of diverse spiritual perspectives for the enhancement of the profession. It organized meetings at NASW and CSWE national conferences. In 1994, under the leadership of Robin Russel, it held its first national conference, bringing together practitioners and educators from a wide variety of religious and nonreligious spiritual views (Derezotes, 2006).

In phase five, *transcending boundaries*, all of these trends have been accelerating. The distinguishing features of this period are the formal recognition of spirituality in U.S. social work educational standards and the movement among scholars and practitioners "to transcend boundaries between spiritual perspectives, academic disciplines, nations, governmental and religious institutions, and between humans and nature" (Canda, 2005a, p. 99).

The 1995 version of CSWE's curriculum guidelines returned attention to belief systems, religion, and spirituality, especially with regard to client diversity (Russel, 1998). Social work practice texts and a human behavior theory text published in the United States and United Kingdom during the next several years set out frameworks for integrating spirituality into social work (Bullis, 1996; Canda, 1998a; Canda & Furman, 1999; Crompton, 1998; Derezotes, 2006a; Ellor, Netting, & Thibault, 1999; Nash & Stewart, 2002; Patel, Naik, & Humphries, 1997; Robbins et al., 1998) .

In the early 2000s, ecophilosophical spiritual views on social work entered our field, mainly through the work of Besthorn (e.g. 2000, 2001) and Coates (2003). The range and numbers of publications on spirituality in general and context-specific understandings have continued to increase until the present. (For example, see the *Journal of Religion and Spirituality in Social Work*, formerly *Social Thought*). Postmodern perspectives (such as feminist, ecophilosophical, transpersonal, and post-colonial) are calling "social work to extend its inclusive approach to spirituality to all people and nations, with special attention to the oppressed and marginalized, to all beings on the planet, and to the earth itself as a living being deserving of honor and respect" (Canda, 2005a, p. 100; Meinert, Pardeck & Murphy, 1998). For example, Derezotes' (2006a & 2006b) approach to spiritually oriented social work calls for an integration of biopsychosocial, spiritual, and environmental paradigms in a way that celebrates spiritual diversity.

Courses, conferences, and symposia on spirituality have been increasing in North America and in other countries. For example, Russel (1998, 2006) noted that spirituality electives in American MSW programs increased significantly in the past 10–12 years; she identified 57 such courses in the country in 2004. The first international conference of the Society for Spirituality and Social Work (SSSW) took place in 2000. In the past several years, international conferences hosted by International Federation of Social Workers (IFSW) and *International Association of Schools of Social Work* (IASSW) have featured many presentations and networking on spirituality. The Centre on Behavioral Health of the University of Hong Kong was established by Cecilia Chan in 2002 "to provide a holistic approach for the promotion and betterment of mental, emotional and behavioral welfare of the community, as well as aspiring towards achieving international recognition in the field" (http://web.hku.hk/~bhealth/index.html). The Canadian Society for Spirituality and Social Work was established in 2002. John Coates, the director, cooperates with Ann Weaver Nichols, the director of the U.S. based SSSW to cohost annual North American conferences. International symposia on spirituality and social work at the Inter-University Center of Dubrovnik, Croatia expanded under the inspiration of Dada Maglajlic. In 2004, I (EC) established the web-based Spirituality and Social Work Resource Center to create interdisciplinary and international linkages and information sharing (see www.socwel.ku.edu/canda). In 2005, Bernard Moss formed the Staffordshire University Centre for Spirituality and Health in England (see http://www.bernardmoss.org.uk/).

Another trend of this phase has been the increase of empirical research about spirituality in social work. Sheridan was the main forerunner of surveys on practitioners' and educators' attitudes about spirituality in social work and has continued to develop these (e.g. Kvarfordt & Sheridan, 2007; Sheridan, 2004; Sheridan & Amato-von Hemert, 1999; Sheridan & Bullis, 1991; Sheridan et al., 1992; Sheridan, Wilmer, & Atchison, 1994). Our national and international surveys rely heavily on her work; they also illustrate the fruits that can come through international collaborations. Qualitative and quantitative empirical studies on the impacts of religious participation as well as spiritually based social work practices have increased (e.g. Hodge, Langer, & Nadir, 2006; Thyer, 2007a). These often draw on interdisciplinary insights and research approaches especially from gerontology, health, and mental health fields (e.g. Ai, 2006; Canda, 2009).

These trends of spiritually sensitive social work are helping to draw the profession farther beyond egocentric, ethnocentric, humanocentric and other limiting, divisive views. These trends intersect with globalization in both its helpful forms (such as promotion of human rights) and its detrimental forms (such as militaristic expansionism and exploitive transnational economies). The challenge now is how spiritually sensitive social work can continue to further personal well-being and social and ecological justice for all people and all beings, as we extend connectedness around this planet and beyond. To paraphrase the Canadian social work scholar John Graham (2006), social workers invested in spirituality need to develop a knowledge base that is both locally and globally compatible, by connecting North and South (and we would add East and West) through collaborations that are nonhegemonic and mutually enriching.

Patterns of Spiritual Orientations among Social Workers

A detailed picture of social workers' demographic and spiritual diversity can be derived from our 2008 National Survey of social workers. The sample was composed of 72.6% (n = 1,309) women and 26% (n = 469) men. The data for gender were missing on 1.4% (n = 26) of the surveys. The gender demographic is very similar to the 1997 sample: 74.4% women; 24.7% men. The average age of the respondents was 58 (standard deviation of 10.7) with a range of 23–89. The age demographic in 1997 was considerably lower, with an average age of 48. There were 40 questionnaires missing data pertaining to age. Most of the 2008 respondents were Caucasian/Euro-American (87.1%, n = 1,572). The rest of the sample were African American (4.2%, n = 75), Latino/Hispanic American (3%, n = 54), Asian American/Pacific Islander (1.5%, n = 27), Native American/First Nations (0.3%, n = 5), mixed heritage/bi-racial (1.3%, n = 23), and other (1%, n = 18). Missing data accounted for 1.7% (n = 30). The ethnic/racial composition of the 2008 National Survey was very similar to the 1997 sample, although the percentages of Caucasian (–3.2%) and Native American (–0.4%) respondents were lower whereas respondents in the other racial groups increased in 2008.

The participants were requested to indicate their current primary religious or spiritual orientation (see Table 4.2). Not surprisingly, by far the largest percentage of the respondents related that they were Christian (56.8%), which is very similar to the 1997 sample (57.5%). Adherents to various forms of Judaism formed the second largest religious category. We had far more Jewish respondents in 2008 (20.2%) than in 1997 (6.1%). There is also a wide variety of other religious orientation affiliations, most notably Buddhism, Goddess religion, spiritism or shamanism, traditional First Nations and Native Hawaiian, and Unitarian. In addition, about 14% of participants indicated a nonreligious orientation as their primary affiliation.

After they selected a primary affiliation, participants were asked to indicate if they have only one religious or spiritual affiliation, a multiple religious orientation (combinations of at least one religion and any other religious or nonreligious spiritual orientation), or a multiple nonreligious orientation (any combination of atheist, agnostic, existentialist, nonaffiliated Jewish, and none) (see Table 4.3). Among Christians, 6% indicated they have a multiple religious orientation. Among those with a primary nonreligious spiritual orientation, 1.6% indicated that they have a multiple religious orientation, and 6.8% have a multiple nonreligious orientation. Overall, 5.9% of the sample indicated a multiple religious orientation and 1.2% indicated a multiple nonreligious orientation, compared with 9.9% and 9.1% respectively, in 1997. This lower proportion of multiple spiritual affiliators in 2008 may be due to the changed questions. This time, we asked respondents to specify their primary affiliation in order to make this clear and to facilitate other statistical analyses. In 1997, on the other hand, we asked respondents to select as many religious and nonreligious spiritual orientations as they wished, without specifying primary affiliation. This resulted in a greater degree of overlapping religious and nonreligious spiritual orientations.

In comparison with ARDA statistics, while a majority of NASW members in our study are Christian (56.8%, including those with multiple affiliations), the percentage is quite smaller than the general population (about 82%). In addition, the percentage of Jewish and Buddhist members is much higher; the percentage of Muslims is much lower; and percentage of nonreligious is slightly higher. In general, as would be expected, those who claimed a religious affiliation were

Table 4.2. National NASW Survey: Religious and Spiritual Orientations of Social
            Workers.

	Percentage	*Frequency*
Primary Religious Orientations		
Buddhism	4.8	86
Christianity:		
Protestantism	26.9	486
Catholicism	17.8	321
Nondenominational	5.8	105
Unspecified	5.6	101
Latter-Day Saints	0.2	3
Eastern Orthodox	0.4	8
Subtotal Christian	**56.8**	**1,024**
Goddess Religion	0.1	1
Hinduism	0.2	3
Judaism:		
Reform	16.2	293
Conservative	2.3	42
Unspecified	1.2	21
Orthodox	0.5	9
Subtotal Jewish	**20.2**	**365**
Islam	0.1	2
Spiritism/Shamanism	0.7	13
Traditional Native American (First Nations)	0.4	8
Traditional Hawaiian	0.1	1
Unitarian Universalism	0.7	13
Wicca	0.2	4
Religious Others[a]	0.5	9
Total Religious	**84.8**	**1,529**
Primary Nonreligious Spiritual Orientations		
Agnosticism	6.5	117
Atheism	2.9	53
Existentialism/Humanism	1.5	27
Nonaffiliated Jewish	3.0	54
Total Nonreligious	**13.9**	**251**
Other		
None (No spiritual affiliation)	0.1	2
Other—Unspecified	0.6	11
Not Reported	0.6	11

Note: [a]Religious others includes unspecified multifaith/interfaith (6 responders), Buddhism/
Christianity (1 responder), Zen/Taoism/Episcopalian (1 responder), and Buddhism/Shamanism/
Existentialism (1 responder).

likely to have an average to high level of involvement in religious or spiritual
activities, such as prayer and attendance at religious services. In contrast, atheists and agnostics were likely to have a low to average involvement in religious
or spiritual activities.

Table 4.3. National NASW Survey: Singular and Multiple Religious and Spiritual Orientations of Social Workers by Primary Affiliation.

	Total	Singular Primary Affiliation Only	Multiple Religious Orientation in Addition to Primary	Multiple Nonreligious Orientation in Addition to Primary
	(n)	% (n)	% (n)	% (n)
Primary Religious Orientations				
Buddhism	(86)	90.7 (78)	9.3 (8)	
Christianity:				
Protestantism	(486)	95.3 (463)	4.7 (23)	
Catholicism	(321)	94.1 (302)	5.9 (19)	
Nondenominational	(105)	90.5 (95)	9.5 (10)	
Unspecified	(101)	92.1 (93)	7.9 (8)	
Latter-Day Saints	(3)	66.7 (2)	33.3 (1)	
Eastern Orthodox	(8)	100 (8)		
Subtotal Christian	**(1024)**	**94.0 (963)**	**6.0 (61)**	
Goddess Religion	(1)	100 (1)		
Hinduism	(3)	66.7 (2)	33.3 (1)	
Judaism:				
Reform	(293)	99.3 (291)	0.7 (2)	
Conservative	(42)	97.6 (41)	2.4 (1)	
Unspecified	(21)	81 (17)	19 (4)	
Orthodox	(9)	100 (9)		
Subtotal Jewish	**(365)**	**98.1 (358)**	**1.9 (7)**	
Islam	(2)	100 (2)		
Spiritism/ Shamanism	(13)	84.6 (11)	15.4 (2)	
Traditional Native American (First Nations)	(8)	100 (8)		
Traditional Hawaiian	(1)	100 (1)		
Unitarian Universalism	(13)	15.4 (2)	84.6 (11)	
Wicca	(4)	100 (4)		
Religious Others[a]	(9)		100 (9)	
Subtotal Primary Religious Orientations	**(1529)**	**93.5 (1430)**	**6.5 (99)**	
Primary Nonreligious Spiritual Orientations				
Agnosticism	(117)	94.0 (110)	1.7 (2)	4.3 (5)
Atheism	(53)	92.5 (49)		7.5 (4)
Existentialism/ Humanism	(27)	74.1 (20)	7.4 (2)	18.5 (5)

Table 4.3. Continued.

	Total	Singular Primary Affiliation Only	Multiple Religious Orientation in Addition to Primary	Multiple Nonreligious Orientation in Addition to Primary
	(n)	% (n)	% (n)	% (n)
Nonaffiliated Jewish	(54)	94.4 (51)		5.6 (3)
Subtotal Primary Nonreligious Spiritual Orientations	(251)	91.6 (230)	1.6 (4)	6.8 (17)
Other				
None (No primary religious/spiritual affiliation)	(2)	50.0 (1)	50.0 (1)	
Other—Unspecified	(11)	45.5 (5)	27.3 (3)	27.3 (3)
Not Reported	(11)	81.8 (9)		18.2 (2)
Percentage and Count for Total Sample	(1,804)	92.8 (1,675)	5.9 (107)	1.2 (22)

Note: [a]Religious others includes unspecified multifaith/interfaith (6 responders), Buddhism/Christianity (1 responder), Zen/Taoism/Episcopalian (1 responder), and Buddhism/Shamanism/Existentialism (1 responder).

Other regional and national studies of social workers (Derezotes & Evans, 1995; Furman & Chandy, 1994; Hodge & Boddie, 2007; Kvarfordt & Sheridan, 2007; Mattison, Jayaratne, & Croxton, 2000; Sheridan et al., 1992) have also shown variations in proportion of spiritual perspectives compared to the general population, for example, fewer Christians, more Jews, more other religious, and more nonreligious. This is a reminder of the necessity for social workers to be able to engage in a spiritually sensitive helping relationship that takes into account similarities or differences of spiritual perspective between worker and client. It is likely that this wider variety of religious and nonreligious spiritual perspectives among social workers contributes to professional commitment to respect spiritual diversity because of the opportunity to interact across differences among students and faculty in educational programs. Conversely, it may also raise a challenge for less traditionally spiritual social workers to be sensitive to more traditionally religious clients.

Ethnic Diversity and Spirituality

We have seen the interconnections between ethnicity and religious affiliations in the review of American history and social work. The spiritual diversity of the

United States has been directly influenced by interactions between Indigenous peoples, people of African descent, and immigrants and refugees from all regions of the world. Even within a single religious tradition or a single religious congregation, ethnic diversity brings different modes of belief and practice. For example, very different patterns of language, worship styles, symbolism, and religiosity can be found among Hispanic Catholics whose families resided in New Mexico for many generations, first generation Catholic immigrants from El Salvador, fourth generation Irish Catholics, and Vietnamese Catholics who came here as refugees in the 1970s and 1980s.

In some cases, there are close associations between ethnicity and spiritual perspective, such as among the Amish, Jews, Eastern Orthodox Christians, Arab-American Muslims, Indian American Hindus, Asian American Buddhists, and traditional spiritual ways of Indigenous peoples (Corbett, 1997). This is not to say that any of the religious traditions are entirely ethnic exclusive; however, some religious communities maintain an intentionally close link between cultural identity and spiritual tradition and may seek to maintain a boundary between themselves and others. Often people in these groups view culture and religion or spirituality as inseparable. They may discourage or limit participation in religious ceremonies by outsiders. Interreligious and inter-ethnic marriage may be perceived as a dilution or threat to the continuance of the group. This voluntary separatism is often complicated and reinforced by involuntary exclusion, ostracism, persecution, and prejudice directed at these groups by so-called mainstream Euro-American Christians. For example, declarations that the United States is a Christian country, anti-Semitism, White racist practices of exclusion and segregation, anti-Arab and anti-Islamic rhetoric, and attack against Indigenous spiritual ways have all contributed to inter-group tensions.

Yet even given these challenges, connections between cultural diversity and religious diversity increase the richness and complexity of patterns of spiritual diversity as portrayed in the metaphor of weaving that began this chapter. In order to illustrate this, we introduce some strengths of spirituality among the two largest ethnic minority groups, as defined by the U.S. census, African Americans, and Hispanic Americans. These discussions provide sources for more detailed explorations of these groups by the reader. They also provide examples for how the reader could explore spiritual diversity within and between ethnic groups not addressed here.

African American Spirituality

Spirituality is a significant aspect of life and source of resilience and mutual support in African American communities (Bacchus & Holley, 2004; Bell & Bell, 1999; Black, 1999; Chaney, 2008; Corbett, 1997; Frame, Williams, & Green, 1999; Grant, 2001; Logan, 2001; Johnstone, 2004; Martin & Martin, 2002; Shiele, 1994). Some African Americans distinguish spirituality from religion in ways similar to our definitions. Religion is more associated with organized rituals, doctrines, and worship forms, while spirituality is a source of meaning, vitality, and divine connection that can give significance to religion or can give significance to life outside religion (Banerjee & Canda, 2009; Chaney, 2008). In many communities the Black church is a focal point for material, emotional, social and spiritual support; social reform efforts; affirmation of self-esteem and cultural integrity, recreation apart from intrusiveness of majority White culture; and education. As an African American spiritual song puts it "In my trials Lord, walk with me...In my sorrows Lord, walk with me...I want Jesus to walk with me" (quoted in Chaney, p. 215).

African Americans participate in a wide range of religious affiliations, most commonly Christianity (75.7% Protestant and 6.5% Catholic), including National Baptist Conventions, African Methodist Episcopal churches, the Christian Methodist Episcopal Church, mainline Protestant denominations such as United Methodism, Roman Catholicism, and nondenominational churches and Islam. 10.6% of African Americans identify as nonreligious (General Social Surveys from 1972–2004, retrieved from http://www.religionlink.org/tip_070108. php#stats, October 27,2008), 81% of African Americans describe themselves as "somewhat religious or religious," which is the highest percent among the racial/ ethnic groups studied (Kosmin, Mayer, & Keyser, 2001). Religious groups with 20% or higher Black membership include Jehova's Witnesses (37%), Baptist (29%), Muslim (27%), Seventh Day Adventist (26%), and Pentecostal (22%).

Mainline Protestant and Catholic African Americans often belong to integrated congregations and their religious worship style generally is not significantly different from their Euro-American fellow congregants (Chalfant, Beckley & Palmer, 1987). However, most African American Christians belong to primarily Black denominations that include more than 13 million members. There are also about 3–5,000 Rastafarians, a religion with roots in Jamaica, and an unknown number of adherents to Vodoun, a blending of African, Haitian, and Catholic religious elements (Payne, 1991). Recent immigration and refugee flight from African countries bring additional forms of Indigenous African, Christian, and Islamic traditions (e.g. Gbemudu, 2003; Shandy & Fennelly, 2006).

The origin of the Black Muslims (which now includes several denominations) can be traced to slaves brought from Africa, among whom about 10% were Muslim. In 1934, Elijah Muhammad became the leader of the Nation of Islam. The 1960s and 1970s saw increasing influence of Black Muslims in the African American community generally as well as the Black Power Movement, one of the heroes of which was Malcolm X. For some African Americans, an advantage of the Black Muslim movement is that it is not associated with the history of slavery and racial oppression in the United States, as was Christianity. There are also many African American members of Islamic groups that originate from the Middle East.

African American Christian congregations have often provided a safe haven and source of community support for Black people throughout their experience of Diaspora (Franklin, 1994; Leashore, 1995; Logan, 2001; White

& Hampton, 1995). During the period of slavery, they provided a way to link traditional African patterns of culture and spirituality with the Christian religious practice mandated by White culture. They drew on Christian themes of perseverance and liberation to provide nurture, mutual support, assistance for escape, and support for the abolitionist movement. After the civil war, churches became major sources for community support and leadership training. Hence, they have been active in promoting and organizing the civil rights movement since the 1950s.

Paris (1995) and Martin and Martin (2002) emphasized the continuity of heritage between African and African American spiritual perspectives and values. Paris stated that a fundamental principle of African and African American spirituality is the interdependency between God, community, family, and person in a holistic and sacramental view of life. Paris identified the following virtues as central to African American spirituality: beneficence to the community; forbearance through tragedy; applying wisdom to practical action; creative improvisation; forgiveness of wrongs and oppression; and social justice as the culmination of these other virtues.

According to Franklin (1994), worship style in many Black Christian congregations is characterized by several common features. Times of intimate, cathartic "altar prayer" are encouraged in which members express pain and vulnerability and celebrate forgiveness and liberation in a public manner, thus joining individual feeling with communal care and support. Some congregations encourage cathartic shouting of praise and triumph, ecstatic dancing, and speaking in tongues. Choir singing and music often help stimulate collective feelings, growing in beat and intensity or calming. Religious education often has a strong political component, emphasizing civil rights, community support, and pride in African identity and culture. In regards to preaching, Franklin said, "Black people expect the sermon, as a word inspired by God and located within the community, to be spiritually profound, politically relevant, socially prophetic, artistically polished, and reverently delivered" (p. 265).

Kwanzaa is a nonsectarian Afrocentric spiritual celebration founded in the 1960s by Maulana Karenga (1995), a civil rights activist and professor of Black Studies. He estimated that about 18 million African Americans and other African people throughout the world now celebrate it. Karenga was inspired by the Black Power Movement's goals of individual and community self-determination, culturally grounded self-respect, and collective capacity to end and prevent oppression. In cooperation with others, Karenga drew on empowering principles, values, and symbols widely shared in traditional African cultures, and adopted Swahili terms, to create the format for Kwanzaa. The Kwanzaa celebration supports and appreciates the strengths of African families, communities, and cultures within the larger context of re-Africanization and African American community empowerment. Seven principles (*Nguzo Saba*), paraphrased below, represent core values to be encouraged in the African American community through Kwanzaa.

1. *Umoja:* **Unity** of the family, community, nation, and race.
2. *Kujichagulia:* **Self-determination** in defining, naming, creating, and speaking for oneselves.
3. *Ujima:* **Collective responsibility** to build and maintain community and solve problems together.
4. *Ujamaa:* **Cooperating economically** to build and maintain the community's own stores, shops, and other businesses for mutual benefit.
5. *Nia:* **Purpose** to build and develop the community and restore our people to their traditional greatness.
6. *Kuumba:* **Creativity** in doing as much as possible to make the community more beautiful and beneficial than how it was received.
7. *Imani:* **Faith** to believe totally in our people, our parents, our teachers, our leaders, and the righteousness and victory of our struggle.

Kwanzaa is a collective nonsectarian celebration of spiritual and cultural renovation, innovation, and liberation. It is an opportunity for African and African American families and communities to come together across Muslim, Christian, Jewish, traditional African, and any other spiritual perspectives to reverence the Creator and give thanks for the gift of life, fruits of the earth, and the support of African heritage and community.

Social Work Implications

In order for social workers to provide culturally competent service with African Americans, it is crucial to engage the supportive and transformative aspects of African American spirituality, since this is so important for most Black people. This requires knowledge about and respect for the historical and contemporary roles of the wide variety of African American religious groups and practices. It requires familiarity with patterns of worship and values. It requires practical ability to assess the particular spiritual style and practices of African American clients and to work collaboratively with their religious community-based relatives, friends, and leaders or with their other nonreligious support systems if they are nonreligious.

For African American social workers working with Black clients, there is an opportunity to build on common experiences and sense of solidarity. It is also important not to assume agreement or commonality on religious practices and beliefs, since there is a great deal of diversity within the African American population. For others working with African Americans, it is important to be able to deal honestly and comfortably with the context of racism as it may affect the current situation of the client and the client's relationship with and perception of the social worker. Euro-American social workers must be especially cautious not to make ethnocentric evaluations of unfamiliar spiritual styles and beliefs. Martin and Martin (2002) provide recommendations for spiritually sensitive and culturally appropriate social work practice within both mainstream contexts and Afrocentric approaches.

They believe that social workers in the African American community now need to address spiritual and cultural fragmentation, as evidenced by collapse of meaning and excessive levels of violence. They lament that many White domi-nated social work agencies do not understand or encourage Black cultural and spiritual values. They suggest five principles to guide practice.

The Principle of Internal Locus of Control proposes that Black people are free and responsible for their own moral, intellectual, and spiritual develop-ment, even when oppression impacts their outer lives. The Principle of Personal Responsibility and Collective Reciprocity emphasizes that Black people should do all they can to care for each other as a spiritual act. The Principle of Social Debt proposes that Black people can repay the debt to their ancestors and to God by helping each other to "grow in decency, dignity, and respect" (p.208). The Principle of Sanctification of Human Life states that each human life is sacred, that even small problems are significant, and that the helping process itself is sacred. The Principle of a Holistic Approach proposes that spirituality is not the exclusive domain of religious leaders and that social workers attend to this sig-nificant aspect of clients' lives. They advocate that social workers learn from the Black helping tradition how to engage spirituality in a nonjudgmental, inclusive, and empowering manner, similar to what we have described as the ideal of spir-itually sensitive social work. Martin and Martin encourage social workers to be attentive to the language of Black clients for allusions to their religious beliefs and themes. Social workers should be attentive when Black people recount spir-itually meaningful dreams that represent insights and warnings from the spirit world. Social workers can build on the spiritual strengths of Black communal life events, such as baptism, weddings, holidays, family reunions, and memori-als for the deceased. Social workers should also assess whether and how Black clients draw on prayer, religious attendance, scriptures, forgiveness, and other religious practices for strength.

A midwestern Micro-Entrepreneurial Training (MET) Program is an exam-ple of some of these practice principles (Banerjee & Canda, 2009). Informal and formal interviews with 60 low-income African American women who partici-pated in the program revealed that spirituality was important in their dealing with the challenges of poverty and welfare to work policy. "It helped them to cope with basic needs, such as persevering while seeking food, clothing, shel-ter, and employment; to deal with health problems and personal and family crises; to grow in relationships with their children and spouses or partners; to enhance self-esteem and sense of inner peace; to develop nonjudgmental and caring attitudes toward others; and to process feelings of anger or frustration with supervisors, case managers, and the general difficulties of navigating the welfare system (p. 247)."

For example, Alicia said that a life without God is being poor, but if you have God, you can accomplish what you need. Monique said that if it was not for "my Lord and Savior, Jesus Christ" she probably would have died from drinking alcohol. Brenda explained how she prayed for God's guidance in setting up her micro-enterprise program. God guided her to join the program and to start a graphic design business. She said, both seriously and humorously, that God is the president of the company and that she is just the sales rep. "When I run across problems in the company, I'd tell people, 'Well, the President isn't in at this moment, but if you leave a message, I'll relay it to Him and if He doesn't get back with you, I'm sure He'll tell me how to handle it." Somber said that praising God in worship lifts you up so that you feel light and free of worries. She said that she knows God will take care of everything if she follows God's directions to work and care for her children. Michelle said that she inherited the abilities to see spirits and to have dreams that foretell the future. Once, following directions from a dream, she gathered a group of 25 people to stand in front of a drug house in order to " pray a young man to come out and change his life."

Participants in the MET program felt that this program was a good match for their spiritual values. They viewed staff as caring and persevering teachers who related as fellow humans with their own struggles. Participants formed a sense of spiritual bond with each other. Even though the MET program did not take a religious approach, participants viewed it as having a spiritual quality, because it helped participants to draw on their own spiritual ways and to support each other in the process of developing micro-enterprise strategies.

On a larger scale of social change, the joining of spirituality and action for justice is well reflected in the nonviolent resistance strategy promoted in this country by Rev. Martin Luther King, Jr. He and countless other known and unknown African American civil rights advocates and their allies made immeasurable contributions and sacrifices for the benefit of this country. King's nonviolent resistance strategy confronted racism and unjust war in an inspired and direct way that sought to overcome evil acts and policies, but not to debase or dehumanize anyone, including the oppressors. He sought a *beloved community* of mutual caring, benefit, and justice for everyone (King, 1992). His approach grew from the Christian stand for love, justice, and forgiveness and it embraced every one in all cultures (see Figure 4.2).

If it were not for him and fellow members of the civil rights movement, I (EC) may not have been able to marry my Korean wife in 1977. It was only 10 years earlier that the Supreme Court struck down so-called antimiscegenation laws as one more step in the ongoing march to achieve freedom for everyone. I believe that the social work profession at large is heavily indebted to the legacy of the African American freedom movement for vitalizing the principles of dignity, respect, and empowerment. Social work could become much greater if we considered more seriously how to apply the nonviolent resistance strategy to current issues of injustice.

I will digress a moment to a small but personally inspiring event. Around 1985, I was invited to teach an introductory world religions course as part of

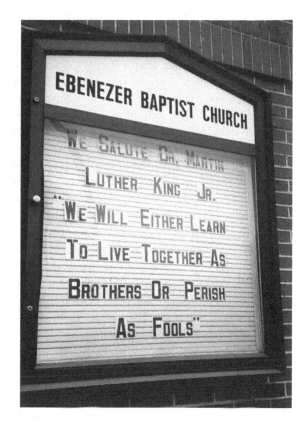

Figure 4.2. Ebenezer Baptist church sign, Atlanta, GA.

an Ohio State University outreach program. African American Christian clergy and lay leaders requested it in order to learn more about religious diversity. During the course, I took special note of the most senior clergy person there. He always spoke with careful thought and deliberation, in few but stirring words. Everyone paid respectful attention when he spoke. For example, one day, when I was covering shamanism and the animistic worldview that honors the spirits in nature, he raised his hand. He said, "Those shamans remind me of how I like to sit on the bank of a river and listen to the water. In the flowing water, I hear God speak to me. That is very powerful, so I know what those shamans are talking about." The sincerity and depth of feeling in his voice moved me. His Christian faith went so deep that it found common root of experience with other religions.

On the last day of class, one of the students approached me as most people had already departed. She noticed how I thanked the reverend as he left. Then she informed me that this man was Reverend King, uncle to Reverend Martin Luther King, Jr. Of course I had known his name, but I didn't realize the relation. I was grateful that Reverend King had touched me with a deep wisdom and peace that connects and reconciles across race, culture, and religion.

Hispanic American Spirituality

The federal government designated the category "Hispanic" in the 1970s to refer to "a person of Mexican, Puerto Rican, Cuban, Central or South American or other Spanish culture or origin, regardless of race" (cited in Castex, 1994, p. 189). This designation implies a cultural or linguistic commonality, which is rather misleading. The federal definition includes people originating from 26 countries with different languages, religions, other cultural patterns, and varied historical relations with the United States. For example, this includes people from countries in North, Central, and South America; people from the Caribbean; and Spain, in Europe. For the 2000 census, anyone who identified as Hispanic, Latino, or Spanish was included. The follow up U.S. Census Bureau American Community Survey of 2006 (http://www.census.gov/population/www/socdemo/hispanic/hispanic.html, retrieved October 31, 2008) showed subgroups from origins in Mexico (64%), Puerto Rico (9%), Central America (7.6%), South America (5.5%), Cuba (3.4%), Dominican Republic (2.8%), and other (7.7%). Between 2000–2006, growth in the Hispanic population accounted for half of the nation's growth. Current Hispanic percentage of total U.S. population is 14.8. There are Hispanic people whose ancestors have resided here since before the U.S. revolutionary war. People classified as Hispanic under this definition may identify as White, African American, First Nations (Indigenous), Asian, or other.

More than two-thirds of Hispanics are Roman Catholic (about 68%), but many are leaving this church to seek more personal forms of worship and experience (Pew Hispanic Project, 2008). Born-again or Evangelical Protestants comprise 15%. About 8% do not identify with a religion. Most view God as important in daily life, pray every day, have a religious object in their home, and attend a religious service at least once a month. Revivalism, or spirit-filled religious experience, is becoming more common. In addition, there are many religious beliefs and practices that are blendings of Christian and African and Indigenous spiritual traditions (Castex, 1994).

Even within a single denomination and ethnic group, there are further complications. For example, many Mexican Americans view the Catholic Church as a source of significant social and spiritual support (Aguilar, 2001; Curiel, 1995). However, there is also some ambivalence rooted in the history of colonialism. Catholicism came to the Americas in cooperation with the Spanish campaign of military, economic, cultural, political, and religious conquest. Thus, many Indigenous peoples were forced to become Catholic. Many of their traditional spiritual places of worship, sacred texts, beliefs, and practices were destroyed, forced into hiding, or melded with Catholic forms of symbolism and ritual. The Catholic Church was opposed to the Mexican War of Reform and 1910 revolution; so after independence, the Mexican government formed an anticlerical policy. After Mexican territory was annexed by the United States, many Spanish-speaking clergy were replaced by Irish and Anglo clergy with a more austere doctrinal approach, less sympathetic to syncretistic practices.

In response to discontent, during the 1960s and 1970s, the American Catholic Church instituted alternative, culturally and linguistically relevant liturgies, appointed more Hispanic bishops, and established more active community-based programs to promote social and economic justice (Curiel, 1995). The American Catholic Church has also been active in recent decades in opposing various human rights violations in Central and South America and in assisting refugees and undocumented entrants who fled war and persecution (Deck, 1989). Grass roots Catholic communities and socially concerned clergy in Latin America have given rise to liberation theology, which influenced social justice action among Hispanics and stimulated similar movements throughout the world (Garcia, 1987; Getz & Costa, 1991; Gutierrez, 1988; Roland, 2007; Sobrino, 1988).

Costas (1991) suggested that Hispanic theology in North America is characterized by the cultural and historical factors of colonialism. It takes into account painful experiences of migration and refugee flight, and dilemmas and struggles pertaining to biculturality, isolation, or assimilation. Bishop Ramirez (1985) provided a summary of common features of Hispanic Christian spirituality. He said that God is often regarded as a compassionate and forgiving yet judging and punishing Father and Creator. Popular piety regards God with love and reverence as well as fear and dread.

Popular spirituality focuses faith on Jesus as Savior, King, and Infant God through special titles and devotional practices (Ramirez, 1985). Mary "the Blessed Virgin" is revered as the merciful, loving, and majestic Mother of God (see Figure 4.3). The Feast of Mary as Our Lady of Guadalupe is of major significance (Aguilar, 2001). Saints are popular as models for behavior as well as miraculous benefactors. Blessed objects, such as depictions or relics of saints, are both symbols and conveyers of divine protection and care. Christian holy days, days of national celebration in the country of origin and family life cycle transition times, such as baptisms and marriages, and coming of age celebrations for girls, may be marked with religious ceremony and major family gatherings.

Hispanic spirituality often combines these Catholic teachings with African and Indigenous spiritual traditions that vary considerably among and between particular Hispanic groups. In the social work literature, several types of spiritually based syncretistic Hispanic support systems have been identified (Delgado, 1977, 1988; Delgado and Humm-Delgado, 1982; De La Rosa, 1988; Paulino, 1995a, 1995b). *Curanderismo*, common among Mexican Americans, and *santiguando* among Puerto Ricans, are forms of healing that combine herbalism and other physical interventions with Catholic beliefs and practices. Among Puerto Ricans and Caribbean immigrants, *espiritismo* (spiritism) is a folk healing practice involving mediumistic healers who employ group dynamics of role-playing and catharsis, with the support of helping spirits. Mediumistic healing also occurs in *santeria*, a religion mainly among Cubans, and Dominican and Haitian forms of *vodoun* (voodoo) which formed from a blending of African traditions and Catholic beliefs. A survey of Mexican American social work students

Figure 4.3. Our Lady
of Guadalupe Tiles,
Cathedral, Santa Fe.

compared Catholics and non-Catholics (Faver & Trachte, 2005). It found that
non-Catholics attend church more often and use a *curarandero/a* half as often;
but both groups have similarly high levels of private religious practices and sense
of being a spiritual person.

Social Work Implications

The Hispanic population is large and fast growing. Given the many variations of culture, language, and spiritual beliefs and practices among Hispanic
Americans, it is clear that social workers who work with Hispanic people need to
learn the particular circumstances of clients' history, culture, and family experience in relation to particular spiritual beliefs and practices. As we pointed out
in the previous section on African American spirituality, competent practice
requires suspending assumptions and ethnocentric judgments while opening up
to the stories of the clients. Clients and their religious or spiritual elders, leaders,

healers, friends, and family are the best sources of information about their particular practices and beliefs. For example, De La Rosa (1988) and Delgado (1988) have given specific suggestions for tailoring social work practice style, setting, and beliefs to work with Puerto Rican clients influenced by spiritism.

The range of spiritual beliefs and practices can be quite startling to unfamiliar social workers. For example, social workers need to be open to learn about culture-specific beliefs addressing the spiritual causes and cures of physical, mental, and social problems. Some practices, such as possession trance among some healers, or animal sacrifice in *vodoun* and *santeria*, may be particularly uncomfortable to social workers who have differing beliefs.

Women and Spirituality

In the United States, women represent the majority of adherents in most religious groups. Women are significantly more likely than men to say that they are absolutely certain in their belief in a personal God and somewhat more religiously engaged, including the likelihood of being affiliated with a religion at all (Pew Forum on Religion and Public Life, 2008). However, their stories are often subsumed and neglected in discussions of religion and spirituality because of the androcentric assumptions of religious research and theology (Braude, 1997). Men have written most religious texts, theological discourses, and scholarly studies of spirituality. Male authors have tended to focus on formal religious doctrines and practices of religious hierarchies which themselves are usually dominated numerically and politically by men. Since most adherents are women, this male perspective presents an inaccurate picture of women's lives. Feminist writing in social work has critiqued similar trends in our profession. However, the topic of women and spirituality has not been addressed often in the social work literature. This section gives a brief introduction to some trends and issues concerning the junction between women, spirituality, and gender justice in the United States. As in the case of ethnic diversity and spirituality, women's spirituality raises many complex and controversial issues concerning both the liberating and oppressing functions of religious traditions.

There is a great variety among women and their situations within and between religions and spiritual perspectives (Holm & Bowker, 1994; Joy & Neumaier-Dargyay, 1995; King, 1987; Sharma, 1994; Sharma & Young, 2007). Generally speaking, women in the Judeo-Christian-Islamic stream of monotheistic traditions operate with conceptions and symbols of God that are usually masculine and have theological justifications for restricting women from formal leadership positions. An interesting case in point is the Catholic veneration of the Virgin Mary (Warner, 1976; Zimdars-Swartz, 1991). Scholars have pointed out that Marion devotion has served to imbue feminine symbols and attributes with sacred significance. It has also provided women (and men) opportunities to honor and emulate these feminine qualities. On the other hand, Marion devotion has been contained within constraints developed by the all male church hierarchy. Critics have contended that Marion devotion actually serves to support patriarchal gender stereotypes and male privilege. Many women scholars emphasize the importance of ordination of women and bringing women into leadership positions within religions to provide a more woman-affirming approach (Roberts, 2004).

Many nontheistic or polytheistic Asian religions, such as Buddhism, Hinduism, and Taoism, have positive feminine and androgynous representations of divinities, cosmic forces, and religious teachers. However, women have also commonly been restricted from leadership positions within these religious institutions. Confucianism and Neo-Confucianism acknowledge the importance of harmony between men and women as well as complementarity of yin and yang qualities of reality, which are often seen as related to feminine and masculine traits. However, in practice the Confucian tradition has often enforced patriarchal social arrangements (Nyitray, 2007). There are efforts to revivify the liberatory potential of Confucianism from feminist and social work standpoints (Canda, 2002a, 2002b; Shim, in press). Many Indigenous tribal religions have positive feminine spiritual conceptions of women, the earth, and various spirit powers; and women have been major leaders within many Indigenous spiritual traditions. However, under the impact of colonialism and Christian missionary influence, many of these more woman-affirming traditions have been eroded. So, despite the wide variety of religious beliefs and spiritual experiences in the United States, it is all too common for women to experience constraints imposed by the very religious traditions to which they may faithfully adhere.

However, most women in the United States belong to conventional Christian and Jewish denominations and most appear generally satisfied with their affiliations (Corbett, 1997). Indeed, many belong to evangelistic, charismatic, and fundamentalist groups that tend to be supporters of traditional patriarchal religious and family arrangements for gender roles in family and religious groups. Many others are movers for reform toward greater participation of women in their religious groups' patterns of ritual and leadership and advocate for gender inclusive theological and scriptural language. Further, there are many women who call for radical restructuring of patriarchal religious institutions. Some have left them altogether for alternative spiritual paths, or as the feminist philosopher, Mary Daly put it in the title of a famous book, to go "beyond god the father" (1973).

Women in Conventional Religions

Corbett (1997) summarized various trends toward greater inclusion and leadership of women within the conventional Christian and Jewish denominations. Jewish and Christian feminist theologians have pointed out that some biblical passages use feminine images to refer to God. For example, the Hebrew word for "spirit" is *ruach* (a feminine word) which is translated as *pneuma* (a gender-neutral word) in the Greek language Bible. God is sometimes described in images relating to bearing and suckling children. God is sometimes referred to as wisdom, with the feminine Greek word *sophia*. Feminist theologians build on these biblical precedents to advocate for gender inclusive language in Bible translations, hymns, and liturgy. Feminist scholars suggest that biblical passages implying subordination of women should be understood within the historical and cultural context of their authors and should be reinterpreted in ways that support the liberation of women in contemporary society. There are many biblical examples that directly affirm the worth of women.

Many religious women are active in making their churches and synagogues more responsive to social issues, such as day care for children and elderly dependents, shelters for battered or homeless women and children, and support of or opposition to legal abortions (Corbett, 1997). Religious laywomen and nuns have been active in the formation of major religiously based social movements, such as antislavery, prohibition of alcohol, religious missions, and social gospel-based activism (Braude, 1997).

In the past 30 years, many mainline Christian churches and Jewish temples and synagogues have provided equal opportunities for women as lay leaders in worship. Some Christian and Jewish denominations allow women to become clergy. Others, such as the Catholic Church, many conservative Protestant denominations, and Orthodox Jewish synagogues, do not allow women to become clergy. Some Christian women have developed their own organizations, such as Church Women United, an ecumenical group with 1,500 local groups.

Alternative Women's Spiritual Perspectives

Some women have decided that the traditional patriarchal religions are not viable spiritual support systems for women and have created alternatives. Some women become agnostics or atheists or form nonsectarian informal spiritual support groups. Some are exploring religions imported from Asia, such as Buddhism, and transforming them by focusing on their traditional feminine or androgynous religious images and expanding their potential for women to become leaders and teachers (Gross, 1994).

Paganism (including Neo-Paganism, Wicca, Goddess worshippers, Druids, Neo-Shamans and others) is a movement that is small but important for growing numbers of women and men (Corbett, 1997; Starhawk, 1979; Yardley, 2008). Some women find it a more congenial spiritual context for its attention to feminine qualities of life and availability of leadership positions. Paganism is a movement rooted in pre-Christian European or other non-Christian religions. It honors nature as sacred, includes male and female aspects of the divine, and promotes improvements in life through magic, that is, "focusing intention and energy toward a goal through the use of symbolic rituals" (Yardley, p. 330). Since there are no formal, centralized Pagan organizations or membership lists, and many members are cautious about identifying their belief out of fear of ostracism, it is difficult to identify numbers of practitioners. The number of Pagans in the United States is probably around 300,000 (Yardley). They are usually organized in local informal small spiritual support groups. The large majority of Pagans are Euro-American.

Wicca means the tradition of "the wise one"; it is also known as Witchcraft, or the Craft. Witchcraft and other pre-Christian religious traditions were maligned and persecuted during the medieval Inquisition (Roberts, 2004). Some accounts suggest that millions of people were killed in Europe under accusations of witchcraft and heresy, most of whom were women, homosexuals, people with disabilities, and others defined as deviant by political and church authorities. Wicca, and paganism generally, continue to be portrayed with superficial or negative stereotypes by conventional religious groups and popular American movies and news media.

Wiccan beliefs emphasize harmony with the earth and balance of female and male spiritual powers. Special attention is given to feminine aspects of life and the spiritual realm. Female characteristics are viewed as good and powerful. Women's experience of biological cycles is related in a positive way to the cycles of the earth, seasonal changes, and the phases of the moon. Women's roles as maiden, mother, and wise elder are honored as reflections of the Goddess in her three forms as Maiden, Mother, and Crone. All living beings, and the earth Herself, are regarded as holy. Therefore, people are enjoined to live respectfully with the planet. Contrary to popular misconceptions, Wiccans do not worship Satan (which is a Christian concept) or put evil spells on people. Rituals are often geared toward seasonal celebrations and emotional and physical healing for individuals.

Social Work Implications

Social workers should consider the impact of gender and gender roles on the spirituality of women and men. Our experiences, perceptions, needs, and goals are likely to vary by our vantage point as men and women, both because of our different experiences of spirituality in relation to our embodiedness and in relation to gender role definitions, empowerments, and restrictions, placed on us by social and religious contexts. We need to avoid assuming or imposing gender-based views on clients. As we have seen, there is a great variety among women with regard to their attitudes toward and participation in conventional religions. Yet, especially in practice with women, whatever her own position regarding patriarchy and feminism, the importance of the distinctness of being a woman is inextricably related with spirituality. Randour (1987) suggested that women in both conventional and alternative spiritual groups tend to share an ideal of healthy connectedness between people and people and the divine, including respect for women's roles and traits.

In clinical practice, women may be trying to work out a sense of resolution between their loyalty to a faith tradition that is patriarchal and their personal aspirations for affirmation of their experience. In extreme cases, women who are victims of spousal abuse might be told by religious leaders to be patient and stay within the relationship, even under risk of serious injury and death. If a woman feels that her affiliation with a religious group is no longer tenable, she may need assistance exploring alternative spiritual support systems and working through feelings of guilt.

Kahn (1995) pointed out how innovations in ritual within conventional religions can affirm and empower women. She discussed the adult *bat mitzvah* as a Jewish life cycle ritual for women that simultaneously helps to clarify identity and commitment as a Jew and as a woman. As Laird (1984) pointed out, social workers can help clients utilize existing rituals or invent new rituals in order to support transition through life crises and to celebrate life cycle transitions. Feminist spiritual innovations, both within and outside of conventional religions, highlight many possibilities for developing symbolism and ritual that affirm women's experience and honor female aspects of the earth and the divine.

Social workers also need to be alert to issues of gender justice and diversity in spirituality. If clients experience ostracism or discrimination because they question patriarchal constraints and oppression within religious groups, or because they adhere to alternative religious groups such as Wicca, social workers may be called on to respond. For example, child welfare workers have sometimes removed children from parents' homes because of prejudice against their Wiccan parents (Yardley, 2008). Children in schools who have Pagan parents may be ostracized. Most Pagans have been raised in other religions, so they might experience tensions with their families of origin. Social workers should uphold clients' spiritual self-determination.

Coholic's (2003) interviews with 20 self-identified feminist social workers in Australia yielded valuable insights for practice in general. Participants expressed that an inclusive approach to spirituality is consistent with feminist values. Both promote a holistic outlook on person (including body, mind, emotions, and spirit) and environment, emphasize the importance of process and relatedness, support diversity, and view social change on both collective and personal levels. They often used generic ways of talking about spirituality with clients and then tailored communication to the specific client situation. Participants pointed out that not all feminists or clients would find spirituality to be relevant. They viewed spirituality as often important in making meaning of work and life and in forming connectedness with one's own spirit and with the universe or God. The helping relationship has a spiritual quality when it involves sharing life stories, sense of deep connection, and feelings of compassion and caring. This relationship should foster the client's ability to experience trust, love, and respect for self and others. They emphasized that it is important to attend to clients' spiritual beliefs as they affect his or her life and spiritual development. Participants' said that these practice principles are congruent with feminism and social work in general, though to remain true to feminist values, they should operate within a context of equity and fairness.

Homosexuality, Sexual Orientation Diversity, and Spirituality

Estimates of the homosexual population in all cultures range from 2%–10%. Obviously, this means that every large religious and spiritual tradition is likely to have some gay or lesbian members. There are distinct issues related to sexual orientation in each tradition (Dynes & Donaldson, 1992; Swidler, 1993). This is further complicated by various definitions of varieties of sexual orientation diversity that go beyond a simple homosexual/heterosexual binary, such as bisexual, transgender, and more fluid self-identifications.

According to Duran (1993), in some religious cultures, same gender sexual contacts are sometimes tacitly accepted in the context of temporary or alternative relationships, as long as the person forms a heterosexual marriage. Scholars have identified religious rationales for tolerance of sexual orientation diversity in Judaism, Christianity, Islam, Confucianism, Taoism, and Buddhism even though the historically prevalent view in these traditions has been to favor heterosexuality (Ellison & Plaskow, 2007). Hinduism is highly diverse so opinions about homosexuality range from intolerance to affirmation of sexual orientation diversity   (http://www.hinduismtoday.com/archives/2004/10-12/30-31_mela_council.shtml, retrieved October 31, 2008). Researchers have documented various forms of sexual orientation diversity in many Indigenous nations of North America (Baum, 1993). The influence of Christian missionaries seems to have made antihomosexual attitudes more prevalent among Native peoples recently; however, in many communities, affirming spiritual perspectives on LGBT people continue.

The link between sexual orientation and spirituality is one of the most controversial aspects of contemporary American society. Conventional American social mores concerning sexuality, sexual identity, and sexual orientation have been shaped by the Judeo-Christian tradition, which has generally maintained that normal and moral sexual relations are only expressed within the context of heterosexual marriage (Cahill, Garvey, & Kennedy, 2006). On the opposite side, some Christians view this belief as heterosexism, defined as a prejudice in favor of heterosexual people and prejudice against others (Hunt, 2007). Hunt describes heterosexism as "a sin against a Divine who created sexually diverse people" (p. 155). Currently, various Christian denominations are struggling and splitting over this issue. The Pew Forum website gives an overview of this wide range of religious views and policies (http://www.pewforum.org/gay-marriage/). In addition, particular attitudes and behavior about homosexuality vary within each religious congregation, and among individuals, beyond the official denominational policies.

For example, within Christian denominations, the range of responses to homosexuality and sexual orientation diversity can be summarized by four alternative views placed on a continuum. Analogous views can be found in many religious and secular contexts. The first three views operate within the Christian framework and the fourth reacts against it. They vary in interpretation of and adherence to biblical passages and denominational doctrine regarding homosexuality and sexual orientation diversity in general (Cahill, Garvey, & Kennedy, 2006; Coleman, 1980; Comstock, 1993; Cromey, 1991; Ellison & Plaskow, 2007; Mickey, 1991; Seow, 1996).

We summarize the four major alternative ideological responses in order of degrees from a strident antigay standpoint to complete rejection of Christian teachings (see Table 4.4). Most American Christians would likely identify themselves with the middle two positions.

The first type of response is *outright condemnation*. This comes from a perspective that posits patriarchy and heterosexuality as divinely ordained aspects of human nature and society. LGBT people are viewed as deviants, criminals, and immoral sinners. Biblical passages that refer to homosexuality are interpreted in the most literal and punitive manner. In such communities, homosexual people may be driven out, punished, or pressured to confess as sinners or to "change" into heterosexuals. In such a religious context, LGBT people may have to contend with guilt-inducing and shaming messages from the social environment and internal homophobic feelings learned from religious upbringing. In extreme cases, antigay Christian militants make a public mission out of harassing LGBT people.

Table 4.4.   Four Christian Ideological Responses to Homosexuality.

Condemnation
  Patriarchy and heterosexuality accepted as divine mandates
  Biblical texts interpreted as punitive toward LGBT people
  Homosexuals and other LGBT people labeled as deviant, immoral, criminal
  Homosexuals in congregation ostracized, defined as sinners; forced to leave congregation
    or subjected to "changing"

Accept the Person, Reject the Behavior
  Patriarchy might be questioned while heterosexuality accepted as normal and divine
    mandate
  Biblical texts interpreted to condemn homosexual sexual acts, but affirm dignity and care
    for all people
  Homosexuals and other LGBT people granted acceptance with inherent dignity and worth,
    yet often not accepted openly as clergy
  Homosexual expression of sexual intimacy labeled as sinful
  Homosexuals in congregation subjected to ambivalence

Affirmation
  Patriarchy and heterosexual privilege criticized as oppressive social constructs
  Biblical texts interpreted to support affirmation and liberation of oppressed
  Homosexuals and other LGBT people affirmed as whole persons, including sexual
    orientation and sexual intimacy
  Homosexuals and other LGBT people in congregation openly accepted, including as clergy
  Congregations advocate for social justice regarding LGBT issues

Reject Christianity
  Patriarchy and heterosexual privilege criticized as oppressive social constructs
  Christianity viewed as an inherently oppressive religious institution
  Biblical texts on homosexuality criticized and rejected
  Homosexuals and other LGBT people and their advocates depart from Christian
    congregations
  New spiritual support groups and religious organizations are formed

The second type of response is *accept the person, reject the behavior*. This perspective also accepts heterosexuality as divinely ordained. However, it advocates for acceptance and respect for people of all sexual orientations, on the basis of inherent human dignity. Biblical passages referring to homosexuality are interpreted as opposing same-gender sexual relations (and other sexual relations outside of heterosexual marriage) in a larger context of affirming God's love for all people. This position separates homosexual orientation from same-gender sexual activity. It leaves open the question of how people become homosexual and acknowledges that this may be a matter of identity, not only a lifestyle or choice. However, while LGBT people are allowed in such Christian communities, they are enjoined not to engage in same gender sexual activity or the issue is politely avoided. Openly LGBT people are prevented from holding leadership positions. In denominations that maintain this "accept the person, reject the behavior" position, it seems inevitable that LGBT people will be subject to ambivalence. This position makes a split between their experience of who they are (which is granted dignity) and how they express intimacy with loved ones (which is defined as sinful).

For example, this is the official position of the Catholic Church. In 1997, the American Catholic bishops released a public statement of apology for the church's frequent mistreatment and rejection of gay and lesbian people. However, the bishops maintained the official teaching against same gender sexual activity. Some Catholic parishes have support groups for LGBT members, such as the organization named DignityUSA. "DignityUSA envisions and works for a time when Gay, Lesbian, Bisexual and Transgender Catholics are affirmed and experience dignity through the integration of their spirituality with their sexuality, and as beloved persons of God participate fully in all aspects of life within the Church and Society" (http://www.dignityusa.org/). This organization seeks to transform the Catholic Church toward the third position, while offering support to LGBT members in the meantime.

The third option is *affirmation of sexual orientation diversity*, viewing every person as loved in the embrace of God. In this view, it is not loving to force a split between who a person is, how that person genuinely expresses intimate love, and what privileges are accorded in religious communities and in society in general. In this view, God would not create LGBT people only in order to condemn them. This position critiques and transforms the Christian tradition in order to move out of what it considers to be a patriarchal, heterosexist, and alienating viewpoint. In this case, biblical denouncements of same-gender sexual behavior are interpreted as an expression of an overall divine ethic of compassion that was distorted through human heterosexism. In other words, various passages in the Bible condemn homosexual acts of exploitation just as it condemns heterosexual exploitive acts and other harmful actions that have nothing to do with sexuality. Some passages are seen as culture bound and outdated. This position views the Christian message as one of affirmation and empowerment of all people, especially those who have experienced social discrimination and persecution, such as

LGBT people. In this context, LGBT people are openly accepted, full members of a congregation. Christian marriage or sacred union ceremonies may be performed for gay or lesbian couples. In some denominations, openly LGBT people are eligible as clergy. Also, Christian denominations with primarily LGBT membership have developed, such as the Metropolitan Community Churches.

The fourth response is to *reject Christianity* as unacceptable or unviable for LGBT people and others who support sexual orientation diversity. In this view, the Christian tradition has demonstrated a long history of persecution and discrimination of LGBT people. Persecution has varied in intensity from widespread murder during the Inquisition to contemporary ostracism. In this position, people might reject the Christian tradition of their upbringing in favor of atheism, agnosticism, exploration of other religious traditions that are more congenial, or creation of new patterns of spiritual belief and support groups. For some people, this could be a comfortable and liberating option. Yet the process of breaking from one's religious heritage and community could also be painful. Lingering feelings of internalized homophobia may still have to be dealt with.

Social Work Implications

The NASW Code of Ethics takes a clear proactive stance with regard to diversity of sexual orientation, as with other aspects of human diversity. Social workers are required to obtain education about diversity and oppression, including sexual orientation (standard 1.05). They are also prohibited from directly or indirectly practicing any form of discrimination on the basis of diversity, including sexual orientation (standard 4.02). These same standards also take a proactive stance on religious diversity. Since many spiritual traditions and groups take a negative stance toward homosexuality, there are many occasions when the two ethical principles of supporting religious diversity and sexual orientation diversity may conflict. Therefore, the most basic social work implication is that we need to be able to deal openly and honestly with different and conflicting spiritual positions on sexual orientation diversity in such a way that constructive dialogue for mutual understanding is created in direct practice settings, professional education, and social advocacy. We believe this dialogue is only meaningful with the full inclusion of LGBT people of a variety of religious and nonreligious spiritual beliefs. Social workers on all sides of the issue should be able to communicate on the basis of respect and dignity.

It needs to be emphasized, though, that the overall ethical stance of the social work profession is to oppose any form of discrimination or oppression and to support self-determination and empowerment for all people. Therefore, it seems to us that there are certain limits on what spiritual perspectives on sexual orientation diversity can be promoted in professional capacities by social workers. The first option above, which is directly antigay and degrading, is clearly inconsistent with social work ethics. If a social worker holds such a view, we believe it is incumbent upon the worker to do some serious thinking about whether he or she can in good conscience affiliate with and practice in the social work profession. It does not seem honest to claim to be a social worker while holding a position that demeans people. The same can be said about any value position, religiously based or otherwise, that demeans and oppresses any person or group of people.

Indeed, Keith-Lucas, who was a prominent writer on Christian social work, identified four patterns of Christian belief in relation to social work ethics (Ressler, 1992). He named one extreme Christianity of Morality, which is judgmental and punitive, and as such, is least compatible with social work. He promoted Christianity of Grace, which views all things created by God as perfect, to be the ideal orientation for social work. This view is most consistent with the second and third types of Christian responses to homosexuality, as described above.

Social workers who hold the second perspective, accept the person, reject the behavior, should also consider how that might influence their practice with LGBT clients. Studies of gay and lesbian sexual identity development and coming out process highlight common developmental challenges that relate to clarification of self-identity and long-term relationships in relation to the societal context of discrimination (Miller, 2008; Morrow, 2008; Robbins et al., 2006). The second theological position is likely to compound identity and relationship confusions by creating a split between self-awareness of sexual orientation, feelings of affinity for others, and restrictions or denigration of honest expressions of intimacy with others. LGBT clients who are working through such developmental issues or experience of tension or conflict with a religious group need assistance from social workers who are able to provide an unambiguous relationship of empathy and respect. If a worker is unable to do so, then the worker needs to refer the client elsewhere and engage in a process of self-examination and professional development in order to move toward an empathic and respectful way of relating with LGBT clients.

On the other hand, social workers who take the fourth position of rejecting Christianity will need to be alert to her or his feelings and behaviors toward religious clients. If the worker has unresolved issues pertaining to the reasons for rejecting Christianity, then feelings of anger, mistrust, or derisiveness could cloud the helping relationship. As above, a worker who is unable to relate empathetically and respectfully with a religious client needs to refer the client elsewhere and engage in personal and professional development.

Different and conflicting positions on homosexuality obviously exist among social workers, often related to rival spiritual and ideological positions (e.g. Adams, 2008; Cain, 1996; Canda, 2003; Hodge, 2002; Parr & Jones, 1996; Spano & Koenig, 2007; Van Soest, 1996). We emphasize that spiritually sensitive social workers should work with LGBT clients in a way that affirms their intrinsic human dignity and helps them to attain their goals for the helping process according to their values and priorities. As professionals who have expressed commitment to uphold the NASW Code, workers need to find ways to relate with empathy and skill through a client-centered position. This means including and transcending the limitations of our personal positions.

A further implication of this debate is that social work education needs to prepare social workers for an astute analysis of the spiritual issues involved in attitudes about sexual orientation diversity and the diverse spiritual opportunities available for LGBT people. For example, many students and faculty seem to accept the mistaken idea that Christianity (or other religions) uniformly opposes LGBT people. As we have seen, there is much variety and debate within and between religions on this issue. Some social work educators and practitioners express hurtful discriminatory views of religious, especially conservative, students and clients (Cnaan, 2006). We also emphasize that this is not appropriate. As Sherwood (2000) put it, "Real tolerance and respect for diversity requires that we figure out how we should deal with ideas, behavior, and persons we genuinely disagree with, some of which we believe to be not simply different but wrong" (p. 5). We recommend that social work educators and practice supervisors mentor their students and supervisees to help them work out areas of disjuncture between their personal values and professional values, to develop more inclusive and widely embracing compassion, and to discern whether social work is the most fitting profession for them.

There is another option beyond the range of ideological positions described. Professionals can get unstuck from any position. In an actual helping relationship, the worker can decenter from a position and recenter on the client. If you predetermine a relationship by an idea, then the relationship is not an encounter of persons—it is a confrontation of ideas. My idea of right confronts my idea of the person, all stuck in my head. In the process, I lose my real self and the real client. There is another way: here and now, real person to real person, in helpful dialogue.

Conclusion

This chapter presented a summary of the history of spiritual diversity in the United States and the American social work profession. We introduced patterns of spiritual belief and practice in the general public and among social workers. We addressed complex intersections between spiritual diversity and ethnicity, women's experience, and sexual orientation. We discussed ways in which spiritual perspectives can enhance human well-being or contribute to discrimination and oppression. Genuine compassion moves us to empathize and join with people who experience suffering and injustice. It stretches us beyond our egocentric, ethnocentric, and religiocentric assumptions in order to meet the other. In doing so, we grow to the point at which no one is "the other" in the sense of a person who seems remote or estranged. Indeed, encounters with diversity inevitably challenge us to broaden and deepen our spirituality, so that we can appreciate both difference and commonality. If we succeed in doing this, then the

potential of spirituality to bring about personal healing and social justice will
surely express in our personal and professional lives.

EXERCISES

4.1. Writing a History of Spiritual Diversity in Your Community

The historical overview in this chapter can be a model for you to study the
historical development and contemporary situation of spiritual diversity in
your community. A history of local spiritual diversity can be useful to acquaint
practitioners and policy makers with the cultural and religious backgrounds
of client populations and constituencies. Source materials can include library
materials such as regional religious historical studies, survey and census data,
and directories of religious organizations. Local newspapers (especially "religion" sections), telephone directories, and social service directories have listings
of religious organizations and religiously affiliated social service organizations.
Internet search engines are powerful tools for exploring religious groups in
your service area as well as the official teachings of religions on a national or
global level. Social service agencies that provide specialized services for eth-
nically diverse groups (such as refugee resettlement programs, ethnic mutual
assistance associations, and universities or colleges with geographical area
studies and international studies programs) can be identified. Chaplains in
hospitals and hospice programs are often very knowledgeable of local spiritual
resources.

4.2. Self-Assessment of One's Own Spiritually Based Attitudes about Sexual Orientation Diversity

One of the most contentious issues in many religious communities, and in the
general public, is the standpoint toward LGBT people. Given the social work
profession's ethical stance of nondiscrimination, this is a good starting point
for self-reflection about our level of openness, empathy, and support regarding
human diversity. Table 4.4 identifies four major Christian ideological positions
toward homosexuality (and by extension, other nonheterosexual orientations)
that can help you reflect on where you stand. Since there are analogous positions
possible within other religious and secular spiritual perspectives, you can adapt
the positions to your own background. As you go through the exercise, consider
how your sexual orientation relates to the ideological position you take on this
issue and how you relate with clients who have similar or different views.

The first step in this exercise is to identify which ideological position is closest to your own and then state your position in your own words. If none of these
positions is an accurate depiction of your view, then articulate your view. Be
aware of feelings that arise in response to this self-questioning. What are areas
of comfort and discomfort? What particular beliefs do you have about sexual

orientation diversity? What sources of religious authority, if any, do you use to support your position, such as sacred texts, traditional doctrines, or spiritual leaders' teachings? How does this position affect your behavior in your private life, within your religious or spiritual community, and in your professional social work practice? Are you able to be client-centered and empathetic in relating with clients who have a different sexual orientation or ideology about sexual orientation from yourself?

Now, consider the degree of fit between your position and the NASW ethical standards cited in this chapter. Do you feel comfortable affirming these ethical standards? Do you feel tension between professional values and ethics and your own personal beliefs?

Once this is clear, it is important to engage in direct respectful dialogue with someone who holds a different ideological position from yourself on this issue. This dialogue is for the purpose of understanding another's perspective; it is not to try to convince someone else of the rightness of your own position. For example, if the social worker holds the second position, "accept the person; reject the behavior," it would be valuable to identify a fellow student, colleague, or community member who holds position 1, 3, or 4. An appropriate person would be someone who is comfortable and willing to discuss this topic openly. Then, in the conversation, each person should take turns sharing one's position and explaining the rationale. Each person should also express honestly one's feelings about the other's position.

It is essential that the conversation take place in a setting that feels safe and private for both parties. Ideally, the conversation could be facilitated among students in a class, with faculty support and guidance, or in some other professional setting. The conversation needs to be based on an explicit expression of mutual respect, willingness to learn, and agreement to disagree.

After the conversation, write a self-reflective essay about one's ideological position, ethical implications for oneself, and the subsequent conversation. Then, areas for one's own personal and professional growth should be identified.

4.3. Self-Assessment of Your Spiritually Based Attitudes about Other Forms of Diversity

A similar procedure to Exercise 4.2 can be used for any topic related to spirituality and human diversity. For example, your can explore your spiritually based attitudes and beliefs regarding women, people with disabilities, people with spiritual perspectives different from yours, or particular racial and cultural groups. Identify the degree of your own acceptance of a particular group that is significantly different from yourself. Reflect on the religious or nonreligious spiritual sources of your attitude. Have a respectful conversation with a person from the selected group about issues of discrimination. Strive to understand the other person's perspective. Then write a self-reflective essay, including implications for your growth.

4.4. Your Personal Experience of Spiritually Based Discrimination

In order to deepen empathy for people who experience spiritually based discrimination, it is helpful to look honestly at your own attitudes and behaviors in concrete examples from your life. We all at some times are on the receiving or giving ends of spiritually based discrimination. When we reflect on the times we experienced it, we can work through painful feelings and consider more effective ways to prevent it or respond to it. When we reflect on the times we have committed it, we can correct our behavior for the future and make amends for the past.

First, jot down one way you have directly or indirectly *experienced* discrimination or oppression toward yourself, based on your spiritual perspective. Then, jot down one way you could prevent this or respond well in the future.

Second, jot down one way you have directly or indirectly *engaged in* discrimination or oppression toward someone different from yourself, based on your spiritual perspective. Then, jot down one way you could prevent this in the future. If possible, make amends for your mistake.

Identify specific steps for your personal and professional growth that will contribute to the mutual well-being of both yourself and others who are different from yourself, but with whom you regularly interact, such as clients, colleagues, and neighbors.

5

Religious Perspectives on Social Service and Their Insights for Social Work Practice

Woe to those who pray
but are heedless in their prayer;
who make a show of piety
and give no alms to the destitute.

The Quran, Islam
(trans. Dawood, 1974, p. 28)

In this chapter, we provide an overview of religious traditions that are currently influencing American social work. Our purpose is to increase readers' knowledge about diverse approaches to social work that have an explicit connection to religious traditions and communities alluded to in Chapter 4. The information in this chapter provides a foundation for the reader's further exploration of traditions that are of particular relevance to personal interest and to clients and their communities. Each religious tradition yields insights for social work practice, both for working with clients within the tradition and for general innovation in social work practice.

We examine seven religious perspectives that have worldwide impact, while focusing on the American social work context. They cover most of the religious believers in the United States and the world, giving both regional focus and international relevance. They are (in alphabetical order) Buddhism, Christianity, Confucianism, Hinduism, Indigenous Religions, Islam, and Judaism.

The next chapter continues this approach by addressing nonsectarian spiritual perspectives. In both chapters, spiritual perspectives are presented according to the following topics: historical origin and contemporary varieties; basic beliefs underlying the approach to service; basic values motivating service; and social work practice implications. We will present more detail on selected spiritually based helping practices in Part III.

These summaries of religious perspectives are vast generalities. It is important to remember that they are only starting points for further exploration of the spiritual perspectives relevant to your clients and your practice approaches.

It is especially important to discuss with clients, whenever relevant, to discover the real significance and practice for that person in her or his family and community. We simplify complexity to help readers move forward into deeper understanding. However, we do not want to be simplistic. There are many different (and sometimes conflicting) interpretations and applications of these basic ideas within each perspective. We must be wary of turning generalizations into stereotypes.

Buddhism and Social Service

Origin and Contemporary Varieties of Buddhism

Buddhism, or the *Buddha Dharma* (Sanskrit), originated around 500 years BCE (before the common era) in what is today Nepal and northeastern India (Canda, 2001; Gethin, 1998; Harvey, 1990; Schuhmacher & Woerner, 1994). Buddha Dharma means "teaching of the awakened one." Its founder was Siddhartha Gautama who lived about 566–486 BCE. Siddhartha was a prince who left the luxury and confines of his royal life to seek understanding of human suffering and how people can become free from suffering. After several years of spiritual disciplines and meditation, he achieved enlightenment, which means awakening into the true nature of self and reality. The Buddha spread his teachings for 45 more years until his death. Since Buddhism emerged from a Hindu context, it uses many Hindu religious terms, symbols, and practices often with different nuances.

During the next five centuries, Buddhism spread throughout India and south Asia, formalized its doctrines, established orders of monks and nuns, and separated into various branches. The Theravada branch (Pali, Way of the Elders) traces to this original form of Buddhism. Theravada is most common today in South and Southeast Asia. Buddhism spread into central and east Asia around 2000 years ago. The Mahayana (Sanskrit, Great Vehicle) branch developed from interaction between Indian Buddhism and philosophical and religious systems of central and East Asia. From China, Buddhism spread to Korea, Japan, and Vietnam. Currently, the Mahayana branch is most common in these countries. Vajrayana (Sanskrit, Diamond Vehicle) Buddhism is related to Mahayana; it is most common in Tibet and Mongolia. These branches of Buddhism have many variations between and within them, shaped by different schools of philosophy and practice as well as the cultural environments in which they have taken root.

Various forms of Buddhism are present in the United States. There are many ethnic-specific forms of Buddhism brought by Asian immigrants and refugees as well as nonethnic-specific (but primarily Euro-American membership) Buddhist meditation centers (Canda & Phaobtong, 1992; Furuto, Biswa, Chung, Murase, & Ross-Sherif, 1992; Prebish, 1999; Tan, 2006; Timberlake & Cook, 1984). Buddhists from Laos, Cambodia, and Thailand are usually Theravadin.

Buddhists from China, Japan, Korea, and Vietnam are usually Mahayanist. Pure Land Buddhism promulgated by Buddhist Churches of America has about 100,000 members in the United States (Corbett, 1997). Zen philosophy and meditation practice was promulgated widely in North America first by Japanese scholars and missionary monks. It started to become popular among American intellectuals, such as artists and poets in the 1950s. Now, there are many different Zen-oriented centers in the United States, founded by Japanese, Korean, Chinese, Vietnamese, and American Zen Masters (Morreale, 1998). Since 1975, many Southeast Asian refugee communities established Buddhist temples and mutual assistance associations. Tibetan Buddhism, headed by the Dalai Lama, has become influential in American Buddhism among Tibetans and the general public.

Zen is the form of Buddhism discussed in social work literature most often. Zen emphasizes the priority of attaining enlightenment through direct personal experience and disciplined effort. Zen originated in China under Indian influence, incorporating elements of Daoism and Confucianism, and spread to Korea, Japan, and Vietnam and on to the West. In the social work literature, general insights and practices influenced by Zen are often presented without restriction to a specific religious affiliation. Zen is commonly portrayed as a way of life and a nonsectarian spiritual approach to social work practice (e.g. Bein, 2008; Brandon, 1976, 2000; Krill, 1990; Martin, 1999).

Basic Beliefs

All forms of Buddhism accept the original teaching of Siddhartha, summarized in the Four Noble Truths (Canda, 2001; Gethin, 1998; Pyles, 2005; Smith, 1991). The first truth is that human existence is characterized by *suffering,* that is, a sense of pervasive unsatisfactoriness due to experiences of pain, injustice, loss, and lack of fulfillment. The second truth is that this suffering arises from *inappropriate desire* that clings to what we have and rejects what we do not want to have. However, nothing is permanent, all conditions change, and all things we have, including the body itself, passes away. Further, we inevitably have things and conditions we do not like, such as illnesses. The third truth is that *suffering can cease* by eliminating inappropriate desires. Ironically, in living a life based on desire, we glue to the situation of suffering. The most basic attachment to stop is the illusion of a separate self. Since all things are interdependent, and coproducing (as in systems theories), the idea of a separate self is faulty. Belief in a separate self is an intellectual error and an emotional trap. Egotistic desire-based clinging or rejecting hinge on this illusion. The fourth truth is that egotistic desire can be stopped by practicing a *disciplined way of life* (the Eightfold Path) based on correct perception, conduct, and meditation. In the process, we realize that there is no separate independent self, since all things co-arise and pass away in interdependency. This complete awareness is called *Nirvana* (Sanskrit) which means "cessation."

Basic Values

The process of enlightenment leads to awareness of the interconnectedness of all beings together with compassionate motivation (*karuna*, Sanskrit) to help them also become free from suffering (Blofeld, 1988; Brandon, 1976; Eppsteiner, 1988; Pyles, 2005). In Mahayana Buddhism, the supreme ideal is the Bodhisattva, a person who attains enlightenment and vows to help all beings do the same (Canda, 1995a; Keefe, 1975). Thus, the Zen-oriented social worker upholds a profound commitment to empathic relations with clients, undistorted by counter-transference (Chamberlayne, 2007; Keefe, 1996). This compassion extends to all beings, not just one's clients and not just human beings.

The central virtues of Buddhism are called *paramitas* (Sanskrit). Paramita literally means "to reach the other shore" of enlightenment. Practicing these virtues is a process of simultaneously helping oneself and others to become enlightened, and hence, saved from suffering. Canda, Shin, and Canda (1993, p. 91) summarized, "The *paramitas* are generous giving, ethical conduct, patient endurance, zealous effort, concentration of the mind, realizing wisdom, and integration of all the virtues in service to others." Thus, compassion flows through them all.

Social Work Implications

In countries with large Buddhist populations, many formal and informal social welfare services are provided through Buddhist temples (e.g. Canda & Canda, 1996; Kubotani & Engstrom, 2005). Many Asian Americans have been influenced directly or indirectly by Buddhism, especially first or second generation immigrants or refugees from East and Southeast Asia. For Asian American Buddhist clients, it is important to identify what particular form of Buddhism they practice and what significance it has for them. Many Southeast Asian refugee communities establish temple-based mutual assistance associations that provide a wide variety of physical, mental, social, and spiritual supports for cultural preservation, dealing with postwar and genocide trauma, and promoting overall well-being (Canda & Phaobtong, 1992; Tan, 2006; Timberlake & Cook, 1984). These can be important environmental resources for collaboration. In addition, many Buddhists of all ethnic backgrounds practice personal-, family-, and community-based rituals and meditation techniques that can assist with stress management, personal insight, and conflict resolution. For example, Nakashima (1995), a Japanese American social worker, described how her upbringing and practice as a Buddhist helped her to deal with issues pertaining to her own mortality and provided her with a nonsectarian framework for helping clients in hospice deal with their own issues around dying and death. Martin (1999) gave a detailed account of how to follow a Zen path through depression, both in personal life and clinical practice.

Some social workers promote Buddhist insights that can guide spiritually sensitive practice in a nonsectarian manner, without using explicit Buddhist language. For example, Brandon, who was a British social work scholar and Zen teacher, blended insights from Zen, Daoism, and humanistic perspectives. In his view, Zen-oriented practice is wary of conceptual constructs, rigid treatment plans, and diagnostic categories because these tend to obstruct direct and spontaneous interactions with the client (Brandon, 1976, 2000). Rather than impose professionally designed interventions that arise from the worker's own desires and conceptual constructs, the Zen-oriented worker strives to merge harmoniously with the spontaneous ongoing process of mutual interaction with the client. Indeed, the Zen approach assumes that the client truly knows the way to resolve his or her suffering, but is unaware or is not implementing it. As Brandon put it, social work is a process of attempting to widen and illuminate people's choices and their costs in order to extend autonomy rather than restrict it (1976, p. 30). Bein (2008) presents an open hearted model of Zen inspired practice that blends skill with spontaneity, celebrates challenges and paradoxes in life, and finds strengths to realize aspirations. As he put it, "Zen is about being intimate with what is. As we enter helping relationships with real people, what could be more important? We offer them our authentic presence, our hearts, and our willingness to muck around in their pain and fear as well as their successes and failures" (p. 1).

Buddhist inspired social workers often highlight therapeutic qualities of mind and relationship that are cultivated through meditation and mindful awareness of each moment. These include radical and unconditional acceptance of what is; nonjudgmentalism; steadying and clarifying the mind; being present in each moment; compassion; patiently witnessing pain; nonattached responsibility; embracing paradox; self-understanding; clear listening; and working through anger (Bein, 2008; Berlin, 2005; Brenner & Homonoff, 2004; Kissman & Maurer, 2002; Pyles, 2005). Socially Engaged Buddhism is a movement to bring Buddhist meditative practice and awareness into the arena of social service (Eppsteiner, 1988; Pyles, 2005). This includes teaching meditation to prisoners, helping dying people in hospice, microenterprise with homeless people, environmental activism, peaceful and collaborative community development, and peace advocacy. The Zen Peacemaker Order is a good example. (See http://www.zenpeacemakers.org/).

Zen inspired practice can make use of meditation training for both the worker and the client (Finn & Rubin, 2000; Keefe, 1996; Mace, 2008; McBee, 2008; Vohra-Gupta, Russel, & Lo, 2007; Wegela, 2003). Zen meditation combines relaxation of the body with focusing of the mind. The meditator learns to be aware of the stream of consciousness without being attached to the thoughts and feelings that pass through. The meditator then becomes able to perceive the world directly, without the distortion of desires and illusions. Traditional meditation is for the purpose of attaining enlightenment. It can be very intense and prolonged, in order to crack the illusion of separate self. In social work and mental health practice, usually a milder form of mindfulness meditation is used with clients, directed toward stress management, enhanced self-awareness, and clear insight into one's situation and how to deal authentically with it (e.g. McBee,

2008). Dialectical Behavior Therapy, popular in mental health settings, is derived from Zen mindfulness practice and cognitive behavioral techniques (Haynes, Follette, & Linehan, 2004). The social worker can benefit from meditation by increasing her or his skills of concentration, attentiveness, accurate listening, empathy, and stress management.

A broad implication of Buddhism for social work is to expand our conception of the person and environment. In Buddhist thought, as in dynamic systems theory, the person does not exist independently from the environment (Macy, 1991; Robbins, Chatterjee, & Canda, 2006). Helping oneself and helping others must be interrelated. Human rights of individuals link with collective responsibility (Abe, 1995; De Silva, 1995; Thurman, 1996). Understanding and action must necessarily address both micro- and macrosystems, as all are woven together. Achieving human aspirations for peace and justice is inextricable from supporting the well-being of the entire planetary ecology and all beings within it (Eppsteiner, 1988). Thus, Buddhist philosophy can inspire social workers to weave together micro- and macropractice, local and global issues, and to seek creative solutions to problems that provide maximum mutual benefit to all human and nonhuman beings (see Table 5.1).

Christianity and Social Service

Origin and Contemporary Varieties of Christianity

Christianity traces its origin to Jesus of Nazareth, who was born in Israel in about the year 4 BCE (Crim, 1981; Nielsen et al., 1993; Smith, 2005). Jesus was a Jewish teacher whom Christians consider the Messiah, born as the incarnation of God to save humanity from sin. The title of Jesus, Christ, is derived from a Greek word meaning Messiah or Anointed One. Early in the 1st century, Christian communities were established in Israel and then spread to Gentiles throughout Asia Minor and parts of Europe. Gentile Christians came to outnumber Jewish Christians as missionary efforts expanded. During this period, Christians were a persecuted minority in the Roman empire. However, the Roman emperor Constantine converted to Christianity and in 380 CE made Christianity the official religion of the Roman empire.

This alliance between the Roman empire and Christianity eventually changed the status of the religion from persecuted minority to the politically and numerically predominant majority. This pattern of alliance between church and state continued in Europe throughout the middle ages. Christianity became referred to as Catholic, in order to indicate its universal scope, under the authority of the Roman pope. In 1054, Christianity underwent a major division between western Catholic Christianity (centered in Rome) and Eastern Orthodox Christianity.

The 1500s began a period of theological and political challenges to reform the western Catholic Church, under such Protestant leaders as Martin Luther (German), John Huss (Czech), and John Wycliffe (English). Many Protestant

Table 5.1. Comparison of Religious Perspectives on Service.

Perspective	Beliefs	Values	Service
Buddhist (esp. Zen)	(1) Nontheistic Buddha Nature. (2) Beliefs from traditions, sutras, direct spiritual experience; Nonattachment to beliefs. (3) Existence is suffering, caused by desire and illusion of separate self; suffering ends through disciplined lifestyle, meditation, and enlightenment.	(1) Primary life task is to seek enlightenment. (2) Commitment to compassionate help toward all beings. (3) Transcendence of self/other dichotomy in virtuous living.	(1) Mutuality and harmony in helping relationship. (2) Aim to help client clarify awareness, act realistically; ultimately attain enlightenment. (3) May use meditation and connect with temple or meditation center based support systems.
Christian	(1) Theistic and trinitarian. (2) Beliefs from Old and New Testaments, church traditions, faith experience. (3) People are prone to sin; relation with loving God yields reconciliation, meaning and purpose.	(1) Primary life task to love God and people. (2) Commitment to charity and justice. (3) Moral relation between individual needs, social welfare, God's will.	(1) Agape love based helping relationship. (2) Aim to help client meet physical and spiritual needs, reconcile with others and God. (3) May use witnessing, prayer, sacrament, clergy/congregation referrals.
Confucian	(1) Nontheistic Dao. (2) Beliefs from Chinese classics, sages and religious teachers, and local traditions. (3) Benevolent human nature must be cultivated for benefit of person, family, society, and world.	(1) Primary life task to cultivate sageliness and benefit society. (2) Commitment to lifelong learning, public service, family/social harmony. (3) Filial piety and complementary reciprocal relationships.	(1) Helping relationship based on benevolence and harmony. (2) Aim to help client learn from life situations and harmonize relationships. (3) May use quiet sitting, self-reflective practices, qigong, acupuncture, herbs.
Hindu (esp. Vedanta)	(1) Nondualistic, with theistic and other forms. (2) Beliefs from Upanishads & Vedas, religious teachers, and local, family traditions. (3) Karmic bonds to suffering and rebirth can be released through spiritual disciplines (e.g. yogas); liberation comes through union with divinity (Brahman).	(1) Primary life task to achieve liberation (moksha). (2) Commitment to respectful nonattached service. (3) Nonviolent means and ends for everyone's attainment of truth and liberation.	(1) Helping relationship honors the divine in all. (2) Aim to achieve welfare of all. (3) May use various yogas, rituals, and cooperative nonviolent community action.

(continued)

Table 5.1. Continued.

Perspective	Beliefs	Values	Service
Indigenous Religions of North America	(1) Animistic, holistic, collectivistic. (2) Beliefs from cultural traditions, teachings of elders, and spiritual insights. (3) Human well-being requires balance and harmony within self, with community, nature, and spirit realm.	(1) Primary life task to balance body/mid/feelings/spirit interrelated with community and world. (2) Commitment to maintain or restore balance and harmony. (3) Honoring family, elders, ancestors, spirits of place, all relations in earth and sky.	(1) Helping relationship based on respect, openness, humility. (2) Aim to help client toward balance, harmony, empowerment, resolving historical trauma. (3) May use symbols and stories of balance and connectedness, culture specific ceremonies and healing.
Islamic	(1) Monotheistic. (2) Beliefs from Quran, community (umma) traditions and teachers, and body of law (shari'a). (3) There is no God but Allah and Mohammed is Allah's prophet; personal and social well-being comes from submission to Allah in all things.	(1) Primary life task is to live in accord with will of Allah and the Islamic community. (2) Commitment to life of prayer and justice. (3) Community responsibility of almsgiving and protection of disadvantaged.	(1) Helping relationship honors God and supports client in community context. (2) Aim to help client meet basic needs, as bases for living in accord with God and community. (3) May use almsgiving (zakat), mutual support in community, reflection on Quran, daily prayer, and religious practice.
Judaic	(1) Theistic. (2) Beliefs from tanakh, halakah, Jewish community. (3) People created in God's image but may be distorted by experience; sinful behavior requires reconciliation.	(1) Primary life task to love God and people, uphold Jewish community. (2) Commitment to loving kindness and justice. (3) Compassion both inner personal quality and behavior.	(1) I-Thou and communally concerned helping. (2) Aim to help client problem-solving in context of Jewish community. (3) May use Jewish role modeling, religious reflection.

Note: Revised and expanded from Canda (1988b); used with permission of publisher.

denominations of Christianity have continued since that time. They tend to hold in common a denial of the authority of the pope and an emphasis on salvation by divine grace rather than human effort. The various denominations of Christianity have engaged in extensive missionary activities, leading to its predominance in the United States and in many other parts of the world.

Most Americans identify as Christians. There are more than 900 denominations, including Catholic, Orthodox, and Protestant denominations that originated elsewhere, and also denominations that have originated in the United States, such as the Church of Jesus Christ of Latter-day Saints, Church of Christ, Scientist, Seventh-day Adventists, and the Watchtower Bible and Tract Society (Jehovah's Witnesses).

Christianity has been extremely influential in the formation and current practice of professional social work (Cnaan, Wineburg, & Boddie, 1999; Garland, 1992, 2008; Loewenberg, 1988; Van Hook, Hugen, & Aguilar, 2001). As we have seen in the National Survey, most American social workers are Christian. Christianity is the most prevalent religion in social work publications in the field of spirituality (Canda, Nakashima, Burgess, Russel, & Barfield, 2003). Many professional and volunteer social services are provided under Christian denominational auspices. Three of the largest Christian organizational providers of social services are Catholic Charities, U.S.A., Lutheran Social Services, and the Salvation Army. The North American Association of Christians in Social Work (http://www.nacsw.org/2008/2008-index.shtml) sponsors conferences, a journal, and book publications. Many of its members are Protestant, from theologically conservative denominations. The National Catholic School of Social Services of Catholic University of America for many years sponsored the journal, *Social Thought*, as a forum for Christian (especially Catholic) and other theological and philosophical approaches to social work. For many years, it has been published by Haworth Press, presenting a nonsectarian orientation to spiritual diversity. It is a membership benefit of the Society for Spirituality and Social Work (http://ssw.asu.edu/portal/research/spirituality).

Basic Beliefs

This presentation emphasizes beliefs and values that are widely shared by Christian social work authors past and present, keeping in mind the great variety among Christians discussed in the previous chapter (e.g. Biestek, 1956; Canda, 2008c; Catholic Charities U.S.A., 2006; Consiglio, 1987; Constable, 2007; Corbett, 1997; Garland, 2008; Keith-Lucas, 1985, 1994; Ressler, 1992; Shank, 2007; Sherwood, 2001; Van Hook et al., 2001).

Christian theology forms through the interaction of several sources: scholarly exegesis of the Old and New Testaments, regarded as the inspired word of God; the traditions and doctrines of various denominations; and personal inspiration of Christian individuals and communities. Basic Christian beliefs can be summarized as follows.

The universe was created by a personal supreme God who loves the world. Humankind was created with the capacity for moral choice. Unfortunately, people often choose sin, asserting their own prideful desires in disobedience to God's will. Jesus Christ became incarnated as both God and human being in order to save humanity from sin through his crucifixion and resurrection from the dead. Christ will come again to usher in the fullness of the Kingdom of God on earth. The Holy Spirit continues to guide and strengthen Christians. These three divine Persons, God the Creator, Christ, and Holy Spirit, are One God. People who turn away from their sinfulness and align their wills with the will of God are promised salvation and eternal reward after death.

The central message of Christianity is that God is love (King, 1965). Jesus said that the most fundamental laws are to love God fully and to love others as oneself (Mathew 22:37–39). Since Christianity teaches that humans were made in God's image, it accords every human being with dignity and respect (Hodge & Wolfer, 2008). Human beings achieve fulfillment through personal and loving relationship with God and each other (McCabe, 1965). When people are open to the grace of God, they discover a sense of meaning, reconciliation between self, the world, and God, and strength and hope in the face of suffering. Reconciliation is expressed and experienced through loving relationships between people and between God and people. As Sherwood (2001) put it, "Christian faith involves a response of gratitude to God's grace to us which leads to our ability to respond in love and grace to other persons" (p. 99). Many Christians emphasize that loving service should extend beyond helping individuals, or Christian communities, in order to promote well-being and justice for family, community, nation, world, and global ecology (Canda, Ketchell, Dybicz, Pyles, & Nelson-Becker, 2006).

Basic Values

The most central value commitment of Christians is to live a life of charity (love). Since this word is distorted in popular usage to mean condescending help, it is important to return to the theological meaning. Charity (*caritas* in Latin; *agape* in Greek) is recognized in the New Testament as the most important virtue (Benton, 1981; see 1 Corinthians 13, New Testament). Charity does not expect gratitude or reward. Charity is a spiritual impulse of love, arising from relationship with God. As Christ is present in all people, the Christians show love of God in service to the needs of people. Charity involves recognizing the essential communion of all people, both in their shared suffering of the human condition, and in their relationship with God. As Tillich (1962) explained, relating to another person in charity involves both unconditional acceptance of the person's worth and caring expression of constructive criticism. As the National Conference of Catholic Charities (1983) asserted, four related primary values are love (as charity), truth, justice, and freedom. The Christian upholds the truth of God's reconciling work in the world. He or she works toward the just ordering of social relationships, respecting the needs of all people. The Christian supports freedom of opportunity for all people to live in a fully human and loving manner. This may involve active opposition to corrupt social policies and social institutions (Scharper, 1975). Shank (2007) summarizes the values of Catholic social teaching as respect for the human person; rights to subsistence, health, and freedom; responsibility to self, others, the larger society, and the common good; the dignity of work as a contribution to God's creation and welfare of family and society; and special regard for the poor and oppressed.

Biestek (1956) drew on Christian social ethics to explain basic social work values. (1) *Acceptance* of the client means that the worker perceives the client accurately, both strengths and weaknesses, while maintaining a sense of the client's innate dignity and worth. (2) *Self-determination* means respecting the client's right to free choice within the context of the client's capacity for constructive decision making, moral reflection, and social responsibility. (3) *Nonjudgmentalism* means that the worker carefully evaluates whether the behavior of the client is helpful or harmful to self and others, without judging guilt or innocence.

Social Work Implications

For the social worker who practices from a Christian perspective, there is an integral connection between life in Christ and professional activity (Hugen, 1998; Keith-Lucas, 1985, 1994; Ressler, 1992; Sherwood, 2001; Van Hook, Hugen, & Aguilar, 2001). For example, Smith (1961) suggested that helping the client to heal emotional wounds requires constant expression of love in the helping relationship as well as in the ongoing daily interactions of agency staff. This modeling and sharing of love involves the personal spiritual growth of the worker as well as the healing of the client. Indeed, for Keith-Lucas (1985, 1994), the empathic helping relationship is a human reflection of the divine love shown by God to people through the incarnation of Christ and the grace of the Holy Spirit. For these reasons, the Christian social worker should use practice methods that affirm the distinctiveness, worth, and capacity for choice of the client.

Tillich (1962) identified four main aims of this love expression in social work. First, the worker helps the client promptly satisfy immediate needs. Second, the worker guides the client toward independence and withdraws from the dependency relationship. Third, the worker communicates to the client a sense of being a necessary and significant person. This provides a perspective of cosmic meaning in which each person has "a necessary, incomparable, and unique place in the whole of being" (p. 16). Finally, the worker helps to fulfill the ultimate goal of humanity and the world that is to integrate each individual aim into the universal aim of being itself. Thus, Christian social work deals with practical material needs in the context of spiritual needs, the two kinds of needs being inextricable (Canda, 1988b).

Essentially, the Christian view explains the fact of human suffering in terms of sin. When sin is understood as alienation from one's authentic self, from others, and from God (King, 1965), it becomes clear that the primary goal of Christian social work is personal and community reconciliation. Keith-Lucas (1985, p. 14) described the helping process in Christian terms, as including four main elements: repentance, which requires that a person recognize a problem needing help; confession, which requires telling someone about the problem; submission, which requires giving up familiar old but unproductive behaviors; and faith in the positive outcome of the change efforts.

One controversial practice method employed by some Christian social workers is witnessing their faith to the client. Keith-Lucas suggested four situations in which witnessing might be appropriate: (1) when a client is a Christian, would like to become one, or wishes to have companionship in prayer; (2) when a client inquires about the worker's motivation for providing caring and helping; (3) when the client's view of Christian faith needs enlargement or theological reflection; and (4) when the client is explicitly asking questions about the purpose of life and suffering. He added that the most effective Christian witness is not talking about religion, "but treating people in a Christian way oneself" (p. 29). In this context, witnessing or other religiously based practices should be done only according to the need and interest of the client (Canda, Nakashima, & Furman, 2004).

Another Christian helping method is seeking help from God for specific situations through prayer in a professional context (Canda, 1990a; Gatza, 1979; Sherman & Siporin, 2008). Prayer may involve petition for help, quiet meditation or contemplation, prayerful scripture reading, ritual and community celebration, and relating to each moment of life prayerfully. According to Gatza, healing prayer involves openness to God's grace that goes beyond ordinary human ability to heal. Gatza recommended using healing prayer to complement ordinary professional knowledge and skill. Sneck and Bonica (1980) pointed out that one need never overtly and explicitly pray with a client in order to help prayerfully. According to them, the Christian worker should trust in the power of God to heal through the therapeutic relationship itself. Their contraindications to praying with clients are when the counselor is inexperienced; when the client is potentially hostile or in danger of being exposed to needless additional pain; or when an act of prayer is a substitute for a more genuine and imaginative intervention. Hodge (2007a) reviewed empirical studies (typically in a health treatment context) on the effects of intercessory prayer, which is a silent or vocal prayer to God or another transcendent or sacred force to benefit another person. He found a trend that reported generally favorable outcomes. He suggested that some workers might find this evidence sufficient to support their praying for clients. He cautioned that use of intercessory prayer should take into account client preferences.

Christian social workers might also engage in prayer to help themselves relieve stress, to clear their minds and set good intentions before meeting a client, and to deepen the sense of connection with God and client throughout the helping relationship. These practices can be private and unobtrusive. Canda (1990a) offered ethical guidelines for use of various kinds of prayer in social work.

Encouraging forgiveness is one of the most common spiritual interventions by psychotherapists, especially those with a theistic orientation (Richards & Bergin, 2005). DiBlasio (1993) summarized research findings that indicate religious ideas and rituals concerning forgiveness can help religious families and individuals to resolve problems and conflicts and to enhance relationships. His study of social workers' religiosity and attitude toward forgiveness indicated that many are not aware of or comfortable with forgiveness theory and practice. He recommended development of more research and clinical applications on the appropriate and effective uses of forgiveness.

All social workers can refer to and cooperate with Christian clergy and church communities in so far as these are sources of support for Christian clients (Bigham, 1956; Furman & Chandy, 1994; Furman & Fry, 2000; Garland, 2008; Hugen, 1998; Joseph, 1975; Loewenberg, 1988; Pepper, 1956). When social workers and pastoral workers understand each other and share basic aspects of worldview, their work can complement each other (Lee & Gorman, 2005). Thus, clients can deal with problems in both psychosocial and spiritual terms. Social workers sometimes provide consultation to Christian congregations to help them enhance their attention to issues of health and well-being for themselves and the wider community (Canda, Ketchell, Dybicz, Pyles, & Nelson-Becker, 2006; Tirrito & Cascio, 2003). However, significant issues of logistics and trust need to be addressed in clergy/social worker collaboration (Bilich, Bonfiglio, & Carlson, 2000). This will be addressed in Part III.

Christian volunteers and professional social workers often engage in community service, social policy advocacy, and social justice activism through Christian church auspices (Brenden, 2007; Breton, 1989; Ellor, Netting, & Thibault, 1999). As we saw in Chapter 4, Christian values and congregations were very active in the civil rights movement. Many Christian congregations provide informal and formal social service supports, including church social work and parish nursing. In fact, Christian (and other) religiously affiliated agencies range considerably in the extent to which Christian teachings explicitly connect with staff hiring, program designs, and work with clients (Tangenberg, 2005). Therefore, services might be provided in a nonsectarian manner, although consistent with basic Christian social ethics. This is even more likely when the program is funded by federal or state money, due to the separation of church and state (Ressler, 1998). Christian philanthropy and social policy advocacy efforts are extensive (Weber & Jones, 1994), for example, by Church World Service, National Council of Churches of Christ, the U.S. Catholic Conference, and Women's Division of the United Methodist Church. As we saw in Chapter 4, Christians vary and conflict in their concepts and goals for social justice, so numerous lobbying and social action groups vie to influence public policy and behavior on such issues as abortion, church/state relations, civil rights, education, poverty relief, foreign policy, pornography, world peace, and gay rights.

Some social work scholars have raised concerns about the role of theologically conservative, especially fundamentalist, Christian groups in promoting judgmental, exclusivistic, patriarchal, and sometimes militant conservative approaches to individual, family, and social issues (see the letters to the editor in *Social Work, 2003, 48*(2), 278–282; plus Denton, 1990; Loewenberg, 1988; Midgely, 1990; Midgely & Sanzenbach, 1989; Sanzenbach, 1989; Swigonski, 2001). By Christian fundamentalism, we mean a movement primarily among Protestant and newer Christian denominations that has the following characteristics: conviction of personal salvation by faith in Jesus; commitment to evangelize others; faith in the inerrancy of the Bible as the literal, authoritative word of God; special interest in the imminent apocalyptic second coming of Christ; practice of exclusion of "unbelievers"; and active opposition to liberalism and secularism (Marty & Appleby, 1991). Denton (1990) distinguished between fundamentalists with a polemical, exclusivist style versus those with a faith nurturing style. In his view, polemical groups' rigid standards of patriarchy and authoritarian discipline may pose risks to women and children in families. On the macrolevel, militant fundamentalists may actively oppose social work values and agendas and spread distrust of social workers and mental health professionals.

On the other hand, conservative religious communities provide many people with positive experiences of social support, forgiveness, reconciliation, and spiritual guidance. Several authors have cautioned against negative stereotyping and ostracism of conservative Christian clients and groups or religions in general (Canda 1989b; Cnaan, 2006; Joseph, 1989; Pon, 2008). Denton (1990) suggested that fundamentalist families be addressed as culturally distinct. Hodge (2004a) proposed guidelines for culturally competent practice with Evangelical Christians (who may or may not be fundamentalist or exclusivist). However, we point out that this does not mean that Christian social workers are permitted to engage in discrimination or oppression against clients. We advocate for spiritual sensitivity, including adherence to ethical standards, for all social workers, religious and nonreligious (Spano & Koenig, 2007).

Confucianism and Social Service

Origin and Contemporary Varieties of Confucianism

Confucianism originated in China about 2500 years ago. Its philosophical, religious, and ethical views spread from China to Korea, Japan, Vietnam, and elsewhere within Chinese cultural influence (Chen, 1990; Takashima, 2000; Yao, 2000; Yip, 2005). The founder was Kongzi or Kong Fuzi, anglicized as Confucius, who lived about 551–479 BCE. Confucius described himself as the transmitter of wisdom from ancient sages. He hoped to restore virtue of leaders during a time of social and political disruption. For many years, he taught students and advised rulers, holding public office only briefly. He tried to clarify principles for applying the Dao (or Way) of humane benevolence to relations with self, family, the wider society, and world. Mengzi (anglicized as Mencius), who lived in China from about 371 to 289 BCE was the second most influential teacher. He elaborated Confucius' teachings about human nature and social justice. Over the centuries, East Asian governments sometimes supported, suppressed, or neglected Confucian teachings. The ruling classes often distorted or selectively applied Confucian social ethics in an authoritarian and rigid patriarchal manner (Canda, 2002a, 2002b; de Bary, 1991; Nyitray, 2007; Yee, 2003). Other Confucian scholars protested social policies that injured social welfare.

Confucianism has taken various forms over the centuries, shaped by its host cultures and historical changes. Neo-Confucianism, which was influenced by Daoist and Buddhist cosmology and meditation practices, became prevalent from the Song dynasty (960–1279) until the early 20th century, especially in Korea where it was the state ideology during the Joseon dynasty (Canda & Canda, 1996; Canda, Shin, & Canda, 1993; Yao, 2000). Neo-Confucianism (and its modern varieties) emphasizes that everyone is capable of becoming a sage through cultivation of their true nature through diligent study and effort. Traditionally, this sage learning was primarily the province of men. In the contemporary period, Confucian scholars are reinterpreting the teachings in light of modernization, democracy, globalization, and feminism (Bell & Hahm, 2003; de Bary & Tu, 1998; Shim, in press). This summary gives ideas from classical Confucianism and Neo-Confucianism that lay the foundation of all current varieties.

Few contemporary people identify as Confucians. However, it is important for social workers to understand Confucianism because it directly or indirectly influences the worldviews, social ethics, and health practices of many millions of people around the world, especially East Asians and Asian Americans (Chu & Carew, 1990; Reid, 2000; Yao, 2000). The influence of Confucianism on clients may not be obvious, since there are no formal Confucian religious institutions in the United States and formal membership in a Confucian religious group is not common. Many people do not think of Confucianism as a religion per se, but rather as a social ethical system. It is most likely to influence traditionally minded people of East Asian descent, whatever their religious or nonreligious affiliation. In popular American culture, many people interested in Asian philosophy are familiar with the Chinese Book of Changes (Wilhelm & Baynes, 1976). This is one of the world's oldest philosophical texts for understanding the cosmic patterns of change and how to live in harmony with them. According to traditional belief, Confucius and a prior sagely ruler wrote some of its commentaries.

Basic Beliefs

The main purpose of Confucianism is to help people become aware of their inherent nature of *ren* (all Chinese terms are rendered in the pinyin system). *Ren* means benevolence or humane-heartedness (Taylor, 1990; Tu, 1979, 1985; Yao, 2000). It is the cardinal virtue to guide living with family, society, the wider world, and all in heaven and earth. For example, Mencius said that anyone who notices that a baby is in danger of falling into a well would naturally rush to save the baby. Confucianism teaches that when we look into our own hearts with sincerity, we recognize that our genuine needs are shared by everyone. The benevolent person strives for mutual benefit and harmony in relationships. People need to use effort to keep the benevolent nature clear in mind and action. This begins by cultivating sincerity and wisdom in ourselves and continues by extending that outward in larger spheres of relationship through family, community, society, and world (Chung, 1992, 2001; Tu, 1989). Benevolence is the basis of other cardinal virtues, such as *li*, which means proper conduct of rituals as well as propriety in daily life.

Well-being is fostered through the cultivation of virtue (*te*), which is both a quality of personal character and a moral power through which we influence social well-being and justice. Mencius explained that the best way to keep our vital energy (*qi*) flowing in a healthy way is to develop our virtue through diligent yet gentle effort.

The human Dao (way of life) interconnects with the cosmic Dao, represented in the metaphor of heaven and earth as humanity's spiritual parents and all things as our brothers and sisters. We owe greatest respect and care to heaven and earth and should treat all things as relatives. However, Confucian philosophers did not promote literal anthropomorphic ideas about heaven. Heaven (*tian*) refers both to the sky and to a metaphysical force. Heaven is regarded as the source of human nature, the creative power behind all things, and the determiner of personal destiny. Earth is respected for its nurturing bounty and beauty.

Everything in heaven and earth operates according to the dynamics of yin and yang, which are qualities or types of vital energy (*qi*). Yin (receptive, yielding, birthing, shadowy, earthy) and yang (creative, proactive, generative, bright, heavenly) are complementary, mutually shaping, and alternating opposites that work together (Yee, 2003). Sometimes yin is more prominent and sometimes yang. For example, each human body has organ and energy systems (addressed in acupuncture and herbal medicine, for example) that are affected by yin and yang. If either energy quality is too extreme or too faint, or if they are not in harmony, illness results. Qi and its aspects of yin and yang emerge from the Supreme Ultimate (*Taiji*), which is boundless and beyond any division, name, or form. Health and social welfare require a practical harmonization of yin and yang in the body and in relationships, plus a profound realization of the oneness of everything in the Supreme Ultimate (Canda, 2002a, 2002b; Chung, 2001; Yao, 2000).

Basic Values

In Confucianism, values and beliefs about cosmology are inseparable, as illustrated above. *Ren* is the heart of all other virtues and ideals for relationships. Traditionally, *ren* expresses strongly through values of reciprocity (*shu*) and filial piety (*xiao*) (Yao, 2000).

Human social relations are organized traditionally in partnerships of related persons, for example, royalty and common people, teacher and student, leader and subordinate, husband and wife, parents and children, elder and younger siblings, and friend and friend (Yee, 2003). Confucianism recognizes the importance of the individual, but it is not individualistic. Indeed, Confucian oriented societies tend to be more familistic and communalistic. In traditional societies, many relationships are hierarchical and patriarchal, with greater authority given to those in the superior position. Ideally, the principle of reciprocity means that those with more authority should use it for the care and benefit of their juniors, while the juniors should relate to their superiors with respect. If people violate this pattern of mutual benefit, then those in lesser positions of power are vulnerable to exploitation or oppression. Therefore, well-being at personal and social levels depends on harmony and benevolent reciprocity (Chung & Haynes, 1993). Government policies should promote the welfare of the people, with special attention to the destitute and solitary (Canda, 2002b; Chen 1993).

Since the relationship between parents and children is the basic building block of traditional East Asian societies, the virtue of filial piety is very important (Yao, 2000). It sets the standard for other types of hierarchical relationships. For example, the king and queen are like the parents of their subjects. A special teacher or mentor is like a parent to her or his students. Parents give the great gift of life to their children, so children should respect and appreciate their parents. When parents are elders, the adult children (especially the oldest son and his wife) should return care and support for their parents. Good parents raise their children with loving attentiveness, using great effort, resources, and personal sacrifice. Traditional people live in extended families, often including grandparents, parents, and adult eldest son with his spouse and children. Other family members remain closely connected. Departed ancestors are also honored as they are the roots of the living family. On the widest level, filial piety means that we treat all people and things with love, since they are our fellow children of heaven and earth.

Social Work Implications

Most contemporary people influenced by Confucianism do not engage in religious institution based practices such as rituals or prayers that were prevalent prior to the 20th century. Some East Asians and East Asian Americans draw on cultural traditions that meld Buddhism, Confucianism, and Daoism, and may not distinguish what is Confucian. Many are members of other religions, such as Buddhism, Christianity, or Daoism, through which they may engage in formal religious practices. Many others are not religious. In these situations, people commonly consider Confucianism to be an ethical or philosophical system rather than a religion. Conversation with the client and family is the only way to know if Confucianism is significant for them. If concepts of filial piety, ancestor honoring, and holistic healing based on yin and yang energies are important to the client, then Confucianism is probably an important influence.

It is also important to note that there is widespread distrust among social workers and general populations in East Asia about rigid patriarchy and governmental authoritarianism that may be attributed to Confucianism (Shim, in press). Others praise Confucianism as the distinctive feature of East Asian heritage that paved the way for contemporary democracy and economic advances. There is polarization around this issue (Canda 2002a, 2002b). For many second or later generation East Asian Americans in the United States, Confucianism is simply irrelevant or little known. Social workers should not assume an East Asian Americans' attitude about Confucianism.

Many practice approaches that draw on traditional Chinese medicine, such as yin/yang and five elements theory, holistic mind-body-spirit-cosmos perspective, and acupuncture, herbal medicines, and qigong can be integrated with social work while connecting them with the spiritual perspective of East Asian American clients however they define it (e.g. Chan, 2001; Lee, Ng, Leung et al., 2009). Although these traditional healing approaches in East Asia are strongly influenced by Chinese medicine, each country has its particular styles.

The Confucian Way approaches each moment as an opportunity for learning, including times of illness and distress. Therefore, there are practices to promote constant learning, such as daily reflecting on the quality and results of one's intentions and actions; maintaining a consistently sincere attitude; seeking to understand both the practical details of how things work and the deeper principles beneath them; intensive study of the writings of sages; and pursuit of formal education that should round the whole person and develop skills for human service (Canda, 2002a, 2002b; Chen, 1993; Chung, 2001; Kalton, 1988; Taylor, 1990).

Many Confucians practice a form of quiet sitting that allows the mind to still and one's true nature to emerge clearly. It does not involve use of strong mental force, extreme postures, or overly intense techniques of concentration. Clients who are comfortable with such practices might be interested in this or similar practices, such as Zen meditation, Christian centering prayer, qigong, yoga, or generic relaxation exercises to help with stress relief, self-understanding, good health, and harmonious relationships. These should be matched with the beliefs and comfort level of the client.

Some Confucian oriented clients may be interested to adjust diet to harmonize with the yin/yang qualities of the person. Some also draw on geomancy (i.e. feng shui) to make their homes' energy conducive to health and harmony. Specialists in traditional Eastern medicine can be sources of information, referral, or collaboration for social workers (Lee et al., 2009). Clients may seek advice and support from respected family elders, mentors, scholars, herbal medicine practitioners, acupuncturists, and diviners who use the Book of Changes to tell fortunes and give advice.

Social workers should be attentive to clients of East Asian descent for whether they celebrate special days. For example, in some countries, Confucians hold a major national celebration to honor the teachings of Confucius, Mencius, and the other sages. These occur at the Spring and Autumn equinoxes, the exact dates of which vary by year according to the lunar calendar. More commonly in the

United States, people influenced by Confucianism perform rites to memorialize their deceased parents, grandparents, and other close deceased relatives. These involve offerings of food and bows of respect before the grave or an offering table set at home. If the grave is far away, this can lead to a feeling of loss and sadness. These rites are performed on anniversaries of the death and on special holidays, such as Autumn Harvest Thanksgiving Day. Social workers engaged in bereavement work with Confucian influenced clients should be aware of these practices.

Many people influenced by Confucianism come from patriarchal cultures and may give preferential treatment to males. Traditionally, adult men are expected to have primary authority and activity outside the home, while adult women are to have primary authority and activity within the home. This may still manifest in men (particularly family elders) being most outspoken in interactions with social workers. However, social workers should not ignore the role of women as family nurturers and behind-the-scenes decision makers. It may be uncomfortable for some men when a female social worker takes on authority in the helping relationship.

Whether or not a Confucian influenced client supports patriarchal relations, it is likely that the person's sense of identity will be closely tied to family and community. In this case, social workers should be alert to the possible importance of reciprocity, harmony, and filial piety for the client in decision making and problem solving. Yip (2004) suggests that the Western concept of empowerment may need to be adapted to Confucian (and Buddhist and Daoist) influenced contexts. Yip indicates that such clients may be more comfortable with helping that promotes mutual empowerment of the individual and significant others; building on complementarity of individual rights and responsibilities; attending to the need for social harmony; and promoting self-cultivation and gradual empowerment rather than disruptively rapid change.

East Asian Americans, especially first or second generation immigrants, often go through rapid culture change. Younger members of families tend to change values and lifestyles significantly from elders, leading to family role confusion and conflict (Furuto et al., 1992). Some people (especially elders and males) may try to maintain traditional patriarchal patterns. Many younger Asians and Asian Americans challenge these patterns and seek to change them. For example, Shim (in press) explains how she worked through a process of rejecting Korean Confucian patriarchy from a feminist vantage, then struggled with a sense of identity confusion and cultural ambivalence, and finally moved to a more self and culture affirming position of feminist style Confucianism with insights for social work. Clients might raise these kinds of intrapersonal issues in East Asian American families.

Finally, some social workers have proposed ways that Confucian social welfare ideals and self-cultivation practices can be applied to contemporary social welfare and social work in a general nonsectarian manner (Canda, 2002a, 2002b; Chung, 1992, 2001; Chung & Haynes, 1993; Imbrogno & Canda, 1988; Lee, 2004). Their approaches draw out important insights from the original cultural and religious contexts and suggest ways to apply them in a culturally diverse society and world. For example, viewing the person, community, and cosmos as interconnected and mutually benefitting can correct excesses of Western individualism, alienation, and narcissism. This approach connects with current social work theory developments related to holistic biopsychosocial-spiritual models, transpersonal theory, and deep ecology. Chung gives practical recommendations for qigong practice within this holistic approach (http://www.geocities.com/bgaughr/).

Hinduism and Social Service

Origin and Contemporary Varieties of Hinduism

Hinduism is the common name for the predominant religion of India and Indian Americans. The term originated from Persian; it literally means "the belief of the people of India" (Nielsen et al., 1993). Sometimes the term Brahmanism, referring to the priestly class, is used to distinguish it from other religions in India. Hindus use the term *Sanatana Dharma* (Sanskrit), meaning eternal cosmic principles that guide human life (Singh, 2001). Hinduism is an extremely varied tradition (Smith, 1991). Certain scriptures are highly regarded, such as the Vedas and Upanishads, but there are many different schools of philosophical orientation and types of religious groups and practices. Hinduism is not organized with a central overarching institution. There is little attempt to regulate conformity of beliefs. Rather, a common Hindu viewpoint is that there are many legitimate spiritual paths, just as there are many paths to the top of a mountain. Hindus may embrace many varieties of monotheism, polytheism, animism, nontheistic philosophy, or combinations of these. There are also many variations based on caste, region, language, and ethnicity. Indeed, each family may have its own traditions and home-based forms of worship dedicated to particular deities (Banerjee, 2005; Singh, 2001). Variations in these aspects of diversity, and various cross-cultural experiences and immigration history, have significant influences on the particular spiritual forms of Hindu Indian Americans (e.g. see Banerjee, 1997a, 1997b).

Early Hinduism emerged from the Indus Valley agricultural cultures, which were established by 2400 BCE (Corbett, 1997; Crim, 1981; Nielsen et al., 1993). By about 1600 BCE, Indo-European people, called the Aryas, colonized the Indus valley region. Mingling between traditions of the original Indus civilization and the Aryas gave rise to historical Hinduism. Between 1200 and 800 BCE, the priestly class compiled the Vedas from a long tradition of oral literature. By around 200 BCE, the main core of the Upanishads (secret teachings) were written. These teachings gave rise to the world view of Vedanta (Veda's End), which is widely considered to be a culmination and refinement of earlier Vedic teachings. The classical language of Hinduism is Sanskrit.

In the United States, there are many varieties of Hindu originated religious systems and practices. For example, Swami Vivekananda was a major proponent of *karma yoga* as an approach to social work in India (Patel, 1987). In 1894, the first American Hindu organization, the Vedanta Society, was founded in the United States by Swami Vivekananda (Corbett, 1997; Melton, 1992). In the United States, the Vedanta Society promotes intellectual study of Vedantic philosophy. In 1965, the International Society for Krishna Consciousness was founded in the United States by Swami Prabhupada. This organization (also called the Hare Krishna movement) promotes a devotional approach to worship for Indian Americans and many Euro-Americans. This group gives special devotion to Krishna, an incarnation or manifestation of God featured in one of the most important Hindu scriptures, the Bhagavad Gita. Maharishi Mahesh Yogi founded the transcendental meditation program that has trained thousands of people since the 1960s. Sathya Sai Baba Centers emphasize performance of service as a form of devotion. There are many other kinds of yoga centers and yoga practice groups throughout the United States. *Yoga* means "union." The practice of yoga is meant to unify body-mind-spirit with the divine, although some American yoga practitioners view it only as a form of healthy exercise. The previously mentioned groups are not limited to Hindus and have a broad spectrum of members in the United States. Besides this, Hindu Americans have established numerous Hindu temples around the country. Aside from formal Hindu related organizations, the primary locus of Hindu practice is the home.

In the social work literature, two forms of Hindu oriented views are most often addressed. One is *karma yoga*, based largely on the teaching of Swami Vivekananda and other yogic traditions (Banerjee, 1972; Battacharya, 1965; Patel, 1987; Seplowin, 1992; Singh, 1992). The other is a Gandhian approach to social work (Capozi, 1992; Dasgupta, 1986; Sharma, 1987; Walz, Sharma, & Birnbaum, 1990). Although Mahatma Gandhi (1869–1948) is well known throughout the world for his spiritually based social activism in India and South Africa, his ideas were not systematically applied to American social work until the mid-1980s. Patel (1987) said that there are many similarities between Gandhian social work and karma yoga. However, she suggested that the Gandhian perspective focuses more on social action goals, while *karma yoga* has *moksha*, or spiritual liberation and union with the divine, as its explicit goal.

In the following presentation, we will focus on ideas from Vedanta, karma yoga, and Gandhian social work. Social work writers advocate these ideas in order to promote nonviolent, spiritually based practice for social workers both for Hindus and for others. They can be applied with explicit religious and cultural features for practice with Hindus. Their principles can also be expressed in a nonsectarian manner for diverse clients.

Basic Beliefs

In general, Vedantic worldview emphasizes a universal, ultimate, nondualistic reality that underlies all things, called Brahman. There are many Gods and Goddesses that are manifestations of this ultimate reality. Vedanta identifies the goal of life as liberation (*moksha*) from the *samsara*, cycle of birth, suffering, death, and rebirth that is rooted in the illusion of separate self. *Moksha* involves realizing the unity of one's true self (*atman*) with Brahman and freedom from the bondage of *karma*. Karma literally means "action." Moral and helpful actions generate beneficial reactions for oneself and others. Immoral or irresponsible actions generate harmful results for self and others. Karma binds the person to the cycle of death and rebirth until he or she attains liberation through moral action and religious practices. Traditional Hindus believe that each person has a *dharma*—a set of duties and obligations linked to family, society, occupation, and the wider sacred *dharma*, that is, the order of the universe (Nimmagadda & Cowger, 1999).

Singh (1992) defined karma yoga as "the realization of the divinity through complete selfless dedication to work and duty" (p. 9). Vivekananda elaborated principles of karma yoga by building on the foundation of Vedantic philosophy (Patel, 1987). Karma yoga is a spiritual discipline of selfless service that leads to the liberation of the social worker from karmic suffering at the same time as helping to relieve others' suffering. Karma yoga cultivates an awareness of the divine (Brahman) as the absolute ultimate reality that envelops everything, including the social worker's true self (atman) and the true selves of clients. Patel (1987) explained that karma yoga means helping others, even to the point of death, without being attached to any outcome.

Gandhian social work rests on similar principles. Although Gandhi was a Hindu, he did not promote divisive sectarianism. He believed that ultimate Truth is beyond the comprehension of any one person or any one religion. He believed that all people should seek the Truth through their various religious and cultural frameworks. This is true self-realization (Pandey, 1996; Walz et al., 1990). Gandhi's approach to social action was based on *satyagraha*, meaning "truth force." Satyagraha means living life as a nonviolent pursuit of Truth, while honoring everyone else's pursuit of truth, even in the midst of conflict.

Basic Values

In Vedantic perspective, all beings are manifestations of the divine Truth. Therefore, every being should be treated with respect. Vedantic beliefs lead directly to three fundamental values to guide practice. First, social workers should maintain clear benevolent purpose toward clients and fulfill their responsibilities in a sacred manner. This is our professional *dharma*. Second, social workers should not be attached to the fruits of their actions. This does not mean being careless or uncaring. It means having motivation free from egotistic attachment to one's own goals for clients. Service is its own reward.

The third value principle is nonviolence (*ahimsa*). In nonviolence, all people are granted unconditional respect and compassion, including people who are one's opponents and oppressors. Nonviolence means refraining from intentional harm while loving the other (Banerjee, 1972). Gandhian *ahimsa* involves dedicated and persevering search for Truth, and assisting others to live with dignity and freedom so they too can pursue Truth. Oppression and dehumanization are to be resisted actively, but in a way that does not oppress or dehumanize others. In Gandhian thought, nonviolence actively promotes individual and social peace such that even one's opponents can progress in their own search for Truth (Dasgupta, 1986; Pandey, 1996; Sharma, 1987, Walz & Ritchie, 2000).

These three values imply the value of seeking mutual benefit in social work. It is not sufficient to benefit only an identified client. Since all people and beings are interconnected by karma, the results of helping actions on clients and others need to be discerned. Harming some to help others is not nonviolence. Further, the process of helping is itself a natural karmic benefit for the social worker. Thus, helping others naturally helps oneself work toward *moksha* or realization of Truth.

There is a paradox inherent in these values. Karma yoga and Gandhian social work both advocate that the social worker should seek the benefit of others without seeking personal benefit. However, selfless action results in spiritual benefits for the social worker. Yet, if one's motivation is solely to accrue material or spiritual benefits, then even apparently good action does not help the social worker toward the spiritual goal of liberation.

Social Work Implications

The helping relationship should reflect these values of respect, selflessness, and nonviolence. The traditional Hindu greeting, *namaste*, meaning "the divine within me greets the divine within you," signifies that the social worker should relate to clients on the basis of their inherent worth.

On a practical level, karma yoga practitioners in India have established educational and social service programs, medical institutions, cultural activities, rural and tribal development programs, and youth training for social service (Patel, 1987). Such formal service organizations based on karma yoga have not been described in the American social work literature. However, the principles of karma yoga could be applied in American social work contexts. Gandhian principles have not been applied widely in American social work, although they were a significant influence on Rev. Martin Luther King Jr.'s, civil rights organizing approach. Advocates suggest that American social work could move toward a more holistic, spiritually attuned, and nonviolent approach by considering Gandhian principles.

Singh (1992) suggested that the Vedantic perspective and traditional helping techniques, such as yoga systems, could provide a culturally familiar framework for many Hindus (and other Asian Americans) in the United States. He identified four types of yoga: karma yoga (as already described); *bhakti yoga*, devotional dedication to a personal God; *raja yoga*, opening awareness of the divinity within oneself through mental and physical exercises; and *jnana yoga*, realizing one's own divine nature through intellectual disciplines. The yogas provide a holistic approach to individuals, by using different means suited to particular talents, personalities, and beliefs, in "application to stress management, mental clarification from confusions, self-unification, emancipation from suffering and enhancement of self-image" (p. 9). Singh also identified some current helping techniques that have similarity to yogic disciplines, such as biofeedback and healing visualization.

Seplowin (1992) recommended meditation in conjunction with group therapy. Logan (1997), gave a personal example of how her practice of an Indian originated meditation practice (siddha yoga) simultaneously helps herself achieve clarity while relating in a clear and open minded way with social work students.

Gandhian principles highlight the importance of spiritually explicit, compassionate approaches to macro-action. The practical techniques of Gandhian community organizing and development can be applied to American social work. This would require reenvisioning the nature of social work (Walz et al., 1990; Walz & Ritchie, 2000). For example, the personal lifestyle of the worker, the consumption patterns of the agency, and efforts for larger social change should all foster material simplicity. Material simplicity reduces violence by performing work simply, limiting environmental damage, and taking only what is needed for service. Helping strategies should seek the welfare of all (sarvodaya) by taking a holistic and systemic understanding of situations and applying a value of compassion for everyone affected by change. Social work should also embody the principle of swadeshi, which means focusing help for those most needy in the local environment while rippling benefits out to wider social systems, including the global context. Swadeshi links local and global dimensions of justice.

In general, the Vedantic inspired approaches to social work suggest innovative possibilities for working with Indian American clients in a culturally appropriate way. In addition, when the principles are extended beyond specific traditional Hindu terminology and religious beliefs, they provide guidelines for developing holistic models of social work in general.

Traditional Hindus emphasize personal identity as interdependent with family, social class, and cosmic design. Decision making in the helping process needs to take into account the client's sense of dharma, including responsibilities within the family and larger social context. Recognized authorities in the family, such as husband or elder males, may have special priority in family meetings with social workers (Hodge, 2004b). Hindu temples may be important sources of psychosocial and spiritual support. However, Hindus with high levels of formal education, multicultural living experience, or preference for egalitarian relationships may not conform to the expectations described for traditionalists.

Since religious beliefs and practices vary widely, spiritual assessment should include identification of particular deities, home- or temple-based worship practices (puja), religious teachers (guru), temple priests, and Indian community celebrations (if any) that are relevant to the client's sources of strength, resilience, and problem solving. Hindu clients may be open to referral to complementary healing and stress management practices rooted in Indian culture, such as Ayurvedic medicine and yogas.

Indigenous Religions of North America and Social Service

Origin and Contemporary Varieties of Indigenous Religions

In this section, we summarize some features of traditional religions among Indigenous peoples of North America, drawing heavily on insights from Indigenous social workers and helping professionals in the United States and Canada. Yellow Bird (2008) defines Indigenous peoples as culturally and linguistically diverse populations who reside on ancestral lands, share ancestry with the original inhabitants, and regard themselves as different from those who colonized and control their lands. Although the terms American Indian and Native American are commonly used in the United States, we wish to avoid the colonialist implications of these terms. The terms Aboriginal or First Nations are used sometimes in Canada, and to a lesser extent in the United States. We will use the terms Indigenous or First Nations (capitalized) to recognize these diverse peoples' status as descendents of the original inhabitants as well as to recognize their sovereignty and special connection with their ancestral and current lands.

The term "Indigenous religion" has many problems from a technical religious studies viewpoint (Cox, 2007). There are so many variations around the world (and within North America) of historical circumstance, population movement, contents of worldview, and social organization among peoples often referred to as Indigenous that is difficult to make a definition that fits all situations. Cox's critical review of the term concludes that the main distinguishing features of Indigenous religions are that group identity is formed by kinship and ancestor relations tied to a particular place and shared traditions. Some authors (e.g. Fleming & Ledogar, 2008) use the term "Indigenous spirituality". Following our definitions, by Indigenous religions (or spiritual perspectives) we are referring to shared features of worldview as recounted by Indigenous peoples of the United States and Canada. Each Indigenous culture has one or more religions in the sense of an organized pattern of spiritual beliefs, values, and practices shared by the community over time in traditions. However, most Indigenous religions of North America are not organized according to bureaucracies or centrally controlled doctrines. For Indigenous people who associate the term religion with this style, or in particular with religions of colonizers, the terms spirituality or spiritual perspective may be preferred. Further, Indigenous spirituality permeates all aspects of individual and community life.

Given the wide range of diversity among Indigenous peoples, it is crucial to remember that the descriptions of shared worldview are very general (Fire, 2006; Gray, Coates, & Yellow Bird, 2008; Voss, White Hat, Bates, Lunderman, & Lunderman, 2005; Weaver, 1999). Social workers should become familiar with Indigenous clients' particular culture (named in their own language), religious beliefs, degree of religiousness or spiritual interest (if any), and other variations based on level of traditionalism or acculturation, reservation, urban, or rural living situation, affiliations with one or more First Nations, and possible membership in nontraditional religions, such as a Christian denomination (McKenzie & Morrisette, 2003). Another significant, but little addressed, religion is the Native American Church (NAC). It is the largest specifically Indigenous, formally organized denomination (i.e. with a charter, formally organized chapters, and legal status as a church) that is widespread across cultures in North America (Prue, 2008). The NAC developed from a blending of use of peyote as a sacrament (stemming from Indigenous Mexican cultures), with American Indigenous spiritual ways and, for some, Christian elements. The English social work literature focuses mainly on Indigenous peoples of Canada and the United States, rather than Mexico, and even within that does not address the full range of Indigenous cultures.

Shamanism is a common feature of many Indigenous religions (Canda, 1983; Gray et al., 2008; Voss, Douville, Little Soldier, & Twiss, 1999). The term shamanism covers a diverse range of religious healing traditions centering around the practices of spirit-guided people within the context of an animistic worldview that regards nonhuman beings (i.e. animals, plants, mountains, etc.) as living persons with whom humans should live respectfully (Anderson, 1996; Eliade, 1964; Lehmann & Myers, 2001). Canda (1983), drawing on anthropology and religious studies, defined shamanism as "a religious style which centers on the helping ministrations of a sacred specialist, the shaman, who utilizes a technique of ecstatic trance in order to communicate with spirits and other powerful forces, natural and supernatural. The shaman obtains sacred power from the spiritual realm to heal and edify the human community in harmony with the nonhuman environment" (p. 15). Gray, Yellow Bird, and Coates said, "Acknowledging the connection between all things, the shaman turns inward to his [sic] personal psyche and also moves laterally and outward into the landscape and its many voices...Today shamanism has come to connote an alternative form of therapy with an emphasis on the curative power of nature and personal insight" (p. 55).

Frey and Edinburg (1978) and Canda (1983) pointed out that shamanistic healing is the historical precursor of social work and other helping professions. Shamanism probably originated within Paleolithic period gathering and hunting bands and tribes. It is the oldest documented religious approach to healing and service in the world. There are currently many hundreds or thousands of forms of shamanism in the world, given the great number of cultures in which it appears. In addition, in many cultures, missionary religions, such as Christianity and Buddhism, have been converged with older Indigenous shamanistic traditions, to form new varieties of shamanism. Unfortunately, shamanism has often been persecuted by missionaries and colonizers throughout the world, including North America.

There is also a recently developed religious movement in many countries, which adapts general cross-cultural themes of shamanism to contemporary urban life, by removing them from traditional culture-specific contexts and formulating generic shamanistic spiritual beliefs and practices. This movement is sometimes referred to as Neo-shamanism to indicate both its origins from and revision of traditional forms of shamanism (Cox, 2007; Doore, 1988). Neo-shamanism began to emerge in the late 1960s with the writings of Carlos Castenada (1968) and other counter-cultural writers. In the 1980s, centers for (neo)shamanistic study expanded, including the Dance of the Deer Foundation (by Brant Secunda), the Foundation for Shamanic Studies (by Michael Harner), the Cross-Cultural Shamanism Network (by Timothy White), and the Sun Bear Medicine Society (by Sun Bear, now deceased). Neo-shamanism involves loose networks of people, mostly Euro-Americans, who are interested in exploring diverse spiritual practices to support personal growth and healing as well as ways of living in harmony with the earth (Townshend, 1988). Two related trends of Neo-shamanism in the United States can be identified. The first has grown directly from the teachings, workshops, and rituals of traditional Indigenous shamans who have decided to share their spiritual ways with people of different cultures from their own. The second trend has grown from mainly Euro-Americans who have studied shamanism from traditional teachers and academic research.

Some Indigenous people are opposed to Neo-shamanism, viewing it as an inappropriate use of Indigenous spirituality by others and self-seeking Indigenous teachers, which furthers the process of colonialism and cultural destruction for Indigenous peoples (Canda & Yellow Bird, 1996; Gray, Coates, & Yellow Bird, 2008). Other traditional teachers from many regions of the world believe it is time to share these teachings in order to change the course of industrial and postindustrial ways of life that are destroying the earth.

This is a topic full of controversy (Buhner, 1997). For our purposes, we believe that social workers should be aware that Neo-shamanism may be important and valuable for some clients, usually Euro American members of alternative spiritual groups. However, Neo-shamanism should not be confused with Indigenous spiritual traditions. The remainder of this discussion will focus on traditional Indigenous religions and their implications for social work.

In social work literature, there are two main approaches to Indigenous religions. The first addresses culture-specific forms of Indigenous helping (e.g. Mokuau, 1990; Nabigon & Mawhiney, 1996; Voss et al., 1999). The second addresses the cross-cultural common features of Indigenous religions and shamanism (e.g. Bullis, 1996; Canda, 1983; Cataldo, 1979; Dumbrill & Green, 2008; Fleming & Lodogar, 2008; Frey & Edinburg, 1978; Gray et al., 2008; Hart, 2008; Laird, 1984; McKenzie & Morrisette, 2003; Weaver, 1999). We pool together their insights, placing first priority on the ideas that come directly from Indigenous peoples.

Basic Beliefs

The traditional Indigenous worldview is a holistic and collectivistic understanding of intimate interdependence between whole person, family, community, and the environment, especially in relation with the ancestors and places of the locale. The natural (nonhuman) world is a source of beauty and inspiration. The earth and sky are often described as our mother and father, with all creatures our relatives, since our lives are sustained by the natural environment. There is a balance and order to the universe (Fleming & Ledogar, 2008; Hart, 2008). Well-being consists of harmonious relation with this order as it permeates family, clan, society, world, and the larger universe. For example, Voss et al. (2005) explained,

> For the Lakota, the sense of self has traditionally been associated with an intimate bond with the group (Lakota Nation) and with a profound sense of kinship with all creation, including the natural universe and ancestral spirits articulated in the Lakota imperative *Mitakuye oyas'in!* which has been translated as "All my relations!" For the traditional Lakota, self-identity does not exist apart from the spiritual world, the nation, and all creation. (p. 214)

Thus Indigenous identity and helping approaches are communal, focusing on holistic and reciprocal relations with other persons and nature (McKenzie & Morrisette, 2003). These authors emphasize that all things connect together with a spiritual essence flowing from its source. Elders are respected as transmitters of traditional wisdom between generations. Indigenous people also seek knowledge through an inner-focused spiritual journey in order to support the harmony and balance between all living things. This understanding is conveyed through stories, symbols, and ceremonies that go beyond linear thinking (McKenzie & Morrisette, 2003; Yellow Bird, 1995).

The Medicine Wheel symbolizes this understanding of the interrelated and cyclical nature of life (Bruyere, 2007; Coggins, 1990; Dumbrill & Green, 2008; Fire, 2006; Nabigon & Mawhiney, 1996; Verniest, 2006). There are many different versions of Medicine Wheels within and between the Indigenous cultures that use them (and not all do), but there are some common insights. Each direction can be related to aspects of existence, such as four human races (red, yellow, black, and white), four seasons, (spring, summer, fall, winter), four aspects of human being (spiritual, emotional, physical, and mental), four elements of creation (earth, air, water, and fire), four cardinal sacred medicines (tobacco, cedar, sage, and sweetgrass), and four aspects of the life cycle (infant, youth, adult, elder). All aspects of persons, community, and universe should balance and harmonize throughout developmental processes. These distinctions are not hierarchical or concrete divisions, but rather an aid to achieve a holistic understanding of interrelatedness and mutual honoring. Healing is a matter of completing and restoring the circle of wholeness for individuals, families, communities, and nation (Baskin, 2006).

Basic Values

Indigenous religions do not merely acknowledge interconnection in a technical sense, as Western science does. They value interconnectedness as a sacred basis of life and of well-being for individuals, communities, nations, and world (Coggins, 1990; Dumbrill & Green, 2008; Saulis, 2006; Waegemakers Schiff & Pelech, 2007). Nature is alive with the mutually sustaining web of all beings. Human and nonhuman beings are persons and relatives, so humans should regard other beings with respect (Bowen, 2005).

Harmony and reciprocity in communal relationships are valued, so that all things fulfill their obligations for mutual benefit (Hart, 2008; McKenzie & Morrisette, 2003). Human life itself is appreciated as a spiritual journey toward balance, harmony, and reciprocity. Humility before elders and the sacred powers is important (Dell, Dell, & Hopkins, 2005). Hart highlights three values: respecting all without imposing our own views; sharing what we have, know, and experience; and recognizing the nonphysical spiritual world in all interactions, including meditation, prayer, and ceremonies.

Social Work Implications

As we have seen, authors commonly recommend that practice with Indigenous people should emphasize culturally appropriate knowledge, respect, use of community based support systems, holistic thinking, and awareness of spirituality imbued in daily life. Weaver (1999, p. 223) provided a set of widely applicable recommendations for social workers to work well with Indigenous clients. Social workers should understand and appreciate diversity among and within Indigenous groups; understand the history, culture, and contemporary ways of the specific groups relevant to clients; employ strong social work skills emphasizing patience, listening, and tolerance of silence; develop self-awareness of biases and needs for well-being; show humility and willingness to learn; be respectful, nonjudgmental, and open-minded; value social justice; and remove colonialistic and ethnocentric thinking from practice approaches.

Traditional healing and helping are not just a matter of reducing symptoms of individuals, but rather maintaining and restoring the relational circle of harmony and balance for individual, family, community, nation, and world. Holistic and transpersonal approaches to social work practice may be appropriate when adapted to the particular cultural patterns of Indigenous clients and communities. Even more importantly, approaches for effective social work with Indigeneous people can best be developed by and with Indigenous social workers and the trusted family members, spiritual teachers, healers, shamans, and elders within specific Indigenous communities, whether based in reservations, rural, or urban areas. This is not indigenization in the sense of starting with Eurocentric social work and adapting it to Indigenous people, but rather building genuinely Indigenous social work up from particular communities (Gray et al., 2008).

Historical trauma and acculturation stress are pervasive issues for many Indigenous people due to the history of colonialization, genocide, and continuing discrimination and oppression, including assaults upon traditional spiritual perspectives and rituals (Cousineau, 2006; McKenzie & Morrisette, 2003;

Verniest, 2006; Weaver, 1999; Yellow Horse Brave Heart, 2001). On the other hand, Indigenous people are exemplars of resilience for surviving, reviving, and thriving as a people in the face of such conditions (Chenault, 1990). Positive participation in traditional activities and spiritual ways has been shown to support resilience (Fleming & Ledogar, 2008). Social work educational programs that take an affirming approach to Indigenous worldview are likely to feel more congruent for Indigenous students and prepare them for effective work in their communities (Dumbrill & Green, 2008; Fire, 2006; Voss et al., 2005).

Social workers should gain knowledge of the regional Indigenous nations and social support systems in order to be prepared to make referrals and to collaborate as relevant to Indigenous clients. Successful referral and collaboration are more likely if the social worker has a respectful relationship with Indigenous community leaders, healers, spiritual teachers, elders, and social service agencies, or, with people who do have such relationships and can serve as brokers and mediators. The details of spiritual practices and contacts of course vary by each culture and community. Only the client can determine what is relevant and whether traditional or other spiritual ways, alone or in combination, are preferred. In general, the literature suggests the following as some potentially beneficial supports: traditional ceremonies, for example the *sweat lodge* that is prevalent in various forms among many nations (Gossage et al., 2003; McCabe, 2008; Smith, 2005; Waegemakers Schiff & Pelech, 2007, elders); understandings of human life development and well-being that are holistic, such as *Medicine Wheels* (Coggins, 1990; Dumbrill & Green, 2008; Gilgun, 2002; Nabigon & Mawhiney, 1996; Verniest, 2006); consultation with respected elders (Bowen, 2005; Broad, Boyer, & Chataway, 2006; Zellerer, 2003); referral to or collaboration with *traditional healers*, such as herbalists and shamans (Beatch & Stewart, 2002; Bucko & Iron Cloud, 2008; Struthers, 2003; Voss et al., 1999); use of narrative and *story telling* (Stewart & Wheeler, 2002; Yellow Bird, 1995); and use of *talking circle* style therapeutic groups (Thomas & Bellefeuille, 2006; Warner, 2003). Other family-based and traditional activities that may be important to Indigenous clients include feasts to honor the deceased; pow wows, seasonal feasts, naming ceremonies, give-aways, and fasting (Fleming & Ledogar, 2008).

Bullis (1996) offered guidelines for referral to and collaboration with shamanistic healers that are useful to consider regarding any type of Indigenous healers. First, he suggested that the social worker should identify the healer's type of expertise, specific beliefs, healing practices, and possible impacts on the client. Second, the social worker should ascertain the reputation of the healer within his or her own community. Third, the expectations of the social worker within the healer's and client's culture should be clarified to enhance cooperation and culturally appropriate behavior. Likewise, the social worker should make clear his or her own professional expertise (or lack thereof) and sense of respect for the client's culture. Fourth, the social worker should seek to establish an ongoing knowledgeable and respectful relationship with the Indigenous culture by approaching it as a learner. Fifth, the social worker should reflect with the client

on the consistency between the healer's assessments and planned helping strategies for the client. Sixth, the social worker should ascertain what protective and
supportive strategies will be used to ensure the well-being of the client.

As we noted, social workers need to be cautious not to impose their own
ethnocentric or religiocentric biases on Indigenous clients. An important case
in point is the Native American Church. Some social workers and substance
abuse counselors mistake the sacramental use of peyote as a form of substance
abuse and dismiss spiritual insights from NAC ceremonies as delusions or hallucinations. On the contrary, research has shown that NAC participation can be
a valuable source of social support, health promotion, and recovery from substance abuse (Bullis, 1996; Prue, 2008). Currently, the federal American Indian
Religious Freedom Act and most states authorize Indigenous people to use peyote within the NAC.

Social work in general can benefit by learning from Indigenous traditions
of helping and healing. The concept of person-in-environment can be given a
more profound significance through the Indigenous ideal of harmony between
all beings as evinced in Medicine Wheel teachings. Although not all social workers believe in spirits or have an animistic worldview, we could all enhance our
relationship with the world by regarding all beings, human and nonhuman as
significant and worthy of respect (Canda, 1983; Gray, Coates, & Hetherington,
2008). Therapeutic practice would also help the client to pay attention to the
quality of relationship with the natural environment, not only in terms of physical resource acquisition but also in terms of the client's openness to the inspiration and beauty of the earth, sky, and all the beings of this universe (Cataldo,
1979).

We can learn from shamanism to utilize a wide range of consciousness
states for both the practitioner and the client (such as meditation and trance to
heighten empathy and stimulate creativity of insights) and ways of stimulating
this through drumming, dance, song, and ritual. The kind and quality of ritual
celebrations of life transitions employed by the client could be examined and
improved where found lacking or dysfunctional (Laird, 1984). The shamanisti-
cally oriented social worker would practice personal disciplines that encourage
constant personal growth and resolution of fundamental existential issues and
crises, so that he or she is prepared to offer assistance for the clients' spiritual
quests from a standpoint of personal experience (Canda, 1983). However, non-
Indigenous social workers should be cautious not to borrow, imitate, or appropriate Indigenous symbols and ceremonies in a thoughtless or colonialist manner
(Canda & Yellow Bird, 1996; Gray et al., 2008). Given our commitment to social
justice, social workers need to be mindful of the history of colonial occupation
and religious persecution directed against Indigenous peoples by Europeans.
Until recently, Indigenous spiritual ways were actively persecuted by governmental and Christian religious authorities. Therefore, suspicion on the part of
Indigenous people is common regarding the borrowing of their traditions by
others. If we are not careful, even well intentioned uses by non-Indigenous social

workers can exacerbate historical trauma and injustice. Indigenous social workers also must be attentive to the particular goals, beliefs, identities, and community affiliations for Indigenous clients, being sure to practice in a manner congruent with that, rather than their own presumptions. For a social worker (Indigenous or otherwise) to employ Indigenous healing practices in a professional capacity raises additional issues, such as how permission from traditional communities can be (or should be) obtained, how the social worker can be properly trained, and how powerful transformative practices can be used safely in a social work setting. Finally, social workers who work with Indigenous people need to be aware of relevant U.S. treaty agreements and laws, such as the Indian Child Welfare Act of 1978, and First Nations' laws and social welfare systems.

Islam and Social Service

Origin and Contemporary Varieties of Islam

Islam originated among Arab Bedouins in the 6th century (Esposito, 1991; Nielsen et al., 1993; Peters, 1982). The word Islam is derived from an Arabic term meaning "surrender, obedience, and peace" (Nadir & Dzieglielewski, 2001; Smith, 1991). Islam is a faith based on the person's and community's submission to the will of God, Allah, in all spheres of life. Islam developed in the monotheistic stream of traditions that includes Judaism and Christianity. Each shares a common basis in the biblical books of Moses (the Torah). Islamic monotheism was in part a reaction against the polytheistic beliefs, preoccupation with striving for wealth and power, and feuding among Arab tribes prevalent at the time of Islam's founder, the Prophet Muhammad (c. 570–632).

Muhammad was born into a wealthy clan of Mecca. As a young man, he spent much time in reflection upon problems of social corruption (Nielsen et al., 1993; Haynes et al., 1997; Smith, 1991). At around the age of 40, while in solitary meditation in a cave, he had a series of revelations. Tradition has it that the angel Gabriel delivered God's messages to Muhammad, and they were set down in the Quran, the Islamic scripture. After 613, Muhammad spread his message to his family and community, especially focusing on disadvantaged groups, such as women, slaves, poor people, and children. Muhammad soon moved to Medina, which accepted him as the prophet of Allah and agreed to fight on his behalf. With support of people from Medina, Muhammad established authority in Medina by 630.

From the time of the Prophet's death in 632–661, his successors led campaigns of conquest and proselytization that extended from north Africa to the Indian frontier (Crim, 1981). Early in this period, a major division occurred between Sunni Islam, the largest group, and the Shiite Muslims. The Shiite Muslims identified Ali, Muhammad's cousin and son-in-law, as the Prophet's successor. Since that time, Islam has spread throughout the world, with large numbers of adherents in the Middle East, Africa, Europe, India, and East and

Southeast Asia. The Muslim population of North America is growing quickly. In most countries except Iran and Iraq, the Sunni Muslims are the majority. Thus among the worldwide community of believers (*ummah*, Arabic), there is a fundamental unity based on common beliefs as well as wide variety based on particular cultural contexts.

As mentioned in Chapter 4, in the United States there are now three major groupings of Muslims: Muslim immigrants and their descendants (mostly Sunni), converts to these traditional forms of Islam, and primarily African American new Islamic groups, such as the Nation of Islam. There is great variety depending on ethnicity and, for immigrants, country of origin. The primary immigrant Muslim national organization is The Islamic Society of North America (Corbett, 1997; Melton, 1992). The American Muslim Mission is the largest organization of American-born Muslims. Sufism, a mystical form of Islam, was brought to the United States in 1910 by Pir Hazrat Inayat Khan. The Sufi Order sponsors many spiritual groups, meditation and ecstatic rituals, and educational programs.

Muslim mosques and student and community organizations in the United States, such as Islamic Relief USA and Islamic Circle of North America Relief, provide social support for Muslims and the wider society (Nadir, 2008). Over 90% of mosques in the United States provide cash assistance to members in need. Many provide counseling, prison outreach, and assistance with food and clothing. The Islamic Social Services Associations of Canada and United States were established in 1999 to increase awareness of social service needs of Muslims (see http://www.issausa.org/).

Basic Beliefs

The primary sources of authority in Islam are the Quran and the Hadith, the traditions based on the life of the Prophet Muhammed (Smith, 1991). Islamic law (*shari'a*) was written as a divinely inspired guide for living, elaborating on the Quran and hadith. The Quran is an unchangeable divine text, whereas *shari'a* is open to interpretation and modification based on different cultural contexts (Crabtree, Husain, & Spalek, 2008). Muslims believe that Muhammad was the last and final prophet, culminating the earlier Jewish and Christian prophetic revelations (Corbett, 1997; Haynes et al., 1997; Smith, 1991). Islam is strictly monotheistic. The central tenet is that there is no God other then Allah, the supreme, incomparable, inconceivable, personal creator deity. Muslims declare their submission to and reliance upon Allah in all things. Since Allah cannot be understood in terms of any created thing, it is strictly prohibited to produce images of the deity. The Six Pillars of Faith (*Iman*) include belief in the one Creator God; reverence for angels, especially Gabriel, who live in obedience to God; belief in all the revealed scriptures, including the Scrolls of Abraham, Psalms of David, Torah, Gospel of Jesus, and the Quran revealed to Muhammad; reverence for all the Prophets of God, for example Adam, Abraham, Moses, David, John the Baptist, Jesus and Mohammad; belief in the after-life in which people return to

God for judgment and relegation to heaven or hell; and belief in human free will limited by divine destiny (Barise, 2005; Nadir & Dziegielewski, 2001).

Muslims regard the Quran as the culmination of the scriptures of Allah. Muhammad is the final prophet. Jewish and Christian scriptures are respected, but if there is disagreement with the Quran, the Quran takes precedence. None of the Prophets are considered divine themselves, as that is a quality of God alone.

The Five Pillars of Islam are the core duties (Barisse, 2005; Corbett, 1997; Haynes, et al., 1997; Nadir, 2001; Smith, 1991). The first is daily declaration of faith (*shahada*) that "There is no God but Allah, and Muhammad is the last Prophet of Allah." The second is prayer (*salat*), which takes place five times daily facing Mecca, and if possible, at a mosque on midday Friday. The third pillar (*zakat*) is the giving of alms (2.5% of annual wealth after expenses) for care of the needy. The fourth pillar is fasting (*sawm*), from sunrise to sunset, during the month of Ramadan that celebrates the revelation to Muhammad and teaches empathy and self-restraint. The fifth pillar is the pilgrimage (*hajj*) to Mecca, which should be done at least once in a lifetime if a person is able. This pilgrimage is a joining of all the diverse peoples of the *ummah* in unity as people who will be judged by God on the basis of their accordance with God's will. These pillars of practice assist the person and community to strive toward self-improvement and welfare in all aspects of life.

Muslims also have beliefs related to distinctive cultural traditions. For example, Al-Krenawi and Graham (2009) give detailed accounts of culture-specific beliefs and appropriate health and mental health practices for Bedouin-Arabs. Crabtree, Husain, and Spacek (2008) address family and community relations issues in relation to health and social work in the United Kingdom and several other countries.

Basic Values

Since the person and community should be wholly oriented toward the will of Allah, there is no separation between religious and secular spheres of life. Individual fulfillment, family life, and community well-being are all related to following the precepts of Islamic law. As Muhammad originally advocated for social reforms on behalf of women, children, and disadvantaged groups, there is a strong social justice value framework in Islam (Barise, 2005; Nadir, 2008; Smith, 1991). Ideally, there should be a reciprocal relationship between individual freedom and community obligations and responsibilities. People should be persistent in their efforts toward self-improvement, both in actions and in feelings. Family roles traditionally involve patriarchal gender roles, but women and men are to respect each other. The aim of all life is to achieve peace through accordance with God's will and human freedom from all contrary forces (Barisse, 2005).The Islamic community of believers has a special mission from Allah to create a just society for its members and to be a model for others (Esposito, 1991).

The Quran recognizes differences in social status, wealth, and tribal origin, but it promotes a unity and equality of all believers under Allah. The Quran condemns exploitation of the poor, widows, women, orphans, and slaves. It denounces economic abuse, such as false contracts, bribery, hoarding of wealth, and usury.

Social Work Implications

Since Islam means that all of life should be oriented toward Allah, social work practice with Muslim clients should respectfully incorporate their beliefs and practices (Hodge, 2005a). The close sense of community connectedness and identity should not be confused with dysfunctional enmeshment, but rather understood as a potentially strong source of support. Its community orientation provides an opportunity for social workers to consult and collaborate with Muslim social support networks, Islamic teachers (*imam*), and friendship support groups. Sometimes problems may be defined in relation to Islamic law, Hadith, and the Quran. In these cases, familiarity with relevant passages, as well as family and ethnic customs, could be developed with guidance from the client and qualified teachers. Almsgiving (*zakat*), has significant social welfare implications. Almsgiving is both an act of worship to God and a service to the community. This payment is owed because people receive their wealth from the bounty of God. *Zakat* reflects a broad concern for ideals of equality, mutual respect, justice, and relief of the disadvantaged.

The Islamic view of social service emphasizes a complementary relation between individual well-being and social welfare. The helping process itself is a spiritually significant action and relationship, not only between worker and clients, but also with the divine.

As our National Survey showed, there are fewer Muslim social workers in proportion to the growing U.S. Muslim population. There is a significant need for more Muslim social workers and Muslim based social service organizations as well as non-Muslim social workers who are sensitive and competent to work with Muslims (Nadir, 2008). After the terrorist attacks of September 11, 2001, anti-Muslim suspicion and discrimination in North America and European countries also increased significantly (Crabtree et al., 2008; Nadir, 2008). Social workers should be especially attentive to violations of human rights and other acts of discrimination or oppression against Muslims. The unfortunate state of conflict and war in many countries, often under the guise of religious and ideological positions of various kinds, presents social workers with a challenge to promote a spirit of peace and tolerance in society and world at large.

As with all religions, social workers need to attend to diversity within Muslim communities. In addition to variations based on sect (e.g. Sunni or Shi'ite), ethnicity and national origin, as mentioned before, there are also variations based on individual and family interpretations and choices. There are degrees of religious observance and conformance with family or community norms. A good example is variety of opinion about Muslim women wearing the veil (*hijab*). Muslims and others variously interpret that as a sign of dignity, disgrace, individual choice and affirmation, or group oppression (Meshal, 2007). Some Muslim women view the veil as an aid to women's liberation from exploitive sexualization; others think it is a tool to enforce male dominance. Traditions for veiling or not veiling vary by cultures and religious groups. The social work principle of self-determination would support the various choices of Muslim women in this matter and encourage social workers to understand the particular meaning given to the veil in a given situation.

Judaism and Social Service

Origin and Contemporary Varieties of Judaism

Judaism originated from the agrarian nomadic Hebrew tribes of Israel around 2000–1000 BCE (Crim, 1981; Neusner, 1979; Nielsen et al., 1993). During this period, the tribal God came to be understood as the one true God, creator transcendent over creation. According to tradition, the Patriarch of Israel, Abraham, migrated from Mesopotamia to Canaan to leave the polytheistic past and to dedicate himself and his descendants to God. Later, Jacob and his people went to Egypt during a time of famine. The people of Israel became oppressed by the pharaoh. Finally, Moses led his people across the wilderness to freedom. Moses received revelation of the Torah from God, confirming the covenant of God's care for the Jews and the Jewish people's commitment to God. The first five books of the Bible are attributed to Moses, though they were probably not completed in their present form until the 5th century BCE. Key themes of Judaism were established during this time: monotheism; a covenant between God and God's chosen people; and endurance of suffering, exile, and liberation.

In 586 BCE, the temple of Jerusalem was destroyed and the Hebrews were exiled to Babylonia. The tradition of the synagogue developed as a place for study and worship. Many Jews returned to Israel around 500 BCE and reestablished the temple in Jerusalem. During this period, priests took responsibility for religious sacrifice at the Temple; scribes studied and interpreted the scriptures; and messianic Zealots struggled against foreign rulers. The core of Hebrew scriptures (*tanakh*, Hebrew) was formed, including the Torah (Pentateuch), Prophetic writings, and other writings.

The Second Temple was destroyed in 70 CE by the Romans. After the destruction of the Second Temple, the rabbis (learned teachers) gradually emerged from and supplanted the priests and scribes. The classical or rabbinical period continued to the 19th century along with dispersion of the Jews to many parts of the world. Jews in the Diaspora struggled with various means of retaining cultural distinctiveness and faithfulness to the Torah, often enduring discrimination and oppression.

During the 19th and 20th centuries, various forms of Zionism emerged, which emphasized the importance of Jews returning to Israel to establish a state and fulfill their religious and cultural aspirations. The holocaust of the Jews amplified this Zionist movement, as the need for state protection and political autonomy became a matter of survival. The holocaust also accelerated immigration of Jews to the United States.

Currently, there are about 5.2 million Jews in the United States (Gelman, Andron, & Schnall, 2008). There are three major groups of religious Jews, Orthodox, Conservative, and Reform; many Jews are not affiliated with a religious group. Since the late 1800s, there have been many forms of Jewish agencies and social services in the United States. The strong Jewish tradition of commitment to education and service is reflected in the percentage of Jews in our 1997 and 2008 National Surveys, which is proportionately much higher than that of Jews in the United States overall.

Basic Beliefs

According to Neusner (1979), Judaism is a tradition built upon the scriptures (*tanakh*, Hebrew), ethical commandments governing daily conduct (*mitzvot*), Talmudic commentaries, faith in God, and membership in the Jewish community. For religious Jews, Jewish law (*halakhah*) dictates that one should live in accord with the covenant between God and the Jewish community. Friedman (2001) summarized the foundation of Judaism as God, Torah, and the Jewish community. Therefore, it follows that a Jewish perspective would emphasize that social work with Jewish people should have an intimate connection with and relevance for the Jewish community. Many Jewish communal service workers view the heightening of Jewish identity and preservation of the Jewish community as key issues in Jewish social welfare, because of the challenges of diaspora and holocaust, and more recently, the large numbers of Jews who choose to live in the United States, and high rates of intermarriage and secularism (Bubis, 1981; Gelman, Andron, & Schnall, 2008).

Judaism is a way of life, not just a religious or philosophical system. However, there is a great variety of lifestyle and belief within the Jewish community pertaining to cultural backgrounds, degree of religiousness, and religious affiliation. Humanistic Judaism focuses on social ethical relations between people (Friedman, 2001). Reform Judaism gives a liberal interpretation to Torah and adapts to American culture. Reconstructionism observes many traditions while adding a more scientific and egalitarian approach. For example, the *Bat Mizvah* for girls to enter adulthood was developed in complement to the traditional *Bar Mitzvah* for boys. Conservative Judaism follows Torah rituals but allows innovation in law. When Conservative Judaism began ordaining women as rabbis, Traditional Judaism grew to preserve more traditional standards. Orthodox Judaism closely adheres to Torah law and practices, but individual congregations vary along with the rabbi's views. Hasidic Judaism uses parables, song, and dance to celebrate the joys of being Jewish. In addition, some Jews identify with their cultural heritage but not with religious practices or theistic beliefs.

In the Judaic religious view, there is an inextricable connection between faith in God and service, because the *tanakh* requires Jews to imitate God through partnership in the ongoing process of creation, including social welfare activities (Eskenazi, 1983; Schecter, 1971). According to Eskenazi, the God of Israel has neither identifiable appearance nor a name that Jews may speak. Yet God sanctifies diverse and authentic emotions as well as fallibility. God transcends human images but also sanctifies the uniqueness of human experience. I-Thou (person to person connection and acceptance) is the proper mode of relationship between people and God.

The details of this relationship are prescribed by the Torah and its commentaries pertaining to diet, Sabbath, morality, civil law, and Torah study (Ostrov, 1976; Friedman, 2001). There are also communal commemorations of annual holidays (Passover, Shavuoth, and Succoth), holy days for repentance and introspection (Rosh Hashanah and Yom Kippur), life events (birth, Bar and Bat Mitzvah, marriage, divorce, death), and historical events (e.g. the Six-Day War). Religious observance is most strict among Orthodox Jews.

According to Ansel (1973), Judaic thought views human nature as essentially good, having been created in the image of God, including an innate need for growth. However, this growth may be blocked by misunderstandings of self or external conditions. When this growth runs contrary to God's purpose and moral relationships, one must practice *t'shuva* (repentance), involving self-awareness and change of heart, to return to God's will. This process may involve a healthy feeling of guilt and reconciliation. Accordingly, Judaic thought includes an understanding of human behavior in terms of sin. Yet the relationship between sin and mental illness is a complex one in the Torah. Identification of a person who has mental health problems as a sinner, in the pejorative sense, is not appropriate (Wikler, 1977). However, Wikler (1986) pointed out that some Orthodox Jews may attach a sense of stigma and community sanction (such as damage to family reputation or reduced marriage prospects) to people with mental illness.

Basic Values

In Judaic thought, since all people are created in the image of God, each person has intrinsic worth. There are many commandments to set forth expectations for social relations and care for the needy. The Torah injunction to love one's neighbor expresses through commitment to standards of righteousness, compassion, and truth with regard to all people (Schecter, 1971). In particular, this value expresses through systematic means of providing help to members of the Jewish community in need. This is based on a sense of responsibility for mutually supportive community obligations, rather then individual acts of kindness (Gelman, Andron, & Schnall, 2008).

The devout Jew performs acts of loving kindness (*hesed*) and righteousness or justice (*tsedekah*) out of a sense of compassion modeled upon the compassion of

God (Linzer, 1979). Therefore, according to Linzer, the Jewish social worker should extend compassionate help to clients while restraining his or her own self-needs that may interfere with the client's benefit. Yet Bubis (1980) asserted that within the context of Jewish communal service, workers should uphold the Jewish community and advocate community values to the Jewish client when those values are demonstrably essential to the continuity and prosperity of that community.

Social Work Implications

Biblical and Talmudic injunctions have supported community based welfare since ancient times. For example, provisions were made for the benefit of the poor, fair treatment of workers, fair credit, and for the care of widows, orphans, strangers, and refugees (Friedman, 2001; Gelman, Andrin, & Schnall, 2008). The value of justice has led American Jews to establish many formal social service programs, most of which are independent from synagogues.

Since at least the late 1800s, numerous Jewish sponsored human service organizations have provided services to indigent people, resettled refugees and helped immigrants adjust to American life, responded to international crises, fought anti-Semitism, and provided professional services for health and mental health of Jews and the wider society. These include Jewish communal service agencies, Jewish fundraising federations, Jewish community centers and family services, hospitals and geriatric facilities, vocational services, and several social work education programs, such as Wurzweiler School of Social Work at Yeshiva University. The Journal of Jewish Communal Service is the most prominent journal dedicated to Jewish perspectives on social work. There has been recent growth in groups of Jews providing material aid, empowerment, and advocacy around the world to vulnerable populations under the principle of *tikkun olam*, which means, to heal or repair the world. Also, many alternative Jewish services have emerged to address underserved groups, such as people with special needs, lesbian, gay, bisexual and transgender (LGBT) people, interfaith couples, orthodox Jews, and new immigrants.

When the focus of service involves issues specific to the Jewish community, it is often helpful for Jewish workers to assist Jewish clients. The Jewish worker who works with Jewish clients affirms Jewish identity, values, and experiences (Berl, 1979). Therefore, the Jewish worker needs to understand Jewish history, ideologies, geography, sociology, religious customs and teachings, and calendar (Bubis, 1980). According to Eskenazi (1983), in order to be a good role model for other Jews, the Jewish worker needs to uphold Jewish values in his or her own life. This does not only apply to adherence to Jewish regulations, but also to the inner cultivation of compassion, kindness, and restraint of egoism as personal attributes (Linzer, 1979). In essence, the committed Jewish worker needs to combine professional knowledge and skill with personal Jewish commitment (Miller, 1980). Sweifach's (2005) survey of social workers in Jewish community centers found that most recognize the importance of literacy with the Jewish community, utilize Jewish practice principles, and generally feel a satisfactory fit between social work and Jewish roles.

It should be emphasized that diversity among Jews, including degrees and types of religiosity, need to be respected by the Jewish worker. Wikler (1986) found that some Orthodox Jews may prefer to see Orthodox workers or non-Orthodox Jewish workers. Matching should be a matter of client preference rather than presumption, as some Orthodox Jews prefer the greater confidentiality possible in agencies outside their community (Lightman & Shor, 2002). Wikler also found that many Orthodox rabbis may not refer people who could benefit from mental health services to agencies. His study suggested that careful work needs to be done to establish good ties of respect, mutual understanding, and cooperation between agencies and Orthodox rabbis and communities. Lightman and Shor (2002) explain how the *askan* (indigenous paraprofessional) can be a valuable mediator and linkperson between ultra-Orthodox communities of Israel and Canada and social work professionals.

While the Jewish helping professional needs to be knowledgeable and sensitive about the religious dimension of clients' needs, he or she must also be able to discern between functional and dysfunctional uses of religiosity (Ostrov, 1976; Spero, 1981). In order to avoid nonconstructive over identification or collusion between the worker and the client's religious resistances, Spero (1981) recommended that therapy begin with the following recognitions: that shared religious beliefs may involve shared distortions of religious expectations; that shared religious belief is not a legitimate motive for positive or negative regard; and that both therapist's and client's religious beliefs will be subject to examination. Ostrov (1976) urged caution in challenging dysfunctional religious practices and beliefs. One approach is to attempt to deal with the underlying psychopathology itself in order to free the client to develop more constructive religious expression. If the religious issue is too great an obstacle to effective treatment, then consultation with a competent religious authority who is sensitive to psychological dynamics is advisable.

The increasingly nonsectarian nature of Jewish communal service demonstrates that the Jewish ethos for service can be extended to non-Jewish people. In this case, particular religious language and regulations would not be applied. However, the spirit of *tsedekah* is relevant to all people.

When social workers who are not Jewish work with Jewish clients, it would be useful to assess the meaning of Jewish identity for the client and the implications of religious or secular orientation. This can be a difficult issue, because of differing qualifications for who is a Jew among different forms of Judaism (Sweifach, 2005). If the client considers this relevant, aspects of Jewish history, customs, community support systems and religion could be affirmed as strengths and resources. Social workers who are not Orthodox Jews may need to be especially careful to connect in a culturally appropriate manner with such clients. For example, Ringel's (2007) study showed how Orthodox Jewish women can feel fulfilled and empowered as primary family caretakers with pervasive traditional religiousness. Danzig and Sands (2007) formulated a group specific model of spiritual development that pertains to Jews who become Orthodox. On the other hand, strongly religious Jews would need to make efforts to relate in a client-centered manner with less or nonreligious Jews.

Conclusion

The religious perspectives we reviewed have significant contrasts in the content of beliefs. But they also have a remarkable similarity in the core of their values with regard to service. The commonalities imply possibilities for finding common ground. The differences provide many insights for various helping strategies in social work. Comparisons and connections between spiritual perspectives will be examined further at the end of Chapter 6. Next, we turn to nonreligious spiritual perspectives on service.

EXERCISES

5.1. Exploring a Religious Perspective on Service

These descriptions of religious perspectives on service only touch the surface. It is important for the reader to explore in more detail the religions that are relevant to clients and communities with whom one is likely to work. It is helpful to include both cognitive and experiential learning in order to increase both "head" knowledge and "heart" understanding.

The first step is to choose one religious tradition that has special personal or professional relevance. Consider whether you have a client or are likely to have a client who could benefit from your increased knowledge. It would be most productive for you to choose a tradition with which you are unfamiliar, uncomfortable, or have a desire to deepen or refresh familiarity.

The second step is to obtain further information about the religion. If it was covered in the chapter, go to the sources cited for further reading. Use internet search engines to check official and authentic websites maintained by these religions as well as scholarly websites about religious studies. You can get a start by going to the online Spiritual Diversity and Social Work Resource Center (www.socwel.ku.edu/canda) and exploring the relevant essays, gallery folders, and internet links. In addition, identify the key religious texts for this tradition and read some of them. You could focus by looking for passages relating to themes of compassion, justice, and service.

In the third step, contact a member of the religious group for personal discussion in a comfortable and confidential location. If permissible, participate in a religious ceremony, or visit a religiously significant place, and learn from your contact person about proper conduct for a visitor and the meaning of the symbols and actions involved.

The fourth step is to think through ways this information can be used to enhance your practice with clients who share the tradition, and for your general social work practice. Clients and people they respect as religious authorities are the best experts on this. Take a respectful and appreciative learner stance in discussing possibilities with the client. You might also establish a focus group of people familiar with the relevant religion and related client population to brainstorm with you and agency staff on possible innovations.

6

Nonsectarian Spiritual Perspectives, Comparisons, and Implications for Cooperation

Life is—or has—meaning and meaninglessness.
I cherish the anxious hope that meaning will
preponderate and win the battle.

Carl Jung, Transpersonal,
Analytical Psychology (1965, p. 359)

In this chapter, we examine two major nonsectarian spiritual perspectives that influence spiritually sensitive social work: existentialism and transpersonal theory. These perspectives grew out of humanistic intellectual developments in Europe and North America. They reflect the concerns of industrialized societies and postmodern movements regarding reaction to dehumanizing aspects of alienating and oppressive social conditions and the threats of global catastrophes, such as world wars, genocide, and environmental degradation. In the contemporary world, all peoples in the global community are interdependent economically, politically, militarily, and spiritually—for better or for worse. Disenchantment with ethnocentrism, patriarchy, colonialism, religious rivalry and violence, and positivistic science led to alternative ways of understanding the spiritual purpose and developmental possibilities of human beings. Thus, existentialism and transpersonal theory deal with basic spiritual issues of meaning, purpose, and response to suffering by drawing on many religious and philosophical views that challenge conventional thinking.

These perspectives are not sectarian or allied exclusively with any religion, although they integrate many insights from religious traditions. Some of their adherents belong to religious or nonreligious spiritual groups; some are atheists or agnostics. They tend to question ethnocentric and religiously exclusive views. They see the global interdependence of all peoples as an opportunity for creative spiritual transformation of individuals and societies through mutual learning and cooperation. They also recognize the all-too-common happenings of exploitation, oppression, and environmental injustice.

The current movement in social work toward inclusive and holistic under-standing of spirituality is a manifestation of postmodern spiritual trends. In fact, social work innovators often draw on these nonsectarian spiritual perspectives (e.g. Besthorn, 2001; Cowley, 1996; Derezotes, 2006). It is possible to connect their insights to many religious and nonreligious spiritual perspectives of clients. In fact, many people who advocate these nonreligious spiritual perspectives in social work are also, in their private lives, adherents to particular religions.

We present existentialism first because it sets historical context and philo-sophical themes for transpersonal theory. After considering these nonsectarian spiritual perspectives, we will compare all the spiritual perspectives on service presented in Chapters 5 and 6. Then, we will consider issues of mutual under-standing and cooperation among people of diverse perspectives within an inclu-sive approach to spirituality in social work.

Existentialism and Social Service

Origin and Contemporary Varieties of Existentialism

Existentialism developed as a social critical school of philosophy in Europe (Bradford, 1969; Dwoskin, 2003; Kauffman, 1956; Robbins, Chatterjee, & Canda, 2006). During the late 1800s to the middle of the 20th century, many intellectu-als began to react negatively to dehumanizing aspects of urban industrial life. The close familiar ties of agriculture and small town life were supplanted by more formal, task-oriented, anonymous modes of living in large industrial cit-ies. Workers became reduced to commodities—labor was sold to produce mass quantities of goods on assembly lines, or to work in health threatening condi-tions in coalmines and oil fields to fuel the industrial life style. The two World Wars and rise of the Nazi movement displayed with horrifying intensity how the efficiency and power of science and technology could be applied to mass produc-tion of weapons and mass destruction of people.

Some existentialists developed their thought primarily in the context of political resistance to tyranny, such as the French atheist philosophers Camus and Sartre. Some focused on critique of religious establishments and social convention while remaining strongly religious, such as the Russian Orthodox novelist Dostoevsky, the Danish Lutheran Soren Kierkegaard, and the Jewish theologian, Martin Buber. Some philosophers, such as Husserl, reacted against the reductionism and mechanistic view of positivistic science by emphasizing the importance of human subjectivity and consciousness. Some psychologists and psychotherapists developed humanistic approaches to therapy, focusing on the human search for meaning and creativity in the midst of suffering, such as Rollo May and Victor Frankl.

The major writing on existential social work has been done by Donald Krill (e.g. 1978, 1986, 1990, 1995, 1996) and Jim Lantz (e.g. 1993; Lantz & Walsh, 2007). Krill drew on existential and humanistic thought as well as insights from

Zen and Christianity. Lantz applied the logotherapy approach of Victor Frankl to family therapy and social work. Although existentialism has been discussed in the social work literature for more than 30 years, its main impact on social work has been through insights and values for practice. For example, unconditional positive regard for clients, therapeutic use of self, emphasis on the empathic quality of the helping relationship, and promoting client creativity in meaning-making help to shape social work, especially in the strengths perspective, social constructionism, narrative therapy, solution focused therapy, and cognitive behavioral therapies.

Basic Beliefs

Existentialists focus on the immediacy of human experience and how people deal with the human condition of impermanence, suffering, death, and the inhumanity of human beings. They are not concerned about abstract ideas of ultimate reality or metaphysics so much as immediate reality, and how we make meaning of it. In particular, existentialists are interested in how people respond to situations that challenge our systems of meaning, such as natural catastrophe and warfare, or, on a more personal level, crises of loss, confusion, and trauma (Lantz, 1993; Lantz & Walsh, 2007). At such times, the socially constructed nature of our meaning systems may become apparent. The hand-me-down truths of social convention and religious tradition are put to a trial by fire. How can we make sense when it seems nothing makes sense anymore? Humanly constructed meaning is similar to a castle made of sand. When a high tide rolls in, the castle washes away. Manufactured meaning is *absurd* in that it lacks absolute, essential, or ultimate meaning or authenticity (Robbins et al., 2006).

Existentialists assert that individuals are responsible to determine the meaning of their own lives. When social norms or religious teachings stand in the way of human freedom to experience life fully and to discover and create meaning, then they should be challenged. Authentic meaning derives from clear awareness of one's identity in relations with others in the constant process of moment-to-moment change (Krill, 1978). The qualities of freedom and individual dignity arise from the distinctive subjectivity of each person. This subjectivity of the individual is not a matter of isolation, however. The human condition involves inextricable intersubjective transactions between the self, other people, and the world (Bradford, 1969; Krill, 1996).

Yet, a person's subjective sense of potential for satisfaction and meaning encounters inescapable human limits and finitude, most intensely with regard to the fact of death and conditions of social injustice. Existential suffering is inevitable because there is a creative force for growth at the core of the person that brings her or him into experience of the conflict between desire and limit, life and death (Krill, 1979). Existential suffering, often manifested in feelings of dread, shame and guilt, is rooted in the problem of alienation within the self, between self and others, and between self and the totality of being. People must deal with the contradictions between the drive to create meaning and the life crises that expose the fragility and inadequacy of meaning systems. This awareness invokes a sense of dread in the face of the absurd. Nonetheless, each person must make choices, create or discover meaning, and learn to survive and thrive through mistakes, obstacles, and social pressures toward conformity.

Being human involves self-responsibility for one's choices in discovering and inventing meaning. To be a free person means never allowing oneself to be trapped in a personal comfort zone or a viewpoint dictated by external rules and authorities (Edwards, 1982). In the view of Christian and religious Jewish existentialists, authentic meaning or authentic faith becomes possible when the individual transcends limitations and anxieties through spontaneous and immediate experience of others and God. Yet in the existentialist view, God is beyond the limits of human concepts. Therefore, the spiritual emphasis is upon experience rather than adherence to doctrines (Imre, 1971).

However, even in a nontheistic or atheistic view, authentic meaning or faith is a crucial element in the successful creation of meaning. Edwards (1982) stated that authentic faith is not belief in illusions or fantasies. Rather, it is an empathic expression of self toward others. It is the moment-to-moment manifestation of a spiritual communion that encompasses the being of individuals in interaction. We forge authentic meaning as we creatively connect our experiences as beings subject to the physical conditions of the world, who choose how to live in it, and who take responsibility to care for others (Lantz & Walsh, 2007).

Basic Values

The existential perspective opposes the influence of depersonalization and conformity in contemporary society (Imre, 1971). In contrast to the pressures of society toward conformity and to the daunting challenges of suffering and injustice, the existentialist asserts human freedom and dignity (Krill, 1978). Each person must take responsibility for one's chosen views of self and the world and their consequences in action (Krill, 1979). Existentialism also asserts that merely rational means of knowing are inadequate, particularly in that they tend to reduce understanding of human relationships to relations between things as though people are mere objects. Satisfying truth arises from intimate genuine interpersonal experiences (Bradford, 1969). In fact, individual determination of meaning should occur through responsible and loving relations with others. Although existentialism emphasizes the inherent worth, dignity, and responsibility of individuals, it is not individualistic. Human being is being together with others. Human being is a process of continual becoming through cocreation of our individual and collective systems of meaning.

Krill (1979) said that human love is the effort to understand, share, and participate in the uniqueness of others. Existentially authentic relationship involves acceptance of a person's intrinsic dignity and worth, expressed through caring and helping. In the terms of Buber's Jewish theological existentialism, this type of relationship is called I-Thou, one subjectivity relating lovingly with another subjectivity. For Buber, loving human relationship is rooted in humanity's relationship with the eternal Thou, the divine source of being. The solidarity of caring people helps them to hold the courage required to affirm meaning and creativity in the face of doubt, suffering, absurdity, and oppression (Imre, 1971; Krill, 1979, 1996; Lantz, 1993).

Social Work Implications

The existential social worker helps the client to overcome both social institutional forms of oppression and psychological barriers that limit the expression of freedom and dignity. Through the solidarity of a therapeutic I-Thou relationship, the client is supported to actualize potential and meaning through clear self-awareness and responsible relations with others (Imre, 1971; Krill, 1979, 1996; Lantz, 1993; Lantz & Walsh, 2007). The helping relationship is intense, open, and intersubjective, genuinely sharing the selfhood of the worker with the client. The therapeutic encounter helps the client to develop keen awareness of self and to tap one's creative possibilities for attaining meaning and satisfying relationships (Bradford, 1969). Given the concern about constraints on human freedom and dignity, existential social work favors action on behalf of the disadvantaged and oppressed; an attitude toward the client of caring, empathy, and affirmation; present-focused, experiential, short-term therapies; and eclectic use of treatment techniques within the spontaneous therapeutic relationship (Krill, 1978, 1996). It discourages rigid diagnostic categorizations, stereotyped treatment plans, and dogmatic uses of theory that strip clients of their distinctiveness and freedom (Krill, 1986, 1990). A significant advantage of an existentialist approach to spirituality in social work is that it sensitizes the social worker to be alert and responsive to themes of meaning, purpose, connectedness, responsibility, and transcendence without requiring explicit discussion of religion or spirituality. This is very useful when clients do not have a religious affiliation or are not comfortable with terms such as religion, spirituality, or faith. Existentialism also reminds us to focus on the quality of the helping relationship as the foundation of spiritually sensitive practice.

The existential therapeutic approach is client-centered, experiential, rapid change focused, and sensitive to issues of values and philosophical or religious perspectives (Krill, 1978, 1979, 1996; Lantz & Walsh, 2007). According to Edwards (1982), some specific treatment approaches that are consistent with an existentialist view are brief and paradoxical therapy, family systems therapy, reality therapy, rational emotive therapy, psychodrama, holistic therapies integrating body and mind, relaxation and meditation methods, client-centered therapy, and existential group therapy. Krill (1978) emphasized the importance of phenomenological, humanistic, reality-oriented, interpersonal and unselfish social action types of helping approaches. He also incorporated insights and techniques from Eastern and Western religious traditions. Krill (1990) developed many exercises for social workers to help us deepen in self-reflection and self-understanding as preparation for authentic, spiritually sensitive relating with clients. These include systematic introspection about our systems of meaning, identification of our highest ideals and aspirations, distinguishing between realistic and unrealistic guilt, and examination of religious images and their change over the life span. Given the deep questions of meaning that commonly arise when people confront serious illness and dying, existential approaches may be especially relevant when social workers help clients deal with issues of illness, violence, cultural disruption, postcombat distress, social isolation, and dying (Gwyther, Altilio, Blacker, Christ, Csikia, et al., 2005; Jones, 2006; Lantz & Walsh, 2007; Wintestein & Eisikivots, 2005).

Lantz (1993) pointed out that the family is the primary locus for persons to encounter each other intimately, to experience both the tragic and joyful possibilities of life, and to receive and reconstruct meaning. He discussed several family therapy techniques that can assist family members to learn to know each other more genuinely and to construct patterns of meaning and relationship that are mutually fulfilling. For example, paradoxical intention encourages the client to do something that is perceived to be anxiety provoking or problem causing, so that by confronting it with explicit awareness and reflection, the problematic behavior can be resolved and the anxiety can be relieved. Paradoxical intention can break a rigid pattern of meaning and behavior, opening up a new possibility. In Socratic dialogue, or "self-discovery discourse," the family therapist asks clients questions that probe the deeper meanings of people's spirituality and aspirations, helping them to discover meaning in the midst of suffering. Lantz emphasized the importance of helping clients to link with sources of strength and revitalization in their environment, such as spiritual support groups, religious communities, and natural places of beauty. Although some existentialist therapeutic techniques involve a directive approach by the therapist, all techniques should be done within the context of a therapeutic relationship of trust, openness, honesty, permission, and sense of camaraderie in the process of making meaning out of suffering.

Transpersonal Theory and Social Service

Origin and Contemporary Varieties of Transpersonal Theory

Transpersonal theory is a perspective on human experience, development, and helping that focuses on our highest potentials for creativity, love, spiritual awareness, and connectedness. It spans many disciplines, such as philosophy, environmental studies, mental health professions, religious studies, medicine, political activism, and social work (Ferendo, 2007; Wilber, 2000, 2006). It draws on ancient insights from diverse Eastern and Western spiritual traditions as well as contemporary scientific research (Canda, 1991; Cowley, 1996; Robbins et al., 2006). Like existentialism, it is a transdisciplinary perspective rather than a religious institution. Also like existentialism, transpersonal theory promotes a nonsectarian, spiritually sensitive approach to social work. Transpersonal theorists share with existentialists a critique of personal and social structural conditions that lead to a sense of alienation, oppression, and meaninglessness (Cowley, 1996; McGee, 1984; Robbins et al., 2006). Transpersonalists believe that the solution to this malaise can be found through a developmental process in which a person works out a sense of individual wholeness and harmony as well as profound connection with other people, other beings, the universe, and the ground of being itself. In this way, transpersonal theory entwines with ecophilosophies such as deep ecology and ecofeminism that recognize and honor human/nature interdependence (Besthorn, 2001).

Transpersonal theory arose in response to limitations of Freudianism, behaviorism, and humanistic psychology. In 1969, Abraham Maslow announced the arrival of the fourth force of psychology that would be dedicated to understanding what he called the farther reaches of human nature. In his view, Freudian theory reduced human beings to neurotic psychological defense mechanisms, desire-based instincts, and unconscious psychodynamics. Freud viewed religion as a social institution based on neurotic reality-denying fantasies and normative controls. In contrast, behaviorism reduced human beings to machine-like or rat-like things at the mercy of inborn response patterns and environmental conditions. For strict behaviorists, religion was considered irrelevant or unscientific and misleading fantasy. Neither Freudianism nor behaviorism distinguished between religion and spirituality.

Humanistic psychology (including existential psychology) emerged in the 1950s and 1960s in order to focus on positive and distinctive aspects of human experience, such as creativity and loving relationships. Maslow and other humanistic therapists and researchers found that many people who reported high levels of life satisfaction also reported important transformative events that moved them to explicit spiritual interests (Robbins et al., 2006). Experiences that move one beyond a sense of limitation to the individual body/ego boundary (persona) can be crucial to self-fulfillment. Transpersonal theory focuses on understanding these experiences, related varieties of altered states of consciousness, spiritual development process, ways of living in accord with transpersonal insights, and therapeutic techniques that facilitate transpersonal awareness.

Contemporary American transpersonal theory has several major influences. There are many varieties of transpersonal theories (that do not always agree with each other), so we are presenting common themes. Many theorists have refined or revised the work of the Swiss psychologist, Carl Jung, who developed the theory of the collective unconscious through study of clinical reports by clients and cross-cultural study of mythology and religious symbolism (Jung, 1959). Since the 1960s and 1970s, many researchers investigated the therapeutic aspects of altered states of consciousness related to drugs, meditation, biofeedback, and hypnosis. Stanislav Grof's transpersonal approach to psychiatry, called holotropic (wholeness-seeking) theory, arose from this (Grof, 1988; Grof & Halifax, 1977). One of the most influential transpersonal writers is Ken Wilber, who draws on many intellectual and religious traditions, developmental theories, systems theorists, postmodern philosophers, and contemplative practices (Wilber, 1995, 1996). Since Wilber's work now encompasses many fields of thought and application, he refers to his work as *integral* (Wilber, 2000, 2006). His work and extensive network of collaborators can be accessed at the Integral Institute website (http://www.integralinstitute.org/). Many other transpersonal theory resources and integral approaches to social work can be found at http://www.atpweb.org/ hosted by The Association for Transpersonal Theory and at http://csisw.cua.edu/ hosted by Catholic University of America's National School of Social Service. The Global Alliance for A Deep Ecological Social Work offers access to the work of Fred Besthorn, John Coates, and other leaders in the movement to bring a deep ecological understanding into social work (http://www.ecosocialwork.org/). Transpersonal perspectives are beginning to shape theory and practice for social work (e.g. Borenzweig, 1984; Canda & Smith, 2001; Coates, 2003; Cowley, 1993, 1996; Cowley & Derezotes, 1994; Derezotes, 2006; Larkin, 2005; McGee, 1984; Smith, 1995; Smith & Gray, 1995; Thomas, 2004).

Basic Beliefs

Transpersonal theorists share an optimistic view of human nature. They believe that people are intrinsically growth oriented. As long as adequate environmental supports exist, people have a natural tendency to strive toward more comprehensive ways of understanding the world, more loving and responsible ways of relating with others, and more creative ways of living (Grof, 1988; Jung, 1938; Maslow, 1968 & 1970; Robbins et al., 2006; Wilber 2006). There is no guarantee that individuals or societies will develop more caring and just ways of living, but this is an inherent developmental potential.

There are two directions of growth for people. One is inward, toward a sense of integration, balance, and wholeness within oneself. One is outward, toward a sense of mutual fulfillment, co-responsibility, and communion between oneself and others. These two trajectories of growth can be thought of as arcs, which curve around to meet each other in a full circle. The complete or true Self is attained when one's awareness and actions encompass this full arc of inward and outward growth.

Transpersonal theories criticize most conventional theories of human behavior and social ideals because they do not honor the full potential of human beings. Conventional developmentalists generally claim that the formation of an autonomous, personal, separate self (ego), bounded by body and social roles, is the epitome of development. In contrast, transpersonalists advocate for further developmental possibilities (Canda, 1988; Cowley, 1996; Robbins et al., 2006). They generally recognize three major phases of development: preegoic (infancy through early childhood) in which the young child has not yet developed a clear sense of ego, distinct from caretakers and the environment; egoic (usually older childhood and beyond) in which a person establishes a clear sense of ego autonomy and capacity for rational thought along with mature social relationships;

and transegoic (most likely in adulthood if at all) in which a person realizes one's fundamental connectedness and unity with all others. The transegoic or transpersonal Self is able to utilize the egoic modes of thought, feeling, and action; but the transpersonal Self is not limited to them. Wilber (2000b, 2006) points out that there are actually many aspects of individual development (e.g. cognitive, moral, spiritual, physical) that usually develop at different rates. With concerted effort, a person can integrate these various aspects into an overall progression into transpersonal levels of consciousness and daily functioning.

The transpersonal Self recognizes that true self-actualization is inseparable from other-actualization. The transpersonal Self develops enhanced skills of intuition, empathy, holistic thinking, and ultimately, a sense of complete unity with all that is. Depending on the spiritual perspective of the person, the ultimate level of development may be described as union with God, unity of true self (atman) with the true nature of the universe (Brahman), enlightenment, or cosmic consciousness.

Deep ecology and ecofeminism include a transpersonal perspective on the fundamental unity of human beings and all other beings (Besthorn, 2001, 2002; Besthorn & Canda, 2002; Besthorn & Pearson McMillan, 2002). The Norwegian ecological philosopher, Arne Naess (1988), explained that people who realize their inseparateness from the earth ecology expand their self-concept to become *ecocentered* rather than egocenric or ethnocentric. This expanded self-identity is called the *ecological self*. While many psychologically oriented transpersonal theorists focus on individual humans as the main concern, ecophilosophers focus on the total planetary ecosystem (as well as bioregions) with humans as one type of being within it.

When I (LF) taught social work students in Norway as a visiting professor in 1998, I found that most students insisted that they were neither religious nor spiritual. On one level, this was understandable because Norway is a very secular country, with low rates of formal religious participation (Zahl, Furman, Benson, & Canda, 2007). However, I suggested that their love of the outdoors and their apparent communion and harmony with nature could be considered spiritual. They then agreed that they were indeed spiritual and transpersonal as they were deeply integrated with their environment.

Basic Values

Transpersonalists believe that human development is purposeful and goal oriented (i.e. toward integration, wholeness, and self-transcendence). However, they also claim that few people ever achieve transpersonal levels of development. This is largely due to restrictions imposed by lack of physical, emotional, and social supports; social pressures toward egotism and conformism; and contemporary materialistic scientific worldview that try to convince people that spiritual and transpersonal experiences are mere fantasies. Therefore, transpersonalists advocate for spiritual empowerment on several levels. They advocate for individuals to demonstrate self-initiative, exploration, creative nonconformity, and effort for growth. They advocate for social structures that provide full access and opportunity for all people to resources that support development. For example, Maslow (1970) criticized religious institutions when they inhibit or punish their members for spiritual experiences that challenge formal teachings. Wilber (1998) decried dominator hierarchies, which are social structures that impose exploitive conditions and restricting beliefs on people. Transpersonal theorists also advocate for local and global initiatives and policies that promote the well-being of the entire planetary ecology (Coates, 2003).

Cowley (1996) provided a summary of key transpersonal values pertaining to the ideal of optimal health or well-being. These include seeking self-transcendence, working toward personal balance and integration of self, and establishing harmony between oneself and others. As a person experiences profound connection with others, the value of compassion naturally arises (Dass & Gorman, 1985). Transpersonal compassion goes beyond the ordinary ideas of selfishness or altruism. True self-actualization is reciprocal with other's actualization; the true Self is not limited to or owned by any one person or culture. The true Self is one with all beings. Therefore, according to transpersonal theory, compassion is to be extended actively toward all beings, not just human beings.

Social Work Implications

The transpersonal helping relationship is modeled on the principles of unconditional love and mutual compassion (Cowley, 1996). All clients are viewed as having unconditional worth and unlimited possibilities for growth, regardless of present difficulties. The social work value of self-determination is extended to mean that each client's self-defined spiritual strengths, resources, and aspirations should be the focus of attention in practice. In this process, starting wherever the client's goals and needs, the potential for growth is encouraged. This is a mutual process, because the social worker grows through this relationship (Forster, McColl, & Fardella, 2007). From a transpersonal perspective, the helping situation is an opportunity for both client and worker to deepen insight and to grow toward their highest potentials (Robbins et al., 2006). Derezotes (2006) draws on transpersonal theory in his model of spiritually oriented social work practice. He says that the spiritually oriented social worker supports the spiritual development of the client according to the client's goals and spiritual beliefs. The social worker also seeks mutual benefit for client, family, community, and natural ecosystem.

Transpersonal social work helps people to address situations of suffering and existential confusion, first by establishing a clear sense of self-esteem and identity, and second, by helping people to go beyond the limits of the ego-bounded self-identity. Crises are opportunities for growth, because crises fracture the person's ordinary psychosocial status quo and open up new possibilities (Canda, 1988c; Canda & Smith, 2001; Smith, 1995; Smith & Gray, 1995). Certain kinds of crises directly relate to spiritual development, such as a crisis of faith, questioning of religious affiliation, or confusion resulting from experience of new states of consciousness through practice of meditation, prayer, or ritual. Even dying can be an opportunity for transpersonal growth (Nakashima, 2007). Transpersonal social work is especially interested in helping clients to optimize the possibility for transformation to an enhanced transpersonal awareness and creative relations with others (Moxley & Washington, 2001; Nixon, 2005).

Transpersonal theory challenges social work to broaden its conception of the person and environment (Canda, 1988c; Canda & Smith, 2001; Robbins et al., 2006). According to transpersonal theory, a person is not just an ego-limited self. The environment is not just the small range of the relationships a client has with significant others, which is usually the focus in practice. Rather the person and environment are viewed as systemically interrelated and fundamentally one. Social work's commitment to assist personal fulfillment is thereby extended to self-transcendence. Social work's commitment to environmental supports and justice is extended to global justice and harmony for the entire life web of the planet. Further, personal strengths are recognized to include intuition, beyond egoistic emotion and thinking (Luoma, 1998). Environmental resources are recognized to include the beauty and inspiration of nature as well as the client's experiences of spiritual beings and the ground of being itself (Besthorn & Canda, 2002).

Cowley (1996) suggested that transpersonalists can utilize any theories or techniques for social work practice that fit the developmental level and interests of the client. Theories that are particularly well suited to address the transegoic levels of development are Jungian archetypal theory, Assagioli's psychosynthesis, Grof's holotropic theory, and Wilber's spectrum model of development. Larkin (2005) and Thomas (2004) offered Wilber's integral model as a way to bring together insights from many different theories to understand both subjective and objective aspects of individual and societal systems.

Transpersonal clinical skills and techniques could include any of those previously listed under existential social work, as well as meditation, yoga, disciplined breathing techniques, guided visualization and healing imagery, holistic body therapies, therapeutic use of symbolism and ritual, biofeedback, self-reflective journaling, art and music therapies, and deep relaxation exercises (Robbins et al., 2006). In addition, transpersonal social workers should assess whether clients utilize any particular religious beliefs, practices, and support systems. If so, religion-specific symbols, rituals, healing practices, and means of seeking reconciliation or support in community can be utilized, either by collaboration and referral with relevant religious helpers, or by direct use by a qualified social worker (Derezotes, 2006a; Derezotes & Evans, 1995). When social workers further recognize the human/nature interrelationship, additional micro- and macropractice issues come to the fore, such as connections between environmental damage and exploitation of low income communities and Indigenous peoples; energy waste and pollution generated through social services provision; anxiety and stress related disorders due to toxic work conditions; and depression related to loss of cherished places (Besthorn & Canda, 2002; Coates, Grey, & Hetherington, 2006; Keefe, 2003; Muldoon, 2006; Ungar, 2002). Clinical practice can attend to therapeutic effects of intimate connections between people, pets, and wilderness. The quality of human/nature connections in the client's living place can be assessed for qualities of human/nature mutual benefit and harmony. Clients who cherish transpersonal experiences of communion with nature can be encouraged to draw on them to sustain well-being in times of distress and crisis.

Comparison of Spiritual Perspectives on Service

Tables 5.1 and 6.1 summarize and compare key ideas of the nine spiritual perspectives on social service reviewed in Chapters 5 and 6. The tables can assist the following comparison. The comparative summary of religious perspectives on beliefs and psychotherapy issues in Richards and Bergin (2000) is an excellent supplement to our discussion.

Comparison of Basic Beliefs

The Beliefs columns are organized according to issues and themes found in all spiritual traditions: (1) the nature of ultimate reality; (2) major authoritative sources for beliefs; and (3) propositions about the nature of human existence, suffering, and ways to resolve suffering. A broad contrast is between spiritual perspectives that invest primary authority for truth in divine revelation and inspired scriptures (i.e. Christianity, Islam, Judaism, and some forms of Hinduism), those that hold certain texts in high esteem as teachings of enlightened or sagely figures (i.e. Buddhism and Confucianism), and those that emphasize direct personal experience, guidance by living spiritual teachers, and unwritten community tradition (i.e. Indigenous religions, Zen Buddhism, some forms of Hinduism, existentialism, transpersonal theory, and contemplative forms of Christianity, Islam, and Judaism).

Some of the perspectives are theistic (i.e. Christianity, Judaism, and Islam; some existentialists and transpersonalists, and some forms of Indigenous religions and Hinduism). Zen Buddhism, particularly as portrayed in the social work literature, neither affirms nor denies theistic concepts, so it may be described as nontheistic. Confucianism acknowledges the influence of heaven's will and cosmic forces (such as yin and yang), but does not formulate an idea of a personal deity. Existentialism encompasses theistic, atheistic, and agnostic variations. Like Zen, it emphasizes the primacy of direct experience. Indigenous religions encompass animistic and theistic beliefs. Transpersonal theory appreciates diversity of belief systems within the context of holistic, inclusive, and integral worldview.

Regarding human nature, all perspectives recognize suffering and alienation as basic to the human condition. Despite contrasting beliefs about whether people are innately good, sinful, or undetermined, each perspective sees that

Table 6.1. Comparison of Nonsectarian Spiritual Perspectives on Service.

Perspective	Beliefs	Values	Service
Existential	(1) Theistic/atheistic/ nontheistic varieties. (2) Beliefs from direct experience and questioning conventions. (3) People are free; experience is intersubjective; people must cope with suffering by authentically making meaning.	(1) Primary life task to take responsibility for making/ discovering meaning. (2) Commitment to uphold freedom and dignity of person. (3) Mutual caring and support between people.	(1) I-Thou and freedom promoting helping relationship. (2) Aim to help client overcome inner and outer barriers to free and responsible action. (3) Uses humanistic, eclectic, change promoting, client-centered, and experiential techniques.
Transpersonal	(1) Theistic/atheistic/ animistic/nontheistic varieties. (2) Beliefs from many cultural contexts; philosophical, scientific, and spiritual inquiry; personal and transpersonal experiences. (3) Human nature is oriented toward growth to establish ego and transcend it, integrating whole self, others, and cosmos.	(1) Primary life task is to attain self integration, ego-transcendence and harmony with all. (2) Commitment to help individuals achieve full potential within just society and balanced world ecology. (3) Mutual benefit between self-actualization and other actualization.	(1) Client-centeredness and mutuality in helping relationship. (2) Aim to help client actualize and transcend self in fulfilling relations with all others. (3) May use religious and nonreligious helping practices as client wishes, e.g. meditation, ritual, body therapies, healing imagery, dream work, collaboration with spiritual community, wilderness retreats, activism for environmental justice.

Revised and expanded from Canda, 1988b; used with permission of publisher.

human beings have an innate drive to stop suffering by developing a sense of meaning, purpose, and fulfilling relationships. For Zen, this involves seeking enlightenment through direct experience. For Confucianism, this requires constant cultivation of one's benevolent nature and expressing it in relationships. For Christianity, Judaism, and Islam, it involves alignment with the will of God in all aspects of life. In Indigenous religions, it involves finding balance and harmony in relationships between individuals, family, community, and all relations of the local place and the earth and sky. Existentialism and transpersonal theory offer a wide variety of ways to confront the fact of suffering with courage, solidarity among people, and transcendence of egotism, ethnocentrism, religiocentrism, and humanocentrism.

All perspectives agree that human existence is intrinsically relational. Individual fulfillment is only possible through moral relations between self, society, the nonhuman world, and ultimate reality. Traditionally, all the religions tend to define standards of moral relationship in terms that are specific to cultural or religious institutional norms and customs. In contrast, existentialism and transpersonal theory emphasize that moral standards naturally arise from authentic moment-to-moment interactions, rather than from norms or regulations. These perspectives, as well as postmodern versions of the religious perspectives, question traditional religious and social norms and encourage people to form their own beliefs based on exploration of alternatives, critical thinking, and accommodation of human diversity in all its forms.

Comparison of Basic Values

The Values columns are organized according to the following themes: the primary purpose or task of human life; commitments to principles of service; and basic moral orientation toward service.

While there is great diversity of beliefs, there is a striking similarity of fundamental values among these perspectives. Each perspective upholds the inherent dignity of people. Some perspectives emphasize individual autonomy and responsibility (American Zen, existentialism, and some versions of transpersonal theory) while traditional religions emphasize interdependency and collectivity. Yet every perspective advocates for caring and just relations between people, the nonhuman world, and ultimate reality. Indeed, each perspective asserts that compassion toward others is the natural outcome of authentic communion in relationships.

However, the monotheistic traditions tend to emphasize compassion toward fellow human beings. Although all of creation should be respected as God's creation, human beings typically are seen as stewards of this creation, set above it. Traditional Indigenous religions emphasize that respect, balance, and harmony should pervade human relations and relations with all things, including the nonhuman plants, animals, and spirit powers. Buddhism, Confucianism, Hinduism, and some forms of transpersonal theory and ecophilosophy extend compassion to all beings in the universe. In these Asian religious traditions, humans are regarded as specially privileged with self-consciousness and capacity for spiritual awakening; concomitantly, this special privilege entails special responsibility to care for the earth.

In each of these perspectives, the prerequisite for genuine compassion toward others is transcendence of one's own selfish desires. In essence, one's own fulfillment requires a life of communion between self, society, the nonhuman world, and ultimate reality. This means that compassion must be joined with justice. Of course, the specific meanings of compassion and justice vary tremendously by traditions, spiritual community, and situational applications. Of course, these values are high ideals that few individuals or spiritual groups attain.

Comparison of Basic Approaches to Service and Social Work

The columns on Service address three themes: (1) the ideal quality of the helping relationship; (2) the basic aim of helping; (3) particular helping strategies and techniques.

Given the common value commitment to compassionate, just, and moral relationships, each perspective approaches the helping relationship as one of mutual growth and benefit. Each perspective is also holistic and ecological in addressing the connection of bio-psycho-social and spiritual aspects of the client and community. Each perspective sees the primary aim of helping as enabling the client to overcome suffering and alienation in terms of both subsistence and fulfillment needs. Therefore, the client is helped to heighten awareness of self and environment in order to establish mutually beneficial relationships.

Each perspective utilizes various techniques of prayer, meditation, ritual, and social supports to assist both client and social worker. Each perspective asserts that the professional helper must engage in his or her own process of coming to terms with suffering and alienation in order to help clients effectively and to model the process successfully for the client. Each perspective is also open to cooperation between social workers and religious specialists. However, some adherents of all religious traditions may be suspicious of social workers who come from different religious or cultural backgrounds. Trust must be earned in order to enjoin religious beliefs and practices and to cooperate with religious specialists of helping and healing. Spiritually derived helping practices can either be in a form specific to a particular perspective matching the client's perspective, or, can be in a generic form without explicit religious content (such as the mindfulness component in general stress management meditation).

Engaging in Dialogue and Cooperation Across Spiritual Perspectives

In Part I, we advocated for an inclusive approach to spirituality in social work that respects diverse religious and nonreligious forms of spirituality through spiritually sensitive and culturally competent practice in accord with professional ethical principles. Inclusion does not mean ignoring differences and disagreements. It does not mean forcing others into artificial or self-serving spiritual assumptions. Rather, inclusion means inviting others into dialogue and cooperation, as whole people, within the helping process.

This is a tall order. As we have seen in Part II, there are numerous variations of spiritual perspectives and associated practice issues and controversies—far too many for any one social worker to master them all. However, each social worker can adopt an inclusive attitude and respectful behavior in each practice situation. The spiritually sensitive social worker should pursue the development of knowledge and skills specific to the spiritual perspectives of particular clients and their communities by following the leads and suggestions provided in this book.

This requires the social worker to form a personal framework of spiritual beliefs, values, and practices that encourage an inclusive approach. An inclusive approach could be established on the basis of any of the spiritual perspectives that we reviewed in Part II. As we noted, each perspective contains implications and insights that can be applied in service to its adherents, both by social workers who share the perspective and by others who wish to cooperate with it. Further, social work writings on each perspective have identified underlying principles and practices that can be applied to innovative conceptions and practices of social work in general, without restriction to sectarian settings or particular religious language.

Significant communication and cooperation with clients and community-based spiritual supports require us to engage in cross-perspective dialogue that facilitates the helping alliance as well as our own continual growth in inclusive consciousness and behavior. A spiritually inclusive approach to social work must be practical. This takes more than lip service. We must be and act in a genuinely inclusive manner.

The goals of the Parliament of the World's Religions (2004) are apropos. Through encounter and celebration among people of widely varied religious and spiritual traditions, we can deepen spirituality and experience personal transformation; recognize the humanity of the other in a broadened sense of community; foster mutual understanding and respect; learn to live in harmony with diversity; seek peace, justice, and sustainability; and actively work for a better world. According to the Parliament, "Too often, religion is misused as an instrument for division and injustice, betraying the very ideals and teachings that lie at the heart of each of the world's great traditions. At the same time, religious and spiritual traditions shape the lives of billions in wise and wonderful ways....When these diverse communities work in harmony for the common good, there is hope that the world can be transformed" (http://www.parliamentofreligions.org/index. cfm?n+1 retrieved August 4, 2008). The organization Religions for Peace (2007, p. 1) puts it this way: "At a time in history when pervasive violence threatens the human family and religion is portrayed in the headlines worldwide as a source of violent conflict and human suffering, religious communities face a stark choice: the *status quo* that leads to escalating violence or the path of multi-religious cooperation for peace." We add that this challenge faces people of all spiritual perspectives, religious or nonreligious. Given social work's commitment to well-being and justice for all people, we believe that the ideals and practical actions of cross-perspective dialogue are extremely pertinent and timely.

The Museum for World Peace in Kyoto, Japan is dedicated to such an ideal of peace through dialogue and cooperation. A large mural there depicts the fire-bird of peace, which like the legendary phoenix, rises from the ashes of wartime conflagrations into a new life of peace among nations (Figure 6.1). Although this image was inspired by World War II, we believe it is a valuable metaphor for the way social workers could contribute to local, national, and global peace.

Figure 6.1. The firebird of peace.

Steps for Dialogue Across Spiritual Perspectives

Raimon Panikkar, an influential figure in the field of interreligious dialogue, offered valuable insights about prerequisites for genuine dialogue between people of different spiritual perspectives. Pannikar is a Catholic priest who was raised by a Spanish Catholic mother and an Indian Hindu father. He considers himself to be fully Catholic and fully Hindu, not either/or a little of one and a little of another. His personal experience gives depth to his approach to dialogue. He said that genuine interreligious dialogue must be based on experiences of deep interaction. "As long as I do not open my heart and do not see that the other is not an other but a part of myself who enlarges and completes me, I will not arrive at dialogue. If I embrace you, then I understand you" (2000, p. 834). His methodology for dialogue can be summarized in seven steps, which we adapt for social work purposes (Krieger, 1996; Idliby, Oliver, & Warner, 2006; Raines, 2004). We add an eighth step, bringing the dialogue into cooperative social service action. Social workers can use these steps to learn from each other and members of the local community. This is a process that can take many encounters. The steps are not linear; they cycle and recycle through each other. While the steps might be modified to support discussion with clients to learn more about their spiritual perspectives, the helping relationship should stay focused on the goals of the client rather than cross-perspective dialogue per se. The eight steps are summarized in Table 6.2.

STEP 1: UNDERSTANDING ONE'S OWN PERSPECTIVE   Spiritual sensitivity to others starts with spiritual sensitivity to oneself. We must know ourselves well at a deep level. We need to be aware and clear about our spiritual beliefs, values, and implications for our practice as a social worker. We need to understand how this is derived from and illuminated by the spiritual tradition or traditions to which we are committed. This requires introspective insight as well as serious study of our inherited or chosen traditions. We also need to be aware and

Table 6.2   Steps for Dialogue Across Spiritual Perspectives.

1. Understanding one's own perspective
2. Learning about another's spiritual perspective
3. Transforming ourselves
4. Engaging in spiritual dialogue with ourselves
5. Engaging in spiritual dialogue with others
6. All partners in dialogue engaging the previous five steps
7. Checking understandings with the partner in dialogue
8. Engaging in active cooperation for service

honest about our stereotypes and misgivings about other spiritual perspectives. We need to process our internal chatter of negative judgments as well as anxiety about encounters with people and situations that are unfamiliar or that stretch us past our comfort zones.

STEP 2: LEARNING ABOUT ANOTHER'S SPIRITUAL PERSPECTIVE   Dialogue presupposes more than one person and more than one perspective. In order to prepare, we need to engage in serious study of another's spiritual perspective and its implications for social work. The summaries of spiritual perspectives and the learning exercises of Part II of this book are helpful as a start. To do this seriously requires concerted research, reading, internet exploration, and visits to sites and teachers relevant to the perspective.

STEP 3: TRANSFORMING OURSELVES   Deep encounter with a new spiritual perspective necessarily engenders self-transformation. If one takes seriously the worldview, rituals, and helping practices of another tradition, and to some extent enters this perspective, one cannot avoid being transformed. This is genuine communication—"communing with." Who we are becomes inclusive of the other spiritual perspective. This is not likely to happen with one encounter, unless we prepare very well ahead of time. In fact, if we are not careful, a single encounter can lead to misunderstandings and reinforce stereotypes. Thorough self-transformation grows as we commit ourselves on a long-term basis to cross-perspective learning. We must be willing to engage with differentness and stretch beyond our comfort zones.

STEP 4: ENGAGING IN SPIRITUAL DIALOGUE WITH OURSELVES   As we continue to engage our own tradition, we engage with another. As we reflect internally on the transformation happening within us, we need to dialogue within ourselves between the two perspectives, to bring them into communion with each other within our own hearts.

STEP 5: ENGAGING IN SPIRITUAL DIALOGUE WITH OTHERS   Genuine encounter with others brings into sharp relief the distinctiveness and disagreements between our positions. It also opens the possibility for finding common ground and empathy. Dialogue with people of different spiritual perspectives, going beyond just reading and thinking about it, makes the encounter very real and practical. This is what happens in social work practice. We must find very practical ways to honor the client's spiritual path, to help him or her along it, or to change course, according to her or his own terms. We stretch our minds, hearts, and actions and broaden our spiritual vantage. This opens the possibility for mutual growth and transformation throughout the helping encounter.

STEP 6: ALL PARTNERS IN DIALOGUE ENGAGING THE PREVIOUS FIVE STEPS   If we extend ourselves in dialogue across spiritual perspectives in the general community and with professional colleagues, all partners in the process need to engage the previous steps. "It takes two to tango" as the saying goes. Otherwise, we have monologue or diatribe designed to control rather than to grow.

This step is different in relation to clients. It is not reasonable (nor often relevant) to expect clients to transform their spiritual perspective in relation to ours. That is not usually what they are seeking. Yet a genuine I-Thou helping relationship is naturally mutually transforming. In some cases, a client is seeking help to address questions, dilemmas, or new possibilities related to her or his spiritual perspective. These steps of dialogue could enhance the therapeutic process as long as they serve the purpose and beliefs of the client.

STEP 7: CHECKING UNDERSTANDINGS WITH THE PARTNER IN DIALOGUE   As we weave through these steps of dialogue, our understanding of the other spiritual perspective will change. We form interpretations of formerly alien ideas to make them understandable to ourselves. We try to find areas of agreement, common purpose, or common language. As we do this, it is necessary to check the understandings with the client or other representatives of the other spiritual perspective. If they do not confirm our understandings, we need to reexamine our views. The purpose of dialogue is not to impose our own understandings on others. We also need to give feedback to the partners in dialogue about their understandings of our own spiritual perspective.

STEP 8: ENGAGING IN ACTIVE COOPERATION FOR SERVICE   For social work purposes, the reason to engage in dialogue is to enhance service. Enhanced understanding, including empathy, knowledge, and skill for connecting with others, should be applied to effective action. Dialogue becomes the basis for cooperation with the spiritual strengths and resources of clients and their communities. Part III explains how to do this.

Personal and Professional Issues Regarding Cross-Perspective Cooperation

We advocate for respectful cooperation within and across spiritual perspectives in social work. We discussed many innovations and benefits that can result from this. We also indicated some dangers in superficial, condescending, coercive, or unskillful attempts to connect across spiritual perspectives. The steps for dialogue just described can help avoid these dangers. I (EC) would like to take this further now by considering more deeply the cultural and political contexts of cross-perspective dialogue and cooperation based on my own experience. I do not suggest that others should follow my spiritual path. But since my experience involves interreligious dialogue and practice to a major degree, it offers an example of possible benefits and concerns.

A Light of Many Colors

I have been blessed as a student, friend, and colleague of teachers and healers from many different spiritual perspectives. I have already mentioned the importance to me of my Roman Catholic heritage. The teaching and guidance of my extended family, Catholic religious teachers, and spiritual directors provided my spiritual foundation. By facing both the positive and negative aspects of Catholic tradition and history, I have learned to become more realistic. Particularly the mystical, activist, and interreligious aspects of the Catholic tradition, as represented by the monk Thomas Merton (1961, 1968a, 1968b), have been the most important to me.

I have also been fortunate to be taught, guided, mentored, and helped along my way by wise friends and elders of other Christian denominations, Confucianism, Buddhism, Korean shamanistic traditions, Indigenous North American spiritual ways, and earth-centered spiritualities. They have nurtured, encouraged, challenged, and helped me. They opened my mind to new ways of experiencing and living. They opened my heart to a greater sense of compassion for all. And they gave me skills of prayer, meditation, and ritual for my own replenishment and for the help of others (Canda, 2009).

I met my wife, Hwi-Ja, in Seoul, Korea when I was a Graduate Fellow of East Asian Philosophy at Sungkyunkwan University from 1976 to 1977. In our personal lives, we have brought insights and practices together from our Euro-American and East Asian spiritual traditions. She grew up in a rather traditional family that drew on Confucianism, Buddhism, and shamanism while encouraging exploration of Christianity, without any sense of tension. I have studied and engaged in Buddhist and Confucian spiritual practices over many years. My wife (who became a Catholic) and I have been members of an inclusive religious community named Shantivanam, the Forest of Peace Catholic House of Prayer, in Kansas since 1989.

My personal life, relationships with family and friends, and professional work have grown from this spiritual diversity. To me, all the insights and helping approaches of these spiritual perspectives are wonderful and precious, including the learning that comes from dealing with tensions and disappointments along the way. Living in harmony with them all feels very natural and ordinary. But that is certainly not the case for everyone I meet along the way. Many people expect me to fit into a particular religious box. Often, if someone asks about my spiritual perspective, they frame the question like a multiple choice test: You must select one and only one answer from the options given, and if you don't pick the correct one, you are wrong. Sometimes this comes from a rigid, authoritarian way of thinking that views all spiritual ways, other than one's own, as wrong. This may also come from people who have a very sincere and admirable commitment to their own tradition, while respecting others. They may feel that to draw on multiple spiritual perspectives can only lead to confusion or dilution.

During my visit to a Lao Buddhist temple in the Midwest, a monk asked me about my practice of Buddhist meditation. I had stayed overnight with the monks and participated in their religious practices, so he wanted to know more about my spiritual orientation. I used the metaphor of sunlight. I said that sunlight appears to be one color that we call white. However, when we hold a prism to the light, we see it displayed as a brilliant array of colors, all finely blended from one to another, even going beyond our ability to see. I said that I understand spiritual truth that way. There is one light of truth that encompasses all. But it can be perceived according to many different colors, each one in its distinctness brilliant and beautiful and yet inseparable from the complete white light. Some people choose to live within one band of spiritual color. Others perceive truth in multiple bands and may even be able to move between them. I explained that this is the spiritual way to which I am committed.

The monk said that unless I followed only one spiritual way, I would never get very far. In a friendly manner, he urged me to dedicate my life to the supreme Buddha Way if I had any hope of attaining enlightenment. His comment was a valuable warning against superficial eclecticism, wishy washy spirituality, or undisciplined wavering between this, that, and the other thing. I have heard similar admonitions from teachers in many religious traditions. However, his comment also missed my point. For me at least, this way of commitment to spiritual diversity, even in my personal life, is itself a particular discipline. In any case, to be authentic, I cannot be any other way.

Although I do not recommend my personal spiritual style to others, I do feel that there are very practical reasons that social workers must be able to at least appreciate the many colors of spiritual insight shining through their clients. Just as practice across different cultural contexts requires a bicultural, multicultural, or even transcultural approach (while remaining faithful to one's own cultural identity and way of life), just so practice across different spiritual perspectives requires an inclusive spiritual approach.

Dialogue and cooperation open the possibility to work for peace even across conflicting views.

Examples of Interreligious Tension and Cooperation

Refugee resettlement serves as an excellent illustration of the practical ramifications of cooperation across spiritual perspectives. Throughout most of the 1980s, one of my (EC) major areas of service was practice, training, and research in regard to Southeast Asian refugees. Although refugee influx to the United States is mainly from other world regions now, the underlying issues of dialogue and cooperation remain. In resettlement and postresettlement services, a complex set of international, national, state, and local organizations must cooperate. The United Nations, International Red Cross, U.S. Immigration and Naturalization Service, Lutheran Immigration and Refugee Services, Catholic Migration and Refugee Services, local Christian congregations, local Buddhist temples, mental health centers, and state human service departments are just a few of those involved. Each organization represents various secular or religious humanitarian values and perspectives that must link for all this to work well.

The principle of separation of church and state complicates this. Much refugee resettlement is channeled through cooperation with religious organizations. When they receive federal funds, they cannot proselytize or impose religious beliefs on the refugee clients. However, the religious ethos of service pervades the entire process of sponsorship and helping. On a practical level, many congregations and family sponsors for refugee families have personal agendas to welcome the refugee into the religious community to offer fellowship. Yet most Southeast Asian refugees came from non-Christian traditions and practices, such as Buddhism, Confucianism, and animism.

In order to explore this complexity, in 1990, I informally interviewed more than 20 active participants in refugee resettlement about their experience with interreligious and sectarian/nonsectarian connections. They represented many vantage points: public refugee program administrators in two states, voluntary religious agency staff, church-based volunteer refugee sponsors, private nationally known consultants, federal Office of Refugee Resettlement administrators, refugee ethnic mutual assistance association leaders, and shamans and monks in Southeast Asian refugee communities. The following discussion is based on these informal interviews, as well as my observations during 9 years of involvement with Southeast Asian refugee services.

I observed three areas of possible tension in interreligious cooperation. First, some representatives of refugee communities told me that they felt torn between loyalty to their original religious beliefs and the expectation of their local Christian sponsor that they convert or participate in the sponsor's religious group. Commonly, Buddhist refugees told me that they felt comfortable combining Christian and non-Christian beliefs and practices, since they all have aspects of truth, caring, and helpfulness. However, if the Christian sponsor had an exclusive view of spirituality, then the refugee was put in a bind. Respondents typically said that they felt gratitude and indebtedness to their Christian sponsors, so they did not want to disappoint or alienate them. Neither did they want to abandon the religious and cultural traditions that were precious to them. So refugee respondents often said, "Please don't tell my sponsor about my continued practice of my traditional religion. I don't want to cause trouble."

Second, some professional refugee resettlement staff told me that they believe some religious voluntary agencies do not want the federal government to know about the religious pressures exerted upon refugees, because that might jeopardize their public funding. So the topic is rarely discussed openly. It should be noted, however, that the official policies of religiously based refugee services, such as Lutheran and Catholic, prohibit imposing religious beliefs on clients. According to interviewees, the difficulty usually comes at the local congregation and family sponsor level.

Third, some staff at refugee service programs, health and mental health organizations, and church volunteers exhibited the belief that Asian religions and traditional healing practices are primitive, superstitious, or even demonic. Therefore, staff may neglect to engage them in cooperative helping or may encourage proselytization and acculturation to Euro-American social conventions.

In one case, a Hmong couple brought their sick infant to a hospital. The physicians diagnosed a cancer in the eyes that would require surgical treatment, resulting in blindness. The parents were shocked and sought traditional shamanistic healing as an alternative. Child welfare workers and physicians became upset about the parents' delay in obtaining conventional treatment. They also regarded the traditional healing as bizarre. They obtained custody of the child by court order. According to news media investigators, the judge said that the parents' religious beliefs (Hmong shamanism) were not common in America, and so did not deserve protection. The primary pediatrician said to me, "They are in our country now so they better do things our way." The infant was placed in the hospital for mandated treatment. By now, the parents felt alienated and persecuted, much as they had under conditions of war and refugee flight in Laos. The professional helpers became the enemy. So the parents "stole" their child from the hospital and fled to a Hmong community in another state. They became "kidnappers!"

When refugee advocates became involved, they discovered that the professional helpers had not used translators and had not collaborated with refugee sponsors or Hmong community leaders. The parents did not fully understand what was happening to them and their baby, except for the obvious threat. The cultural and spiritual arrogance on the part of the helpers destroyed the helping relationship. Fortunately, the parents found a set of professional helpers in the new community who engaged a multicultural and spiritually sensitive approach. The child received necessary treatments while the family also benefited from the Hmong community supports and traditional religious practices.

Despite these three areas of tension, it has been inspiring to see the generally high level of cooperation across spiritual perspectives and religious institutions in refugee resettlement. Many Southeast Asian refugees are comfortable combining beliefs and religious practices from different traditions in their personal lives. Sometimes, this is based on a philosophical principle, such as the view of many Buddhists that all spiritual paths can lead to truth. Sometimes, this is a matter of doing "whatever works" as when an ill Cambodian refugee consults a shaman, a Buddhist monk, a Christian minister, and a Western style physician in order to find a cure for an intractable problem.

Spiritual diversity calls for creative responses within refugee families as well. For example, a Cambodian community leader told me that Buddhism is very important to him as an integral part of cultural heritage and as a source of spiritual guidance. Yet, he explained, his children, who have grown up in the United States, have become more comfortable practicing within a Christian context, because most of their peers and friends are Christian and Christianity is a major aspect of the American cultural milieu. This father encouraged his children to attend the local Methodist church and often accompanies them. In addition, he educated them about Cambodian traditional culture and religion. He encouraged them to attend the Buddhist temple for special religious festivals and for learning Cambodian language and traditional arts. He viewed the Christian message of love and the Buddhist message of compassion to be compatible. The family has learned to combine both spiritual ways.

Some health and mental heath centers had traditional Asian medicine practitioners on staff and would refer clients to shamans, monks, and traditional healers as needed. Many Christian sponsors felt that the best way they can witness to their faith is to help the client on her or his own terms, rather than to impose their own religious agenda. For example, one of my Lao Buddhist clients was having severe cross-cultural adjustment stress. He participated in the sponsor's church services comfortably. But he felt that the local Buddhist temple could help him through his crisis. So the Christian sponsor, who was also a pastor, gladly arranged for him to live for a time at the temple. There, the monks counseled the Lao client, guided his practice of meditation, and performed healing rituals for him.

A more recent project illustrates the importance of the social worker placing the common good above personal issues in interreligious cooperation. From 2000 to 2005, The United Methodist Health Ministry Fund of Hutchinson, Kansas provided generous funding for me to create the Project for Health Through Faith and Community. This project developed curricular materials to help adult members of Christian congregations to link their personal faith with health and well-being in the family, community, nation, and world. It also developed online resources promoting broad understanding of spiritual diversity and its contributions to health and social welfare (Canda, Ketchell, Dybicz, Pyles, & Nelson-Becker, 2006; Spiritual Diversity and Social Work Resource Center via www.socwel.ku.edu/canda). The Fund's conception of and support for this project showed how Christian faith and dedication to service can bring people of many spiritual perspectives together.

Although the Fund promoted this inclusive approach, not everyone I met shared it. For example, when I was giving a presentation at a United Methodist conference on spirituality and health, I briefly alluded to insights from Tibetan Buddhism to help people prepare spiritually for dying. A pastor strongly objected that non-Christian ideas should not be introduced. Another member of the group leaned over toward me and whispered, "They are all going to hell anyway!" Others in the group disagreed with them and indicated interest. In this situation, I had to be aware of my internal feeling of being offended so that I could hold my reaction in abeyance. This allowed me to listen to all views and to help discussion and cooperation continue. The important thing was not my own opinion or feeling reaction, but rather how I could facilitate a valuable learning experience and helpful outcome for the group. During the 5 years of the project, I had to study the nuances of theological differences between and within denominations and how these played out in Kansas communities. I had to learn how to work with a religiously diverse and multidisciplinary advisory group. My project team had to stretch beyond our comfort zones in order to help increase the health, peace, and justice zone in the wider community.

Conclusion

Part I established fundamental values and concepts for spiritually sensitive social work practice. Part II presented a more detailed base of knowledge regarding spiritual diversity and implications for practice. Part III builds on this material to apply a spiritually sensitive approach to social work practice.

EXERCISES

6.1. *Exploring Nonsectarian Spiritual Perspectives on Service*

Return to the exercise at the end of Chapter 5 (5.1) on exploring religious perspectives on service. Apply the steps to learn more about the nonsectarian existential or transpersonal perspectives on social work.

6.2. *Dialogue Across Spiritual Perspectives*

Think through the eight steps for dialogue across spiritual perspectives to help you refine your exploration begun in Exercises 5.1 or 6.1. Reexamine how you have begun to explore one of the perspectives in light of these steps for dialogue. Engage in a dialogue process with a person or group, completing as many of the steps as possible. If you only meet once for this purpose, keep your goals for the discussion modest. Do not engage in controversial or painful discussion, since one meeting is not enough to work through those issues. Focus on respectful questioning, listening, and sharing. It is not likely you can achieve deep mutual understanding, but you could at least raise mutual awareness and respect. The discussion can alert you to ways you can learn more about spiritual perspectives relevant to your clients. If possible, meet the person or group at least two or three times. Keep a journal that helps you process feelings and think about how to improve each meeting. Consider how to apply your learning to enhance your social work practice.

If you wish to extend this further, you could invite a small group of people to meet on an ongoing basis for mutual exploration of spiritual perspectives. Idliby, Oliver, and Warner (2006) present excellent suggestions and examples for how to create what they call a Faith Club for more personal, intimate, and extended activities. While their suggestions focus on dialogue among people of monotheistic religions, the principles could be adapted more broadly. Their book tells the story of how three women—Muslim, Christian, and Jewish—came to know each other and work through the difficulties and joys of sustained transformative interfaith dialogue.

6.3. Extended Dialogue in Established Organizations

If you wish to pursue long-term interreligious dialogue and cooperation, explore organizations dedicated to this purpose. For example, you could join initiatives of the Parliament of the World's Religions or Religions for Peace as mentioned in this chapter. You may also discover local interreligious dialogue groups by doing an internet search using key terms interfaith, ecumenical, or interreligious together with nearby cities' names. If you are near a university, check if there is a Department of Religious Studies or a university based ecumenical or interfaith organization. You could also become involved with a social service community network that includes representation of a variety of religious and secular sponsored agencies.

PART III

Spiritually Sensitive Social Work in Action

7

Creating a Spiritually Sensitive Context for Practice

You shall love your neighbor as yourself.

Leviticus 19:18, Judaism and Christianity
(Holy Bible, Revised Standard Version)

The purpose of Part III is to develop a general inclusive framework for spiritually sensitive practice that is applicable to a wide range of religious and nonreligious clients. This general framework can then be tailored to the particular spiritual perspective of a given client and her or his community.

Mencius, the Confucian sage, said that if an archer shoots an arrow at a target and misses, the archer should not blame the target, but rather look to oneself for the mistake (Lau, trans., 1970). Spiritually sensitive practice stems from the social worker's close examination of self, the helping relationship, and the human service organization as the context for helping. If the context for helping is not spiritually sensitive, then success in supporting the client's spiritual growth can only come despite it. A shaky arm shooting an arrow at a target is a dangerous thing! As Sheridan (1997) encouraged, social workers can nurture the soul of social work by recognizing the spiritual aspect in all that we do. Then we can encourage collaborating among colleagues, leading creatively, organizing to improve the human condition, supporting workers to enjoy their work, regarding clients as respected partners in the helping process, and being stewards of the earth. Accordingly, in this chapter we describe a spiritually sensitive approach to the helping relationship and process and their organizational and environmental context.

The Helping Relationship and Process

All the spiritual perspectives on service that we reviewed emphasized that the helping relationship is the foundation of spiritually sensitive service. The full humanity of both client and worker should be honored in the nature of the relationship itself. Talk about spiritual ideals is empty without embodying those ideals in action and relationship. Principle and practicality need to join. We begin our discussion of spiritually sensitive practice with five guiding principles for all aspects of the helping relationship and context. These principles draw on the values and ethical guidelines established in Part I, as well as the common themes of the spiritual perspectives presented in Part II. We offer suggestions and examples for putting each principle into action. These illustrations make clear that spiritually sensitive practice is not merely a matter of discussing religion or spirituality with clients. *Spiritually sensitive practice is a way of being and relating throughout the entire helping process.* Every social work helping activity, from providing access to food, shelter, and cash assistance, to in-depth discussion of life goals, to community development work, can be conducted in a spiritually sensitive manner without necessarily mentioning religion, faith, or spirituality. In our view, spiritual sensitivity is the foundation of all good practice.

You will notice that many of these principles are consistent with standard social work practice values and the values that pervade this book. We believe that social work's basic values reflect spiritual sensitivity, though they are not always described as such. Further, these principles are eminently practical. For example, over the past few decades, hundreds of empirical studies about factors associated with enhanced client outcomes have shown that the helping relationship is significant (Cooper, 2004; Elkins, 2005; Fitzpatrick & Irannejad, 2008; Messer & Wampold, 2006; Pargament, 2007). As Elkins (p. 140) put it, "But what does it mean that the relationship heals? From a spiritual perspective, I believe this is another way of saying that the therapist nurtures the client's soul, and through this nurturing the client is healed. Love is the most powerful healer of the suffering soul, and in the therapeutic relationship love takes the form of empathy, respect, honesty, caring, and acceptance."

In 1999, the American Psychological Association Division of Psychotherapy Task Force conducted the largest ever review of empirical research on the therapeutic relationship involving the feelings and attitudes shared and expressed between therapist and client (Cooper, 2004). The study concluded that the therapy relationship makes substantial contributions independent of type of treatment and that practice guidelines should address these qualities. Three relational qualities have especially strong research support: *collaborative relationship* between client and therapist; *consensus and cooperation on treatment goals*; and therapist *empathy*. Seven additional qualities of therapists in relation with clients were found to be promising and probably effective: positive regard; genuineness; repairing tensions and breakdowns in relationship; appropriate professional self-disclosure; giving feedback on clients' ways of relating with others; and ability not to act out toward clients with countertransference. Estimates of the impact of relationship quality on variance in outcomes range from 7% to 30%. Miller, Hubble, and Duncan's (2008) review of numerous empirical studies on qualities of excellence emphasizes the importance of getting clear ongoing feedback from clients about the relationship and progress toward outcomes, responding authentically and practically to the feedback, and continually practicing to improve performance throughout one's career. This is a behavioral enactment of positive relationship qualities. All of this suggests that skills and techniques should flow from a nurturing helping relationship and fit the specific circumstances and goals of clients.

Value Clarity

The spiritually sensitive helping relationship is characterized by value clarity. The worker needs to be clear about his or her feelings, opinions, beliefs, and moral commitments that shape the approach to practice. One's own strengths and resources, including those based on spiritual and religious perspectives, need to be identified and linked to social work in a way that is congruent with the NASW Code of Ethics (see Chapter 2). One's own limitations, biases, prejudices, and negative attitudes also need to be identified, so that one can grow beyond them. Major value commitments of the worker and agency that have an impact on clients should be disclosed so that the client can exercise informed consent or refusal of service.

For example, some social workers identify their mode of practice primarily in religious terms, such as a "Christian social worker in a private group practice". In such a case, the name of the group practice, informational materials, and the worker's business card, should identify this clearly so that clients can decide whether this is appropriate for her or him. But "Christian social worker" can mean many different things. So the specific meaning of this and implications for service should be explained in a brochure and initial meeting with the client.

Value clarity is a quality that should pervade the entire helping process. Self reflection by the worker and by the client and ongoing dialogue about the process of helping should enhance each other. Value clarity requires openness to explore and refine one's values and moral and ethical understandings of oneself, the client, and the helping process in an ongoing manner. This is the basis of what existentialists call authentic faith.

Value clarity and ongoing self-reflectivity can be enhanced by regular activities of introspection. Traditional process recording can be very helpful (Wilson, 1980). We suggest that reflections on the interplay between the values, feelings, thoughts, and actions of the worker and client include explicit attention to religious, moral, and spiritual concerns and dynamics.

The format for journaling that we explained in the exercises for Chapter 1 can be adapted to the practice setting. For example, the social worker can identify a particular interaction with a client as a topic for reflection. The worker should obtain clear feedback from the client about the interaction and what the client perceives as helpful or not helpful. Then, the worker can go through each step of identifying: (1) What predisposes me to this way of interacting? (2) What did the client find helpful or not helpful and why? (3) What does this suggest about my strengths and limitations in general and in relation to this particular helping situation? (4) What are specific implications for personal and professional growth? (5) What are the steps I will take to accomplish this growth? (6) How will I use this self-understanding, behavioral change, and growth to help this person immediately and to improve in my future work with clients? (7) What is my timeline for working on this within the current helping relationship and in my ongoing development as a professional?

Respect

Spiritual perspectives have many ways of describing a respectful helping relationship: affirming inherent dignity and worth; nonjudgmental acceptance; recognizing the divinity or sacredness of each person; upholding an I-Thou relationship; being mindful of the essential unity between worker and client. In each case, the client is not to be perceived merely as an object or thing. In spiritually sensitive social work, no client or client system is reduced to a label, diagnosis, number on a chart, or demographic stereotype. Each person, group, or community is given unconditional positive regard.

This may not be so easy, though. Partly as a matter of convenience, or pressures from funders, insurance companies, and governmental and agency policies, clients tend to be processed in terms of fixed categories, with predetermined expectations, eligibility options, and services attached. The danger is that the client becomes subjugated by this categorization. Imagine that a clinical social worker learns that her or his new client has a diagnosis of borderline personality disorder. On the basis of previous experience and stereotypes, she or he might feel anxiety at anticipated frustration and mentally write off the client as hopeless, without even meeting the client. Respect means encountering the client with a fresh mind, unhindered by presumptions, and open to the mystery and possibility of the person.

One way to encourage this *fresh mind* is to treat the first meeting with a client as a precious opportunity not to be wasted. This first encounter involves mutual uncertainty and testing. This also means many possibilities are open. In order to keep the possibilities as open as possible, if appropriate to the helping situation, avoid reading any assessment or diagnostic material about the client beforehand. If it is necessary to read it, or you have heard information from another source, avoid creating a mental foreclosure. Do not use standardized intake or assessment forms as a checklist or rigid format for closed questions. If you need to complete them, wait until after you have had a conversation with the client. Invite the client to tell his or her story in the most open-ended way. Once a rapport and basic understanding of the client's goals and interests is established, more specific assessment tools can be used as relevant. We will say more about assessment in the next chapter.

At all times, avoid being carried away by *inner mental chatter* (Krill, 1990). Our inner chatter labels, analyzes, categorizes, and judges ourselves and our clients. In the process, we miss what is really happening. In Chapter 10, we will present basic relaxation and meditation techniques that can help you to avoid the distraction of inner chatter. For now, whenever you notice your mind waiver, become drowsy, or full of chatter, return awareness to the flow of your breath. Then pay special attention to the sound of the client's voice, the color of his or her clothes, the nuances of body posture and motion, and the emotional tone of his or her words. Perceive these details like you would smell a fresh cut flower or taste a new kind of food. This simple activity can quickly cut through the mental fog and open us up to the here-and-now experience of ourselves in relation with the client.

Client Centeredness

Spiritually sensitive social work gives the value of client-centeredness special nuances. If we truly respect the client, we honor her or his aspirations, self-understandings, beliefs, and values. We recognize, as Gandhi put it, that we are all on a search for truth. Professional education prepares social workers to assist clients in achieving their aspirations, but it does not make us experts about what is best for the client. Nor does it make us authorities about the nature of reality or the validity of spiritual beliefs and practices. Client-centeredness means taking the client's worldview and spiritual experiences seriously. When we have disagreements, detect signs of clients' delusion or self-deception, or feel a responsibility to intervene to protect the client or others, we still need to relate in a way that respects the client. Proselytization or moralistic judging of clients based on religious, political, theoretical, or other ideological positions is not an appropriate activity for a professional social worker.

For example, social workers in mental health settings often encounter clients who report visionary experiences with religious imagery and meaning. As we will discuss in Chapter 8, assessment of such reports needs to be done in the context of the client's own spiritual and cultural context, just as the *Diagnostic and Statistical Manual of Mental Disorders, fourth edition, text revision* (DSM-IV-TR) guidelines indicate (APA, 2000). Suppose that a person reports that he or she has recently had an important conversation with her or his grandmother, who has been deceased for several years. The significance of this experience can only be ascertained by a careful open-minded dialogue with the client. Even if the worker believes that such an experience must be a hallucination, the worker's belief is irrelevant to the actual significance for the client. It may well be that the conversation with the spirit of her or his grandmother has yielded an important insight and sense of spiritual support for the client. Indeed, within her or his religious community, such experiences may be considered quite ordinary and commonplace.

I (LF) recently experienced a situation in which the principle of client-centeredness was violated (Furman, 2007). A woman I knew well, whom I will refer to as Joy, was admitted to an in-hospital hospice due to having an advanced stage of a virulent form of cancer. A hospice social worker discussed the diagnosis with Joy and her husband. They had been Lutheran missionaries in Brazil for 30 years. They recently returned to live permanently in the United States with their adult children and grandchildren. They told the social worker that, although they were devastated, they believed God would give them the strength to accept the cancer situation and that God would empower them to follow His will just as He had in the past. "Are you *sure* about that?" the social worker asked. Joy responded, "Yes, for me to live is Christ, and to die is gain." The social worker responded incredulously, "Do you *really* believe that?" "Yes" she said. The social worker then burst out crying and ran out of the room. When talking about this incident with me, Joy said "It made me feel like the hospice social worker didn't approve of my religious faith even though that is all I have left now. I felt as if she was challenging my faith. And when she ran out of my room in tears, I thought she must feel my case is hopeless!" Joy died two weeks later.

Inclusivity

Spiritually sensitive practice goes beyond tolerance of spiritual diversity among clients. It moves us to appreciation and advocacy for clients' religious freedoms and spiritual self-determination and the many variations of spiritual expression. We have discussed in previous chapters the importance of this value and have suggested guidelines for cross-perspective dialogue. For example, inclusivity was demonstrated when Southeast Asian refugee resettlement took place through interreligious cooperation and collaboration, bringing together governmental and nongovernmental agencies and staff, local religious communities, and refugees of various religious and cultural backgrounds.

One of the most difficult challenges is to be able to address *exclusive* spiritual perspectives in practice. Some clients and community members believe that their way is the only right way. They may reject dialogue and cooperation. They may operate in a coercive or punishing manner toward people who don't conform to their beliefs. Some clients use religious rationales to justify child abuse, ethnocentrism, racism, homophobia, or violence against women. Some religious communities, such as the Amish, wish to live separate from others in order to maintain a unique lifestyle and moral commitments. In any of these situations, there will be additional challenges for the social worker to establish trust, mutual understanding, and cooperation. But there is hope for this connection if the social worker himself or herself truly values inclusion and connection. We need to have a broad enough sense of respect and compassion that we can genuinely engage with clients and their spiritual communities, even when some aspects are contrary to our own beliefs and values. Even if we don't agree, we need to create a relationship that encompasses agreement to disagree. If we advocate for change of spiritual beliefs and values, change needs to occur in the context of the client's goals and a dialogue in which we also are open to learning and change as the interaction continues.

There may be four caveats to this. First, if the behaviors of clients are demonstrably threatening to safety of self or others, then we have a duty to follow professional standards and laws for protection and mandatory reporting. Second, our practice could itself involve advocacy for empowerment of groups in the community who experience discrimination or oppression. Then, our work involves opposition to unjust behaviors and policies. We discuss this issue in the next section on implementing change. Third, a client might express such severe hostility or prejudice toward us that it is not tenable to work with him or her. In that case, referral may be required. Fourth, in nonprofessional roles as members of the general public, we advocate for our views of health and welfare in the public arena. We suggest that this can be done in a spiritually sensitive, peaceful manner along the lines of Rev. Martin Luther King, Jr. and Mahatma Gandhi, as described previously. In all four situations, we can treat the people involved respectfully.

In a class on spirituality and social work, one of my (EC) students was a charismatic and theologically conservative Christian. When she first introduced herself and her beliefs in an unusually fervent way, my gut reaction was to become cautious, expecting that she might try to proselytize or inhibit free discussion and experiential exercises. There was a practitioner of Wicca who mentioned misgivings with Christianity, so I expected a conflict between them to develop. Fortunately, we were able to let go of our presumptions and just relate to each other person to person. As class participants came to know each other better, we became impressed by both students' inner spiritual life, deep sense of intuition and inspiration, vivid experience of personal relationship with the sacred, and resources of support in their spiritual communities. The two students who began feeling polarized and suspicious of each other developed mutual understanding, appreciation, and support. By the end of the course, they literally embraced each other in a spirit of mutual acceptance.

Whenever I (EC) facilitate courses, intensive workshops, or dialogue groups on spiritual diversity, I begin with an explicit statement of the ground rules that are necessary for a fruitful experience. The following explanation could be adapted in the formation phase of a course, intensive workshop, dialogue group, family therapy, or groupwork.

> The subjects of religion, faith, and spirituality can be very controversial. We each have beliefs, values, and traditions that we hold dear. As we get to know each other, we will discover common ground as well as areas of difference and disagreement. In this course (or workshop, group, etc.) we need to create a climate in which each person's spiritual commitments are honored. Therefore, I am asking that all of us make an explicit agreement to relate in a manner that encourages open dialogue and mutual learning. This means that we demonstrate appreciation for religious and spiritual diversity among us. On occasions when we may disagree, we need to agree to disagree, while still respecting each other. In this course (or workshop, group, etc.), we will not engage in proselytization. We may well challenge each other to pursue

new understandings of truth, but we may not coerce or denigrate each other on the basis of our own versions of truth. (Group discussion follows until a sense of closure and agreement is reached.) Now that we have agreed on this mutual respect, let's applaud ourselves to celebrate our beginning of this time together that promises to be very rich and enjoyable.

Creativity

The spiritually sensitive helping relationship is creative. Possibilities for growth, problem solving, crisis resolution, and solution finding are encouraged. All spiritual traditions identify that human suffering is only one aspect of our condition. There is also the aspect of healing, reconciliation, salvation, enlightenment. As we will see in Chapter 9, even in crises, breakdown of the person's sense of security, safety, and meaning opens an opportunity for transformation toward an enhanced way of being (Canda, 1988a). This is not seeing the world with rose-colored glasses or naive optimism. It is a recognition that every person has a mysterious capacity for resilience and that there are creative possibilities in every situation. To achieve transformation may well require pain and sacrifice. To use a religious notion, the term sacrifice comes from the Latin root words meaning "to make sacred." By going through the hazardous tunnel of ego disintegration, we may be able to come through to ego-transcendence (Smith, 1995; Smith and Gray, 1995).

Creative possibilities need to be nurtured. The creative social worker encourages creativity in the client. The spiritually sensitive social worker is like a midwife, who provides a supportive, caring environment, helpful skills and knowledge, and positive enthusiastic energy to help the client to give birth to a new self and situation. The creative social worker needs to be flexible and spontaneous, clearly present in the moment with the client. The creative social worker may feel inspired, as if "breathing-in" wisdom and energy from a sacred or transpersonal source and then sharing that in empathic flow of being with the client.

In fact, following one's breath is one of the simplest ways to keep the mind clear, to stay focused with the client, and to encourage a creative process. I (EC) once was called by a refugee resettlement agency to consult on a case of potentially violent conflict between two Lao men who were roommates. One man had threatened the other with a knife during an argument. Fortunately, I also had the excellent assistance of a multilingual and multicultural Thai international student, Thitiya Phaobtong (see Canda & Phaobtong, 1992). Thitiya and I went to the apartment of the Lao clients to meet them and their church sponsor. We were apprehensive, given the volatile nature of the situation.

Conversation proceeded through Thitiya's interpretation. Disagreements were aired, the knife incident was recounted, and threats were made. Heat of anger and frustration mounted. I felt my stomach tightening. I became hyper-alert, checking the closest exit, palms sweating. Thitiya ably relayed messages between people, but the complexity of conversation between five people and the growing tension also strained her. Yet, I sensed the possibility for a resolution behind the overt conflict. The roommates had shared goals and good times. The church sponsor was supportive and open to any possibility to help. As soon as I realized that I was feeling carried away into the tension of the conflict, I was able to return awareness to my breathing. While Thitiya interpreted, I focused on drawing deep and gentle breaths, releasing all tension, taking in the feelings and possibilities of the situation with clarity. The obvious suddenly hit me— everyone involved was spiraling out of control into tension, magnifying each other's anxiety. So I asked for a glass of water. I knew that customary politeness would require the roommates to pause while one of them left the room to fill the glass. That gave us all a moment of quiet. I followed my breath, feeling as though the room itself settled down to a gentler quality of energy.

Those simple acts—following my breath and asking for water—made a shift in the interactions. Afterward, we were able to reflect on the goals and aspirations of the roommates, reaffirm their friendship, and discover a solution that would meet their goals. After the session, Thitiya and I reflected on our feelings. We had shared an unspoken connection in the process of mounting tension and release. We felt that the pause, quiet, and breathing had averted a small disaster and felt quite grateful for the small miracle of transformation that happened. Thitiya and I had a rapport in the situation that allowed an intuitive sensitivity to each other's cues so we could flow toward a resolution. Often, creativity, intuition, and transformation arise from just such simple things as breath, awareness, and a glass of water.

The creative social worker attends also to the aesthetics of helping. We can fill the place of helping with colors, sounds, and images with which the client resonates. The helping relationship can put the client in touch with the aspects of the human and nonhuman environments that feel like a boon or blessing. The beauty and inspiring qualities of art and nature can be engaged.

A nurse for the Navajo (Diné) Nation once told me (EC) about the reaction of many traditional Navajo people to a hospital there when it was first opened some 30 years ago. The hospital was built in a conventional manner with the usual standards of efficiency, cleanliness, and technological proficiency. But many traditional people did not want to go there. The building was made of squares and rectangles. The rooms were barren and cold. Patients were expected to divest themselves of clothing and daily items that lend a sense of identity, community connectedness, and sacred support. Inside those square barren rooms, people felt cut off from the healing powers of earth and sky. The natural beauty way moves in circles and cycles: the curve of earth, the roundness of moon and sun, the rotations of day, night, and seasons. Hence, traditional homes (*hogans*) and healing places are circular. Traditional lifeways are intimately connected with the beauty and harmony of all around us and within us. The sacred spirit beings are invited into the healing ceremonies and places. The hospital was just the opposite of all that—cut off from beauty, circularity, community, harmony. In order to avoid this problem, many current leaders in the health, mental health, and social service systems of the Diné Nation advocate for culturally congruent and spiritually sensitive programs for treatment and prevention.

The boxed-in hospital is a great metaphor for the way helping in general, and social work in particular, often happens. And the Diné spiritual perspective reminds us to welcome back all the places, powers, beauties, relationships, colors, sights, sounds, smells, tastes, dances, songs, and memories that can have an inspiring, healing, and helping significance for our clients.

Teaching can also be enhanced this way. For example, each year from 2002 to 2006, I conducted an intensive study abroad course on spiritual diversity in Korean social work for American students. (See http://www.socwel. ku.edu/candagrant/korea/KAS%202002–06%20compressed.pdf.) Professor Park Seung-Hee of Sungkyunkwan University was co-teacher and guide. Students often expressed how their learning was enhanced by his creative approach that included information together with humor, artistry, and sensitivity to the beauty of places we visited. As one of the students put it:

> Professor Park explained how we can use our six senses to learn about nature and life in general. He told us that we first look at the mountain with our eyes to see its beauty. Next, we hear all the noises the mountain has to offer; we can hear six or seven noises at the same time if we listen carefully enough. Third, we smell all of the scents of the mountain. Then we can taste the mountain if we put bits of flowers and plants into our mouths. Fifth, we can touch the trees, rocks, and dirt on the mountain with our hands and feet. Finally, he explained that we can feel the mountain with our souls. This is how I believe I truly learned the important lessons of how to look and listen.

A Holistic Approach to Social Work Practice

If we take together all the implications of these five principles for spiritually sensitive practice, we can see many challenges to innovate holistic ways of understanding and doing social work. The words heal, whole, and holy all have the same root meaning. *Holistic helping is healing*—making and restoring wholeness with clients, ourselves, our agencies, and educational institutions. In order to clarify some of these possibilities, we suggest models for holistic understanding of the person and environment and for a holistic approach to social work activity.

Holistic Understanding of the Person and Environment

Social workers often say that we want to address the whole person in the environment. But usually in practice what we really mean by that is to pay attention to some small parts of the person and his or her immediate social environment that are relevant to our specialization or agency function. Spiritually sensitive practice means reconsidering what is the whole person and what is the whole environment.

Spirituality encompasses and transcends the biological, psychological, socio-logical, and spiritual aspects of a person. It engages the relationships between an individual and his or her family, community, nation, the global community, the planetary ecology, the cosmos, and ultimate reality, however understood. From this vantage point, the "and" in "person and environment" should not be under-stood as a separator, but rather as an interconnector. Person is always with, in, and of environment. Person cannot exist without environment. Human nature is human/nature. By connecting insights from traditional religions, existential-ism, deep ecology, and transpersonal theory we can move toward an ecospiritual (Coates, Gray, & Hetherington, 2006) or trans/ecological (Besthorn, 2001) under-standing. For example, Indigenous and East Asian philosophical perspectives on interconnectedness, balance, harmony, and dynamism among all aspects of the person and world, as reflected in Medicine Wheels, mandalas, and Chinese yin/yang, five elements theory can help us to envision and act holistically. Systems theories can help us think about these various types and levels of systems and to map them with genograms and ecomaps. We can draw creatively on insights from many human behavior theories and practice models that address various aspects of the whole person and environment, including transpersonal levels of con-sciousness and functioning (Larkin, 2005; Robbins, Chatterjee, & Canda, 2006).

Robbins et al. (2006) emphasized that application of theories to social work practice should be based on careful critical reflection on their assumptions and their implications for practice. Holistic practice can gain many insights by inte-grating useful complementary aspects from many theories and perspectives, whether rooted in science, philosophies, religions, or cultures. No one perspec-tive can encompass all aspects of human experience adequately. Each one has various advantages and disadvantages. Each one reveals important features of human life and ways to enhance it. But each one obscures or omits important features as well. As they put it:

> The critically reflective approach (to theory) involves cultivating clear aware-ness of one's own values, goals, practice commitments, strengths, and limi-tations. It also involves developing a thorough knowledge of a wide range of theories that deal with the whole person and the environment. It requires mak-ing informed evaluations about the strengths and shortcomings of each theory, and it requires careful professional discernment about the relevancy of theories to a particular situation in collaboration with the client. (p. 424)

For example, Kim and Canda (2006) developed a holistic model for social work practice with people with disabilities by critiquing the limitations and integrat-ing the complementary insights of the social model and the conventional med-ical model of disability. These two models draw on different theories and are often posed in opposition to each other. The social model emphasizes empow-ering responses to structural barriers, social injustice, and socially constructed stigma. The medical model emphasizes preventive or corrective responses to indi-vidual functional impairments, psychosocial problems, and medical symptoms.

The social model alone can lead practitioners into an adversarial mentality and neglect of individual level challenges. The medical model alone can lead practitioners into an authoritarian, pathologizing mode that neglects sociocultural and structural issues and injustice. By bringing the useful insights of the two models together in a strengths oriented holistic approach, the social worker partners with the client in a way that addresses both the individual and collective aspects of empowerment according to the client's own aspirations and values. This holistic approach respects and engages the whole person in her or his life context.

Robbins et al. (2006) use the metaphor of musical performance to describe the harmonious joining of preparation in theory and skill with spontaneous interaction with the client that should characterize good practice, what we refer to as spiritually sensitive practice.

> Indeed, in that moment of inspired performance, the theory and skill are, in a sense, forgotten at the same time that they give form to the beauty and spontaneity of the music. In order to achieve such a harmonious expression of theory, skill, and spontaneity, the performer must engage in a continuous process of training, self-reflection, and performance. In social work, this quality of rapport, harmony, and spontaneous insight during helping is often called practice wisdom. (Krill, 1990, p. 423)

Holistic Activity in Social Work

Imbrogno and Canda (1988) and Canda (1998c) developed a conceptual model for viewing social work activity as a holistic system. Many times we get bogged down in dichotomistic thinking and debates: cause versus function; process versus outcomes; logic versus feeling; objective versus subjective; strengths versus pathologies; qualitative research versus quantitative research; and on and on. By drawing on insights from Chinese philosophy in the Book of Changes (Wilhelm & Baynes, trans., 1967) and principles of general dynamic systems theory, they developed a model of social work activity that shows the connections between all stages of the helping process, as well as complementary aspects within each stage. Koenig and Spano (1998) and Lee et al., (2009) discuss similar ideas related to Daoism, Buddhism, the strengths perspective, and traditional Chinese medicine theory. We modify and expand Imbrogno and Canda's model here as on overall orientation to holistic social work practice, including the organizational context.

The stages in this model are (1) understanding the situation, (2) designing and planning action, (3) implementing service, (4) evaluating the process and results, and (5) integrating all these activities within a coherent system of activity. Each stage involves two complementary and contrasting aspects, analogous to yin and yang (as described in Chapter 5 regarding Confucianism), which need to be converged. All stages are interconnected. Although we may emphasize stage related activities at certain times in practice, actually each stage and their related activities influence each other and may repeat recursively throughout the helping process. Each individual social worker needs to integrate each stage and activity in her or his work. Each human service organization needs to integrate the stages and activities of helping among its staff. As we grow and improve as individual practitioners and as helping organizations, we spiral upward in creativity and proficiency. Therefore, this model should be understood as cyclic and spiral rather than linear. The vertical and horizontal cross lines show the interconnections between all stages. The encompassing circle shows the essential unity of all the stages in the flow of helpful change. Each direction is labeled with the appropriate stage and two complementary and contrasting aspects of activity relevant to that stage. One aspect (the yang side) of each stage is commonly addressed in social work education, so we will focus more on the yin aspect that is typically neglected, so that both aspects can be brought together. As you look at Figure 7.1,

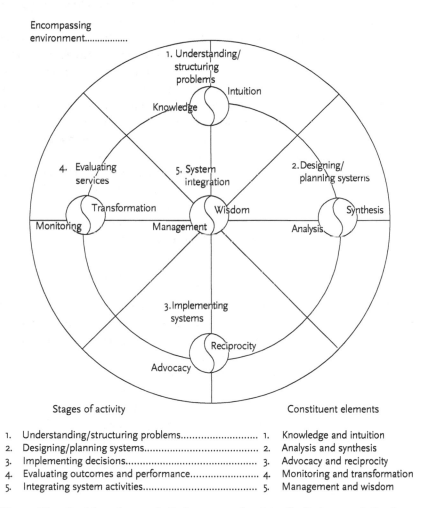

Stages of activity		Constituent elements
1. Understanding/structuring problems.............................	1.	Knowledge and intuition
2. Designing/planning systems..	2.	Analysis and synthesis
3. Implementing decisions..	3.	Advocacy and reciprocity
4. Evaluating outcomes and performance.......................	4.	Monitoring and transformation
5. Integrating system activities......................................	5.	Management and wisdom

Figure 7.1. Social work as an holistic system of activity (by Imbrogno & Canda, 1988; used with permission of the publisher).

which is flat on the page, image that there is a spiral coming up off the page to represent the growth and improvement of the professional and human service organization as they cycle through the holistic process of helping.

Stage 1: Understanding

Usually in social work education, we are taught to seek *knowledge* by establishing facts through empirical observations, logical reasoning, and learning of facts and theories from established experts and scholars. This type of knowing is necessary, but not sufficient. We also need to pay attention to nonlinear, nonrational, and spontaneous modes of awareness. We need to have an intuitive grasp of the client and his or her situation. Intuition, in this context, refers to a holistic way of knowing, which derives from rapport with the client as a whole person in his or her situation. To achieve this, we need to become a participant in the client's world, listen to his or her stories, and relate to his or her feelings with empathy. When rapport is established, we can experience the world from his or her perspective and realistically anticipate reactions. Intuitive awareness can give rise to unexpected insights for what to do at just the right time. This is what Thitiya and I felt in our meeting with the conflicting roommates. Koenig and Spano (1998) described *intuition* as "all-at-once knowing," that comes from immersion in the moment and perspective of the client. Luoma (1998) discussed intuition as a process of direct knowing derived from a sense of merging between the subject (the knower) and the object (the known). Intuition arises before and beyond analytic thinking that splits subject and object and operates in linear terms.

One simple technique that can encourage intuitive, creative insight into a client situation is to ask for a dream or day dream about it. Before taking a nap, going to sleep for the night, or just resting, become aware of your breath and settle into a relaxed feeling. If you enjoy drawing, painting, or writing poetry, try this before beginning your artwork. Then, call to mind the client situation or relation with colleagues about which you feel a question or blockage. Recall vividly your sense of sincere caring and connection with the other persons involved. According to your own belief system, ask your deep self, your unconscious, inspiring spirit, or God for a dream or symbol that relates to it. Be sure to do this in a way that feels safe and comfortable. Don't try to make it happen or to grab at it. Just prime yourself for the possibility. Then, let go of it. It may well be that something will occur to you at that time or maybe when you least expect it— in sleep, in a daytime reverie, or while taking a shower. Most often, these insights spontaneously arise when we are relaxed and receptive.

Stage 2: Designing

Understanding opens possibilities for action. When we creatively design a helping plan, we need to apply both analysis and synthesis. *Analysis* involves rational evaluation of alternative results of actions, based on the best information available. The situation is broken down into components and characteristics such as assessment categories, system levels, action steps, professional roles, and alternative outcomes. In analytic thinking, we link empirical observations and information about the actual situation with starting assumptions, values, and theoretical and policy models that seem relevant. If we use evidence-based practice, we might work according to manuals that prescribe interventions in a certain way with certain types of clients. This is the conventional mode of planning taught in academia. Analytic understanding is necessary but not sufficient. When we break a picture into its parts, we have a puzzle to be solved, but no longer the actual picture.

Analysis needs to be converged with synthesis. In this context, *synthesis* means that we use our immersion in the helping situation and our rapport with the people involved to connect alternative and even opposing perspectives and feelings. We don't limit ourselves to neat roles, categories, theories, and rational plans. Like a child having fun in a sandbox, we get into the messiness and unpredictability of the situation. We seek possibilities of synergy, that is, creative interaction between contrasting people and perspectives, so creative outcomes that cannot be anticipated are possible. Analytically derived information and possibilities can be brought into the dialogue and action, to be synthesized with the spontaneous and messy realities of everyone involved. In agency planning meetings and case reviews, we encourage divergent opinions and work them through for a more comprehensive view. We engage clients as partners in the helping process and take seriously their feedback about what works. We involve community representatives and consumer advocates in planning and reviewing agency goals and policies.

Brainstorming is a helpful approach to this. In brainstorming, no idea is rejected. No possibility is impossible. Every sincere idea is given expression and considered by the participants. For example, in a family therapy session, each member could be asked to imagine her or his ideal family. How would each member of the family be the same or different compared to how they are now? What are the goals, aspirations, hopes, and dreams that color this picture of the ideal family? Each member of the family could be asked to present her or his ideal with a rule that no one interrupts, except for asking for clarification or examples. Then, the social worker could help everyone consider the points of each person's ideal that are similar or different. The family can brainstorm about how to create a collective ideal that incorporates the hopes and dreams of each member.

Stage 3: Implementing

Designing opens up possibilities for various roads we can travel. But we have to travel down a particular road to get somewhere. Change requires implementing the planned designs. Often, implementation of social work plans is called "intervention" and helping activities are called "interventions." Intervention implies that an external force intrudes upon some client system and directs it. The same term is used in military strikes against enemies. To us, a metaphor more consistent with spiritually sensitive practice is *cultivation*. The difference between these two approaches to implementation is well illustrated by the metaphor of gardening.

The intervention mode of social work is like the common American practice of lawn care. Suppose a homeowner has a patch of earth to take care of. He or she may think she "owns" this earth, so it is his or her job to control it, to make it look like the neighbors expect it should. Cultural convention dictates that this patch of earth should be covered with green grass, ideally to look like a miniature golf course. If the grass is too long or too weedy, neighbors may complain or even ask the city government to fine the owner and cut the grass. Heaven forbid that lovely yellow dandelions should sprout up, lest they turn to seed. Wind or fun-loving children might blow those seeds around to contaminate other people's lawns. For some reason, it doesn't occur to this kind of gardener that dandelions are lovely or that they can be used to make salads or wine. Instead, grass is planted for the desired texture and color. Since the grass often isn't well suited to the local growing conditions, the homeowner has to give the lawn frequent water and fertilizer. If anything undesirable appears, like weeds, grubs, or moles, out come the herbicides and pesticides. So in the process of keeping an ideal lawn, that which grows well is killed and that which does not grow well is maintained by willpower, hard effort, and time. Toxic runoff from lawns joins the toxic runoff from farms, and then we drink the poisons from our tap-water.

Too often, we view clients like this. They and their situations appear to be weedy with problems. We think we know how they should look, think, and act in order to be "normal," "functional," "reality-based," "healthy," and "adaptive." We try to make clients fit into the artificial socially constructed standards of normality within our mental health, social welfare, and criminal justice systems. We weed, prune, pull, and poison the behaviors, thoughts, and attitudes that don't meet our standards. This is the "social worker as expert" model of intervention.

But social workers can operate more like organic gardeners. In this case, we identify the strengths, aspirations, and resources of clients. When clients focus on problems and obstacles, we partner with them in working through challenges toward opportunities. We help them to discern how these relate to their loved ones, the workplace, the larger social environment, and the natural environment. We help them to cultivate the natural growth potential already inherent within them and their situations. We may not know what the end product will look like. But we can experience directly that the process of getting there is affirming to everyone involved. This kind of helping action has been called *Daoistic change* (Brandon, 1976; Maslow, 1968), meaning that help flows along with the natural course and potential of the client system in their situation. This is not passivity. It is creative, harmonious action.

When the Confucian sage, Mencius, encouraged help and support between people, he warned against two common mistakes (Lau, trans., 1970). He said that a rice farmer must be caring and attentive in cultivating rice. One mistake is to do nothing; the other mistake is to be impatient and intrusively forceful. If the farmer ignores the seedlings, they might be destroyed by lack or excess of water or by feeding birds. On the other hand, if the farmer is impatient with the speed of growth, he or she might tug on the seedling, to stretch it and encourage it. Of course, the seedling will be uprooted.

Daoistic change means that the social worker joins with the client system and situation, understands it with empathy and rapport, and encourages the growth potential already there or helps the client to discover it. This is consistent with the strengths perspective on social work (Saleebey, 2008). "Harmony with" does not mean avoiding conflict, however. It means relating authentically and realistically with situations as they are, conflict or not, and flowing with the creative process.

There was an American student who had learned the Japanese nonviolent defensive martial art of aikido (Dass & Gorman, 1985). His teacher had always told him that aikido was for spiritual discipline, not for picking fights. Still he longed to encounter a situation of threat when he would feel justified to try out his skills in actual combat. One day, he was riding a train in Japan. A drunken angry man became belligerent and intimidating to passengers. The student became alert, ready for a fight in which he could rescue everyone. While the student was poised to strike, an elderly gentleman called out to the drunken man: "Come over here. What are you drinking?" "Sake," answered the man. This caught his attention and he lumbered over to the elderly gentleman.

The old man said, "Ah, I love to sit with my wife and sip a cup of sake." Then the drunken man began to cry. He said that his wife had died and that he was deeply sad. His anger and threat disappeared. He sat and commiserated with the elderly gentleman, who had subdued him without flexing a muscle. The elderly man, not the brash student, was the real master of aikido.

The gardening metaphor reminds me of a quandary that my wife and I (EC) faced with my neighbors. Several years ago, we landscaped our backyard with stone terraces, flower gardens, wild medicinal plants, a small pond, and Korean style natural stone towers. The unusual project attracted so much attention that strangers sometimes wandered around. I imagined we were making a private meditation park but instead we had more intrusions than before. I was also worried that a curious child might fall in the pond. We did not want to close everything off with a large fence, so we wondered how to solve this problem. Then it struck us to try a Daoist approach. Rather than resisting public attention, my wife and I invited all the neighbors and many friends to gather for a garden opening party with tea and desserts. Many people came. Once they satisfied their curiosity, no one intruded again. Nonresistance and going with the flow succeeded.

This does not deny that there are occasions that call for forceful action to protect someone's safety. In a crisis, the client may feel overwhelmed, confused, or disoriented. If the person is a danger to self or others, then temporary protection, restraint, or support might be necessary. This is a naturally compassionate response. But compassion also means that we help the client to become empowered, reoriented, and proficient again, so that her or his aspirations can be achieved in relationship with others.

We can summarize this by referring to two complementary aspects of helping: *advocacy* and *reciprocity*. As an advocate, we identify a client or client system and assist the accomplishment of the clients' goals. In this process, we often identify problems, barriers, opponents, and enemies that block the clients' goal achievement. While commitment to the client and zeal for justice are important and necessary, these qualities become dangerous when they are pursued in a one sided manner. One danger is that we don't pay attention to harmful impacts on other people or the natural environment that result from our advocacy. To use a Christian expression, this is a sin of omission, that is, harming others by not paying attention or caring. Another danger is that we act from an enemy-mentality. We identify some persons or situations as enemies to be combated. This is the militaristic implication of "intervention" taken to an extreme. We might even feel glee at our victory over the opponent. In this enemy-mentality, we perceive the other only as enemy. He or she is no longer precious or even important. Ironically, if we exploit, damage, or diminish others in our efforts for victory on behalf of the client system, we become exactly what we opposed. This is a sin of commission, that is, committing acts of violence or dehumanization. We despised the opponent for the indignities and harm they caused for the client. And in returning indignity and harm to that opponent, we become just like the enemy. This approach does not afford any possibility of reconciliation or mutual benefit.

Jesus said that we should love our enemy; we should do unto others as we would have them do unto us. Confucius said we should not do to others what we would not have them do to us. All spiritual traditions proclaim their highest aspirations as love and compassion. If we take this seriously, there are major implications for spiritually sensitive practice. In order to avoid falling into an enemy-mentality, it is helpful to complement advocacy with reciprocity. In *reciprocity*, we seek mutual growth and benefit through creative solutions. We respect all parties involved, even when we disagree or conflict. When conflict is unresolvable, we find ways to continue the conflict in a humane manner, or to forgive and move on. Mohandas Gandhi and Martin Luther King, Jr. were excellent examples of social activists who strove to put this ideal into action.

Of course, this is easier said than done. In 1997, I (EC) presented at a symposium on spirituality and social work at the Inter-University Centre in Dubrovnik, Croatia. Another presenter was Arun Gandhi, grandson of Mohandas Gandhi and director of the M.K. Gandhi Institute for Nonviolence in Memphis. Many of the presentations addressed the ideals of compassion, forgiveness, reconciliation, service, and nonviolence. The fact that our building had only recently been rebuilt since prolonged bombings on the city added an intensity and urgency to

Table 7.1.   Principles and Steps for Win/Win Solution Making.

1. Bring all parties into a dialogue based on mutual respect and willingness to understand each other.
2. Do not reduce people to problems or enemies—get to know each other as fellow people.
3. Identify the positions of all parties and the most important principles and aspirations underlying them.
4. Identify what each party feels will result in success from their point of view.
5. Identify the common interests and different standards for success.
6. Freely discuss to discover alternative solutions in which all parties would feel gain, based on their various aspirations and standards.
7. Select solutions acceptable to all parties.
8. Develop an action plan and roles, involving cooperative teamwork by representatives of all parties.
9. Follow up implementation of the plan, evaluating success in terms of common interests and different standards.
10. Examine collaboratively the long-term impacts of the change and revise activity as necessary.

our discussions. Croatian participants struggled with how to act on these ideals while recovering from emotional trauma and the physical destruction of many of their homes, loved ones, and social infrastructure. But at the same time that the difficulty of this was shown, the importance was equally clear. Somehow, we must all keep going on the way of peace in order to get out of the cycles of violence and victimization that all too often characterize human life.

A related trend in conflict mediation is called *win/win problem solving or solution making* (McLaughlin & Davidson, 1994). In win/win strategies, victory is not at the expense of others. It is intended for the mutual benefit of both sides in the disagreement or conflict. Table 7.1 summarizes the major principles and steps of the win/win approach.

The remainder of this book will give many more practical suggestions for implementing spiritually sensitive practice.

Stage 4: Evaluating

Spiritually sensitive evaluation is an ongoing process of discernment. We reflect gently yet consistently upon ourselves and clients in their situations so that we recognize the impacts of our activity in both the process and outcomes of helping. But this is not an egocentric type of reflection. To borrow an insight from karma yoga, spiritually sensitive evaluation cares about helpful results but is not egotistically attached to them. Evaluation is not for the purpose of guaranteeing that clients conform to the expectations of social workers or their agencies. It is for the purpose of helping the client to be aware of and encouraged by beneficial change and to avoid the pitfalls of mistakes or ineffective helping strategies.

The conventional aspect of evaluation is *monitoring*. We keep track of continuities or changes in the client's functioning in relation to helping activities and objectives. We adjust the help as needed to seek the most effective helping approach. We learn many professional mechanisms for monitoring, such as clinical dialogue, helping contracts, psychological measuring instruments, single subject research designs, and consumer satisfaction surveys. We may have standards of progress dictated by agency programs or funding sources. This is all useful. But if that is all we do, there are dangers. We may simply be measuring client conformity, rather than genuine growth. As Imbrogno and Canda (1988) put it, "All too often it happens that assessment of service delivery leads to a quantitative increase of clients served or income earned (i.e. as an indicator of change) with a decrease in the quality of service and client satisfaction" (p. 26).

Monitoring needs to be complemented by a process of *transformation*, in which the client system and help provider system mutually shape each other. Evaluation then is not just for imposing change on clients. It is for mutual reflection on the partnership of helping, in which both client and worker change each other. The social worker and the agency are open to self-transformation of goals, strategies, technologies, rules, and policies, based on learning from the clients, community representatives, and consumer advocates.

I (EC) have often seen the ineffectual result in agencies when this is not the case. I have done many trainings for cultural competence and spiritual diversity in mental health and social service agencies and social work education programs. One aspect of the training is a study of the preparedness of the social workers and the organizational setting. We may do surveys of clients, staff and administrators, direct observation of organizational performance, brainstorming sessions and cultural awareness exercises. We might provide examples and guidelines and bring in guest speakers. Enthusiasm raises as new possibilities for providing services are identified. However, once this monitoring has finished, the process of innovation often fizzles out. Genuine transformation may entail long-term discussions about difficult issues such as racism, prejudice, religious discrimination, and factionalism in the workplace. It may call for greater efforts for recruitment, retention, and promotion of staff who are well qualified to work with a wide range of diverse clients. It may require creating new multicultural and spiritually diverse teams and community networks. It may require fundamental rethinking of the theories and policies that structure practice and education. It might require redistribution or generation of funding for new initiatives. These changes challenge the status quo of the organization and the daily patterns of the service providers. It may not be easy to engage in such transformation especially if the agency or educational unit is already struggling for survival in the face of threatened funding cuts or some other organizational crisis. But without self-transformation, evaluation can hardly be authentic or fruitful. Inauthentic evaluation may create the illusion of change, for public relations purposes, but it only serves to maintain a helping system more dedicated to the benefit of the agency than the clients.

Holistic evaluation relies upon modes of inquiry and research methods that can tap into many different ways of knowing and a wide variety of spiritual perspectives and worldviews. This is consistent with heuristic and transpersonal research approaches (Braud & Anderson, 1998; Tyson, 1995). These approaches recognize that there are many ways of knowing that draw on human capacities for thinking, feeling, sensing, and intuiting. There are many techniques for gaining knowledge, each with advantages and disadvantages, such as qualitative and quantitative methods and contemplative practices that foster clear mindedness and creativity. There are many different worldviews that shape assumptions about what can be known and how it is best to know it. Holistic understanding requires bringing together (synergizing) many different ways and methods of knowing.

Conventional social scientific research has long been rooted in the philosophical tradition of *positivism*. Positivism asserts that reliable knowledge must be based upon sensory experience subjected to logical analysis (Lincoln & Guba, 1985). Research methods most often associated with positivism are controlled experiments, quantitative surveys, highly structured detached observations, and statistical analysis. This is valuable as an advance over prejudice, untested assumptions, or sloppy thinking. But the shortcoming of positivistic research is that it does not utilize the full range of ways of knowing and it also presents an overly simplified, reduced understanding of the world. Figure 7.2 illustrates that the positivist domain of inquiry only addresses one quadrant of possibilities for ways of knowing.

Spiritually sensitive research needs to be holistic, encompassing the full circle of ways of knowing and addressing both process and outcomes of helping. Depending on the nature of the research question and the aspects of spirituality studied, experiments and statistical studies could be useful. But we also

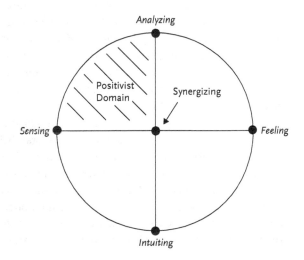

Figure 7.2. Synergizing ways of knowing.

need detailed case studies, narratives, field research, ethnography, historical and hermeneutic studies, phenomenological research, contemplative methods, and qualitative analysis.

Even if a social worker is not doing formal research, the evaluation of practice involves some kind of systematic questions, information gathering, and interpretation. Spiritually sensitive evaluation should emphasize the active involvement of clients and other research participants in the formation, conduct, and interpretation of the research design. The process and outcomes of research should directly and indirectly benefit participants and/or people who have similar issues. This approach to research is often called empowerment or participatory action research (Chesler, 1991; Lincoln, 1995; Rapp, Shera, & Kisthardt, 1993; Suarez-Balcazar & Harper, 2004).

Stage 5: Integrating

All stages and aspects of the helping process need to be integrated. Imbrogno and Canda (1988) placed system integrating at the center of the holistic helping model in order to symbolize that it must pervade and connect the other four functions of understanding, designing, implementing, and evaluating. Management and wisdom are the complementary aspects of integrating holistic social work activity. The integrating function is most closely connected with the administrative and executive levels within human service organizations. However, this does not mean that those involved with management are at the center of importance. Clients and consumers of services are at the center of importance. Management is at the functional center in order to bring the resources of the agency to bear for the benefit of clients and for the support of workers' well-being.

In conventional bureaucratic models of administration, the administrative function is located at the top of a pyramidal shaped organizational structure. There are fewer people at the top of the agency hierarchy, but they wield greater power in forming policy, making decisions, governing staff behavior, and distributing resources (Netting, Kettner, & McMurty, 1998). The executive administrator oversees all the operations of the organization in order to maintain order and integration of activities. If there is input from direct service staff and clients, the executive and administrators have predominant power and authority to decide what to do with this input.

The bureaucratic *management* model is designed to maximize efficiency by rational determination of goals and objectives. Staff behaviors are controlled to be in conformance with achievement of the goals. The danger of this model is that the power hierarchy may engender administrative exploitation of workers, remoteness of administrators from clients and direct service staff, and inflexibility of rules and roles. It does not emphasize the importance of I-Thou relations between all staff, clients, community, and nature. It does not attend to the human growth and fulfillment needs of its members. It neglects creativity in favor of conformity. When managers recognize that productivity and spiritual fulfillment are complementary, then spiritually sensitive administration is likely.

Spiritually sensitive practice is more likely to flourish in an organizational culture and structure that actively support creativity, flexibility, person-to-person respect, input from all stakeholders in decisions, human development needs, and well-being of the natural environment as well as organizational goal attainment needs. For example, interviews with 11 social workers in a variety of work settings found that that they felt it necessary to go around agency policies and procedures in order to meet client needs, especially pertaining to spirituality (Svare, Hylton, & Albers, 2007). When human service organizations (HSOs) fail to address spirituality explicitly in their organizational culture, time and energy may be wasted while workers circumvent or resist dehumanizing and distressing policies, procedures, and management behaviors.

Managers and leaders are in key positions to inspire and support spiritually sensitive HSO culture. In order to do so, they need to complement traditional management approaches with *wisdom*. As Imbrogno and Canda (1988) explained, the central position of an executive (or administrative level of an HSO) entails responsibility for the integrity of the service providing system as a whole through appraising and connecting the performance of professionals at all phases of activity in a constant creative development process of the service system in interaction with its environment. This brings administration back to the root meaning of "administer," which is "to serve."

Indeed, many empirical studies in business and human services demonstrate that effective organizations have leaders who promote well-being and empowerment for both workers and clientele by engaging spiritual qualities of meaning, purpose, sense of connectedness, integration of personal and work life, and inspiration by higher ideals or sense of divine purpose (Benefiel, 2005; Chamiec-Case & Sherr, 2005; Damianakis, 2006; Doe, 2004; Kinjerski & Skrypnek, 2008; Marques, Dhiman, & King, 2007; Mitroff & Denton, 1999; Moss, 2005; Svare, Hylton, & Albers, 2007). *Effective leaders* listen well to staff, regard them as coworkers rather than subordinates, encourage participatory decision-making with stakeholders inside and outside the organization, activate wide communication and collaboration, delegate to small groups for creative teamwork, maintain manageable workloads, provide flextime and opportunities for worker stress-management, support worker self-esteem, provide strengths-based evaluative feedback, seek wisdom and knowledge from consultants for implementing spiritually inclusive policies and practices, and ensure that organizational mission, objectives, and actual daily behaviors are congruent.

Organizations that have these qualities tend to experience greater profit, lower worker turnover, lower absenteeism, and higher employee satisfaction. The claim that humane management practices are too expensive is not borne out by evidence. Therefore, humane spiritually sensitive approaches to management are becoming more popular in business, challenging the traditional bureaucratic authoritarian style that places profit or material productivity over the well-being of employees, clientele, and the natural environment. These studies show that organizations that view the well-being of all stakeholders as having primary importance actually tend to be more successful. Damianakis (2006) described how workers in a small woman-centered agency felt that consciousness raising (in the sense of critiquing oppression) and transpersonal awareness of interconnectedness complement each other in affirming, respectful, and empowering relationships. Chamiec-Case and Sherr (2005) presented the views of Christian social work administrators who felt more fulfilled when they regarded their work and relations with staff and clients as an expression of God's will through loving, accepting service. This type of organizational culture is referred to in business as *spirituality in the workplace* or *soul at work*. In social work contexts, Doe (2004) referred to this approach as *spiritually based macropractice in human service organizations* and Aldridge, Macy and Walz (no date) developed a model named *humanocracy*. Marques et al. (2007, p. 89) said: "Spirituality in the workplace is an experience of interconnectedness among those involved in a work process; initiated by authenticity, reciprocity, and personal goodwill; engendered by a deep sense of meaning that is inherent in the organization's work; and resulting in greater motivation and organizational excellence."

Social work administrators can generate many innovations in organizational culture by converging insights from spirituality focused management approaches and expanding them with consideration of the transpersonal and nonhuman natural aspects of organizational life. Given that this is becoming more popular in the business sector, and that empirical studies support the effectiveness of spirituality in the workplace, it is curious why social work has been slow to pay attention to this. If we are to practice in a manner consistent with professional values (as well as good evidence), we should become active in the movement for spiritually sensitive administration in HSOs.

In our approach, the spiritually sensitive human service organization's (HSO) mission and its productivity goals should be designed to serve personal well-being and social justice primarily. Economic considerations of income and profit should be directed to maintaining services, subsidizing low income clients, and supporting staff. Policies, rules, and roles should not foster alienation or dissatisfaction among workers, clients, or the community. For example, if third party payers require use of DSM-IV diagnoses in a mental health setting, the diagnostic process should include client input and full consideration of the cultural and spiritual beliefs and experiences of the client.

Innovation should be the shared responsibility of all staff, with meaningful involvement of clients and other stakeholders. Administrators are in a special position to be aware of all the facets of the organization. Therefore, they can be especially valuable as facilitators of this innovation process. Table 7.2 lists principles for spiritually sensitive organizational culture with brief examples of innovations that would support them. Accompanying Table 7.3 adapts the principles from Table 7.2 as a rating instrument for assessing the degree of spiritual

Table 7.2. Principles and Activities for Spiritually Sensitive Human Service Organizational Culture.

General Structure and Functioning

Spiritually Attuned Mission, Goals, and Objectives. The mission of the HSO should reflect its primary values and service priorities, in the context of a vision for peace, well-being, and justice. If the HSO is religiously affiliated, the mission may reflect its particular religious beliefs and values. If it is not religiously affiliated, or if it prefers a broadly inclusive approach, the mission can address its spiritual commitments without use of religious language in a spiritually sensitive manner. The mission should also indicate respect for spiritual and cultural diversity of the HSO's clientele and community. The mission should link explicitly to spiritually sensitive goals, objectives, and specific organizational behaviors, including hiring policies and program designs.

Human scale. The size and complexity of the HSO should be limited to a scale in which all personnel can be familiar with each other personally and professionally. In large organizations, such as state human service systems, area offices and departments should reflect human scale; communication should flow smoothly between offices and departments.

Functional flexibility and integration. Staff should be prepared to be competent in multiple organizational tasks, so that they can cooperate and shift roles across specializations as needed. Responsibility for organizational goals should be shared between all administrative levels. Examples of activities are cross-training, job sharing, interdisciplinary teamwork, and shared worker/administrator ownership of the organization.

Rule flexibility. Agency policies, procedures, rules, and roles should be clear yet flexible. They exist to serve people; people do not exist to serve them. Staff, clients, and other stakeholder representatives are involved in the ongoing assessment and revision of all rules. Rules are adapted to fit unusual staff and client circumstances. Examples are procedures for revision and appeal of rules, client-centered procedures for assessment of their challenges and strengths, and periodic reviews of agency manuals.

Work environment aesthetics. The physical work environment should be designed in a way that promotes health and well-being. Staff and clients should be consulted to assess and design the work environment. Examples are ergonomic work stations, artwork, live plants, aquariums, personalized decoration of work spaces and photos of places and events fond to clients and staff, display of symbols that are significant and relevant to the spiritual perspectives of workers and clients, comfortable waiting rooms, and avoidance of overt or subtle cues that indicate religious or cultural biases that would offend or exclude staff and clientele.

Convivial technology. Technologies and information management systems should be simple to operate and repair for most staff or conveniently accessible consultants. They should be used to increase staff and client comfort and goal achievement. Technologies should be periodically evaluated with staff and client input. Examples are worker safety protocols for technology use, user-friendly copy machines and computers, ergonomic work stations, and multi-media technology that enhance the content and aesthetic quality of formal presentations, printed matter, and online resources.

Preparedness for spiritually sensitive practice. Policies, programs, and direct helping activities should address clients' spiritual needs and goals, if any, in a culturally appropriate manner within the context of their religious or nonreligious perspectives and community support systems. Practitioners are educated, supervised, and supported for including spirituality in assessment, implementation, and evaluation of services. Ethical guidelines and dilemmas are addressed systematically and explicitly.

(continued)

Table 7.2. Continued.

Meaningful Interconnectedness

Staff composition. Hiring and work task allocation should take into account the special talents and aspirations of workers and should reflect a match between the cultural and spiritual perspectives of clientele and the competencies of workers. For example, if there are many Muslim clients or members of the community in the service area, the agency should include workers who are respected members of the local Muslim community or who have training and comfort for working with Muslim clients and collaborating with Muslim community support systems.

Meritorious shared leadership. Formal leadership positions should be filled by people who have the respect of staff and leadership of the service area community. Staff should be meaningfully involved in selection of leaders. Staff could rotate through various leadership positions. Informal leadership, based on qualities of innovation, collaboration, and communication skills, should be recognized and rewarded officially. Leaders should have good communication and listening skills, inspire colleagues, and encourage their self-esteem. Examples are rotating directorships, rotating team leadership, and egalitarian collaborations and teamwork.

Participatory decision making. All people who will be impacted by a significant decision including staff, clients, and community members, should be included directly or indirectly in the decision-making process. Examples of activities are brainstorming, anonymous suggestion boxes, rewards for beneficial suggestions and critiques, surveys, inclusion of representatives from all levels of staff and clients and community on advisory and planning groups, and staff retreats for reflection on possible innovations. Decision-making meetings should be conducted in an atmosphere of trust, encouragement of risk-taking, and willingness to work through tensions or disagreements. Moments of meditation or quiet reflection can facilitate mindful and respectful interaction.

Spiritual diversity innovation planning group. A committee should be formed to focus on planning and implementation of spiritual diversity innovation on an ongoing basis. (See Chapter 9 for related recommendations.) This group encourages and monitors the ongoing spiritual innovation processes of the overall organization.

Interpersonal communication. All personnel in small agencies or in departments of large agencies should be able to communicate with each other directly and personally on a regular basis. If memos or email modes of communication are used, they should supplement and enhance personalized communication rather than replace it. Communication should emphasize respect, affirmation, honesty, enjoyment, and willingness to work through disagreements.

Holistic satisfaction of personnel aspirations. Aspirations for personal growth of staff should be ascertained so that programs can be designed to support them. Satisfaction of growth aspirations should be reflected in specific organizational objectives. Personnel should be regarded as whole persons with opportunities for making personal and work life situations complementary. Supervisory evaluations focus on identifying and building on strengths and self-esteem while striving for excellence in performance. Patterns of staff stress, burnout, absenteeism, and turnover should be tracked in order to develop preventive and responsive activities. Examples of supportive activities are creative and challenging work assignments that promote workers' professional development, flex time, on-site day care for children, stress management activities, subsidies for continuing education, medical insurance that covers preventive and holistic care, and places and times for quiet reflection and centering.

Climate among colleagues. Staff of all levels and specializations should relate with each other in a collaborative, respectful manner. Staff should appreciate each other for the value of particular roles and talents that complement each other for the good of the organization. Relations are not based on rigid hierarchy, condescension, coercive authoritarianism, or destructive competition.

Social and cultural environment rapport. The community environment of the HSO should be enhanced by all aspects of organizational activity. Professional and grass roots community leaders should be involved in program design and evaluation. Interagency and community-based networks and teams should be established through formal interagency agreements, task forces, and informal cooperative arrangements. Religious and nonreligious spiritual leaders, helpers, and healers should be included in service collaboration, as relevant to clients. Empowerment and justice principles relevant to the community should be demonstrated clearly in work objectives and behaviors.

Natural environment rapport. The natural environment of the HSO should be enhanced by all aspects of organizational activity. Damaging impacts should be identified and eliminated or minimized. Nurturing and inspiring human/nature connectedness should be evident within the HSO. Inspiring places of natural beauty should be included in programs for staff and clients as desired. Examples are energy efficient vehicles and lighting, car pooling and recycling programs, use of biodegradable materials for cleaning, safe disposal of toxic materials, developing neighborhood organic gardens, landscaping the grounds around the organization with organic methods, indoor placement of live plants or aquariums, opening window views and walking areas in the HSO location, client opportunities for pet therapy or wilderness therapy, and arranging staff and client visits to nature parks.

---

sensitivity in the organization. See also Chapter 10 for related recommendations on spiritual diversity innovation in HSOs.

We recommend that staff development meetings should be held periodically for open discussion about agency policies, procedures, and behaviors in relation to these qualities of spiritually sensitive HSO culture. Staff members at all levels (e.g. management, direct service workers, support staff), client representatives, community advisory board members, and any other stakeholders could complete this assessment form in an anonymous and confidential manner, or the form could be used as a basis for individual and focus group interviews. Information and suggestions gleaned from this study can inspire specific recommendations for HSO innovation.

Benefiel (2005) pointed out that this involves a long-term commitment to reflection, dialogue, planning, implementation, and review. Organizations sometimes are provoked into this type of self-reflection through crises, such as business failures or lawsuits. Even after setting out on this path, crises may challenge the organization again. Working through these crises can be a valuable process of transformation. Mitroff and Denton (1999) recommended that organizations should start with small, achievable changes and build on successes and proceed in a gentle, soft way that respects all spiritual vantage points, in order to avoid causing offense or being overwhelmed by the scale of challenge. They recommended ongoing spiritual audits of the organization. Organizations should expend as much energy in the process of integrating spirituality as they would dedicate to any other significant goal. They recommended that these audits be honest in identifying strengths on which to build and mistakes in principle and practice that should be discarded or corrected. Mitroff and Denton emphasized

Table 7.3.   Rating Form for Assessing Spiritual Sensitivity in Human Service
Organization Culture.

Instructions: Rate your organization for the level it meets on each quality criterion
(see Table 7.2 for explanation) on a scale of 0–5, from 0 [nonexistent] to 5 [excellent].
Think of your reasons for each rating and an example and write brief notes. Tally the
total score. In discussing your rating with colleagues, feel free to include musings or
disagreements regarding any of the criteria. Discuss your overall impression of the
organization's spiritual sensitivity. Identify at least one specific suggestion for innovation by building on the HSO's strengths or addressing its limitations.

General Structure and Functioning

1.	*Spiritually Attuned Mission, Goals, and Objectives.*	RATING (0–5)——
2.	*Human scale.*	RATING (0–5)——
3.	*Functional flexibility and integration.*	RATING (0–5)——
4.	*Rule flexibility.*	RATING (0–5)——
5.	*Work environment aesthetics.*	RATING (0–5)——
6.	*Convivial technology.*	RATING (0–5)——
7.	*Preparedness for spiritually sensitive practice.*	RATING (0–5)——

Meaningful Interconnectedness

8.	*Staff composition.*	RATING (0–5)——
9.	*Meritorious shared leadership.*	RATING (0–5)——
10.	*Participatory decision making.*	RATING (0–5)——
11.	*Spiritual diversity innovation planning group.*	RATING (0–5)——
12.	*Interpersonal communication.*	RATING (0–5)——
13.	*Holistic satisfaction of personnel aspirations.*	RATING (0–5)——
14.	*Climate among colleagues.*	RATING (0–5)——
15.	*Social and cultural environment rapport.*	RATING (0–5)——
16.	*Natural environment rapport.*	RATING (0–5)——

TOTAL SCORE (0–80)——

NOTES ON RATINGS AND OVERALL IMPRESSIONS:

RECOMMENDATION FOR ONE INNOVATION, WITH SPECIFIC ACTION PLAN:

that spiritually oriented organizations take into account both short-term mutual
benefits of all stakeholders and long-term implications for future generations.

Conclusion

In this chapter, we presented an overall revisioning of the helping relationship and
its organizational context. We drew from insights of many spiritual perspectives

and empirical studies as well as humanistic and transpersonal approaches to human service and organizational behavior. We emphasized that spiritually sensitive practice is not just a matter of including religious or spiritual topics in social work activity. Spiritually sensitive practice is a whole way of being and relating within all aspects, stages, and environments of helping. Our suggestions here open many possibilities for innovation, but they are a small beginning. We hope that they encourage readers to examine themselves and their service settings in order to find creative ways of enhancing their practice.

In the following chapter, we will consider spiritually sensitive ways to understand and support human development through clinical practice.

EXERCISES

7.1. Linking Self-Understanding to Practice with Clients

This chapter includes many exercises in the body of the text designed to help you link self-understanding to practice with clients. We suggest that you choose one to carry out. We list them here. Return to the text for explanation about how to do the exercises.

A. Journaling about a practice situation.
B. Experiencing the client with a fresh mind.
C. Dissolving inner chatter.
D. Developing an introduction on inclusivity for groupwork.
E. Asking for an intuitive insight.
F. Brainstorming.

7.2. Planning for Innovation in the Context of Practice

Each table and figure listed here depicts ideals, principles, guidelines, or suggestions for creating a spiritually sensitive context for practice. We suggest that you review each table and figure and reread the relevant section of text. Make a commitment to one significant innovation and then write out a plan for how you can accomplish it in your practice. The plan should include your objective for enhancing practice, a specific course of action, and a timeline for implementing the activity.

A. Making win/win solutions (Table 7.1).
B. Organizing social work activity in a holistic system (Figure 7.1).
C. Synergizing different ways of knowing (Figure 7.2).

Write out a plan for how you can accomplish this in your practice. The plan should include your objective for enhancing practice, a specific course of action, and a time line for implementing the activity. After you have completed the activity, evaluate the impact on yourself, the clients, colleagues, and any relevant stakeholders. Then refine further use of the activity based on this evaluation. Continue this process.

7.3. Assessing Spiritual Sensitivity of Organizational Culture

Use Table 7.3 as a tool for rating the spiritual sensitivity of your human service organizational culture.

Quick Version. Complete the rating instrument yourself. For each principle, write a brief explanation of why you rated the organization this way and give an example. Then identify one way to begin enhancing the organization's spiritual sensitivity. State your plan in clear action steps. This could serve as the basis for more extensive innovation.

Ongoing Spiritual Auditing and Innovation. Conduct a staff in-service training session to begin group thinking about innovation in organizational culture. Ask each person to complete the rating instrument after you explain the meaning of each principle. The total possible score is 80 points. Ask for volunteers to explain why they gave their ratings, asking for examples. Note the overall range of scores (minimum to maximum) and invite participants to discuss why they rated the organization differently. As discussion proceeds, help the group reflect on emerging consensus or areas of disagreement. Identify specific suggestions for enhancing spiritual sensitivity for each principle. Explore the level of interest for the agency to commit to an ongoing process of spiritual auditing and innovation. If there is interest, see Chapter 9 for more suggestions about creating an ongoing planning and innovation process through transcultural teamwork.

8

Understanding and Assessing Spiritual Development

Wake up!
It is time to wake up!

The Dhammapada, Buddhism
(trans. Lal, 1967, p. 134)

The conceptual models of spirituality formed in Chapter 3 suggest two major ways of thinking about human development. First, when we think of spirituality as an aspect of the person that strives for a sense of meaning, purpose, connection, and transcendence, our attention focuses on the way people develop meaning through immersion in spiritual groups and belief systems and through questioning of meaning systems due to personal doubts and life challenges, such as crises.

Second, when we think of spirituality as the wholeness of what it is to be human, our attention focuses on how people develop toward a sense of integration and integrity between all aspects of themselves (bio-psycho-social-spiritual) and in relation with other beings and the universe. For people who believe in a divine ultimate reality, this actualization of wholeness is seen as an accomplishment of communion between oneself, others, and the divine.

These two ways of thinking about human development are closely related. The existential quest for meaning can motivate a person toward actualization of wholeness and communion. Thus, the existential quest can lead us into the transpersonal realm. Among those who believe in a divine plan or transcendent goal for human existence, some would say that God, spiritual beings, or our true self, of which the ego is yet latently aware, can reach out to us, reveal truths to us, and call us onward toward integrity and wholeness.

These two developmental metaphors have been discussed widely by humanistic and transpersonal developmentalists (Robbins, Chatterjee, & Canda, 2006). The first is the metaphor of innate human potential. In this metaphor, the potential for spiritual unfoldment is like a seed with which we are born. When environmental conditions are sufficiently supportive and nurturing, the seed of spirituality sprouts and grows. Our innate drives for meaning, purpose, and loving relationships express as we grow throughout the life span. Eventually, we might form a clearly integrated individual self and move beyond it into transpersonal awareness.

The second developmental metaphor is that of striving toward perfection or a spiritual ideal. The person is like a green plant that naturally orients itself toward light and grows to reach it. As the plant encounters light, it receives energy from above that sustains and replenishes it. In this metaphor, the ideal of wholeness, encompassing personal integrity and universal communion, is like the sun to which we are drawn. For people who believe in divine beings, a cosmic order, or a Supreme Being, they may feel that they are called toward perfection and wholeness to rise up out of their ego-limited self into transpersonal awareness. In theistic and animistic belief systems, this spiritual calling (vocation) may be initiated by sacred powers, including nonhuman or nonphysical beings, such as spirits, angels, deities, or a Supreme Being.

Both of these metaphors are related. The earth nurtures the seed of our spiritual potential, allowing it to sprout and grow, but rain and light from the sky are also necessary to feed and draw forth that growth. The first metaphor emphasizes that innate and immanent qualities of spirituality require nurturance by a supportive environment. The second metaphor emphasizes ideals and transcendent qualities of spirituality that draw forth human potential. It emphasizes the importance of the social, natural, and transpersonal environment not only as a support, but also as a catalyst and even initiator of developmental breakthroughs.

This chapter explores these themes of individual spiritual development. First, we consider how spiritual development relates to everyday life. Second, we discuss types of developmental phases and events, including gradual growth and sudden transformational breakthroughs. Third, we relate these to life span developmental theories. Then we provide assessment practices that can help clients to reflect on their spiritual development and to discern the difference and relationship between growthful spiritual experiences and psychopathology.

Spiritual Development and Everyday Life

In Canda's (1988b, 1988c, 1990c) study of social work educators' views of spirituality, participants often emphasized that spirituality should be understood in relation to everyday life, including the ordinary events and circumstances of our personal lives and our professional work with clients. As Zen and existentialism emphasize, people enhance the quality of their lives when they pay attention to the preciousness of each moment day to day. Of course, there may be occasions of powerful insights, spiritual crises, and breakthroughs. There may be experiences of trances, visions, and revelations. People may feel powerfully moved by sacred powers and divine beings. Yet these extraordinary events and realities must be integrated into ordinary everyday life, or they disappear like a flash in the pan.

Social workers have a mandate for practical action. We recognize that spiritual development is an ongoing process, day to day, night to night. The nitty gritty tasks of obtaining food and shelter, washing the dishes, and raising children are the spiritual ground upon which we walk during our spiritual journeys. To borrow Maslow's (1968, 1969) concept of the hierarchy of needs, the satisfaction of subsistence, security, and self-esteem needs is the basis for the emergence of loving connections with others, creativity, and transpersonal experience.

Unfortunately, Maslow's idea is too often used superficially to imply that spiritual development only starts after all these so-called lower needs are satisfied. Maslow's point was that when a person's energy and attention are preoccupied with survival needs and fending off dangers or threats, it is natural that there will be less energy and time available for artistic and mystical pursuits. So when a homeless client states that her present goal is to find a shelter from the winter cold, then that is the appropriate point to help. By starting where the client is, by joining with the client's present concern, we are already being spiritually sensitive. We are acknowledging the significance of her priorities and the preciousness of who she is just at this moment. Indeed, by relating with her in terms of her own aspirations, we create an opportunity for a profound connection and reflection. In pursing shelter, the client is already on the path of spiritual development. When the shelter for homeless people reflects a humane, caring, and uplifting physical appearance and social climate, the provision of the shelter service nurtures the spiritual potential of the residents and staff.

It is often the times of greatest deprivation and oppression that call forth a response of creativity, discovery of meaning, and sense of divine support. As Victor Frankl, the founder of logotherapy (therapy of meaning) pointed out, when people get in touch with an inner source of spiritual support and hold dear the sense of their own and others' integrity, they may find surprising sustenance and resiliency in the face of tragedy (Frankl, 1969; Lantz, 1993). For example, during the period of slavery, African American anti slavery abolitionists drew on Christian hymns, both to glorify God and to proclaim their secret hopes and strategies for winning freedom (Harding, 1990). The underground railroad was not made of rails, but rather of prayer, song, risk, courage, mutual support, sacrifice, and tremendous effort.

When we realize that spirituality encompasses the wholeness of what it is to be human, we become aware of the precious and wonderful nature of every moment and interaction. There is a Zen expression that Zen mind is simply: "When hungry, eat; when sleepy, sleep." This does not mean that habitual, mindless routines and actions promote spiritual growth. Rather, the simplest act, when done with mindful awareness, is an occasion for realizing the amazing and mysterious quality of the moment (Welwood, 1992). Every day, as we work, play, love, become sick, heal, flame in anger, speak words of forgiveness, or go through the process of dying, we can be moving along a spiritual journey toward meaning and wholeness if we realize what we are doing.

Spiritual development is not one aspect of life. Rather, spiritual development *is* everyday life. By calling human development *spiritual*, we are calling attention to the potential for deep meaning and realization of wholeness inherent in human life. When we wake up to this potential, and dedicate ourselves to actualizing it, then our lives become explicitly spiritual in orientation.

In 1976, while I (EC) waded in gentle waves lapping on the shore of the East Sea of South Korea, I had an experience that made this point unforgettable. Suddenly, a tall wave came rushing in. It knocked me down into the water and an undertow pulled me out to the deep. I am not a good swimmer, but I strove to keep my head above water. Each time I surfaced, another wave washed me under. I could not find my way to the shore. This bobbing and submerging continued for what seemed an endless time. I felt that I was being swallowed into a pitiless void to die before my proper time.

Finally, my cries for help brought a Korean friend to my aid. He tried to take my arms around his neck and swim us both back to shore, but the crushing waves overcame us, so he had to release me back into the water to save himself and to look for rescue on the beach. My hopeless bobbing continued. To my amazement, my mind and body shifted into a state of strength and endurance that seemed impossible. An inexplicable energy filled me. Everything in the universe collapsed into each intense moment, no hope for the future, no help from the past. Finally, a Korean soldier who was stationed on the beach responded to my friend's summons and rushed to me with an inflated inner tube. He swam me back to the beach, pushed the water out of my lungs and stomach, and put me to rest in his encampment.

I lay on a cot, acutely aware of the miracle of my survival. All my senses were heightened. The sounds of the soldiers talking about me, the radio music playing in the background, the shining sunlight—all struck me as absolutely amazing, precious, and wonderful. In contrast to the pitiless void from which I had been rescued, each simple moment of life was brilliant and fantastic. A soldier asked me, with a humorous tone of voice, "How does it feel to come back from hell?" I said, "Wonderful!"

About a week later, I was rushed to a hospital in Seoul, due to an attack of acute pancreatitis, which is an excruciating abdominal disorder that may have been triggered by the physical trauma of drowning and life saving efforts. When I came out of the hospital about a week later, again I was amazed at the glory of life.

Almost exactly 22 years later, a Korean colleague kindly brought me back to that place for a rapprochement. I squatted on the beach just out of water's reach, looked over the ocean, and contemplated. I put out my hand as if coaxing the waves to approach near enough for me to touch them fondly. I thanked God and the ocean for that near death lesson about the wonder of life. I gave thanks for the 22 years I lived since then and renewed my commitment to use my remaining life in the way I feel called. I gave thanks for my wife, the friend and stranger who helped rescue me, and all the tiny and major events of my life that would not have happened if I had succumbed in 1976.

This experience showed me was how each moment—whether dramatic or boring, whether intense or gentle—is amazing and precious. The gentle lapping of the waves; the drowning and rescue; the feeling of pitiless void; the mysterious life sustaining energy; the medical crisis; the care and love I received from friends and strangers; the recovery and return to ordinary life; every subsequent moment of 22 years—all were amazing.

I recount this experience to remind you of any experiences you may have had that woke you up to the wonder of the ordinary. If you have not had such an experience, we hope that you can wake up to how wonderful each moment is without going through some catastrophe. This bright awareness can guide practitioners in work with clients as they flow through the moments of their lives.

Spiritual Emergence and Emergencies

Stanislav and Christina Grof coined the term *spiritual emergence* to refer to the developmental process in which people learn to orient themselves to their daily lives with clarity and appreciation, to work out a sense of authentic meaning and purpose and relationship with other people and the world, and to open up to transpersonal awareness (Bragdon, 1990; Grof & Grof, 1989, 1990; Watson, 1994). As Robbins et al. (2006, p. 398) summarized, "*Spiritual emergence* is an experience of relatively gradual, but progressive expansion of a sense of wellness, freedom, responsibility, and connection with the cosmos. The related experiences and insights are rather easy to integrate into ordinary life." Of course, there are many twists and turns, steps forward and back, and leaps and falls on this journey of spiritual emergence, but the overall trend is toward meaning, wholeness, and communion.

Although spiritual emergence is usually a relatively gradual process, there are variations of intensity during various developmental phases and transpersonal experiences. Spiritual awakenings sometimes occur to us in the most mundane and ordinary circumstances and through gradual unfolding of spiritual potential. Maslow (1970) described the *plateau experience* as a sense of profound yet gentle happiness and enjoyment that elevates our awareness of the moment beyond the taken-for-granted. He gave the example of a mother who watches her baby playing and marvels at the preciousness and loveliness of this young life.

In general, people who say that they have a general sense of spiritual well-being report a preponderance of positive feelings, such as joy, peace, love, self-esteem, and rapport with other people, nature, and God or other spiritual beings and forces, as well as the ability to work through serious life challenges with resilience (Canda, in press). On the other hand, *spiritual distress* comes in many forms. For example, after a parent or significant other dies, some children develop serious anxiety about death and troubling spiritual questions about the fragility of life and possibilities of an afterlife (Crompton, 1998). Children's excessive anxiety, shame, and guilt can be provoked by parents and religious authorities who convey punitive, threatening, or blaming ideas about God or other supernatural powers. These kinds of patterns can persist into adulthood and emerge in adult therapeutic settings. Young adults might experience spiritual distress when they encounter challenges to their received spiritual teachings from peers, from widening formal education, and meeting people from outside their communities of childhood (Roehlkepartain, King, Wagener, & Benson, 2006). Adults who develop strong questions about their spiritual beliefs, consider converting to a different faith, or who become life partners with a person of a different spiritual perspective or style can experience distress while working this through. Older adults and people with serious illnesses may experience spiritual distress as they come to terms with mortality and dying (Moberg, 2001; Nelson-Becker, Nakashima, & Canda, 2006). These periods of spiritual distress can, when addressed as opportunities for growth, become gateways into enhanced life and well-being in the midst of dying.

Sometimes we experience startling breakthroughs that are exhilarating and enjoyable, as in periods of unusually fluid creativity, especially profound loving connections with other people, or meditative experiences of expanded consciousness. When we are able to integrate these experiences relatively easily, then our spiritual growth accelerates without any sense of crisis. But sometimes the intensity is overwhelming. Our life's status quo may be severely disrupted. We may feel lost, disoriented, or panicked. When spiritual development becomes a crisis, the Grofs refer to it as a *spiritual emergency* (Bragdon, 1990; Grof & Grof, 1990; Watson, 1994). They explain:

> When spiritual emergence is very rapid and dramatic, however, this natural process can become a crisis, and spiritual emergence becomes spiritual emergency. People who are in such a crisis are bombarded with inner experiences that abruptly challenge their old beliefs and ways of existing, and their relationship with reality shifts very rapidly. Suddenly they feel uncomfortable in the formerly familiar world and may find it difficult to meet the demands of everyday life. They can have great problems distinguishing their inner visionary world from the external world of daily reality. Physically, they may experience forceful energies streaming through their bodies and causing uncontrollable tremors. (Grof & Grof, 1990, p. 35)

Like any crisis, a spiritual emergency is fraught with both danger and opportunity. The danger is that the person may feel destroyed. But the opportunity is that the person's de-structuring can open the possibility of reconstructing a new, more fulfilling way of living. Ego shattering opens the way to ego-transcendence. Spiritual emergency, when successfully resolved, propels us rather suddenly into transpersonal realms of experience.

Grof (1988) contrasted two modes of consciousness that help to clarify this process. The first mode is called *hylotropic*. This term literally means "moving toward matter." It characterizes typical ordinary waking states of consciousness in which awareness of reality is limited to input through physical senses, physical boundaries of the environment and body, and three dimensions of time and space. This mode characterizes the typical mental orientation of egoic development.

The second mode of consciousness is called *holotropic*. This term literally means "moving toward wholeness." This mode involves transegoic experiences that become more common and typical as a person's spiritual emergence moves into the transpersonal levels. We will discuss the transpersonal levels of development in more detail later in this chapter. For now, it is important to note that spiritual emergencies involve sudden openings to transpersonal experiences that can be a shock to the ego and to one's significant others. The person's sense of identity and reality, and his or her usual strategies for living and relating, may be thrown into doubt and confusion. Gradual emergence of transpersonal awareness allows for a smoother transition to new ways of experiencing and relating with the world while spiritual emergencies may temporarily overwhelm us with a flood of mind-blowing insights, visions, sensations, and feelings.

Table 8.1 lists examples of various transpersonal experiences (Faiver, Ingersoll, O'Brien, & McNally, 2001; Fontana, 2003; Grof, 1988; Marquis, 2008; Yang, Lukoff, & Lu, 2006). These can be considered transpersonal in that they involve surpassing the ordinary limits of the body/ego and ordinary sense of time, space, and causality. However, as Wilber (2000b, 2006) often points out, delusions, hallucinations, or preegoic fantasies might be confused with these. Although most of these transpersonal experiences might appear to be positive (e.g. experiencing profound joy), there can be distressing, frightening, confusing, and painful versions. For example, in most traditional religions and cultures, people believe in harmful spirit beings, magical attack, and other damaging transpersonal forces.

Maslow (1968, 1970) made a useful distinction between two types of spiritual breakthrough events. The *peak experience* is an intense life-changing event that propels a person into a profound sense of communion with oneself, other people, the universe, or divinity. A peak experience loosens or dissolves the limiting ego-boundary, opening the person to transpersonal awareness and experiences. For example, quite literally, a mountain hiker might suddenly come out from a forest onto a peak and look out to an expansive valley far below. Standing poised between heaven and earth, looking out to the vastness, the hiker might feel swept away with awe at the beauty and magnitude all around. He might feel suddenly at one and at peace with the universe. After such an experience, one's perspective on life can never be the same.

A peak experience is a sudden developmental breakthrough, but it does not necessarily lead to a sense of emergency. Although the emotional valence of the peak experience is positive, it may be so intense and contrary to expectations

Table 8.1. Examples of Transpersonal Experiences.

- Expanded consciousness
- Profound and intense experiences of peace, joy, or love
- Sense of timelessness and spacelessness
- Identification or merging with other people
- Communication with plants, animals, and other beings of nature
- Communication with spirits of ancestors, deceased loved ones, and spirit powers associated with nature
- Communication with deities, angels, saints, and spirit guides
- Communication with God or awareness of God's presence and grace
- "Gifts of the Spirit" such as speaking in tongues
- Oneness with the universe or ultimate reality
- Remembrance of past incarnations
- Remembrance of planetary or cosmic evolution
- Awareness of subtle energies, such as qi or kundalini
- Experiences of influence by magic, ritual, prayer, or other nonphysical or supramundane interventions
- Out of body travel
- Insight into universal symbolic meanings (archetypes)
- Extrasensory perceptions such as precognition, telepathy, and telekinesis
- Near death experiences
- Experience of the sacredness of daily life

that one's sense of self and reality is shattered. Then it becomes a spiritual emergency.

There is also the spiritual breakthrough event that Maslow called the *nadir experience*. This is an intense life-changing event that plunges one into a pit of confusion, despair or grief. If a loved one has died, one's very sense of self, formerly closely connected with this person, could be shattered. The bereaved may feel lost and hopeless. He or she may feel bewildered that a supposedly loving God could allow such a thing to happen. Like Job in the Bible story, one's sense of reality and rightness may be dashed in a way that seems incomprehensible and unjustifiable. But when a person is able to work out of this pit, one becomes able to reorient self and relationships and to understand the meaning of life and connection to the sacred in a more realistic, resilient, and profound manner. This is the existentialist path of confronting the absurdity of life in order to come to an authentic and more fulfilling sense of meaning.

This is the kind of pivotal experience that I (LF) experienced when my husband Phil, was dying of cancer. It was inconceivable that my husband, an ENT (ears, nose, and throat) specialist who had surgically removed cancers from others, now had an inoperable cancer himself. What happens when the silver bullet of modern medical technology no longer provides the cure?

For Phil, it was not his renaissance intelligence that gave him courage or his material estate that consoled him. What sustained him was his unwillingness to give up hope that a cure would be found at the same time as he accepted the inevitability of his death. The operant factor in this dual perspective was his discovery of a profound faith in a very personal God who could empower him in his own physical and spiritual vulnerability. Phil's deep faith through this experience was a personal gift to all of us, especially to me. Death or the threat of death has been called the decisive teacher because it goads us into appreciating what we have or what we can do. We can create our own opportunities from the same raw materials from which other people create their defeats.

Initially I felt that I could not face the inevitable. I remember one evening I was feeling angry that I had been given this bitter slice of life. Why was this happening to me? Why was my husband dying, and how could I possibly live without him? I did not have the strength to face the future—the terrifying short term or the lonely long term. That moment of utter despair was the definitive moment in my life. The reality of death was present there in our home, in our very bedroom. But somehow, looking at Phil and seeing his incredible calmness, I was able to enter into his dying experience. In a certain way, his cancer and his response reached into my psyche and my soul and stimulated them to growth.

I realized that what I needed was to return to the foundations of my youth, my religious and spiritual heritage. I needed to seek guidance in the Christian Holy Scriptures and to find empowerment in personal and communal prayer. I also knew that I needed the support of other human beings. Phil and I would go through this experience together, but we needed guidance, and so we sought pastoral counseling. I realized that grief issues would be most important for us to process. I would be saying goodbye to a marriage of 25 years and preparing to be without him. Phil was saying good-bye to his family he loved so well and to his medical practice. We both needed help transitioning from the known to the unknown.

Phil's illness had a profound impact on our marriage. Before his diagnosis, our marriage and love for each other was like most other long-term marriages— anything but perfect. There were times when we misunderstood each other, were insensitive to each others' needs, or demanded too much of each other. During our first 23 years together, I realized that I did not know Phil very well. He was busy with his career and I with mine and the raising of our sons. Marital quid pro quo (you do for me, and I'll do for you) was also prevalent in our marriage, as it is in most other marriages. During the last years of Phil's life, this type of thinking totally stopped. Through Phil's spiritual journey, he began to open up to me and share his innermost feelings—his greatest joys and his deepest fears. I really got to know him, and I fell in love with this wonderful, brilliant man all over again.

During those last years, our marriage had no visible quid pro quo. I was the primary caregiver for Phil because I loved him, expecting nothing in return. But Phil and his illness gave me psychological and emotional maturity. I experienced a total acceptance of my husband, including the breakdown of his body and all of its functions. In most relationships, it is easier to live in a fantasy of how we wish the other person to be or how we think she or he is. These images may be more positive or more negative than the person really is. They do not identify the person in reality. As Phil lay dying, there was no room for an inaccurate image of him. I saw the plain truth of his deteriorating body, the shutdown of his intellectual mind, and his inevitable death.

On the day of Phil's funeral, I realized how far I had come up out of the pit of confusion and despair. Phil's example, his courage, honest intimacy with his death, and my religious faith had worked a profound change in me. This crisis tapped a source of spiritual support within me and revealed the integrity of Phil's life and his most dignified death.

It is never really possible to predict how we will react in a crisis. As in combat, it is often unknown who will have the courage to stay and fight. I am thankful that I chose to stay and fight because Phil's illness and his courageous response to his inevitable death presented me with enduring gifts. I have no feelings of guilt for not doing enough; I did all I could. Not only am I no longer afraid of death, I am no longer afraid of life. I have a fearlessness to tackle almost anything.

The unconditional acceptance of my husband as he lay dying carried over into other areas of my life. As I examined what was most important in my own particular beliefs and spiritual practices and as I began to put them to work through the events of my husband's illness and death, I was allowed to get out of my own frame of reference and learn to see other people from their own perspectives. This has resulted in taking a less critical stance toward those whose worldviews are considerably different from mine. I have learned to be less judgmental and am cultivating more empathy and understanding. Most important, I have moved away from being dependent on what others think and being concerned with conformity towards an independence of spirit and a recognition of my own individuality. The myth of my not being strong enough was peeled away by this experience. However, as much as I value my independence and solitude now, I still recognize a need for others in my life. Without interpersonal connections, I would not have been able to grow throughout this life crisis nor would I be able to continue to discover more about myself, deepen my personal experience with God, and find ways to be of service within my community. For me, spirituality has become an intimate communication with God and others.

The experience of the death of my husband from cancer motivated me to explore the importance of religion and spirituality during a life crisis from a professional and ethical position in both my teaching and international research. In reflecting back over the years, I realize that for those who have experienced and adjusted to the death of a loved one, positive life changes can result from the event even though it has caused them great suffering.

Yet Maslow emphasized that the peak and pit types of experiences do not necessarily result in an enhancement of life. We could try to deny the revelation or forget the insight. In so far as we are dramatically changed by these experiences, our customary patterns of relationships with other people will be challenged as well. In order to fit back into our psychosocial status quo, we might try to deny and hide our profound experiences and insights. Our loved ones, and helping professionals, might brand our spiritual emergency as a form of pathology to be squelched by therapy and medications. Sometimes, even our spiritual or religious support groups oppose us for daring to have insights, revelations, visions, or communications with the divine that go outside the constraints of their regulated beliefs. So integration of our transpersonal experiences into our ordinary lives may pose a challenge to our social environment.

On the other hand, some people become spiritual thrill seekers. They become so enamored of the intense highs or lows of peak and pit experiences that they seek to repeat them on demand. In this case, ordinary life and relationships may be discarded in order to chase after the next transpersonal thrill. In some cases, this leads to abuse of drugs and self-damaging extremes of spiritual disciplines. This approach can eventually lead to addiction or burnout. If the spiritual insights are not integrated into ordinary life, they are merely fireworks displays at night that wink out and leave only the darkness.

Even if a person is conscientious in the pursuit of spiritual growth, or does not seek it at all, sometimes a spiritual emergency comes with such suddenness and overwhelming force that it is impossible to cope with it or integrate it personally or socially. Spiritual emergency in the form of a debilitating crisis imposes a serious risk for physical illness, psychopathology, and social disruption. According to some belief systems, such as shamanism, nonphysical entities might disrupt our bodies and minds for the purpose of calling us into a new way of life. Although this presents a great opportunity for growth, it can also be a frightening and dangerous process.

When we are able to integrate transpersonal insights into our ongoing daily life, we grow to an enhanced level of functioning and fulfillment. Maslow referred to this as another kind of *plateau experience*. This is a way of being that is oriented toward compassion, beauty, wisdom, responsibility, creativity, and profundity (Maslow, 1970). This is a developmental ideal and a major goal of spiritually sensitive practice. In other words, we can support people not only to recover from crises (restore the status quo), we can also support them to learn and grow through the process.

Spiritual Emergence throughout the Life Cycle

Spiritual emergence occurs in the context of our growth through the life cycle, from birth to death, and possibly beyond. Therefore, in this section we will draw on three life cycle theories that shed light on the relation between spiritual emergence and stages of the life cycle: Erik Erikson's (1962, 1963, 1968, 1969, 1982) psychosocial development theory, James Fowler's (1981, 1996, 2000) cognitive-structural faith development theory, and Ken Wilber's (1995, 1996, 1998; 2000a, 2000b, 2006) integral model of development. Although there are many spiritual development theories, these three provide helpful examples of different approaches. For our purpose, it is not necessary to reiterate the details of each stage in their theories. We are more concerned with their insights about the overall flow and dynamics of spiritual development through the life cycle. However, for the reader's convenience we include Table 8.2, which summarizes the names, stages, and major themes for each of these theorists by drawing on

Table 8.2. Qualities of Spiritual Development Emerging Through the Life Cycle in Three Stage Theories.

Usual Age of Emergence (if at all)	Erikson: Ego Challenge Stage and Virtue	Fowler: Faith Stage and Quality	Wilber: Consciousness Stage and Quality
Older Adulthood	Ego Integrity vs. Despair: Wisdom	Universalizing Faith: Nonjudgmental, Transcendent, Inclusive View	Nondual: Union of Ultimate and Ordinary
			Causal: Formlessness, No Separation
			Subtle: Communion with Divinity
			Psychic: Communion with World
Middle Adulthood	Generativity vs. Stagnation: Care	Conjunctive Faith: Complex and Pluralistic View	
			Vision Logic: Holistic Inclusivity
Early Adulthood	Intimacy vs. Isolation: Love	Individuative-Reflective Faith: Critical Reflection	
			Formal Operational: Sophisticated Rationality
Adolescence	Ego Identity vs. Role Confusion: Fidelity	Synthetic-Conventional Faith: Personalized Peer Referenced Beliefs	Concrete Operational: Autonomous But Conformist Perspective
Older Childhood	Industry vs. Inferiority: Competence	Mythic-Literal Faith: Loyalty to Community Beliefs	
Middle Childhood	Initiative vs. Guilt: Purpose		Late Preoperational: Symbolic Representational Thinking
Early Childhood	Autonomy vs. Shame, Doubt: Will Power	Intuitive-Projective Faith: Creative Fantasy	Preoperational: Fantasy-Emotional Centeredness
Infancy	Trust vs. Mistrust: Hope	Primal Faith: Trust in the Universe & Divinity	Sensori-physical: Body-Oriented Awareness

these sources. For further information, see the human behavior theory textbook by Robbins et al. (2006) and the sources cited here.

Erikson's View of Spiritual Development

Erikson's psychosocial development theory is based on an *epigenetic perspective* that views development as a process of psychosocial responses to age related changes in the body (i.e. physical maturation) and socially defined transitions (e.g. marriage or retirement) that occur in sequential stages. Epigenesis means that each stage presents particular tasks, opportunities, and challenges. Development at each stage builds upon the accomplishments of the prior stages. As the person responds to these challenges successfully, he or she accrues coping skills, ego strengths, and social resources. When these challenges are not met successfully, due to inadequate coping or lack of support from the social environment, the person fails to learn effective coping patterns and carries on the burden of unresolved issues.

Erikson's theory reminds us to be aware of relatively predictable age related challenges that may affect spiritual emergence, as determined by physical changes and socially programmed transitions. For example, the adolescent, according to Erikson, typically is dealing with the challenge of forming a clear sense of personal identity in relation to socially available roles, increasing emotional ties to peers outside the family of origin, and exploration of budding sexuality. Therefore it is expectable that many adolescents will be dealing with spiritual challenges pertaining to reevaluation of family-based religious beliefs and practices. Also, in so far as a society demarcates significant life cycle transition points, such as birth, marriage, child birth, retirement, and death, it is expectable that people will have a heightened sense of preoccupation with existential issues of meaning and purpose, as well as practical behavioral responses determined by spiritual and religious reference groups, such as rituals. When a person experiences a lack of guidance from spiritual support systems at important life cycle transition points, it is expectable that the person will have greater difficulty meeting the challenge. However, when a person has accrued a wide repertoire of internal strengths (which Erikson called virtues) and skills in utilizing external spiritual support systems, then we can expect greater creativity, sense of positive self-esteem, and resiliency in confronting crises, including spiritual emergencies.

Erikson suggested that people in late adulthood (after age 50) often review their lives with increased interest and concern as the facts of mortality and physical decline become more evident. He believed that most people have a heightened sense of spiritual concern at this stage, because there is greater urgency to establish a sense that one's life has been meaningful and worthwhile. Questions about the nature of death and the possibility of an after-death existence naturally increase. The wise elder moving toward to end of life incorporates and reworks insights gleaned from earlier stages of life, so that basic trust of infancy becomes appreciation of human interdependence, learning control over the body in stage two replicates as bodily deterioration in old age occurs, childlike playfulness manifests as good humor, sense of life accomplishments is balanced with humility, complexity of life is more appreciated, love and empathy become more deep, and the sense of wholeness of personhood transcends physical deterioration (Robbins et al., 2006).

Erikson also suggested that some people have a precocious and unusually strong interest in spiritual matters throughout life. Even in childhood, such a person focuses on questions about the meaning and purpose of human life. He presented Martin Luther and Mohandas Gandhi as examples of such extraordinary people, and referred to them with the Latin term *homo religiosus*, which means "the religious person" (Erikson, 1962, 1969). In adulthood, the *homo religiosus* extends the sense of responsibility to connection with other people beyond family and one's own society to all humanity and even the entire cosmos. Such personalities are more likely to experience peak and pit experiences at early ages and throughout the life cycle. Their approach to life overall is to integrate these insights into ever increasing levels of spiritual plateaus. They are more likely to build on unfolding psychosocial virtues to develop an overall way of living committed to joining personal edification with benefit for others. Therefore, they often have an unusually high degree of facility with both inner self-reflection (wisdom) and humane relations with others (compassion) leading to effective action (service).

James Fowler's Faith Development Theory

Fowler is a Christian theologian and developmental theorist who built on the structural-cognitive perspective of Piaget and Kohlberg in addition to psychosocial theory. In the cognitive-structural perspective, development reflects the process of learning increasingly sophisticated and comprehensive ways of mentally comprehending the world. Stages of development represent levels of cognitive complexity achieved, rather than age determined tasks.

Fowler's theory focuses on the formation and transformation of faith throughout the life cycle. As we mentioned in Chapter 3, by *faith*, Fowler meant, "the pattern of our relatedness to self, others, and our world in light of our relatedness to ultimacy" (1996, p. 21). "Ultimacy" refers to that which a person gives a sense of first importance and greatest profundity in orienting his or her life with fundamental values, beliefs, and meanings. Just as we have defined spirituality, faith may take religious or nonreligious forms. Fowler depicted faith as a universal aspect of human nature that gives coherence and meaning to life, connects individuals together in shared concerns, relates people to a larger cosmic frame of reference, and enables us to deal with suffering and mortality. As Robbins et al. (2006) summarized, "A *stage of faith* is a pervasive pattern of knowing and valuing that orients us to ourselves, the world, and ultimacy. Transition through stages is affected by challenges to the prevailing faith orientation that require more complex, sophisticated, and comprehensive understandings" (pp. 281–282). Challenges may appear from physiological changes, such as maturation or injury, significant changes and losses in the environment, and God's grace.

Ideal faith development is portrayed as a progression from childhood conformity to expectations of belief and behavior set by family and society with relatively simplistic and concrete images of God or other spiritual realities; through adolescent questioning and formation of a more personally tailored faith; to critically reflective, flexible, and even inclusive forms of faith. Fowler described a mature faith stance as one that upholds one's own particular beliefs and practices at the same time as being able to empathize and cooperate with people who have other faith commitments.

Fowler provided a helpful set of categories to understand various contents of a person's developing faith. These are (1) the things or *qualities with greatest value* to us; (2) the *master stories* that we use to guide and explain our lives; (3) the *images of sacredness or power* that sustain us; and (4) our *locus of authority* for what we consider moral and right (Robbins et al., 2006). Over time, people refine and change their contents of faith, both within stages (at the same level of complexity and sophistication) and by moving to a more advanced stage of faith. The latter case is called *conversion*, which is sometimes rather sudden (Fowler, 1981). Sudden conversions can involve what transpersonalists call peak or pit experiences, including spiritual emergencies. Given Fowler's Christian perspective, he suggested that conversion may sometimes result from an unpredictable revelation of God's grace and intentions for us to reform our lives (Fowler, 1996, 2000).

Fowler's (2000) second highest stage, *conjunctive faith*, reveals the ideals he holds for spiritual development of adults. The term conjunctive faith is derived from the insights of the Christian mystic, Nicholas of Cusa (1401–1464) and the depth psychologist Carl Jung, who both emphasized the way spiritually mature people are able to reconcile apparent contradictions, polarities, and paradoxes within a unifying consciousness. For example, the wise elder is able to hold together in awareness polar tensions between youth and old age, masculine and feminine, and constructive and destructive aspects of life. The wise elder views truth as multiform, varied, and paradoxical rather than concrete and singular. The wise elder is open to the truths of varied traditions and cultures. While having a clear commitment to one's faith, the wise elder is humble, open to correction, and appreciative of other views.

People who attain this ability to decenter from self and take others' perspectives might move to the highest stage of *universalizing faith*. As Fowler put it, "This process reaches a kind of completion in universalizing faith, for there a person decenters in the valuing process to such an extent that he or she participates in the valuing of the Creator and values other beings—and being—from a standpoint more nearly identical with the love of the Creator for creatures than from the standpoint of a vulnerable, defensive, anxious creature" (2000, p. 56). Mahatma Gandhi is Fowler's exemplar for this stage.

Ken Wilber's Integral Model of Development

Like Fowler, Wilber draws on the cognitive-structural theories of development. But unlike Fowler, his spiritual assumptions are more influenced by Vedantic Hinduism and Buddhism, while taking into account mystical contemplative insights from many religious traditions. Wilber refers to his approach as *integral* because it addresses human development across four quadrants or vantage points (i.e. interior-individual; exterior-individual; interior-collective; and exterior collective) and also through all levels of consciousness development from preegoic through egoic into transegoic. This means that the subjective awareness, objective/behavioral, cultural, and social dimensions of human experience (in connection with everything else) coevolve and interface. In order to account for this complex process, Wilber draws on thinking and evidence from more than 100 developmental theorists across many scientific, philosophical, and religious fields (1980, 1993, 1996, 2000a, 2000b, 2006). His theory posits that human development is a process of evolution toward increasingly comprehensive scopes of consciousness with concomitant standards of well-being and justice becoming more and more inclusive. His view of spiritual development is similar to Fowler's except that it goes into more detail with the transpersonal levels that relate to Fowler's universalizing faith. For Wilber, the goal of development is for each person, culture, and eventually the human species as a whole, to attain nondual consciousness integrated with individual and societal functioning. Each level of consciousness includes yet transcends the capacities and points of view of the lower levels. As we develop increasingly complex, comprehensive, and inclusive modes of spirituality, we move from a preegoic orientation (early childhood), to an egoic orientation (typically established firmly in adolescence or young adulthood), and (less commonly) to a transegoic orientation in adulthood.

Wilber is most interested in the transegoic levels of development, which some people achieve in a stable manner during adulthood. He does not separate adulthood into age-linked stages of spiritual development. The transpersonal stages of consciousness progress through the way individuals take on the challenges of life, incorporate insights from transpersonal states of consciousness, engage in diligent cultivation of consciousness by spiritual practices such as contemplative prayer and meditation, and then influence each other and society at large through dialogue and innovations in politics and other socially engaged activities.

Wilber refers to his model as a *holarchy*, that is, an ordering of increasingly comprehensive wholes. Although the model is often portrayed as a linear sequence of stages, that is a simplification. One might better portray each stage as a circle that encompasses the earlier stages as smaller circles. If one imagines this three dimensionally, the circles of expanding consciousness spiral upward more and more widely. In other words, at each stage, the person's consciousness is able to incorporate more aspects of reality and more modes of functioning. Each stage (or level) is epigenetic as are those of Erikson and Piaget. Each stage has a *structure* or holistic pattern of experience, awareness, and functioning. Each stage can be thought of as a *wave* to highlight the fact that all stages are fluid, flowing, and overlapping developmental processes that include regress, progress, and wavering. In addition, there are many *lines of development* that are interrelated but distinct, such as physical, cognitive, moral, spiritual, and emotional. A person can be well developed in one line and less developed in another line. For example, an inspiring spiritual teacher could be emotionally immature with poor sense of social boundaries, and thus be prone to exploit or abuse students or congregation members.

At the stage of transition from egoic to transegoic consciousness (vision-logic), the person learns to perceive the world holistically and globally. In the early transegoic stages (psychic and subtle and causal), the person realizes that the self is not limited to ordinary space-time limits or ego boundary. Transpersonal experiences such as extra-sensory perceptions and mystical experiences become more common and consistent. Ultimately, the person's identity may grow beyond the confines of the self and culture-bounded ego, body, and social roles until it becomes unified with the divine or totality of the universe.

The ultimate stage of development is called the *nondual*. The nondual stage is characterized by a consciousness beyond all separations and distinctions. It is really a nonstage, because it is experience of Pure Consciousness, the source, process, and goal of all development. In the nondual stage, a person realizes that every moment is already complete. Every particular thing including oneself, is fundamentally one with all. Ordinary life becomes infused with awareness of the sacredness of every experience. Wilber (1995, p. 301) proclaimed that the nondual is "the Ground or Suchness or Isness of *all* stages, at all times, in all dimensions: the Being of all beings, the Condition of all conditions, the Nature of all natures."

Wilber recognized that peak and pit experiences sometimes propel one into the transegoic levels of consciousness, even while one is operating regularly at an egoic or preegoic level. However, he noted that it takes time, effort, and practice to develop proficiency and regularity of functioning at the transegoic levels. In Maslow's terms, temporary peak experiences can catalyze transegoic development, but it takes dedicated and consistent work to stabilize at a transpersonal plateau of functioning.

Critique of Stage Theories of Spiritual Development

We make use of insights from these theories for assessment and helping activities. However, there are weaknesses and controversies that limit their usefulness for a client-centered spiritually sensitive approach to social work. Wilber's ongoing work is the most elaborately formulated and is attentive to many of these concerns. We think that his work is useful to help social workers develop a holistic, integral, and spiritually sensitive approach, as long as it is tempered by our professional values, critical thinking, practice wisdom, and empirical testing.

One of the limitations of the stage theories is that they overemphasize the emergence of spiritual issues in adulthood. Coles' (1990) narrative interview studies with children from many cultural backgrounds shows a great richness and profundity of spirituality that needs to be explored further. Sometimes, adult views of religion and spirituality become jaded and routine, as compared with childhood open-mindedness and spontaneity. Wilber (2000b) acknowledged that children may be more in touch with imaginative and emotional modes of spiritual experience and can even have peak experiences. However, they typically experience spirituality in a fantasy-based or egocentered mode. Adult development hopefully can recapture the positive features of childhood spirituality that may have been repressed during early formation of the young adult ego and social roles, while moving forward in more sophisticated modes of spirituality. The importance of childhood as a key formative period for development of spiritual propensity was demonstrated in our U.S.A. National Surveys. According to scatter plot analyses for both 1997 and 2008 surveys, the more a social worker participated in religious (e.g. church) services and felt positive about religious and spiritual experiences in childhood and adolescence, the more likely the person would continue to participate and feel positive in adulthood. Spiritual development through childhood and youth needs much deeper exploration (Roehlkepartain, King, Wagener, & Benson, 2006).

All stage theories present an oversimplified picture of development because they try to capture a highly complex and multifarious process in static models. These models are useful as heuristic devices. They sensitize practitioners to themes and questions to explore with clients who wish to pursue spiritual development. But practitioners need to remember that the map is not the territory (Robbins, Chatterjee, & Canda, 2008). Since the models are standardized, they cannot accommodate the tremendous individual and cultural diversity of developmental experiences and paths. Although Erikson, Fowler, and Wilber have all addressed concerns about diversity to some extent, there continue to be many problems when trying to take into account diversity of gender, culture, religion, sexual orientation, and cognitive abilities. Wilber's integral approach is the most fully developed, but there are metaphysical assumptions embedded in it that are not congruent for all clients. Also, as religious studies scholars commonly emphasize, it is important for us to understand individual and group specific forms and histories of religious and spiritual experience, rather than generalized and abstract ideas about it. Further, despite Wilber's profound calls for expanded consciousness, compassion, and justice, his tone of argument is sometimes arrogant and demeaning toward different views (Robbins et al., 2006).

On a practical level, if social workers take a stage theory too seriously, there is the risk that we will not be open to the unique developmental story of each client. We might assume that, at a certain age, a person *should* act and think in such and such way, and then impose our prejudice upon the nonconforming client. Instead of listening carefully for the particular themes, plots, sequences of events, and interpretations within the client's life story, we might be listening to our internal dialogue based upon our own ideal version of a life story.

In addition, many people recount unexpected and complicated twists, turns, detours, reversals, revelations, and breakthroughs that couldn't fit any preconceived notion of how development should proceed. We recommend that spiritually sensitive practitioners become very knowledgeable about spiritual development theories (stage based and otherwise) and use them to open up possibilities for understanding and working with clients. However, they should never be used to close down possibilities or drive a rigid or judgmental style of helping. Therefore, in the following discussion of assessment, we draw on the previously described theory base to formulate an individualized and contextualized approach to understanding a client's spiritual journey.

Assessing Spiritual Experiences and Development

Social workers may encounter spiritually interested clients in many situations such as working through the gradual unfolding of spiritual awareness; drawing on spiritual beliefs, experiences, values, practices, and social support systems as strengths and resources for growth and resilient response to adversity; recounting important peak or pit experiences in the context of understanding their life story; being overwhelmed in a state of crisis; coping with abuse or discrimination in religious communities; or dealing with connections between spirituality and mental illness. It is therefore very important that we assess clients' spirituality during the beginning of the helping relationship or as needed while the helping process progresses. Table 8.3 lists a variety of purposes for spiritual assessment by drawing on advice from social work, counseling, psychology, and medicine (Ellor, Netting, & Thibault, 1999; Faiver et al., 2001; Frame, 2003; Gorsuch & Miller, 1999; Helmeke & Sori, 2006; Hodge, 2001a; Marquis, 2008; Nelson-Becker, Nakashima, & Canda, 2006, 2007; Pargament, 2007; Puchalski, 2006; Sperry & Shafranske, 2005). These sources contribute significantly to our assessment guidelines.

According to our U.S.A. National Surveys, most social workers are likely to be open to spiritual assessment. For example, a majority of respondents reported that they helped clients consider the helpfulness (in 1997 = 94%; in 2008 = 92%) or harmfulness (in 1997 = 71%; in 2008 = 66%) of their religious or spiritual support systems. We explore social workers' views on assessment and practice further in the next chapter.

There are many different approaches to spiritual assessment. The specific nature of the assessment process and questions are likely to vary by a client's goals and spiritual perspective, the theoretical perspective of the worker (Sperry & Shafranske, 2005), the mandates of the agency, and the nature of the helping relationship. There are many structured tools for spiritual assessment, ranging from intake forms (Marquis, 2008) to instruments for assessing qualities and degrees of individual well-being or for inclusion of the client in studies of the effects of religion and spirituality. For many examples, see the section on measuring spirituality and spiritual well-being in Chapter 3 as well as resources listed in Frame (2003, p. 112), Gorsuch and Miller (1999); Helmeke and Sori (2006), and Pargament (2007, pp. 234–236).

Here we present approaches to spiritual assessment that are more open ended and flexible so they can be adapted to many different practice settings

Table 8.3.   Purposes for Spiritual Assessment.

Spiritual assessment can be therapeutic in itself, engendering client insight.
Spiritual assessment can identify:
- *Importance* of spirituality in the client's life and family, community context
- *Components of the client's spiritual perspective* relevant to the focus of helping
- The spiritual aspect of the person/environment in a *holistic strengths oriented assessment*
- Client's *interest* in addressing spirituality within the helping process
- *Proper fit* between client's spiritual perspective and the social worker or agency
- Client's *desire for referral to or collaboration with* spiritual mentors of particular religious or nonreligious spiritual perspectives and styles
- Ways in which the client's past and present spiritual beliefs, values, practices, and group participation (if any) are *helpful or harmful* to self-esteem, coping, well-being, and to dealing with the presenting issue
- Specific *spiritual strengths*, such as inspirational religious or philosophical texts, music, art; enjoyable participation in religious or nonreligious spiritual support groups; personal practices of prayer, meditation, rituals; spiritually motivated healthy lifestyles; nurturing connection with God, nature, and other sources of profound meaning, sacredness, or transcendence; sense of life meaning and purpose; sources of joy, peace, harmony; qualities of empathy, compassion, wisdom, kindness, generosity, and other virtues; ability to forgive and be forgiven; effective ways of working through crises; spiritual mentors, healers, and friends; commitment to benefit family, society and world
- Spiritually based *complementary or alternative health care* practices (such as prayer, ritual, healing visualization, yoga, acupuncture, herbs) that might interact with possible helping activities and medications
- Attitudes about *death and the afterlife*, especially in bereavement counseling and hospice
- The nature of past or recent *peak or pit experiences* that shape the presenting issue
- Intergenerational and current *family patterns* pertaining to spiritual perspective and relationship dynamics
- Complications of *mental disorders* due to religious beliefs, such as in delusions, hallucinations, unrealistic fears
- Struggle with *spiritual problems* not necessarily related to mental disorders, such as spiritual emergencies; feeling of estrangement from God; religiously based inappropriate anxiety, shame, guilt; loss of life meaning or purpose; deep moral perplexity; loss of faith; loss of hope; sense of attack by harmful spirits or magic; abuse by clergy or other spiritual authorities; abuse by parents or caregivers under religious rationales; experience of religiously or ideologically based discrimination or oppression; alienation from or conflict with religious groups; collective persecution and genocide based on membership in an oppressed spiritual (religious or nonreligious) group

and clients spiritual perspectives. We do not recommend assessment approaches that are overly structured, religiously or ideologically biased, or ethnocentric. For example, an agency intake form that limits exploration of spirituality to religious affiliation by asking "Are you Christian, Jewish, or other" gives several counterproductive messages: religious diversity is not appreciated; spirituality is reduced to religion; nonreligious spiritual perspectives are not of interest; and spirituality in general is of little consequence. In any case, the information obtained is too vague to be useful. We suggest that practitioners review the intake forms and assessment practices in one's work setting in light of the following guidelines.

General Guidelines for Spiritual Assessment

Spiritually sensitive assessment should be done in a collaborative manner with clients within the context of a respectful, empathic, and client-centered relationship and dialogue. The client has the primary role in defining and interpreting the meaning and value of his or her spirituality. The client's experiences and behaviors should be understood within the context of his or her culture and spiritual perspective. Assessment should be ongoing and dynamic, since self-understanding and life circumstances continually change.

The topic of spirituality should not be imposed when the worker has no information about its relevance to the client or when the client is not ready or interested. Spiritual assessment should begin in the least intrusive and open ended way. On the basis of the client's responses, more detailed assessment could be pursued or skipped. Wording of assessment questions should demonstrate willingness to learn from the client's cultural and spiritual views. If discussion of spirituality continues, adjust terminology to fit the client's cues about relevant words. Themes related to spirituality (e.g. meaning, purpose, morality, connectedness, transcendence, most significant sources of support, or profound experiences of joy, peace, and life turning points) can be discussed without use of the terms religion, faith, or spirituality if they are not relevant or comfortable to the client.

Spiritual assessment should never be a matter of hasty jumping to conclusions. If the client poses a danger to self or others, a quick risk assessment and appropriate action can be conducted in a respectful manner. If and when more detailed assessment is possible, these full guidelines can be used.

We advocate for spiritual assessment within a holistic strengths perspective on social work (Eichler, Deegan, Canda, & Wells, 2006; Saleebey, 2008). For example, the life domains within the strengths model of mental health case management are daily living, financial/insurance, vocational/educational, social supports, health, leisure/recreational supports, and spirituality. Marquis (2008) places spiritual assessment within a comprehensive integral intake that covers the four quadrants of Wilber's model; this is similar to our holistic model of spirituality in Chapter 3. In strengths assessment, the client is never reduced to problems, pathologies, diagnostic labels, or pieces. If clients are dealing with specific problems or disabilities, these are addressed within the context of the whole person/environment, including spirituality. Clients are assisted to draw on their talents, abilities, hobbies, capacities, and community connections to meet their aspirations. Their spiritual strengths and resources are brought to bear on ideals for growth or identified problems to achieve growth, recovery, and resilience. Focus is kept on the present, but past strengths are recalled and future hopes are invoked to catalyze growth.

When clients describe transpersonal experiences or experiences unique to particular religious beliefs and practices, social workers must be wary of imposing irrelevant, ethnocentric, or religiously biased assumptions and judgments.

The social work dictum, "start where the client is," means that social workers need to take seriously the client's current reality, even if it seems quite alien to their own. Jung (1938, 1953, 1959, 1963) said that each person lives in a world of mental experiences that are vivid and real to him or her, although they may appear strange and bizarre to another. He referred to this as a person's *psychic reality* (i.e. the reality of the psyche). For example, if a client says that he is being punished by God for some behavior he believes to be sinful, this is the reality that must be the starting point for help. It does not matter if the social worker does not believe in God, or thinks guilt is an inappropriate feeling, or objects to the idea of a punishing God. To work with this client's psychic reality means that the social worker can help him explore the helpful and harmful implications of his concepts of God, morality, punishment, and forgiveness.

Suppose that the client is an estranged Methodist and has not gone to church for many years. In the course of therapeutic dialogue, it is possible that the client will seek rapprochement with the church as part of the process of dealing with the burden of sin and guilt. The social worker could help the client to find a faith community that would be supportive and comfortable.

In the context of the strengths perspective, the social worker needs to suspend disbelief in order to connect with the reality of the client. If a client feels he or she is supported by a guardian angel, then this sense of support can be enlisted at times of spiritual crisis. If a client believes he or she is under attack from a demon, then collaboration with an exorcist in that client's tradition may be useful if this is not merely a case of delusion or the exorcism procedures are not contraindicated for medical reasons. The important thing is to enable clients to tell their stories unhindered and to help them discover the themes, plots, characters, and developments within these stories. However, starting where the client is does not mean staying stuck there. It may well be that the client will change the story, or reinterpret it, as the process of self-reflection and discernment continues. Patterns of spiritual development vary widely and may or may not move to transpersonal awareness. Spiritual emergence is a process of growth, including ups and downs, and variations of intensity. It may include climbing to peaks, descending into pits, and efforts to incorporate these experiences into our ongoing daily lives. Sometimes these peak and pit experiences are so sudden, drastic, and overwhelming that we cannot cope. We need assistance from loved ones, healers, and helpers. But with assistance and our own effort, we can progress on our travel toward even higher plateaus. Spiritual growth is the total process of development of meaning, morality, relationships, and orientation toward ultimacy throughout the life span.

Implicit Spiritual Assessment

The least intrusive approach to assessment is implicit. First of all, by cultivating a spiritually sensitive relationship with the client, without talking explicitly about religion or spirituality, we cue the client to our openness, receptivity, interest, and respect for whatever is important to her or him. We cue the client with our mannerisms, clothing or jewelry, decorations in the agency or office, word choice, or landscaping around the agency. If there is a home visit, then comments of interest about items of obvious importance to the client can stimulate conversation about spiritual matters. If a client feels comfortable with the helping relationship and setting, then it is more likely she or he will bring up relevant spiritual issues.

For example, during a rural home visit to a foster family with a Vietnamese refugee unaccompanied minor, I (EC) noticed that the young man liked to spend time in a tree house. I also noticed that he was reticent to talk in front of his foster parents. So I mentioned that I really enjoyed tree houses when I was younger. He invited me into the tree house. We sat with many moments of quiet and conversation off and on. We talked about the vegetation and squirrels and how they compared to nature in Vietnam. The subject of recent movies came up. My client mentioned that he had seen the movie Gandhi and was very inspired. He said that he would like to live with that kind of dedication to peace. He reflected on his own experience of war, refugee flight, trauma, and cross-cultural transition. He hoped to learn to deal with these challenges as Gandhi would. That gave me an opportunity to explore further his spiritual beliefs and ideals for his life. This put his current foster care situation into a more profound and inspiring perspective. This likely would not have been possible if I had used a structured and intrusive style of questioning.

Implicit spiritual assessment can be facilitated by open-ended questions that tap themes related to religion and spirituality through use of everyday nonreligious language. Clients' responses will give cues about whether and how to proceed into explicit spiritual assessment. Table 8.4 shows some sample questions for implicit spiritual assessment, especially drawn from Eichler, Deegan, Canda, and Wells (2006) and Pargament (2007).

Brief Explicit Spiritual Assessment

Social workers often work in settings with very limited time for interaction with clients, such as managed care, hospitals, acute mental health settings, solution focused therapy, other brief therapies, and adoption and foster care home studies. In these situations, brief assessments can quickly clarify whether spirituality is important to the client and relevant to the practice situation. Then the social worker can decide with the client whether to engage spirituality directly or to refer to clergy or other spiritually oriented helpers of interest to the client. Caution should be used even in brief assessment not to pressure the client into spiritually focused discussion or activities, especially given that clients often feel less powerful or at the mercy of health care providers.

Since medical personnel typically work in outpatient or inpatient situations of brief interaction with patients, some guides have been developed for spiritual assessment in health care settings. These usually consist of a few easy

Table 8.4.   Questions for Implicit Spiritual Assessment.

- What currently brings a sense of meaning and purpose to your life?
- What helps you feel more aware and centered?
- Where do you go to find a sense of deep inspiration or peace?
- When do you feel times of great peace, joy, and satisfaction with life?
- What are the most important sources of strength and help for you in getting through times of difficulty or crisis?
- Please describe some recent experiences when you felt a sense of important new insight, such as an "aha" moment?
- Who are your most important mentors and why?
- For what are you most grateful?
- In what way is it important or meaningful for you to be in this world (or in this situation)?
- What are your most cherished ideals?
- Who is most important in your life?
- In what do you put your sense of trust and hope?
- With whom or what do you feel love?
- When do you feel most fully alive?
- What are the deepest questions your situation raises for you?
- What causes you most distress and confusion?
- What is it about this situation that shakes your sense of what is true and right?
- What is it about this situation that shakes your sense of who you are?
- What were your sources of deep meaning, peace, joy, and strength in time of past trouble that helped you get through and how can they be applied to this situation?
- How can you draw on any of the past or present strengths and resources you identified in order to respond better to this situation (or to achieve your goal)?
- If you had a magic wand, what would you change to make your life more meaningful and fulfilling?
- What is your goal for the near future and how can we work together to help you get there?

to remember topics with open-ended questions, including terms that refer to spirituality or religion both implicitly and explicitly. This is important because The Joint Commission on Accreditation of Healthcare Organizations as well as nursing guidelines require health care professionals to assess patients' spiritual interest and to address their spirituality if requested (Anadarajah & Hight, 2001; Anonymous, 2002; Hodge, 2006; Koenig, 2007; Puchalski, 2006). In 2004, The Joint Commission instituted a requirement that "Spiritual assessment should, at a minimum, determine the patient's denomination, beliefs, and what spiritual practices are important to the patient. This information would assist in determining the impact of spirituality, if any, on the care/services being provided and will identify if any further assessment is needed" (Retrieved from http://jointcommission.org/AccreditationPrograms/HomeCare/Standards/FAQs). This is a useful guideline for brief social service settings as well, unless spirituality is clearly irrelevant to the service required.

By bringing together insights from health care assessment tools, guiding questions about spirituality in gerontological social work (Nelson-Becker, Nakashima, & Canda, 2006), and assessment themes in this chapter, we develop a set of questions for brief spiritual assessment in social work settings. For easy recall, we use the acronym MIMBRA, for Meaning, Importance, Membership,

Table 8.5. MIMBRA: Questions for Brief Explicit Spiritual Assessment.

Preamble: I am interested to know what is most meaningful and important in your life that might be relevant to our work together. Please feel free to respond or not respond to the following questions in any way that makes sense to you.

1. What helps you to experience a deep sense of *meaning*, purpose, morality, hope, connection, joy, or peace in your life?
2. Are spirituality, religion, or faith *important* to you? Please explain why or why not.
3. Are you a *member* of any groups or communities (such as a religious group, support group, or cultural group) that give you a sense of belonging and help you find meaning and support in life? Please explain.
4. Please describe any important *beliefs*, practices (such as prayer, meditation, rituals, or holistic therapies), or values that shape your understanding and response to your current situation.
5. From what we discussed so far, what if anything is *relevant* to your current situation and your goals for our work together?
6. Is there anything we discussed that you would like us to *act* on in our work together? For example, is there anything that has been helpful that we could apply or unhelpful that we should avoid or deal with? Are there close friends, relatives, mentors, clergy, or spiritual teachers whom I should be aware of or contact? Please explain. Thank you.

Beliefs, Relevance, and Action (Table 8.5). Please be sure to adapt wording to the situation, the client's background and goals, and any clues about the client's spiritual perspective and culture you have from prior contact.

Detailed Explicit Spiritual Assessments

When clients express that they want to pursue detailed exploration of religion, spirituality, or faith in relation to their situation and goals, social workers should be prepared to respond effectively. Sometimes clients may desire referral to religious specialists, traditional healers, clergy, or spiritual mentors for this exploration. However, if the exploration is important to successful response to the presenting situation, the social worker can engage detailed spiritual assessment directly. The best way is to pursue leads given by the client through spontaneous questions that follow up comments of the client.

Assessing domains of spirituality. In order to give suggestions for topics and questions that might stimulate your thinking about assessment possibilities, Appendix A presents possible questions based on domains and issues identified in our operational model of spirituality as an aspect of the person in Chapter 3.

Spiritual development timeline. Our review of transpersonal theory provides us with a way to help clients recount their spiritual development over periods of time or even their entire life span. By thinking about gradual phases of spiritual growth, rapid transformational periods (peak and pit experiences), including their expression as spiritual emergencies, and plateaus of relatively stable functioning at enhanced levels in relation to preegoic, egoic, and transegoic stages of development, we create a diagrammatic and pictorial presentation of the client's spiritual autobiography. In order to depict this development, we expand on the concepts of a spiritual development timeline (Bullis, 1996) and spiritual life map (Hodge, 2005b).

The spiritual development timeline is useful for clients who want to put their current situation in the context of their earlier life and hopes for the future. Like in narrative therapy, the client is asked to tell stories about the plot, pivotal life events, main characters, themes, and significance of their spiritual journey. Clients can thus recall the learning from past experience, apply it to the present, and draw insights to guide the future. In order to make life patterns clear, the client draws a timeline that depicts spiritual development. Then the client explains the meaning of the drawing. In this process, the social worker explains and facilitates the timeline procedure, provides quiet time and drawing materials, and encourages the client to adapt it however she or he chooses.

On the bottom horizontal axis, time points at even intervals are specified. For example, if the span of life review is an entire life, then each interval could be a year. If the client wants to think about a shorter timeframe, each interval could be a day, a week, or month. The shorter timeframe allows going into much greater detail of events. The life long timeframe gives the big picture. If the client rather not be limited by time intervals, the line could be labeled with a desired starting date on the left and an ending date (or the present) on the right.

The left vertical axis shows the three main phases of preegoic, egoic, and transegoic consciousness development. The social worker can briefly and simply explain the meaning of each phase, so the client can think about particular states of consciousness and general patterns of functioning that relate to the three phases. If this concept is too complicated or unfamiliar to the client, then the transpersonal development phases need not be indicated. The vertical axis can refer to the ups and downs and steady phases of spiritual life, however the client understands that. Technical jargon should be avoided. Then the client draws a line that shows the ups, downs, swerves, gradual slopes, and steady plateaus of development. The topics listed at the bottom of Figure 8.1 can help the client to think about this along with key events, people, and spiritual strengths. In addition to the line, the client may wish to draw symbols and pictures, use various colors, and write in descriptive words or names of important people or events. Then the client explains the flow of spiritual development and tell stories to illustrate.

There are infinite possible variations on this timeline. Periods of gradual growth, gradual decline, sudden peaks and pits, and steady plateaus can all alternate in any order and duration. By using the spiritual timeline as a basis for life review, we can form an assessment of spiritual development in a way that is entirely congruent with the person's own spiritual orientation, cultural background, and personality. We do not need to start with any particular theoretical assumptions or religious beliefs about how development should occur. We can discover the person's own self-understanding.

Figure 8.1 depicts a graph of a segment of a person's life, from the age of 10–30 years. We name the fictional person Alice. The graph indicates that Alice shifted from preegoic to transegoic plateaus of consciousness during this time.

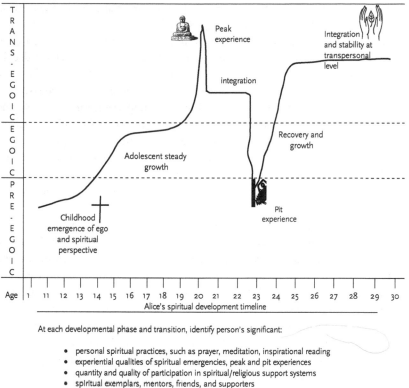

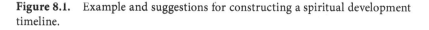

At each developmental phase and transition, identify person's significant:

- personal spiritual practices, such as prayer, meditation, inspirational reading
- experiential qualities of spiritual emergencies, peak and pit experiences
- quantity and quality of participation in spiritual/religious support systems
- spiritual exemplars, mentors, friends, and supporters
- key beliefs, symbols, rituals that support transformation

Explore how all this relates to the person's overall life narrative and guiding story of spiritual transformation.

Figure 8.1. Example and suggestions for constructing a spiritual development timeline.

Ages 10 through 19 show a period of consistent, increasingly rapid growth. In mid- to late childhood, Alice incorporated the beliefs and values of her parents and religious community into her sense of identity and worldview. As an adolescent and young adult, Alice began to question her Presbyterian religious upbringing. Although the religious stories and images of childhood provided a sense of security, she had come to feel that they were too narrow to address her interests in extra-sensory perception, mystical experiences, and religious diversity. She felt that her family's way of understanding religious doctrines and rituals did not help her to experience directly the sacred realities to which they referred. Her locus of spiritual authority was shifting away from family, church, and Bible toward her own inner experience and a few trusted friends.

At the age of 18, Alice joined a Zen meditation group recommended by one of her close friends. She began practicing meditation on a regular basis. As she became more adept at the technique, she felt herself becoming more centered and calm. When challenging events occurred, she was better able to deal with them and could let go of any distress quickly. She felt herself changing in subtle but important ways. She felt more empathetic in her relationships with loved ones. And she was able to enjoy the beauty of nature during morning walks more deeply. During this time, she found a job as an office receptionist that supplied her with necessary income but also left time for her to pursue her spiritual interests.

Her values began to emphasize caring and compassion for all people and beings. She became a vegetarian and an active volunteer in a hospice program. The life story of the Buddha, Siddhartha Gautama, became her guiding story encouraging her to keep up consistent effort to attain enlightenment. She appreciated the Zen emphasis on coming to conclusions about the nature of self and reality through direct personal experience rather than unquestioning acceptance of beliefs.

This phase ended rather abruptly after 2 years, at the age of 20, when she went on an intensive meditation retreat. This meditation retreat precipitated a peak experience. For 3 days, she and a group of retreatants practiced meditation for 15 hours each day, punctuated by brief meals, and periods of silent work. The first 2 days were very difficult to endure, as they caused a dramatic break from customary patterns of sleep, eating, and communicating. The prolonged periods of meditation and silence intensified her awareness of her mental chatter. As she learned to let go of it, she experienced times of profound peace and clarity. On the third day, Alice had a breakthrough in her meditation. She suddenly realized that the person she had believed herself to be was not substantial and had no lasting value. The self she defined in terms of physical appearance, social roles and expectations, social status, and various possessions no longer seemed very real. Alice became acutely aware that all this would disappear with death and maybe even sooner.

This was somewhat frightening. Both her Christian upbringing and her Buddhist learning did not prepare her for the intense and perplexing quality of her experience. She suddenly experienced a tremendous doubt about the validity of all values, beliefs, and religious images from any source.

However, she also experienced a deeper truer sense of self beneath all this transitory surface. She came to call this her true self. She had heard such an expression in Zen teaching, but until this it was just a fascinating concept. Her realization was very exhilarating. Though she did not understand exactly what this would mean, she committed herself to change her life to be more in accord with this true self. After the retreat, she returned to her job as a receptionist and to her hospice volunteer work. Although she was not able to keep the same vivid awareness of her true self as during the retreat, she was able to retain the insight at a transegoic level and began changing her life.

Until the age of 23, Alice continued her meditation practice. She made moderate changes in her daily life to reflect her new insights. Overall, she felt a greater sense of well-being than before the peak experience. Her friendships became more satisfying. She decided to go to college and major in social work so that she could obtain a job that matched her growing interest in human service. Thus, she had arrived at a plateau of beginning transpersonal awareness in daily life (Wilber's Vision Logic to Psychic stages).

A pit experience began with a tragic precipitating event when Alice was 23 years old. Alice was in a car accident that caused a severe spinal injury. It took several months of intense effort, medical care, and physical therapy to regain health and mobility. This accident shocked her terribly. Up to the point of the accident, she was feeling quite content with her life. She felt that she had a meaning and purpose that she was able to express through her work and friendships. She began to feel protected and nourished by the universe. But the accident shockingly reminded her of her earlier peak experience insight with great starkness—all this could pass at any moment, unpredictably. The universe no longer felt safe. She questioned her sense of meaning and purpose. Overwhelmed with physical pain and emotional turmoil, she gave up on her meditation practice. She felt at a very low point in life, confused and disoriented at a preegoic level.

However, Alice never forgot about her meditation and transpersonal experiences. This gave her a feeling of positive possibility, although it took about 6 months for this to come to the forefront of her awareness as she began to work her way out of this pit experience. Alice dedicated herself to physical therapy and met with a social worker for counseling. The social worker recognized that Alice viewed her life as a spiritual journey and that Alice was working hard to make sure that this crisis would not be a dead end. The social worker helped Alice to recall the benefits that she had received from meditation practice and connection with her Zen meditation group. Alice decided to begin her meditation practice again and to seek the comradeship and support of her friends in the meditation group. This supported her physical and emotional resiliency. Gradually but relatively quickly, she healed to the point of being able to return to university at the age of 24.

Alice reestablished her precrisis range of activities and relationships. However, as she continued to reflect on the implications of her accidental injury, she decided to begin an even more concerted effort to transform her lifestyle, relationships, and meditation practice so that there would be greater congruence with her transpersonal insights. She was on guard against complacency or taking anything for granted. Life seemed both more precious and more vulnerable. She felt that there was a new strength emerging as she shifted her sense of identity and reality more consistently in accord with her true self. This process of recovery and growth took 3 years. During this period, Alice completed her BSW degree. She found a social work job as a case manager for people with disabilities. She felt good that she could use insights from her own experience with a temporary disability to enhance her rapport with clients.

By the age of 26, Alice felt that she had stabilized with an even deeper understanding about her true self through all of this. She learned to be comfortable with the unpredictability of life and to sense a mysterious yet significant purpose behind all of it. Now she is 30 years old. For the past 4 years, she has been rather consistent in her spiritual practice and daily lifestyle. This does not mean she has been stagnant. On the contrary, she has felt highly creative and energetic. She did not feel adrift or chaotic. She now feels confident that she will be able to deal with any unforeseen challenges with even greater resiliency than she ever had before.

Alice's values of compassion and respect for diverse peoples helped her blossom as a social worker. She felt a high level of congruence between her personal values and the social work profession's commitment to individual well-being and social justice. She also developed a more comprehensive story of her life that encompassed her Presbyterian upbringing and more recent Zen practice. She found ways to connect these two traditions in her daily life. Alice started a local spiritual support group for people who wanted to discuss the challenges around linking various spiritual perspectives and practices. Recently, Alice arranged for a Presbyterian minister who was also an authorized Zen teacher to lead a meditation retreat for her support group.

Other narrative and pictorial assessments. Two exercises from earlier chapters can be adapted to help clients depict their spiritual development. Exercise 2.3 (Symbols of Compassion, Chapter 2) can help clients identify their highest ideals of compassion, caring, and justice as they developed from childhood, as they exist now, and as they are growth goals for the future. Exercise 3.1 (What Does Spirituality Mean to You?, Chapter 3) helps clients to define spirituality on their own terms, to consider how their understanding developed over time, and how they wish to grow spiritually.

There are other narrative and pictorial ways of representing spiritual life and development that may be useful for social workers (Hodge, 2005c; see also the online resource on assessment at http://www.socwel.ku.edu/candagrant/Bib/ BibliographyGrant.htm#Assessment). For example, the *spiritual genogram* depicts kinship based and intergenerational patterns of spiritual development (Dunn & Massey, 2006; Frame, 2003; Hodge, 2001b). The *spiritual ecomap* focuses on the client's present situation by depicting the client in relation to important social groups (e.g. family, friends, and spiritual communities), nature, and God or other spiritual beings and forces (Hodge, 2005c). Hodge developed the *spiritual ecogram* that combines features of the ecomap and genogram.

The explicit assessment tools tend to be more suitable for adults. For children, all of the previous assessment approaches can be adapted to their age, maturity, patience, and interest (Crompton, 1998). For example, children could be asked to tell favorite stories, bring in favorite toys or religious symbols, or draw pictures that help illustrate their spiritual views and experiences, including those that give them happiness or distress. Assessment exercises that require complicated explanations or extended time would not likely be useful.

Considering Spiritual Propensity

Spiritual propensity is the degree and manner for which spirituality is expressed for a person. We adapt this from the concepts of intrinsic and extrinsic religiosity

(Koenig, McCullough, & Larson, 2001; Paloutzian & Park, 2005) by changing the terms and concepts to be consistent with our definitions of spirituality and religion. All of the assessment approaches we presented can shed light on the spiritual propensity of the client.

Religious spiritual propensity (often called religiosity or religiousness) refers to the degree and manner of expressions of a person's spirituality given a primarily religious orientation. *Nonreligious spiritual propensity* refers to the degree and manner of expressions of a person's spirituality given a primarily nonreligious orientation. There are two styles of each of these: extrinsic and intrinsic. *Extrinsic spiritual propensity* means that the person's spiritual values, beliefs, and behaviors are primarily embedded in external social groups or communities (that may be religious or nonreligious) in conformance with group norms, consensus, and group leaders' directions. An extrinsically oriented person uses spiritual involvement mainly for instrumental, utilitarian purposes of personal benefit. *Intrinsic spiritual propensity* means that the person's spiritual values, beliefs, and behaviors (that may be religious or nonreligious) are integrated flexibly in daily life, demonstrate inclusiveness and respect for others, and show commitment to authenticity in spiritual growth. For the intrinsically oriented person, the spiritual search and experience of connection are rewarding in themselves. There is a stronger orientation toward compassion and altruism.

This results in a classification of four types of spiritual propensity (see Table 8.6). These types should not be taken as absolute categories, but rather as starting points for understanding the spiritual propensity of the client. Keep in mind that religious persons can express spirituality through both religious and nonreligious contexts and can have multiple spiritual affiliations. The distinctions about types of spiritual propensity are useful to identify a client's interest and patterns of participation in religious or spiritual groups and activities before planning explicitly spiritually based practice activities. For example, a client who is nonreligious should not be approached in a religious manner. A client who is

Table 8.6. Types of Spiritual Propensity.

	Religious	*Nonreligious*
Extrinsic	Person's spiritual orientation primarily tied to religious group membership, conformity, and personal benefits.	Person's spiritual orientation primarily tied to nonreligious spiritual group membership, conformity, and personal benefits.
Intrinsic	Person's spiritual orientation primarily tied to religious group membership, and, integrates spirituality into daily life with flexibility, inclusiveness, caring for others, and commitment to ongoing spiritual growth.	Person's identity and spiritual orientation primarily privatized or tied to nonreligious spiritual group membership, and, integrates spirituality into daily life with flexibility, inclusiveness, caring for others, and commitment to ongoing spiritual growth.

religious would more likely be interested in religiously based social work practice, referral, or collaboration.

A client who has an extrinsic spiritual propensity is more likely to rely heavily on beliefs, values, and practices prescribed by spiritual reference groups and authority figures (whether religious or nonreligious). She or he will more likely be averse to social work practices that are unfamiliar or that are prohibited or held suspect by the spiritual reference group. In contrast, a client who has an intrinsic spiritual propensity is more likely to be willing to engage in self-reflection, to explore new spiritual insights, and to try new spiritual helping activities, even if these are not officially approved by the spiritual reference group (whether religious or nonreligious). Appendix A includes questions for exploring a client's spiritual propensity.

Assessing Helpful or Harmful Impacts of Participation in Spiritual Groups

Clients sometimes wish to address issues of discomfort with their spiritual communities, consider ways to enhance their involvement or the functioning of their community, sort through a process of spiritual searching or conversion, or process trauma from religiously based abuse or discrimination. It may be appropriate to help the client reflect on the quality of fit between her or his needs and the spiritual group as long as the practitioner is not steering the client according to his or her own biases. For example, some social workers might have an elevated concern about the possibility of harm for clients resulting from participation in unfamiliar or alternative spiritual groups, especially when the worker brands them as extremist, strange, or cultish. Unfortunately, discrimination and stereotyping is sometimes directed against new or alternative spiritual groups in the mental health and social work fields (Lewandowski & Canda, 1995; Robbins, 1997). For this reason, we do not use pejorative terms such as *cult* or *superstition*. One person's cult is another's religious innovation. One person's superstition is another's dearly held belief.

It is best for social workers to help clients assess helpful or harmful impacts of spiritual group participation without prejudices about the validity of beliefs. For this purpose, we present in Table 8.7 a set of suggested questions to facilitate discussion, based on guidelines from Lewandowski and Canda (1995) and Canda, Ketchell, Dybicz, Pyles, and Nelson-Becker (2006). Questions should be selected and worded to fit the client's presenting issues and spiritual perspective.

Differentiating between Spiritual Emergencies and Psychopathology

When a person is in an acute state of crisis, such as a spiritual emergency, he or she may be cognitively disoriented, extremely anxious, overwhelmed by real or imagined events, and incapable of making rational decisions and engaging in

Table 8.7. Questions for Assessing Client's Views on Spiritual Group Characteristics.

- How satisfied are you with the *leadership style* of your group? Are you satisfied with how leaders allow participation of community members in decision making? Do you have trust and confidence in the leaders? How inspiring and supportive are they?
- How is *recruitment* of new members done? Is the community welcoming and supportive of new members? Does it ever bring in participants under false pretenses?
- How do you feel about the *sense of community* or fellowship in the group? To what extent do you feel supported in the group? When members are having personal difficulty, how does the group respond?
- How does your involvement in this group *impact your family and friends*?
- How does the group respond to *diversity* of spiritual opinions, lifestyles, gender, political views, culture, disability or other issues important to you?
- Have you ever experienced or observed *abuse, neglect, discrimination or oppression* in this group? Please give examples.
- How do you feel about the sources of *authority for spiritual beliefs*, such as sacred texts, spiritual teachers, or structures of authority?
- To what extent do you agree with this group's *spiritual beliefs, values, and practices*? Please give examples of agreements or disagreements.
- How does this group relate to the *surrounding community and natural environment*? Are you satisfied with its involvement with community service, sense of justice, and caring for others and nature?
- What are your group's positions about *social and economic policies* and how much do you agree with them? Please give an example.
- How well does your group address internal *changes* or changes in the environment? Please explain.
- Are members free to leave the group if they wish to? How does your group deal with issues of *departure* of leaders and other members? Please give an example.
- Are there ways you would like your spiritual group to be *involved* and supportive of our work together? Please explain.
- Are you questioning the nature of your *participation* in this group and wish to explore how you can enliven your participation or consider alternatives? Please explain.
- If there are any issues that came up in this discussion that you would like to discuss in our *work together*, please let me know.

effective action (Golan, 1981; Simos, 1979; Yang, Lukoff, & Lu, 2006). The person might experience anomalous perceptions and striking visions. Many of these characteristics are shared with mental disorders. However, in contrast to most forms of mental disorder, spiritual emergencies usually are characterized by a combination of sudden onset, limited duration, and intense temporary distress. Usually the person in crisis returns to a precrisis level of functioning, or grows through the experience, within several months of onset. Although crisis resolution sometimes requires assistance from social workers or other professional helpers, people's established coping patterns, resilience, creativity, and social supports are the primary forces in healing. The helper works with these natural healing capacities. When directive techniques or medications are used, they are temporary measures designed to enable the client to restore self-sufficiency.

If the temporary symptoms of spiritual emergency are mistaken for mental disorder, antipsychotic medications might be used inappropriately, causing more harm than good. Indeed, the symptoms of crisis are indicators of dramatic change and potential for growth. If these symptoms are suppressed or pejoratively labeled by the actions of professionals, the person's growth potential and capacity to learn from the experience may be jeopardized.

Professional helpers who are unfamiliar with the special issues and symptoms of spiritual emergencies may be likely to misunderstand them as expressions of a mental disorder. As is well known, for example, schizophrenia and other psychotic disorders, severe mood disorders, and severe substance-related disorders often involve delusions, hallucinations, and preoccupations with religious themes or images similar to transpersonal experiences. Many forms of mental disorder and personality disorders involve a sense of confused identity, impairment of reality testing, and loosening of the boundary between ego and others. Dissociative disorders may include experiences of involuntary trance or other alterations of consciousness. So when clients in spiritual emergency talk about peak or pit experiences that entail ego transcendence, questioning the nature of reality, and visions, alarm bells may go off in the mind of the mental health worker. Contrarily, if a client is known to have a chronic and persistent mental disorder, mental health professionals may be prone to dismiss all of her or his ideas and feelings about religion and spirituality as nothing more than symptoms of the illness.

However, studies of mental health service consumers' views about the strengths and resources that are most helpful to them in dealing with a mental disability show that many people feel their spiritual and religious insights and support systems are very important (Corrigan, McCorkle, Schell, & Kidder, 2003; Fallot, 1998; Ridgway, McDiarmid, Davidson, Bayes, & Ratzlaff, 2002; Starnino, 2009; Sullivan, 1992). Unfortunately, consumers often report that their spiritual and religious experiences and supports are ignored or dismissed by professional helpers.

In our National Survey, more respondents stated that is appropriate to raise the topic of spirituality (52%) than religion (37%) with a client who has a chronic mental illness. These figures are within 1% of the 1997 findings. Given that 50% of respondents (i.e. 908/1804) work in mental health settings, this indicates that many clinical social workers might not be assessing clients' spirituality and most might not be assessing their religious involvement. This is counter to consumer's views on the importance of spirituality, guidelines for strengths assessment in mental health case management, and instructions in The Diagnostic and Statistical Manual of Mental Disorders, Fourth Edition, Text Revision (DSM-IV-TR) that cultural and religious factors should be considered in making a diagnosis and treatment plan. Spiritually sensitive social workers in mental health settings need to attend to the religious or nonreligious spirituality of mental health service consumers, if consumers so desire. Guidelines for mental health assessment using DSM-IV-TR can facilitate this.

Through the last few editions of the DSM, there has been a general trend to emphasize diagnosis as a process that examines symptoms in the context of the person's overall psychosocial functioning, experience of stressors, and relevant medical/physical conditions. There has been greater attention to variations in cultural and religious patterns, variability of norms, and the importance of the meaning that individuals attribute to their experiences. Even the concept of mental disorder is recognized to be overly simplistic, because it implies an artificial division between physical and mental aspects of the person. It is helpful to restate the definition of mental disorder used in the DSM-IV-TR (APA, xxxi). A mental disorder:

> is conceptualized as a clinically significant behavioral or psychological syndrome or pattern that occurs in an individual and that is associated with present distress (e.g. a painful symptom) or disability (i.e. impairment in one or more important areas of functioning) or with a significantly increased risk of suffering death, pain, disability, or an important loss of freedom. In addition, this syndrome or pattern must not be merely an expectable and culturally sanctioned response to a particular event, for example, the death of a loved one.

Spiritual emergencies do meet the criteria in the first sentence (i.e. a clinically significant pattern in an individual, involving distress and risks). However, not all spiritual emergencies meet the criteria of the second sentence. Some spiritual emergencies are expectable reactions to dramatic life changes (such as diagnosis of a terminal illness, traumatic loss, or sudden opening to transpersonal awareness in peak or pit experiences). Most have a limited duration, as with other crises. A spiritual emergency includes the potential for growth as one works through the process. In addition, there are peak and pit experiences that catalyze rapid spiritual growth, but do not cause the debilitation of a crisis, and hence do not qualify as spiritual emergencies.

For example, a peak experience, by definition, involves intrinsically pleasant, even euphoric feelings, rather than distress. In theory of stress, this is called *eustress*. Eustress is still stress, and too much of a good thing can cause overload and become distress. However, eustress mobilizes excitement, enthusiasm, and creativity, rather than anxiety, hopelessness, and despair. Since peak experiences may involve dramatic changes of states of consciousness and extraordinary thoughts and feelings, care must be taken not to confuse them with hallucinations or delusions.

Pit experiences, by definition, always involve intensely unpleasant feelings. However, the associated psychosocial disruption may be manageable through a person's ordinary coping skills and resources. In this case, the pit experience would neither qualify as a spiritual emergency nor as a mental disorder, but it might involve struggle with a spiritual problem.

There is another important qualifier in the second sentence of the concept of a mental disorder. The syndrome or pattern must not be a *culturally sanctioned* response to a particular event. The DSM-IV-TR states:

> A clinician who is unfamiliar with the nuances of an individual's cultural frame of reference may incorrectly judge as psychopathology those normal

variations in behavior, belief, or experience that are particular to the individual's culture. For example, certain religious practices or beliefs (e.g. hearing or seeing a deceased relative during bereavement) may be misdiagnosed as manifestations of a Psychotic Disorder. (p. xxxiv)

This means that behaviors and beliefs held to be "normal" in one religious or cultural context could be viewed as "abnormal" in another context. When a practitioner does not share the spiritual framework of the client, there is an increased danger of biased and inaccurate diagnosis related to the ethnocentrism, religious assumptions, and theoretical beliefs of the practitioner.

This matter of so-called normality is further complicated by the fact that every spiritual and cultural group has variations within it. It is quite possible that a person could have a valuable, life enhancing peak experience that is deemed abnormal by members of his or her religious reference group. If the practitioner merely takes the position that the standard of normality of the group should be imposed upon the person, then practice becomes nothing more than norm enforcement rather than spiritually sensitive helping. Maslow (1970) pointed out that religious organizations can promote and support peak experiences. But they also can inhibit and punish them. So spiritually sensitive dialogue with the client is crucial in helping him or her to sort this out.

Although DSM-IV-TR takes into account cultural and religious variation, there are still biased assumptions embedded within it. For example, the peyote cactus is referred to as a hallucinogen. Although the manual mentions that peyote may be used within established religious practices (implying this is normal in that context), no guidelines are given for distinguishing this. As we mentioned in Chapter 5, Native American Church participants regard peyote as a sacred plant. Consciousness changes, insights, and visions in this context are religious revelations rather than signs of hallucinogen intoxication. Peyote is better described as an *entheogen*, which means a substance that opens consciousness to the divine (Smith, 2003). On a broader level, transpersonal visionary experiences (with or without use of entheogenic substances) are branded as hallucinations (i.e. false perceptions), albeit "normal" ones if approved by the religious group of the person.

This assumes that the diagnoser knows what *is* a true perception. Sometimes this is an obvious issue of incongruence between reported perceptions and physical observation, for example, a tactile hallucination of insects crawling on the skin when none are present. But sometimes nonordinary perceptions raise important spiritual questions. As we have seen in the review of various religious and nonsectarian spiritual perspectives, there are many different views of the nature of reality, many of which contradict each other. Social workers (and all other helping professionals) are not trained to be master metaphysicians and we certainly have no authority to dictate spiritual beliefs to clients. So we urge great caution in making any such judgments during assessment.

The same dilemma appears when trying to decide what constitutes a *delusion*, an erroneous belief usually involving misinterpretation of perceptions or experiences. How is the social worker to determine what is an erroneous belief pertaining to spirituality? It is indeed an important question for people of all spiritual perspectives to distinguish between false (but apparently real) perceptions and genuine perceptions—*within the context of their own understanding of reality as it is influenced by personal experience and their cultural and spiritual group contexts.* It is not important for people to make this decision based on the social worker's understanding of reality. This determination is up to clients, not mental health professionals. In many Asian originated spiritual systems, the common Western belief in the autonomy of an individual ego is considered to be a delusion at the heart of greed, violence, egocentrism, ethnocentrism, and environmental destruction. We mention this to point out the difficulties and profundities that loom as soon as we try to make absolute judgments about the nature of reality in a professional helping context.

Further, there are many states of consciousness besides ordinary waking states (Robbins et al., 2006). A state of consciousness is an organized pattern and style of overall mental functioning at any given time (Tart, 1975). An *altered state of consciousness* is a pattern of mental functioning that is significantly different from the ordinary alert waking state. These include states associated with dreaming, deep relaxation, various types of meditation, biofeedback, sensory deprivation (e.g. fasting and isolation), sensory hyperstimulation (e.g. intense drumming or dancing), and psychoactive drug use (Achterberg, 1985; Fontana, 2003; Grof & Halifax, 1977; Masters & Houston, 1966; Pelletier & Garfield, 1976; Robbins et al., 2006; Winzeler, 2008). Many kinds of altered states of consciousness are actively promoted in religious groups so that they give access to more profound understandings of reality, not "false" beliefs or "hallucinations." Perhaps the DSM-IV-TR should recognize this wider variety of states of consciousness when making a distinction from hallucinations.

Actually, the DSM-IV-TR includes some categories of spiritually oriented problems and mental syndromes that are unique to spiritual contexts. For example, Appendix A includes a glossary of many culture-bound syndromes, that are perceived as problematic within particular cultures, but may not be recognized or present in others. Many of these have an explicit spiritual or religious connotation. Some of these are ghost sickness (among some Indigenous Americans), evil eye (*mal de ojo*) among Mediterranean peoples, spirit sickness (*shin-byung*) among Koreans, and soul loss (*susto*) among Latinos.

Unfortunately, the descriptions are brief and often misleading. For example, *shin-byung* is described as a Korean folk label for a syndrome characterized by anxiety and somatic complaints leading to dissociation and possession by ancestral spirits. However, *shin-byung* is better understood as a culture-specific shamanic form of a spiritual emergency. The disorders associated with shin-byung are manifestations of a call by spirits (not necessarily ancestors) to a person to become a shaman. Therefore, it is not a mental disorder or syndrome, but rather a transformational spiritual crisis, which, when successfully resolved, leads to a new social role as a shaman and skills in applying transpersonal states of consciousness in this role (Canda, 1982).

Spiritual problems and crises that do not involve mental disorders can be categorized under a V Code that was introduced in DSM-IV: V62.89 *Religious or Spiritual Problem* (p. 741). It is described as follows:

> This category can be used when the focus of clinical attention is a religious or spiritual problem. Examples include distressing experiences that involve loss or questioning of faith, problems associated with conversion to a new faith, or questioning of spiritual values that may not necessarily be related to an organized church or religious institution.

Advocates for this new category distinguished between a religious problem and a spiritual problem (Lukoff, Lu, & Turner, 1992, 1995; Turner, Lukoff, Barnhouse, & Lu, 1995). According to them, a *religious problem* relates to distressing experiences pertaining to participation in formal religious institutions and adherence to their beliefs. Their examples include distress relating to changes in religious membership or belief, unusually intense adherence to religious beliefs and practices, loss or questioning of religious faith, guilt at committing a transgression against religious principles, and participation in destructive religious groups.

A *spiritual problem* relates to distressing experiences of a transpersonal nature or that involve powerful questioning of one's fundamental spiritual values that underpin the sense of self and reality. These include peak and pit experiences and spiritual emergencies. Their examples include distress associated with mystical experiences, near death experiences, meditation-associated difficulties, and crises of meaning associated with terminal illness and addictions. These could be related to participation in a religious institution, but may not. The differentiating factor is the transpersonal nature of the experiences that become distressing. The distinction in DSM-IV-TR is simpler and less specific: religious problems pertain to religious institutional participation and spiritual problems relate to spiritual issues outside of a religious context.

For our purposes, one crucial distinction is between a troubling spiritual crisis (which should be designated by the appropriate V Code) and that which contributes to or coexists with a mental disorder (which should be indicated by the V Code along with the relevant mental disorder). Another important distinction is between a spiritual growth experience or emergency that superficially resembles a mental disorder and bona fide mental disorders. The Religious or Spiritual Problem V Code acknowledges that a religious or spiritual growth issue or crisis merits clinical assistance, but it is not regarded as pathology.

As Lukoff and colleagues pointed out, religious or spiritual problems may coexist and interact with mental disorders or physical illnesses. For example, a person with schizophrenia, paranoid type, who also grew up with an idea of a wrathful punishing God, may have delusions of being persecuted by God.

This would suggest that long-term treatment should address the mental disorder through appropriate combinations of medication, psychosocial support, and community and strengths-based case management. As the person with schizophrenia feels safe, coherent, and ready to engage in dialogue, the religious problem could be addressed through spiritually sensitive discussion and collaboration with the client's spiritual support system. This approach takes mental disorders and disabilities seriously, but it does not reduce the person to the disorder. Rather, the person is helped to deal with the disability as well as possible religious and spiritual strengths and resources for recovery.

Nelson (1994) cautioned against two extreme forms of argument. One extreme is represented by the antipsychiatry movement, which views all psychiatric diagnoses and treatments as arbitrary, coercive, and spiritually destructive. In some versions of this, mental disorders are seen as nothing more than social constructions that justify enforcement of social conventions. Psychoses are seen as mystical experiences that are misunderstood. In this view, preegoic or ego-confused experiences are represented as transegoic experiences. Wilber (2000a) refers to this as a kind of pre/trans fallacy, in which a preegoic (or confused egoic) experience is confused with a transegoic experience.

The other extreme argument is to say that all transpersonal experiences are nothing more than delusions and hallucinations, involving regression to preegoic modes of irrational functioning, flights of fantasy to avoid uncomfortable realties, or delusions related to inability to clearly distinguish between the egoic self and the environment. This mistake reduces transegoic experiences to preegoic (or confused egoic) experiences. This is another kind of pre/trans fallacy.

Nelson presented a detailed examination of mental disorders in relation to transpersonal experiences and spiritual emergencies. He advocated for a holistic approach to assessment and treatment of people with chronic and persistent mental disorders, from a transpersonal theoretical perspective. His book would be valuable for those who are working in the mental health field, especially regarding schizophrenia, bipolar disorder, and borderline personality disorder. Table 8.8 draws on the transpersonal psychology literature cited here to show common contrasting qualities of severe mental disorders and spiritual crises. This is meant to suggest ways that clinicians can explore differential assessment with clients. However it is not intended as a checklist. Each mental health assessment needs to be tailored to the individual in her or his life context. The following discussion elaborates on these characteristics.

The assessment process should help the client to tell her or his story of spiritual development in the terms of her or his own spiritual perspective, unfettered by the presumptions of the social worker. Therefore, we summarize topics that could be used to help clients assess the nature and significance of transpersonal experiences.

Describe the immediate situation. Initially, it is important to assess whether the client perceives the transpersonal experience as a spiritual emergency. Is it

Table 8.8. Common Qualities of Severe Mental Disorders and Spiritual Crises.

Contrasts	
Severe Mental Disorders	Spiritual Crises
Underlying biochemical/organic pathology	Absence of underlying physical pathology
Long-term duration	Short-term duration
Meaningless chaos	Meaningful transformation
Functional disabilities	Brief functional disabilities with intensified perceptual sensitivities and insights
Incoherent communication	
Religious delusions	Poetic, metaphoric, and paradoxical communication
Hallucinations	
Involuntary dissociation	Spiritual inspirations and insights
Ego confusion or inflation	Mystical visions or heightened consciousness
Psychosocial debilitation	
	Spontaneous or induced trance
	Ego transcendence and expanded love
	Psychosocial reorganization

Issues of Further Complexity
Psychopathology, medical crises, and spiritual crises can intersect
Mental and physical illnesses can be opportunities for spiritual growth
Standards for normality vary by cultural and religious context
Interpretations of transpersonal experiences may shift over time
Spiritual import of a mental illness or crisis may unfold over a lifetime
Thorough assessment requires in-depth dialogue with client

a peak or pit experience? If so, does it constitute a crisis? If not a crisis, the discussion can continue without a sense of urgency or danger.

If the client identifies the experience as a crisis, then a safety assessment is necessary immediately. Is the person able to communicate coherently? If the person is feeling overwhelmed, what can be done to provide a sense of security, reassurance, and support by professionals, loved ones, and supportive community members? Is the person at risk of harm to self or others? Is there suicidal ideation, intent, or a suicide plan? Where there is immanent risk of harm, then protective measures should be taken until the person establishes sufficient emotional balance and cognitive function to enable continued therapeutic dialogue.

Once safety is assured, the story of the transpersonal experience can be explored in more detail. What occurred specifically? What was the physical place of the event? What precipitated the experience? Was it entirely spontaneous? Did it feel like a revelation or incoming of an insight or influence from a transcendent or supernatural source? Was it associated with a specific practice, such as prayer, meditation, visualization technique, group ritual, or use of a psychoactive substance or entheogen? What was the experiencer's state of consciousness? Were there any paranormal or mystical experiences? What senses were involved?

Identify predisposing factors. What factors prepared the person to be open to this experience? What inner spiritual strengths and coping skills had the person developed that may have encouraged this experience? For example, is the person very introspective? Has he or she been generally preoccupied with spiritual questions and quests? What environmental resources has the person been utilizing in support of spiritual development, such as spiritual reading material, religious group participation, being in touch with nature, feeling close to God? Are there life stage developmental issues influencing this experience and its interpretation?

Are there any distressing predisposing factors, such as physical or mental disorders that could generate alterations of perception and consciousness? Has the person been experiencing intense distress, related to a life stage transition or psychosocial crisis? If yes, then medical and psychological assessment should rule out pathogenic hallucinations or delusions. Even if physical or mental disorders are involved in the experience, the possible meaningful aspects of the experience need to be explored.

Explore interpretations of the event. How does the person interpret the meaning and significance of the experience? Were there important insights or messages inherent within the experience? What values were conveyed? What images, symbols, metaphors, paradoxes, or parables best relay the nature of the experience? Are there religious stories familiar to the client that provide understanding? What are the implications of the experience for understanding and relating with oneself, other people, other beings, and ultimate reality? Are there immediate fruits of the experience, such as enhanced energy, creativity, insights into life problems, deepened sense of rapport?

If the experience has a strong negative tone, as in a pit experience, or sense of dread, or attack by demonic forces, then special care should be taken. Again, sense of safety should be assured. What spiritual or religious practices and support systems could lend a sense of protection? Does the person wish to be referred to a religious specialist who can perform a necessary prayer or ritual for protection? What is the potential for resolution and growth through this negative experience?

Locate the experience within a complete spiritual development narrative. If the person wishes to explore more deeply how this experience relates to his or her overall path of spiritual development, the timeline for graphing spiritual emergence can be used to help illustrate the client's life story. First, identify other key spiritual turning points in life by date and mark them on a long sheet of paper to demarcate life phases. Consider how these turning points relate to gradual emergence experiences, gentle breakthroughs of awareness, or pit or peak experiences. Were any of these crises? How did they relate to life cycle events and stages of physical or psychosocial growth? Each of the significant spiritual turning point events could be assessed using the topics above.

Then, long-term patterns of development can be identified by observing trends, themes, major characters, changes of spiritual styles, master stories, spiritually influential people and sources, key values, new or recurring symbols, and altered states of consciousness. The pattern of flow from preegoic through egoic to transegoic experiences and modes of consciousness can be identified.

What is the future potential implied by the current experience in relation to one's overall spiritual emergence story? Are there indications about possible changes of vocation? Is there any sense of what one should do next, in the near or long-term future? In the case of a crisis, is there any indication of a "light at the end of the tunnel?" How can the learning of the past and present be applied to enhance one's future spiritual development?

Conclusion

In this chapter, we applied insights from many religious and nonsectarian spiritual perspectives to the assessment of a person's spirituality and its development. We wish to emphasize the importance of a sense of humility for helping professionals. It is a privilege for a person to invite a social worker into the intimate details of her or his spiritual journey. People often have a sense of mystery, sacredness, destiny, or fate in the events and flow of spiritual emergence. People may even feel propelled by spiritual forces beyond our understanding and drawn to spiritual realities beyond their ken. In our efforts to provide guidance for understanding and assessing spiritual development, we do not wish to diminish or discount this mystery. Rather, we wish to honor it.

EXERCISES

8.1. Sharing a Transpersonal Experience

This chapter discussed many kinds of transpersonal experiences. However, it is not common to discuss them in public, even though many people have them. This exercise is intended to raise your awareness of such experiences and to extend your comfort level about discussing them. Then you will feel more prepared to discuss them with clients if they are relevant. See Table 8.1 as a reminder of various kinds of transpersonal experiences.

Find a trusted friend, relative, or colleague to discuss this. You and your discussion partner should each share a story of a transpersonal experience that each of you directly experienced or heard someone else recount in your professional practice or personal life. You should begin by telling a story while your partner listens nonjudgmentally, asking only questions to help you expand on the story. Then your partner can tell a story while you take the listening and questioning role. Finally, discuss what you find especially interesting and similar or different in your stories. As a last step, write a brief essay about what you learned from this discussion that might enhance your practice with clients.

8.2. Assessing One's Own Spiritual Development

Before trying to assess clients' spiritual development, it is best to have a clear understanding of one's own development. Self-understanding provides a basis for rapport with clients on their own spiritual journeys. In addition, it is best to practice the developmental assessment approaches in order to become familiar and comfortable with them before using them with clients. Review Table 8.3 about purposes for spiritual assessment.

Choose one of the assessment approaches presented in this chapter. First, conduct the assessment on yourself, if it is relevant to your life. Then, conduct it with a trusted colleague. Ask for feedback from your colleague about what worked well or could be improved in your procedure. Write up a brief assessment report for each, including suggestions for how you could apply this in work with clients. We recommend that you find ways to practice thoroughly any assessment approach prior to using it with clients, but for now start with one.

A. Implicit spiritual assessment (see Table 8.4)
B. MIMBRA assessment (see Table 8.5)
C. Assessing impacts of spiritual group participation (see Table 8.7)
D. Distinguishing between psychopathology and spiritual emergency (see Table 8.8)
E. Spiritual development timeline (see Figure 8.1)
F. Detailed assessment of domains of spirituality and spiritual propensity (see Appendix A)

8.3. Assessing a Client's Spiritual Development

Now you are ready to try the selected assessment approach with a client who wishes your assistance in understanding his or her spiritual experiences and development. Be sure to adapt the assessment approach to the goals, interests, beliefs, and comfort level of the client.

When you become familiar and comfortable with additional assessment approaches, incorporate them into your practice.

9

Ethical Guidelines for Spiritually Sensitive and Culturally Appropriate Practice

The beginning of wisdom is this:
Get wisdom,
and whatever else you get,
get insight.

Proverbs, 4:7, Judaism and Christianity
(The Bible, New Revised Standard Version)

In this chapter, we focus the principles and values of spiritually sensitive social work down to the level of application in practice. We present ethical guidelines for engaging spirituality in social work practice, indicating relevance to a wide variety of helping activities. Then we offer suggestions for fulfilling the ethical requirement for culturally competent practice through transcultural teamwork applied to spiritual diversity.

Ethical Guidelines for Using Spiritually Oriented Activities

Practitioners' Behaviors and Attitudes about Spiritually Oriented Activities

In order to set the context for our ethical guidelines, it is useful to consider the range of spiritually oriented helping activities employed by social workers in the field as well as practitioners' views on their appropriateness. Our 1997 and 2008 U.S.A. National Surveys identified a wide range of spiritually oriented helping activities employed by social workers and practitioners' attitudes about whether they are appropriate (see 2008 results in Table 9.1). These include activities done directly with clients (e.g. spiritual assessment, prayer, meditation, or rituals), activities suggested to clients as "homework" assignments outside of the session (e.g. reading of scripture or inspirational material, journaling), activities done by the social worker privately to prepare for practice (e.g. private prayer or meditation), and connecting with religious helpers and spiritual support systems.

Table 9.1. National NASW Survey: Practitioners' Views on Spiritually Oriented Helping Activities.

Question	Have Personally Done with Clients		Is an Appropriate Social Work Helping Activity (Intervention)	
	(%)	(n)	(%)	(n)
8. Use or recommend religious or spiritual books or writings	55.8	985	76.5	1308
9. Pray privately *for* a client	56.4	1003	68.3	1168
10. Pray privately *with* a client	27.1	478	44.8	750
11. Meditate to prepare *for* a client	66.3	1175	86.3	1478
12. Meditate *with* a client	30.5	539	60.4	1020
13. Use religious language or concepts	66.0	1169	73.3	1265
14. Use nonsectarian spiritual language or concepts	84.2	1491	90.7	1581
15. Recommend participation in a religious or spiritual support system or activity	77.2	1373	85.3	1485
16. Touch clients for "healing" purposes	14.1	250	22.3	382
17. Help clients develop religious/spiritual rituals as a clinical intervention (e.g. house blessings, visiting graves of relatives, celebrating life transitions)	57.8	1030	77.1	1333
18. Participate in a client's religious/spiritual rituals as a practice intervention	17.5	311	32.3	553
19. Encourage clients to do regular religious/spiritual self-reflective diary keeping or journal keeping	51.1	905	78.8	1371
20. Discuss role of religious or spiritual beliefs in relation to significant others	75.3	1332	88.2	1536
21. Assist clients to reflect critically on religious or spiritual beliefs or practices	57.4	1009	73.2	1253
22. Help clients assess the meaning of spiritual experiences that occur in dreams	40.6	714	67.9	1155
23. Help clients consider the spiritual meaning and purpose of their current life situations	69.3	1224	81.9	1417
24. Help clients reflect on their beliefs about what happens after death	71.1	1258	88.1	1526
25. Help clients consider ways their religious/spiritual support systems are *helpful*	92.2	1621	96.2	1667
26. Help clients consider ways their religious/spiritual support systems are *harmful*	65.5	1150	82.0	1403
27. Refer clients to a clergy person, or other religious/spiritual helpers or leaders	74.8	1319	89.5	1551
28. Collaborate with a clergy person or other religious/spiritual leaders	59.2	1045	85.9	1473

Note: Valid percentages and frequencies are reported; missing cases have been excluded.

Respondents in both years were similar in their use and approval of these activities. It is interesting to note that a higher percentage of respondents both years indicated it is *appropriate* to use every spiritually oriented activity than those who actually did use them.

More than two-thirds of 2008 respondents believed it is appropriate to use all but four activities: pray with a client, meditate with a client (new item in 2008), touch clients for healing purposes, and participate in the client's religious/spiritual rituals as a practice intervention.. Among these, meditating with a client had a rather high level of approval (60%). Also, except for the four least approved activities and dream assessment, more than half of respondents have actually performed these helping activities. This finding shows that most social workers are likely to recognize the usefulness and ethical appropriateness of a wide range of spiritually oriented practices. The four least approved practices are most directive and intimately involved with a client's personal life space and boundary, so it is understandable that workers would be cautious about them. Similarly, regarding assessment, in our 1997 National survey, 35% agreed that the worker should introduce the subject of religion and spirituality, whereas 52% felt that the client should take the lead on such matters. Respondents in our 2008 National Survey once again reflected this concern. Only 33% ($N = 586$) of respondents agreed that they should introduce religion or spirituality by their own discretion; nearly 54% ($N = 949$) felt that the client should first express interest. Other regional studies of social worker attitudes have found a similar pattern of widespread approval of spiritually based helping practices, with lower (but still significant) rates of use, along with concern about intrusive practices, such as healing touch (e.g. Sheridan, 2004; Stewart, Koeske, & Koeski, 2006).

In 2008, a minority of responders agreed that "integrating religion and spirituality in social work practice conflicts with the NASW Code of Ethics" (12.5%, $N = 220$) or "social work's mission" (13.2%, $N = 232$). Over 84% ($N = 1511$) of responders believe that church-state separation does not prevent them from dealing with religion in practice. Over 91% ($N = 1636$) believe it does not prevent them from dealing with nonsectarian spirituality in practice. Although 2008 respondents did not differ significantly from the 1997 sample in terms of dealing with nonsectarian spirituality in practice, respondents in the current National Survey were significantly more likely ($p < 0.001$) to believe that church-state separation does not prevent workers from dealing with religion in practice. Compared with the 1997 National Survey, a larger minority of respondents in 2008, however, were significantly more likely to express neutrality or to agree that integrating religion and spirituality conflicts with the NASW code of ethics ($p < 0.001$) and social work's mission ($p < 0.01$). Overall, these attitudes about spirituality, ethics, and values show that most social worker respondents feel that dealing with spirituality and religion in practice is consistent with professional values at similar but slightly larger percentages than in 1997.

On the one hand, Table 9.1 shows that that there is a wide repertoire of spiritually oriented helping activities that may be appropriate. As Part II of this book pointed out, social workers can learn much about these and other helping activities from religious and nonreligious spiritual perspectives. Also, as we pointed out in Part I, spirituality and religion are important for understanding the person in environment holistically. Indeed, if a social worker ignored or denigrated the religious or nonreligious spiritual perspective of clients, this would be a form of discrimination prohibited by the NASW Code of Ethics and other international standards for social work.

On the other hand, although there was rather strong support among our respondents for using spiritually oriented activities, the table shows there is not unanimity about any of them. Ninety percent or more of respondents approved only two activities: using nonsectarian spiritual language or concepts and considering ways that religious/spiritual support systems are helpful. Curiously, there was a slight downward trend in approval of some activities from 1997 to 2008. Respondents in the current survey were significantly less likely (based on chi-square test) to use ($p < 0.05$) or approve of ($p < 0.01$) recommending religious or spiritual books or writings, to approve of praying with clients ($p < 0.001$), to use ($p < 0.01$) or approve of ($p < 0.05$) using nonsectarian spiritual language and concepts, to recommend ($p < 0.01$) participation in a religious or spiritual support system or activity, to use ($p < 0.01$) or approve of ($p < 0.01$) helping clients develop rituals, to approve of ($p < 0.01$) participating in client rituals, to approve of ($p < 0.05$) journaling, to use ($p < 0.001$) or approve of ($p < 0.05$) discussing the role of religious and spiritual beliefs in relation to significant others, to use ($p < 0.001$) or approve of ($p < 0.01$) critical reflection on religious or spiritual beliefs or practices, to use ($p < 0.05$) or approve of ($p < 0.05$) activities that help clients consider ways their religious and spiritual support systems are helpful, and to use ($p < 0.001$) and approve of ($p < 0.001$) activities that help clients consider ways their religious and spiritual support systems are harmful. The respondents in 2008, however, were significantly more likely to have used dream assessment ($p < 0.05$).

For many of the helping activities, respondents in 2008 who had not received education and training in religion and spirituality were significantly less likely to use or approve of helping activities than 1997 respondents who also had not received educational content. This finding may indicate that education and training is even more crucial in helping social workers to assess and utilize religious and spiritual helping activities should the need arise in the helping relationship. It should be noted that the profession only began to attend much to education and training in religion and spirituality within the last 15 years. Perhaps for this reason, respondents below the mean age of 58 were significantly more likely to use and to approve of most of the helping activities than those respondents at or above the mean age of 58. Exceptions include touching clients for healing purposes and dream assessment for which no significant differences occurred.

In the 1997 survey, respondents were given the opportunity to add comments to open ended questions. These comments shed considerable light on practitioners' ethical considerations about spirituality (Canda, Nakashima, & Furman, 2004). Overall, about 660 comments stressed the importance of upholding the NASW Code of Ethics. Numerous comments addressed broad ethical principles such as not imposing the social worker's perspective (551); necessity of worker competency (332); fitting the timing and goals of clients' developmental process (179); establishing a helping relationship of empathy, respect, and mutual understanding about spirituality prior to explicit engagement on the topic (85); and having clear self-awareness (44).

Eighty-five of 87 comments supported assessing spirituality in initial assessment. Most who commented about assessment (468/480) viewed spiritual assessment favorably. For example, consistent with our recommendations in the previous chapter, spiritual assessment was approved as a way of learning about positive and negative impacts of spirituality. Some reasons for initial spiritual assessment included identifying strengths and resources within a holistic assessment, exploring sources of resilience and recovery, deepening knowledge related to cultural diversity and human development, identifying harm and vulnerability engendered by spirituality (especially religion), differential mental health assessment, and generally understanding the meaning and significance of spirituality for clients. These approving comments, as well as some disapproving comments, emphasized the importance of maintaining professional ethical principles of starting where the client is, respecting the dignity of the person, cultural competency, client self-determination, nonjudgmentalism, avoiding harm, and obtaining necessary training to address spirituality.

These ethical concerns were reflected in comments about spiritually oriented helping activities other than assessment. Most comments about helping activities were favorable, with caveats for how to be client-centered. Consistent with the quantitative data, controversial practices included using prayer, meditation, visualization, or similar practices (i.e. 47 supporting comments vs. 22 opposing). For example, several comments supported prayer with a client only when the client requests it, believes in it, is comfortable with the specific form, and is dealing with crisis or an anxiety attack. Some opposing comments objected to clients relying on prayer or faith alone and to practitioners crossing church/state separation, imposing spiritual assumptions, and overstepping their role.

We agree that it is very important to use explicit spiritually based practices on the basis of careful ethical reflection. We are very encouraged by the ethical reflection indicated by the comments of practitioners in the 1997 survey. However, there is little evidence that many social workers are receiving educational preparation for how to engage in ethical decision making about using spiritual-based helping practices. Therefore, we offer guidelines adapted and expanded from Canda's (1990a) ethical criteria for use of prayer in social work. These were presented in the first edition (Canda & Furman, 1999). Since then, the usefulness of the guidelines has been supported by Moore (2003), Sheridan and Amato-von Hemert (1999), and Sheridan (2004). We expand our original guidelines with insights from Nelson-Becker, Nakashima, and Canda (2006).

First, we identify a range of options for activities. Then, we suggest conditions under which these options might be appropriate. We offer these guidelines to help you engage in your own ethical decision making. We recognize that ethical decision making often occurs in fluid and unpredictable situations presenting dilemmas that require taking into account general ethical principles (such as client self-determination), determination of ethical priorities (e.g. protection of public safety vs. client self-determination), and caring for everyone impacted by a decision (Horner & Kelly, 2007). We propose our guidelines as starting points for contextual decision making through dialogue with clients, rather than as absolute or unilateral standards. Like spiritually sensitive assessment, spiritually sensitive ethical decision making should occur in partnership with clients whenever possible. Discussion with wise supervisors and colleagues can help sort this through. Also, ethical reflection is not necessarily an individualistic process. A client could be an individual, couple, family, group, community, or any other system. In addition, many clients belong to collectivist religious or cultural groups, so they might view individual identity and decision making to be inextricably linked with family and community.

Options for Spiritually Based Helping Activities

In Table 9.2, the options for using spiritually based activities are ordered according to the degree to which the worker directly and explicitly utilizes them with a client, from least to most direct and explicit. Listing activities in this order highlights the increasing level of care and caution necessary as we increase the risk of infringing on clients' self-determination and stretch our level of competence.

The first option, *private spiritually based activities by the worker*, refers to the social worker's use of religiously or spiritually based activities in his or her private life, as preparation and support for doing social work practice. For example, a worker might practice a form of relaxing meditation to relieve stress after a difficult day and to clarify the mind in preparation for practice. Indeed, we encourage spiritually sensitive social workers to engage in stress relieving and spiritual growth-promoting activities in private life to develop a solid spiritual foundation in daily life that will naturally infuse professional work with vitality and insight and prevent burnout and compassion fatigue.

Some workers privately pray for their clients' well-being, believing that this supports their resilience and opens up a divine source of support for helping. These private activities do not infringe on the client and may enhance the worker's ability to help. So when the social worker is committed to a spiritual path and practice, it seems artificial and unnatural to exclude such activities.

However, a caveat is in order. People pray for help and healing of clients because they believe this is effective in some way. Indeed, there is mounting evidence that prayer can impact health outcomes (Hodge, 2007a) and even that people may be influenced by prayer at a distance without their knowledge (Dossey, 1993). Whatever the empirical evidence, if a social worker believes that a client

Table 9.2.   Ethical Considerations for Using Spiritually Based Helping Activities in
Social Work.

Conditions for Determining When Activities are Appropriate

A. Client has not expressed interest in spirituality (religious or nonreligious)
B. Client has expressed interest in spirituality
C. Spiritually sensitive relationship is well established
D. Worker has relevant qualifications for particular spiritually based activities

Options for Activities

1. Private spiritually based activities by worker to enhance readiness for practice
e.g. prayer, meditation, relaxation, journaling, receiving spiritual mentoring
2. Implicit spiritually sensitive relationship, context, assessment, and helping activities
e.g. strengths-based case management, existential therapy, mindfulness, dialectical
behavior therapy, art therapies, or wilderness retreats
3. Brief explicit spiritual assessment
e.g. MIMBRA assessment
4. Referral to outside spiritual support systems
e.g. spiritually sensitive colleagues in interdepartmental and interagency networks or
community-based clergy, spiritual mentors, traditional healers, or other resources matching client interests
5. Cooperation with outside spiritual support systems
e.g. coordinated helping activities with spiritually sensitive colleagues or community-based
resources matching client interests
6. Direct use of spiritual activities by client's request
e.g. any activities in Table 9.1 or others matching client request
7. Direct use of spiritual activities by worker's invitation
e.g. any activities in Table 9.1 or others matching client interest

Conditions Present	*Appropriate Options*
A	1,2; 3 and 4 with caution
B	1, 2, 3, 4; 5 with caution
B and C	1, 2, 3, 4, 5; 6 with caution
B, C and D	1, 2, 3, 4, 5, 6; 7 with caution

Significantly revised and expanded from Canda (1990). Used with permission.

can be influenced by prayer or other remote spiritual helping practices, there
is an important ethical consideration—Is it proper to influence clients without
their informed consent?

Without the client's informed consent, spiritual techniques to manipulate
the client are egocentric and presumptuous. If one were to pray for a specific outcome, such as that a client should undergo a religious conversion or become free
of an affliction, this would imply that the social worker somehow had superior
knowledge, foresight, and power over the client. What human can really know
what is ultimately best for the client's spiritual development? What the worker
ascertains to be an erroneous spiritual belief may really be the most appropriate place for the client to be. Even with seemingly good intentions, such as to
relieve pain or distress, how can we know what role this affliction plays in the

client's spiritual unfolding? A hidden manipulative agenda is certainly not what we mean by spiritually sensitive practice. In scientific research settings, covert experimental manipulation of people is highly suspect and is usually prohibited. We believe the same caution should be exercised with spiritual manipulation.

Some healing traditions recommend that helping prayer, without the client's permission, should be of an open, humble, and compassionate nature. For example, one might pray for the client's support and healing according to the client's own best interests and spiritual path. One leaves it to the wisdom of the divine and the choices of the client to work out the specifics. We recommend that social workers maintain a consistent stance of humility and client-centeredness regarding private prayer, healing visualizations, or other remote or undisclosed spiritual practices directed at clients.

The second option is engaging *an implicit spiritually sensitive relationship, context, and helping activities.* By *implicit*, we mean that there is no overt reference to religion or spirituality in the helping situation. Neither the worker nor the client raises spiritual issues in an overt manner. For example, the presenting issues may be practical, such as employment assistance or housing, or they may involve existential or transpersonal matters, but the client does not use explicitly religious or spiritual language to describe them.

As we pointed out in Chapters 7 and 8, it is not necessary to use overt religious or spiritual language in order to cultivate a spiritually sensitive relationship and context for helping or to do an initial implicit spiritual assessment. When the client is not interested in discussing religion or spirituality, it is certainly better not to. But, in our view, establishing at least an implicit spiritually sensitive relationship and context for helping is a prerequisite for competent practice of any kind. Genuine respect; empathy; rapport; compassion; understanding of centrally important beliefs and sources of meaning and support; alertness to transformative possibilities; incorporation of inspiring places, people, and symbols; building on clients' capacity for resilience, creativity, and mutual support; attending to the impacts of practice on clients and their social and natural environments; creating agencies and practice settings that are humane, empowering, and ecologically responsible—all of these qualities are essential to good practice. Further, as we saw in Chapters 5 and 6, there are certain approaches to practice that are closely allied with or derived from religious or nonreligious spiritual sources but have been detached from explicit religious language, such as strengths-based case management with spiritual assessment, existential therapy, mindfulness meditation, dialectical behavior therapy, many art therapies, many transpersonal therapies, and ecospiritual practices such as wilderness retreats. These or other approaches that are congruent with spiritually sensitive practice may be especially useful with a wide range of clients since they do not require explicit use of religious or spiritual language. Indeed, any helping activities relevant to the client should be infused with spiritual sensitivity.

The ethical issue here is one of risk incurred when *not* relating in a spiritually sensitive manner. Here, the onus is on the worker to justify why one would *not* do this, since not to do so reduces the client to an "it" rather than a full human being. Not doing so treats workers as expendable human resources rather than respected and cherished colleagues. Not doing so denies our responsibility as social workers for our part in the larger picture of social justice and human/ nature interdependence. Therefore, we advocate that an implicit spiritually sensitive relationship and context for practice are relevant under all practice conditions and circumstances.

Yet we wish to express an important caveat. There is a difference between being implicitly spiritually sensitive and acting on a hidden agenda. For example, if a transpersonally oriented social worker believed that all clients *should* view their crises as "opportunities for growth," this would lead to surreptitious or incompetent manipulations. If a person is overwhelmed with grief, despair, or anger, there is nothing worse than telling her or him, "Don't feel bad; in the long run you will grow from this." If the social worker had a favorite transpersonal technique, such as healing visualization, and sought every opportunity to insinuate it into practice, this would also be a problem for those for whom the practice is irrelevant or objectionable.

The third option is *brief explicit spiritual assessment.* We discussed procedures and guidelines for spiritual assessment in the previous chapter. Here we remind readers that brief spiritual assessment should be conducted when relevant to the client situation and in the least intrusive manner. Often implicit spiritual assessment will naturally lead into more explicit discussion of spirituality for interested clients. Certain settings may require at least brief explicit spiritual assessment, such as hospice, health care settings, substance abuse treatment, and strengths-based case management. Workers' familiarity and comfort with client-centered, strengths oriented, or holistic assessment will usually be sufficient background skill for conducting brief explicit spiritual assessment.

The fourth option is *to refer the client to outside spiritually based social support systems.* These might include spiritually sensitive colleagues within other departments or work teams in a large human service organization (HSO), such as a child welfare agency or hospital. This might also include members of the clients' social network such as clergy, religiously based healers, friends, family members, spiritual mentors, or wise elders. These might include support groups such as religious communities, 12 Step programs and other nonsectarian spiritual mutual support groups, spiritual friendship groups, and groups for learning and practicing various types of meditation, prayer, ritual, and spiritually oriented physical disciplines, such as hatha yoga or taiji. Referral could also be to places and things, such as beautiful natural parks, retreat centers, and inspirational readings. Our summaries of social work practice implications from religious and nonreligious spiritual perspectives gave numerous examples of possible resources for referral.

This option presumes that the client has expressed interest and that the referral is congruent with the client's beliefs and interests. It might involve helping the client to utilize a current support system more effectively, to restore connection with a support that has been discontinued, or to create a new support system. Competent referral also requires that the worker know to whom or what the client is being referred and that an assessment has been made that the outside support will serve the interests of the client. Follow up should clarify that the contact has been made successfully and that it is working well for the client.

Option five, *cooperation with an outside spiritually based social support system*, involves a cooperative relationship (but not necessarily active collaboration) between the spiritually based helper or support group and the social worker. For example, the social worker might, with a Christian client's permission, inform the client's pastor about goals and progress in counseling so that the pastor can coordinate pastoral counseling and congregational activities, social supports, prayer, and ceremonies.

Option six is *direct use of spiritually based activities by the client's request*. By this we mean that the activities are utilized directly within the social work relationship and setting. This could be the case with forms of collaboration in which there is a multidisciplinary team operating within an organization, such as chaplains, social workers, nurses, and physicians in a hospital. The social worker and the religious helper might function as cotherapists or coworkers. This option also includes the possibility that the social worker employ any of the explicit spiritually based activities on his or her own with the client in the helping session. This presumes that the client has expressed interest, that a spiritually sensitive relationship is well established, and that the social worker is authorized and adequately prepared to cooperate in this way.

This situation could also occur when a client requests a worker to pray with her or to help him design a ritual that would mark an important life transition. In community-based practice, social workers might interact with clients within the context of their religious support systems or within a faith-based service organization. So this option requires an even greater degree of specialized training on the part of the worker. For example, if a client asks a social worker for advice about transpersonal experiences related to the practice of Zen meditation, the worker would need relevant knowledge and skill of this particular practice, as well as comfort, to respond directly. If the social worker is not prepared, then referral or collaboration are more appropriate responses.

Of course, regardless of familiarity, a social worker should be very wary of assuming the role of a religious leader with the client, even if the social worker is authorized as such (e.g. is both a social worker and a pastor) since this risks serious role confusion. This would require careful discernment with the client to ascertain whether and how this dual role could be necessary and beneficial and whether there are any better alternatives. For example, some social workers in Indigenous communities might be authorized to lead sweat lodges. Indeed, some tribally based substance abuse treatment programs include sweat lodge. In culturally approved and congruent situations, rigid role separations might not make sense. This is a good illustration of the need for situational, culturally appropriate, community-based ethical reflection, rather than rigid standards imposed from the outside.

It is also possible that a client might feel an immediate need for spiritual solace and support that can best come from a spiritual practice dear to him or her. Yet the worker might feel unprepared or uncomfortable engaging in this. For example, if a client invites a social worker to engage in Christian prayer to support the work at hand, but the worker does not share that belief or practice, the social worker could offer to be with the client respectfully, with an attitude of quiet support, while the client prays. This response avoids a rude cutting off of the client. It also respects the beliefs and level of comfort and competence of the worker. It would certainly be inappropriate to share a spiritual activity without sincerity and honesty.

Option seven, *direct use of spiritually based activities by the worker's invitation*, is the most controversial and risky. In this situation, a client has not requested an explicitly spiritually based activity, but the worker might assess that it could be helpful. Here danger of abrogating the client's self-determination or inappropriate proselytization is greatest. Even when clients seem amenable, the social worker should be cautious about the possibility of undue (even unintended) influence due to the perceived or actual power difference in the helping relationship. For this reason, we only consider this option feasible if the client has expressed at least general interest in exploring spirituality in practice, a spiritually sensitive helping relationship and context are well established (including thorough assessment of the client's spiritual interests), and the worker has specialized qualifications related to the spiritually based activity. In any case, we believe that it is better to err on the side of caution.

This option is most safe when the practice is nonreligious in nature. For example, the social worker may be familiar with a meditation technique that has been derived from Zen mindfulness meditation (Keefe, 1996). This technique involves quiet sitting, watching the breath, and awareness of the contents of ones' thoughts and feelings without being attached to them. This technique could be applied without using any Zen specific religious language or imagery. Similar practices are used in the systematic desensitization technique of behavior modification for teaching people to overcome phobic responses. Chapter 10 includes similar nonreligious (though religiously derived) helping practices.

As another example, Jungian psychotherapists have often recommended a technique of symbol amplification to help clients explore the possible meanings of a dream symbol (Jung, 1963; Sandner, 1991). Suppose a person is going through a spiritual emergency. He feels that he is going through a major and tumultuous life change but is not sure of the direction. He is trying to sort out whether there is growth potential in the process. Then he dreams that he is being dismembered by spirits, who tell him that he must change his life or die. Although the dream is frightening, the man is intrigued by this message that the dismemberment may have something to do with his life purpose. Since he has no religious or cultural stories to explain this dream, it seems rather anomalous and confusing. So in symbol amplification, the social worker could explore the possible symbolic meanings of this dismemberment by spirits, first with the client himself. It emerges that the client sees the possibility that the dream may be a portent of an important vocational transformation. In this case, the worker might describe the model of therapeutic transformation in relation to spiritual emergencies. She could further suggest books that describe the symbolism of dismemberment and reconstruction of the self as part of a life transformation, as in many shamanistic cultures (e.g. Halifax, 1982). The client could read these books as part of a process of self-reflection, to determine whether any of these associations are significant to him.

Note that in both these examples, the social worker's invitation to the client is tentative, is centered in the client's own beliefs and goals, and is open to rejection by the client. We do not recommend introducing any religious practice without a foundation of interest expressed by the client.

The Ethical Mandate for Cultural Competence

Culturally Appropriate Practice

Our approach to spiritually sensitive practice includes within it the more common idea of *cultural competence*. We have in many ways pointed out the importance of being knowledgeable, respectful, and skillful in working within and between diverse religious and nonreligious spiritual perspectives. We have noted that spiritual diversity is interwoven with all other aspects of human diversity. We would like to discuss some special ethical considerations pertaining to spirituality and cultural competence.

The NASW Code of Ethics includes many principles pertaining to respect for human diversity. In fact, in 2008 NASW revised four items to strengthen this (1.05 on cultural competence, 2.01 on respect, 4.02 on discrimination, and 6.04 on social and political action; retrieved December 13, 2008 from http://www.socialworkers.org/pubs/Code/code.asp). NASW's (2007) standards for cultural competence, building on the Code of Ethics, recognize the importance of religion and spirituality in the lives of clients. It also recognizes that culture involves patterns of behavior and values that relate to social groups (not just groups defined by ethnicity or national origin) including religious groups. Several authors have emphasized the connection between spiritual diversity and cultural competence (e.g. Bullis, 1996; Canda, 1998b; Hodge, 2007b; Nash & Stewart, 2002; Raines, 1996; Rey, 1997). We concur with NASW's (2007, p. 12) view that cultural competence is "the process by which individuals and systems respond respectfully and effectively to people of all cultures, languages, classes, races, ethnic backgrounds, religions, and other diversity factors in a manner that recognizes, affirms, and values the worth of individuals, families, and communities, and protects and preserves the dignity of each." American social workers are enjoined to promote social conditions of respect for human diversity in the

United States and globally. This is similar to the position of the global standards for social work discussed in Part I. Cultural competence, in this sense, is an essential quality of spiritual sensitivity. Spiritual sensitivity and cultural competence involve a never-ending process of living and learning to expand one's values, knowledge, skills, and relationships toward these ideals. We do not imply that cultural competence means that an outsider becomes a technical expert in another cultural group and imposes views or that culture is a static thing to which one can adjust (Gray, Coates, & Hetherington, 2008). We regard cultural competence as a process of social workers engaging self-awareness and professional growth, humble acknowledgment of limitations, searching for mutual understanding with clients, and engaging in empowering partnerships with clients and communities. It is a process of expanding consciousness and behavior through self-cultivation and respectful dialogue and collaborations with others, based on the priorities and aspirations of our clients and their communities. In order to emphasize a client and relationship-centered focus, it might be better to use the term *culturally appropriate* practice, since the term "culturally competent" implies a focus on the social worker's level of ability, rather than the transactional helping relationship.

In order to promote culturally appropriate practice with spiritual diversity, we advocate for a *transcultural perspective* (Canda, 1998b; Canda, Carrizosa, & Yellow Bird, 1995), for which insight I (EC) am especially grateful to Professor Daniel B. Lee of Loyola University in Chicago. This goes beyond cultural competence if that is understood only as developing tolerance, knowledge, and skills for cross-cultural interaction. As Canda (1998b, p. 101) explained:

> A transcultural spiritual perspective would embrace diversity and commonality. Transcultural spirituality goes to the heart or center of what it is to be a human being. When we "center" ourselves, we come to a clear awareness of who we are most deeply and fundamentally, before and beyond cultural constructions, social roles, and personal idiosyncracies. We discover that our own true nature involves a common-heartedness with all others. We realize that all people are on a spiritual search for meaning. In keeping with the value of mutual benefit, we realize that we all need to support each other on this quest. When our disagreements and differences about truth encounter each other in a respectful way, we can all embrace each other.

A transcultural approach to spiritual diversity embeds in social workers' particular spiritual and cultural experiences of self, culture, and world; it connects with other particular contexts relevant to the client, the helping process, and wider movements for global ecojustice; and it transcends limitation to any particular context. Thus it includes both emic and etic vantage points.

Figure 9.1 illustrates a transcultural perspective on spiritual diversity. The outer circle represents a transcultural perspective that includes and honors particular spiritual views and also embraces them from a wider consciousness. The four small circles around the rim of the inner circle represent the variety of

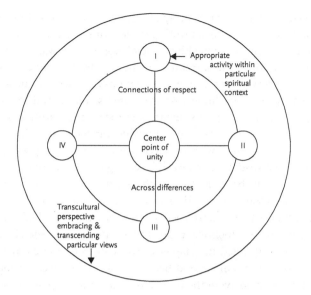

Figure 9.1. A transcultural perspective on spiritual diversity.

particular spiritual views that social workers and clients might hold. A social worker needs to learn how to interact appropriately within each view relevant to clients while also honoring her or his own view. When dealing with spiritual diversity, this means that social workers who have multicultural competence are able to connect across different spiritual perspectives in an appropriate and respectful manner. The circle in the center shows the common connection point among spiritual perspectives that is our shared humanity and common cause in promoting well-being and justice. A transcultural perspective enables social workers to develop relevant self-awareness, knowledge, values, skills, and relationships that facilitate mediating, connecting, collaborating, and reconciling across cultural and spiritual contexts. As Fowler's and Wilber's theories of spiritual development point out, this is not easy or common to achieve. However, we believe that it is important for social workers who are committed to spiritually sensitive practice to work toward this ideal, since the process of growth itself makes it more likely that helping professionals will relate in a spiritually sensitive and culturally appropriate manner with a wide range of clients. Next, we address some thorny value and ethical issues that arise when social workers interact across different spiritual and cultural perspectives.

Cross-Tradition Exchange of Spiritual Practices

The use of spiritually based helping activities in social work raises a social justice dimension of ethics, in addition to the direct practice considerations we emphasized so far. The review of religious and spiritual traditions of service in Part II demonstrated that there is a vast array of insights, institutions, and helping practices available to enhance social work practice. In some cases, these spiritually based practices might be applied by a social worker who was raised with them and has been authorized in a traditional manner by a spiritual community to employ them. However, we are often in situations in which the client and worker have different spiritual traditions. Appropriate use of, referral to, or collaboration with practices and support systems from the client's tradition might be necessary for spiritually sensitive and culturally competent practice. In addition, some social workers might wish to develop innovative theory and practices by learning from the wisdom of many different spiritual traditions. Finally, some social workers might be invited by teachers from spiritual traditions different from their own to learn the practices and to share them with others.

In all of these situations, we need to address some special ethical issues that relate to the macro-sociopolitical context of spirituality and social work. On the one hand, as we suggested in Chapter 6, we wish to promote a respectful dialogue and cooperation among and between spiritually diverse people. On the other hand, we wish to avoid the pitfalls of "superficial exploitive borrowing or misuse of spiritual activities" (Canda & Yellow Bird, 1996, p. 1). In order to assist in ethical reflection about cross-tradition exchange of spiritual practices, we consider how the exchange is done and what is the political relationship between individuals or groups involved in the exchange.

There are six common kinds of exchange between people: banning, stealing, borrowing, sharing, selling, and gifting. The first two options, banning and stealing, occur in the context of overt exploitation and oppression. *Banning* means that a powerful individual or group prohibits a spiritual practice or belief of another group. For example, Euro-American dictated governmental and religious policies prohibited many traditional African and Indigenous spiritual practices in the United States for hundreds of years in the context of cultural genocide and slavery. Even today, there are attempts by social workers to ban, denigrate, or pathologize spiritual experiences and practices that they consider superstitious or irrational. Sometimes this takes on a legal struggle, as when human service administrators in Oregon punished an employee, a member of the Native American Church, for using peyote as a sacrament (Bullis, 1996), causing legal repercussions through the Supreme Court and Congress. Banning is clearly not consistent with the NASW Code of Ethics principles of justice and nondiscrimination, nor is it consistent with the principles of spiritually sensitive practice. The long history of spiritual banning and persecution, often of religious adherents who are people of color or politically marginalized groups, gives rise to a great deal of continuing suspicion toward social workers who want to engage in cross-tradition spiritual exchange.

Stealing means that we take without permission for the purpose of our own benefit at someone else's expense. This might be tempting when a social worker admires a spiritual practice from another tradition and seeks to appropriate it for professional use. However, to make a play on words, appropriating something is not appropriate. Suppose a social worker wished to develop a ritual of forgiveness for a client overwrought with guilt. The social worker heard of a Catholic practice, called the Sacrament of Reconciliation, and thought it might be useful to adapt. So the social worker donned the garment of a priest, told the client to confess his sins, and then pronounced absolution. Any Catholic would think this ridiculous and offensive. The problem is not in learning about the dynamics of confession and reconciliation from Catholic tradition. The problem is not in helping the client to work through feelings of guilt and to seek forgiveness, perhaps through referral to a priest, if the client wishes. The problem is in mimicking the sacrament, taking a religion specific form out of its religious context, and using it without proper training or authority. Likewise, from a Zen Buddhist perspective, no matter how enamored of Zen meditation, a social worker cannot proclaim himself or herself a Zen Master (whether or not one is a Zen Buddhist).

Borrowing means that a social worker asks permission to use or adapt a spiritual activity in professional practice. Borrowing also implies that one return something. So, for example, I (EC) studied Korean percussion from a teacher in the shamanistic tradition of *nongak* (agricultural music) from 1976 to 1977 (Canda, 1993). I experienced that the music of drums and gongs, when employed in a meditative and ritual manner, can enhance therapeutic transformation for people. By incorporating my learning from this Korean teacher together with training in social work and cross-cultural religious studies, I developed a musical performance technique that can be applied in practice to facilitate transpersonal insights. As I was developing this, I corresponded with my Korean teacher, to seek his advice and permission. In 1987, I was able to see him again shortly before his death. I told him in detail about what I was doing and he gave me his encouragement. He hoped that I would promote respect and understanding of Korean *nongak*. By his permission, and the encouragement of other Korean friends and relatives, I have sometimes employed percussion with clients, students, and colleagues. When doing so, I explain the purpose, indicate where I use traditional Korean forms or adapt them, honor my teacher, and give participants an opportunity to decide whether to participate. Whenever I can, I express my appreciation for Korean culture and encourage others to learn about it, as my teacher requested. I sometimes perform traditional Korean percussion for Korean American community festivals. I also lecture and write about Korean *nongak* percussion, as my teacher hoped, so that more people can appreciate it as an artistic and spiritual form. Genuine borrowing leads to returning, and "paying forward," so that the circle of mutual benefit extends outward through sharing.

Sharing is a mutual exchange of learning and support that benefits both parties, and others, directly. It is a collaborative approach, in which people involved share each others' knowledge and help. For example, in my (EC) work with Southeast Asian refugee communities, I developed panels to educate helping professionals about the varieties of traditional healing practices and systems available, such as acupuncture, herbalism, shamanic rituals, and Buddhist meditation. The panels were composed of presenters from conventional helping professions and a variety of Southeast Asian backgrounds, including professional physicians and social workers as well as traditional shamans and monks. The purpose was to generate mutual knowledge and respect so that cross-referral and cooperation could be enhanced. This meant that people from various religious, cultural, and helping perspectives connected to learn from each other.

Selling means that a person gives spiritual help in return for a specified payment. This is a controversial and complicated issue. Professional social workers usually sell their help. Professionals expect to be reimbursed for services. On a practical level, social workers hope to make a living for ourselves and our loved ones through our work. In fact, state licensure boards may not even recognize free (voluntary and pro bono) service as professional activity in qualification for licensure. Yet some people feel that selling spiritually based help (including social service) demeans it, by attaching it to materialistic or selfish gain. For example, some Indigenous people consider it to be a violation of sacred trust to sell spiritually based helping and healing through professional service, workshops, and retreats (Bullis, 1996; Gray, Coates, & Yellow Bird, 2008).

When spiritually sensitive social workers function in a professional paid capacity, we need to be mindful of this problem. First of all, even if we are paid, we should have service as the first priority. Ideally, we want to work ourselves out of a job. Wouldn't it be wonderful if no one needed social workers any more! If we need to make a choice between profit and caring, caring comes first. In general, we should always seek ways for clients to receive needed services through social policy changes (such as those governing private or governmental insurance and other third party payments), sliding fee scales, subsidy by philanthropic individuals and groups, and pro bono work.

Regarding explicitly religiously based helping practices in social work, whenever appropriate, social workers need to consider the feelings and wishes of recipients in a given case. For example, if an Indigenous social worker is involved in a substance abuse treatment program for Indigenous participants, it may well be appropriate for a qualified social worker to conduct a sweat lodge purification ritual for interested people going through the recovery program. But many Indigenous people would consider it necessary to separate this from the formal social work context and not to have a fee charged for the sacred ritual.

We also need to consider the risk of cooptation in professionalism. If we view our vocation as nothing more than a paying job, or if we view our "spiritual" helping activity as nothing more than a new technical gimmick, then we lose the sense of sacredness in our service. Our capacity for compassionate action and justice might be compromised by limiting our work to pay, for, as the saying goes, "you shouldn't bite the hand that feeds you." This gives pause to consider why is it that some of the most noteworthy social reformers in recent decades, such as Mahatma Gandhi, Rev. Martin Luther King, Jr., Mother Teresa, and President Nelson Mandela all did their most powerful work outside the confines of a formal paying job, often under extremely difficult and life-threatening conditions.

Gifting means that a person gives without any expectation of return. Spiritual teachers of many different traditions have done this and made their insights available to all. So we have an incredible array of spiritually based helping systems, strategies, and activities available for social work. However, accepting a gift means being respectful to the giver. So, especially when spiritual practices are offered for help across cultural or spiritual traditions, it is important that social workers use them according to the guidance, intentions, and highest purposes of those who contributed them. Further, the first principle of the NASW Code of Ethics encourages social workers to provide some pro bono services.

The Political Context of the Helping Relationship

Some of our examples indicate that ethical decision making requires taking into account the political context of the helping relationship between worker and client. For example, if a Euro-American social worker wishes to explore the possibility of an Indigenous client's use of traditional spiritual practices, such as the sweat lodge purification ritual, the political context should not be ignored. Many First Nations people are understandably suspicious when Euro-Americans inquire about their spirituality. The long history of insults, attacks, and prohibitions against their spirituality makes it understandable for the client to have a healthy mistrust. Self-protection requires caution. Further, some First Nations people feel that the current interest among Euro-Americans in Native spirituality can be problematic (Bullis, 1996; Canda & Yellow Bird, 1996; Gray et al., 2008). Sometimes sacred teachings and rituals are taken out of context, adapted, and sold, without due regard for the feelings and intentions of Indigenous people. This is a case of inappropriate appropriation.

However, we are not implying that social workers (including Euro-Americans) should not learn from other spiritual traditions, convert across religions, follow their own genuine sense of spiritual calling into innovative paths, or utilize new insights to help people. This is a matter of personal conscience and religious freedom (Buhner, 1996, 1997). Indeed, despite the controversy about this, many Indigenous elders have chosen to share their teachings widely, including with social workers (Indigenous and non-Indigenous), in order to promote understanding and respect for their traditions and to enhance services for their communities. I (EC) have been privileged and honored to receive mentoring and teaching from spiritual teachers and friends in many traditions beyond my cultural upbringing, especially East Asian and Indigenous North American. My life has been enhanced tremendously by this, so I am very grateful. We recommend that when social workers act in a professional capacity, professionals should consider the ethical and justice issues we have described in order to be consistent with professional standards of ethics.

Special care and attention should be applied when the historical relationship between cultural or religious groups represented by worker and client has been one of oppression, colonialism, genocide, slavery, racism, discrimination, exploitation, homophobia, sexism, classism, disabling stigmas, prejudice, or any other form of systematic harm. Even if an individual worker is not directly responsible for the systematic harm of present or past, the memory, wounds, and anger may still loom in the mind of the client. Posttraumatic stress, both for individuals and for communities, takes a long time to process. Further, those of us in relatively privileged social positions, despite good intentions, continue to reap differential benefits from discriminatory, oppressive, and hierarchical social structures (Pewewardy, 2007). In keeping with our professional value to promote justice, the social worker has a special responsibility to work for the redress of wrongs and the empowerment of disenfranchised people.

For example, a Japanese American worker would need to be mindful of the possible sensitivity of a Korean American client, given Koreans' experience of Japanese colonialism. If a Mormon client is suspicious of a non-Mormon's inquiries about private spiritual practices and beliefs, again, one shouldn't be surprised given the history of persecution of the Mormons. Of course, the specific action to be taken depends on the particular experiences, feelings, and attitudes of worker and client. But we recommend that the worker tread lightly, especially because spiritual matters can be so precious and private for people. Many times, the spirituality of an oppressed people is one of the last areas of traditional value and practice that has survived cultural persecution, and so it is protected carefully.

Transcultural Teamwork for Spiritually Sensitive Practice

Transculturally aware, culturally appropriate, spiritually sensitive practice involves more than mere tolerance of diversity. It involves active appreciation for diversity and proactive advocacy for empowerment and justice at both individual and collective levels. If the ethical principle of cultural competency is to be more than rhetoric, HSOs (including individual and group private practices) need to institute ongoing policies, programs, and procedures to address diversity. We touched on this critical component for forming spiritually sensitive HSOs in the previous chapter. Here, we give additional practical suggestions for how to develop a transculturally astute HSO in relation to spiritual diversity. We believe that this effort should be connected with an overall process of developing HSOs that are responsive to all forms of human diversity.

We propose eight steps of spiritual diversity innovation, summarized in Table 9.3. These are based on prior cited works, especially my (EC) experience consulting with child welfare agencies, adult mental health centers, refugee serving agencies, and Christian congregations for enhancing engagement with human diversity (Canda, 1988d; Canda, Carrizosa, & Yellow Bird, 1995; Canda, Ketchell, Dybicz, Pyles, & Nelson-Becker, 2006). Our suggestions are geared toward agency-based practice. They will need to be adapted by social workers in private practice by emphasizing community linkages and interagency cooperation to compensate for the limited resources and personnel available.

Table 9.3. Eight Steps for Spiritual Diversity Innovation through Transcultural Teamwork.

1. Create an ongoing spiritual diversity innovation team and action plan.
2. Designate a team coordinator.
3. Identify the range of spiritual diversity in the service area.
4. Include service recipient and community representatives in the process.
5. Identify current preparedness of staff to respond to spiritual diversity.
6. Evaluate organizational policies, programs, and procedures for responsiveness to spiritual diversity.
7. Establish a directory of spiritual resources in the community.
8. Form cooperative cross-site teams and partnerships.

(1) Create an ongoing team within the HSO for development, implementation, and monitoring of spiritually sensitive practice.

In our experience, most HSOs do not have a formal plan for spiritually sensitive practice. Even if an agency has a plan to address cultural diversity, it is unlikely that religious and spiritual issues have been a major focus. Sometimes health care settings include a chaplain and a list of clergy resources in the community. While this is a good start, it is usually not sufficient to build a spiritually sensitive HSO that is ready to address the full range of spiritual perspectives among clientele and community, especially in urban areas. Although religiously affiliated agencies are more likely to address religious issues than secular agencies, most do not have a formal plan for addressing spiritual diversity. This means that most agencies will have a great deal of work to do if they wish to develop a full-fledged approach to spiritual diversity. Therefore, an ongoing formal team effort is important for sustained innovation.

Representatives from administrative and direct service staff in all agency departments should be involved. In addition, membership should include staff persons who have diverse spiritual perspectives and contacts with diverse types of religious and nonreligious spiritual groups in the community. This range of representation will make it more likely that the team can anticipate both agency-based and community-based issues.

Of course, identification of staff persons' religious or spiritual group affiliation should be voluntary. The most important qualification is not simply group membership, but rather enthusiasm for the task and personal familiarity and mutually respectful relationships with members of community-based religious and nonreligious spiritual groups. If a cultural diversity innovation committee already functions in the agency, its mission could be expanded to address religious and spiritual diversity.

The spiritual diversity innovation team should be authorized to create, guide implementation, and monitor action plans. The team itself should consider how to function in a spiritually sensitive manner, so that the process and outcomes of change are congruent. It is best to start with easily achievable goals, related to behavioral objectives and timelines for completion. Successes lead to further confidence, expanded goals, and more successes. For concrete suggestions about forming organizational innovation groups, see "Congregational Social Action Committees: Suggestions for Formation and Planning" (Canda & Dybicz, 2006, available at http://www.socwel.ku.edu/candagrant/CSAC.pdf). Although these suggestions are written for religious congregation-based planning committees, they can be adapted to social service agencies.

In private practice settings, the practitioner and partners (if any) would all need to be dedicated to this effort. So in effect, the "team" would be solo or the entire group.

(2) Designate a staff person to coordinate the team and to oversee the overall process of innovation.

Responsibility for ongoing professional education and innovation about spiritual diversity should be shared by all staff. However, the team and agency's wide efforts need to be coordinated by a particular person so that momentum does not fade. This should be a person with special interest (and ideally, preparation) for addressing spiritual diversity. If there is already a staff person designated for cultural competence innovation, it might be feasible to have this person incorporate spiritual diversity, or to cooperate with another team member who takes on spiritual diversity as a focus of work.

If there is no staff member with formal preparation to address spiritual diversity, it could be helpful for the team coordinator to go through the exercises in this book.

(3) Identify the range of spiritual diversity in the service area.

In order to plan a response to spiritual diversity, it is necessary to know what variety exists in the service area of the agency. It would be an overwhelming task to prepare to address the full range of spiritual diversity present in the United States. For local agencies, that is neither feasible nor necessary. So a study of the current service recipients' spiritual perspectives should be done. If the agency keeps records of recipients' spiritual affiliations or other aspects of spirituality, these should be reviewed and a client population profile can be constructed. As a next step, a richer profile of spiritual characteristics of service recipients can be developed by adapting a uniform intake assessment from the MIMBRA assessment tool.

A profile of service consumers does not necessarily reveal the full range of perspectives in the service area, however. In order to be proactive, and to prevent last minute responses in cases of emergencies, spiritual groups of all potential service consumers should be identified. Diversity team members can find this information by exploring through several kinds of sources: ask members of the spiritual diversity team about any groups with which they are familiar in the community; ask clients about the spiritual resources in the community important to them; contact city government or university-based demographers;

explore religious listings in directories available in city phone books, newspapers, university phone books, and online directory services; use internet search engines about local organizations by using key terms (e.g. religion, faith, spirit, interfaith, interreligious, and names of specific spiritual perspectives); contact local clergy and community leaders who are active in interreligious organizations or social workers who are involved with interagency networks; if there is a social work education program nearby, contact the director of field education to inquire about social service agencies that attend to religious and spiritual issues and culturally diverse populations; explore insights from staff of hospice programs and hospitals that are likely to have multiple religious contacts. As you identify knowledgeable people, ask them to refer you to other good contacts. In this way, you can branch out until you are likely to have identified the full range of spiritual diversity in the community.

A community profile of spiritual diversity can be developed by indicating the range of religious and nonreligious spiritual groups as well as important variations of spiritual groups pertaining to ethnicity, gender, sexual orientation, disability, or other pertinent aspects of human diversity. Table 9.4 lists examples of types of environmental spiritual support systems that could be explored.

(4) Include service recipient and community representatives in the innovation process.

People who are affected by decisions should be involved in making them. This is an important ingredient in empowerment and spiritually sensitive practice generally. This can bring a practical benefit to the agency, since staff persons can not be expected to know or anticipate all the needs and goals of recipients and community members. Once the range of spiritual perspectives in the service

Table 9.4. Types of Possible Environmental Spiritual Supports.

- Family members and friends who contribute spiritual encouragement
- Informal spiritual support groups, such as philosophical/religious reading groups, informal meditation or prayer groups, regular friendship groups for spiritual discussion
- Semi-formal spiritual support groups, such as classes for yoga, reiki, or taiji or short-term spiritual retreat groups
- Formal nonreligious spiritual support groups, such as 12 Step programs
- Formal religious congregations and groups
- Religiously affiliated human service organizations
- Community-based traditional healers and helpers, such as shamans, faith healers, herbalists, acupuncturists
- Professional helpers with a spiritual focus, such as spiritual directors and counselors, pastoral counselors, chaplains, transpersonal mental health therapists, spiritually sensitive social workers, parish nurses
- Places, mountains, valleys, lakes, oceans, rivers, plants, animals, the earth as a whole, and other beings of nature experienced as helping, healing, replenishing, inspiring, or sacred
- Nonphysical beings within a person's system of belief and experience, such as God, spirits, saints, angels, Bodhisattvas, souls, ancestors

area is identified, then representatives can be recruited as team members and consultants. In communities with a large number of different spiritual groups, it may not be possible to include representatives from every one. In that case, it is a good idea to seek representatives from highly contrasting perspectives. Representatives of community groups should be people who are formal or informal leaders, with a positive reputation among their constituents.

> (5) Identify the current level and range of preparedness to address spiritual diversity among the service providers.

The spiritual diversity innovation team should conduct a study of agency staff persons' level of interest and preparation for addressing spiritual diversity. Some staff may have specialized training in ministry, pastoral care, or academic religious studies. Some may have taken courses and continuing education workshops dealing with various aspects of spirituality in human service. Many will have developed personal familiarity pertaining to their own religious or spiritual group affiliation. Staff who have formal experience with interreligious dialogue or clergy-social worker collaboration would be especially helpful.

Expertise in particular types of spiritual development issues or helping skills would also be desirable, for example, training and experience to help people deal with spiritual emergencies. Staff members who are familiar with spiritual practices and therapeutic techniques that promote transpersonal development, such as meditation, could also be helpful.

A directory of agency staff expertise could be compiled from this study. This way, relevant staff people can be consulted on an as-needed basis for planning and implementation or for helping with a particular case.

All staff can be encouraged to engage in continuing education and reading to expand their competency to address spiritual diversity. As new areas of expertise are developed, those staff persons can be added to the directory. Unfortunately, our National Survey showed that nearly 65% of social workers responding reported that they received no content on religion or spirituality in their social work education. Although this shows an 8% improvement from responses on the 1997 survey, it still shows that most social workers are likely to lack educational preparation, reinforcing the need for continuing education about spiritual diversity.

> (6) Evaluate organizational policies, programs, and procedures for their responsiveness to spiritual diversity.

Part III of this book gives many suggestions for policies, programs, and procedures for spiritually sensitive practice. Agency mission, goals, and objectives should be examined to identify the extent to which issues of spirituality and spiritual diversity are addressed formally or informally. If spiritual issues are not addressed sufficiently, modifications can be made. Policies, programs, procedures, and service activities should also be evaluated and modified. Special care should be taken to be sure that the policies, programs, and procedures are appropriate to the full range of spiritual diversity among clientele and in the community.

(7) Establish a spiritual resource directory for the community.

The previous steps will identify the spiritual resources and key link people in the community. The spiritual diversity innovation team can compile this information. Information from Step 3 can be used to identify basic information about religious and spiritual groups, including addresses, telephone numbers, and other contact information. Community representatives on the spiritual diversity innovation team could help make contacts with other spiritual group leaders in the area.

(8) Form cooperative cross-site service teams and partnerships.

In many communities, it would be impossible for agency staff to have personal familiarity and expertise regarding the full range of spiritual diversity in the service area. However, staff can engage in cooperation and mutual learning with other people in the community who do have the relevant experience. So teamwork begins within the agency and extends into the community.

When there are likely to be frequent occasions of referral and collaboration between agency staff and community-based spiritual groups, formal cooperative arrangements should be made. Spiritually based clergy, healers, and helpers can cross-train or at least meet together with social workers and other agency staff in order to learn about each others' perspectives and procedures, to facilitate cross-referral and collaboration, and to establish ongoing partnerships that can be quickly and easily activated on a case-by-case basis. In practice settings in which sustained cooperation is necessary, as in refugee resettlement, hospice, substance abuse treatment, and health care, formal multisystem teams (including secular and religiously based service systems) can be established to coordinate community wide planning and activity involving spiritual diversity. The steps for cross-perspective dialogue (Chapter 6) could facilitate this relationship building.

Cooperation with Clergy and Religiously Affiliated Organizations

As we saw in the review of U.S. religious demographics, a majority of people have ongoing contact with a local or community church or other religious group, whereas they typically do not have such relationships with human service providers. Therefore, clergy are often the clients' first contact for help and serve as "gatekeepers" to other service resources (Henderson, Gartner, Greer, & Estadt, 1992). Indeed, many congregations provide social services to their members and even the larger community, such as soup kitchens, preschool programs, health clinics, day care centers, food and clothing aid, disaster relief, and many others (Bilich, Bonfiglio, & Carlson, 2000; Cnaan, Wineburg, & Boddie, 1999; Furman, Perry & Goldade, 1997; Tirrito & Cascio, 2003; Wineburg, 2001). Community-based religious organizations, as well as nonreligious spiritual support groups such as 12 Steps programs, should be recognized as potentially valuable partners for social workers. They can be sources of beliefs that support meaning, purpose, hope, and connectedness; authoritative motivators for service and justice; individual and group practices that promote spiritual development; volunteers; space for meetings and service activities; funding; creative ideas; and focal points for community-based networking and organizing. Collaboration between social workers and clergy can avoid duplication of services (Turner, 1984) and integrate psychological and theological perspectives which allows for more breadth and depth in the healing process (Danylchuk, 1992) while providing an opportunity to develop creative models of service delivery.

Since cooperation with religious or spiritual leaders is an important component of spiritual diversity teamwork, it is instructive to consider findings from our U.S.A. National Surveys on social workers' use of referral and collaboration with clergy. In 1997, 71% of respondents had referred a client to a clergyperson or spiritual leader. Among those who responded in 2008 (see Table 9.1), a higher percentage (74.8%, $N = 1319$) had referred clients to a clergyperson or other religious or spiritual leader than in 1997. Also, 89.5% ($N = 1551$) indicated that referring clients to clergy was an appropriate helping activity. Over 59% ($N = 1045$) among those who responded had also collaborated with clergy or other religious or spiritual leaders, and 85.9% ($N = 1473$) believed that collaboration was an appropriate helping activity. These findings are encouraging in that a large majority of social workers may be receptive to referral and collaboration as appropriate helping activities. However, social workers and clergy vary in the comfort level and ability to cooperate with each other (Furman & Chandy, 1994; Furman & Fry, 2000; Loewenberg, 1988).

For example, Furman and Fry (2000) studied the patterns of referral between social workers and clergy in an upper mid-western state. The random samples consisted of 640 social workers and 876 clergy who represented major Christian denominations. Among those who responded, 209 were social workers and 305 clergy. Of the social workers, 41% had referred individuals with marriage and family problems to clergy, 30% had referred individuals with mental or physical health problems, and 50% had referred individuals with religious and spiritual problems to clergy. More clergy had referred their congregational members to social workers. Sixty-four percent of the clergy members had referred congregational members with marriage and family problems and 39% had referred individuals with mental or physical health problems to social workers. Clergy were not asked if they had referred congregational members with spiritual and religious issues to social workers. Forty-seven percent of the clergy and 50% of the social workers said that barriers such as conflicting values, issues of confidentiality, and differing religious belief systems prevented them from making referrals.

Table 9.5 summarizes special considerations for social workers who work with religiously affiliated HSOs, especially those funded under the Faith-Based and Community Services Act H.R. 7. These considerations take into account

Table 9.5. Special Considerations for Working with Religiously Affiliated Human Service Organizations (HSOs).

- Connect in a spiritually sensitive and culturally appropriate manner with the organization, including its distinctive religious character
- Note the type and degree of the HSO's connection to a religious auspice, for example, congregation-based with religion infused in staffing and services, focused on member services only or including community outreach; or professional social work agency with mixed religious/state funding and with spiritually inclusive approach or inattentive to spirituality
- Work to establish mutual understanding, trust, and practical collaborations between the HSO leadership and social workers, if not already present
- Promote clients' voluntary access to services, free from enforced proselytization or discrimination
- Promote adequate training and preparation for volunteer and professional staff as relevant to clients' issues and spiritual and cultural backgrounds
- Promote accountability and transparency of HSO operation
- Balance legal principles of separation of church and state and freedom of religion
- Encourage service planning in collaboration with local leaders, rather than top down governmental agendas
- Prevent governmental neglect of social responsibility via diversion to underfunded and underprepared religious organizations

recommendations from NASW's (2002) position on faith-based services and insights from Tangenberg (2005), Tirrito and Cascio (2003), and Wineburg (2007).

We hope that our transcultural teamwork approach will encourage social workers to reach out to community-based spiritual leaders, teachers, mentors, and support groups.

Conclusion

In this chapter, we discussed social workers' attitudes about and ethical guidelines for using spiritually oriented helping activities in social work. Then we recommended a transcultural perspective in response to the ethical mandate for culturally competent practice in relation to spiritual diversity. We considered value and political concerns in cross-tradition exchange of spiritual practices in social work. Finally, we presented practical steps for spiritual diversity innovation in HSOs. In the next chapter, we will discuss additional spiritually explicit social work practice activities.

EXERCISES

9.1. Ethical Decision Making about Using Spirituality in Practice

Identify a past or present situation in which you have encountered an ethical question about whether to include an explicitly religious or nonreligious spiritual helping activity. Review Table 9.1 as a reminder of possible activities you might have considered or actually used. Then, use the guidelines in Table 9.2 to help you clarify what you should have done or what you plan to do in the future. Write an essay that explains the practice situation, the spiritually oriented activity (e.g. related to self-preparation for practice, assessment, cooperation, referral, collaboration, or direct use of activities), reasons for why you decided whether this was (or would be) appropriate, and how you engaged the client and other relevant persons in the decision-making process. How well do these guidelines work for you? Is there any way you believe they should be changed?

9.2. Cultural and Political Issues in Cross-Tradition Exchange of Spiritual Practices

Reflect on the types of practices that you currently use (if any) that have been inspired or learned from a spiritual or cultural tradition different from the one in which you were raised. Are there any issues of a cross-cultural, interreligious, or political nature that you feel you should pay more careful attention to? How have you obtained or conveyed this practice (i.e. banning, stealing, borrowing, sharing, selling, gifting)? If you have exerted influence on a client to restrict or discourage a spiritually based practice (i.e. banning), reflect on whether your decision can be justified. How do you demonstrate respect and support for the people or group from whom you received this practice?

9.3. Developing a Transcultural Team for Spiritual Diversity Innovation

Review the eight steps for spiritual diversity innovation through transcultural teamwork (Table 9.3). Put this in the context of a transcultural perspective (Figure 9.1). Think about how you can cooperate with current efforts or initiate new efforts in your professional practice setting. Gather a small group of staff persons who share this interest and begin the steps.

9.4. Creating a Profile and Resource Directory of Spiritual Diversity in the Community

One of the major initial projects for spiritual diversity innovation is to create a profile and directory of spiritual diversity recourses in your community. See Table 9.4 for examples of possible resources. Follow the recommendations in Steps three and seven of spiritual diversity innovation to begin this project.

9.5. Evaluating Relations with Clergy and Religiously Affiliated Organizations

Reflect on the types and quality of partnerships you and your HSO have with clergy, spiritual leaders, and religiously affiliated organizations in your community. What are the patterns of cooperation, referral, or collaboration? To what extent are the resources in your community (Exercise 9.4) actually utilized? What is the level of trust, mutual, understanding, and practical cooperation between social workers and religious personnel and organizations? How do you address social work professional issues in working with religiously affiliated organizations (Table 9.5)? Make a list of at least five ways that these relationships could be improved to enhance service for your clients. Then, make an action plan with a timeline for completion to implement these innovations.

10

Spiritually Oriented Transformational Practice

*The way of the Creative works through change and
transformation,
so that each thing receives its true nature and destiny
and comes into permanent accord
with the Great Harmony.*

*The I Ching or Book of Changes
(trans. Wilhelm & Baynes, 1976, p. 371)*

In this chapter, we present a conceptual model for understanding the flow of therapeutic transformation in social work and also selected spiritually oriented helping activities that are conducive to clients' spiritual growth. Actually, all forms and types of social work activities can be consistent with spiritually sensitive practice when conducted within a framework of spiritually sensitive values and contexts for helping. Everything that furthers the fulfillment and well-being of people, individually and collectively, is spiritually sensitive *when the practitioner is aware of and intentional about this.* Again, this does not necessarily require that the practitioner speak explicitly about this with clients—this decision should reflect the best interests of clients. However, it does require a keen spiritual vision of human capacity and possibility. This vision helps us to breathe new life (literally, to inspire or to fill with spirit) into all our social work activities.

Social Work Practice as a Transformational Process

Social workers often describe themselves as change agents. Of course, spiritually sensitive social work practice may be geared toward maintaining, supporting, and celebrating existing personal and societal conditions that are beneficial. However, since people often involve in social work services because they desire a change in themselves, relationships, and social structural conditions, spiritually sensitive social work often promotes growth, empowerment, and justice in ways that challenge an existing status quo. Indeed, spiritual growth and crises, such as through peak and pit experiences, include in their nature a fracturing of the status quo. In addition, social workers might proactively advocate for change in social conditions, institutions, and policies to promote peace, justice, and environmental sustainability. So spiritually sensitive practice involves creating conditions and activities that are conducive to growth and transformation for individuals and communities and their natural environments. This means that spiritually sensitive social work practice includes but is *more than* problem solving or conflict resolution. It includes but is *more than* promoting coping, adapting, or maintenance. In keeping with the strengths perspective, spiritually sensitive practice identifies people's talents, skills, capacities, and resources and mobilizes them in the service of both their immediate goals and their highest aspirations and potentials.

When change is *transformational*, it moves people forward on their life paths. Transformational practice recognizes challenges and crises as opportunities for growth. This does not mean that a social worker should hold a presumption about what the client's aspirations should be. Rather, the spiritually sensitive social worker helps in a way that supports the potential for growth that is inherent within the client and his or her context.

When we pay attention to the transformational dynamics within the helping process, we can flow with them like a rafter moving with the river current. The social worker does not originate the transformational energy, but he or she can help steer and channel the raft of change along with it. By drawing on cross-cultural studies of transformational rituals for healing and life transition, we present a conceptual model for understanding and working with the transformational process. Of course this model is a simplification; but as a guide, it can help us to flow more confidently on the river current of transformation (Figure 10.1).

Therapeutic Transformation and Ritual Studies

The cross-cultural study of rituals has yielded a great deal of insight into the ways that people create dramatic, artistic, and religious formats to mark important life transitions. Contemporary ritual studies embrace many fields, ranging from anthropology to the dramatic arts and religious studies (Bell, 1992; Bowie, 2006; Grimes, 1995, 2000a, 2000b; Heimbrock & Boudewijnse, 1990; Turner, 1992; Winzeler, 2008). These studies point out the great variety of rituals and their purposes. They caution against over-generalization about universal patterns of action and symbolism in ritual process, and urge us to be attentive to variations by culture, situation, purpose, gender, and other aspects of human diversity. However, they acknowledge that one of the remarkable commonalties among human beings is our tendency to mark and to facilitate important life transitions, such as a shift through a stage in the life cycle, changes in social status or role, healing processes, and periods of personal and community crisis.

Preparation	Separation	Flux	Aggregation	Congregation
Life disruption or proactive goal that motivate help seeking and anticipation of therapy	Separation from status quo; incorporation into helping process	Liminal phase maximizing expectations and possibilities for change	Reconstruction of enhanced condition; plan to integrate changes into ongoing life; closure of helping process	Creativity and ongoing growth as changes are integrated into ongoing life and relationships
"Falling apart"	"Taking apart"	"Neither here nor there; betwixt and between"	"Getting it together"	"Having it together"
Disturbing sense of chaos or compelling desire for life change	Protective order	Creative chaos	Creative order	Ongoing creative balance of chaos and order
Spontaneity		Formal helping process		Spontaneity

Figure 10.1.   A conceptual model of therapeutic transformation.

This is not to say that all rituals are benign. Well-intended rituals can fail their purposes. Rituals can sometimes be violent or serve to impose injurious and oppressive social conditions and expectations on disadvantaged members of a society or on members of other societies.

Therefore, our conceptual model emphasizes insights from ritual studies for helpful transformation of individuals and groups. In keeping with our transcultural and transperspectival approach, we intend this model as a heuristic device to open creative ways of understanding and enhancing the helping process. We do not intend it to serve as a universal description of all rituals across cultures or as a prescription for formulaic practice. However, we hope that it will encourage readers to explore the specific forms of rituals within their own and others' cultures with genuine interest, respect, and willingness to connect with the particular beliefs, values, and practices of the people for whom the rituals are significant. As we will show later in this chapter, the model also provides a theoretical basis for helping clients to utilize and design rituals and ceremonies.

Rituals not only mark transitions, they also create them, celebrate them, and help us to pass through them safely. Indeed, many rituals of healing and helping can be understood as rites of passage that help a person to pass from a condition of distress to a new condition of restored or enhanced life (Eliade, 1971; Frank, 1963; Kiefer & Cowan, 1979; Kiev, 1972; Lincoln, 1981; Scheff, 1979; Turner, 1965, 1969, 1974, 1992; Van Gennep, 1960; Wallace, 1966). Therefore, theory of ritual process provides us with keen insight into the transformational process that is so important in spiritually sensitive social work.

Grimes (2000a, pp. 5–6) summarizes this well:

> Life passages are rough, fraught with spiritual potholes, even mortal dangers.
> Some passages we know are coming; others happen upon us. Birth, coming of
> age, marriage, and death are widely anticipated as precarious moments requir-
> ing rites for their successful negotiation. But there are other treacherous occa-
> sions less regularly handled by ritual means: the start of school, abortion, a
> serious illness, divorce, job loss, rape, menopause, and retirement.... Even a
> single rite of passage can divide a person's life into "before"" and "after." An
> entire system of such rites organizes life into stages.... Effective rites depend on
> inheriting, discovering, or inventing value-laden images that are driven deeply,
> by repeated practice and performance, into the marrow.... The primary work
> of a rite of passage is to ensure that we attend to such events fully, which is to
> say, spiritually, psychologically, and socially. Unattended, a major life passage
> can become a yawning abyss, draining off psychic energy, engendering social
> confusion, and twisting the course of life that follows it.

By drawing on ritual studies, we present a model of therapeutic transformation that can guide our planning of activities in the helping process (adapted
from Canda, 1988a). The model supplements more conventional models of the
helping process by adding a focus on the potential for spiritual growth that is
inherent within social work processes.

A Conceptual Model of Therapeutic Transformation

Social work practice often produces therapeutic change, that is, an enhancement
of a person's or social system's situation. From the standpoint of spiritually sensitive practice, we recognize that each enhancement is a move in the life process
of spiritual emergence. So we need to consider more carefully what we mean by
these two key terms: therapeutic and transformation.

There is a significant nuance of the expression "therapy," which is generally
omitted from common usage in social work. The Greek word *therapeutes* meant
a healer who serves both the human and the divine (Hillman, 1975). So when we
refer to *therapeutic* transformation, we do not restrict ourselves to thinking of
social work as a form of psychotherapy, for social work's scope is much greater
than that. Rather, we wish to emphasize a spiritual orientation to the helping process in all forms of social work practice. To improvise with Grof's term "holotropic," *therapeutic transformation* is change that moves people toward wholeness
in relation with oneself, other people, the earth, the universe, and the ground of
being itself, however people understand it.

As the Chinese Book of Changes (I Ching) points out, there are many
types, degrees, and speeds of change in human life (Wilhem & Baynes, 1976).
The wise person understands the particular kind of change involved at any point
in life and works with the potential inherent in the flow of change to maximize
the possibility of enhanced living in relationship. Some periods of change are

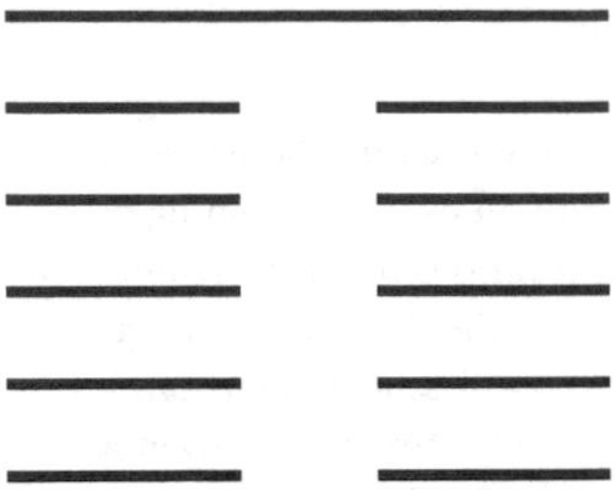

Figure 10.2. Hexagram #23, splitting apart.

transformational—occasions of greater danger as well as opportunity. They call for greater wisdom. By *transformation*, we mean a significant relatively rapid or concentrated change of condition, such as developmental leaps through peak and pit experiences. In this sense, especially as social work increasingly uses brief modes of helping, such as solution-focused therapy, we are midwifing clients through transformational processes.

For example, I Ching hexagram number 23, named "splitting apart," symbolizes a time of life in which the status quo is breaking up (see Figure 10.2). The five lower lines, which are broken, represent the walls of a house that are crumbling down. The roof is ready to fall in. This can be frightening. It is definitely time to move! The symbolism of the hexagram includes advice for how to respond to this situation. The upper three lines symbolize a mountain; the lower three lines symbolize earth. So if one can keep a mind that is well grounded, clear, virtuous, and open to insight (like a mountain resting on earth and rising toward heaven), then the splitting apart can be an opening to something greater. Another way to look at the symbolism of the hexagram is that the single unbroken line at the top is a ripened fruit in a tree. When change goes to its maximum, the fruit falls to the earth. This apparent death of one situation actually plants the seed for the future.

As we have seen in the discussion of spiritual emergencies, transformational experiences have great potential for enhancing a person's insight, vitality, sense of purpose, and way of life. However, getting to that point of breakthrough may depend on first going through a period of breakdown. Transformational processes often occur spontaneously, as in crises. Healing and helping rituals are procedures to help bring a person through the passage to enhanced life. In this sense, social work encounters with clients can be considered rituals. Note that in common usage, the word ritual sometimes means something rote, stale, or meaninglessly repeated. That is actually the opposite of the meaning of ritual in the context of therapeutic rituals, which are lively, dynamic, intentional, and careful.

The conceptual model divides the therapeutic transformation process into five phases that are like flowing waves rather than discrete steps. The preparation phase involves all that has gone before the helping encounter, especially whatever precipitates the client's need for help and whatever the client does in anticipation of the beginning of the helping process. Formal helping begins at contact with the social worker and moves through three phases: separation, flux, and aggregation. After formal helping, the person continues with life in a more spontaneous way, hopefully more resilient and reliant on his or her strengths and resources (congregation).

Therapeutic transformation is like the process of moving to a new home. In phase one, some series of events and responses leads to the decision to move. Sometimes the decision is proactive and agreeable. Sometimes, like in an eviction, natural disaster or war, the decision is forced upon us. Moving one's home often is a significant life event, since the move disrupts the established patterns of behavior, relationships, and comforts. Even if the status quo is problematic and we have incentive to move, old habits and relationships connected to home may be hard to break or alter. Once we decide to move, we need to make advanced preparations. If we are forced out of home suddenly, then the lack of preparation complicates the move. In phase two, we dismantle our belongings and pack them in boxes, hopefully with sufficient order that we can retrieve and reorganize them later. In phase three, we go on a journey to a new place, uncertain of the future. New possibilities emerge, bringing both hope and anxiety. If friends, family, or a moving company are helping, this journey to the new home can be relatively quick and safe. In phase four, we move into the new home, unpack, and reorganize in a way that suits our new situation and purposes. In phase five, hopefully, we reestablish life in the new home, with reorganized relationships and daily activities. Social workers are like specialists in moving who facilitate the packing, unpacking, and reorganizing of life.

PHASE ONE: PREPARATION (PRETHERAPY PRECIPITATING EVENTS)
English idioms portray the transformation process vividly. In a time of crisis, we might say that "I am falling apart." This is the spontaneous phase of crisis in which we feel overwhelmed and out of control. When this experience is intense, we might seek help from someone who can help us to "get it together." Our previous life experiences predispose us to perceive and respond to a crisis or life transition in a certain way. We are prepared by our learning of problem solving strategies and acquisition of strengths and resources. However, when a life challenge or proactive goal for change goes beyond our usual means and resources, we are more likely to consult a professional helper. When a person anticipates beginning a therapeutic process, she or he will begin to form expectations, hopes, and worries. In some traditional rituals, the healer advises the person to prepare by creating a hopeful anticipation and by reflecting on cultural stories and patterns for successful transformation. The spiritually sensitive social worker should be attentive to ways that oneself or the agency cues clients (subtly or overtly) about what to anticipate and how to prepare. When there is an opportunity to encourage a client to prepare, it would be useful to provide some guidance about what to expect and how to use the helping process in a

way that would best serve his or her interests. For example, in a medical setting, a social worker who discusses a patient's transition into hospice care could refer the patient and family to online and written materials about the principles and practice of hospice. This could make the transition to work with a hospice team more smooth.

PHASE TWO: SEPARATION (INCORPORATING INTO FORMAL HELPING)   In social work practice, the worker first welcomes a client into the helping relationship. A space, such as an office or the client's home, is designated for a special kind of encounter dedicated to helping. We cue the person that she or he is being separated from the ordinary life situation in which they feel stuck. We indicate our intentions to help. We identify the person's story, troubles, and aspirations. This is the phase of assessment and analysis, which literally means "to take apart." We help the client to deconstruct the situation and open up new possibilities. At this phase, it is important to assure the client of respect, trust, and safety in the helping relationship. If he or she had been feeling overwhelmed by chaos, this phase of helping emphasizes restoration of a sense of protection, cognitive understanding, and hope for the future.

PHASE THREE: FLUX (DYNAMIC CHANGING)   Disorder has its advantages; chaos can be creative. The very fact that a client's status quo is shaken up means that she or he is likely to be more amenable to change and growth. As the helping process continues, it is important for the social worker to help the client open up more possibilities, new ways of looking at things, unforeseen solutions, and to summon up all the personal strengths and environmental resources that can support the change process. This means that old rigid patterns need to be dismantled.

This is the phase of flux, in which maximum possibilities for creativity are opened up. Idiomatic expressions for this are being "neither here nor there" or being "betwixt and between." The anthropologist Victor Turner (1965, 1969, 1974), drawing on the work of Arnold Van Gennep, referred to this as the liminal phase, which literally means the passageway phase. When a person stands in a passageway, he or she is not in any particular room (which can feel ambiguous and disconcerting), but he or she has possibility to move from one room to another (which can feel hopeful and empowering).

Turner pointed out that healing rituals and rites of passage emphasize two dimensions of this phase. One is the sense that ordinary personal or cultural structures, habits, norms, and expectations are temporarily altered or suspended. Many possibilities open. People who are going through this antistructural process together tend to form a sense of community bond or egalitarian mutual support, which he termed *communitas*. However, this lack of structure needs to be complemented by careful protection, support, and guidance by the helpers and healers. Creative chaos is complemented by supportive order, thus catalyzing the transformational process.

The complementarity of antistructure and structure is similar to the concepts of morphostasis and morphogenesis in dynamic systems theory (Robbins, Chatterjee & Canda, 2006). *Morphostasis* means "form maintaining." It is the process of living systems that protects and restores the integrity of a living system, so that it can survive over time. *Morphogenesis* means "form generating." It is the process that adapts, changes, and creates new patterns in a living system, so that it can develop and grow over time. Morphostasis and morphogenesis are complementary and necessary aspects of the dynamic transformation process in living systems, called *homeokinesis*. Morphostasis alone results in stagnation. Morphogenesis alone results in destructive chaos.

PHASE FOUR: AGGREGATION (REINTEGRATING) It is necessary, but not sufficient to open up possibilities. If a person's life is only deconstructed, then it is destroyed. It is critical that social workers help clients to continue through to reconstruction at an enhanced level of functioning and fulfillment. This is the third phase of helping—aggregation. In this phase, social workers help clients to incorporate insights, to stabilize lifestyle changes, and to work through these implications with significant others. This is the phase of "getting it together." A sense of closure is reached and the client is helped to prepare for reentry into ongoing living. In effect, this three-phase helping process assists the client to rise above a constraining situation, journey to a peak of new possibilities, and then integrate this new learning at a plateau of enhanced living.

PHASE FIVE: CONGREGATION (POST-THERAPY ONGOING LIVING) When clients achieve a sense of successful passage, their lives are again characterized by spontaneous creativity and enjoyment. The person no longer relies on professional helpers (at least until another serious challenge). So one might say with satisfaction, "I feel like I have it together." During the aggregation phase, social workers can prepare clients to incorporate the learning from the helping process into self-help and mutual support in ongoing daily life in enhanced relationships with others. In anticipation of congregation, clients might be encouraged to commit to continuing new ways of thinking, feeling, acting, and relating after the helping relationship ends. When individual changes are linked to familial, friendship, and community support systems, then continuing of learning and growth is more likely. This is also an opportunity for the social worker to occasionally follow up with the client to help her or him continue to incorporate the changes.

The Flow of Transformation

So far we described the process of transformation with reference to individual growth over the course of an entire helping relationship. Whether the relationship lasts an hour, a day, 10 weeks, or a year, it can be understood in terms of this flow from spontaneous experience of life challenge through the helping process of separation, flux, and aggregation, and on to ongoing spontaneous living. Of course, a person might seek help with transformation many times throughout life, so this process would recur. In addition, there are often life events of transformation and growth that do not involve professional helpers.

Within the total span of the helping process, there are many small transformational experiences. For example, each helping encounter proceeds through a rite of helping, from initial greeting, through therapeutic work, to planning for future work and how to make headway, for example through therapeutic homework assignments, and closure of the session.

Within each helping encounter, there can be moments of powerful insights or catharses that break through habitual ways of thinking, feeling, and acting. The model of therapeutic transformation reminds us to be careful about these cathartic experiences. *Catharses* involve recalling and releasing painful memories and feelings. Therefore, social workers should only evoke them in the context of a safe and supportive environment. The released pain needs to be converted into creative energy that catalyzes growth. Cathartic episodes need to be processed, and integrated emotionally, physically, intellectually, and spiritually so that a sense of closure is reached before concluding a session.

The division of the formal helping process into three phases is an artificial simplification of a flowing experience. We feel this flow in a musical composition that builds theme and rhythm, crescendos, and then resolves. We sense it in the plot of a story, in which a narrative world is created, tensions are introduced, and then there is a denouement. Within each musical composition or story, as in all transformational forms, there are many variations of this flow.

We can relate this model to the familiar stages of therapeutic group development, from group formation and norm establishment (separation), through conflict resolution and synergistic interactions (flux) to completion of goals and reaching closure (aggregation) (Hutchison, 1999). And we know that in music and story, as well as in therapeutic work, conflict, complications, and catharses can occur at any time. As each of these breakthrough events are worked through, the sense of dynamic energy is enhanced.

Using Metaphors, Stories and Artistry in Therapeutic Transformation

This model of therapeutic transformation encourages us to draw on metaphors and stories pertinent to clients that demonstrate the spiritual growth potential inherent in their experiences. Once we identify the spiritual perspective of the client, we can ask her or him to identify symbols and stories of transformation and crisis resolution that are inspirational and encouraging. For example, Christians might look to the story of the passion, death, and resurrection of Jesus. Jews might reflect on the exodus from servitude in Egypt. Hindus might consider the story from the Bhagavad Gita about the crisis of the hero Arjuna confronting battle and how the divine Krishna advised him. Many people are familiar with the legend of the magical phoenix that bursts into flame and rises out of its own ashes into new life.

If no stories of transformation are familiar or appealing to the client, this itself is an important indicator. It is much easier to wander aimlessly when we do not have a map to guide us at a time of feeling lost. In this case, especially if the client is not religious, nonreligious metaphors for transformation could be explored, for example, the butterfly emerging from a cocoon, a baby bird hatching from it egg, the moon moving through its phases, the setting and rising of the sun, or the passage from coldness of winter to new vitality of spring. Sometimes symbols of transformation appear to clients spontaneously in dreams, daydreams, and visions.

In any case, it is important to personalize these metaphors and stories. Discussion with the client can explore how he or she has experienced transformation previously. One could ask the client to recall important dreams that depicted an experience of struggle and victory or resolution. Previous life experiences of challenge and courage can be recalled, identifying successful strategies and calling up reserves of resilience and courage. People who have been inspirational to the client for their ability to grow, overcome crises, and transform themselves and other people can be reflected upon. When these are ancestors, relatives, and friends, a sense of spiritual kinship and solidarity can be mobilized. If these inspiring figures are deceased ancestors or sacred beings, clients might find insight by engaging in an inner dialogue with them, asking for guidance and support. If they are living spiritual helpers, relatives and friends, clients can consider reconnecting or deepening their relationship with these significant people. People may also have special inspirational relationships with plants, animals, and other natural beings and places.

When we consider social work practice in the light of transformational ritual, we are reminded to pay attention to its creative, aesthetic, emotive, and dramatic qualities. If we work in a bland square office and approach helping only as an analytic discussion or problem solving task, our helping will hardly be vibrant, beautiful, inspiring, or conducive to transformation. Symbols of transformation and artistic modes of expression can be embedded within a therapeutic narrative and drama of resilience and growth. Siporin (2009, p. 1) said: "It is from such an aesthetic, artistic perspective that social workers are to be recognized as artists who create works of art through their knowledge and skills of social work practice. A group of family members may be helped to resolve a hostile, destructive set of relationships and to achieve an enduring state of an acceptable level of mutual trust, affection and working together. Such a state may be viewed as aesthetically beautiful, good and true, and thus as a work of art. Social work practice is essentially and primarily an art, and it is valid to consider it to be a scientific art. It is a way of seeking experiential, meaningful truth and producing aesthetic, transformative, helping actions and results." The following example illustrates spiritually sensitive practice as an artistic and transformational process.

An Example of a Transformational Helping Process

In spiritually sensitive practice, it is important to attend to these occasions of transformation, both at particular moments of breakthrough and in the overall process of helping. By supporting this transformational potential, we encourage the ongoing spiritual development of our clients. The transformational power of social work can be enhanced when the client's personal experience is connected with a spiritual tradition and community of support for the transformational process. I (EC) composed the following example from several of my experiences with former clients so that there is no identifying information.

Amy was experiencing stressors related to her personal spiritual development at the same time as dealing with disruptive behaviors of her teenage son and tensions with her husband. Although raised as a Catholic, she had recently begun practicing Buddhist meditation and attending intensive meditation retreats. I met with Amy and other members of her family over a period of several months, sometimes with Amy or her son alone and sometimes with the family together.

Amy had a series of dreams during this period in which she was trapped in a house with no windows. In an early dream, she looked through a keyhole in the door to the outside and saw a beautiful field. She longed to go out to this field, but could not open the door. In another dream, the house in which she was trapped was burning to the ground. These dreams were frightening. They symbolized Amy's feelings of being stuck, hopeless, and helpless in a tension fraught home and family life. However, Amy's view of another world outside conveyed the possibility that there was an alternative, if only she could find out how to open that door. This did not mean that Amy wanted to depart the family. Rather, it meant she wanted to find a way to transform the situation for the benefit of her whole family.

Since Amy was familiar with meditation and various visualization techniques, we agreed to create a meditation experience that would explore the possibility of liberation from this burning house. She began with her usual meditation practice in order to relax and center herself. I then suggested that she reenvision herself within the house from her dreams. She asked for inspiration about how to find a way out. As she explored the house more carefully, she realized that there was a trap door in the floor and she knew that she should go below.

Although she was nervous, she called upon her higher spiritual self for help. I reminded her that while she was in this waking dream, she could call on any powers needed to help her, just as in a sleeping dream. Feeling encouraged, she opened the trap door and climbed down a dark stairway. Along a long passageway, she encountered some frightening creatures that blocked her way. However, when she regarded them with compassion and let her spiritual light shine, the creatures disappeared, opening the way ahead. Deep below, she discovered an illuminated cavernous room with a pool of water. As she approached, she noticed an old bearded man with a kindly and reassuring manner. The old man beckoned her to enter the water. She did so, and felt renewed and strengthened, as though she had returned to her baptismal water of infancy. Afterward, the old man led her through a passageway that brought her up through a hole in the ground. She emerged into a beautiful sunlit field of flowers.

After this meditation journey, Amy felt that she rediscovered an inner reserve of spiritual vitality and strength as well as a more vivid sense of divine help. She felt confident that there would be a way out of her current crisis, although to get there would require the courage to go deep into a dark place of uncertainty. Amy decided to connect her personal experiences of transformation into her Buddhist practices of meditation and group retreats. She understood the Tibetan Buddhist concept that clear compassionate mind can transform poisons of affliction into elixirs of enlightenment.

The dreams, meditation experiences, and religious practices did not make Amy's problems and worries disappear suddenly and magically. However, they infused her efforts with a sense of hope, strength, and support. She was not going through this alone or aimlessly. Rather, she was following a meaningful pattern of suffering and transformation with the support of her social worker, her family, Buddhist community, and her personal meditation practice.

Amy's teenage son, Jim, was a focal point of family tension. In a sense, his disruptive behavior was an expression of the family system difficulties. Marital dyad tensions triangulated with the teenage son's defiant behavior. Although his mother's strong meditation practice was a comfort to her, he felt that the style was too restrictive. Jim was a drummer for a rock band. He liked to be with his friends, playing rock music, and partying. Sometimes he got into trouble. For example, he and his friends were driving down a street and noticed that someone left television equipment outside while in the process of moving into the house. On an impulse, he and his friends stole the television and sped away.

I met with Jim individually a few times. At first, Jim was not interested in talking about spirituality or doing meditation. Since I am also a percussionist, we found common interest. I asked him to think about what it was like when he played with his band. He reflected that in order to perform well, everyone had to practice extensively and to form synergy as a group. He was able to see that family life could also be like that. He had to learn to express himself fully while at the same time complementing and synergizing with all the family members.

I asked Jim to think about how he felt when he had a sudden impulse to do something dangerous, such as stealing. He described the energy rush of excitement. But he also acknowledged the painful consequences that came later. We discussed how his strong energy and impulses were good—they fed his creativity in music. His rapid action and high energy channeled into drumming resulted in good music rather than harmful consequences to himself or others. Since he recognized that, I asked if he would like to hear about how I use drumming to improve centering, focus, and creative energy, based on something I learned from my studies of meditative and ritual percussion.

326 SPIRITUALLY SENSITIVE SOCIAL WORK

Jim thought this was a good idea. He was intrigued with the idea of drumming spontaneously to express feelings, rather than playing preestablished music. This could become a kind of meditation suited to his personality, skill, and interest. We drummed together this way so that Jim could become comfortable with it. Jim began the drumming by paying attention to his feelings and expressing them. I joined in and together we flowed with the rhythms that emerged until we settled down into quiet. In this way, Jim experienced how he could be aware of his impulses and channel them in a creative way that gave him an energy rush without extremes of unbalanced feelings or harmful rash actions.

In this example of family based social work, the overall time of working with the family flowed through a transformational process. There were also particular transformational events that fueled and inspired the overall transformation process, for example, the waking dream meditation exercise with Amy and the drumming meditation with Jim. In addition, we connected these in-session transformational activities with out of session transformational processes, for example, Amy's meditation practice and Jim's rock band performances. Although the husband did not share interests in meditation or drumming, he was open to discussing the insights of his wife and son, and sharing his own views, within the family counseling sessions. This way, the particular spiritual interests and talents of family members were engaged within a whole family process. Our helping activities also matched my familiarity and training with Buddhist meditation, visualization exercises, and drumming.

Spiritual Growth Oriented Helping Activities

As discussed in Chapter 9, our National Survey of Social Workers showed that a large percentage of social workers utilize a wide range of spiritually oriented helping activities. Also, the spiritual perspectives on service (Part II) offer many other helping techniques. The next section of the chapter provides a more detailed introduction to the practice of some of these techniques to encourage greater use of these valuable ways of helping.

Note that there are many spiritually oriented psychotherapy and social work approaches that have specific theoretical presuppositions and concomitant implications for the helping relationship and specific therapeutic techniques (Sperry & Shafranske, 2005). For example, helping practices could be embedded within any of the religious or nonsectarian perspectives presented in Part II (e.g. Buddhist, Christian, deep ecological). They might be rooted in particular psychotherapeutic traditions such as spiritually-oriented cognitive-behavioral therapy, spiritually oriented psychoanalysis, existential therapy, or transpersonal therapies such as holotropic breathwork. They might be very specific to particular communities, such as the social work approaches that have been found useful with Beduoin Arab communities (Al-Krenawi & Graham, 2009). Practitioners should be clear about matching their practices with the cultures, spiritual perspectives, and comfort of clients and their communities. They also should consider the issue of congruence between client background, chosen helping practices, and the theoretical assumptions behind them. It is beyond the scope of this book to present detailed descriptions of techniques for the full range of client backgrounds and theories. So we refer the reader to our extensive citations for these details. We present techniques that may be relevant to self-care of the social worker as well as a wide range of clients and contexts, keeping in mind the importance of selecting or adapting them as appropriate.

We selected helping techniques according to several criteria. First, they *promote spiritual development.* They help clients move in a sense of healing and wholeness on their chosen paths and aspirations. Second, their practice *results in an immediate perception of benefit,* in the forms of clarified awareness of self and others, reduction of tension and distraction, and new insights. Third, they are *conducive to transpersonal awareness and experiences.* Fourth, they are so *basic to being human* that there are versions in most, if not all, religious traditions and cultures. For example, all people breathe and all religious traditions recognize the significance of intentional, careful breathing. Indeed, many languages have words that associate spirit with vital force and breath; for example, *spiritus* (Latin), *ruach* (Hebrew), *pneuma* (Greek), *prana* (Sanskrit), and *qi* (Chinese).

Fifth, the techniques are *nonreligious in form,* although they may have been derived from or inspired by religious traditions. Sixth, they *can be linked to specific religious versions* of the practice, if a client so desires. Seventh, they *can be applied to many different practice situations.* Eighth, they are relatively *easy to learn.* Ninth, they *do not require extensive formal training,* unless they are taken to a refined level or they are practiced in the context of a specific tradition or manualized therapy. Tenth, they *involve low risk to clients.* Eleventh, their effectiveness is supported by extensive *scientific evidence and/or long-standing traditions.*

Regarding this last point, although the scientific evidence base about these practices is growing, social work and allied professions are still at a relatively early stage of research (Ai, 2006; Cook, Becvar, & Pontius, 2000). Also, most of the empirical studies use quantitative measures of outcomes and report findings based on group trends. The evidence based practice movement encourages that a specific treatment be well defined and described in a manual so that practitioners can be trained in precise and consistent application of the treatment. Research on outcomes with particular client groups can be conducted. When numerous studies are completed, findings can be compared and conclusions about effectiveness can be made. For example, Pargament (2007) presents a list of nine manualized treatments that have an explicit spiritual focus, varying in religious or nonsectarian orientation, dealing with such issues as addiction, coping with medical illnesses such as HIV/AIDS, anxiety disorders, sexual abuse, eating disorders, and forgiveness. This kind of evidence can give helpful indications about possible relevance and effectiveness, but it does not guarantee relevance or effectiveness for a particular practice situation or particular individuals, cultures, communities, or situations. Manualization can enhance faithfulness of application of tested treatments, but it can also sacrifice situation specificity, cultural appropriateness, and spontaneity. Of course, if a client agrees to a manualized treatment, it is necessary for the practitioner to apply it faithfully. However, we emphasize the importance of applying any technique, manualized or otherwise, within the context of a spiritually sensitive and culturally appropriate helping relationship. In tandem with this, we emphasize the importance of evaluating client satisfaction and impact of practices in each situation, through research methods that are themselves spiritually sensitive and culturally appropriate.

We will present some general contraindications and cautions. Then, we will present four ingredients of many spiritually oriented therapeutic practices: paying attention, intentional breathing, equipoise, and consistency. These are prerequisites for the other spiritually oriented helping activities to be described: focused relaxing, caring for the body, doing ritual and ceremony, and practicing forgiveness. These activities can be tailored to specific purposes and spiritual beliefs as needed. Of course, when clients are interested in religion-specific spiritual practices, they can be incorporated into practice according to the ethical guidelines described in Chapter 8. In describing these practices, we draw on many works that the reader may wish to consult for greater detail (e.g. Bullis, 1996; Canda, 1990a; Chan, 2001; Hanh, 1987; Keefe, 1996; Krill, 1990; Lee, Ng, Leung et al., 2009; Mace, 2008; Marlatt & Kristeller, 1999; McBee, 2008; McKay, Wood, & Brantley, 2007; Press & Osterkamp, 2006).

General Contraindications, Cautions, and Indications

Any practice, no matter how ordinary or common, can lead to unexpected and sometimes difficult experiences. Especially if a client is on the verge of a crisis or spiritual emergency, any practice that opens up awareness to the inner world of deep feelings or loosens the ego boundary can catalyze a breakthrough or breakdown. For example, a simple deep relaxation exercise could put a person in touch with a repressed traumatic memory. This could result in a valuable cathartic experience. However, people sometimes need support for breakdown to lead to breakthrough. It is important that practitioners stay alert to this, obtain feedback from the client about progress, and offer support and opportunity to work things through as necessary.

We presume that the social worker is following the ethical guidelines presented in the previous chapter. For example, the NASW Code of Ethics requires that practitioners have established competency before applying any particular helping activities. So, one should not apply any of these spiritually oriented practices with clients without first having significant personal experience and sufficient formal training with them. Therefore, we introduce the practices as exercises for the reader to do, before considering using them with clients.

If a client has a serious physical or mental condition that involves fragile health or psychological instability, special precautions should be taken. For example, in the case of mental disorders or personality disorders, keep in mind a simple principle of transpersonal therapy. Generally, adults should have a relatively well-established ego, with sense of self esteem and positive relationships, before it is safe to challenge and transcend the ego. Promoting transpersonal (transegoic) experiences does not mean destroying the ego or denigrating it. It means including and transcending it. So, for example, if someone already is confused about who he or she is, it would not be appropriate to use a relaxation technique for the purpose of dis-identifying with the individual body and mind (Assagioli, 1965). If a person is experiencing uncontrollable and unpleasant hallucinations, it wouldn't be wise to induce further altered states of consciousness. It would be better to engage a practice that helps to ground and center the person.

However, the simple practices described here could also be helpful in dealing with mental disorders. For example, people with anxiety disorders could learn relaxation techniques. People experiencing depression could learn to do meditative self-affirmations. People coping with certain types of schizophrenia might be able to ground themselves and relieve hallucinatory or delusional episodes through paying attention exercises. A person with bipolar disorder might benefit from paying-attention exercises and relaxation, so that he or she can be more alert to the beginning of mood swings in order to take preventive action (such as changing medication) and in order to reduce the extremes of the swings. Our point is that special care and training on the part of the practitioner is needed to attend to serious acute or chronic physical or mental distress or disability (Nelson, 1994).

In general, it is helpful to choose spiritual practices that build on clients' strengths and provide a balancing complement to their problematic extremes. For example, highly introspective clients would likely be comfortable with quiet sitting, while the same activity might be frustrating to an extrovert. The extrovert might be more comfortable with body focused therapies and meditative practices done during physical activity like jogging, listening to music, or driving a car.

A person's problematic extreme could be balanced by learning a new skill. For example, if a person who is extremely introverted used introspective meditation defensively to avoid dealing with physical issues or social interactions, this would not help her or him to integrate whatever benefits come from meditation into daily life. So physical exercise routines learned and practiced in a group, such as *hatha yoga* or *qigong* might help the person to integrate spiritual learning with the physical and social realms.

We have to be very respectful of clients' spiritual beliefs and related attitudes about spiritual practices. For example, some theologically conservative Christians believe that forms of systematic relaxation or guided visualization are tantamount to New Age brainwashing or demonic tricks. As always, our practice decisions need to be client-centered. So we have to find out what the client believes about these things.

Although it is unlikely with the exercises to be described here, it is possible that someone might report an unusually intense or frightening experience that goes beyond the understanding, worldview, or experience of the social worker. An obvious example would be a sense of attack by evil forces. Our advice—don't pretend you know what you are doing and don't minimize or discount the experience. Take it very seriously, whatever your own belief system. If this experience is clearly a symptom of a mental disorder, then of course appropriate mental health consultation is necessary. However, such an experience can occur in situations that have nothing to do with mental disorders. If necessary refer to or collaborate with a competent spiritual support person or religious leader who shares a perspective similar to the client. And also, take care of your own feelings.

I (EC) recall an emotionally charged consulting visit to a mental health center dealing with this in the early 1990s. Staff members asked me and a colleague to talk with staff about an increasing incidence of clients who claimed to have been traumatized in satanic rituals. This is a very controversial and complex subject, that gained considerable attention in the 1980s and 1990s (e.g. see Melton, 1993; Peck, 1983; Robbins, 1997). However, official satanic organizations disavowed violence and police investigations in my state did not uncover any satanic conspiracies, as had been alleged. Yet the bottom line was that some staff people in this agency felt distressed and confused.

The major issue that emerged was that a few staff people were experiencing similar frightening things. They were worried that somehow they could be under physical or even magical attack. They were confused about the possible reality of the clients' reported experiences and the demonic forces and dangerous people that were allegedly involved. Yet they had not been talking to one another out of fear of embarrassment or sounding unprofessional. During our discussion, it became clear that staff people found various ways of dealing with the stress that made sense within their own religious beliefs and personal styles. Talking about this openly relieved the feelings of isolation and strangeness. Staff decided that they needed to be more open with each other, to help each other ventilate and process feelings, to share effective coping strategies, and to give each other affirmation and support. These are excellent recommendations for any practitioners in stressful working conditions!

On the other hand, techniques that open oneself up to transpersonal experiences could lead to amazingly wonderful but surprising events, such as peak experiences and revelations. As we noted in Chapter 7, even positively perceived peak experiences can shake the foundations of one's sense of self and reality. If a peak experience generates a spiritual emergency, then the social worker certainly needs to help the client work this through to a plateau of enhanced living.

Practicing Mindfulness and Meditation

Mindfulness practice originates from the Buddhist tradition in which clear awareness of subjective experiences and their roots in subtle mental conditions can engender freedom from the bonds of attraction, aversion, and ignorance that keep one enmeshed in suffering while also opening up a nonjudgmental compassionate orientation to relieve the suffering of others (Hanh, 1987; Mace, 2008). The qualities of mindfulness can be found in many religious traditions of meditation and contemplation, such as Christian centering prayer, Kabbalistic Judaism, Sufism, and Confucianism (Sherman & Siporin, 2008). As Marlatt and Kristeller (1999, p. 68) said in regard to mindfulness related meditation, "The full value of meditative practices is best understood as tapping into the universal potential for the human mind to transcend its preoccupation with negative experiences—with fears, anxiety, anger, and obsessions—and to become more comfortable with the experiences of compassion, acceptance, and forgiveness."

In the mental health and health fields, mindfulness is an important ingredient in dialectical behavior therapy, spiritually oriented cognitive therapy, and mindfulness based stress reduction therapy (Baer, 2006). Many mindfulness related meditation practices are utilized to reduce stress and promote resilience for both clients and practitioners in health, mental health, and social work fields (Coholic, 2006; McBee, 2008; Press & Osterkamp, 2006; Sherman & Siporin, 2008). In a more holistic sense, mindfulness is an important quality of nonreligious Zen inspired approaches to social work (e.g. Bein, 2008) and spiritually sensitive practice, as we have described in this book.

Meditation and Mindfulness Defined

Meditation refers to a wide range of practices that involve intentionally focusing attention, commonly joined with balanced well-poised posture (e.g. while sitting or walking), letting go of ordinary preoccupations, distractions, and ruminative thinking, and deepening one's insight or experience of consciousness (Fontana, 2003; Fuller, 2008; Newberg & Newberg, 2005; Press & Osterkamp, 2006). Three broad types of meditation can be distinguished by the intention behind them although they are not necessarily mutually exclusive (Shapiro, Schwartz, & Santerre, 2005). *Concentrative meditation* focuses awareness on a single object. *Mindfulness meditation* attends nonjudgmentally to internal and external stimuli without being caught up in them. *Contemplative meditation* opens and surrenders oneself to a higher self, God, or benevolent other. Many concentrative and contemplative techniques include qualities of mindfulness.

Mindfulness means paying attention to the present moment with a clear mind that acknowledges what is without judgment (Coholic, 2006; Mace, 2008; McBee, 2008). Orsillo, Roemer, Lerner, & Tull (2004, p. 77) define mindfulness as "a process that involves moving toward a state in which one is fully observant of external and internal stimuli in the present moment, and open to accepting (rather than attempting to change or judge) the current situation." There are a variety of mindfulness related techniques that can be joined with specific therapeutic systems that are tailored to particular health or mental health issues.

Many meditative and mindfulness practices incorporate relaxation. However, *relaxation training* intends to create a condition of low autonomic arousal. Meditation and mindfulness add the purposes of deepening insight into the nature of mental processes, consciousness, one's true identity, the nature of reality, and developing optimal well-being or spiritual awakening.

Empirical Support for Beneficial Effects of Meditation and Mindfulness

Specific types of meditation have specific related effects. There are more than 2000 published empirical studies of meditation, including mindfulness (Fontana, 2003; Koenig, McCullough, & Larson, 2001; Newberg & Newberg, 2005; Shapiro, Schwartz, & Santerre, 2005). In general, therapeutic meditation is associated with decreased stress, anxiety, nonclinical depression, cardiovascular disease, pain; heightened capacity for sense of control, spiritual experiences, creativity, positive affects, empathy, and acceptance; and heightened perception, reaction time, and concentration. For example, some types of meditation can alter the autonomic nervous system to decrease heart rate, blood pressure, and respiratory rate, and oxygen metabolism. Certain types of meditation can induce significant changes of consciousness states, including mystical experiences, which may be associated with changes in the neurochemical systems. It is now easy to obtain biofeedback equipment, such as a galvanic skin response device, to show immediate physiological changes that correspond to subjective changes of relaxation. More advanced equipment, such as PET scans and EEG monitors, reveal changes in brain waves and activity in specific areas of the brain in relation to various meditation techniques. Mindfulness practices have been shown to be effective with regard to a wide range of issues, including personality disorders, mood disorders, severe mental disorders (psychosis), pain management, partner violence, and coping with serious illness (Baer, 2006; Dimeff & Koerner, 2007).

We present basic meditative practices conducive to mindfulness, relaxation, and mental clarity without Buddhist specific language and religious practice. This has an advantage of making the benefits of meditation practice available to a wide range of people, without discrimination on the basis of religion or culture. Many helping professionals who advocate mindfulness in this nonreligious form (including both the authors) have received training by Buddhist teachers who encouraged broad application for helping others.

However, it should be kept in mind that the application of mindfulness and meditation practices outside of their original religious contexts and purposes changes them in a profound way. For example, mindfulness is one practice in a total Buddhist path of religious disciplines and lifestyle designed to lead to enlightenment. In contrast, mindfulness within a mental health therapy is a technique designed to promote mental health outcomes, such as reduced symptoms of anxiety or depression, reduction of harmful behaviors such as binge eating, or promotion of self-esteem and positive feelings such as peace and joy. These benefits do not necessarily lead to enlightenment. Attachment to such benefits are actually hindrances to enlightenment in the Buddhist view. Indeed, some Zen meditation practices are designed to induce intense doubt and question about the nature of self and reality in order to break through to deeper realization. This can be quite the opposite of relaxation. As another example, Christian centering prayer, as a meditative practice, includes beneficial health and mental health effects, but those are not the aim. The aim is to rest in loving awareness of God without attachment to results. Yet, we believe therapeutic application of mindfulness and meditation is congruent with the spiritual virtue of compassion. For clients who wish to connect therapeutic goals with a deeper sense of spiritual development, then meditation can support both narrow benefits and the quest for enlightenment or spiritual awakening understood in other spiritual ways.

Paying Attention

The simple act of attention has a healing and restoring effect. When we notice something, we are more acutely affected by it. When we pay attention without attachment, we are acutely aware but not controlled by the object of attention. When we pay attention to ourselves, we are alert to our thoughts, feelings, sensations, and intuitions. When we pay attention to others, we can perceive them accurately and empathize. When we pay attention to the world, the amazing quality of each moment becomes clear. When we notice very carefully, we discover new things and we experience even very familiar things freshly and vividly. Paying attention is free and leads to freedom of mind. It is a practice that is always available.

Mindful paying attention involves clear awareness, moment to moment: accepting without judging. We can be aware of our feelings, thoughts, and sensations without being carried away by them. We can appreciate them without being inappropriately attached to or enmeshed in them. We can liberate ourselves from them without being inappropriately averse or rejecting them.

For example, if someone insults or contradicts you at a staff meeting, you might feel angry and reply in an angry manner. This might trigger an ongoing argument, elevating your own stress, emotionally injuring the other party, and damaging the communication process of the group. This sequence of escalating unpleasant and counter productive actions can be prevented. By practicing gentle clear awareness of communications in the meeting, as well as your own internal responses, it will become possible to hear each person without judgmentalism and knee-jerk reactions. It will be easier to take the other's point of view. It will also be easier to express your own view with clarity and to facilitate a constructive communication process in the group.

When I (EC) was director of our school's Ph.D. program in social work for the past 8 years, I practiced this skill in meetings with students and faculty members many times. The more mindful I was, the better the process and outcome of the meetings. Fellow faculty persons and doctoral students often said they felt respected and listened to. There were few outbursts and arguments in meetings. People often remarked that they felt more peaceful and centered when we met, especially when they entered the space of my office. However, I was not (and am not) always mindful. When I became unfocused and carried away by my own internal reactions and judgmentalism, I felt scattered and swayed and had difficulty facilitating solution-oriented communication dynamics. On rare occasion, I was the object of vociferous disagreement that rattled my composure. But that kind of experience also is just part of the flow of human interaction. So eventually I processed my feelings, moved on, and returned to mindfulness practice later.

A simple exercise to begin with is to pay attention to any common object. Suppose you are ready to eat an orange. Before beginning, look at it closely. Notice the subtle colors of its peel. Do not assume what it looks like. Note every shade of color, every rumple. Touch it and note its texture. Smell it. Then, open the peel as if you are opening up a gift. Allow yourself to be surprised by what is wrapped within. Be vividly aware of the pungent smell, the soft texture, the dripping liquid, veins running through the flesh. Then, taste. Move the piece of orange around in your mouth to sense it with every part of your tongue. Discover the variations of flavor that come with each piece. If you do this, you will discover a new kind of orange, even if you have eaten a thousand of the same kind before!

Now, apply this learning to all aspects of life. While walking, savor the walk. While conversing, savor the conversation. While showering, savor the cleansing shower. While keeping company with a loved one, savor the loving connection. Each moment is so precious yet it immediately disappears. Our enjoyment of life can be greatly enhanced by such a simple thing as paying attention.

In my (EC) MSW course on spirituality in social work practice, I often extend this exercise through a kind of mindful walking. For example, I often bring students to a nearby pond. I ask the students to walk silently and individually around the pond, paying attention to each moment through open senses. If they feel drawn to a place to stop and quietly sit, they may do so. All the while, they just perceive. At the beginning, I say that I will ask them when they return to report one experience they never had before. When we gather together after the walk, I invite students to take turns recounting their experiences, while we all listen with quiet nonjudgmental awareness. One person might notice how they suddenly became quiet and peaceful inside. Another might perceive the glint of sunlight on the water with greater vividness than ever before. Another might express wonder at a butterfly that followed him or her around. Someone else might report intrusive inner chatter and worries that he or she was unable to release. Some notice how things that usually seemed mundane and taken for granted became more lovely and significant.

A more difficult version of this is to pay attention to some uncomfortable sensation. We suggest you start with something mild. Suppose you feel tired from a long day of work. Try lying down in a comfortable position and just pay attention to all the details of what it feels like to be tired out. Soon, the tiredness will be relieved. If not, this tells you to attend even more carefully to your need for rest. Or, to go back to the example of a business meeting, practice just seeing and hearing every other person in the room. Notice their tone of voice, what they are wearing, the feeling they put into their comments. If you have a pen or pencil, pay attention to its color, shape, size, and weight. Just notice these things and qualities without judgment. Then, as someone makes a comment that you find irritating or disagreeable, just notice the comment and your reaction. But do not react to your reaction. Just be aware and let it go. Only respond after you are able to accept the moment and the person with clear awareness.

It is important that paying attention be done gently and nonjudgmentally. Especially if you are paying attention to a painful feeling or sensation, regard yourself gently, lovingly, and soothingly. If you pay attention with harshness, anger, or self-condemnation, you will surely intensify the negative experience.

Intentional Breathing

Of course, our lives depend on breathing. Yet we often take breathing for granted unless our oxygen is cut short by lack of air in a stuffy room or by a respiratory problem. When we pay attention to breathing, more benefits emerge. Of course, it is perfectly natural to breathe automatically most of the time. However, taking periods through the day to watch the breath and settle into it can instantly relieve stress and clarify the mind. It is easier to be mindful when our breathing is smooth and peaceful.

In intentional breathing, we first pay attention to the fact that we are breathing. This practice is easiest to begin by setting aside several minutes without distraction. Find a position in which you are not physically strained, such as sitting upright or laying down. Just notice that you are breathing. Notice the rate of breaths in and out. How deep or shallow are the breaths? How do the abdomen and chest move? Notice how changes of posture affect your breathing.

Now, take in a gentle but deep breath from the abdomen. Bring in the breath to a comfortable extent, then release it slowly and gently for about twice the length of time as the inhalation. Notice how your body and mind feel, already calming and clearing of distractions and distress.

Take 10 breaths in and out like this. You may find it helpful to pause slightly in between each inhalation and exhalation, noticing the quiet moment in between. After 10 breaths, rest for a few moments in a sense of peace and calm. Let your breathing settle into a gentle natural rhythm. Now, return to your previous activity, but bring with you the rest and clarity from this breathing exercise.

If you notice an increase of distractions or uncomfortable sensations, that is a cue that you should pay attention to that uncomfortable feeling. As soon as you can, take care of whatever physical, mental, emotional, or spiritual issue arose. But when you do, try beginning with three intentional relaxing breaths.

Equipoise

Another quality conducive to meditation and mindfulness that is consistent with many spiritual practices is mental and physical balance. The body and mind are poised free of strain or exaggerated motions. Even in some vigorous physical practices, like trance dancing or ritual drumming, the body can be moved in a way that does not strain or harm it. Otherwise, you will be worse off afterward. There are exceptional practices that are designed to rapidly induce transpersonal experiences or to sacrifice one's comfort for others' spiritual well-being, such as enduring extreme austerities or intense physical stimulation and pain. But they require special guidance and support (Achterberg, 1985).

Generally, balance of body and mind are important qualities to prepare for spiritual practices. Literally, the body can be held in postures that are balanced and free of strain. The mind can be poised in a state that balances relaxation with alertness. This combination encourages moving into altered states of consciousness, such as relaxed introspection, heightened awareness of the environment, or deeper meditative states.

It is best to do this in a quiet place at a time when you are not likely to be disturbed and when your stomach is neither too full nor too empty. It is easy for most people to begin this practice by sitting in a comfortable position. Many people find it comfortable to sit on a low cushion with legs crossed. Some people prefer to sit on a comfortable chair, with ankles crossed. In either case, it is best, when possible, to keep the spine straight (but not forced) and to find a natural balancing point. This is aided by being sure that there are solid points of rest for your body: your seat on the cushion or chair and your legs or feet on the floor. Hands can be folded in the lap or rested on the knees. The head rests in a balanced way atop the neck and shoulders. The eyes can be gently closed or half open.

Adjust the posture for your own comfort and body type. When you find a sense of physical equipoise, you will notice that it is easier to calm the mind. The breath will also flow more smoothly. Once you are familiar with the feeling of equipoise while quietly sitting, extend the practice of finding equipoise while walking, jogging, and engaging in other postures and activities. Indeed, the experience of physical equipoise can open you to a sense of equipoise in how you conduct your life in general, for example, in well-poised relationships.

Consistency

In order to become proficient in any practice, consistency is necessary. Also, while there are immediate beneficial effects of these practices, benefits accumulate and grow with consistent repetition. So it is best to set aside a quiet place and time at least once every day, for at least 10 minutes, to practice these exercises. Actually, the exercises all fit nicely together. You can combine them by finding a comfortable, balanced posture, intentionally breathing, and paying attention to your experience. Once you become familiar with this, you will be able to move into a relaxed but alert state very quickly, within a few moments.

Then you can extend the complete practice into your daily activities more easily. When sitting at a boring meeting, try finding a comfortable posture and pay attention to your breath. Soon the meeting will become more interesting or at least bearable. When sitting with a client, try these exercises to help you listen and respond more accurately, empathetically, and intuitively. The ideal is to infuse all of life with these qualities of attention, breath (inspiration), and equipoise.

These basic exercises provide a foundation that can be applied to many other practices conducive to spiritual growth. We next discuss four such practices that can be further be applied to various purposes in social work practice: focused relaxation meditation, mindful caring for the body, ritual practice, and forgiveness.

Focused Deep Relaxation

Once you have learned to combine paying attention with intentional breathing and equipoise, you already have begun focused relaxing. Focused relaxing means there is a combination of focus and relaxation. The mind is neither wandering aimlessly nor tightly controlled. The body is neither limp nor strained. Most people find that sitting is the easiest posture for focused relaxing, because laying down increases the risk of falling asleep. But once one learns the technique, it can be used with any posture, depending on your purpose.

Many people find it comforting to begin with a brief affirmation of intention or prayer that centers one in a sense of goodwill and protection. As we discuss later, it is important to set a purpose for the focused relaxation, as that can determine the specific technique of relaxation to use as well as the internal activity while one is relaxed. Find a posture of equipoise, establish harmonious breathing, and pay attention mindfully. This sets the foundation for more extended relaxation or meditation.

There are some common techniques for maintaining focus during extended sitting. One is to follow the breath, as we already discussed. You might try counting on each inhalation: one... two... three... up to ten; and then start over again. If you lose count, your attention has wavered. No problem. Go back to one.

A common mistake in focused relaxing is being too impatient or judgmental. All you need to do is just let yourself *be* relaxed. It is natural for people to settle into relaxation when given the chance. There is no need to force yourself to relax. Suppose you notice that you've lost count. Then, in your mind, you complain to yourself for being so distracted. That is a sure way to become more distracted! Just return to one and begin counting again or you may become tense because you are not yet relaxed enough. Just return to one.

This is very simple and natural. Watch a cat stretch and settle into relaxation. No one had to teach the cat how to do that. Learn from a cat to just relax naturally.

Another common focusing technique is to use a word or brief phrase that you repeat to yourself silently. Often this is termed a *mantra*, meaning sacred word, from Hindu and Buddhist traditions. But there are versions of focusing words in all religious meditation traditions. It is often best if you choose a word or short phrase that feels like it fits you well. It might have a special spiritual significance to you. It might come from a spiritual teacher or tradition. Or it might have no literal meaning. It should be short enough so that you can harmonize its repetition with the inflow and outflow of breath. For example, breathe in "peace;" breathe out "for all."

If any distracting or disturbing thoughts, feelings, or sensations arise, just be gently aware of them, remind yourself that you will remember them if important after the session so you can attend to them. Then let them go. Best results are obtained with a minimum of 10–20 minutes at a sitting.

If we add an intention to use relaxation as an entry for developing deeper insight, then it transitions to meditation. An important ingredient of any meditation or relaxation practice is *purpose*, such as just relaxing or cultivating insight. A purpose is necessary to focus the practice's direction and specific use. There are three common directions for focus of awareness in various relaxation and meditation techniques: outward, inward, and at the boundary in between. These directions of focus can link with purposes for a meditation session.

If you want to clarify your awareness of the outside world, then an outward focus of awareness will affect your technique. So, in quiet sitting, outward focusing techniques include keeping your eyes open and gazing gently at an attractive or significant but mild stimulus, such as a candle flame, or symbol, or a meaningful picture. One could listen to music or natural sounds that are inspiring. One could chant aloud a focusing word or phrase. Outward focus can also be used to enhance walking, driving, or any other physical or social activity.

If you want to enhance awareness of your inner thoughts, feelings, sensations, intuitions, or stillness and quiet, then it would be helpful to close the eyes, or keep them only slightly open, and to avoid loud or distracting sounds. Use an inner focus, such as the breath or a silent focusing word.

You might also wish to cultivate an awareness that is not fixed in either the internal or external worlds, but is restfully clear between them. In this case, you can follow the breath and/or a focusing silent word, keep the eyes gently and slightly open, and let your attention rest at the border between inside and outside yourself. For example, you could rest your gaze at a spot on the floor a foot or two in front of you, without fixing on the spot but also without losing awareness of it.

Purpose also directs what you want to accomplish with your chosen practice. Actually, it is often very restful not to try to accomplish anything, but just to dwell in the peace of the experience. But we might have a particular helping or healing purpose in mind, or a spiritual practice for deepening insight that could lead to other adjunct techniques. In this case, focused relaxation is a gateway into some other practice. Here are several examples.

Inward directed focus can prepare one for various kinds of self discovery. There are many learning exercises in this book based on *self-reflection*. So, inward focused relaxation can clarify awareness of one's feelings, thoughts, sensations, and intuitions and the reasons behind them, through introspective self-reflection. It can also prepare one to explore the creativity of imagination. For example, in the Jungian *active imagination* technique, the person relaxes and pays attention to the spontaneous flow of images and inner dialogue in relation to some important life theme. One might seek out conversation with an inner guide, or an important inspirational figure, to seek advice. In the Jungian form of practice, these are conversations with deep and wise aspects of the transpersonal True Self. Active imagination can be applied to *exploring the meaning of dreams*, as well, by reentering the dream situation and letting the dream play out further, or by dialoguing with the dream figures.

One could also use inward focused awareness to prepare for religion specific forms of *prayer* that involve getting in touch with the divine within yourself. Some forms of *contemplation* or *meditation* involve going within oneself into an experience of quiet and stillness that involves no contents of thought, feeling, sensation, self, or object. In theistic traditions, such as Christian centering prayer, this is described as a communion with God beyond all limiting images and thoughts of God.

Outward focused awareness can lead directly into self-reflective *journaling* or diary keeping, reading of *inspirational books or scriptures*, or *artistic expressions* such as poetry, drawing, dance or musical performance. When applied in therapeutic contexts, these practices can help clients open up many sources of insight into self, one's life situation, and creative ways of solving problems, working through crises, or growing.

In-between focused awareness has the advantage that it can prepare one for activities that move in either direction, inward or outward. Of course, any directional focus can prepare one for any type of activity, if you shift direction while continuing the experience of clarity. Indeed, focused relaxation is an excellent skill to incorporate into the following practices.

Caring for the Body

Although we often say that, as social workers, we want to deal with the whole person, bio-psycho-social (and now spiritual) aspects in all, we too often neglect the body (as well as the spirit). Clients who feel stressed, hurt, and confused also may tend to neglect their bodies. So caring for the body is an important ingredient in holistic spiritually sensitive practice. In some religious traditions, this notion is embodied (pun intended) in such expressions as "the body is the temple of the divine." Whatever our beliefs, we know that we can't live without the body, so let's make the best of it.

Everyone has occasions when they crave caring attention to their bodies. For example, at a time of illness or dying, the body is especially tender and in need of care. At such times, if we are able, we should tend to our own bodies with the same kind of careful paying attention as we use to prepare for focused relaxation. Indeed, practice in focused relaxation can help put us in touch with inner reserves of resilience and it can relieve pain and distress. When our loved ones or clients are physically distressed, we can also help them to find the physical comfort and care they need. We intend that this goes beyond the technical aspects of medical care. Medical treatments, unfortunately, may be given without caring attention. Caring attention is the more fundamental medicine.

We also suggest that caring for the body is a practice that should be done everyday, whatever the state of physical health. This promotes overall well-being and helps to prevent stress. There are many such practices possible; for example, regular *exercise, sports activities, walking in beautiful places*, following a *healthy eating pattern, gardening*, taking a *relaxing shower or bath*. One could learn *physical exercise* systems that have an explicit spiritual orientation, such as taiji or hatha yoga. There are many types of body therapies that can be received from trained professionals (or loved ones), such as *therapeutic touch* and *massage*. Any type of physical care can be conducive to spiritual growth when it involves paying caring attention and is placed within the context of the person's spiritual aspirations.

We need to make a cautionary note on body therapies that involve touching clients. There is a great deal of potential for misuse or abuse of touching clients. Even a simple gesture intended as a sign of friendliness, such as touching a client's shoulder, can be an unwanted intrusion. In some cultures, touching the head is considered rude and jarring. More intimate kinds of touch, like massage, are even more risky. If a social worker wishes to incorporate these practices within his or her own work (rather than making referrals), it is important to have clear, explicit, informed consent from clients as well as appropriate training. It is crucial to be sure that psychodynamic issues don't complicate and confuse the meaning of touch if both psychotherapy and massage are combined. As we mentioned in Chapter 9, touching clients for healing purposes was the least used or approved helping activity by respondents in our National Survey. This is a little explored area in social work so far. A quote regarding physical contact from the NASW Code of Ethics (standard 1.10, p. 13) is noteworthy here:

> Social workers should not engage in physical contact with clients when there is a possibility of psychological harm to the client as a result of the contact (such as cradling or caressing clients). Social workers who engage in appropriate physical contact with clients are responsible for setting clear, appropriate, and culturally sensitive boundaries that govern such physical contact.

This statement is vague as to what specific types of contact are prohibited. However, it is clear that the onus is placed on the social worker to establish competency, minimal risk for the client, and a good rationale for the practice.

Table 10.1.   General Qualities of Mindfulness, Meditation, and Systematic
Relaxation.

Paying Attention
• Gently focused, consistent awareness
• To specific objects or inner focus
• Throughout the flow of daily life, moment to moment

Intentional Breathing
• Simple awareness of breathing and gratitude for life with
• Special attention to inhalation and exhalation
• That can be aided by counting breaths, or
• Synchronizing breaths with mantra, prayer, or any brief word/phrase of significance

Equipoise
• Balance of body in unstrained coordinated posture
• Balance of mind in equanimity, unswayed by extremes, preoccupations, or aversions
• Ongoing balance in care for body, mind, spirit, relationships, and overall well-being

Consistency
• Regular practice, daily if possible, at least 10 minutes
• Developing proficiency and cumulative benefits

Focused Systematic Relaxation
• Letting go
• Going with the flow
• Nonjudgmental awareness

Purpose
• Setting sincere intention and practical purpose for a particular meditation session
• Clarifying link with a tradition of spiritual or therapeutic practice, if relevant
• Specifying focus of attention: within, outer world, border between

Specific Techniques
• Practicing techniques for specific spiritual and therapeutic forms of meditation,
  if necessary, under guidance of experienced teachers
• Being responsible about indications and contraindications for yourself and clients
• Exploring what works best for the person in situation

Life as Meditation
• Extending benefits of meditation to pervade your life
• Regarding life itself as a meditative process
• Meditating everywhere, at all times

Further Possibilities
• Meditative music listening
• Meditative walking and movement
• Meditative dance
• Meditative chanting and singing
• Meditative group activities

We summarize the main generic qualities of meditation, mindfulness, and relaxation practices in Table 10.1. Table 10.2 offers three brief meditation exercises that can be learned quickly. Table 10.3 presents directions for a more in-depth systematic relaxation exercise.

Table 10.2. Three Brief Meditation Exercises.

These exercises are especially useful to generate quickly a sense of rest and regeneration, to release tensions and distractions, and to heighten clarity for helping self and others. Practitioners might find them useful to prepare for a clear fresh mind before meeting a client, for releasing residual feelings after a session, and for replenishment any time. The exercises could be taught to clients who wish to augment their stress management skills.

1. Letting Go of Stress

   - Sit in a comfortable position, balanced but without physical strain
   - Close the eyes gently
   - Notice how you feel in the moment as you settle into quiet
   - Take in one deep but gentle breath from the lower abdomen
   - Release the breath and let yourself settle into a gentler, smooth flow of breathing in and out
   - Remind yourself to settle into peaceful relaxation together with clear bright mind
   - Then begin a special breathing and visualization practice
   - With each breath in, imagine you are filled with replenishing, refreshing air and energy. If you wish, add a visualization that you are filled and surrounded with a light of your favorite healing or soothing color
   - With each breath out, imagine you are releasing all tension and distraction. If you wish, add a visualization that all tension and distraction are drifting up and away, like evaporating mist
   - Breathe like this for 5 minutes
   - Just before concluding, sit quietly without special breathing or visualization, simply being aware of yourself in the moment
   - Finish by reminding yourself to bring with you any benefits from the relaxation session to help yourself and to enhance your beneficial interactions with others

2. Breathing Peace

   - Sit in a comfortable position, balanced but without physical strain
   - Close the eyes gently
   - Notice how you feel in the moment as you settle into quiet
   - Take in one deep but gentle breath from the lower abdomen
   - Release the breath and let yourself settle into a gentler, smooth flow of breathing in and out
   - Remind yourself to settle into peaceful relaxation together with clear bright mind
   - Then begin a special breathing and mantra practice
   - On each breath in, silently repeat the word "peace" or another word conducive to peace and well-being
   - On each breath out, silently exhale gently but about twice as long as the inhalation, while quietly releasing the breath along with all tensions or distractions
   - If you wish, on the breath out, silently repeat the words "for all" or some other expression of compassion for others
   - Breathe like this for 5 minutes
   - Just before concluding, sit quietly without special breathing or mantra, simply being aware of yourself in the moment
   - Finish by reminding yourself to bring with you any benefits from the relaxation session to help yourself and to enhance your beneficial interactions with others

3. Instant Release Meditation

This mindfulness practice aids relaxation and freedom from control by habitual reactivity. As soon as you notice an internal indicator of distress, distraction, or loss of clarity (e.g. sweating palms, hampered or excessive breathing, moment of anxiety, self-defeating thought,

(continued)

342

Table 10.2. Continued.

other-attacking thought, demeaning judgment of self or other, wandering internal chatter, or loss of awareness of the moment):

- Notice the indicator without judgment
- Observe it gently
- Realize that you do not have to be controlled by it
- Take in and release a breath, letting go of the feeling, thought, or chatter
- Settle into a smooth exchange of breathing, in and out
- Just observe the breathing process, accepting the moment without judgment
- Open your senses and pay attention to whatever is right before you in the moment
- If there is someone (including yourself) or something that you find disturbing, regard it with gentle kindness
- When you feel ready, respond to the situation out of clarity and compassion

---

Table 10.3. Systematic Deep Relaxation Exercise.

This exercise is likely to take 20–30 minutes. It is designed to increase general relaxation, mental clarity, and awareness of the body. In this exercise, you will focus awareness on various parts of your body in order to be aware of their condition and to release tension or discomfort. This is especially useful to thoroughly release tensions and to become more aware of physical and mental issues that may require attention later. If the purpose is to enhance relaxation and clarity during the daytime, then maintain alertness throughout the exercise. If the purpose is to assist falling asleep, then let yourself naturally drift off to sleep as you go through the exercise.

- Sit in a balanced well-supported comfortable position, or, lie on your back on a flat comfortable surface
- Close your eyes
- Just be aware of your feelings and sensations in this moment
- Notice that as you become quiet and pay attention to yourself, you already begin to relax
- Remind yourself to settle naturally into physical relaxation together with bright clear mind
- Next, gently pay attention to your right foot, noticing its position and sensations
- Then, gently curl the toes of your right foot, slightly tensing the muscles of your entire foot. Hold the tightness gently for several seconds, saying to yourself, "hold it, hold it, hold it, and…release." Release all tension and distraction from your right foot. Let it float away like evaporating mist. Feel the waves of relaxation flowing through your body. Feel any distractions from your mind lift away and disappear
- Repeat the practice for your left foot
- As you continue, notice any sensations, thoughts, feelings, insights that come to you. If this is just a pointless distraction, let it go. If it is a valuable message for something to attend to (such as need for sleep or relief from pain in some part of the body, a reminder of something important to take care of, or a valuable insight), gently tell yourself that you will remember this for later and let it go. After the relaxation session, you can take appropriate action
- Pay attention to your right leg, scanning awareness from your ankle, to your knee, and your hip. Then, slightly tense the muscles of your right leg. Hold it, hold it, hold it, and…release, letting go of any tensions or distractions from your right leg, noticing waves of relaxation flowing through your body, and letting your mind be clear and bright
- Repeat the practice for your left leg
- Pay attention to your buttocks, following the same practice of gently tensing and releasing
- Pay attention to your right hand and arm, gently curling your fingers into a fist and tensing the muscles of your right arm. Follow the practice of releasing tension

(continued)

343

Table 10.3. Continued.

- Repeat the practice with your left hand and arm
- Notice your back, scanning awareness from the base of your spine, up the spine, around the small of the back, up to the shoulder blades. Then, gently arch your spine at the small of the back, slightly tensing the muscles. Hold it, hold it, hold it, and... release all tension and distraction from your back, feeling the waves of relaxation moving through your body, with mind clear and alert
- Notice your breathing. Be aware of the movement of your abdomen and chest with each breath
- Now, take in one deep breath from the abdomen and hold it, hold it, hold it, and... release. Let your breathing settle into an even deeper, gentler rhythm. Be aware with each inhalation of the refreshing, replenishing air and energy you receive. Be aware with each exhalation of releasing any remaining tensions or distractions, floating away like mist. Be aware of the quiet pause in between each breath in and out. Let your breathing settle and continue naturally
- Pay attention to your neck, all the way around, from the base of your neck to the meeting point with the head
- Then, scan your awareness up the back of the head, over the scalp, down the forehead, around the eyes and nose and mouth. Be aware of how your neck and head feel
- Gently, close your eyes and your lips a little more tightly, slightly tensing the muscles of your face. Hold it, hold it, hold it...and release. Let all remaining tension and distraction float away. Feel the waves of relaxation moving freely throughout your body, cleansing and clearing body and mind
- Rest quietly in this relaxed condition as long as you wish
- Before concluding, remind yourself to bring back whatever insights and benefits you received to help yourself and to enhance your interactions with others
- As you prepare to finish and reenter ordinary activity, gently flex your fingers and toes and adjust your posture. Pay attention to your sensations in the moment. When you are ready, gently open your eyes and look around the room
- Let yourself return to ordinary alertness and movement, bringing with you refreshment and insights from the relaxation exercise. (If your purpose was to fall asleep, then you probably fell asleep by this point.)

Engaging Ritual and Ceremony

As we discussed in the section on ritual studies, all cultures and religions include ceremonies and rituals. They are ubiquitous features of human behavior, reflecting our capacity for symbolism, narrative, and meaningful group interaction. Ritual and ceremony have not been discussed extensively in the helping professions. However, their importance is recognized implicitly in psychodrama, certain family therapy techniques, narrative therapy, and art therapies. We believe that ritual and ceremony deserve much more attention, study, and application in social work.

Ritual and Ceremony Defined

Victor Turner (1965), a cultural anthropologist who had major influence on ritual studies, made a helpful distinction between ritual and ceremony. *Ceremony* refers to celebrations and confirmations of existing situations and conditions.

Ritual refers to procedures that bring about a fundamental transformation of existing situations and conditions. We will use the terms in this way. Traditional rituals and ceremonies are well established and authorized within particular cultural or religious communities. As we discussed earlier, clients might wish to connect their social work process with them. However, sometimes clients would like alternatives.

Laird (1984) pointed out that some people do not have well established rituals (or ceremonies) to celebrate important life events and to encourage transitions. For example, there is no ritual to mark the passage from adolescence to adulthood that is generally accepted by most Americans. There are some religious rituals, such as Jewish Bar Mitzvah and Bat Mitzvah (Kahn, 1995) that can help a person to make a clear statement of identity and to have that affirmed and supported by others. But all too often, adolescents may take up activities that are not necessarily beneficial in order to claim adult status, such as smoking or drinking alcohol. For another example, divorce is a major life transition for many married people, but the legal and economic rituals marking this change generally are not set up to help people grow through the process. Other occasions of serious loss or wonderful life transitions often have no standard means of celebrating or assisting. The opposite problem is when people have a ritual or ceremony that is too routine, rigid, or taken for granted. It no longer has a sense of meaning or power for the client. So Laird suggested that social workers might sometimes be called on to help clients to celebrate accomplishments and to move through critical life passages safely.

Further, the model of therapeutic transformation suggests that all social work practice situations promoting change can be viewed as a form of ritual. We can enliven them by applying ritual techniques, if clients are so inclined.

Empirical Support for Beneficial Effects of Ritual and Ceremony

Most empirical studies of ritual and ceremony are qualitative and ethnographic. As we saw in the review of ritual studies, field research around the world for several decades has demonstrated the ubiquity, variety, and importance of ceremony and ritual. These studies have shown that benign rituals and ceremonies can lead to feelings of peace, joy, meaningfulness, reassurance, and even ecstasy for participants. They also serve to reinforce social cohesion and collective feelings of meaningfulness, or, transform and enhance personal and relational patterns. In general, ritual and ceremony can enhance individual and collective sense of control, harmony, balance, and order, as well as connectedness with the sacred. Ceremony and ritual can connect with prayer and meditation, thus tapping their beneficial effects (Spilka, 2005). With regard to our recommendations for helping clients engage ritual and ceremony, there is no formal research of the particular practices. However, we can infer that engaging the therapeutic qualities of a spiritually sensitive relationship, meditation, and meaning-making (which are widely studied) within a ritual or ceremonial process is likely to be beneficial.

Most importantly, client's views are paramount in determining whether engaging ritual or ceremony would be appropriate and beneficial.

Designing a Ritual or Ceremony

Designing ritual or ceremony can be emotionally moving and enjoyable. It links clients' self-reflection and dialogue with significant people whom they wish to be present. It can involve joining with existing ritual and ceremonies in one's spiritual group to find affirmation and support there. It can involve renewing lost ties to a spiritual group, to rediscover a community of spiritual caring. It can involve creating an entirely new or personally tailored event, suited to private and particular beliefs and circumstances. Actually performing the ritual or ceremony, especially with a sense of support from loved ones, spiritual mentors, one's community, and (if believed) sacred or supernatural beings can be very powerful events cherished for a long time.

In order to clarify this, I (EC) would like to give an example from a former student who was a social worker for a Lutheran Social Services agency during the 1980s. He had established a peer support group for Cambodian refugee youth who were resettled as unaccompanied minors. These youth were dealing with many compounded stressors related to loss of homeland, family and friends; experience of the genocidal killing fields; the dangerous and uncertain flight from Cambodia; stay in refugee camps; and cross-cultural transition in the United States.

Over the course of support group meetings, it became clear that the youth needed to tell their stories for healing, not only to each other but also to the general public. Speaking the truth, including the pain, was an important step in honoring the memories of loved ones lost, releasing the traumatic pain, and moving on. Therefore, the group meetings became a multimedia event. Participants told stories, drew pictures, wrote stories and spoke to newspaper reporters. The social worker recognized that a dramatic ritual of transformation was unfolding. He documented this in records kept for the youth participants.

But there was still a lot of pain and much hope for the uncertain future to address. The youth were Buddhist and so they asked to have a Cambodian Buddhist monk visit them to perform a formal religious ritual of healing. They worked with the social worker and the monk to tailor a ritual that focused all the energy of healing from the entire process.

The youth found a beautiful location for the ritual in a field. They dug a hole in the ground. They symbolically placed all their pain, grief, and loss into the hole. The monk prayed for their help and blessed the process and the earth. Then the youth planted a sapling in the hole, so that new life would grow up from it. This tree symbolized their new life in the United States in which they would continue to honor their culture of origin and their memories, but would also forge a new identity and way of life. This ritual simply yet powerfully represented their healing transformation. This example beautifully reflects the guidelines we offered for ethical use of religiously based activities and transcultural teamwork.

Table 10.4. Guidelines for Designing Ritual and Ceremony in Social Work
Contexts.

- Ascertain client's interest
- Clarify relevance to client's spiritual perspective and helping goals
- Assess client's prior experience with rituals and ceremonies, e.g.
  - Traditional cultural or religious forms, if any, and level of satisfaction with them
  - Established family-based or personal forms, if any, and level of satisfaction with them
  - Coordinate with, refer to, or collaborate with client's ritual traditions or personal practices, if client prefers
  - Dialogue with client about designing a new ritual, if client prefers, and move on to next steps
- Clarify client's purpose for the event, such as affirmation and celebration of a life situation or transformation into a new hoped for situation
- Codesign ritual or ceremony
  1. Establish specific intent and hoped for outcomes (why)
  2. Identify key themes, symbols, meaningful actions, music, art, decorations, or objects for the event (what)
  3. Clarify intended participants (who)
  4. Decide timing of event (when)
  5. Identify safe and conducive setting (where)
  6. Compose process and structure (how)
     - Create opening of event
     - Plan activities marking transition or affirmation
     - Plan activities establishing sense of closure and way to carry benefits into ongoing life
- Client conducts ritual or ceremony with or without social worker
- Follow up results

In order to help you to design helping rituals or ceremonies for yourself or your clients, we include a list of suggestions influenced by ritual studies and practical suggestions by Paladin (1991) (see Table 10.4).

Ritual and ceremony need not be mutually exclusive; we see this as a matter of emphasis. But we think it can be helpful to be clear about the general purpose of your event. For example, you might wish to design a ceremony that emphasizes themes and symbols of celebration, confirmation, appreciation, dedication, affirmation, and continuation. You might wish to design a ritual that emphasizes themes and symbols of transformation, movement, discontinuity, and newness. At the conclusion of a ritual, it would be important to have an ending that confirms and celebrates the change and assists incorporation of benefits into ongoing life.

Friends sometimes ask me (EC) to help them design and perform rituals. Although I do that as a friend, there is usually a therapeutic quality to the event. For example, a family who moved into an old house was experiencing some transition difficulties. The family was composed of father and mother and their 7-year-old daughter. Since I would be visiting their city, the parents asked me if I would help them do a "house blessing" ritual to help the family feel better connected with the house and their new life situation. The parents had been doing remodeling and encountered many structural problems. This was frustrating on a practical level. In addition, they said that various things were suddenly malfunctioning in the house, moving in a line from the front of the house to the back. During this period, the daughter had difficulty sleeping due to nightmares. Overall, the family was happy about their move and new home, but there was an unsettling feeling.

We had done meditative drumming together many times. So we decided to adapt that familiar activity to this ritual. I came to the house on an afternoon when all members were available. We discussed each family member's feelings about their situation in the house. We discussed various possibilities for how to mark a sense of deepened good relationship with the house as a home.

We decided to sit together in the living room, near the front of the house, where things had started to go awry. I gave each person a drum or rattle and I had a variety of percussion instruments. First, we sat in quiet meditation, setting an intention to make a good relationship with the house. Then we talked a short time about what we experienced during the meditation. The daughter said that she saw, in her mind's eye, a wolf appear. The wolf snarled angrily. She didn't know why the wolf was angry. But she and the parents said this reflected their uneasy feelings.

I began drumming with a heartbeat like rhythm. Everyone joined in. When we formed a good musical pulse and synergy as a group, we stood up, continuing to play our instruments. The father had a rattle and a bowl with incense. The mother had her rattle and a flash light. The father and mother went ahead, leading us in a line around the living room and on through every room of the house. I kept a steady pulse on a small Korean gong as we moved along. As we proceeded, we kept good intentions for making a relationship with each area of the house. The sound and incense smoke spread our good intentions and cleansed the space. In every room, the parents opened every door and drawer as we processed along. The mother shined a light into every nook and cranny and under every bed. The daughter played along with their instruments and looked into all the spaces, relieving worry about anything hidden or creepy.

After we covered the entire house, the yard, and garage, we circled back to the living room. We sat back down, continuing to play together. I brought the pulse down to quiet. We sat quietly in meditation for several minutes.

Then I asked how everyone felt about the experience. Everyone said they felt better connected with the house; it felt more like a home. The daughter said that when she meditated at the end, the wolf reappeared. But this time, the wolf was smiling. Everyone was happy and said this reflected their feeling of resolution.

I visited them again several years later, since we lived far apart. They talked about their lives since my last visit and how good they felt about living in this house. We reminisced about the house-blessing ritual. Then it suddenly occurred to me that their pet dog, whom they adopted not long after the ritual, looked like a wolf. In fact, the father explained, the dog was part wolf. The family had not thought about this before, but they agreed it was significant that the dog they all felt attracted to adopt resembled the wolf in the daughter's vision. The father said that when they first saw the dog in the pet store, they were concerned about the wolf ancestry and wondered if it would be a suitable family pet. But they all felt such a good connection to the dog that they brought it home.

In this ritual, it was not necessary to analyze anything formally. We engaged in a creative process of play, music, and meditation, letting the literal and symbolic actions work on their own. Every family member and the house itself were connected in a process that transformed the relationship. Amazingly, although it was not planned consciously, even the daughter's vision of making relationship with a wolf came to be true as they bonded with their home.

Practicing Forgiveness

Forgiveness is addressed in many religious traditions as an important virtue for self-healing, social reconciliation, and restoration of community and cosmic harmony (McCullough. Bono, & Root, 2005; McCullough & Worthington, 1999). Many religions have values and rituals encouraging forgiveness of self, others, and sense of forgiveness by God, other spiritual beings, or one's fellow religious community members. Not surprisingly then, several studies suggest that highly motivated religious people tend to be more willing and active to forgive themselves and others (Mullet, Barros, Frangio, Usai, Neto, & Shafighi, 2003; Toussaint, Williams, Musick, & Everson, 2001). However, forgiveness does not necessarily have a religious intention or context.

Forgiveness is now widely appreciated and included in the helping professions and social sciences (Frame, 2003; Griswold, 2007). For example, we asked two questions that dealt with forgiveness issues in our 2008 National Survey. Among those who responded, 63.8% (n = 1,127) indicated that it is important to help clients assess whether they wish to work on forgiveness while 72.3% (n = 1,271) of the respondents use techniques in their practice that deal with forgiveness. This finding is similar to the 1997 National survey. At that time, 60% of respondents believed it was important to assess whether a client would benefit from work on forgiveness, and another 74% used forgiveness techniques. These findings show that most respondents address forgiveness. Yet it appears that some do so without assessing whether the client wishes to do so. This puzzling result calls for a reminder of the importance of assessment and matching a helping technique to the client's preference. The following discussion presents considerations for addressing forgiveness at micro and larger community levels of practice.

Defining Forgiveness

The etymology of the word forgiveness refers to giving up anger, resentment, and desire for revenge (Sanderson & Linehan, 1999). McCullough, Paragament, and Thoreson (2000) defined forgiveness as an "intraindividual, prosocial change toward a perceived transgressor that is set within a specific interpersonal context" (p. 9). Forgiveness of self or others can be an important step in releasing pain and preoccupation with feelings of guilt, shame, or anger toward oneself and anger and hostility toward others (Garvin, 1998). Generally, forgiveness is grounded in a moral relation between two individuals, one of whom has wronged the other. The work of forgiveness is facilitated by communication and reciprocity between injurer and injured. Forgiveness is not necessarily altruistic, but when it is, it is a deep expression of concern, compassion, and love for others, even when the other is an undeserving and blameworthy transgressor (Witvliet & McCullough, 2007). Forgiveness, can take many forms, such as forgiving a person who directly offended oneself; third party forgiveness, in which wrongs done to others are forgiven, including wrongs done to victims no longer living; forgiving oneself; forgiving the dead or unrepentant; forgiving God for perceived unfairness of life or divine will; seeking God's forgiveness for one's own offenses; judicial pardon; restorative justice in a criminal case; political apology; economic forgiveness; political pardon; and metaphysical forgiveness (Griswold, 2007). People can forgive and still bring legal justice to bear as required by the situation. Also forgiveness alone is distinguished from reconciliation in that forgiveness is one person's response to injury whereby reconciliation involves both forgiveness and two people (and possibly a community) coming together again. The injurer must realize his or her offense, see the damage done, and take steps to rectify the problem (Enright, Freedman & Rique, 1998).

Empirical Support for Beneficial Effects of Forgiveness

Forgiveness is an increasingly researched topic in psychology because of its potential enhancement of psychosocial functioning. From 1998 to 2005, published scientific studies on forgiveness increased from 58 to 950 (Doblmeir, Juday & Schmidt, 2007). Forgiveness may be associated with psychosocial benefits by reducing negative emotions and cognitions such as anger, depression, cynicism, and resentment and by fostering qualities of affirmation, compassion, and prosocial behaviors (Hebl & Enright, 1993; Witvliet & McCullough, 2007). Forgiveness is connected to physical health in that reduced feelings of hostility, revenge, and anger may lower distress and associated physiological (especially cardiovascular) damage (Koenig, McCullough, & Larson, 2001; Witvliet & McCullough, 2007). Much of the research on forgiveness has focused on specific instances of forgiveness, namely *state forgiveness*, which represents the extent to which a person has forgiven a specific offender for a specific offense, and *trait forgiveness*, which represents a person's general tendency to grant forgiveness across a variety of instances and relationships. The expression of *anger-out*, such as raising one's voice, sarcasm, or confrontation, was less positively associated with good health than assertiveness in telling the offender how one honestly feels, working on the problems with the offender, and expressing feelings openly (Kamat, Jones, & Row, 2006). Research and computer simulations also demonstrate that mutually supportive, cooperative, and collaborative strategies of social relations, which forgiveness can support, are conducive to personal well-being, satisfaction in close relationships, and wider social group benefits (Sanderson & Linehan, 1999).

Lawler-Row, Karremans, Scott, Eddis-Matityahou & Edwards (2008) have identified several findings associated with forgiveness and health. For example, lower forgiveness was associated with poorer health habits such as alcohol and cigarette use. Overall, the evidence supports the contention that both state and trait forgiveness tend to be positively correlated with healthier physiological responses, as measured by cardiovascular responses like lower blood pressure and lower heartbeat. The authors also found strong negative correlations between both state and trait forgiveness and number of medications taken, poor quality of sleep, fatigue and somatic symptoms. In a sample of adults over 55 years of age, trait forgiveness was associated with higher levels of health behaviors. In summary, forgiveness appears to be an important psychological factor that has an impact on physiological and health responses.

Worthington, Mazzeo, & Canter (2005) have developed a detailed protocol for forgiveness therapy, including empirical testing of its effectiveness.

Therapeutic Forgiveness at the Microlevel

Therapeutic forgiveness of a transgressor does not mean "forgive and forget" because it is often impossible and undesirable to forget an injustice or outrage. Elder (1998) defined interpersonal forgiveness as "a willingness to abandon one's right to resentment, negative judgment and indifferent behavior toward one who unjustly injures us, while fostering the undeserved qualities of compassion, generosity and perhaps even love" (p. 151). We need to take proactive stands against indignity or injustice against ourselves and others, but without being stuck in an adversarial mentality and way of life. Indeed, forgiveness can open up energy and insight for more effective action. Thus, forgiveness can be a powerful therapeutic intervention (Fitzgibbons, 1986) that facilitates the client's process of "letting go of the need for vengeance and releasing associated negative feelings such as bitterness and resentment" (DiBlasio, 1993, p. 163).

Studzinske (1986) listed reasons a client may not wish to work on forgiveness. These included lack of time and energy, preoccupation with the wrongdoer's guilt, and a bias against forgiveness because of its association with religious traditions. In addition, Smede (1996) posited that some people mistakenly believe that if they forgive, they must reunite with the offender. Therefore, it is important to assess whether clients wish to work on forgiveness. The social worker should be aware, however, that although a client may not be interested in *full forgiveness* (i.e. the diminishment of negative affect and full restoration of the relationship), he or she may wish to work toward *detached forgiveness* (i.e. reduction of negative affect, but no restoration of the relationship), or *limited forgiveness* (i.e. reduction of negative affect and partial restoration of the relationship) (Flanigan, 1998, p. 101).

Regarding forgiveness of self, Krill (1990) made a helpful distinction between appropriate and inappropriate feelings of guilt. In practice, a client can be encouraged to reflect on feelings of guilt without self-punishing judgmentalism. This opens the possibility for distinguishing between appropriate guilt (i.e. remorse for one's harmful acts) and inappropriate guilt induced by harsh evaluations of self, low self-esteem, or blaming by others. Honest acknowledgment of appropriate guilt can shift a person from self-defeating preoccupation with mistakes to constructive acts of acceptance of self, correction of mistakes, and restitution. Recognition of inappropriate guilt can lift the weight of blame and open up energy and insight for positive self-concept and refusal to accept inappropriate judgments from self and others. Hope (1987) suggested that when the therapist models an accepting attitude toward the client, the experience of being valued in the present in spite of failures in the past may encourage clients to forgive themselves for past mistakes and to develop a more forgiving attitude in the present.

Regarding forgiveness of others, we construct seven phases of the forgiveness process based on several models (Coleman, 1998; Frame, 2003; Krause & Ingersoll-Dayton, 2001; McCullough, Paragament, & Thoreson, 2000; Sanderson & Linehan, 1999; Worthington, Mazzeo, & Canter, 2005). The first phase involves *identifying the hurt*, including feelings of shock or denial at the offense and ensuing anger or resentment. The second phase involves *sorting through* the pros and cons of forgiving, including reflection on the negative effects on oneself from holding on to anger and resentment. The third phase involves *confronting the wrongdoer* either by letter, which may or may not be mailed, by therapeutic exercises, or face to face. Powerful healing effects come from writing or speaking about one's loss or injury. People who only thought about their injury suffered more negative mental and physical health symptoms than those who wrote about or discussed their injury. If the client decides it is desirable and possible to dialogue with the offender, the offender is sincere in apology, and gives a clear explanation for her or his behavior, then the client can validate the offender's remorse and change of behavior. The fourth phase incorporates *dialogue to understanding*. It is important in the healing process to make sense of one's suffering and the offender's behavior, if possible. If the offender is willing to engage in this process, then dialogue can include the offender's following up expressions of remorse with commitment not to reoffend and clear changes of behavior. The fifth phase is *expression of forgiving*, which can be an awkward leap of faith, although it does not mean that the client has to trust the injurer. The sixth phase involves *letting go* of the pain and resentment. However, for many the memory of having been hurt will reappear now and again. The seventh phase is *reconstructing one's life and relationships* on the basis of forgiveness. There is a possibility of meaningfulness, a possibility that in spite of suffering or even because of it, people will grow to a higher quality of well-being than they might have otherwise known. If the forgiveness process included a restoration of relationship, then the one who forgives can engage in conciliatory behavior and the relationship can be restored. This entire transformational process could be very long and go beyond the confines of the professional helping relationship.

According to Worthington and DiBlasio (1990), it is necessary to evaluate whether the client and the offender have sufficient ego capacities to seek or grant forgiveness. These ego capacities include the ability of the client to empathize with his or her offender and the ability of the offender to demonstrate remorse. Holmgren (1993) said that the aggrieved must complete a series of tasks that are central to his or her self-esteem and self-respect before he or she can forgive. Worthington and DiBlasio (1990) emphasized that when clients demonstrate defensive posturing and continuous denial, they are not ready to work on forgiveness. In addition, DiBlasio (1993) stated that whether forgiveness is appropriate depends solely on the beliefs, feelings, attitudes, and decisions of the aggrieved person. If the client does not wish to forgive the offender, then the client's right to self-determination must be respected.

Sometimes clients feel anger and resentment toward God or the universe due to the unfair and miserable conditions of life. Why do infants die? Why are thousands of people swallowed up by tsunamis or volcanic eruptions? Why do deceivers and cheats sometimes prosper while the righteous sometimes suffer adversity? Why do groups wage war and commit genocide? And why does God allow such things to happen? *Metaphysical forgiveness* is the effort to give up resentment caused by the manifold imperfections of the world. It comes down to forgiving the world for harboring natural adversities and moral evils such as disaster, death, illness, physical decay, and all the wrongs people do to each other (Griswold, 2007).

The activities of mindfulness, relaxation, and meditation can help clients to get in touch with painful feelings gently, in the process of working through to forgiveness. The social worker could also help an interested client to design a ritual of forgiveness for self and/or others at an appropriate time. If the client participates in a religious tradition or spiritual practice with an established ritual for forgiveness, an authorized spiritual helper could be involved in the process through referral or direct collaboration.

Restorative Justice and Political Forgiveness or Reconciliation

Restorative justice is a means of settling disputes, often in a criminal justice context, in which aiding victims, forgiveness, reconciliation, and community restoration are sought rather than simply retributive punishment (Von Wormer, 2004; Zehr, 1995). This does not mean that perpetrators of crime do not receive punishment. But if punishment occurs, it is within a context of communication and mediation that seeks to uphold the humanity and dignity of all involved and to restore the integrity of the larger community impacted by wrongdoing. The restorative justice movement is influenced by Indigenous cultural practices and religious forms of justice, such as Mennonite practices. Restorative justice emphasizes face-to-face communications, truth telling, personal empowerment, and healing by all parties to the wrongdoing. Around the globe, such restorative processes are offering hope for more constructive responses to harm inflicted by humans on one another.

Restorative initiatives are not limited to work with individuals and families, but also can be successfully applied to the unjust treatment of whole populations where the violator would be the state. Wartime persecutions, widespread destruction of the land of the people, slave labor, mass murder, and genocide are forms of crimes against humanity and the earth that demand some form of comprehension and reparation for survivors and their families even generations after the initial events. The Truth and Reconciliation Commission in South Africa is one of the most powerful examples of restoration, which often included monetary exchange in addition to public acknowledgment of responsibility for the crimes against humanity that occurred during the apartheid period. Other examples of reparation are U.S. compensation to families of Japanese Americans held in concentration camps during World War II and German compensation to survivors of slave labor camps (Von Wormor, 2004).

Political apology and forgiveness include apology offered in a political context and may or may not be accompanied by reparation. The relevant institutions or organizations include corporations, churches, and other civic organizations. Social workers can play a role in facilitating this process. The 20th and 21st century challenges to social justice and human rights posed by transnational capitalism, growing global inequality, and social exclusion along with multiple forms of violence confront the limits of the social work imagination and call for creative and critical interventions that focus on social justice (von Wormer, 2004).

Archbishop Desmond Tutu (1998), as chair of the South African Truth and Reconciliation Commission, remarked that "the world is on the brink of disaster if we don't forgive, accept forgiveness and reconcile. Forgiveness does not mean amnesia. For that is a most dangerous thing, especially on a community, national or international level. We must forgive, but almost always we should not forget that there were atrocities, because if we do, we are then likely to repeat those atrocities" (p. xiv). Tutu (1999) declared that in South Africa there was to be no general amnesty for members of the previous government. General amnesty would victimize the victims of apartheid a second time around. Rather, the victims had to tell their stories, which in a sense rehabilitated and affirmed the dignity and personhood of those who for so long had been silenced and had been turned into anonymous, marginalized people. Perpetrators were also expected to tell their stories honestly and to participate in social reconstruction. So, the Truth and Reconciliation Commission granted amnesty to individuals in exchange for a full disclosure relating to the crime for which amnesty was being sought. A genuine truth and reconciliation process can support people's resilience, enabling them to survive, and emerge still human despite all efforts to dehumanize them.

In cases such as in South Africa, to the extent that the reconciliation process reveals a public account of who did what to whom, and where some attempt is made for restitution, important elements of justice have been achieved. South Africa's Truth and Reconciliation Commission (TRC) is a prime example of where political forgiveness puts its faith in truth and the people are capable to forgive in order to aid in the peaceful transformation of a regime. The South African TRC went beyond most other such commissions by including public disclosures by perpetrators, respectful public hearings for victims, individualized amnesty hearings, and a focus on national reconciliation (Sacco & Hoffman, 2004). However, political forgiveness is not about clearing the victim's heart of resentment. Rather, it entails clearing a debt that the transgressor or debtor owes to the victim or the creditor and revealing the truth of crimes and responsibilities as part of a process of social and national reconstruction. Unfortunately, in situations of catastrophic oppression and genocide, such as in South Africa or Rwanda, given the nature of crimes, the scale of oppressions and atrocities, the amount of restitution needed, and the absence of punishment, full sense of justice and reconciliation will not likely be attained (Digeser, 2000). Yet political apology and forgiveness can facilitate forgiving a debt (including *economic forgiveness* whereby the debtor is released from the obligation of repayment), reconciling the past, and restoring the civil and moral equality of transgressors and their victims.

Enright and North (1998) said that forgiveness between nations, forgiveness between cultural groups, and forgiveness between communities are all possible once the necessary steps have been taken. These steps include being completely honest in the recognition that harm has been inflicted by one party on another, expressing a willingness to forgo prolonging the hostility through the acts of revenge, developing empathy and understanding between the parties, and finally, renewing the community in the future. What is annulled in the act of forgiveness is not the crime or wrongdoing but the distorting effect that this wrong has upon one's relations with the wrongdoer and perhaps with others (North, 1998).

Sacco and Hoffman (2004) brought forth a statement of the social work profession's complicity in apartheid for the South African TRC process. This was formulated by some social work educators at the University of Witwatersrand as part of the national truth telling and disclosure process. "Social work educators stated unequivocally that they were sorry for not challenging apartheid's vicious policies and outcomes sooner and with more vigour" (p. 163). The statement itemizes ways that the school's efforts to educate social work students and address issues of diversity and justice fell short of fully challenging apartheid and its impacts on black students. Sacco and Hoffman propose that social work educators around the world engage in a reconciliation and reparation discourse concerning their roles in indirect or direct complicity with injustice and oppression. We concur that this is an important process for social work to move to a deeper level of promoting national and international justice.

Table 10.5. Facilitating Therapeutic Forgiveness.

Assess the Situation (At outset and ongoing throughout the process)

Client's Perspective

- Interest, readiness, and willingness to invest time and energy
- Relevant religious or personal values
- Willingness to work toward letting go of resentment and preoccupation with wrongdoer's guilt
- Level of self-acceptance and self-esteem
- Ability to empathize with the offender or let go of the relationship
- Intention and possibility for engaging the offender in the process
- The level of intended forgiveness (e.g. detached, limited, or full)
- Desire for working on forgiveness solely with the social worker or in collaboration with or referral to a spiritual mentor and established traditional ritual
- If client and offender are willing to work together, assess:

Offender's Perspective

- Interest, readiness, and willingness to invest time and energy
- Relevant religious or personal values
- Willingness and ability to engage in sincere communication and acknowledge wrongdoing
- Ability to empathize with the client

Support the Forgiveness Process

- Model acceptance within the helping relationship
- Identify the client's hurt, including nature of the offense and client's feelings of shock, denial, anger, resentment
- Sort through the pros and cons of forgiving
- Help client confront the offender directly or indirectly
  - If directly, facilitate the offender's expression of sincere apology, remorse, reparation, commitment not to reoffend, and follow through with changed behavior
  - If indirectly, help the client devise a way to symbolically communicate with the offender and work toward forgiveness
- Continue dialogue through to understanding or acceptance of situation
- Facilitate a decision and action of forgiveness
- Help the client let go of resentment, anger, and desire for revenge
- Facilitate the client's restructuring of life and relationships, including with the offender, if desired and possible

Table 10.5 summarizes assessment and implementation issues in therapeutic forgiveness of others. Although the focus is on forgiveness within a clinical social work context, many ingredients may contribute to the interpersonal level of forgiveness within larger social contexts, as in restorative justice and a national truth and reconciliation process.

Conclusion

This chapter presented a conceptual model for therapeutic transformation along with theoretical and practical guidelines for using meditation, ritual, and forgiveness. The following chapter provides concluding reflections on further directions for spiritually sensitive social work in a worldwide view.

EXERCISES

Before you attempt to employ any of these practices with clients, you should learn how to do them well yourself. Practice them repeatedly with yourself or colleagues until they feel familiar and natural. Seek training and supervision from experienced practitioners if necessary. Once you are certain of your competence with a practice, you might employ it with clients who express interest. Evaluate the impact of the practices on the helping relationship and the client. The following exercises are designed to help you manage stress, enhance your preparedness for a spiritually sensitive relationship, and prepare for possible use with clients.

10.1. Social Work as Transformational Practice

Review the conceptual model of therapeutic transformation. Consider the purposes and qualities of each phase. Reflect on how it is relevant to your own experience of important life transitions. Choose a practice situation for which the model is relevant. Write an essay that presents a case example according to what happened in each phase, the metaphors or stories that were significant to the client, and how you approached the helping process artistically as an opportunity for creative change. Then consider how the model was helpful in gaining insight into the helping process and how this suggests ways you could enhance the transformational process in future work. Describe any limitations of the model and how you would improve it.

10.2. Basic Meditation Related Practices

Review the general qualities of meditation related practices in Table 10.1. Reread the explanations in the chapter for Paying Attention, Intentional Breathing, Equipoise, Consistency, and Caring for the Body. Choose one of these practices to try out. Try it at least three times. Reflect on what happened and how you could improve the experience. If you decide that the practice was not suitable for you, then reflect on the reason. Then try a different practice at least three times. Repeat this until you find one that works well for you.

10.3. Quick Meditation Exercises

Review the general ingredients of meditation related practices in Table 10.1 and also the instructions for three meditation related brief exercises in Table 10.2. Choose one exercise and try it at least three times. Reflect on what happened and how you could improve the experience. If you decide that the practice was not suitable for you, then reflect on the reason. Then try a different practice at least three times. Repeat this until you find one that works well for you. If you do not find any that works well for you, review the chapter for other possibilities and explore further.

10.4. Deep Relaxation Exercise

Review the general ingredients of meditation related practices in Table 10.1 and also the instructions for deep relaxation in Table 10.3. Try the exercise at least three times. Reflect on what happened and how you could improve the experience. If you decide that the practice was not suitable for you, then reflect on the reason. Review the chapter for other possibilities and explore further.

10.5. Doing Ritual and Ceremony

Review the explanations of transformational process and ritual and ceremony, including Table 10.4. First, design a ritual or ceremony for yourself that addresses some significant life event or transition, or, engage in a traditional ritual or ceremony with an intention to focus on this life event or transition. Reflect on the experience and its impact on you. Consider the implications of your experience for how to help clients engage ritual or ceremony in their own growth process.

Before helping a client to design a ritual or ceremony, be sure you have done this for yourself several times until you are comfortable with the activity. Then consider the assessment and implementation issues in Table 10.4.

10.6. Practicing Forgiveness

Review the explanation of forgiveness along with Table 10.5. Think of an issue in your life in which forgiveness would be important. Work through the forgiveness process around this issue. Reflect on the personal journey from experiencing hurt to letting go or reconciliation. Use this experience to enhance your empathy for clients and your ability to help clients work through forgiveness when appropriate.

11

A Worldwide View

The world before me is restored in beauty.
The world behind me is restored in beauty.
The world below me is restored in beauty.
The world above me is restored in beauty.
All things around me are restored in beauty.
My voice is restored in beauty.
It is finished in beauty.

Healing Ritual Concluding Prayer, Diné (Navajo)
(cited in Sandner, 1991, p. 193)

In this final chapter, we complete the framework for spiritually sensitive practice. We have come a long way—from defining central values and concepts, to portraying the wide range of religious and nonsectarian expressions of spirituality in social work, to setting a context for understanding, assessing, and practicing spiritually sensitive social work, and to providing ethical and practical guidelines for spiritually oriented helping activities. Now we present an overview of our recommendations for spiritually sensitive helping activities and resources related to various fields of practice. Then we reflect on spirituality in social work within a worldwide view.

Spiritually Oriented Helping Activities Revisited

We offered suggestions for many spiritually oriented helping activities throughout this book. For your convenience, we list them together in Table 11.1. You can find their locations by consulting the index.

We would like to reemphasize that these helping activities are not just tools. For example, forgiveness is not just a hammer that we can use any time we find a loose nail of grievance or remorse. Forgiveness is a process that engages people deeply, heart to heart, in vulnerability, courage, and healing. A social worker who facilitates forgiveness must have a rapport with the client and willingness to engage his or her own deep feelings, process unresolved issues, and work through a profound healing relationship and process with the client and other involved

Table 11.1. Examples of Spiritually Oriented Helping Activities.

Activities with Individuals, Families, and Groups
- Active imagination
- Art therapies and artistic qualities of practice
- Assessing spiritual emergencies
- Assessing spiritual propensity
- Assessing attitudes about sexual orientation diversity
- Biofeedback
- Brief explicit spiritual assessment (MIMBRA)
- Caring for the body, e.g. healthy lifestyles
- Complementary and alternative healing, such as acupuncture
- Cooperation with clergy, religious communities, and spiritual support groups
- Cooperation with traditional healers
- Creating a spiritual development timeline and narrative
- Detailed explicit spiritual assessment
- Developing and using transcultural teams
- Developing mutually beneficial human/nature relationships
- Developing or collaborating with rituals and ceremonies
- Dialoguing and cooperating across spiritual perspectives
- Differentiating between spiritual emergencies and psychopathology
- Dissolving inner chatter and distractions
- Distinguishing between religious visions and hallucinations or delusions
- Dream reflection
- DSM diagnosis, spiritually sensitive and culturally appropriate
- Ethical decision making about spirituality in practice
- Existential practice
- Exploring family patterns of meaning and ritual
- Exploring sacred stories, symbols, and teachings
- Family brainstorming
- Focused relaxation
- Forgiveness
- Guided visualization
- Identifying client's definitions of spirituality and religion
- Implicit spiritual assessment
- Intentional breathing
- Intuition
- Journaling and diary keeping
- Measuring aspects of religiousness and spirituality
- Meditation
- Mindfulness
- Nature retreats
- Paying attention
- Physical disciplines for spiritual cultivation, such as hatha yoga or taiji
- Prayer
- Reading scripture and inspirational materials
- Reflecting on beliefs regarding death and afterlife
- Reflecting on helpful or harmful impacts of religious group participation
- Reflecting on ideals and symbols of compassion
- Reflective reading
- Refugee resettlement
- Religious tradition specific helping activities and resources (numerous, see Chapter 5)
- Spiritual development timeline and related assessment tools, such as spiritual genogram
- Transpersonal practice
- Win/win solution making

(continued)

Table 11.1.   Continued.

Activities with Organizations, Communities, and World
- Advocacy for spiritual sensitivity in health and social service policy
- Almsgiving and donations
- Cooperation with clergy, religious communities, and spiritual support groups
- Cooperation with traditional healers
- Creating a spiritually sensitive administration and organizational culture
- Developing spiritual diversity innovation planning group
- Developing and using transcultural teams
- Developing mutually beneficial human/nature relationships
- Developing or participating in rituals and ceremonies
- Dialoguing across spiritual perspectives
- Exploring sacred stories, symbols, and teachings of spiritual communities
- International networking
- Lobbying and social activism by religious groups
- Promoting ecojustice and opposing environmental racism
- Reflecting on beliefs regarding death and after life
- Refugee resettlement
- Religious tradition specific helping activities and resources (numerous, see Chapter 5)
- Restorative justice
- Truth and reconciliation commissions
- Voluntary agency assistance to redress poverty and justice issues
- Win/win solution making

---

persons. Spiritually oriented helping activities should flow out of a spiritually sensitive helping relationship and human service organizational context. This is why we focused on developing a foundation of spiritually sensitive values, concepts, knowledge, and context before going into detail on particular practices.

Linking Micro and Macro in Practice

In this book, there is greater emphasis on micro and mesolevels of practice (referred to as micro hereafter) rather than macro, because those are the system levels in which most American social workers practice. However, micro and macro really go together in spiritually sensitive practice. When social workers expand their sense of identity and compassion to include others widely, the near and the far are both close in mind.

In Table 11.1, we categorize helping activities according to their focus on scale of human relational systems, including social work practice with individuals, families, and groups on the one hand and social work practice with organizations, communities, ecosystems, and international connections on the other hand. As we said, "on the one hand...on the other hand." We encourage the reader to put together both hands in a gesture honoring the whole person/world. Effective micropractice needs to take into account larger systems. The hallmark of social work is its commitment to both individual well-being and social justice.

Many activities have relevance to both micro- and macrosystems, so they are listed in both sections. Some activities focus on the individual and also set a foundation for well-being at all system levels. For example, starting with the "hand" of micropractice, mindfulness focuses on the individual social worker and/or client. However, mindfulness is a quality that can help the social worker to approach any practice situation at any system level with clarity, centeredness, and compassion. Likewise, forgiveness can facilitate individual and relational healing both in clinical therapeutic settings and in restorative justice and national or international reconciliation processes.

Starting with the other "hand" of macropractice, all helping activities that promote justice and well-being for larger human systems and earth ecosystems help to generate conditions of living that are conducive to the fulfillment of individuals, families, and local communities. Indeed, as we described a holistic view in Chapter 3, individual, community, and universe form a unity within profoundly deep and wide spirituality.

NOT JUST A PRIVATE MATTER   In our use of the term spirituality, it is not merely a private or individual matter. Human beings are relational beings. We live only because of our interrelatedness with other people and all other beings. Certainly, there is a private dimension of spiritual experience, some of which a person might never share openly with others. But even that could not exist without others. Individual spirituality grows in the field of community: family and friends; religious institutions or nonsectarian spiritual social groups; neighborhoods and cities; cultures and nations; ecosystems of plants, animals, stones, air, sunlight, moonlight, and clouds; the planet earth; the cosmos; and perhaps, as many believe, communities of spiritual beings and the divine Ground of Being Itself. Many religious traditions of service acknowledge and honor this relatedness and it would be well for us to do so also.

CORESPONSIBILITY   As we grow in our awareness of this interrelatedness, we realize with gratitude our fundamental reliance on others. Our capacity for empathy and our zeal for justice ripen. We experience that our own well-being cannot be separated from the well-being of others. Our sense of compassion extends from self and those familiar to us; out to others of different cultures, religions, and ways of life; and out to other beings. A principle of coresponsibility guides us. *Spiritual responsibility is response-ability.* As the saying goes, together we rise, separate we fall.

On a practical level, *spiritually sensitive helping requires a supportive context of organizations and communities.* So we need to attend to the way our human service organizations (HSOs) are structured. We need to examine programs, policies, and procedures for the extent to which they humanize and support people's highest aspirations and transpersonal potential. We seek modes of social change that nonviolently promote solutions for the benefit of all involved, including the nonhuman beings with whom we share this planet.

SOCIAL POLICY AND POLITICS   Social workers need to be very astute about the use and abuse of spirituality in the political process (Canda & Chambers,

1994). Since social policies determine key social values and the distribution of resources, we need to examine them for whether they empower people and support them on their individual and collective spiritual paths. The value and moral dimensions of policy making are spiritual. They are best examined explicitly and openly in the context of public dialogue and critical reflection, lest particular religious or spiritual agendas dominate and harm people who are less influential in the policy-making process. Some politicians and activists openly appeal to divine sanction, religious authorities, and politically charged religious groups to bolster their positions and sway the public. Sometimes religious and nonreligious spiritual ideologies are used to promote peace, justice, and reconciliation. They also are used to foment divisiveness, terrorism, and war.

In order to avoid this danger, as well as to incorporate the positive insights of careful spiritual reflection, we recommend that social workers assist people of diverse and contrasting spiritual perspectives to become active in national and international policy-making processes. We can work to create settings and processes for policy debate based on win/win strategies and the value of mutual respect. We view the ideal policy-making process as a societal and global movement toward creating conditions that are conducive to all people's spiritual development.

Solidarity and Spiritual Renewal Accomplishing large-scale social change requires many people working together. So it is crucial that each person in the effort is also working out her or his spiritual development. If a person feels spiritually empty, one's energy and motivation for justice, especially in the mode of nonviolence, will be hard to sustain.

In 1979, I (EC) had a memorable conversation with two African American activists, Dr. Vincent Harding, who was a theology professor at Iliff School of Theology, and his wife Rosemarie (in memoriam), who was a social worker. They were personal friends and associates of Rev. Dr. Martin Luther King, Jr. I met them when I was a graduate student in religious studies at the University of Denver, before I went into social work. Dr. Harding is now director of the Veterans of Hope Project: A Center for the Study of Religion and Democratic Renewal (http://veteransofhope.org/). The project mission is to share wisdom and encouragement for compassionate and spiritually attuned personal and social transformation that come from people who have been oppressed and marginalized. We highly recommend this website as a source of sayings and video clips from wise and experienced social activists.

Vincent and Rosemarie told me of their heady times at the peak of the civil rights movement. When the movement was going strong, there were tremendous collective energy and mutual support. Charismatic leadership, group enthusiasm, and optimism carried them along. But after Rev. King and Malcolm X were killed, the movement lost some steam and direction. Hopes and dreams began to waiver. Some of the group momentum and energy seeped away. But the need for justice and social change continued. They said that many, like them, went through a period of discontent and emptiness. They needed new energy and inspiration to help them keep on.

They realized that they had over relied on outside forces and group momentum to sustain them. They realized that they needed more inner spiritual strength and vibrancy to sustain them over the long haul. So they took some time to reconnect with their spirituality, to nurture it, and to gain new perspective. This spiritual rejuvenation not only restored energy and direction for their continuing local, national, and international peace and justice work for many decades, it also deepened their grounding in compassion as a guide to their action.

They pointed out the wisdom of Black spirituals, the hymns of divine praise and human liberation, so important in the African American community. These hymns bond individuals into community and they sustain masses of people in collective action for social transformation. They tap a power for perseverance by joining spirituality and justice in a spirit of celebration.

The Hardings' advice stayed with me so long, and I share it here, because it is a valuable reminder for social workers to stay in touch with our inner spiritual centers as we go out to do our work in the world.

Spirituality in Fields of Practice

Many times my (EC) MSW students have mentioned that it is difficult to broach the subject of spirituality in their agency settings. They say that many of the professional staff and their field instructors are not familiar with the topic, have suspicions about it, and are stuck in long established routines of practice. I have also found this to be true when I consult at agencies and social work education programs about how to address spirituality in practice and education. Even when there is some openness to the possibility, there are often feelings of being habit bound or blocked by colleagues and administrators.

For example, a social worker in a psychiatric hospital setting said that the social workers feel they are too busy to deal with spirituality (assuming that takes too much time) and that the psychologists, psychiatrists, and physicians with greater authority insist on using a reductionist medical pathology model. The social worker says that the staff use an intake assessment form that only focuses on DSM type diagnostic criteria. There is one vague question about whether the client belongs to a religion, but most people do not bother to ask about that.

I found that an effective way to begin or expand innovation is to start with the professional standards and resources that are accepted in a given setting. Fortunately, in the United States, many social work fields of practice, as well as the profession as a whole, do have standards and resources relevant to spirituality (see Appendix C). The problem is often that professionals are not aware of them or simply do not bother complying. When an innovator points out the standards and offers suggestions for how to meet the standards, then interest and cooperation are more likely to grow.

In regard to the psychiatric hospital setting, as we discussed earlier, the Joint Commission for accrediting healthcare organizations JCAHO sets requirements that healthcare settings must address the spiritual needs of patients. Failure to do so can result in penalties or loss of accreditation. Regarding the mental health issues in this setting, the DSM itself requires that diagnosis take into account religious, spiritual, and cultural factors. Failure to do so is a violation of diagnostic standards and can result in erroneous and injurious mental health interventions, such as the mistaken diagnosis and prolonged hospitalization of the Tarahumara Mexican woman mentioned in Chapter 1. In addition, for social workers, lack of respect for religious diversity and spirituality is a violation of the NASW Code of Ethics and the NASW standards for culturally competent practice. Social workers who violate the Code of Ethics and/or state licensing regulations can be publically sanctioned or have their licenses to practice suspended or removed. Further, the mental health consumers advocacy movement continues to grow, emphasizing strengths and recovery approaches that recognize spirituality as significant (Ridgway, McDiarmid, Davidson, Bayes, & Ratzlaff, 2002; Starnino, 2009). This movement is increasingly calling for mental health service providers to address spirituality.

As a negative motivator, when professionals realize that failure to address religion and spirituality (or to do so in a negative discriminatory manner) can open them to professional and legal sanctions, they may be more willing to invest resources in innovation. I have seen several occasions when agencies were sued by clients or consumer rights organizations for lack of proper attention to spiritual and cultural diversity. When embarrassing stories appear in the press and when legal pressures are applied, suddenly the supposedly unavailable resources for innovation come forth to address the situation. When I do consultation for HSOs, I recommend that it is best not to wait for negative consequences of spiritually insensitive or culturally incompetent practice. A proactive approach addresses spiritual diversity within the context of professional standards and expectations in the nest interests of clients and their communities. When social workers act on the basis of positive motivators (such as striving for professional excellence, spiritual sensitivity, cultural competence, cultural appropriateness, and justice), enthusiasm moves staff and the HSO forward to pursue spiritual diversity innovation and transcultural teamwork, as we presented in Chapters 8 and 9.

But for innovation to succeed, staffs need more than negative or positive motivators. Innovation is much easier when innovators have access to resources about spiritual diversity in their field of practice, so they can build on professional values, empirical evidence, and practical experience. In order to assist individuals and HSOs to engage in spiritual diversity innovation, we include Appendix C. Appendix C presents a concise list of documents citing professional standards addressing religion and spirituality, selected books, articles, or specialized journals that give comprehensive reviews of the field and relevant organizational websites. We are not endorsing everything listed. But we hope the appendix will give readers a helpful place to start their explorations of these fields of practice. The reader should also consult the index for these and other fields of practice.

Actually there are thousands of publications and relevant websites available. Appendix C and our references list serve as entry points. We recommend that you begin with these materials, consult them for more resources and internet links, and then expand your search from there. Keep in mind that website addresses change and internet links break on websites. So examine the resources for terms to use in internet search engines. Also, we recommend using websites with reputable academic sponsorships or official websites of religions, HSOs, and professional societies. Many internet sites put up erroneous information or have biased agendas.

MANAGED CARE ISSUES   Much social work practice takes place in the context of managed care systems, restrictive insurance policies, and government-based standards of utilization review. This creates pressures toward short-term, technocratic ways of service. To the extent that these pressures are inimical to spiritually sensitive practice, social workers can be active in movements for health care reform, mental health policy reform, and advocacy with insurers and other third party reimbursers. Actually, some third party payers are supporting holistic and complementary approaches to health care, such as acupuncture and stress management programs. Accreditation standards in many managed care settings, such as health care, include spiritual needs. We can work creatively with these trends to find ways to incorporate spiritually oriented helping activities.

Even when managed care requires short-term modalities of service, that does not preclude spiritually sensitive helping. For example, brief solution focused therapies are very consistent with both a strengths perspective and spiritual growth issues (Hoyt, 1996). There are many therapeutic activities derived from humanistic and transpersonal theories that are conductive to rapid breakthroughs in spiritual awareness, such as holotropic breathwork (Grof, 1988). Many helping activities in this book can be taught to clients to be done as self-directed "homework" outside of paid sessions (e.g. focused relaxation and journaling). Many religiously affiliated HSOs include volunteers, pro bono professionals, and philanthropic donations to make services affordable for those who do not have ability to pay. Careful discharge planning with clients in short-term settings, such as hospitals, can include ongoing spiritual practices and referral to community-based spiritual support systems, if clients wish.

Managed care pressures can be an incentive to find ways for clients to work on solutions and growth in their home and daily life settings, free from the often stultifying confines of hospitals, mental health centers, and social work agencies. For instance, a medical social worker could assist a person with a chronic physical illness to access home-based health care and to draw on the loving, beautiful, and supportive qualities of family, friends, spiritual support groups, the natural environment, and activities such as meditation, prayer, or ritual.

Finally, spiritual sensitivity can pervade all situations and modalities of practice. Clients can be treated with humanity, compassion, and concern for justice in managed care or any other setting. This depends on the quality of the helping relationship more than on any particular technique.

A Worldwide View of Spiritually Sensitive Practice

We advocate for a worldwide view of spirituality in social work that embraces micro- and macro-approaches to practice as well as local and global issues. Part 1 presented a foundation of values and concepts for spiritually sensitive practice that took into account a variety of national and international viewpoints on professional ethics and meanings of spirituality. Parts II and III, up to this point, developed a detailed framework of values, knowledge, and practices, primarily within an American (and to some extent Canadian) context, but always with a mind toward the world. Indeed, the discussion of spiritual diversity in the United States showed how this country became a microcosm of the world through the interactions of Indigenous and immigrant spiritual perspectives. The experience of the American social work profession in dealing with cultural and spiritual diversity, and its successes and failures, might serve as an example to critique for social workers in other countries to develop culture and country specific approaches to social work, including dealing with spiritual diversity within the given country.

To be sure, many of the issues and examples of practice we presented are rooted in a distinctively American context—as is necessary for our primary reading audience. However, we hope that our overall approach to spiritually sensitive practice, including its underlying principles and many particulars that draw on spiritually and culturally diverse inspirations, may be of use for international dialogue and collaboration. As we said in Part I, we encourage social workers around the world to adapt what is of use and to discard what is not. We also encourage North American social workers to do the same—and one of the best ways to begin is by expanding point of view to global reach. Indeed, we believe that this is one of the most exciting features of this fifth phase of professional development on spirituality in social work, Transcending Boundaries (Chapter 1).

Growing International Perspective in Social Work

Changing social conditions and service populations due to globalization have had a profound impact on professional standards and social work education during this fifth phase (Butcher, 2004; Hayes & Humphries, 2004; Morris-Compton, 2006; Gray & Fook, 2004; Moss, 2005; Sewpaul & Jones, 2004; Williams & Sewpaul, 2004). Hokenstad and Midgley (2004) noted that "global interdependence is a reality of the 21st century. Economic and social interdependence are now equally important to political interdependence" (p. 1). While calls for stronger Indigenous and local approaches to social work grow (Gray, Coates, & Yellow Bird, 2008), many personal and social problems in any given country are becoming increasingly interconnected and generic, as the issues presented in Link and Healy's (2005) survey of curriculum resources for international social work demonstrate.

The U.S. Council on Social Work Education's (CSWE, 2008) Educational Policy and Accreditation Standards (EPAS) expects programs to include a global perspective and prepare students to develop global awareness of oppression and human rights and to comply with IFSW/IASSW ethical standards. The predatory nature of global capitalism and its detrimental impact on humans and the environment, the spread of infectious diseases, the drug trade, international terrorism and reactive racial profiling and wars, and the increasing number of refugees due to poverty and ethnic and religious conflicts have placed demands on educators to prepare students who can effectively address discriminatory and oppressive social, economic, and health practices (Hokenstad & Midgley, 2004; Link & Healy, 2005). In recognition of the increasingly international scope of social work, the CSWE established the Katherine A. Kendall Institute for International Social Work Education (NASW, 2005) to guide and motivate future researchers, practitioners, and educators in the field. This trend has also generated more collaborations between U.S.-based professional organizations and international organizations such as IASSW and IFSW.

There has been a growing collection of research on international social work. Representative publications include Midgley (1995), Healy (1995), and Hokenstad and Kendall (1995), who have identified the state of international social welfare research, activities, organizations, and social work education in the mid-1990s. Alcock and Craig (2001) compiled a volume of comparative studies on welfare provision and social policy in 12 developed nations. Hokenstad and Midgley (2004) have also assembled a similar volume designed to impart innovations in practice and social welfare policy from other countries to a U.S. audience. Link and Healy (2005) compiled an indispensable collection of sample courses and syllabi for educators that focus on international social work.

As global phenomena challenge the profession to define its worldwide role, Midgley's (1995) observation that the social work knowledge base can be enhanced by investigating social phenomena in other societies, by testing propositions in different cultural contexts, and by cross-national application of social science findings is especially relevant to spiritually sensitive social work in this fifth phase. Hokenstad and Midgley (2004) noted that "it is today generally accepted that mutuality and the reciprocal sharing of knowledge and practice approaches should characterize international exchanges in social work. This implies that social workers in all parts of the world can learn from each other" (p. ix).

Tripodi and Potocky-Tripodi (2007) identified a typology of approaches to international social work research and examples of each approach. *National research* addresses problems and issues within national boundaries, and does not frame the research question, make reference to, or discuss implications for other countries. *Supranational research* studies a population within one country but frames the research question and discusses implications beyond the country in question. *Intranational research* focuses on immigrant or refugee populations within one country, but incorporates literature from, and discusses implications for, the country of origin. *Transnational research* studies populations within two or more countries, utilizes literature from the countries in question, and discusses implications for the countries involved.

Transnational Studies of Spirituality in Social Work

Most English language publications on spirituality in social work so far have been of the first kind; lesser numbers have been of the second and third kinds; and very little transnational study of spirituality in social work has yet been done. Graham (2006) encourages social work scholars who write about spirituality to move beyond North American vantage point and to address it from the perspective of the Global South, or "Asia, Africa, Central and South America, and elsewhere" (p. 63). Indeed, a 2007 content analysis of items dealing with religion in Social Work Abstracts and Social Service Abstracts confirmed that the vast majority of publications were by global North authors and dealt mostly with Judaism and Christianity (Graham & Shier, 2009). Furman and Benson (2006) advocate for the development of globally sensitive curricula and practice interventions, and for more large-scale national and transnational quantitative and qualitative studies that examine the role of religion and spirituality in practice and education. As a step in this direction, our approach to spiritually sensitive practice incorporates materials from all four kinds of studies. We encourage much more work of all four kinds and emphasize the importance of increasing the third and fourth kinds that are most neglected.

An outstanding example of the fourth kind, transnational research, is Al-Krenawi and Graham's (2009) in-depth study of social work practice with Bedouin-Arab people of the Negev, Israel. This study weaves together detailed culture-specific understanding and practices that honor Bedouin Arab and Islamic traditions, together with theoretical and practical guidance for culturally appropriate social work from various countries, and yields implications for social work more widely. Another outstanding example is the development of an Integrative Body-Mind-Spirit approach to social work with global relevance that draws on insights from Chinese traditional medicine and philosophy, an interdisciplinary body of theory and knowledge from East and West, case examples, and empirical studies of effectiveness (Lee, et al., 2009).

Our 2008 National Survey is part of a larger transnational study, that so far included collaborative ventures between researchers in the United States, Norway, Aotearoa New Zealand (ANZ), and the United Kingdom (Canda, Nakashima, & Furman, 2004; Furman, Benson, & Canda, 2004a; Furman, Benson, Canda, & Grimwood, 2005; Furman, Benson, Grimwood, & Canda, 2004b; Furman, Zahl, Benson & Canda, 2007; Stirling, Furman, Benson, Canda, & Grimwood, 2009; Zahl & Furman, 2005; Zahl, Furman, Benson, & Canda, 2007). These studies have provided a platform for interdisciplinary conversation, new theoretical understandings, and multiple perspectives on religion and spirituality. See the website, International Study of Religion and

Spirituality in Social Work Practice (http://spiritualityreligionsurvey.com/default.aspx) for executive summaries. We would like to share some insights from social workers across these four countries.

Raising the Topic of Religion and Spirituality.

This issue was explored in-depth via 22 questions that dealt with raising the topic of religion or spirituality with clients dealing with specific practice issues. These issues included terminal illness, substance abuse, foster parenting, sexual abuse, partner violence, natural disaster, bereavement, mental illness, unemployment, difficult family relations, and criminal justice (e.g. see Table 11.2 for the U.S. responses).

Three scales examined the relationships between religion, spirituality, and client issues. The Religion Practice Issues Scale (RPIS) was constructed for the U.K. (Cronbach's alpha = 0.96), Norway (Cronbach's alpha = 0.95), and the ANZ, U.S. 1997, and U.S. 2008 studies (Cronbach's alpha = 0.97, respectively) by summing the 11 items on religion. The Spirituality Practice Issues Scale (SPIS) was constructed for the U.K., Norway, ANZ, U.S. 2008 (Cronbach's alpha = 0.97, respectively), and the U.S. 1997 (Cronbach's alpha = 0.96) studies by summing the 11 items on spirituality. The range for the RPIS and SPIS is 11–55. Finally, a third scale, the Religion and Spirituality Practice Issues Scale (RSPIS), summed the 22 religion and spirituality items for the U.K., Norway, ANZ, U.S. 1997 (Cronbach's alpha = 0.97, respectively) and the U.S. 2008 (Cronbach's alpha = 0.98) surveys. Given the strong coefficient alphas, the scale demonstrates good validity and reliability, even across cultural contexts and in translation (English/Norwegian).

In summary, U.S. social workers in 1997 and 2008 felt somewhat comfortable about raising the topics of religion and spirituality when dealing with several practice issues. In comparison, the U.K. and ANZ social worker respondents were significantly ($p < 0.01$) more cautious, and Norwegians even more significantly ($p < 0.001$) skeptical. This might be influenced by the degree of secularization of social work and society across the countries, with the United States being least secularized and Norway the most secularized. Further, Norwegian social workers have been dealing with the topic only since 1999 or later. Although ANZ is quite secularized, national legislation and social work standards give special recognition and importance to Indigenous Maori worldview, which is highly spiritual, though distinct from the colonially imported Christian denominations.

HELPING ACTIVITIES   The respondents were presented with a list of 17 helping activities and asked to indicate which they had personally used with clients or approved of the activities. For example, praying privately for a client, using religious language or concepts, using nonsectarian spiritual language or concepts, helping clients develop religious/spiritual rituals, and encouraging the client to do regular religious/spiritual self-reflective diary keeping or journal keeping (e.g. see Table 9.1 for U.S. responses).

Less than 2% of the U.S. respondents in 1997 and 2008 who responded to these 17 questions had not used any interventions, compared with 3% in ANZ, 8% in the United Kingdom, and 10% in Norway. This shows a relatively high level of use of at least some spiritually oriented practices, even though there are cautions in every country. Overall, respondents in New Zealand, the United Kingdom, and Norway were significantly less likely ($p < 0.001$) to approve of the helping activities as interventions compared with the 1997 and 2008 U.S. national surveys. The higher rates of actual use in the United States and ANZ may reflect the high level of spiritual interest in the United States (including high level of religiousness) and the high level of recognition of Maori spirituality in ANZ.

SIGNIFICANCE OF SPIRITUALITY The national surveys each explored whether or not respondents agreed that spirituality is a fundamental aspect of being human. More than 75% of respondents in each country agreed or strongly agreed that it is (see Table 11.2). Further, more than half of all respondents across countries agreed or strongly agreed that social workers should become more knowledgeable about spiritual matters. This indicates that despite misgivings, especially in the more secular countries, many social workers now recognize the importance of spirituality and education about it.

VALUES AND ETHICAL ISSUES The survey instruments included items regarding ethical concerns related to the topic of religion and spirituality (see Table 11.2). Among those who responded, a majority of ANZ (60.5%, $n = 98$), U.S. 1997 (74.7%, $n = 1529$), and U.S. 2008 (66.7%, $n = 1176$) respondents indicated that integrating religion and spirituality in social work practice did not conflict with social work's mission, compared with Norway (43.3%, $n = 257$) and the United Kingdom (47.7%, $n = 369$). Many respondents in ANZ (24.1%, $n = 39$), Norway (31.9%, $n = 189$), the U.K. (32%, $n = 248$), and the U.S. surveys (1997: 16.5%, $n = 337$; 2008: 20.1%, $n = 355$) remained neutral on this issue.

Nearly 64% ($n = 1120$) of U.S. 2008 respondents indicated that integrating religion and spirituality in social work practice is compatible with the code of ethics, compared with New Zealand (39.5%, $n = 64$), Norway (39.8%, $n = 235$), the U.K. (46.8%, $n = 358$), and the U.S. 1997 study (68%, $n = 1397$). Again, a large minority in New Zealand (31.5%, $n=51$), Norway (36.2%, $n = 214$), the U.K. (37.6%, $n = 288$), and the U.S. studies (1997: 22.2%, $n = 449$; 2008: 23.6%, $n = 415$) remained neutral on this topic. Greater acceptance in the United States on this topic may be due to changes since the 1990s in standards for education and practice that include recognition of religious diversity and spirituality (see Appendix C).

It is curious that most respondents in every country recognize the significance of spirituality as a fundamental aspect of being human and the need for education, yet many outside the United States are skeptical of dealing with this on the basis of professional ethics and mission. This may be related to a general

Table 11.2 Values, Ethics, and Educational Issues in the Transnational Surveys.[a]

Variable	U.S. 2008 (N=1804) (%)	(n)	ANZ 2006 (N=162) (%)	(n)	Norway 2002 (N=601) (%)	(n)	U.K. 2000 (N=789) (%)	(n)	U.S. 1997 (N=2069) (%)	(n)
Spirituality is a fundamental aspect of being human										
Strongly Disagree	1.6	28	0.6	1	0.7	4	2.3	18	1.0	20
Disagree	2.9	51	1.9	3	1.7	10	4.5	35	2.1	43
Neutral	14.6	258	11.7	19	18.2	108	16.7	131	9.1	186
Agree	43.9	776	34.6	56	55.6	330	41.9	328	40.4	830
Strongly Agree	37.1	656	51.2	83	23.9	142	34.6	271	47.5	976
Integrating religion and spirituality in social work practice *conflicts* with social work's mission										
Strongly Disagree	18.5	326	9.9	16	7.4	44	10.2	79	20.3	415
Disagree	48.2	850	50.6	82	35.9	213	37.5	290	54.4	1114
Neutral	20.1	355	24.1	39	31.9	189	32.0	248	16.5	337
Agree	9.3	164	12.3	20	19.1	113	13.7	106	6.4	130
Strongly Agree	3.9	68	3.1	5	5.7	34	6.6	51	2.4	50
Integrating religion and spirituality in social work practice *conflicts* with the code of ethics										
Strongly Disagree	16.5	290	8.6	14	6.1	36	8.0	61	17.1	346
Disagree	47.3	830	30.9	50	33.7	199	38.8	297	47.3	1051
Neutral	23.6	415	31.5	51	36.2	214	37.6	288	23.6	415
Agree	9.3	164	24.1	39	19.5	115	10.1	77	9.3	164
Strongly Agree	3.2	56	4.9	8	4.6	27	5.6	43	3.2	56
In your social work education, have you received content on religious or spiritual issues?										
No	64.7	1128	46.5	74	55.6	324	76.5	599	73.3	1516
Yes	35.3	616	53.5	85	44.4	259	23.5	184	26.7	553

Social workers should become more *knowledgeable* than they are now about *spiritual matters*

	%	n	%	n	%	n	%	n	%	n
Strongly Disagree	2.2	39	0.6	1	2.3	14	3.6	28	1.7	34
Disagree	6.5	114	8.6	14	3.7	22	9.8	77	5.9	120
Neutral	25.2	445	27.8	45	22.0	132	29.3	229	23.6	483
Agree	41.9	739	37.0	60	54.8	328	37.1	290	39.1	801
Strongly Agree	24.2	428	25.9	42	17.2	103	20.2	158	29.7	608

Social workers, in general, *do not* possess the skill to assist clients in *religious or spiritual matters*

	%	n	%	n	%	n	%	n	%	n
Strongly Disagree	8.2	145	1.9	3	2.7	16	2.6	20	3.1	64
Disagree	40.2	710	22.8	37	24.9	149	16.5	128	23.5	479
Neutral	26.7	471	25.3	41	30.4	182	23.0	178	36.0	735
Agree	21.3	376	40.7	66	37.0	221	45.1	349	32.3	658
Strongly Agree	3.5	62	9.3	15	5.0	30	12.8	99	5.1	104

[a]Missing values have been excluded from the results.

trend of responses in the surveys that showed greater caution whenever the term "religion" was included compared to items about "spirituality." This suggests that increased international dialogue about a concept of spirituality that includes diverse religious and nonreligious expressions, and an approach to spiritually sensitive practice grounded in professional ethics and mission, may be very useful.

Education and Curriculum Issues

Among those who responded, a larger percentage of social workers in ANZ (53.5%, n = 85) and Norway (44.4%, n = 259) had received content on religion and spirituality in their social work education, compared with the U.K. (23.5%, n = 184) and the U.S. studies (1997: 26.7%, n = 553; 2008: 35.3%, n = 616) (see Table 11.2). Nearly 25% (n = 438) of U.S. 2008 respondents agreed that social workers in general *do not* possess the knowledge to address religious and spiritual issues, compared with ANZ (50%, n = 81), Norway (42%, n = 251), the U.K. (57.9%, n = 448), and U.S. 1997 (37.4%, n = 762). This is very interesting, because it shows that social workers in countries with higher levels of secularization and social work skepticism about religion may actually be receiving more content about religion and spirituality in their education than in the United States. It is possible that this content is provided within the context of antioppressive and antiracist education, which is stronger in these other countries compared to the United States. This puzzling finding merits further discussion among social work scholars and practitioners in these countries, in order to discover how religion and spirituality are addressed within the more secular nations. Perhaps we can learn from each other more about how to approach the topic even with skeptical social workers.

SECULARIZATION   We speculated that patterns of secularization might account for some of these international differences. Secularization refers to a historical process in which a society increases differentiation and autonomy between religious authority and governmental and public life and also emphasizes a rational, utilitarian, and scientific/empirical outlook on life (Roberts, 2004). Since the European Rational Enlightenment, some social theorists have predicted that religion would fade under the impact of secular trends within science, industrialism and postindustrialism, capitalism, and socialism, but this prediction has not materialized (Berger, 1999; Repstad, 1996).

There are many complicated variations on secularization. For example, the United States constitutionally separates church and state and the social work profession disavows specific religious bases for its values, knowledge, and practice. However, in the general population, religious participation is the highest rate among industrialized countries, civil religion is pervasive, and many social services are provided under religious auspices. Further, counter-secularization trends, such as religiously conservative political movements, are strong.

In comparison, in the United Kingdom and Norway, there are state churches (Anglican and Lutheran) although religious participation in the population is much lower than the United States and the social work profession is highly secularized. In ANZ, the society and social work profession are highly secularized, but there is official state and professional recognition and support for Indigenous Maori worldview and spirituality. United Kingdom, Norway, and other northern and western European countries are experiencing rapid increases in religious and cultural diversification, especially due to immigration from Africa, Asia, and the Middle East. Many of these immigrant groups are more actively and pervasively religious than the general populations (Hayes & Humphries, 2004; Modood, 2005). This is giving rise to more attention to spiritual diversity as an aspect of cultural diversity in these countries.

Regarding Norway, Zahl (2003) and Zahl and Furman (2005) have observed that religion and spirituality are still not areas of emphasis in social work practice and education. Norwegian professional social work never had a strong religious orientation. Norway's occupation by the Nazis during World War II also halted and negatively impacted the profession's development. Furthermore, during the 1960s and 1970s, schools of social work were strongly influenced by Marxist ideology. Religion and spirituality, however, are beginning to be considered due to the most recent governmental General Plan for health and social work education (1999:14). The General Plan mandates that the helping professions are to work in accordance with a holistic view of clients, which embraces the physical, psychological, social, cultural, and spiritual aspects of human existence.

Professional social work trends in the United States, United Kingdom, Norway, and ANZ are moving toward standards for holistic perspectives on human well-being and justice, which international organizations such as NASW, CSWE, IFSW, IASSW, the United Nations (1948), World Health Organization (2006), and the European Union (2006) may reinforce. This is consistent with our holistic model of spirituality for social work that points out spirituality is a universal aspect of human experience not limited to religious forms and that religious and nonreligious forms are due respect within holistic and culturally appropriate practice. Indeed, whatever the ways of secularization and counter-secularization in various countries, there will always be a need for spiritually sensitive social work practice (as long as social work exists).

Conclusion

In this book, we have offered a framework of values, concepts, knowledge, and activities that are conducive to spiritually sensitive social work practice. Our framework springs out of our profession's mission to promote a holistic perspective and the well-being of individuals, families, communities, and world. But by reenvisiong our profession's conception of the whole person-in-environment, we hope we have extended the range of that vision to bio-psycho-social-spiritual-ecological.

We stretched the conventional mindset toward transperspectival, transdisciplinary, transcultural, transnational, and transpersonal awareness. We hope that this book encourages you, the readers, to continue your inner work on spiritual development to inspire your service on behalf of others. We also hope this book helps you to extend the range of your service vision to take in people of all religions, spiritual paths, cultures, and ways of life, and further, to regard with compassion and gratitude all beings and the total planet and cosmos in which we live.

By way of concluding, we would like to convey our appreciation to you for reading this book. We designed the book so that reading it would usher you through your own transformation process, your own journey of spiritual development. We appreciate your willingness to participate in this.

As we know from the nature of therapeutic transformation, the end is the beginning. So we leave you with a parting wish.

***

> May any benefit you received
> from reading this book
> ripple throughout your life
> like a pebble dropped into a pond.
>
> And may the ripples of benefit extend
> to all those whom you serve
> to all people whom you meet
> and to all beings
> with whom you share this life.

***

EXERCISES

11.1. Linking Micro- and Macrodimensions of Spiritually Sensitive Practice

Review the list of spiritually oriented helping activities in Table 11.1 and the discussion of interconnections between micro- and macropractice. Reflect on your social work activity at micro- and/or macrolevels. Does your work emphasize one over the other or even exclude one side? Identify one helping activity that is currently part of your work and think of a way to connect it to the other side. For example, if you use mindfulness practice in clinical work, how could you bring this also into administrative or community action work? Or, if you are involved in restorative justice work, how could the principles and practice of individual forgiveness enhance the restorative justice process? Establish a plan for implementing your innovation.

11.2. Enhancing Spiritual Sensitivity in a Field of Practice

Review the nine fields of social work practice listed in Appendix C. Choose one that is closest to your own. If you are a U.S.-based reader, explore the relevant professional standards and select some readings or websites to explore. Consider how well your practice and HSO currently fulfill the professional standards. If these standards are not yet known in your practice setting, bring them to the attention of your colleagues and supervisors. Initiate a discussion of how practice in your setting can better fulfill the professional standards and make use of the resources you have identified.

If you are not a U.S.-based reader, then consider whether the U.S.-based standards are relevant to your field of practice in your country. Also, explore whether there are field of practice-specific professional standards in your country and whether they address religion or spirituality. Also consider whether the IFSW/IASSW standards have relevance. Critique any relevant standards (or lack thereof) regarding the fit with your local context. Bring your ideas to colleagues in your practice setting to initiate a discussion of how spirituality might be addressed more thoroughly.

11.3. Expanding Your View Worldwide

Review the section on a worldwide view of spiritually sensitive practice. Explore the internationally related websites and professional standards in the first part of Appendix C, especially the IFSW/IASSW standards. Also, do an online search for social work Codes of Ethics in at least two countries. Compare them for similarities and differences. Consider implications for your own social work.

11.4. Making International Connections

If you would like to take this to the next step of engaging international dialogue, visit the Directory of International Contacts in the Spiritual Diversity and Social Work Resource Center (http://www.socwel.ku.edu/candagrant/HFC4.htm) as well as websites listed in the first part of Appendix C pertaining to a country different from your own. Or, identify the author of an article or book listed in References who lives in another country and locate her or his professional email address by internet search. In one of these ways, identify someone or an organization in another country and send an email message with a question of interest. Most likely, you will receive a friendly and encouraging response. This is important for extending and growing international networks and collaborations on spiritual diversity in social work.

APPENDIX A

Discussion Guide for Detailed Spiritual Assessment

Note: Begin with an implicit spiritual assessment or brief explicit spiritual assessment to identify if a detailed explicit assessment is relevant to the client. Make sure that a spiritually sensitive relationship is established. Select and modify these suggested questions as relevant to the client and the helping situation. Avoid professional jargon. The introductory explanation and subsequent questions should be modified according to the client's responses to the implicit or brief explicit assessments.

Introduction

I am interested to learn about your experiences about spirituality and religion as they may be relevant to our work together. For the purpose of our discussion, I am defining spirituality as the way you experience life meaning, morally fulfilling relationships, and priorities for what has greatest significance to you. This may or may not involve belief in God or a supernatural aspect of the world. I am defining religion as a set of beliefs, values, and practices that is shared by a community and focused on spirituality. Therefore, a person's spirituality may or may not be expressed through a religion. I would be glad to replace these terms and

Refer to guidelines for spiritually sensitive assessment in Chapter 8. This guide is adapted from Appendix A of this book's first edition and draws on insights from Table 74.1 of Nelson-Becker, Nakashima, & Canda (2006, pp. 801–802).

definitions with any that make more sense to you. Please feel free to answer or not answer my questions in any way that is comfortable to you. I am interested in hearing your story in your own words.

Spiritual Group Membership and Participation

- Do you belong to or participate in any spiritual or religious groups? If so, please name them.
- If you have more than one spiritual affiliation, what is your primary affiliation?
- Would you describe yourself as religious or nonreligious? Please explain.
- How important is religion or spirituality to you?
- Would you be interested in exploring how your spirituality or religion might be related to our work together? Please explain.
- If you do not participate in any spiritual or religious groups, do you have other ways of expressing spiritual needs or interests? Please explain.

Spiritual Beliefs

- What religious or spiritual beliefs are relevant to our work together?
- What beliefs give you a sense of comfort or hope?
- What beliefs do you question or find upsetting?
- Do you believe in God, a spiritual Higher Power, or some other sacred force? Please describe.
- What are the most significant stories, teachings, or symbols that give you guidance? Please describe them.

Spiritual Activities

- How often do you attend a place for religious or spiritual practice, such as a church, temple, mosque, or a ceremonial site in nature? Please describe.
- What kinds of spiritual or religious activities do you perform together with a spiritual group? These might include prayer, meditation, ritual, ceremony, reading sacred texts, telling and listening to inspirational stories or speeches, participating in social support groups, etc. Please describe them and indicate how often you do them.
- In what ways do you find these activities helpful?
- In what ways do you find them unhelpful?

- What kinds of spiritual or religious activities do you perform together with your family at home? Please describe them and indicate how often you do them.
- In what ways do you find these activities helpful or unhelpful?
- What kinds of spiritual or religious activities do you perform by yourself privately? Please describe them and indicate how often you do them.
- In what ways do you find these activities helpful or unhelpful?

Spiritual Experiences and Feelings

- When have you had feelings of great peace, joy, contentment, and being loved? Please give examples.
- What have been the most profound and moving experiences that gave you a sense of peace, wisdom, insight, or grace? Please describe them.
- What kind of feelings do you usually have when you participate in religious or spiritual activities, if any? Please give examples of positive and negative feelings.
- When you have felt times of loss, grief, or crisis, how did your religion or spirituality help or hinder you in dealing with that?
- Do you experience a sense of connection with spiritual forces, such as God, angels, saints, ancestors, nature, or deceased loved ones? Please explain.
- Are your dreams ever significant or insightful for you? If so, please give an example.
- Have you ever had surprising, troubling, or confusing spiritual experiences and feelings? If so, please explain.

Moral and Value Issues

- What are the main moral principles and values that guide your life?
- Where do these principles and values come from?
- Are there any moral or value issues or questions that are especially relevant to your current situation?

Spiritual Development

- Please describe your understanding and practice of religion or spirituality when you were a child. How did you learn these?
- Please describe your current understanding of religion or spirituality.

- How is this similar or different from childhood?
- Describe your spiritual developmental path from childhood to now.
- What is your ideal for spiritual development in the future and how would you like to achieve it?
- Who have been your most important spiritual friends and mentors? Please describe them.
- When you have been at a time of crisis previously, what spiritual or religious supports helped you most? Please describe them. Would these supports be helpful to you now?
- When you have been at a time of great satisfaction and joy, what spiritual or religious supports contributed most? Please describe them. Would these supports be helpful to you now?
- Describe any times of spiritual breakthrough or pivotal life events that are relevant to you now.

Spiritual Sources of Support

- On the basis of the previous discussion, what spiritual sources of support would be useful for you now? These might relate to your inner strengths, spiritual practices, family, religious or spiritual communities, nature, or the sacred realm, however you understand that.
- When you have religious or spiritual concerns, whom do you talk to or whom would you talk to if you could?
- What religious or spiritual sources give you a sense of protection, comfort, and reassurance?
- Have spiritual or religious groups provided you with material things like food or shelter when you were sick or in difficult times? Please explain.
- Have spiritual or religious teachings or communities hindered you? Please explain.

Spiritual Sources of Transformation

- What spiritual or religious sources help you to grow, change, and thrive?
- What spiritual or religious sources help you to break through at times when you feel stuck in life?
- What helps you to forgive and to experience forgiveness?
- What helps you to work through feelings of loss, grief, anger, despair, or crisis into recovery, joy, hope, and new life?

Spiritual Well-being

- How clear is your sense of meaning and purpose in life? Please explain how your spirituality or religion relates to this.
- How often do you feel like life is joyful and worthwhile? Please explain how your spirituality or religion relates to this.
- How strongly do you feel a connection with something inspiring that is greater than yourself, like God, nature, or sacredness? Please explain.

Extrinsic/Intrinsic Styles of Spiritual Propensity

- How often do you agree with the teachings and values of your spiritual or religious groups? Please explain and give examples.
- If you ever disagree or are uncomfortable with any aspect of your spiritual or religious groups, how often do you address the issue or tell people? Please explain and give examples.
- How much are your spiritual or religious principles and practices integrated into your daily life? Please explain and give examples.
- In what ways, if any, do your family and work activities relate to your spiritual development?
- When you meet someone from a different religious or spiritual perspective from your own, do you feel that you should persuade that person to change to your perspective? Please explain.
- In our work together, are you interested in exploring ways to enhance your religious or spiritual activities or to find new ones that might help you deal with your situation?

APPENDIX B

Methodological Summary for the 2008 National Survey of NASW Members (U.S.A.) on Spirituality and Religion in Practice

This national study explored the attitudes of NASW members in direct practice regarding their ideas about professional use of religion and spirituality. The questionnaire defined *religion* as "an organized, structured set of beliefs and practices shared by a community, related to spirituality" and *spirituality* as "involving the search for meaning, purpose, and morally fulfilling relations with self, other people, the encompassing universe and ultimate reality, however a person understands it." According to these definitions, spirituality also can be expressed through religious forms but is not limited to them.

The study followed the sampling methods used in the 1997 National Survey of NASW members (For more details, see Canda & Furman, 1999). A stratified-random sample of 8000 practicing social workers was selected from NASW membership lists ($N = 78,879$). This survey population was limited to social workers in the following areas of professional practice: child/family welfare, criminal justice, medical/health care, mental health, occupational, social work-eap, school social work, and other. The survey population was stratified by states into four U.S. Census Bureau Regional Divisions (Northeast, Midwest, South, and West). Two thousand questionnaires were mailed to each area.

Respondents had two options to complete the survey. Respondents could complete a paper survey as in 1997, or respondents could complete the survey online rather than returning it via postal service. The online version of the questionnaire was made as similar to the paper version as possible. A parallel mixed-mode approach was used to accommodate budget constraints, to decrease response time, and to give respondents the convenience of another option to complete the survey (Meckel, Walters, & Baugh, 2005).

Respondents who completed the survey online were directed to go to www. spiritualityreligionsurvey.com, click on the survey link on the homepage, and then enter a personal access code to begin the online survey process. Three hundred respondents chose to complete the survey online, compared with 1504 who completed the paper survey. The resultant 1804 completed surveys provided a 23% overall response rate with a sampling error of ± 2.3% at the 95% confidence interval. Gay, Mills, and Airasian (2006) have provided guidelines for determining the sample size needed to be representative of a given population, including the observation that "beyond a certain point (about $N = 5000$), the population size is almost irrelevant and a sample size of 400 will be adequate" (p. 110). Generally speaking, the resultant NASW sample exceeds the minimum sample size needed to be generalizable, or representative of the opinions of the NASW membership in direct practice. Additional information on sampling can be obtained at www.spiritualityreligionsurvey.com.

The 126-item questionnaire built upon and refined the survey instrument originally used in the 1997 National Survey of NASW Members (Canda & Furman, 1999). The 2008 survey instrument included items for demographic, educational background, and practice information; past and current religious and spiritual affiliation and involvement; and items regarding forgiveness and referral to clergy. Other items explored possible conflicts between religion and spirituality with the social work mission, the Code of Ethics, and separation of church and state. Respondents were also given the opportunity to provide personal definitions of religion, spirituality, and faith, and to indicate their level of religiosity and spirituality. Furthermore, the questionnaire requested information about spiritually based "helping activities" that social workers used in their practice and that they felt were appropriate to use. In addition, items on raising the topic of religion and spirituality with clients from vulnerable populations were added to the 2008 instrument. The items focused on ethnicity/national origin, gender, sexual orientation, older adulthood, political beliefs, religious beliefs, disability, and poverty.

Reliability and Validity

Reliability

A scale developed in 1997 that separated religion from spirituality was used to assess social workers' agreement with raising these topics in practice. Originally, selected items had been used in previous investigations (Bullis, 1993; Dudley & Helfgott, 1990; Sheridan & Bullis, 1991; Sheridan, Bullis, Adcock, Berlin,& Miller,1992; Sheridan,Wilmer, & Atcheson,1994), but the 1997 instrument had no track record. At that time, coefficient alphas were calculated for scales made up of religion items (R), spirituality items (S), and a combined religion-spirituality scale (RS). The R alpha was 0.97, while those for S and RS were 0.96 and 0.97, respectively, which suggested that the religion and spirituality items included in the 1997 instrument may be useful in future investigations as measurement scales (Canda & Furman, 1999). The R (0.97), S (0.97), and RS (0.98) alphas calculated for the 2008 instrument strongly suggest that the spiritually based and religiously based items measure a trait we have called RS (religion/spirituality), which deals with spirituality and religion as they manifest in social work practice. Similar results with the R, S, and RS scales have been achieved in Norway, United Kingdom, and New Zealand.

Validity

Several sets of items were culled from past research, where their utility was at least established through the peer review process (Bullis, 1993; Dudley & Helfgott, 1990; Sheridan et al., 1991, 1992, 1994). Reworkings of items from past studies and newly developed items were subjected to content and wording analysis by 13 members of a university social work department. Items that faculty members found conceptually confusing (validity) or difficult to understand (reliability) were reworked in the light of their comments. Reviewers were asked to comment on whether items tapped attitudes of social workers toward religion, spirituality, and social work practice. The instrument evolved over several weeks and permutations until the instrument was deemed satisfactory in terms of content validity.

Given that the religion and spirituality items could reliably be combined into a scale (or scales), it is possible to use this scale as an initial check on the criterion-referenced/concurrent validity of some of the other items. If the combined RS scale is in fact tapping fundamental attitudes of social workers toward raising these issues in their practices, then the scale should covary with other items where the content is related.

For example, RS correlated positively with the number of religious/spiritual helping activities reportedly performed (r_{xy} = 0.449, p < 0.001 in 2008, compared with r_{xy} = 0.44, p < 0.001 in 1997) and with the number of religious/spiritual activities nominated as appropriate for use with clients (r_{xy} = 0.468, p < 0.001 in 2008, compared with r_{xy} = 0.46, p < 0.001 in 1997). Social workers reporting a higher level of personal spiritual involvement are more willing (and perhaps able) to introduce religion and/or spirituality into their practice. In 2008, the RS scale was significantly correlated with respondents' participation in religious activities (r_{xy} = 0.185, p < 0.001) and spiritual practices (r_{xy} = 0.237, p < 0.001).

A check on the discriminant validity of the R scale (and thus R items) in 2008 can be conducted by comparing the scores of atheists and agnostics with those of Christians. Christians scored significantly higher on the R scale (M = 38.31, SD= 9.65 versus agnostics/atheists M = 31.9, SD = 11.54; t, d.f. = 203.53, = 6.75, p < 0.001), suggesting that those identifying themselves with a specific religion also responded to items dealing with religion in a predictable manner.

It also means that Christians are significantly more likely to discuss the topic of religion with clients than are agnostics or atheists.

Please refer to www.spiritualityreligionsurvey.com for executive summaries of this study and the other national surveys, including more information on reliability and validity.

APPENDIX C

Resources for Addressing Spirituality in Various Fields of Practice

Social Work in General

Professional Standards

INTERNATIONAL FEDERATION OF SOCIAL WORKERS (IFSW) AND INTERNATIONAL ASSOCIATION OF SCHOOLS OF SOCIAL WORK (IASSW)

Ethics in Social Work, Statement of Principles

http://www.apss.polyu.edu.hk/iassw/index.php?option=com_content&
    task=view&id=7&Itemid=50
- 3 International Conventions
- 4.1 Human Rights and Human Dignity
- 4.2 Social Justice

NATIONAL ASSOCIATION OF SOCIAL WORKERS (NASW)

Code of Ethics, 1996 & 1999

http://www.socialworkers.org/pubs/code/code.asp
- 1.05 Cultural Competence and Social Diversity
- 4.02 Discrimination
- 6.04 Social and Political Action

NASW Standards for Cultural Competence, 2001

http://www.socialworkers.org/practice/standards/NASWCultural
Standards.pdf
- Introduction, p.8
- Cultural Competence, p. 11
- Standard 4 Cross-Cultural Skills

NASW Peace Policy Toolkit, 2007

http://www.socialworkers.org/diversity/peacetoolkit/peaceToolKit.pdf
- Numerous allusions to religion and spirituality

COUNCIL ON SOCIAL WORK EDUCATION (CSWE)

Educational Policy and Accreditation Standards, 2008

http://www.cswe.org/NR/rdonlyres/2A81732E-1776-4175-AC42-
65974E96BE66/0/2008EducationalPolicyandAccreditationStan-
dards.pdf
- Educational Policy 2.1.4—Engage diversity and difference in
practice
- Educational Policy 2.1.7—Apply knowledge of human behavior
and the social environment
- Educational Policy 3.1—Diversity

See other country specific Social Work Codes of Ethics and educational standards via internet search
In U.S.A., see state specific social work licensure standards via internet search

Comprehensive Reviews and Specialized Journals

See Canda, Nakashima, Burgess, Russel, and Barfield (2003) for more than 700
social work publications, with many annotations, organized by fields of practice,
textbooks, and other topics.
See extensive references in the back of this book.

Journal of Jewish Communal Service

Journal of Religion and Spirituality in Social Work: Social Thought

The Social Work Forum (Jewish communal service focus)

Social Work and Christianity

Society for Spirituality and Social Work Forum

Websites

Aboriginal and Indigenous Social Work
- http://www.aboriginalsocialwork.ca/

Canadian Society for Spirituality in Social Work
- http://w3.stu.ca/stu/sites/spirituality/index.html

Centre for Spirituality and Health (Social Work focus for the UK)
- http://www.bernardmoss.org.uk/centre_for_health_&_spirituality.htm

Center for Spirituality and Social Work
- http://csisw.cua.edu/resources.cfm

Centre on Behavioral Health, Hong Kong
- http://cbh.hku.hk/

Global Alliance for a Deep Ecological Social Work
- http://www.ecosocialwork.org/

International Study of Religion and Spirituality in Social Work Practice
- http://spiritualityreligionsurvey.com/default.aspx

Islamic Social Services Association
- http://www.issaservices.com/

North American Association of Christians in Social Work
- http://www.nacsw.org

Research Guides to Jewish Studies: Social Work
- http://www.jtsa.edu/Library/Library_Services/Research_Guides_to_Jewish_Studies/Jewish_Studies_and_Social_Work.xml

Social Work for Social Justice (Catholic Social Teaching)
- http://www.stthomas.edu/socialwork/socialjustice/principles/socialJusticePrinciples.html

Society for Spirituality and Social Work
- http://ssw.asu.edu/spirituality/sssw/

Spiritual Diversity and Social Work Resource Center
- http://www.socwel.ku.edu/candagrant/IIFC4.htm

Child Welfare and Positive Youth Development

Professional Standards

NASW Standards for Social Work Practice in Child Welfare

http://www.socialworkers.org/practice/standards/NASWChildWelfareStandards0905.pdf

See Community/local systems, p. 15, and
- Standard 8. Cultural Competence
- Standard 14. Out of Home Care
- Standard 15. Permanency

NASW Standards for the Practice of Social Work with Adolescents

http://www.socialworkers.org/practice/standards/NASWAdolescents
Standards.pdf
- Standard 3. Knowledge of Family Dynamics
- Standard 6. Understanding Adolescents' Needs

Comprehensive Reviews and Specialized Journals

Canda and Cheon (forthcoming); Crompton (1998); Roehlkepartain, King, Wagener, and Benson (2006).

International Journal of Children's Spirituality

Websites

- The Center for Spiritual Development in Childhood and Adolescence, social work reading list
- http://www.spiritualdevelopmentcenter.org/Display.asp?Page=SWreadinglist

Research Resources on Children's Spirituality
- http://childfaith.net/database/

Disabilities

Professional Standards

General social work standards

Comprehensive Reviews and Specialized Journals

Gaventa and Coulter (2001); Vash (2001)

Journal of Religion, Disability, and Health

Websites

None located

See also resources on health, gerontology, and mental health.

Disaster Relief and Trauma Work

Professional Standards

Brief mention in NASW Standards for Palliative & End of Life Care

http://www.naswdc.org/practice/bereavement/standards/standard-s0504New.pdf

Comprehensive Reviews and Specialized Journals

Koenig (2006).

Websites

The Institute for the Study of Spirituality and Trauma
- http://www.geocities.com/frbobparlotz/drbobparlotz.html

Faith-Based Human Service Organizations

Professional Standards

NASW Priorities on Faith-Based Human Services Initiatives, 2002

http://www.socialworkers.org/advocacy/positions/faith.asp

Comprehensive Reviews and Specialized Journals

Cnaan, Wineburg, and Boddie (1999); Cnaan and Boddie, (2006); Tirrito and Cascio (2003); Wineburg (2001).

Websites

Faith and Service Technical Education Network
- http://www.baylor.edu/social_work/FASTEN/

Faith-based Community Initiatives
- http://www.faithbasedcommunityinitiatives.org/fbci_members.htm

Harford Institute for Religion Research: Faith based Social Services/ Charitable Choice
- http://hirr.hartsem.edu/research/charitable_choice.html

Gerontology/Aging

Professional Standards

NASW Standards for Social Work Services in Long-Term Care Facilities, 2003; see introduction, p. 5

http://www.socialworkers.org/practice/standards/NASWLongTerm Standards.pdf

Comprehensive Reviews and Specialized Journals

McBee (2008); Moberg (2001); Nelson-Becker, Nakashima, and Canda (2006, 2007);

Nelson-Becker and Canda (2008).

Journal of Religion, Spirituality & Aging

Websites

Gerontological Society of America, Interest Group on Religion,
    Spirituality, and Aging
    • http://www.geron.org/Resources/Interest%20Groups/Formal
      %20Interest%20Groups#religion

University of Kansas Office on Aging and Long-Term Care

Chapin, Nelson-Becker, Gordon, Landry, and Peng (2004). Spirituality
    Resource.
    • http://www.oaltc.ku.edu/gerorich/Reports/Spirituality.pdf

Health

Professional Standards

NASW Standards for Social Work Practice in Health Care Settings

http://www.socialworkers.org/practice/standards/NASWHealthCare
    Standards.pdf; see the following sections:
    • Social Work Guiding Principles, p. 8
    • Biopsychosocial-spiritual Perspective, p. 9
    • Case Management, p. 10
    • Health Care Settings, p. 12
    • Standard 3. Cultural Competence
    • Standard 5. Knowledge
    • Standard 6. Assessment
    • Standard 7. Intervention and Treatment Planning

The Joint Commission on the Accreditation of Healthcare Organizations
    (JCAHO)

Spiritual Assessment, 2008

http://www.jointcommission.org/AccreditationPrograms/HomeCare/
    Standards/09_FAQs/PC/Spiritual_Assessment.htm

Comprehensive Reviews and Specialized Journals

Greenstreet (2006); Koenig (2007); Koenig, McCullough, and Larson,
    (2001); O'Brien (2008).

Websites

The Center for Spirituality, Theology and Health
- http://www.dukespiritualityandhealth.org/

National Center for Complementary and Alternative Medicine
- http://nccam.nih.gov/

Spiritual Diversity and Social Work Resource Center
- http://www.socwel.ku.edu/candagrant/HFC4.htm

The George Washington Institute for Spirituality and Health
- http://www.gwish.org/

The University of Minnesota's Center for Spirituality and Healing
- http://www.csh.umn.edu/

Hospice and Palliative Care

Professional Standards

NASW Standards for Palliative & End of Life Care, 2004

http://www.socialworkers.org/practice/bereavement/standards/standards0504New.pdf; See the following sections:
- End of Life Care Definition, p. 9
- Palliative Care, p. 10
- Hospice and Palliative Care, p. 11
- Grief, p. 12
- Standard 1. Ethics and Values
- Standard 2. Knowledge
- Standard 3. Assessment
- Standard 4. Intervention/Treatment Planning
- Standard 6. Empowerment and Advocacy
- Standard 9. Cultural Competence

Comprehensive Reviews and Specialized Journals

Berzoff and Silverman (2004).

Gwyther, Altilio, Blacker, et al. (2005).

American Journal of Hospice and Palliative Medicine

Journal of Near-Death Studies

Journal of Social Work in End-of-Life & Palliative Care

Omega: Journal of Death and Dying

Websites

The Social Work in Hospice and Palliative Care Network

http://swhpn.org/lhp/index.html

(This site includes additional standards.)

Mental Health

Professional Standards

US DHHS Substance Abuse and Mental Health Services Administration

Consensus Statement on Mental Health Recovery; See section on Holistic Perspective, p.1 and Professional Social Work and Health sections

http://www.power2u.org/downloads/SAMHSA%20Recovery%20 Statement.pdf

Comprehensive Reviews and Specialized Journals

Fallot, (1998); Frame (2003); Helmeke and Sori, (2006); Koenig (2005); Miller (2003); Pargament (2007); Paloutzian and Park (2005); Ridgway, McDiarmid, Davidson, Bayes, an& Ratzlaff (2002); Sperry and Shafranske (2003); Swinton, (2001).

Journal of Spirituality in Mental Health

Websites

Congregational Resource Guide on Mental Health
   • http://www.congregationalresources.org/ShowCat.asp? CN=35&SCN=49&SSCN=197

National Alliance on Mental Illness FaithNet
   • www.nami.org/namifaithnet

Spiritual Competency Resource Center
   • http://www.spiritualcompetency.com/

Spiritual Emergence Network
   • http://www.cpsh.org/

Substance Abuse

Professional Standards

NASW Standards for Social Work Practice with Clients with Substance Use Disorders, 2005

http://www.socialworkers.org/practice/standards/NASWATOD
Statndards.pdf; See following sections:
- Standard 3. Screening, Assessment, and Placement
- Standard 5. Advocacy and Collaboration

National Quality Forum, National Voluntary Consensus Standards
for the Treatment of Substance Use Conditions: Evidence-Based
Treatment Practices

http://www.qualityforum.org/pdf/reports/sud/sudexesummary.pdf;
See:
- Table 1. Practice Specifications for Treating Substance Use
Conditions

Comprehensive Reviews and Specialized Journals

Coggins (1990); Kus (1995); McGovern and Benda (2006).

Websites

12Step.org
- http://www.12step.org/

Inner Substance (Integral Alternative to 12 Steps)
http://www.innersubstance.com/philosophy.html

REFERENCES

Abe, M. (1995). A Buddhist view of human rights. In A. A. An-Na'im, J. D. Gort, H.
J. & H. M. Vroom (Eds.), *Human rights and religious values: An uneasy relationship?* (pp. 144–153). Grand Rapids, MI: William B. Eerdmans Publishing Company.

Achterberg, J. (1985). *Imagery in healing: Shamanism and modern medicine.* Boston: Shambala.

Adams, P. (2008). The code of ethics and the clash of orthodoxies: A response to Spano and Koenig. *Journal of Social Work Values and Ethics, 5(1)*. Retrieved from http:// www.socialworker.com/jswve/content/view/94/65/

Aguilar, M. A. (2001). Catholicism. In M. Van Hook, B. Hugen, & M. Aguilar (Eds.), *Spirituality within religious traditions in social work practice* (pp. 120–145). Pacific Grove, CA: Brooks/Cole Thomson Learning.

Ai, A. L. (2006). Faith matters, empirical research, and professional practice: Current needs and future steps. *Arete, 30(1)*, 30–41.

Alcock, P., & Craig, G. (2001). The United Kingdom: Rolling back the welfare state? In P. Alcock & G. Craig (Eds.), *International social policy: Welfare regimes in the developed world.* New York: Palgrave Macmillan.

Aldridge, M. J., Macy, H., & Walz, T. (no date). *Beyond management: Humanizing the administrative process.* Iowa City, IA: School of Social Work, University of Iowa.

Al-Krenawi, A., & Graham, J. R. (2009). *Helping professional practice with Indigenous peoples: The Bedouin-Arab case.* Lanham, MD: University Press of America.

Amato-von Hemert, K. (1994). Should social work education address religious issues? Yes! *Journal of Social Work Education, 30(1)*, 7–11 and 16–17.

American Psychiatric Association. (2000). *Diagnostic and statistical manual of mental disorder, fourth edition, text revision).* Washington, DC: Author.

Ammerman, N. T. (Ed.). (2007). *Everyday religion: Observing modern religious lives.* New York: Oxford University Press.

Anadarajah, G. & Hight, E. (2001). Spirituality and medical practice: Using the HOPE questions as a practical tool for spiritual assessment. *American Family Physician, 63* ,81–89.

Anderson, R. (1996). *Magic, science, and health: The aims and achievements of medical anthropology.* Fort Worth, TX: Harcourt Brace College Publishers.

Angel, L. (1994). *Enlightenment east and west.* Albany, NY: State University of New York.

Anonymous (2002). Diagnosis review committee: New and revised diagnoses. *Nursing Diagnosis, 13*(2), 65, 68–96.

Ansel, E. (1973). T'shuva--parallels to the existential growth process. *The Jewish Social Work Forum, 10*(2), 36–47.

Arnal, W. E. (2000). Definition. In W. Braun & R. T. McCutcheon (Eds.).(2000). *Guide to the study of religion (pp. 21–34).* New York: Cassell.

Ashencaen Crabtree, S., Husain, F., & Spalek, B. (2008). *Islam and social work: debating values, transforming practice.* Bristol, Great Britain: The Policy Press.

Assagioli, R. (1965). *Psychosynthesis: A collection of basic writings.* New York: Penguin.

Axinn, J., & Levin, H. (1982). *Social welfare: A history of the American response to need* (2nd ed.). New York: Harper & Row.

Bacchus, D. N. A., & Holley, L. C. (2004). Spirituality as a coping resource: The experiences of professional Black women. *Journal of Ethnic & Cultural Diversity in Social Work, 13*(4), 65–84.

Baer, R. A. (Ed.). (2006). *Mindfulness-based treatment approaches: Clinician's guide to evidence base and applications Burlington, MA: Elsevier.*

Banerjee, M. M. (1997a). Strengths despite constraints: Memoirs of research in a slum in Calcutta. *Reflections: Narratives of Professional Helping, 3*(3), 36–45.

Banerjee, M. M. (1997b). Frozen feta cheese lasagna with crushed hot peppers. *Reflections: Narratives of Professional Helping, 3*(4), 44–54.

Banerjee, M. M. (2005). Allah, Kali, Jesus: Reflections on my own and respondents' spirituality. *Reflections: Narratives of Professional Helping, 11*(3), 46–61.

Banerjee, M. & Canda, E. R. (in press for 2009). Spirituality as a strength of African American women responding to welfare reform. *Journal of Religion and Spirituality in Social Work,* 28(3), 239–262.

Banerjee, G. R. (1972). *Papers on social work: An Indian perspective.* Bombay, India: Tata Institute of Social Sciences.

Barise, A. (2005). Social work with Muslims: Insights from the teachings of Islam. *Critical Social Work, 6*(2), Retrieved August 4, 2008, from http://www.uwindsor.ca/units/socialwork/critical.nsf/inToc/04A251D4FCF201308525701B,.

Barry, W. A., & Connolly, W. J. (1982). *The practice of spiritual direction.* New York: The Seabury Press.

Baskin, C. (2006). Aboriginal world views as challenges and possibilities in social work education. *Critical Social Work, 7*(2). Retrieved from http://www.uwindsor.ca/units/socialwork/critical.nsf/982f0e5f06b5c9a285256d6e006cff78/

Baum, R. M. (1993). Homosexuality and the traditional religions of the Americas and Africa. In Arlene Swidler (Ed.), *Homosexuality and world religions* (pp. 1–46). Valley Forge, PA: Trinity Press International.

Beane, W. C., & Doty, W. G. (Eds.). (1975). *Myths, rites, symbols: A Mircea Eliade reader.* New York: Harper & Row.

Beatch, R., & Stewart, B. (2002). Integrating Western and Aboriginal healing practices. In M. Nash & B. Stewart (Eds.), *Spirituality and social care: Contributing to personal and community well-being* (pp. 151–170).London: Jessica Kingsley Publishers.

Beckford, J. A., & Demerath, N. J. (Eds.). (2007). *The Sage handbook of the sociology of religion*. Los Angeles: Sage Publications.

Bein, A. (2008). *The Zen of helping: Spiritual principles for mindful and open-hearted practice*. Hoboken, NJ: John Wiley & Sons.

Bell, C. M. (1992). *Ritual theory, ritual practice*. New York: Oxford University Press.

Bell T. R., & J. L. Bell. (1999). Help-seeking in the black church: An important connection for social work to make. *Social Work and Christianity, 26*(1), 144–154.

Bell, D. A. & Hahm, C. (Eds.). (2003). *Confucianism for the modern world*. Cambridge, UK: Cambridge University Press.

Bellah, R. N. (1991). *Beyond belief: Essays on religion in a post-traditional world*. Berkeley, CA: University of California Press.

Benefiel, M. (2005). *Soul at work: Spiritual leadership in organizations*. New York: Church Publishing Inc.

Benson, P. L., Donahue, M. J., & Erickson, J. A. (1993). The faith maturity scale: Conceptualization, measurement, and empirical validation. In M. L. Lynn & D. O. Moberg (Eds.), *Research in the social scientific study of religion* (Vol. 5, pp. 1–26). Greenwich, CT: Jai Press, Inc.

Benton, J. F. (1981). A theology of charity for Christian social agencies. *Social Thought, 7*(4). 2–13.

Berger, P. L. (1999). The desecularization of the world: A global overview. In P. L. Berger (Ed.), *The desecularization of the world: Resurgent religion and world politics* (pp. 1–18). Washington, DC: Ethics and Public Policy Center.

Berl, F. (1979). Clinical practice in a Jewish context. *Journal of Jewish Communal Service, 55*(4), 366–368.

Berlin, S. B. (2005). The value of acceptance in social work direct practice: A historical and contemporary view. *Social Service review, 79*(3), 484–510

Berry, D. (2005). Methodological pitfalls in the study of religiosity and spirituality. *Western Journal of Nursing Research, 27*, 628–647.

Berzoff, J., & Silverman, P. R. (Eds.). (2004). *Living with Dying: A Handbook for End-of-life Healthcare Practitioners*. New York: Columbia University Press.

Besthorn, F. H. (2000). Toward a deep-ecological social work: Its environmental, spiritual and Political dimensions. *The Spirituality and Social Work Forum, 7*(2), 1, 6–7.

Besthorn, F. H. (2001). Transpersonal psychology and deep ecological philosophy: Exploring linkages and applications for social work. In E. R. Canda & E. D. Smith (Eds.), *Transpersonal perspectives on spirituality in social work* (pp. 23–44). Binghamton, NY: Haworth Press.

Besthorn, F. H. (2002). Radical environmentalism and the ecological self: Rethinking the concept of self-identity for social work practice. *Journal of Progressive Human Services, 13*(1), 53–72.

Besthorn, F. H., & Canda, E. R. (2002). Revisioning environment: Deep ecology for education and teaching in social work. *Journal of Teaching in Social Work, 22*(1/2), 79–101.

Besthorn, F. H., & Pearson McMillen, D. (2002). The oppression of women and nature: Ecofeminism as a framework for an expanded ecological social work. *Families in Society, 83*(3), 221–232.

Bhaktivedanta, A. C. (Trans.). (1968). *The Bhagavad Gita*. New York: Collier Books.

Bhattacharya, V. (1965). Swami Vivekenanda's message of service. *Social Welfare, 12*(1), 1–3.

Biestek, F. P. (1956). Religion and social casework. In L. C. DeSantis (Ed.), *The social welfare forum* (pp. 86–95). New York: Columbia University Press.

Bigham, T. J. (1956). Cooperation between ministers and social workers. In F. E. Johnson (Ed.), *Religion and social work* (pp. 141–154). New York: Institute for Religious and Social Studies, Harper and Brothers.

Bilich, M., Bonfiglio, S., & Carlson, S. (2000). *Shared grace: Therapists and clergy working together.* New York: Haworth Press.

Black, H. K. (1999). Life as gift: Spiritual narratives of elderly African American women living in poverty. *Journal of Aging Studies, 13*(4), 441–455.

Black, P. N., Jefferys, D., & Hartley, E. K. (1993). Personal history of psychosocial trauma in the early life of social work and business students. *Journal of Social Work Education, 29*(2), 171–180.

Blofeld, J. (1988). *Bodhisattva of compassion: The mystical tradition of Kuan Yin.* Boston: Shambhala.

Boddie, S. (2008). Faith-based agencies and social work. In T. Mizrahi & L. E. Davis (Eds.), *Encyclopedia of Social Work* (e-reference edition). Oxford University Press. University of Kansas. Retrieved 29 July, 2008, from http://www.oxford-naswsocial-work.com.www2.lib.ku.edu:2048/entry?entry=t203.e139

Borenzweig, H. (1984). *Jung and social work.* New York: University Press of America.

Bowen, D. E. (2005). Honoring the elders: Interviews with two Lakota men. *Journal of Sociology and Social Welfare, 32*(1), 125–134.

Bowie, F. (2006). *The anthropology of religion: An introduction* (2nd ed.). Malden, MA: Blackwell Publishing.

Brackney, B., & Watkins, D. (1983). An analysis of Christian values and social work practice. *Social Work and Christianity, 10*(1), 5–20.

Bradford, K. A. (1969). *Existentialism and casework.* New York: Exposition Press.

Bradley, C., Maschi, T., & Gilmore, K (2007). One woman's life journey: A case study of spirituality and activism. *Journal of Religion and Spirituality in Social Work, 26*(4), 21–47.

Bragdon, E. (1990). *The call of spiritual emergency: From personal crisis to personal transformation.* San Francisco: Harper and Row.

Braise, A. (2005). Social work with Muslims: Insights from the teachings of Islam. *Critical Social Work, 6*(2), Retrieved from http://www.uwindsor.ca/units/social-work/critical.nsf/EditDoNotShowInTOC/5540260065

Brandon, D. (1976). *Zen in the art of helping.* New York: Delta/Seymour Lawrence.

Brandon, D. (1979). Zen practice in social work. In D. Brandon & B. Jordon (Eds.), *Creative Social Work* (pp. 30–35). Oxford, England: Basil Blackwell.

Brandon, D. (2000). *Tao of survival: Spirituality in social care and counseling.* Birmingham, England: Venture Press.

Braud, W., & Anderson, R. (Eds.). (1998). *Transpersonal research methods for the social sciences.* Thousand Oaks, CA: Sage.

Braude, A. (1997). Women's history is American religious history. In Thomas A. Tweed, (Ed.), *Retelling U.S. religious history* (pp. 87–107). Berkeley, CA: University of California Press.

Braun, W. & McCutcheon, R. T. (Eds.).(2000). *Guide to the study of religion.* New York: Cassell.

Brave Heart, M. Y. H. (2001). Lakota—Native people's spirituality. In M. Van Hook, B. Hugen, & M. Aguilar (Eds.), *Spirituality within religious traditions in social work practice* (pp. 18–33). Pacific Grove, CA: Brooks/Cole Thomson Learning.

Brenden, M .A. (2007). Social work for social justice: Strengthening social work practice through the integration of Catholic social teaching. *Social Work & Christianity, 34*(4), 471–497.

Brenner, M. J., & Homonoff, E. (2004). Zen and clinical social work: A spiritual approach to practice. *Families in Society, 85*(2), 261–269.

Breton, M. (1989). Liberation theology, group work, and the right of the poor and oppressed to participate in the life of the community. *Social Work with Groups, 12*(3), 5–18.

Brinkerhoff, M., & Mackie, M. (1993). Nonbelief in Canada: Characteristics and origins of religious nones. In W. E. Hewitt (Ed.), *The sociology of religion: A Canadian focus* (pp. 109–131). Toronto, Canada: Butterworths.

Broad, G., Boyer, S., & Chataway, C. (2006). We are still the Aniishnaabe nation: Embracing culture and identity in Batchewana First Nation. *Canadian Journal of Communication, 31,* 35–58.

Brower, I. C. (1984). The 4th ear of the spiritual-sensitive social worker, Union for Experimenting Colleges and Universities. Ann Arbor, MI: University Microfilms International, 8500785.

Brown, J. E. (Ed.). (1971). *The sacred pipe: Black Elk's account of the seven rites of the Oglala Sioux.* New York: Penguin Books.

Brown, L. B. (Ed.). (1994). *Religion, personality, and mental health.* New York: Springer-Verlag.

Bruyere, G. (2007). Making circles: Renewing First Nations ways of helping. In J. Coates, J. R. Graham, B. Swartzentruber, & B. Ouelette (Eds.), *Spirituality and social work: Selected Canadian readings* (pp. 259–272). Toronto: Canadian Scholars' Press.

Bubis, G. B. (1980). The Jewish component in Jewish communal service —from theory to practice. *Journal of Jewish Communal Service, 56*(3), 227–237.

Bubis, G. B. (1981). Professional trends in Jewish communal practice in America. *Journal of Jewish Communal Service, 57*(4), 304–311.

Buck, H. G. (2006). Spirituality: Concept analysis and model development. *Holistic Nursing Practice,20*(6), 288–292.

Bucko, R. A., & Iron Cloud, S. (2008). Lakota health and healing. *Southern Medical Journal, 101*(6), 596–598.

Buhner, S. H. (1996). *Sacred plant medicine: Explorations in the practice of indigenous herbalism.* Boulder, CO: Roberts Rinehart Publishers.

Buhner, S. (1997). *One spirit/many peoples.* Boulder, CO: Roberts Rinehart Publishers.

Bullis, R. K. (1993). *Religious/spiritual factors in clinical social work practice: An examination of assessment, intervention and ethics.* Unpublished doctoral dissertation, Virginia Commonwealth University.

Bullis, R. K. (1996). *Spirituality in social work practice.* Washington, DC: Taylor & Francis.

Butcher, A. P. (2004). Educate, consolidate, immigrate: Educational immigration in Auckland, New Zealand. *Asia Pacific Viewpoint, 45*(2), 255–278.

Cahill, L. S., Garvey, J., & Kennedy, T. F. (Eds.). (2006). *Sexuality and the U.S. Catholic church: Crisis and renewal.* New York: The Crossroad Publishing Company.

Cain, R. (1996). Heterosexism and self-disclosure in the social work classroom. *Journal of Social Work Education, 32*(1), 65–76.

Canda, E. R. (1982). Korean shamanic initiation as therapeutic transformation: A transcultural view. *Korea Journal, 22*(11), 13–26.

Canda, E. R. (1983). General implications of shamanism for clinical social work. *International Social Work, 26*(4), 14–22.

Canda, E. R. (1986). A conceptualization of spirituality for social work: Its issues and implications (Doctoral dissertation, The Ohio State University, 1986). *University Microfilms No. 8625190.*

Canda, E. R. (1988a). Therapeutic transformation in ritual, therapy, and human development. *Journal of Religion and Health, 27*(3), 205–220.

Canda, E. R. (1988b). Conceptualizing spirituality for social work: Insights from diverse perspectives. *Social Thought, 14*(1), 30–46.

Canda, E. R. (1988c). Spirituality, religious diversity, and social work practice. *Social Casework, 69*(4), 238–247.

Canda, E. R. (1988d). *Southeast Asian refugees in Iowa: Cultural background, needs, and services.* Des Moines, IA: Refugee Training and Family Service Project, Iowa Department of Human Services Bureau of Refugee Programs.

Canda, E. R. (1989a). Religious content in social work education: A comparative approach. *Journal of Social Work Education, 25*(1), 36–45.

Canda, E. R. (1989b). Religion and social work: A response to Sanzenbach. *Social Casework, 70*(9), 572–574.

Canda, E. R. (1990a). An holistic approach to prayer for social work practice. *Social Thought, 16*(3), 3–13.

Canda, E. R. (1990b). Afterword: Spirituality re-examined. *Spirituality and Social Work Communicator, 1*(1), 13–14.

Canda, E. R. (1990c). Spiritual diversity and social work values. In J. J. Kattakayam (Ed.), *Contemporary social issues* (pp. 1–20). Trivandrum, India: University of Kerala.

Canda, E. R. (1991). East/West philosophical synthesis in transpersonal theory. *Journal of Sociology and Social Welfare, 18*(4), 137–152.

Canda, E. R. (1993). Gripped by the drum: The Korean tradition of nongak. *Shaman's Drum, 33,* 18–23.

Canda, E. R. (1995a). Bodhisattva, sage, and shaman: Exemplars of compassion and service in traditional Korean religions. In H. Kwon (Ed.), *Korean cultural roots: Religion and social thoughts* (pp. 31–44). Chicago: Integrated Technical Resources.

Canda, E. R. (Ed.). (1995b). *Reflections: Narratives of Professional Helping, 1*(4), Spirituality: A Special Issue.

Canda, E. R., (Ed.). (1998a). *Spirituality and social work: New directions.* Binghamton, NY: Haworth Press.

Canda, E. R. (1998b). Afterword: Linking spirituality and social work: Five themes for innovation. In E. R. Canda (Ed.), *Spirituality and social work: New directions* (pp. 97–106). Binghamton, NY: Haworth Press.

Canda, E. R. (1998c). Spiritually sensitive social work: Key concepts and ideals. *Journal of Social Work Theory and Practice, 1*(1), 1–15. Retreived 10 February, 2009 from http://cj.bemidjistate.edu/sw_journal/issue1/contents.html

Canda, E. R. (2001). Buddhism. In M.Van Hook, B. Hugen, & M. Aguilar, (Eds). *Spirituality within religious traditions in social work,* (pp. 53–72). Pacific Grove, CA: Brooks/Cole.

Canda, E. R. (2002a). Toward spiritually sensitive social work scholarship: Insights from classical Confucianism. *Electronic Journal of Social Work, 1*(1), second article, 23 pages. Retrieved 15 March, 2009 from http://www.socwel.ku.edu/canda/Articles/TowardSpirituallySensitiveSocialWorkScholarship.pdf

Canda, E. R. (2002b). Wisdom from the Confucian classics for spiritually sensitive social welfare. *Currents: New Scholarship for the Human Services, 1*(1), 31 pages. Retrieved 15 March, 2009 http://207.34.118.41/fsw/currents/articles/index

Canda, E. R. (2003). Social work and evangelical Christians. *Social Work, 48*(2), 278–282.

Canda, E. R. (2005a). The future of spirituality in social work: The farther reaches of human nurture. *Advance in Social Work, 6*(1), 97–108.

Canda, E. R. (2008a). Religion and spirituality. In T. Mizrahi & L. E. Davis (Eds.), *Encyclopedia of Social Work* (e-reference edition). Oxford University Press. University of Kansas. Retreived 29 July, 2008, from http://www.oxford-naswsocial-work.com.www2.lib.ku.edu:2048/entry?entry=t203.e188-s4

Canda, E. R. (2008b). Spiritual connection in social work: Boundary violations and transcendence. *Journal of Religion and Spirituality in Social Work, 27*(1–2), 25–40).

Canda, E. R. (Ed.). (2008c). Religious views on personal and social health. Retrieved from http://www.socwel.ku.edu/candagrant/Papers/Papers2.htm

Canda, E. R. (2008d). Foreword. In A. Bein, *The Zen of helping: Spiritual principles for mindful and open-hearted practice* (pp. ix-xi). Hoboken, NJ: John Wiley & Sons.

Canda, E. R. (2009). Chronic illness and transilience along my spiritual path. In D. Saleebey (Ed.), *The strengths perspective in social work practice* (5th ed.) (pp. 72–92). Boston: Pearson A and B.

Canda, E. R. (in press). Spiritual well-being. In S. J. Lopez (Ed.), *Encyclopedia of Positive Psychology*. London: Blackwell Publishing.

Canda, E. R., & Canda, H. J. (1996). Korean spiritual philosophies of human service: Current state and prospects. *Social Development Issues, 18*(3), 53–70.

Canda, E. R., Carrizosa, S., & Yellow Bird, M. (1995). *Cultural diversity in child welfare practice: A training curriculum for cultural competence.* Lawrence, KS: The University of Kansas, School of Social Welfare.

Canda, E. R., & Chambers, D. (1994). Should spiritual principles guide social policy? Yes. In H. J. Karger & J. Midgley (Eds.), *Controversial issues in social policy* (pp. 63–70 and 74–78). Boston: Allyn and Bacon.

Canda, E. R. & Cheon, J. (Eds.). (in press). Special Issue of *Currents* on Spirituality, Social Work, and Positive Youth development. http://www.ucalgary.ca/currents/

Canda, E. R. & Furman, L. D. (1999). *Spiritual diversity in social work practice: The heart of helping.* New York: Free Press.

Canda, E. R., Ketchell, A., Dybicz, P., Pyles, L., & Nelson-Becker, H. (2006). *Health through faith and community: A study resource for Christian faith communities to promote personal and social well-being.* Binghamton, NY: Haworth Pastoral Press.

Canda, E. R., Nakashima, M., Burgess, V. L., Russel, R., & Barfield, S. T. (2003). *Spiritual diversity and social work: A comprehensive bibliography with annotations* (2nd ed.). Alexandria, VA: Council on Social Work Education.

Canda, E. R., Nakashima, M., & Furman, L. D. (2004). Ethical considerations about spirituality in social work: Insights from a national qualitative survey. *Families in Society, 85*(1), 1–9.

Canda, E. R., & Phaobtong, T. (1992). Buddhism as a support system for Southeast Asian refugees. *Social Work, 37*(1), 61–67.

Canda, E. R., Shin, S., & Canda, H. (1993). Traditional philosophies of human service in Korea and contemporary social work implications. *Social Development Issues, 15*(3), 84–104.

Canda, E. R., & Smith, E. D. (Eds.). (2001). *Transpersonal perspectives on spirituality in social work*. New York: Haworth Press.

Canda, E. R., & Yellow Bird, M. J. (1996). Cross-tradition borrowing of spiritual practices in social work settings. *Society for Spirituality and Social Work Newsletter, 3*(1), 1, 7.

Capozzi L. (1992). Nonviolent social work and stress reduction: A Gandhian cognitive restructuring model. *Spirituality and Social Work Journal, 3*(1), 13–18.

Capps, W. H. (1995). *Religious studies: The making of a discipline*. Minneapolis, MN: Fortress Press.

Caroll, M. (1998). Social work's conceptualization of spirituality. In E. E. Canda (Ed.), *Spirituality in social work: New directions* (pp. 1–13). Binghamton, New York: Haworth Press.

Casteneda, C. (1968). *The teachings of Don Juan: A Yaqui way of knowledge*. New York: Ballantine.

Castex, G. M. (1994). Providing services to Hispanic/Latino populations: Profiles in diversity. *Social Work, 39*(3), 288–296.

Cataldo, C. (1979). Wilderness therapy: Modern day shamanism. In C. B. Germain (Ed.), *Social work practice: People and environments* (pp. 46–73). New York: Columbia University Press.

Catholic Charities USA (2006). *Poverty in America: A threat to the common good*. Alexandria, VA: Catholic Charities, USA.

Cave, D. (1993). *Mircea Eliade's vision for a new humanism*. New York: Oxford University Press.

Chalfant, H. P., Beckley, R. E., & Palmer, C. E. (1987). *Religion in contemporary society* (2nd ed). Palo Alto, CA: Mayfield Publishing Company.

Chalfant, H. P., Heller, P. L., Rogerts, A., Brioner, D., Aguirre-Hochbaum, S., & Farr, W. (1990). The clergy as a resource for those encountering psychological distress. *Review of Religious Research, 31*(3), March, 305–315.

Chamberlayne, D. (2007). Case experience: 'dancing shoes', a Buddhist perspective. *Journal of Social Work Practice, 21*(1), 61–75.

Chamiec-Case, R. & Sherr, M. E. (2005). Exploring how social work administrators integrate spirituality in the workplace. In R. Chamiec-Case (Ed.), Proceedings of NACSW's 55th Annual Convention and Training Conference October 27–30, 2005, Retrieved from http://www.nacsw.org.www2.lib.ku.edu:2048/Publications/Proceedings2005/Proceedings2005.htm

Chan, C. L. (2001). *An eastern body-mind-spirit approach: A training manual with one-second techniques*. Hong Kong: The University of Hong Kong Department of Social Work and Social Administration.

Chaney, C. (2008). Religiosity and spirituality among members of an African American church community: A qualitative analysis. *Journal of Religion & Spirituality in Social Work: Social Thought, 27*(3), 201–234.

Chen, J. (1993). *Confucius as a teacher*. Selangor Darul Jaya, Malaysia: Delta Publishing Sdn Bhd.

Chenault, V. (1990). A Native American practice framework. *Spirituality and Social Work Communicator, 1*(2), 5–7.

Cheng Yen (1999). *The sutra of the Bodhisattvas' eight realizations: Lectures by Dharma Master Cheng Yen.* Taipei: Tzu Chi Cultural Publishing Company.

Chesler, M. A. (1991). Participatory action research with self-help groups: An alternative paradigm for inquiry and action. *American Journal of Community Psychology, 19*(5), 757–768.

Chu, K. F. & Carew, R. (1990). Confucianism: Its relevance to social work with Chinese people. *Australian Social Work, 43*(3), 3–9.

Chung, D. (1992). The Confucian model of social transformation. In S. M. Furuto et al., (Eds.), *Social work practice with Asian Americans* (pp. 125–142). Newbury park, CA: Sage.

Chung, D. (2001). Confucianism. In M. Van Hook, B. Hugen, $ M. Aguilar (Eds.), *Spirituality within religious traditions in social work practice* (pp. 73–97). Pacific Grove, CA: Brooks/Cole.

Chung, D. & Haynes, A. W. (1993). Confucian welfare philosophy and social change technology: An integrated approach for international social development. *International Social Work, 36*, 37–46.

Clark, J. (1994). Should social work education address religious issues? No! *Journal of Social Work Education, 30*(1), 11–16.

Cnaan, R. A. (2006). Faith in the closet: Reflections of a secular academic. *Arete, 30*(1), 19–29.

Cnaan, R. & Boddie, S. C. (Eds.). (2006). *Faith-based social services: Measures, assessments, and effectiveness.* Binghamton, NY: Haworth Press.

Cnaan, R. A., Wineburg, R. J., & Boddie, S. C. (1999). *The newer deal: Social work and religion in partnership.* New York: Columbia University Press.

Coates, J. (2003). *Ecology and social work: Toward a new paradigm.* Halifax, NS: Fernwood Publishing.

Coates, J., Gray, M., & Hetherington, T. (2006). An 'ecospiritual' perspective: Finally, a place for Indigenous approaches. *British Journal of Social Work, 36*, 381–399.

Coates, J. (2007). From ecology to spirituality and social justice. In J. Coates, J. R. Graham, B. Swartzentruber, & B. Ouelette (Eds.), *Spirituality and social work: Selected Canadian readings* (pp. 213–228). Toronto: Canadian Scholars' Press.

Coates, J., Graham, J. R., Swartzentruber, B., & Ouellette, B. (Eds.). (2007). *Spirituality and social work: Selected Canadian readings.* Toronto: Canadian Scholars' Press.

Coates, J., Grey, M., & Hetherington, T. (2006). An 'ecospiritual' perspective: Finally, a place for Indigenous approaches. *British Journal of Social Work, 36*, 381–399.

Coggins, K. (1990). *Alternative pathways to healing: The recovery medicine wheel.* Deerfield Beach, FL: Health Communications, Inc.

Coholic, D. (2003). Incorporating spirituality in feminist social work perspectives. *Affilia, 18*(1), 49–67.

Coholic, D. (2006). Mindfulness meditation practice in spiritually influenced group work. *Arete, 30*(1), 90–100.

Coleman, P. (1980). *Christian attitudes to homosexuality.* London, England: SPCK.

Coleman, P. W. (1998). The process of forgiveness in marriage and the family. In R. D. Enright & J. North (Eds.), *Exploring Forgiveness* (pp. 75–94). Madison, WI: University of Wisconsin Press.

Coles, R. (1990). *The spiritual life of children.* Boston: Houghton Mifflin Company.

Coles, R. (1993). *The call of service*. Boston: Houghton Mifflin Company.

Comstock, G. D. (1993). *Gay theology without apology*. Cleveland, OH: The Pilgrim Press.

Consiglio, W. E. (1987). *Spirit-led helping: A model for evangelical social work counseling*. St. Davids, PA: North American Association of Christians in Social Work.

Constable, R. T. (1983). Values, religion, and social work practice. *Social Thought, 9*(4), 29–41.

Constable, R. (2007). Catholic social thought and the caring professions: Social work. *Journal of Religion & Spirituality in Social Work: Social Thought, 26*(3), 81–100.

Cook, C. A. L., Becvar, D. S., & Pontious, S. L. (2000). Complementary alternative medicine in health and mental health: Implications for social work practice. *Social Work in Health Care, 31*(3), 39–57.

Cooper, M. (2004). Towards a relationally-oriented approach to therapy: Empirical support and analysis. *British Journal of Guidance & Counselling, 32*(4), 451–460.

Corbett, J. M. (1997). *Religion in America* (3rd ed.). Upper Saddle River, NJ: Prentice Hall.

Corrigan, P., McCorckle, B., Schell, B., & Kidder, K. (2003). Religion and spirituality in the lives of people with serious mental illness. *Community Mental Health Journal, 39*(6), 487–499.

Costas, O. E. (1991). Hispanic theology in North America. In L. M. Getz & R. O. Costa, (Eds.), *Struggles for solidarity: Liberation theologies in tension* (pp. 63–74). Minneapolis, MN: Fortress Press.

Council on Social Work Education (CSWE). (2008). *Educational policy and accreditation standards*. Washington, DC: Council of Social Work Education.

Cousineau, P. (Ed.). (2006). *A seat at the table: Huston Smith in conversation with Native Americans on religious freedom*. Berkeley, CA: University of California Press.

Cowley, A. (1993). Transpersonal social work: A theory for the 1990s. *Social Work, 38*(5), 527–534.

Cowley, A. S. (1996). Transpersonal social work. In F. J. Turner (Ed.), *Social work treatment: Interlocking theoretical approaches* (pp. 663–698). New York: The Free Press.

Cowley, A. S., & Derezotes, D. (1994). Transpersonal psychology and social work education. *Journal of Social Work Education, 30*(1), 32–41.

Cox, J. L. (1996). *Expressing the sacred: An introduction to the phenomenology of religion*. Harare, Zimbabwe: University of Zimbabwe Publications.

Cox, J. L. (2007). *From primitive to indigenous*. Burlington, VT: Ashgate Publishing.

Crabtree, S. A., Husain, F., & Spalek, B. (2008). *Islam and social work: Debating values, transforming practice*. Bristol, UK: The Policy Press.

Crim, K. (Ed.). (1981). *The perennial dictionary of world religions*. San Francisco: HarperSanFrancisco.

Cristi, M. & Dawson, L. L. (2007). Civil religion in America in global context. In J. A. Beckford & N. J. Demerath, (Eds.). *The Sage handbook of the sociology of religion* (pp. 267–292). Los Angeles: Sage Publications.

Cromey, R. W. (1991). *In God's symbol: Christian witness to the need for gay/lesbian equality in the eyes of the church*. San Francisco: Alamo Square Press.

Crompton, M. (1998). *Children, spirituality, religion and social work*. Suffolk, Great Britain: Ipswich Books.

Curiel, H. (1995). Hispanics: Mexican Americans. In R. L. Edwards, (Ed.), *Encyclopedia of social work* (19th ed., pp. 1233–1244). Washington, DC: NASW Press.

Daaleman, T. P., & Frey, B. B. (2004). The Spirituality Index of Well-Being: A new instrument for health-related quality-of-life research. *Annals of Family Medicine, 2*(5), 499–503

Daly, M. (1973). *Beyond god the father: Toward a philosophy of women's liberation.* Boston: Beacon Press.

Damianakis, T. (2006). Seeking the spiritual in anti-oppressive organizational change. *Critical Social Work, 7*(1), retrieved from http://cronus.uwindsor.ca/units/social-work/critical.nsf/main/E69344834B819BFB852571

Danylchuk, L. S. (1992). The pastoral counselors as mental health professional: A comparison of the training of AAPC fellow pastoral counselors and licensed clinical social workers. *The Journal of Pastoral Care, 46*(4), Winter, 382–391.

Danzig, R. A., & Sands, R. G. (2007). A model of spiritual transformation of *baalei teshuvah. Journal of Religion & Spirituality in Social Work, 26*(2), 23–48.

Dasgupta, S. (1986). Gandhi and the new society. *Social Development Issues, 10*(1), 1–10.

Dass, R., & Gorman, P. (1985). *How can I help? Stories and reflections on service.* New York: Alfred A. Knopf.

Davis, C. F. (1989). *The evidential force of religious experience.* New York: Oxford University Press.

Dawood, N. J. (Trans.). (1974). *The Koran.* London: Penguin.

de Bary, W. T. (Ed.). (1969). *The Buddhist tradition in India, China and Japan.* New York: Vintage Books.

de Bary, W. T. (1991). *The trouble with Confucianism.* Cambridge, MA: Harvard University Press.

de Bary, W. T. & Tu, W. (Eds.). (1998). *Confucianism and human rights.* New York: Columbia University Press.

De La Rosa, M. (1988). Puerto Rican spiritualism: A key dimension for effective social casework practice with Puerto Ricans. *International Social Work, 31*(4), 273–283.

De Silva, P. (1995). Human rights in Buddhist perspective. In A. A. An-Na'im, J. D. Gort, H. Jansen & H. M. Vroom (Eds.), *Human rights and religious values: An uneasy relationship?* (pp. 133–143). Grand Rapids, MI: William B. Eerdmans Publishing Company.

Deck, A. F. (1989). *The second wave: Hispanic ministry and the evangelization of cultures.* New York: Paulist Press.

Delgado, C. (2005). A discussion of the concept of spirituality. *Nursing Science Quarterly, 18*(2), 157–162.

Delgado, M. (1977). Puerto Rican spiritism and the social work profession, *Social Casework, 58*(8), 451–458.

Delgado, M. (1988). Groups in Puerto Rican spiritism: Implications for clinicians. In C. Jacobs & D. D. Bowles, (Eds.), *Ethnicity & race: Critical concepts in social work* (pp. 34–47). Silver Spring, MD: National Association of Social Workers, Inc.

Delgado, M., & Humm-Delgado, D. (1982). Natural support systems: Source of strength in Hispanic communities. *Social Work, 27*(1), 83–89.

Dell, C. A., Dell, D. E., & Hopkins, C. (2005). Resiliency and holistic inhalant abuse treatment. *Journal of Aboriginal health, March,* 4–12.

Deloria, V., Jr. (1994). *God is red: A native view of religion.* Golden, CO: Fulcrum Publishing.

Demerath, N. J. (2007). Religion and the state; Violence and human rights. In J. A. Beckford & N. J. Demerath III (Eds.), *The Sage handbook of the sociology of religion* (pp. 381–395). Thousand Oaks, CA: Sage Publications.

Denton, R. T. (1990). The religiously fundamentalist family: Training for assessment and treatment. *Journal of Social Work Education, 26*(1), 6–14.

Derezotes, D. S. (2006a). *Spiritually oriented social work practice.* Boston: Pearson Education.

Derezotes, D. S. (2006b). Individual consciousness and social responsibility: Spirituality in new-century social work. *Arete, 30*(1), 8–18.

Derezotes, D. S., & Evans, K. E. (1995). Spirituality and religiosity in practice: In-depth interviews of social work practitioners. *Social Thought, 18*(1), 39–56.

DiBlasio, F. A. (1993). The role of social workers' religious beliefs in helping family members forgive. *Families in Society, 74*(3), 167–170.

Digeser, P. E. (2000). *Political forgiveness.* Ithaca, NY: Cornell University Press.

Dimeff, L. A. & Koerner, K (Eds.). (2007). *Dialectical behavior therapy in clinical practice: Applications across disorders and settings.* New York: The Guilford Press.

Doblmeir, M. (Producer/Director), Juday, D. (Producer), & Schmidt, A. (Producer). (2007). *The power of forgiveness* [Documentary film]. United States: Journey Films.

Doe, S. S. (2004). Spiritiually-based social work values for empowering human service organizations. *Journal of Religion & Spirituality in Social Work, 23*(3), 45–65.

Doore, G. (Ed.). (1988). *Shaman's path: Healing, personal growth, and empowerment.* Boston: Shambhala.

Dossey, L. (1993). *Healing words: The power of prayer and the practice of medicine.* San Francisco: Harper.

Dowdy, T. E. (1991). Invisibility and plausibility: An analysis of the relationship between forms of privatization and individual religiosity. In M. L. Lynn & D. O. Moberg (Eds.), *Research in the social scientific study of religion* (Vol. 3) (pp. 89–114). Greenwich, CT: Jai Press Inc.

Dudley, J. R., & Helfgott, C. (1990). Exploring a place for spirituality in the social work curriculum. *Journal of Social Work Education, 26*(3), 287–294.

Dumbrill, G. C., & Green, J. (2008). Indigenous knowledge in the social work academy. *Social Work Education, 27*(5), 489–503.

Dunn, A. B., & Massey, R. F. (2006). The spiritually-focused genogram: A tool for exploring spirituality and the spiritual resources of individuals, couples, and families in context. In Karen B. Helmeke & Catherine Ford Sori (Eds.), *The therapist's notebook for integrating spirituality in counseling: Homework, handouts, and activities for use in psychotherapy* (pp. 77–87). New York: The Haworth Press.

Dupre, L. (1987). Mysticism. In *The encyclopedia of religion* (pp. 245–261). New York: Macmillan Publishing Company.

Duran, K. (1993). Homosexuality and Islam. In Arlene Swidler (Ed.), *Homosexuality and world religions* (pp. 181–197). Valley Forge, PA: Trinity Press International.

Dwoskin, J, (2003). Hannah Arendt on thinking and action: A bridge to the spiritual side of social work. *Journal of Religion in the Social Services, 22*(1), 105–123.

Dynes, W. R., & Donaldson, S. (Eds.). (1992). *Homosexuality and religion and philosophy.* New York: Garland Publishing, Inc.

Easwaran, E. (Trans.). (1985). *The Bhagavad Gita.* Tomales, CA: Nilgiri Press.

Edwards, D. G. (1982). *Existential psychotherapy: The process of caring.* New York: Gardner Press Incorporated.

Eichler, M., Deegan, G., Canda, E. R., & Wells, S. (2006). Using the strengths assessment to mobilize spiritual resources. In Karen B. Helmeke & Catherine Ford Sori (Eds.), *The therapist's notebook for integrating spirituality in counseling: Homework, handouts, and activities for use in psychotherapy* (pp. 69–76). New York: The Haworth Press.

Elder, J. W. (1998). Expanding our options: The challenge of forgiveness. In R. D. Enright & J. North (Eds.), *Exploring Forgiveness* (pp. 150–164). Madison, WI: University of Wisconsin Press.

Eliade, M. (1959). *The sacred and the profane: The nature of religion.* New York: Harcourt, Brace & World, Inc.

Eliade, M. (1964). *Shamanism: Archaic techniques of excstasy.* Princeton, NJ: Princeton University Press.

Elkins, D. N. (2005). A humanistic approach to spiritually oriented psychotherapy. In L. Sperry & E. P. Shafranske (Eds.)., *Spiritually oriented psychotherapy* (pp. 131–151). Washington, DC: American Psychological Association.

Eliade, M. (1963). *Myth and reality.* (W. R. Trask, Trans.). New York: Harper & Row.

Eliade, M. (1964). *Shamanism: Archaic techniques of ecstasy.* Princeton, NJ: Princeton University Press.

Eliade, M. (1971). *The myth of the eternal return, or, cosmos and history.* W.R Trask, trans., Bollingen Series, no. 46. Princeton, Princeton University Press, Bollingen Paperback.

Ellison, M. M., & Plaskow, J. (Eds). (2007). *Heterosexism in contemporary world religion: Problem and prospect.* Cleveland, OH: The Pilgrim Press.

Ellor, J. W., Netting, F. E., & Thibault, J. M. (1999). *Religious and spiritual aspects of human service practice.* Columbia, SC: University of South Carolina.

Emmons, R. A., & Paloutzian, R. E. (2003). The psychology of religion. *Annual Review of Psychology, 54,* 377–402.

Enright, R. D., Freedman, S. & Rique, J. (1998). The psychology of interpersonal forgiveness. In R. D. Enright & J. North (Eds.), *Exploring Forgiveness* (pp. 46–62). Madison, WI: University of Wisconsin Press.

Enright, R.D. & North, J. (1998). Introducing forgiveness. In R. D. Enright & J. North (Eds.), *Exploring Forgiveness* (pp. 3–8). Madison, WI: University of Wisconsin Press.

Eppsteiner, F. (Ed.). (1988). *The path of compassion: Writings on socially engaged Buddhism.* Berkeley, CA: Parallax Press.

Erricker, C., & Erricker, J. (Eds.). (2001). *Contemporary spiritualities: Social and religious contexts.* New York: Continuum.

Erikson, E. H. (1962). *Young man Luther: A study in psychoanalysis and history.* New York: Norton.

Erikson, E. H. (1963). *Childhood and society* (2nd rev. ed, enlarged). New York: Norton.

Erikson, E. H. (1968). *Identity: Youth and crisis.* New York: Norton.

Erikson, E. H. (1969). *Gandhi's truth: On the origins of militant nonviolence.* New York: Norton.

Erikson, E. H. (1982). *The life-cycle completed.* New York: Norton.

Erriker, C., & Erriker, J. (Eds). (2001). *Contemporary spiritualities: Social and religious contexts.* New York: Continuum.

Eskenazi, D. (1983). God concepts and community structure. *Journal of Jewish Communal Service, 59*(3), 217–227.

Esposito, J. L. (1991). *Islam: The straight path.* New York: Oxford University Press.

European Union (2006). *Fundamental rights within the European Union.* Retrieved August 1, 2007, from http://europa.eu/scadplus/leg/en/s20000.htm

Fallot, R. (1998). *Spirituality and religion in recovery from mental illness.* San Francisco: Jossey-Bass Publishers.

Famighetti, R. (Ed.). (1995). *The world almanac and book of facts, 1996.* New York: World Almanac Books.

Faver, C. A. (1986). Religion, research, and social work. *Social Thought, 12*(3), 20–29.

Faver, C. A. (2004). Relational spirituality and social caregiving. *Social Work, 49*(2), 242–249.

Faver, C. A., & Trache, B. L. (2005). Religion and spirituality at the border: A survey of Mexican-American social work students. *Journal of Religion and Spirituality in Social Work, 24*(4), 3–18.

Faiver, C., Ingersoll, R. E., O'Brien, E., & McNally C. (2001). *Explorations in counseling and spirituality.* Belmont, CA: Brooks/Cole Thomson Learning.

Feng, G. & English, J. (Trans.) (1972). *Lao Tsu: Tao Te Ching.* New York: Vintage Books, Random House.

Ferendo, F. (2007). *Holistic perspectives & integral theory.* Westerly, RI: Process Publishing Company.

Fetzer Institute/National Institute on Aging Working Group (1999). *Multidimensional measurement of religiousness/spirituality for use in health research.* Kalamazoo, MI: John E. Fetzer Institute.

Finn, M., & Rubin, J. B. (2000). Psychotherapy with Buddhists. In P. S. Richards & A. E. Bergin (Eds.), *Handbook of psychotherapy and religious diversity* (pp. 317–340). Washington, DC: American Psychological Association.

Fire, A. (2006). Recommendations to enhance educational experience of aboriginal social work students. *Critical Social Work, 7*(2). Retrieved from http://www.uwindsor.ca/units/socialwork/critical.nsf/982f0e5f06b5c9a285256d6e006cff78/

Fischer, L. (1950). *The life of Mahatma Gandhi.* New York: Harper & Row, Publishers.

Fitzgibbons, R. P. (1986). The cognitive and emotive uses of forgiveness in the treatment of anger. *Psychotherapy, 23*(4), 629–633.

Fitzpatrick, M. R. & Irannejad, S. (2008). Adolescent readiness for change and the working alliance in counseling. *Journal of Counseling & Development, 86*, 438–445.

Flanigan, B. (1998). Forgivers and the unforgivable. In R. D. Enright & J. North (Eds.), *Exploring Forgiveness* (pp. 95–105). Madison, WI: University of Wisconsin Press.

Fleming, J., & Ledogar, R. J. (2008). Resilience and Indigenous spirituality: A literature review. *Pimatisiwin: A Journal of Aboriginal and Indigenous Community Health, 6*(2), 47–64.

Fontana, D. (2003). *Psychology, religion, and spirituality.* Malden, MA: BPS Blackwell.

Forster, D., McColl, M. A., & Fardella, J. (2007). Spiritual transformation in clinical relationships between social workers and individuals living with disabilities. *Journal of religion & Spirituality in Social Work, 26*(1), 35–51.

Fowler, J. W. (1981). *Stages of faith: The psychology of human development and the quest for meaning.* San Francisco: Harper & Row.

Fowler, J. W. (1996). *Faithful change: The personal and public challenges of post-modern life.* Nashville, TN: Abingdon Press.

Fowler, J. W. (2000). *Becoming adult, becoming Christian: Adult development and Christian faith.* San Francisco: Harper & Row.

Frame, M. W. (2003). *Integrating religion and spirituality into counseling.* Pacific grove, CA: Brooks/Cole Thomson Learning.

Frame, M. W., Williams, C. B., and Green, E. L. (1999). Balm in Gilead: Spiritual dimensions in counseling African American women. *Journal of Multicultural Counseling and Development, 27*(4), 182–192.

Frank, J. D. (1963). *Persuasion and healing.* New York: Schocken Books.

Frankl, V. E. (1969). *The will to meaning: Foundations and applications of logotherapy.* New York: World Publishing Co.

Franklin, R. M. (1994). The safest place on earth: The culture of Black congregations. In J. P. Wind & J. W. Lewis (Eds.), *American congregations* (Vol. 2) (pp. 257–284). Chicago: University of Chicago Press.

Frey, B., Daaleman, T. P., & Peyton, V. (2005). Measuring a dimension of spirituality for health research: Validity of the Spirituality Index of Well-Being. *Research on Aging, 27*(5), 556–577.

Frey, L. A., & Edinburg, G. (1978). Helping, manipulation, and magic. *Social Work, 23*(2), 89–93.

Friedman, B. (2001). Judaism. In M.Van Hook, B. Hugen, & M. Aguilar, (Eds), *Spirituality within religious traditions in social work,* (pp. 98–119). Pacific Grove, CA: Brooks/Cole.

Fromm, E. (1966). *Marx's concept of man.* New York: Frederick Ungar Publishing Co.

Fuller, A. R. (2008). *Psychology and religion: Classical theorists and contemporary developments.* New York: Rowman & Littlefield Publishers.

Furman, L.D., Perry, D., & Goldade, T. (1996). Interaction of evangelical Christians and social workers in the rural environment. *Human Services in the Rural Environment, 19*(2/3), 5–8.

Furman, L. D. (2007). Grief is a brutal but empowering teacher: A social worker's reflections on the importance of spiritual assessment and support during the bereavement process. *Illness, Crisis & Loss, 15*(2), 99–112.

Furman, L. & Benson, P. (2006). Practice and educational considerations: Cross-national perspectives from the United States, United Kingdom, and Norway. *Arete, 30*(1), 53–62.

Furman, L., Benson, P., & Canda, E.R. (2004a). Religion, spirituality, and geographic region in the USA: An examination of regional similarities and differences among social workers in direct practice. *Social Work & Christianity: An International Journal, 31*(3), 267–294.

Furman, L., Benson, P., Canda, E. R., & Grimwood, C. (2005). A comparative international analysis of religion and spirituality in social work: A survey of UK and US social workers. *Social Work Education, 24*(8), 813–839.

Furman, L., Benson, P., Grimwood, C., & Canda, E.R. (2004b). Religion and spirituality in social work education and direct practice at the millennium: a survey of UK social workers. *British Journal of Social Work, 34*(6), 767–792.

Furman, L. D., & Chandy, J. M. (1994). Religion and spirituality: A long-neglected cultural component of rural social work practice. *Human Services in the Rural Environment, 17*(3/4), 21–26.

Furman, L. D., & Fry, S. (2000). Clerics and Social Workers: Collaborators or Competitors. *Arete, 24*(1), 30–39.

Furman, L., Zahl, M.A., Benson, P., & Canda, E.R. (2007). American and Norwegian social workers' views on spirituality in education and practice: An international comparison. *Families in Society, 88*(2), 241–254.

Furuto, S. M., Biswas, R., Chung, D. K., Murase, K., & Ross-Sherif, F. (Eds.). (1992). *Social work practice with Asian Americans.* Newbury Park, CA: Sage Publications.

Gandhi, A. (no date). *M. K. Gandhi's wit and wisdom.* Nashville, TN: Gandhi Institute.

Gandhi, M. (2000). The message of the Gita by Mohandas K. Gandhi. In S. Mitchell (Trans. & Ed.), *Bhagavad Gita: A new translation* (pp. 211–221). New York: Three Rivers Press.

Garcia, I. (1987). *Justice in Latin American theology of liberation.* Atlanta, GA: John Knox Press.

Garland, D. R. (Ed.). (1992). *Church social work: Helping the whole person in the context of the church.* St. Davids, PA: North American Association of Christians in Social Work.

Garland, D. R. (2008). Christian social services. In T. Mizrahi & L. E. Davis (Eds.), *Encyclopedia of Social Work* (e-reference edition). Oxford University Press. University of Kansas. Retrieved August 11, 2008, from http://www.oxford-naswso-cialwork.com./entry?entry=t203.e55

Garvin, C. (Ed.) (1998). Special issue: Forgiveness. *Reflections: Narratives of Professional Helping, 4*(4), 1–72.

Gatza, M. (1979). The role of healing prayer in the helping professions. *Social Thought, 5*(2), 3–13.

Gaustad, E. S., & Schmidt, L. E. (2002). *The religious history of America* (rev. ed.). New York: HarperSanFrancisco.

Gaventa, W. C.& Coulter, D. L. (Eds.). (2001). *Spirituality and intellectual disability: International perspectives on the effect of culture and religion on healing body, mind, and soul.* Binghamton, NY: Haworth Press.

Gay, L.R., Mills, G.E., & Airasian, P. (2006). Educational Research: Competencies for Analysis and Applications. Upper Saddle River, NJ: Pearson.

Gbemudu, I. (2003). *West African spirituality in social work practice.* Unknown: 1st Books.

Gelman, S. R., Andon, S., & Schnall, D. J. (2008). Jewish communal services. In T. Mizrahi & L. E. Davis (Eds.), *Encyclopedia of Social Work* (e-reference edition). Oxford University Press. University of Kansas. Retreived August 12, 2008, from http://www.oxford-naswsocialwork.com/entry?entry=t203.e213

General Plan for health- and social work education. (1999). Kirke-, utdannings-og for-skningsdepartementet. Oslo, Norway.

Gethin, R. (1998). *The foundations of Buddhism.* Oxford, England: Oxford University Press.

Getz, L. M., & Costa, R. O. (Eds.). (1991). *Struggles for solidarity: Liberation theologies in tension.* Minneapolis, MN: Fortress Press.

Gieben, S. (1980). *Christian sacrament and devotion.* Leiden, The Netherlands: E. J. Brill.

Gilgun, J. F. (2002). Completing the circle: American Indian Medicine Wheels and the promotion of resilience of children and youth in care. *Journal of Human Behavior in the Social Environment, 6*(2), 65–84.

Golan, N. (1981). *Passing through transitions.* New York: Free Press.

Gorsuch, R. L., & Miller, W. R. (1999). Assessing spirituality. In W. R. Miller (Ed.), *Integrating spirituality into treatment: Resources for practitioners* (pp. 47–64). Washington DC: American Psychological Association.

Gossage, J. P., Barton, L., Foster, L., Etsitty, L., LoneTree, C., Leonard, C., et al. (2003). Sweat lodge ceremonies for jail-based treatment. *Journal of Psychoactive Drugs, 35*(1), 33–42.

Graham, J. R. (2006). Spirituality and social work: A call for an international focus of research. *Arete, 30*(1), 63–77.

Graham, J R. & Shier, M. (2009). Religion and social work: An analysis of faith traditions, themes, and global north/south authorship. *Journal of Religion and Spirituality in Social Work: Social Thought, 28*, 215–233.

Graham, J. R., Coholic, D., & Coates, J. (2007). Spirituality as a guiding construct in the development of Canadian social work Past and present considerations. In J. Coates, J. R. Graham, B. Swartzentruber, & Ouelette, B. (Eds.), *Spirituality and social work: Selected Canadian Readings* (pp. 23–46). Toronto: Canadian Scholar's Press.

Grant, D. (2001). The African American Baptist tradition. In M. Van Hook, B. Hugen, and M. Aguilar, (Eds.), *Spirituality within Religious Traditions in Social Work.* (pp. 205–227). Pacific Grove, CA: Brooks/Cole.

Gray, M., Coates, J., & Heatherington, T. (2008). Hearing Indigenous and local voices in mainstream social work. In M. Gray, J. Coates, & M. Yellow Bird (Eds.), *Indigenous social work around the world: Towards culturally relevant education and practice* (pp. 257–269). Burlington, VT: Ashgate.

Gray. M., Coates, J., & Yellow Bird, M. (Eds.). (2008). *Indigenous social work around the world: Towards culturally relevant education and practice.* Burlington, VT: Ashgate.

Gray, M., & Fook, J. (2004). The quest for a universal social work: Some issues and implications. *Social Work Education, 23*(5), 625–644.

Greeley, A. M. (1989). *Religious change in America.* Cambridge, MA: Harvard University Press.

Greeley, A. M. (1995). *Religion as poetry.* New Brunswick, NJ: Transaction Publishers.

Greenstreet, W. (Ed.). (2006). *Integrating spirituality in health and social care* (pp. 89–100). Oxford, England: Radcliffe Publishing.

Griffin, D. R. (Ed.). (1988). *Spirituality and society: Postmodern visions.* Albany, NY: State University of New York Press.

Grimes, R. L. (1995). *Beginnings in ritual studies* (rev. ed.). Columbia, SC: University of South Carolina Press.

Grimes, R. L. (2000a). *Deeply into the bone: Re-inventing rites of passage.* Berkeley, CA: University of California Press.

Grimes, R. (2000b). *Ritual.* In W. Braun & R. T. McCutcheon (Eds.). *Guide to the study of religion.* New York: Cassell.

Griswold, C. L. (2007). *Forgiveness: A philosophical exploration.* New York, NY: Cambridge University Press.

Grof, S. (1988). *The adventure of self discovery.* Albany: State University of New York Press.

Grof, S., & Grof, C. (Eds.). (1989). *Spiritual emergency: When personal transformation becomes a crisis.* Los Angeles: Tarcher.

Grof, S., & Grof, C. (1990). *The stormy search for the self.* New York: G. P. Putnam's Sons.

Grof, S., & Halifax, J. (1977). *The human encounter with death.* New York: Dutton.

Gross, R. (1994). Buddhism. In J. H. & J. B. (Eds.), *Women in religion* (pp. 1–29). New York: Pinter Publishers.

Gutierrez, G. (1988). *A theology of liberation: History, politics and salvation.* Maryknoll, NY: Orbis Books.

Gutierrez, L., Parsons, R., & Cox, E. O. (Eds.). (2003). *Empowerment in social work practice: A sourcebook*. Pacific Grove, CA: Wadsworth Publishing Company.

Gwyther, L. P., Altilio, T., Blacker, S., Christ, G., Csikai, E. L., Hooyman, N., et al. (2005). Social work competencies in palliative and end-of-life care. *Journal of Social Work in End-of-Life & Palliative care, 1*(1), 87–120.

Halifax, J. (1982). *Shaman: The wounded healer*. New York: Crossroad.

Hanh, T. N. (1987). *The miracle of mindfulness: A manual on meditation* (Rev. ed.). Boston: Beacon Press.

Harding, V. (1990). *Hope and history: Why we must share the story of the movement*. Mary Knoll, NY: Orbis Books.

Hart, M. A. (2008). Critical reflections on an Aboriginal approach to helping. In M. Grey, J. Coates, & Yellow Bird, M. (Eds.), *Indigenous social work around the world: Towards culturally relevant education and practice* (pp. 129–139). Burlington, VT: Ashgate.

Harvey, P. (1990.). *An introduction to Buddhism: Teaching, history and practices*. Cambridge, England: Cambridge University Press.

Hayes, D., & Humphries, B. (Eds.) (2004). *Social work, immigration and asylum: Debates, dilemmas and ethical issues for social work and social care practice*. London: Jessica Kingsley.

Haynes, A. W., Eweiss, M. M. I., Mageed, M. A., & Chung, D. K. (1997). Islamic social transformation: Considerations for the social worker. *International Social Work, 40*, 265–275.

Haynes, S. C., Follette, V. M., & Linehan, M. M. (Eds.). (2004). *Mindfulness and acceptance: Expanding the cognitive-behavioral tradition* (pp. 66–95). New York: The Guilford Press.

Healy, L. M. (1995) Comparative and international overview. In T. D. Watts, D. Elliott and N. S. Mayadas (eds). *International handbook on social work education* (pp. 421–440). Westport, CT: Greenwood Press.

Hebl, J. H., & Enright, R. D. (1993). Forgiveness as a psychotherapeutic goal with elderly females. *Psychotherapy, 30*(4), 658–667.

Heimbrock, H., & Boudewijnse, H. B. (Eds.). (1990). *Current studies on rituals: Perspectives for the psychology of religion*. Amsterdam, The Netherlands: Rodopi.

Helmeke, K. B., & Sori, C. F. (Eds.). (2006). *The therapist's notebook for integrating spirituality in counseling: Homework, handouts, and activities for use in psychotherapy*. New York: Haworth Press.

Helminiak, D. A. (1996). *The human core of spirituality: Mind as psyche and spirit*. Albany, NY: State University of New York Press.

Henderson, D. C., Gartner, J. D., Greer, J. M. G., & Estadt, B. K. (1992) Who sees a pastoral counselor? An empirical study of client characteristics. *Journal of Pastoral Care, 46*(2). Summer, 210–217.

Hick, J. H. (1990). *Philosophy of religion* (4th ed.). Englewood Cliffs, NJ: Prentice Hall.

Hill, P. C., & Pargament, K. I (2003). Advances in the conceptualization and measurement of religion and spirituality. *American Psychologist, 58*(1), 64–74.

Hill, P. C., Pargament, K. I., Hood, R. W., McCullough, M. E., Swyers, J. P., Larson, D. B., et al. (2000). *Journal for the Theory of Social behavior, 30*(1), 51–77.

Hill, P. C., & Hood, R. W. (Eds.). (1999). *Measures of religiosity*. Birmingham, AL: Religious Education Press.

Hillman, J. (1975). *Re-visioning psychology.* New York: Harper and Row, Harper Colophon Books.

Hinton, D. (1998). (Trans.). *Mencius.* Washington, D.C.: Counterpoint.

Hodge, D. R. (2001a). Spiritual assessment: A review of major qualitative methods and a new framework for assessing spirituality. *Social Work, 46*(3), 203–214.

Hodge, D. R. (2001b). Spiritual genograms: A generational approach to assessing spirituality. *Families in Society, 82*(1), 35–48.

Hodge, D. R. (2002). Does social work oppress Evangelical Christians? A new class society analysis of society and social work. *Social Work, 47,* 401–414.

Hodge, D. R. (2004a). Developing cultural competency with Evangelical Christians. *Families in Society, 85*(2), 251–260.

Hodge, D. R. (2004b). Working with Hindu clients in a spiritually sensitive manner. *Social Work, 49*(1), 27–38.

Hodge, D. R. (2005a). Social work and the house of Islam: orienting practitioners to the belief and values of Muslims in the United States. *Social Work, 50*(2), 162–173.

Hodge, D. R. (2005b). Spiritual lifemaps: A client-centered pictorial instrument for spiritual assessment, planning, and intervention. *Social Work, 50*(1), 77–87.

Hodge, D. R. (2005c). Developing a spiritual assessment toolbox: A discussion of the strengths and limitations of five different assessment methods. *Health & Social Work, 30*(4), 314–323.

Hodge, D. R. (2006). A template for spiritual assessement: A review of the JCAHO requirements and guidelines for implementation. *Social Work, 51*(4), 317–326.

Hodge, D. R. (2007a). A systematic review of the empirical literature on intercessory prayer. *Research on Social Work Practice, 17*(2), 174–187.

Hodge, D. R. (2007b). The spiritual competence scale: A new instrument for assessing spiritual competence at the programmatic level. *Research on Social Work Practice, 17*(2), 287–295.

Hodge, D. R., & Boddie, S. C. (2007). Social workers' personal spiritual characteristics and their characterizations of spirituality and religion: A mixed method study. *Journal of Religion and Spirituality in Social Work, 26*(1), 53–70.

Hodge, D. R., Langer, C., & Nadir, A. (Eds). (2006). *Arete, Special Issue: Spirituality and Social Work Practice, 30*(1).

Hodge, D. R., & Wolfer, T. A. (2008). Promoting tolerance: The imago dei as an imperative for Christian social workers. *Journal of Religion & Spirituality in Social Work: Social Thought, 27*(3), 259–274.

Hokenstad, M. & Kendall, K.A. (1995). International social work education. In R. L. Edwards (Ed.), *Encyclopedia of Social Work,* 19th ed. (pp. 1511–1520). Washington, DC: NASW Press.

Hokenstad, M. C. & Midgley, J. (Eds.). (2004). *Lessons from abroad: Adapting international social welfare innovations.* Washington, DC: NASW Press.

Hollenback, J. B. (1996). *Mysticism: Experience, response, and empowerment.* University Park, PA: The Pennsylvania State University Press.

Holm, J., & Bowker, J. (Eds.) (1994). *Women in religion.* New York: Pinter Publishers.

Holmgren, M. R. (1993). Forgiveness and the intrinsic value of persons. *American Psychological Quarterly, 30*(4), 341–352.

Hope, D. (1987). The healing paradox of forgiveness. *Psychotherapy, 24*(2), 240–244.

Horner, R., & Kelley, T. B. (2007). Ethical decision-making in the helping profession: A contextual and caring approach. *Journal of Religion & Spirituality in Social Work,* *26*(1), 71–88.

Hoyt, M. F. (Ed.). (1996). *Constructive therapies 2.* New York: Guilford Press.

Hugen, B. (Ed.). (1998). *Christianity and social work: Readings on the integration of Christian faith and social work practice.* Botsford, CT: North American Association of Christians in Social Work.

Hugen, B. (2001). Spirituality and religion in social work practice: A conceptual model. In M. Van Hook, B. Hugen, & M. Aguilar, M. (Eds.). *Spirituality within religious traditions in social work practice* (pp. 9–17). Pacific Grove, CA: Brooks/Cole.

Hunt, M. E. (2007). Eradicating the sin of heterosexism. In M. M. Ellison & J. Plaskow. (Eds.), *Heterosexism in contemporary world religion: Problem and prospect* (pp. 155–176). Cleveland, OH: The Pilgrim Press.

Hutchison, E. D. (1999). *Dimensions of human behavior: Person and environment.* Thousand Oaks, CA: Sage.

Idliby, R., Oliver, S., & Warner, P. (2006). *The faith club: A Muslim, a Christian, a Jew—Three women search for understanding.* New York: Free Press.

Ife, J. (2001). *Human rights and social work: Toward rights based practice.* Cambridge, United Kingdom: Cambridge University Press.

Imbrogno, S., & Canda, E. R. (1988). Social work as an holistic system of activity. *Social Thought, 14*(1), 16–29.

Imre, R. W. (1971). A theological view of social casework. *Social Casework, 52*(9), 578–585.

James, W. (1982). *The varieties of religious experience.* New York: Penguin Books.

Johnston, W. (1995). *Mystical theology: The science of love.* London: Harper Collins Publishers.

Johnstone, R. L. (2004). Religion in society: A sociology of religion (7th ed.). Upper Saddle River, NJ: Pearson Prentice Hall.

Jones, B. L. (2006). Companionship, control, and compassion: A social work perspective on the needs of children with cancer and their families at the end of life. *Journal of Palliative Medicine, 9*(3), 774–788.

Jones, C., Wainwright, G., & Yarnnold, E. (Eds.). (1986). *The study of spirituality.* New York: Oxford University Press

Jones, L. N. (1991). The organized church: Its historic significance and changing role in contemporary African American experience. In W. J. Payne (Ed.), *Directory of African American religious bodies* (pp. 1–19). Washington, DC: Howard University Press.

Joseph, M. V. (1975). The parish as a social service and social action center: An ecological systems approach. *Social Thought, 1*(2), 43–59.

Joseph, M. V. (1987). The religious and spiritual aspects of social work practice: A neglected dimension of social work. *Social Thought, 13*(1), 12–23.

Joseph, M. V. (1988). Religion and social work practice. *Social Casework, 60*(7), 443–452.

Joseph, M. V. (1989). Response to Sanzenbach. *Social Casework, 70*(9), 574–75.

Joy, M., & Neumaier-Dargay, E. K (Eds.). (1995). *Gender, genre, and religion: Feminist reflections.* Waterloo, Ontario, Canada: Wilfrid Laurier University Press.

Jung, C. (1938). *Psychology and religion.* New Haven, CT: Yale University Press.

Jung, C. G. (1953). *The structure of the unconscious.* Princeton: Princeton University Press.

Jung, C. (1959). *The Concept of the Collective Unconscious*. Princeton, NJ: Princeton University Press.

Jung, C. (1963). *Memories, dreams, reflections*. New York: Random House.

Kahn, N. E. (1995). The adult bat mitzvah: Its use in the articulation of women's identity. *Affilia, 10*(3), 299–314.

Kalton, M. C. (Ed. and Trans.). (1988). *To become a sage: The ten diagrams on sage learning by Yi T'oegye*. New York: Columbia University Press.

Kamat, V. I., Jones, W. H., & Row, K.L. (2006). Assessing forgivness as a dimension of personality. *Individual Differences Research, 4*(5), 322–330.

Karenga, M. (1995). Making the past meaningful: KWANZAA and the concept of Sankofa. *Reflections: Narratives of Professional Helping, 1*(4), 36–46.

Kauffman, W. (1956). *Existentialism from Dostoevsky to Sartre*. Cleveland: The World Publishing Company.

Keefe, T. (1975). A Zen perspective on social casework. *Social Casework, 56*(3), 140–144.

Keefe, T. (1996). Meditation and social work treatment. In F. J. Turner (Ed.), *Social Work Treatment: Interlocking Theoretical Approaches* (4th ed) (pp. 434–460). New York: The Free Press.

Keefe, T. W. (2003). The bio-psycho-social-spiritual origins of environmental justice. *Critical Social Work, 4*(1), Retrieved from http://www.uwindsor.ca/units/social-work/critical.nsf/982f0e5f06b5c9a285256d6e006cff78/

Keith-Lucas, A. (1985). *So you want to be a social worker: A primer for the Christian student*. St. Davids, PA: North American Association of Christians in Social Work.

Keith-Lucas, A. (1994). *Giving and taking help* (rev. ed.). St. Davids, PA: North American Association of Christians in Social Work.

Keller, R. R. (2000). Religious diversity in North America. In P. S. Richards & A. E. Bergin (Eds.), *Handbook of psychotherapy and religious diversity* (pp. 27–55). Washington, DC: American Psychological Association.

Kiefer, C. W., & Cowan, J. (1979). State/context dependence and theories of ritual. *J. Psychological Anthropology, 2*(1), 53–83.

Kiev, A. (1972). *Transcultural psychiatry*. New York: Free Press.

Kim, K. M., & Canda, E. R. (2006). A holistic view of health and health promotion in social work for people with disabilities. *Journal of Social Work in Disability and Rehabilitation, 5*(2), 49–67.

King, M. L. Jr. (1992). Facing the challenge of a new age. In J. M. Wshington (Ed.), *I have a dream: Writings and speeches that changed the world*. New York: HarperCollins.

King, N. (1965). Some perspectives on theology and social work. In P. C. McCabe & F. J. Turner (Eds.), *Catholic social work: A contemporary overview* (pp. 6–27). Ottawa: Catholic Charities Council of Canada.

King, U. (Ed.) (1987). *Women in the world's religions, past and present*. New York: Paragon House.

Kinjerski, V., & Skrypnek, B. J. (2008). The promise of spirit at work: Increasing job satisfaction and organizational commitment and reducing turnover and absenteeism in" long-term care. *Journal of Gerontological Nursing, 34*(10), 17–25.

Kissman, K., & Maurer, L. (2002). East meets west: Therapeutic aspects of spirituality in health, mental health and addiction recovery. *International Social Work, 45*(1), 35–43.

Koenig, H. (2005). *Faith and mental health: Religious resources for healing*. Philadelphia, PA: Templeton Foundation Press.

Koenig, H. G. (2006). In the wake of disaster: Religious responses to terrorism and catastrophe. Philadelphia, PA: Templeton Foundation Press.

Koenig, H. G. (2007). *Spirituality in patient care: Why, how, when, and what.* Philadelphia: Templeton Foundation Press.

Koenig, H. G., McCullough, M. E., & Larson, D. B. (2001). *Handbook of religion and health.* New York: Oxford University Press.

Koenig, T. L., & Spano, R. N. (1998). Taoism and the strengths perspective. In. E. R. Canda (Ed.), *Spirituality in social work: New directions* (pp. 47–65). Binghamton, NY: Haworth Press.

Kosmin, B. A., Mayer, E., & Keysar, A. (2001). *American Religious Identification Survey.* New York: The Graduate Center of the City University of New York.

Krause, N., & Ingersoll-Dayton, B. (2001). Religion and the process of forgiveness in late life. *Review of Religious Research, 422*(3), 252–276.

Krieger, D. J. (1996). Methodological foundations for interreligious dialogue. In Joseph Prabhu (Ed.), *The intercultural challenge of Raimon Panikkar* (pp. 201–223). Maryknoll, NY: Orbis Books.

Kreitzer, L. (2006). Social work values and ethics issues of universality. *Currents: New Scholarship in the Human Services,* Retrieved from: http://www.ucalgary.ca/SW/ currents/articles/kreitzer_v5_n1.htm, August 2, 2008

Kreutziger, S. S. (1995). Spirituality in faith. *Reflections: Narratives of ProfessionalHelping, 1*(4), 28–35.

Kreutziger, S. S. (1998). Social work's legacy: The Methodist settlement movement. In B. Hugen (Ed.), *Christianity and social work: Readings on the integration of Christian faith and social work practice* (pp. 27–40). Botsford, CT: North American Association of Christians in Social Work.

Krill, D. F. (1978). *Existential social work.* New York: Free Press.

Krill, D. F. (1979). Existential social work. In F. J. Turner (Ed.), *Social work treatment: Interlocking theoretical perspectives* (pp. 147–176). New York: Free Press.

Krill, D. (1986). *The beat worker: Humanizing social work and psychotherapy.* Lanham, MD: University Press of America.

Krill, D. F. (1990). *Practice wisdom: A guide for the helping professional.* Newbury Park, CA: Sage.

Krill, D. F. (1995). My spiritual sojourn into existential social work. *Reflections: Narratives of Professional Helping, 1*(4), 57–64.

Krill, D. F. (1996). Existential social work. In F. J. Turner (Ed.), *Social work treatment: Interlocking theoretical approaches* (4th ed.) (pp. 250–281). New York: Free Press.

Kubotani, T., & Engstrom, D. (2005). The role of Buddhist temples in the treatment of HIV/AIDS in Thailand. *Journal of Sociology and Social Welfare, 32*(4), 5–21.

Kus, R. J. (Ed.). (1995). *Spirituality and chemical dependency.* Binghamton, NY: Haworth Press.

Kvarfordt, C. L, & Sheridan, M. J. (2007). The role of religion and spirituality in working with children and adolescents: Results of a national survey. *Journal of Religion and Spirituality in Social Work, 26*(3), 1–23.

Laird, J. (1984). Sorcerers, shamans, and social workers: The use of ritual in social work practice. *Social Work, 29*(2), 123–128.

Lal, P. (Trans.). (1967). *The Dhammapada.* New York: Farrar, Straus & Giroux.

Lantz, J. (1993). *Existential family therapy: Using the concepts of Victor Frankl.* Northvale, NJ: Jason Aronson Inc.

Lantz, J., & Walsh, J (2007). *Short-term existential intervention in clinical practice.* Chicago, Ill: Lyceum Books.

Larkin, H. (2005). Social work as an integral profession. *AQAL Journal of Integral Theory and Practice, 1*(2), 2–30.

Lawler-Row, K. A., Karremans, J.C., Scott, C. Eddis-Matiyahou, M., and Edwards, L. (2008). Forgiveness, physiological reactivity and health: The role of anger. *International Journal of Psychophysiology, 68,* 51–58.

Lau, D. C. (Trans.) (1970). *Mencius.* New York: Penguin Books.

Leashore, B. R. (1995). African Americans overview. In R. L. Edwards, (Ed.), *Encyclopedia of social work 19th edition* (pp. 101–115). Washington, DC: National Association and Social Workers.

LeCroy, C. W. (2002). *The call to social work: Life stories.* Thousand Oaks, CA: Sage.

Lee, J. (2001). *The empowerment approach to social work practice (2nd ed.).* New York: Columbia University Press.

Lee, M. Y., Ng, S. M., Leung, P. P. Y., Chan, C. L. W., & Leung, P. (2009). *Integrative-body-mind-spirit social work: An empirically based approach to assessment and treatment.* New York: Oxford University Press.

Lee, D., & O'Gorman, R.(Eds.). (2005). *Social work and divinity.* Binghamton, NY: Haworth Press.

Lehmann, A. C., & Myers, J. E. (2001). *Magic, witchcraft, and religion: An anthropological study of the supernatural* (5th ed.). Mountain View, CA: Mayfield Publishing Company.

Leiby, J. (1985). Moral foundations of social welfare and social work: A historical view. *Social Work, 30*(4), 323–330.

Lessa, W. A., & Vogt, E. Z. (Eds.). (1972). *Reader in comparative religion: An anthropological approach* (3rd ed.). New York: Harper & Row, Publishers.

Letendre, J., Nelson-Becker, H., & Kreider, J. (2005). Teaching spirituality in the classroom. *Reflections: Narratives of Professional Helping, 11*(3), 8–19.

Lewandowski, C. A., & Canda, E. R. (1995). A typological model for the assessment of religious groups. *Social Thought, 18*(1), 17–38.

Lightman, E. S., & Shor, R. (2002). Askanim: Informal helpers and cultural brokers as a bridge to secular helpers for the ultra-Orthodox Jewish communities of Israel and Canada. *Families in Society, 83*(3), 315–324.

Lincoln, B. (1981). *Emerging from the chrysalis: Studies in rituals of women's initiation (pp. 100–103).* Cambridge: Harvard University Press.

Lincoln, Y. S. (1995). Emerging criteria for quality in qualitative and interpretive research. *Qualitative Inquiry, 1*(3), 275–289.

Lincoln, Y. S., & Guba, E. G. (1985). *Naturalistic inquiry.* Beverly Hills, CA: Sage.

Lindsay, R. (2002). *Recognizing spirituality: The interface between faith and social work.* Crawley, Western Australia: University of Western Australia Press.

Link, R.J. & Healy, L.M. (2005). *Teaching international content: Curriculum resources for social work education.* Alexandria, VA: Council on Social Work Education.

Linzer, N. (1979). A Jewish philosophy of social work practice. *Journal of Jewish Communal Service, 55*(4), 309–317.

Lippy, C. H., & Williams, P. W. (Eds.). *Encyclopedia of American religious experience: Studies of traditions and movements.* New York: Charles Scribner's Sons.

Loewenberg, F. M. (1988). *Religion and social work practice in contemporary American society.* New York: Columbia University Press.

Logan, S. L. (Ed.). (2001). *The Black family: Strengths, self-help, and positive change* (2nd ed.). Boulder, CO: Westview Press.

Logan, S. L. (1997). Meditation as a tool for linking the personal and professional. *Reflections: Narratives of Professional Helping,3*(1), 38–44.

Logan, S. L., Freeman, E. M., & McCroy, R. G. (1990). *Social work practice with black families: A culturally specific perspective.* New York: Longman.

Lovheim, M. (2007). Virtually boundless? Youth negotiating tradition in cyberspace. In N. T. Ammerman (Ed.), *Everyday religion: Observing modern religious lives* (pp. 83–100). New York: Oxford University Press.

Lukoff, D., Lu, F. G., & Turner, R. (1992). Toward a more culturally sensitive DSM-IV: Psychoreligious and psychospiritual problems. *The Journal of Nervous and Mental Disease, 180*(11), 673–682.

Lukoff, D., Lu, F. G., & Turner, R. (1995). Cultural considerations in the assessment and treatment of religious and spiritual problems. *Cultural Psychiatry, 18*(3), 467–485.

Luoma, B. (1998). An exploration of intuition for social work practice and education. In E. R. Canda (Ed.), *Spirituality in social work: New directions* (pp. 31–45). Binghamton, NY: Haworth Press.

Lyon, W. S. (1996). *Encyclopedia of Native American healing.* Santa Barbara, CA: ABC-CLIO.

Marques, J., Dhiman, S., & King, R. (2007). Spirituality in the workplace. Fawnskin, CA: Personhood Press.

Mace, C. (2008). *Mindfulness and mental health: Therapy, theory and science.* New York: Routledge.

Macy, J. (1991). *Mutual causality in Buddhism and general systems theory.* Albany, NY: State University of New York Press.

Marlatt, G. A., & Kristeller, J. L. (1999). Mindfulness and meditation. In W. R. Miller (Ed.), *Integrating spirituality into treatment: Resources for practitioners* (pp. 67–84). Washington, DC: American Psychological Association.

Marquis, A. (2008). *The integral intake: A guide to comprehensive ideographic assessment in integral psychotherapy.* New York: Routledge.

Marshall, J. (1991). The spiritual dimension in social work education. *Spirituality and Social Work Communicator, 2*(1), 12–15.

Martin, E. P., & Martin, J. M. (2002). *Spirituality and the Black helping tradition in social work.* Washington, DC: NASW Press.

Martin, P. (1999). *The Zen path through depression.* New York: Harper Collins Publishers.

Marty, M. E. (1980). Social service: Godly and godless. *Social Service Review, 54*(4), 4463–4481.

Marty, M. E., & Appleby, S. (Eds.). (1991). *Fundamentalisms observed.* Chicago: University of Chicago Press.

Maslow, A. (1968). *Toward a psychology of being* (2nd ed.). New York: D. Van Nostrand.

Maslow, A. (1969). The farther reaches of human nature. *Journal of Transpersonal Psychology, 1*(1), 1–9.

Maslow, A. (1970). *Religions, values and peak experiences.* New York: Viking.

Masters, R. E. L., & Houston, J. (1966). *The varieties of psychedelic experience.* New York: Delta.

Matthews, D. A., Larson, D. B., & Barry, C. P. (1993). *The faith factor: An annotated bibliography of clinical research on spiritual subjects.* Rockville, MD: National Institute for Healthcare Research.

Mattison, D., Jayaratne, S., & Croxton, T. (2000). Social workers' religiosity and its impact on religious practice behaviors. *Advances in Social Work, 1*(1), 43–59.

McBee, L. (2008). *Mindfulness-based elder care: a CAM model for frail elders and their caregivers.* New York: Springer.

McCabe, G. (2008). Mind, body, emotions and spirit: reaching to the ancestors for healing. *Counselling Psychology Quarterly, 21*(2), 143–152.

McCabe, P. C. (1965). Sectarian social work--necessity or luxury. In P.C. McCabe & F. J. Turner (Eds.), *Catholic social work: A contemporary overview* (pp. 28–43).

McCullough, M. E., Bono, G., & Root, L. M. (2005). Religion and forgiveness. In R. F. Paloutzian & C. L. Park, C. L. (Eds.), *Handbook of the psychology of religion and spirituality* (pp. 394–411). New York: The Guilford Press.

McCullough, M. E., Pargament, K. I., & Thoreson, C. E. (2000). The psychology of forgiveness: History, conceptual issues, and overview. In M. E. McCullough, K. I. Pargament, & C. E. Thoreson (Eds.), *Forgiveness: Theory, research, and practice* (pp. 1–14). New York: The Guilford Press.

McCullough, M. E., & Worthington, E. L. (1999). Religion and the forgiving personality. *Journal of Personality, 67,* 1141–1164.

McGee, E. (1984). The transpersonal perspective: Implications for the future of personal and social development. *Social Development Issues, 8*(3), 151–181.

McGovern, T. F., & Benda, B. (Eds.). (2006). *Spirituality and religiousness and alcohol/other drug problems: Treatment and recovery perspectives.* Binghamton. NY: Haworth Press.

McKay, M., Wood, J. C., & Brantley, J. (2007). *The dialectical behavior therapy skills workbook.* Oakland, CA: New Harbinger Publications.

McKenzie, B., & Morrissette, V. (2003). Social work practice with Canadians of aboriginal background: Guidelines for respectful social work. *Envision: The Manitoba Journal of Child Welfare, 2*(1), 13–39.

McLaughlin, C., & Davidson, G. (1994). *Spiritual politics.* New York: Ballantine.

McSherry, W., & Cash, K. (2004). The language of spirituality: An emerging taxonomy. *International Journal of Nursing Studies, 41,* 151–161.

McSherry, W., Cash, K., & Ross, L. (2004). Meaning of spirituality: Implications for nursing practice. *Journal of Clinical Nursing, 13,* 934–941.

Meckel, M. Walters, D. & Baugh, P. (2005) Mixed-mode surveys using mail and web questionnaires. *The Electronic Journal of Business Research Methodology, 3*(1), 69–80.

Meinert, R. G., Pardeck, J. T., & Murphy, J. W. (Eds.). (1998). *Postmodernism, religion, and the future of social work. Binghamton, NY: Haworth Press.*

Melton, J. G. (1992). *Religious bodies in the United States: A directory.* New York: Garland Publishing, Inc.

Melton, J. G. (Ed.). (1993). *Encyclopedia of American religion.* Detroit: Gale Research.

Merton, T. (1961). *New seeds of contemplation.* New York: New Directions Books.

Merton, T. (1968a). *Conjectures of a guilty bystander.* Garden City, NY: Image Books.

Merton, T. (1968b). *Zen and the birds of appetite.* New York: New Directions Books.

Meshal, R. A. (2007). Miniskirts and fundamentalist fashions: Clothing the Muslim Canadian woman. In A. Sharma & K. K. Young (Eds.), *Fundamentalism and women in world religions* (pp. 157–177). New York: T & T Clark International.

Messer, S. B., & Wampold, B. E. (2006). Let's face facts: Common factors are more potent than specific therapy ingredients. *Clinical Psychology: Science and Practice, 9*(1), 21–25.

Meystedt, D. M. (1984). Religion and the rural population: Implications for social work. *Social Casework, 65*(4), 219–226.

Mickey, P. A. (1991). *Of sacred worth.* Nashville, TN: Abingdon Press.

Midgely, J. (1990). The new Christian right, social policy, and the welfare state. *Journal of Sociology and Social Welfare, 17*(2), 89–106.

Midgley, J. (1995). International and comparative social welfare. In R. L. Edwards (Ed.), *Encyclopedia of Social Work 19th Edition.* Washington, DC: NASW Press.

Midgely, J., & Sanzenbach, P. (1989). Social work, religion, and the global challenge of Fundamentalism. *International Social Work, 32*(4), 273–287.

Miller, C. (1980). Commitment, ideology, and skill. *Journal of Jewish Communal Service, 57*(1), 30–36.

Miller, G. (2003). *Incorporating spirituality in counseling and psychotherapy: Theory and technique.* Hoboken, NJ: John Wiley & Sons.

Miller, R. L. (2008). Gay men. In T. Mizrahi & L. E. Davis (Eds.), *Encyclopedia of Social Work (e-reference edition).* Oxford University Press. University of Kansas. Retrieved August 12, 2008. from http://www.oxford-naswsocialwork.com/entry=t203.e159-s2

Miller, T. (Ed.). (1995). *America's alternative religions.* Albany, NY: State University of New York Press.

Miller, W. R. (Ed.). (1999). *Integrating spirituality into treatment: Resources for practitioners.* Washington, DC: American Psychological Association.

Miller, W. R,. & Thoreson, C. E. (2003). Spirituality, religion, and health: An emerging research field. *American Psychologist, 58*(1), 24–35.

Miller, S. D., Hubble, M., & Duncan, B. (2008). *Psychotherapy in Australia, 14*(4), 14–22.

Mitroff, I. I., & Denton, E. A. (1999). A spiritual audit of corporate America: A hard look at spirituality, religion, and values in the workplace. San Francisco: Jossey-Bass Publishers.

Moberg, D. O. (Ed.). (2001). *Aging and spirituality: Spiritual dimensions of aging theory, research, practice, and policy.* New York: Haworth Pastoral Press.

Modood, T. (2005) *Multicultural Politics: Racism, Ethnicity, and Muslims in Britain,* Minneapolis, MN, University of Minnesota Press.

Mokuau, N. (1990). A family-centered approach in native Hawaiian culture. *Families in Society, 7*(10), 607–613.

Moore, R. J. (2003). Spiritual assessment. *Social Work, 48*(4), 558–561.

Moreira-Almeida, A. & Koenig, H. G. (2006). Retaining the meaning of the words religiousness and spirituality: A commentary on the WHOQOL SRPB group's "A cross-cultural study of spirituality, religion, and personal beliefs as components of quality of life". *Social Science & Medicine, 63,* 843–845.

Morreale, D. (Ed.). (1998). *The complete guide to Buddhist America.* Boston: Shambhala.

Morris, C. S. (1991). African Americans and Methodism. In W. J. Payne (Ed.), *Directory of African American religious bodies* (pp. 238–247). Washington, DC: Howard University Press.

Morris-Compton, D. (Sept./Oct. 2006). Immigration divides nation, unites social workers. *Social Work Today, 6*(5), 38. Retrieved August 2, 2007, from http://www.socialworktoday.com/archive/swsept2006p39.shtml

Morrow, D. F. (2008). Lesbians. In T. Mizrahi & L. E. Davis (Eds.), *Encyclopedia of Social Work (e-reference edition).* Oxford University Press. University of Kansas. Retrieved

August 12, 2008, from http://www.oxford-naswsocialwork.com/entry?entry=t203.
e223-s2

Moss, B. (2005). *Religion and spirituality.* Dorset, England: Russell House Publishing.

Moss, B., & Tjhompson, N. (2008). *Meaning and values: Developing empowering practice.* Dorset, England: Russell House Publishing.

Moxley, D. P., & Washington, O. G. M. (2001). Strengths-based recovery practice in chemical dependency: A transpersonal perspective. *Families in Society, 82*(3), 251–262.

Muldoon, A. (2006). Environmental efforts: The next challenge for social work. *Critical Social Work, 7*(2), Retrieved from http://www.uwindsor.ca/units/socialwork/critical.nsf/982f0e5f06b5c9a285256d6e006cff78/

Mullaly, B. (2006). *The new structural social work.* New York: Oxford University Press.

Mullet, E., Barros, J., Frongia, L., Usai, V., Neto, N., and Shafighi, S.R. (2003). Religious involvement and the forgiving personality. *Journal of Personality, 71*(1), 1–19.

Nabigon, H., & Mawhiney, A. (1996). Aboriginal theory: A Cree medicine wheel guide for healing First Nations. In F. J. Turner (Ed.), *Social work treatment: Interlocking theoretical approaches* (4th ed.) (pp. 18–38). New York: Free Press.

Nadir, A., & Dziegielewski, S. F (2001). Islam. In M.Van Hook, B. Hugen, & M. Aguilar, (Eds.), *Spirituality within religious traditions in social work* (pp. 146–166). Pacific Grove, CA: Brooks/Cole.

Nadir, P. A. (2008). Muslim social services. In T. Mizrahi & L. E. Davis (Eds.), *Encyclopedia of Social Work* (e-reference edition). Oxford University Press. University of Kansas. Retreived August 12, 2008, http://www.oxford-naswsocial-work.com./entry?entry=t203.e255.

Naess, A. (1988). Self-realization: An ecological approach to being in the world. In J. Seed, J. Macy, P. Fleming, & A. Naess (Eds.), *Thinking like a mountain: Towards a council of all beings* (pp. 19–31). Santa Cruz, CA: New Society Publishers.

Nakashima, M. (1995). Spiritual growth through hospice work. *Reflections: Narratives of Professional Helping, 1*(4), 17–27.

Nakashima, M. (2007). Positive dying in later life: Spiritual resiliency among sixteen hospice patients. *Journal of Religion, Spirituality, & Aging, 19*(2), 43–66.

Nakashima, M., & Canda, E.R. (2005). Positive dying and resiliency in later life: A qualitative study. *Journal of Aging Studies, 19*(1), 109–125.

Nash, M., & Stewart, R. (Eds.). (2002). *Spirituality and social care: Contributing to personal and community well-being.* London: Jessica Kingsley.

National Association of Social Workers (1999). *The NASW code of ethics.* Washington, DC: NASW.

National Association of Social Workers (NASW). (2005). Council creates Kendall education institute. *NASW News, 50*(6), 5.

National Conference of Catholic Charities (1983). *A code of ethics.* Washington, DC: Author.

Nelson, J. E. (1994). *Healing the split: Integrating spirit into our understanding of the mentally ill* (rev. ed.). Albany: State University of New York Press.

Nelson-Becker, H. (2003). Practical philosophies: Interpretations of religion and spirituality by African-American and Jewish elders. *Journal of Religious Gerontology, 14*(2/3), 85–99.

Nelson-Becker, H., Nakashima, M., & Canda, E. (2006). Spirituality in professional helping interventions. In B. Berkman & D'Ambruoso, S. (Eds.), *Handbook of social work in health and aging* (pp. 797–807). New York: Oxford University Press.

Nelson-Becker, H., Nakashima, M., & Canda, E. R. (2007). Spiritual assessment in aging: A framework for clinicians. *Journal of Gerontological Social Work, 48*(3/4), 331–347.

Nelson-Becker, H., & Canda, E. R. (2008). Spirituality, religion, and aging research in social work: State of the art and future possibilities. *Journal of Religion, Spirituality & Aging, 20*(3), 177–193.

Netting, F. E., Kettner, P. M., & McMurty, S. L. (1998). *Social work macro practice second edition*. New York: Longman.

Neusner, J. (1979). *The way of Torah: An introduction to Judaism* (3rd ed.), North Scituate, MA: Duxbury Press.

Newberg, A. B., & Newberg, S. K. (2005). The neuropsychology of religious and spiritual experience. In R. F. Paloutzian & C. L. Park, C. L. (Eds.), *Handbook of the psychology of religion and spirituality* (pp. 199–215). New York: The Guilford Press.

Newsome, C. G. (1991). A synoptic survey of the history of African American Baptists. In W. J. Payne (Ed.), *Directory of African American religious bodies* (pp. 226–237). Washington, DC: Howard University Press.

Niebuhr, R. (1932). *The contribution of religion to social work*. New York: Columbia University Press.

Nielsen, N. C. Jr., Hein, N., Reynolds, F. E., & Miller, A. L. (1993). *Religions of the world* (3rd ed.). New York: St. Martin's Press.

Nimmagadda, J. & Cowger, C. D. (1999). Cross-cultural practice: Social worker ingenuity in the indigenization of practice knowledge. *International Social Work, 42*(3), 261–276.

Nixon, G. (2005). Beyond "dry drunkenness": facilitating second stage recovery using Wilber's "Spectrum of Consciousness" developmental model. *Journal of Social Work in the Addictions, 5*(3), 55–71.

Nyitray, V. (2007). Fundamentalism and the position of women in Confucianism. In A. Sharma & K. K. Young (Eds.), *Fundamentalism and women in world religions* (pp. 47–76). New York: T&T Clark.

Oakley, V. (1955). *Cathedral of compassion: Dramatic outline of the life of Jane Addams 1860–1935*. Philadelphia, PA: Press of Lyon and Armor.

O'Brien, M. E. (2008). *Spirituality in nursing: Standing on holy ground* (3rd ed.). Boston: Jones and Bartlett Publishers.

Orsillo, S. M., Roemer, L., Lerner, J. B., & Tull, M. T. (2004). Acceptance, mindfulness, and cognitive-behavioral therapy: Comparisons, contrasts, and application to anxiety. In S. C. Haynes, V. M. Follette, & M. M. Linehan (Eds.), *Mindfulness and acceptance: Expanding the cognitive-behavioral tradition* (pp. 66–95). New York: The Guilford Press.

Ostrov, S. (1976). A family therapist's approach to working with an Orthodox Jewish clientele. *Journal of Jewish Communal Service, 63*(2), 147–154.

Otto, R. (1950). *The idea of the holy* (2nd ed.). (J. W. Harvey, Trans.). London: Oxford University Press.

Paden, W. E. (2003). *Interpreting the sacred: Ways of viewing religion* (rev. and updated ed.). Boston: Beacon Press.

Paden, W. E. (1994). *Religious worlds: The comparative study of religion.* Boston: Beacon Press.

Paladin, L. S. (1991). *Ceremonies for change: Creating rituals to heal life's hurts.* Walpole, NH: Stillpoint.

Paloutzian, R. F., & Park, C. L. (Eds.). (2005). *Handbook of the psychology of religion and spirituality.* New York: The Guilford Press.

Pals, D. L. (1996). *Seven theories of religion.* New York: Oxford University Press.

Pandey, R. S. (1996). Gandhian perspectives on personal empowerment and social development. *Social Development Issues, 18*(2), 66–84.

Panikkar, R. (2000). Eruption of truth: An interview with Raimon Panikkar. *The Christian Century, August 16–23,* 834–836.

Pargament, K. I. (2007). *Spiritually integrated psychotherapy: Understanding and addressing the sacred.* New York: Guilford Press.

Paris, P. J. (1995). *The spirituality of African peoples: The search for a common moral discourse.* Minneapolis, MN: Fortress Press.

Parliament of the World's Religions (2004). 2004 Parliament of the World's Religions Summary Report. Retrieved from http://www.parliamentofreligions.org/_includes/FCKcontent/File/2004report-rev.pdf

Parr, R. G., & Jones, L. E. (1996). Point/Counterpoint: Should CSWE allow social work programs in religious institutions an exemption from the accreditation nondiscrimination standard related to sexual orientation? *Journal of Social Work Education, 32*(3), 297–313.

Patel, I. (1987). *Vivekananda's approach to social work.* Mylapore, India: Sri Ramakvishna Math.

Patel, N., Naik, D., & Humphries, B. (Eds.). (1997). *Visions of reality: religion and ethnicity in social work.* London: Central Council for Education and Training in Social Work.

Patton, M. Q. (2002). *Qualitative research and evaluation methods* (3rd ed.). Thousand Oaks, CA: Sage.

Paulino, A. M. (1995a). Death, dying, and religion among Dominican immigrants. In J. Parry & A. R. Shen, (Eds.), *A cross-cultural look at death, dying, and religion* (pp. 84–101). Chicago: Nelson Hall Publishers.

Paulino, A. (1995b). Spiritism, santeria, brujeria, and voodooism: A comparative view of indigenous healing systems. *Journal of Teaching in Social Work, 12*(1/2), 105–124.

Payne, W. J., (Ed.). (1991). *Directory of African American religious bodies.* Washington, DC: Howard University Press.

Peck, M. S. (1983). *People of the lie: The hope for healing human evil.* New York: Simon & Schuster, Inc.

Pelletier, K., & Garfield, C. (1976). *Consciousness east and west.* New York: Harper and Row.

Pepper, A. R. (1956). Protestant social work today. In F. E. Johnson (Ed.), *Religion and social work* (pp. 17–27). New York: Institute for Religious and Social Studies, Harper and Brothers.

Peters, F. E. (1982). *Children of Abraham: Judaism/Christianity/Islam.* Princeton, NJ: Princeton University Press.

Peterson, C. & Seligman, M. E. P. (2004). *Character Strengths and Virtues: A handbook and classification.* Washington, DC: American Psychological Association.

Petr, C. G., & Walter, U. M. (2005). Best practices inquiry: A multidimensional, value-critical framework. *Journal of Social Work Education, 41*(2), 251–267.

Pew Forum on Religion and Public Life (2008). U. S. Religious landscape survey report II. Retrieved from http://www.pewforum.org/events/?EventID=190

Pew Hispanic Project (2008). Changing faiths: Latinos and the transformation of American religion: Executive summary. Retrieved from http://www.pewforum.org/surveys/Hispanic/

Pewewardy, N. (2007). *Challenging white privilege: Critical discourse for social work education.* Alexandria, VA: Council on Social Work Education.

Pon, G. (2008). Becoming lost and found: Peace, Christianity, and anti-oppression. *Critical Social Work, 8*(1), Retrieved from http://uwindsor.ca/units/socialwork/critical.nsf/main/35322CBC105B639D85257370

Powell, L. H., Shahabi, L., & Thoreson, C. E. (2003). Religion and spirituality: Linkages to physical health. *American Psychologist, 58*(1), 36–52.

Praglin. L. J. (2004). Spirituality, religion, and social work: An effort towards interdisciplinary conversation. *Journal of Religion and Spirituality in Social Work, 23*(4), 67–84.

Prebish, C. S. (1999). *Luminous passages: The practice and study of Buddhism in America.* Berkeley: University of California Press.

Press, A. N., & Osterkamp, L. (2006). *Stress? Find your balance*, 4th edition. Boulder, CO: Preventive Measures, Inc.

Pribenow, P. (2008). *Augsburg College President's Perspective.* Minneapolis, MN: Augsburg College.

Proudfoot, W. (1985). *Religious experience.* Berkeley, CA: University of California Press.

Prue, R. E. (2008). *King alcohol to chief peyote: A grounded theory investigation of the supportive factors of the Native American Church for drug and alcohol abuse recovery.* Ph.D. Dissertation, University of Kansas, AAT 3336488.

Puchalski, C. (2006). Spiritual assessment in clinical practice. *Psychiatric Annals, 36*(3), 150–155.

Pyles, L. (2005). Understanding the engaged Buddhist movement: Implications for social development practice. *Critical Social Work, 6*(1). Retrieved from http:www.windsor.ca/units/socialwork/critical.nsf/8c20das9flc4be3a8256d6e006d1089

Raines, J. C. (1996). Toward a definition of spiritually-sensitive social work practice. *Society for Spirituality and Social Work Newsletter, 3*(2), 4–5.

Raines, J. C. (2004). Emotional themes in cross-faith encounters among MSW students: A qualitative exploration. *Journal of Religion & Spirituality in Social Work, 23*(3), 109–152.

Ramirez, R. (1985). Hispanic spirituality. *Social Thought, 11*(3), 6–13.

Randour, M. L. (1987). *Women's psyche, women's spirit: The reality of relationships.* New York: Columbia University Press.

Rapp, C., Shera, W., & Kisthardt, W. (1993). Research strategies for consumer empowerment of people with severe mental illness. *Social Work, 38*(6), 727–735.

Reamer, F. G. (1992). Social work and the public good: Calling or career? In P. Nelson Reid & P. R. Popple (Eds.), *The moral purposes of social work* (pp. 11–33). Chicago: Nelson-Hall Publishers.

Reamer, F. G. (2001). *The social work ethics audit.* Washington, D.C.: NASW Press.

Reamer, F. G. (2005). Social work values and ethics: Reflections on the profession's odyssey. *Advances in Social Work, 6*(1), 24–32.

Reid, T. R. (2000). *Confucius lives next door: What living in the east teaches us about living in the west.* New York: Vintage Books.

Reid, P. N., & Popple, P. R. (Eds.). (1992). *The moral purposes of social work: The character and intentions of a profession.* Chicago: Nelson-Hall Publishers.

Religions for Peace (2007). Strategic Plan, Religions for Peace Different Faiths, Common Action. Retrieved from http://www.wcrp.org/resources/reports/annual-report-2007

Rennie, B. S. (1996). *Reconstructing Eliade: Making sense of religion.* Albany, NY: State University of New York Press.

Repstad, Paal (Ed.) (1996). *Religion and modernity. Modes of co-existence.* Oslo: Scandinavian University Press.

Ressler, L. (1992). Theologically enriched social work: Alan Keith-Lucas' Approach to social work and religion. *Spirituality and Social Work Journal, 3*(2), 14–20.

Rey, L. D. (1997). Religion as invisible culture: Knowing about and knowing with. *Journal of Family Social Work, 2*(2), 159–177.

Richards, P. S., & Bergin, A. E. (Eds.). (2000). *Handbook of psychotherapy and religious diversity.* Washington, DC: American Psychological Association.

Richards, P. S., & Bergin, A. E. (2005). *A spiritual strategy for counseling and psychotherapy* (2nd ed.). Washington, DC: American Psychological Association.

Ridgway, P., McDiarmid, D., Davidson, L., Bayes, J., & Ratzlaff, S. (2002). *Pathways to recovery: A strengths recovery self-help workbook.* Lawrence, KS: Supported Education Group at the University of Kansas School of Social Welfare.

Ringel, S (2007). Identity and gender roles of Orthodox Jewish women: Implications for social work practice. *Smith College Studies in Social Work, 77*(2/3), 25–44.

Robbins, S. P. (1997). Cults. In R. L. Edwards (Ed.), *Update for the Encyclopedia of Social Work* (19th ed.). Washington, D.C.: National Association of Social Workers Press.

Robbins, S. P., Chatterjee, P., & Canda, E. R. (1998). *Contemporary human behavior theory: A critical perspective for social work.* Boston: Allyn & Bacon.

Robbins, S. P., Chatterjee, P., & Canda, E. R. (2006). *Contemporary human behavior theory: A critical perspective for social work* (2nd ed.). Boston: Pearson Education.

Roberts, K. A. (2004). *Religion in sociological perspective* (4th ed.). Belmont, CA: Wadsworth Publishing Company.

Roehlkepartain, E. C., King, P. E., Wagener, L., & Benson, P. L. (Eds.). (2006). *The handbook of spiritual development in childhood and adolescence.* Thousand Oaks, CA: Sage Publications

Rodwell, M. K. (1998). *Social work constructivist research.* New York: Garland Publishing, Inc.

Roland, C. (Ed.). (2007). *The Cambridge companion to liberation theology* (2nd ed.). New York: Cambridge University Press.

Roof, W. C. (1993). *A generation of seekers: The spiritual journeys of the baby boom generation.* San Francisco: HarperSanFrancisco.

Rosemont, H. (2008). The summation. In H. Rosemont & Smith, H., *Is there a universal grammar of religion?* (pp. 77–94). Chicago: Open Court.

Russel, R. (1998). Spirituality and religion in graduate social work education. In E. R. Canda, (Ed.), *Spirituality and social work: New directions* (pp. 15–29). Hazleton, PA: Haworth Press.

Russel, R. (2006). Spirituality and social work: Current trends and future directions. *Arete, 30*(1), 42–52.

Sacco, T., & Hoffman, W. (2004). Seeking truth and reconciliation in South Africa: A social work contribution. *International Social Work, 47*(2), 157–167.

Saleebey, D. (Ed.). (2009). *The strengths perspective in social work practice.* (5th edition). Boston: Allyn & Bacon.

Salomon, E. L. (1976). Humanistic values and social casework. *Social Casework, 48*(1), 26–31.

Sanderson, C., & Linehan, M. M. (1999). Acceptance and forgiveness. In W. R. Miller (Ed.), *Integrating spirituality into treatment: Resources for practitioners* (pp. 199–216). Washington, DC: American Psychological Association.

Sandner, D. (1991). *Navaho symbols of healing.* Rochester, VT: Healing Arts Press.

Sanzenbach, P. (1989). Religion and social work: It's not that simple. *Social Casework, 70*(9), 571–572.

Saulis, M. A. (2006). Program and policy development from a holistic Aboriginal perspective. In A. Westhues (Ed.), *Canadian social policy: Issues and perspectives* (pp. 115–130). Waterloo, Ontario, Canada: Wilfred Laurier University Press.

Scharper, P. J. (1975). The theology of liberation: Some reflections. *Social Thought, 1*(1), 59–66.

Schecter, M. (1971). A value system model in Jewish social welfare. *The Jewish Social Work Forum, 8*(2), 5–22.

Scheff, T. J. (1979). *Catharsis in healing, ritual and drama.* Berkeley, University of California Press.

Scherer, B. (2006). Faith and experience: Paradigms of spirituality. In W. Greenstreet (Ed.), *Integrating spirituality in health and social care* (pp. 89–100). Oxford, England: Radcliffe Publishing.

Schiff, J. W., & Pelech, W. (2007). The sweat lodge ceremony for spiritual healing. *The Journal of Religion and Spirituality in Social Work, 26*(4), 71–93.

Schumacher, S., & Woerner, G. (Eds.). (1994). *The encyclopedia of eastern philosophy and religion: Buddhism, Hinduism, Taoism, Zen.* Boston: Shambhala.

Seow, C. L. (1996). *Homosexuality and Christian community.* Louisville, KY: Westminster John Knox Press.

Seplowin, V. M. (1992). Social work and karma therapy. *Spirituality and Social Work Journal, 3*(2), 2–8.

Sessana, L., Finnell, D., & Jezewski, M. A. (2008). Spirituality in nursing and health-related literature: A concept analysis. *Journal of Holistic Nursing, 25*(4), 252–262).

Sewpaul, V., & Jones, D. (2004). Global standards for social work education and training. *Social Work Education, 23*(5), 493–513.

Shafranske, E. P. (Ed.). (1996). *Religion and the clinical practice of psychology.* Washington, DC: American Psychological Association.

Shandy, D. J., & Fennelly, K. (2006). A comparison of the integration experiences of two African immigrant populations in a rural community. *Journal of Religion & Spirituality in Social Work, 25*(1), 23–45.

Shank, B. W. (2007). The call to justice: Social work in Catholic higher education. *Social Work & Christianity, 34*(1), 2–17.

Shapiro, S. L., Schwartz, G. E. R., & Santerre, C. (2005). Meditation and positive psychology. In C. R. Snyder & S. J. Lopez (Eds.), *Handbook of positive psychology* (pp. 639–908). New York: Oxford University Press.

Sharma, A. (Ed.). (1994). *Today's woman in world religions.* Albany, NY: State University of New York Press.

Sharma, A. (2005). *Religious studies and comparative methodology: The case for recipro-cal illumination.* Albany, NY: State University of New York Press.

Sharma, A., & Young, K. K. (Eds.). (2007). *Fundamentalism and women in world religions.* New York: T & T Clark.

Sharma, S. (1987). Development, peace, and nonviolent social change: The Gandhian perspective. *Social Development Issues, 10*(3), 31–45.

Sheng-Yen (1987). *Faith in mind: A guide to Ch'an practice.* Elmhurst, NY: Dharma Drum Publications.

Sheng-Yen & Stevenson, D. (2001). *Hoofprint of the ox: principles of the Chan Buddhist path as taught by a modern Chinese master.* New York: Oxford University Press.

Sheridan, M. J. (1997). If we nurtured the soul of social work. *Society for Spirituality and Social Work Newsletter, 4*(2), 3.

Sheridan, M. J. (2004). Predicting the use of spiritually-derived interventions in social work practice: A survey of practitioners. *Journal of Religion & Spirituality in Social Work, 23*(4), 5–25.

Sheridan, M. J. & Amoato con-Hemert, K. (1999). The role of religion and spiritiuality in social work education and practice: A survey of student views and experiences. *Journal of Social Work Education, 35*(1), 125–141.

Sheridan, M. J., & Bullis, R. K. (1991). Practitioners' views on religion and spirituality. *Spirituality and Social Work Journal, 2*(2), 2–10.

Sheridan, M. J., Bullis, R. K., Adcock, C. R., Berlin, S. D., & Miller, P. C. (1992). Practitioners' personal and professional attitudes toward religion and spirituality: Issues for education and practice. *Journal of Social Work Education, 28*(2), 190–203.

Sheridan, M. J., Wilmer, C. M., & Atcheson, L. (1994). Inclusion of content on religion and spirituality in the social work curriculum: A study of faculty views. *Journal of Social Work Education, 30*(3), 363–376.

Sherman, E., & Siporin, M. (2008). Contemplative theory and practice for social work. *Journal of Religion & Spirituality for Social Work: Social Thought, 27*(3), 259–274.

Sherwood, D. A. (2000). Pluralism, tolerance, and respect for diversity: Engaging our deepest differences within the bond of civility. *Social Work & Christianity, 27*(1), 1–7.

Sherwood, D. A. (2001). Integrating faith and practice: Growing up into the image of Christ through the practices of faith. *Social Work & Christianity, 28*(2), 95–105.

Sherwood, D. A. (2002). Ethical integration of faith and social work practice evangelism. *Social Work & Christianity, 29*(1), 1–12.

Schiele, J. H. (1994). Afrocentricity as an alternative world view for equality. *Journal of Progressive Human Services, 5*(1), 5–25.

Shim, W. (in press). Gender balance with Confucian philosophy: My own experience with empowerment.. *Reflections: Narratives of Professional Helping..*

Simkhovitch, M. K. (1950). The settlement and religion. In L. M. Pacey, (Ed.), *Readings in the development of settlement work* (pp. 136–142). Freeport, NY: Books for Libraries Press.

Simos, B. G. (1979). *A time to grieve: Loss as a universal human experience.* New York: Family Service Association of America.

Singh, R. N. (1992). Integrating concepts from Eastern psychology and spirituality: A treatment approach for Asian-American clients. *Spirituality and Social Work Journal, 3*(2) 8–14.

Singh, R. (2001). Hinduism. In M.Van Hook, B. Hugen, & M. Aguilar (Eds.), *Spirituality within religious traditions in social work,* (pp. 34–51). Pacific Grove, CA: Brooks/Cole.

Singletary, J., Harris, H. W., Myers, D. R., & Scales, T. L. (2006). Student narratives on social work as a calling. *Arete, 30*(1), 188–199.

Siporin, M. (1982). Moral philosophy in social work today. *Social Service Review, 56*(4), 516–538.

Siporin, M. (1983). Morality and immorality in working with clients. *Social Thought, 9*(4), 10–27.

Siporin, M. (1985). Current social work perspectives on clinical practice. *Clinical Social Work Journal, 13*(3), 198–217.

Siporin, M. (1986). Contribution of religious values to social work and the law. *Social Thought, 12*(4), 35–50.

Siporin, M. (1990). Welcome to the Spirituality and Social Work Communicator. *Spirituality and Social Work Communicator, 1*(1), 3–4.

Siporin, M. (2009). *Artistry in social work practice.* iUniverse.com.

Sloan, R. P., Bagiella, E., VandeCreek, L., Hover, M., Casalone, C., Hirsch, T.J., Hasan, Y., & Kreger, R (2000). Should physicians prescribe religious activities? *New England Journal of Medicine, 342,* 1913–1916.

Smede, L. B. (1996). *The art of forgiving: When you need to forgive and don't know how.* New York: Ballantine Books.

Smith, D. P. (2005). The sweat lodge as psychotherapy: Congruence between traditional and modern healing. In R. Moodley & W. West (Eds.), *Integrating traditional healing into counseling and psychotherapy* (pp. 197–209.). Thousand Oaks, CA: Sage Publications.

Smith, E. D. (1995). Addressing the psychospiritual distress of death as reality: A transpersonal approach. *Social Work, 40*(3), 402–412.

Smith, E. D., & Gray, C. (1995). Integrating and transcending divorce: A transpersonal model. *Social Thought: Journal of Religion in the Social Services, 18*(1), 57–74.

Smith, H. (1991). *The world's religions: Our great wisdom traditions.* New York: HarperOne.

Smith, H. (1995). *The illustrated world's religions: A guide to our wisdom traditions.* New York: HarperCollins Publishers.

Smith, H. (2003). *Cleansing the doors of perception: The religious significance of entheogenic plants and chemicals.* Boulder, CO: Sentient Publications.

Smith, H. (2001). *Why religion matters.* New York: HarperSanFransisco.

Smith, H. (2005). *The soul of Christianity: Restoring the great tradition.* New York: HarperCollins Publishers.

Smith, J. E. (1994). *Quasi-religions: Humanism, Marxism and nationalism.* New York: St. Martin's Press.

Smith, R. (1961). Spiritual, ethical and moral values for children in foster care. *Child Welfare, 40*(1), 20–24.

Smithline, C. (2000). *Spirituality as a protective factor against adolescent substance abuse.* Ann Arbor, Michigan: Unpublished Dissertation, United States International University.

Sneck, W. J. & Bonica, R. P. (1980). Attempting the integration of psychology and spirituality. *Social Thought, 6*(3), 27–36.

Snyder, C. R. & Lopez, S. J. (2007). *Positive Psychology: The scientific and practical explorations of human strengths*. Thousand Oaks, CA: Sage.

Sobrino, J. (1988). *Spirituality of liberation: Toward political holiness* (R. R. Barr, Trans.). Maryknoll, NY: Orbis Books.

Spano, R., & Koenig, T. (2007). What is sacred when personal and professional values collide? *Journal of Social Work values and Ethics, 4*(3), 5–23. Retrieved from http://www.socialworker.com/jswve/content/view/69/54/

Spencer, S. (1956). Religion and social work. *Social Work, 1*(3), 19–26.

Spencer, S. (1961). What place has religion in social work education? *Social Service Review, 35*, 161–170.

Spero, M. H. (1981). A clinical note on the therapeutic management of "religious" resistances in Orthodox Jewish clientele. *Journal of Jewish Communal Service, 57*(4). 334–331.

Sperry, L., & Shafranske, E. P. (Eds.). (2005). *Spiritually oriented psychotherapy*. Washington, DC: American Psychological Association.

Spilka, B. (2005). Religious practice, ritual, and prayer. In R. F. Paloutzian & C. L. Park (Eds.), *Handbook of the psychology of religion and spirituality* (pp.365–377). New York: The Guilford Press.

Sprecher, S., & Fehr, B. (2005). Compassionate love for close others and humanity. *Journal of Social and Personal Relationships, 22*(5), 629–651.

Starhawk (1979). *The spiral dance: A rebirth of the ancient religion of the Great Goddess*. San Francisco: Harper & Row, Publishers.

Starnino, V. (2009). Best practices for helping clients diagnosed with a serious mental illness utilize spirituality as a recovery tool. In C. G. Petr (Ed.), *Multidimensional evidence-based practice: Synthesizing knowledge, research, and values* (pp. 179–203). New York: Routledge.

Steen, T. A., Kachorek, L. V., & Peterson, C. (2003). Character strengths among youth. *Journal of Youth and Adolescence, 32*(1), 5–16.

Stewart, C., Koeske, G. F., & Koeske, R. D. (2006). Personal religiosity and spirituality associated with social workers' use of religiously-based intervention practices. *Journal of Religion and Spirituality in Social Work, 25*(1), 69–85.

Stewart, R., & Wheeler, R. (2002). Talk story. In M. Nash & B. Stewart (Eds.), *Spirituality and social care: Contributing to personal and community well-being* (pp. 171–188). Philadelphia: Jessica Kingsley Publishers.

Stirling, B., Furman, L. D., Benson, P. W., Canda, E. R., & Grimwood, C. (2009). A Comparative survey of Aotearoa New Zealand and UK social workers on the role of religion and spirituality in practice. *British Journal of Social Work* Advance Access published on February 13, 2009, DOI 10.1093/bjsw/bcp008, http://bjsw.oxfordjournals.org/cgi/reprint/bcp008v1.

Struthers, R. (2003). The artistry and ability of traditional women healers. *Health Care for Women International, 24*, 340–354.

Studzinski, R. (1986). Remember and forgive: Psychological dimensions of forgiveness. In C. Floristan & D. Duquoc (Eds.), *Forgiveness*. Edinburgh, Scotland: T. & Clark Ltd.

Suarez-Balcazar, Y & Harper, G. (Eds.). (2004). *Empowerment and Participatory Evaluation in Community Intervention: Multiple Benefits*. Haworth Press.

Sullivan, P. (1994). Should spiritual principles guide social policy? No. In H. J. Karger & J. Midgley, (Eds.), *Controversial issues in human behavior in the social environment* (pp. 69–74). Boston: Allyn and Bacon.

Sullivan, W. P. (1992). Spirituality as social support for individuals with severe mental illness. *Spirituality and Social Work Journal, 3*(1), 7–13.

Svare, G. M., Hylton, M., & Albers, E. (2007). On our own: Social workers talk about spiritually-sensitive practice within an organizational context. *Journal of Religioni & Spirituality in Social Work, 26*(4), 95–113.

Sweifach, J. (2005). Social work in Jewish community centers: A question of compatibility. *Social Work, 50*(2), 151–160.

Swidler, A. (Ed.). (1993). *Homosexuality and world religions.* Valley Forge, PA: Trinity Press International.

Swigonski, M. E. (2001). Human rights, hate crimes, and Hebrew-Christian scripture. *Journal of Gay and Lesbian Social Services, 13*(1/2), 33–45.

Swinton, J. (2001). *Spirituality and mental health care: Rediscovering a forgotten dimension.* London: Jessica Kingsley.

Takaki, R. (1993). *A different mirror: A history of multicultural America.* Boston: Little, Brown and Company.

Takashima, S. (2000). An aspect of the Japanese regime of social welfare especially in the "ie" (family) system of pre-Second World War period. *Japanese Journal of Social Services, 2,* 111–116.

Tan, P. P. (2006). Survivors of the killing fields: Spirituality and religious faith as protective factors against the impact of trauma. *Arete, 30*(1), 112–123.

Tangenberg, K. M. (2005). Faith-based human services initiatives: Considerations for social work practice and theory. *Social Work, 50*(3), 197–206.

Tart, C. T. (1975). Science, states of consciousness, and spiritual experiences: The need for state-specific sciences. In Charles T. Tart (Ed.), *Transpersonal psychologies* (pp. 9–58). New York: Harper & Row.

Taylor, R. L. (1990). *The religious dimensions of Confucianism.* Albany, NY: State University of New York Press.

Thomas, P. E. (2004). Toward the development of an integral approach to social work: Implications for human behavior theory and research. *Journal of Human Behavior in the Social Environment, 9*(3), 1–19.

Thomas, W., & Bellefeuille, G. (2006). An evidence-based formative evaluation of a cross-cultural Aboriginal mental health program in Canada. *Australian e-Journal for the Advancement of MentalHealth, 5*(3), www.auseinet.com/journal/vol5iss3/thomas.pdf

Thurman, R. A. F. (1996). Human rights and human responsibilities: Buddhist views on individualism and altruism. In I. Bloom, J. P. Martin, & W. Proudfoot (Eds.), *Religious diversity and human rights* (pp. 87–113). New York: Columbia University Press,

Thyer, B. (Ed.). (2007a). *Special Issue of Research on Social Work Practice, 17*(2).

Thyer, B. (2007b). A note from the editor. *Research on Social Work Practice, 17*(2), 169–170.

Tillich, P. (1962). The philosophy of social work. *Social Service Review, 36*(1), 13–16.

Timberlake, E. M., & Cook, K. O. (1984). Social work and the Vietnamese refugee. *Social Work, 29*(2), 108–114.

Tirrito, T., & Cascio, T. (Eds.). (2003). *Religious Organizations in Community Services: A Social Work Perspective,* New York: Springer Publishing Company.

Toussaint, L.L., Williams, D.R., Musick, M.A., & Everson, S.A. (2001). Forgiveness and health: Age differences in a U.S. probability sample. *Journal of Adult Development, 8*(4), 249–257.

Towle, C. (1965). *Common human needs* (rev. ed). Washington, DC: National Association of Social Workers Press.

Townshend, J. (1988). Neo-shamanism and the modern mystical movement. In G. Doore (Ed.), *Shaman's Path: Healing, personal growth, and empowerment* (pp. 73–83). Boston: Shambhala.

Tripodi, T., & Potocky-Tripodi, M. (2007). *International social work research: Issues and Prospects.* New York: Oxford University Press.

Turner, E. (1992). *Experiencing ritual: A new interpretation of African healing.* Philadelphia, PA: University of Pennsylvania Press.

Turner, K. A. (1984). Local churches and community social work providers as collaborators in rural social service deliver. *Rural Roots, 3*(2), July/August.

Turner, R., Lukoff, D., Barnhouse, R. T., & Lu, F. G. (1995). Religious or spiritual problem: A culturally sensitive diagnostic category in the DSM-IV. *The Journal of Nervous and Mental Disease, 183*(7), 435–444.

Turner, V. W. (1965). Betwixt and between: The liminal period in rites of passage. In W. A. Lessa & E. V. Vogt, (Eds.), *Reader in comparative religion: An anthropological approach* (3rd ed.). New York: Harper and Row.

Turner, V. W. (1969). *The ritual process: Structure and anti-structure.* Ithaca, NY: Cornell University Press, Cornell Paperbacks.

Turner, V. W. (1974). *Dramas, fields and metaphors: Symbolic action in human society.* Ithaca, NY: Cornell University Press.

Tutu, D. (1998). Forward. In R. D. Enright & J. North (Eds.), *Exploring Forgiveness* (p. xiv). Madison, WI: University of Wisconsin Press.

Tutu, D. (1999). *No future without forgiveness.* New York, NY: Image Doubleday.

Tyson, K. (1995). *New foundations for scientific social and behavioral research: The heuristic paradigm.* Boston: Allyn and Bacon.

Underwood, L. G. (2002). The human experience of compassionate love: Conceptual mapping and data from selected studies. In S. G. Post, L. G. Underwood, J. P. Schloss, & W. B. Hurlbut (Eds.), *Altruism and altruistic love: Science, philosophy, & religion in dialogue* (pp. 72–88). New York: Oxford University Press.

Underwood, L. G. (2005). Interviews with Trappist monks as a contribution to research methodology in the investigation of compassionate love. *Journal for the Theory of Social Behavior, 35*(3), 285–302.

Ungar, M. (2002). A deeper, more social ecological social work practice. *Social Service Review, 76*(3), 480–497.

United Nations. (1948). *Universal declaration of human rights.* New York: United Nations. Retrieved August 1, 2007, from http://www.un.org/Overview/rights.html

Van Gennep, A. (1960). *The rites of passage.* (M.B. Vizedom & G.L. Caffee, Trans.). Chicago, University of Chicago Press.

Van Hook, M. P. (1997). Christian social work. In R. L. Edwards (Ed.), *Encyclopedia of social work 19th edition 1997 Supplement* (pp. 68–77). Washington, DC: National Association of Social Workers.

Van Hook, M., Hugen, B., & Aguilar, M. (Eds.). (2001). *Spirituality within religious traditions in social work practice.* Pacific Grove, CA: Brooks/Cole.

Van Os, H. (1994). *The art of devotion in the late middle ages in Europe: 1300–1500.* Princeton, NJ: Princeton University Press.

Van Soest, D. (1996). The influence of competing ideologies about homosexuality on nondiscrimination policy: Implications for social work education. *Journal of Social Work Education, 32*(1), 53–64.

Van Kaam, A. (1983). *Fundamental formation.* New York: Crossroad.

Vardey, L. (Ed). (1995). *Mother Teresa: A simple path.* New York: Ballantine Books.

Vash, C. (Ed.). (2001). Special Issue of *Journal of Rehabilitation, 67*(1), on Spirituality and Disability.

Verniest, L. (2006). Allying with the Medicine Wheel: Social work practice with Indigenous peoples. *Critical Social Work, 7*(1). Retrieved from http://cronus.uwindsor.ca/units/socialwork/critical.nsf/main/9979F6E595E176DB8525717

Vohra-Gupta, S., Russell, A., & Lo, E. (2007). Meditation: The adoption of eastern thought to western social practices. *Journal of Religion & Spirituality in Social Work, 26*(2), 49–61.

Von Wormer, K. (2004). Restorative justice: A model for personal and societal empowerment. *Journal of Religion & Spirituality in Social Work, 23*(4), 103–120.

Voss, R. W., Douville, V., Little Soldier, A., & Twiss, G. (1999). Tribal and shamanic-based social work practice: A Lakota perspective. *Social Work, 44*(3), 228–241.

Voss, R. W., White Hat, A., Bates, J., Lunderman, M. R., & Lunderman, A. (2005). Social work education in the homeland: Wo'Lakota Unglu'su'tapi. EPAS or Impasse? Operationalizing accreditation standard 6.0. *Journal of Social Work Education, 43*(2), 209–227.

Wagemakers Schiff, J., & Pelech, W. (2007). The sweat lodge ceremony for spiritual healing. *Journal of Religion & Spirituality in Social Work, 26*(4), 71–93.

Wallace, A. F. C. (1966). *Religion: An anthropological view* (pp. 240–242). New York: Random House.

Walsh, R. N. (1990). *The spirit of shamanism.* New York: G. P. Putnam's Sons.

Walz, T., & Ritchie, H. (2000).Gandhian principles in social work practice: Ethics revisited. *Social Work, 45*(3), 213–222.

Walz, T., Sharma, S., & Birnbaum, C. (1990). Gandhian thought as theory base for social work. *University of Illinois School of Social Work Occasional Paper Series I.* Urbana-Champaign: University of Illinois.

Warner, J. C. (2003). Group therapy with Native Americans: Understanding essential differences. *Group, 27*(4), 191–202.

Warner, M. (1976). *Alone of all her sex: The myth and the cult of the Virgin Mary.* New York: Pocket Books.

Watson, K. W. (1994). Spiritual emergency: Concepts and implications for psychotherapy. *Journal of Humanistic Psychology, 34*(2), 22–45.

Watts, F., & Williams, M. (1988). *The psychology of religious knowing.* Cambridge, England: Cambridge University Press.

Weaver, H. (1999). Indigenous people and the social work profession: defining culturally competent services. *Social Work, 44*(3), 217–225.

Weber, P. J., & Jones, W. L. (1994). *U.S. religious interest groups: Institutional profiles.* Westport, CT: Greenwood Press.

Wegela, K. K. (2003). Nurturing the seeds of sanity: A Buddhist approach to psychotherapy. In S. G. Mijares (Ed.), *Modern psychology and ancient wisdom: Psychological healing practices from the world's traditions* (pp. 17–42). New York: Haworth Press.

Weisman, E. R. (1997). Does religion and spirituality have a significant place in the Core HBSE curriculum? No. In M. Bloom & W. C. Klein (Eds.), *Controversial issues in human behavior in the social environment* (pp. 177–183). Boston: Allyn and Bacon.

Weitzmann, K. (1978). *The icon: Holy images--Sixth to fourteenth century.* New York: Braziller.

Welwood, J. (Ed.). (1992). *Ordinary magic: Everyday life as spiritual path.* Boston: Shambhala.

White, B. W., & Hampton, D. M. (1995). African American pioneers in social work. In R. L. Edwards, (Ed.), *Encyclopedia of social work 19th edition* (pp. 101–115). Washington, DC: NASW Press.

Wikler, M. (1977). The Torah view of mental illness: Sin or sickness? *Journal of Jewish Communal Service, 53*(4), 338–334.

Wikler, M. (1986). Pathways to treatment: How Orthodox Jews enter therapy. *Social Casework, 67*(2), 113–118.

Wilber, K. (1980). *The Atman project: A transpersonal view of human development.* Wheaton, IL: Quest.

Wilber, K. (1993). *Grace and grit: Spirituality and healing in the life and death of Treya Killiam Wilber.* Boston: Shambhala.

Wilber, K. (1996). *A brief history of everything.* Boston: Shambhala.

Wilber, K. (1998). *The marriage of sense and soul: Integrating science and religion.* New York: Random House.

Wilber, K. (2000a). *Sex, ecology, spirituality: The spirit of evolution* (2nd ed.). Boston: Shambhala.

Wilber, K. (2000b). *Integral psychology: Consciousness, spirit, psychology, therapy.* Boston: Shambhala.

Wilber, K. (2006). *Integral spirituality.* Boston: Integral Books.

Wilhelm, R., & Baynes, C. F. (Trans). (1976). *The I Ching or book of changes* (3rd ed.). Bollingen Series, no. 19. Princeton, Princeton University Press.

Williams, L. & Sewpaul, V. (2004). Modernism, postmodernism and global standards setting. *Social Work Education, 23*(5), 555–565.

Williams, M., & Smolak, A. (2007). Integrating faith matters into social work education. *Journal of Religion and Spirituality in Social Work, 26*(3), 25–44.

Williamson, W. B. (Ed.). (1992). *An encyclopedia of religions in the United States.* New York: Crossroad.

Wilson, M. (2002). *Practice unbound: A study of secular spiritual and religious activities in work with adolescents.* Boxboro, MA: New England Network for Child, Youth and Family Services.

Wilson, S. J. (1980). *Recording guidelines for social workers.* New York: The Free Press.

Wineburg, B. (2001). *A limited partnership: The politics of religion, welfare, and social service.* New York: Columbia University Press.

Wineburg, B. (2007). *Faith-based inefficiency: The follies of Bush's Initiatives.* Westport, CN: Praeger.

Wingren, G. (1994). *Lutheran vocation.* Evansville, IN: Ballast Press.

Winzeler, R. L. (2008). *Anthropology and religion: What we know, think, and question.* Lanham, MD: Altamira Press.

Witvliet, C. V. O., & McCullough, M. E. (2007). Forgiveness and health: A review and theoretical exploration of emotion pathways. In S. G. Post (Ed.), *Altruism and health: Perspectives from empirical research* (pp. 259–276.). New York: Oxford University Press.

World Health Organization (2006). Health and human rights. Retrieved August 1, 2007, from http://www.who.int/hhr/en/

Worthington, E. L., Jr., & DiBlasio, F. A. (1990). Promoting mutual forgiveness within the fractured relationship. *Psychotherapy, 27*(2), 219–223.

Worthington, E. L., Jr., Mazzeo, S. E., & Canter, D. E. (2005). Forgiveness-promoting approach: Helping clients REACH forgiveness through using a longer model that teaches reconciliation. In L. Sperry & E. P. Shafranske (Eds.), *Spiritually-oriented psychotherapy* (pp. 235–257). Washington, D.C.: American Psychological Association.

Wulff, D. M. (1991). *Psychology of religion: Classic and contemporary views.* New York: John Wiley & Sons.

Yao, X. (2000). *An introduction to Confucianism.* Cambridge, UK: Cambridge University Press.

Yang, C. P., Lukoff, D., & Lu, F. (2006). Working with spiritual issues of adults in clinical practice. *Psychiatric Annals, 36*(3), 168–174.

Yardley, M. (2008). Social work practice with pagans, witches, and wiccans: Guidelines for practice with children and youths. *Social Work, 53*(4), 329–336.

Yee, C. S. (2003). The Confucian concept of gender in the twenty-first century. In D. A. Bel & C. Hahm (Eds.). (2003). *Confucianism for the modern world* (pp. 312–333). Cambridge, UK: Cambridge University Press.

Yellow Bird, M. (1995). Spirituality in First Nations story telling: A Sahnish-Hidatsa approach to narrative. *Reflections: Narrative of Professional helping, 1*(4), 65–72.

Yellow Bird, M. (2008). Terms of endearment: A brief dictionary for decolonizing social work with Indigenous peoples. In M. Grey, J. Coates, & Yellow Bird, M. (Eds.), *Indigenous social work around the world: Towards culturally relevant education and practice* (pp. 275–291). Burlington, VT: Ashgate.

Yellow Horse Brave Heart, M. (2001). Lakota—Native people's spirituality. In M.Van Hook, B. Hugen, & M. Aguilar, (Eds.), *Spirituality within religious traditions in social work,* (pp. 18–33). Pacific Grove, CA: Brooks/Cole.

Yip, K. (2004). A Chinese cultural critique of the global qualifying standards for social work education. *Social Work Education, 23*(5), 597–612.

Zahl, M. A. (2003). Spirituality and social work: A Norwegian reflection. *Social Thought, 22*(1), 77–89.

Zahl, M. A., & Furman, L. (2005). Koblingen sosialt arbeid og religion/livssyn: et tilbakelagt stadium eller del av et helhetssyn. [Combining social work and religion/spirituality: better left in the past or included in a contemporary holistic view]. *Nordisk Sosialt Arbeid, 25*(2), 98–100.

Zahl, M. A., Furman, L. D., Benson, P. W., & Canda, E. R. (2007). Religion and spirituality in social work practice and education in a cross-cultural context: Findings from a Norwegian and UK study. *European Journal of Social Work, 10*(3), 295–317.

Zehr, H. (1995). *Changing lenses: A new focus for Crime and justice.* Scottdale, PA: Harold Press.

Zellerer, E. (2003). Culturally competent programs: The first family violence program for Aboriginal men in prison. *The Prison Journal, 83*(2), 171–190.

Zimdars-Swartz, S. L. (1991). *Encountering Mary: Visions of Mary from La Salette to Medjugorje.* New York: Avon Books.

Zinnbauer, B. J., & Pargament, K. I. (2005). Religiousness and spirituality. In R. F. Paloutzian & C. L. Park (Eds.), *Handbook of the psychology of religion and spirituality* (pp. 21–42). New York: The Guilford Press.

INDEX